FR - 8235/6
ML

 **University of the West of England** **BOLLAND LIBRARY**

MEDIUM LOAN COLLECTION

Please ensure that this book is returned by the end of the loan period for which it is issued.

UWE, BRISTOL 7555B 3.95
Printing & Stationery Services

03. DEC 2002	27. FEB 2007
18/12/02	25. MAR 2009
08. DEC 2003	
02. MAR 2004	UWE BRISTOL
14. MAY 2004	WITHDRAWN
	LIBRARY SERVICES
12. OCT 2004	
20. MAY 2005	
23 MAY 2005	
26 MAY 2005	
31 MAY 2005	

Telephone Renewals: 0117 344 3757
Library Web Address: http://www.uwe.ac.uk/library/

Human Rights Protection for Refugees, Asylum-Seekers, and Internally Displaced Persons

A Guide to International Mechanisms and Procedures

The Procedural Aspects of International Law Institute

Human Rights Protection for Refugees, Asylum-Seekers, and Internally Displaced Persons

A Guide to International Mechanisms and Procedures

Joan Fitzpatrick
Editor

Transnational Publishers, Inc.
Ardsley, New York

Published and distributed by *Transnational Publishers, Inc.*
Ardsley Park
Science and Technology Center
410 Saw Mill River Road
Ardsley, NY 10502

Phone: 914-693-5100
Fax: 914-693-4430
E-mail: info@transnationalpubs.com
Web: www.transnationalpubs.com

Library of Congress Cataloging-in-Publication Data

Human rights protection for refugees, asylum-seekers, and internally displaced persons : a guide to international mechanisms / Joan Fitzpatrick, editor.
    p. cm. — (Procedural aspects of international law series)
  Includes bibliographical references and index.
  ISBN 1-57105-061-2
  1. Refugees—Legal status, law, etc. 2. Asylum, Right of.
3. Migration, Internal. 4. Human rights. I. Fitzpatrick, Joan (Joan M.) II. Series.

K3230.R45 H865 2001
341.4'81—dc21

                                                2001052220

Copyright © 2002 by Transnational Publishers, Inc.

All rights reserved. This book may not be reproduced, in whole or in part, in any form (beyond that copying permitted by U.S. Copyright Law in Section 107, "fair use" in teaching and research, Section 108, certain library copying, and except in published media by reviewers in limited excerpts), without written permission from the publisher.

Manufactured in the United States of America

Contents

Acknowledgments	*xxi*
Editor's Foreword	*xxiii*
Contributors	*xxv*
Table of Abbreviations	*xxix*

Chapter 1. The Human Rights of Refugees, Asylum-Seekers, and Internally Displaced Persons: A Basic Introduction
JOAN FITZPATRICK — 1

1. Introduction — 1
2. Who Are Refugees, Asylum-Seekers, and Internally Displaced Persons? — 3
3. Identifying Rights at Risk and Framing a Human Rights Claim — 6
   - 3.1 The Right to Life and to Physical Integrity — 8
   - 3.2 Equality and Non-Discrimination — 9
   - 3.3 Personal Liberty — 10
   - 3.4 Other Civil and Political Rights — 11
   - 3.5 Freedom of Movement — 11
   - 3.6 The Right to Family Life — 13
   - 3.7 Social and Economic Rights — 14
   - 3.8 The Need for Documents — 14
   - 3.9 Property Rights — 15
4. A Basic Primer on the Nature of International Human Rights Law and the Varied Functions of Enforcement Bodies — 15
   - 4.1 The Nature of International Human Rights Law — 16

		4.1.1	Treaties	16
		4.1.2	Customary Law	18
	4.2	\multicolumn{2}{l}{Differing Mandates and Powers of Human Rights Mechanisms}	18
5.	\multicolumn{3}{l}{Conclusion}	20
\multicolumn{4}{l}{*Bibliography*}	21

Chapter 2. Protection Under the Complaint Procedures of the United Nations Treaty Bodies — 23

ANNE BAYEFSKY, STEPHANIE FARRIOR,
KAREN HANRAHAN, AND ANDREW LANGHAM

1.	\multicolumn{3}{l}{Brief Overview of Individual Complaints Under International Human Rights Treaties}	23
2.	\multicolumn{3}{l}{Admissibility Criteria for Individual Complaints}	26
	2.1	\multicolumn{2}{l}{Jurisdiction Ratione Personae— Eligible Complaints}	26
		2.1.1	Who Can Bring a Complaint?	26
		2.1.2	Against Whom May a Complaint Be Filed?	30
	2.2	\multicolumn{2}{l}{Jurisdiction Ratione Materiae— What Must the Complaint Concern?}	31
	2.3	\multicolumn{2}{l}{Jurisdiction Ratione Temporis—When Must the Alleged Violation Have Occurred?}	33
	2.4	\multicolumn{2}{l}{Jurisdiction Ratione Loci—Where Must the Violation Have Occurred?}	35
	2.5	\multicolumn{2}{l}{Must Domestic Remedies Have Been Exhausted?}	36
	2.6	\multicolumn{2}{l}{Are There Any Time Limits for Bringing a Complaint?}	41
	2.7	\multicolumn{2}{l}{Concurrent and Successive Jurisdiction}	41
	2.8	\multicolumn{2}{l}{Other Admissibility Criteria}	43
		2.8.1	Anonymity	43
		2.8.2	Abuse of the Right to Submit a Communication	44
		2.8.3	Incompatibility with the Provisions of the Treaty—Manifestly Ill-Founded Complaint	44
	2.9	\multicolumn{2}{l}{Checklist for Submissions}	44
3.	\multicolumn{3}{l}{Substantive Rights and Significant Jurisprudence}	45
	3.1	\multicolumn{2}{l}{Protection Under the 1966 International Covenant on Civil and Political Rights}	45
		3.1.1	The Right to Life and Physical Integrity	48

	3.1.2	Equality and Non-Discrimination	52
	3.1.3	Personal Liberty	56
	3.1.4	Right to a Fair Trial and Due Process of Law	59
	3.1.5	Right to Vote and Participate in the Political Process	60
	3.1.6	Freedom of Religion	60
	3.1.7	Freedom of Expression	61
	3.1.8	Freedom of Association	62
	3.1.9	Freedom of Movement	63
	3.1.10	The Right to Family and Private Life	68
	3.1.11	Right to a Nationality	70
	3.1.12	Recognition as a Person Before the Law	70
	3.1.13	Prohibition of Trafficking of Women and Girls and Exploitation of Prostitution	71
	3.1.14	Economic and Social Rights of the Child	72
	3.1.15	Economic and Social Rights Through Equality Before the Law and Equal Protection of the Law	73
3.2	Protection Under the 1984 Convention Against Torture and Other Cruel, Inhuman or Degrading Treatment or Punishment		73
	3.2.1	The Right to Physical and Mental Integrity—Prohibition Against Torture	76
	3.2.2	Equality and Non-Discrimination	82
	3.2.3	Personal Liberty	83
	3.2.4	Right to a Fair Trial and Due Process of Law	83
	3.2.5	Freedom of Movement	83
3.3	Protection Under the 1965 Convention on the Elimination of All Forms of Racial Discrimination		84
	3.3.1	The Right to Life and Physical Integrity	87
	3.3.2	Equality and Non-Discrimination	88
	3.3.3	Personal Liberty	89
	3.3.4	Right to a Fair Trial and Due Process of Law	89
	3.3.5	Right to Vote and Participate in the Political Process	89

	3.3.6	Freedom of Religion	89
	3.3.7	Freedom of Expression	89
	3.3.8	Freedom of Association	90
	3.3.9	Freedom of Movement	90
	3.3.10	Right to Family and Private Life	91
	3.3.11	Right to a Nationality	91
	3.3.12	Right to Shelter/Housing	92
	3.3.13	Right to Health Care	92
	3.3.14	Right to Education	92
	3.3.15	Right to Work	92
	3.3.16	Right to Social Support	93
	3.3.17	Property Rights	93
	3.3.18	Additional Issues	94
3.4	Protection Under the 1979 Convention on the Elimination of All Forms of Discrimination Against Women and the 1999 Optional Protocol		95
	3.4.1	Definition of "Discrimination Against Women"	95
	3.4.2	The Right to Life and Physical Integrity	97
	3.4.3	Equality and Non-Discrimination	99
	3.4.4	Right to a Fair Trial and Due Process of Law	101
	3.4.5	Right to Vote and Participate in the Political Process	101
	3.4.6	Freedom of Religion	101
	3.4.7	Freedom of Expression	102
	3.4.8	Freedom of Association	102
	3.4.9	Freedom of Movement	102
	3.4.10	The Right to Family and Private Life	102
	3.4.11	Rights Regarding Nationality	103
	3.4.12	Right to Food, Clothing and Shelter	104
	3.4.13	Access to Health Care	104
	3.4.14	Right to Education	105
	3.4.15	Employment Rights	106
	3.4.16	Equal Rights in Economic Life	107
	3.4.17	Property Rights	107
3.5	Additional Relevant Articles in the Women's Convention		107
	3.5.1	Temporary Measures to Accelerate Equality	107

		3.5.2	Obligation to Modify Social and Cultural Patterns of Conduct	108
	3.6	Other Relevant International Human Rights Treaties		108
		3.6.1	1989 Convention on the Rights of the Child	108
		3.6.2	1966 International Covenant on Economic, Social and Cultural Rights	110
4.	Additional Considerations			111
	4.1	Interim Measures		111
	4.2	Remedies		114
	4.3	Confidentiality		118
	4.4	Legal Aid		119
5.	Strengths and Weaknesses of the UN Treaty Mechanisms for Individual Complaints			119
	5.1	Finding of a Violation by an International Body		120
	5.2	Publicity		120
	5.3	Moral Vindication		120
	5.4	Role for Individuals		121
	5.5	May Prevent Expulsion or Deportation		121
	5.6	Limits on Availability of Mechanism		121
	5.7	Lengthy Time Between Filing and Decision		122
	5.8	The Issue of the Binding Nature of Opinions		123
6.	Other Advocacy Possibilities			123
	6.1	State Reporting Procedure		124
	6.2	General Comments and Recommendations of the Treaty Bodies		125
	6.3	Inquiry Procedure		126
		6.3.1	Torture Convention	126
		6.3.2	Women's Convention	127
Bibliography				128

Chapter 3. The United Nations Charter-Based Mechanisms — 137

CAMILLE GIFFARD AND MEAGAN HRLE

1.	Introduction		137
2.	Setting the Context		138
	2.1	Context in Which the Charter-Based Mechanisms Function	138
	2.2	Why Are Charter-Based Mechanisms Relevant to Refugees, Asylum-Seekers, and Internally Displaced Persons?	143

		2.2.1	As Individual Complaint Mechanisms	144
		2.2.2	As Advocacy Tools	144
3.	How Do The Charter-Based Mechanisms Work and What Can You Achieve by Using Them?			144
	3.1	What Are the Special Procedures of the Commission on Human Rights?		145
	3.2	How Do the Special Procedures Work?		146
	3.3	What Can You Achieve by Submitting Information in the Context of the Special Procedures?		148
4.	What Mechanisms Are Available and How Can You Identify Which Ones May Apply in Your Case?			150
	4.1	Available Mechanisms		150
	4.2	Identifying Applicable Mechanisms: Case Studies		156
5.	Once You Have Identified the Available Mechanisms, How Do You Go about Using Them?			163
	5.1	Common Aspects		163
		5.1.1	Practical Considerations	163
		5.1.2	General Characteristics of a Communication	165
		5.1.3	Submitting Information in Cases of Imminent Deportation	168
	5.2	The Special Procedures of the Commission on Human Rights		169
		5.2.1	Thematic Procedures	169
		5.2.2	Country-Specific Procedures	220
6.	How Effective Are the Mechanisms?			222
	6.1	Thematic Procedures		222
	6.2	Country-Specific Procedures		226
	6.3	Concluding Note		226
7.	Other Advocacy Possibilities in the Context of the UN Charter Organs			223
	7.1	Additional Mechanisms		223
		7.1.1	1503 Procedure	223
		7.1.2	Sub-Commission on the Promotion and Protection of Human Rights	232
		7.1.3	Commission on the Status of Women	234
	7.2	Advocacy and Lobbying: Influencing the UN Charter Organs at the Decision-Making Level		235

	7.2.1	Where Does an Advocacy Campaign Begin?	236
	7.2.2	What Are the Potential Results of Advocacy Efforts?	239
	7.2.3	How Can NGOs Intervene in the Commission and Sub-Commission?	244
Bibliography			248

Chapter 4. African Regional Mechanisms That Can Be Utilized on Behalf of the Forcibly Displaced 259

CHIDI ANSELM ODINKALU AND MONETTE ZARD

1. Introduction 259
2. African Regional Mechanisms 262
   - 2.1 The Organization of African Unity (OAU) 262
     - 2.1.1 The 1981 African Charter on Human and Peoples' Rights 263
     - 2.1.2 The African Commission on Human and Peoples' Rights 267
     - 2.1.3 African Court of Human and Peoples' Rights 275
     - 2.1.4 The African Committee of Experts on the Rights and Welfare of the Child 277
   - 2.2 The OAU Division for Refugees, Displaced Persons, and Humanitarian Assistance 279
   - 2.3 The OAU Mechanism for Conflict Prevention, Management, and Resolution 282
3. Sub-Regional Mechanisms 283
   - 3.1 The Economic Community of West African States (ECOWAS) 283
     - 3.1.1 Aims and Objectives of the ECOWAS 285
     - 3.1.2 Institutions of the Community 287
     - 3.1.3 The ECOWAS, Human Rights, and Migration 287
     - 3.1.4 The Community Court of Justice 289
   - 3.2 L'Union Économique et Monétaire de l'Afrique de l'Ouest (UEMOA) 290
     - 3.2.1 Aims and Objectives of the UEMOA 291
     - 3.2.2 Institutions of the Union 291
     - 3.2.3 The UEMOA, Human Rights, and Migration 292

		3.2.4	The Community Court of Justice	283
	3.3	\multicolumn{2}{l	}{The Inter-Governmental Authority on Development (IGAD)}	297
		3.3.1	The IGAD Institutions	297
		3.3.2	The IGAD, Human Rights, and Migration	298
		3.3.3	The IGAD Conflict Resolution Mechanism	299
	3.4	\multicolumn{2}{l	}{The East African Community (EAC)}	299
		3.4.1	The EAC Institutions	300
		3.4.2	The EAC, Human Rights, and Migration	300
		3.4.3	The EAC Community Court of Justice	301
	3.5	\multicolumn{2}{l	}{The Southern African Development Community (SADC)}	302
		3.5.1	Aims and Objectives of the SADC	302
		3.5.2	Institutions of the SADC	303
		3.5.3	The SADC, Human Rights, and Migration	304
		3.5.4	The SADC and Gender	305
		3.5.5	The SADC Tribunal	306
	3.6	\multicolumn{2}{l	}{The African Economic Community (AEC)}	308
		3.6.1	Objectives	308
		3.6.2	Institutions	308
	3.7	\multicolumn{2}{l	}{The African Union}	309
4.	\multicolumn{3}{l	}{Conclusion}	310
Bibliography				310

Chapter 5. European Human Rights Mechanisms — 315
DIANE ATKINSON-SANFORD

1.	Introduction			315
	1.1	\multicolumn{2}{l	}{Avenues of Redress in Europe}	316
	1.2	\multicolumn{2}{l	}{A Note on the Charter of Fundamental Rights of the European Union}	316
2.	\multicolumn{3}{l	}{Advocacy}	318
	2.1	\multicolumn{2}{l	}{Individual Petition Mechanisms in Europe: The European Court of Human Rights}	318
	2.2	\multicolumn{2}{l	}{Some Background on the ECHR and the Court}	318
		2.2.1	Institutional Framework of the Court	319
		2.2.2	Checklist: Are You Ready and Willing to Bring a Case Before the Court?	320

		2.2.3	Interpreting the Checklist: What Do These Considerations Mean?	321
		2.2.4	Interim Measures	321
		2.2.5	Friendly Settlement	322
		2.2.6	Just Satisfaction	324
		2.2.7	Other Considerations: Legal Aid	330
		2.2.8	Legal Representation	331
		2.2.9	Language Considerations	331
		2.2.10	Enforcing the Court's Judgments—Effectiveness of Remedies	332
	2.3	Admissibility Criteria		334
		2.3.1	Jurisdiction Ratione Personae—Who Is Liable and Who Can Be Sued?	334
		2.3.2	Jurisdiction Ratione Materiae—What Must the Complaint Concern?	334
		2.3.3	Jurisdiction Ratione Temporis—When Must the Alleged Events Have Occurred?	345
		2.3.4	Jurisdiction Ratione Loci—Where Must the Alleged Violation Have Occurred?	346
		2.3.5	Must Domestic Remedies Have Been Exhausted?	347
		2.3.6	Other Admissibility Criteria	353
		2.3.7	Submitting the Application to the Court	353
		2.3.8	Timeline for Making an Application to the Court	354
3.	ECHR Jurisprudence and Refugees, Asylum-Seekers, and IDPs			359
	3.1	The Right to Life and Physical Integrity		362
		3.1.1	The Prohibition on the Taking of Life	363
		3.1.2	Positive Obligations under Article 2—Failure to Enforce the Criminal Law	369
		3.1.3	Failure to Investigate or Prosecute	371
		3.1.4	Extradition, Expulsion, and Article 2	373
	3.2	Torture and Inhuman and Degrading Treatment		373
		3.2.1 Standard of Proof		374
		3.2.2 Torture		374

	3.2.3	Inhuman Treatment	374
	3.2.4	Degrading Treatment	375
	3.2.5	Article 3 and Extradition, Expulsion, and Deportation—Non-Refoulement	376
	3.2.6	Non-Derogability of Article 3	379
	3.2.7	Capital Punishment and Article 3	380
	3.2.8	Health Care and Article 3	381
3.3	Article 8—The Right to Private Life		382
3.4	Equality and Non-discrimination		282
3.5	Personal Liberty		385
	3.5.1	Article 5 and Internally Displaced Persons	385
	3.5.2	Article 5 and Asylum-Seekers and Refugees	385
3.6	Right to a Fair Trial and Due Process of Law		388
	3.6.1	Article 6—The Right to a Fair Trial and Asylum Applications	388
	3.6.2	Procedural Protections for Aliens Facing Expulsion, Article 1 Protocol 7	389
	3.6.3	The Right to a Fair Trial	390
3.7	The Right to Vote and to Participate in the Political Process		391
	3.7.1	The Right to Vote and Citizens	391
	3.7.2	The Right to Vote and Non-Citizens (Refugees and Asylum-Seekers)	392
3.8	Freedom of Religion, Thought, and Conscience		392
	3.8.1	Article 9 and Proof of a Subjective Belief	392
	3.8.2	Limitations on the Ability to Manifest a Religious Belief	393
	3.8.3	Article 9 and Non-State Actors	393
3.9	Freedom of Expression		394
	3.9.1	Establishing the Existence of an Interference with Article 10	395
	3.9.2	Justification for the Interference	395
	3.9.3	Positive Duties Under Article 10	401
3.10	Freedom of Assembly and Association		401
	3.10.1	Freedom to Assemble Peacefully	402
	3.10.2	Restrictions on the Right to Assemble Peacefully	402
	3.10.3	Freedom of Association	403

		3.10.4	The Freedom to Form and Join Political Parties	403
	3.11	Freedom of Movement		404
		3.11.1	Expulsion of Nationals	404
		3.11.2	Collective Expulsion of Aliens	404
		3.11.3	The Right to Asylum	405
	3.12	The Right to Family and Private Life		405
		3.12.1	Limitations on Article 8	405
		3.12.2	The Home	406
		3.12.3	The Right to a Personal Identity	407
		3.12.4	Article 8, Deportation, and Expulsion	408
		3.12.5	The Right to Reunification	411
	3.13	The Right to Marry		413
	3.14	The Prohibition Against Slavery, Servitude, and Forced or Compulsory Labor		414
	3.15	Access to Food, Clothing, Social Support and Shelter		415
	3.16	Access to Education		415
	3.17	Protection of Property: The Right to the Enjoyment of One's Possessions		416
		3.17.1	Meaning of "Possessions"	416
		3.17.2	A "Deprivation" of Property	416
		3.17.3	Limitations on the Enjoyment of One's Property	417
		3.17.4	State Control of Property	418
		3.17.5	International Law and Expropriation of the Property of an Alien	419
		3.17.6	Compensation	419
4.	Other European Human Rights Mechanisms			420
	4.1	The 1961 European Social Charter		420
		4.1.1	Collective Complaints Mechanism	422
	4.2	The 1987 European Convention for the Prevention of Torture and Inhuman and Degrading Treatment or Punishment		422
	4.3	The 1995 Framework Convention for the Protection of National Minorities		424
	4.4	Commissioner for Human Rights		425
	4.5	Organization for Security and Cooperation in Europe (OSCE)		425
	4.6	The European Union		427
		4.6.1	The European Union and Human Rights	428
		4.6.2	Individuals and the ECJ	429

		4.6.3	EU Policies on Refugees and Asylum-Seekers	430
5.	Conclusion			431
Bibliography				431

Chapter 6. The Inter-American Mechanisms — 439
BETH LYON AND SOREN ROTTMAN

1.	The Major Bodies		439
	1.1	The Organization of American States (OAS)	439
	1.2	The Inter-American Commission on Human Rights	440
	1.3	The Inter-American Court of Human Rights	441
	1.4	Inter-Institutional Coordination	442
2.	Admissibility Criteria for Individual Complaints		443
	2.1	Jurisdiction Ratione Personae—The Parties to an Individual Complaint	444
		2.1.1 Who Can Bring a Complaint?	444
		2.1.2 Against Whom Can a Complaint Be Brought?	448
	2.2	Jurisdiction Ratione Materiae—What Must the Complaint Concern?	450
		2.2.1 Rights Protected by Regional Instruments	450
		2.2.2 Acts or Omissions Committed by a State, Its Agents, Officials, Etc.	452
		2.2.3 Court of the Fourth Instance Rule	452
	2.3	Jurisdiction Ratione Temporis	452
	2.4	Jurisdiction Ratione Loci	453
	2.5	Must Domestic Remedies Have Been Exhausted?	453
		2.5.1 Due Process of Law	457
		2.5.2 Denial of Access to Domestic Remedies or Prevention	457
		2.5.3 Unwarranted Delay of Domestic Remedies	458
	2.6	Once Domestic Remedies Have Been Exhausted, Is There a Time Limit Within Which a Complaint Must Be Brought in Order to Be Admissible?	459
	2.7	Concurrent Jurisdiction—If Another International Body Is Examining the Matter, Can the Mechanism in Question Still Admit It?	460

		2.8	Other Admissibility Criteria	461
	3.	Substantive Rights and Important Jurisprudence		462
		3.1	Civil and Political Rights	462
			3.1.1 Right to Seek and Receive Asylum	462
			3.1.2 The Right to Family and Private Life	473
		3.2	Social and Economic Rights	474
			3.2.1 Access to Food, Clothing, and Shelter	474
			3.2.2 Access to Health Care	475
			3.2.3 Access to Education	475
			3.2.4 Property Rights	475
	4.	Effectiveness of the Inter-American Mechanisms		477
	5.	Other Avenues for Advocacy		481
		5.1	On-Site Visits and Country Reports	481
		5.2	The Inter-American Court Advisory Opinion	482
	6.	Specific Guidance for Advocates		483
		6.1	Framing the Complaint	483
		6.2	Supportive Documentation	483
		6.3	Confidentiality	483
		6.4	Settlements	484
		6.5	Temporary Protective Orders	484
		6.6	Amicus Curiae ("Friend of the Court") Briefs	485
	Bibliography			485

Chapter 7. International Criminal Tribunals: Refugees and Internally Displaced Persons Who May Be Witnesses Before the Tribunals 495

ÅSA RYDBERG AND KELLY ASKIN

1. Introduction 495
2. The Establishment of the *Ad Hoc* Tribunals 497
3. Investigation and Pre-Trial Stages 499
4. The Victims and Witnesses Section 503
5. Trial Phase 504
6. Post-Trial Phase 512
7. Restitution of Property and Victim Compensation 513
8. The International Criminal Court 514

Bibliography 518

Chapter 8. Internationalized Legal Structures and the Protection of Internally Displaced Persons 521

MARCUS COX AND CHRISTOPHER HARLAND

1. Introduction 521

2. Human Rights Issues in Population Displacement 523
     2.1 The Right to Return Home 523
         2.1.1 Property Rights 525
         2.1.2 Personal Security 525
         2.1.3 Discrimination 525
     2.2 Restitution and Transitional Justice 526
  3. Institutional Models for the Protection of IDPs 528
     3.1 Mass Property Title Determination: The Property Commission 529
     3.2 Human Rights Standards Setting: The Human Rights Chamber and Ombudsman 530
     3.3 Human Rights Advocacy: The Federation Ombudsmen 533
     3.4 Managing Housing Stocks: Municipal Housing Offices 535
  4. Assessing the Institutional Choices 536
  Bibliography 538

Appendices

Appendix 1A   Relevant Human Rights Manuals/Resources   541
Appendix 1B   Participants at the Consultation on the International Human Rights Complaints Mechanisms Available to Refugees and Internally Displaced Persons   543
Appendix 1C   The Relevance of the Guiding Principles on Internal Displacement to the Individual Complaints Mechanisms of Human Rights Treaties in the United Nations System   545
Appendix 1D   List of States Parties to Selected Human Rights Treaties   557

Appendix 2A   Contact Information for UN Treaty Bodies   565
Appendix 2B   Information on Complaints to the Human Rights Committee   567
Appendix 2C   CAT Fact Sheet and Complaint   571
Appendix 2D   Information on Complaints to the Committee Against Torture   583
Appendix 2E   Information on Complaints to the Committee on the Elimination of Racial Discrimination   587

Appendix 3A   Contact Information (Charter-Based Bodies)   589
Appendix 3B   Model Complaints   591
              3B1   Working Group on Arbitrary Detention   591

	3B2 Working Group on Enforced and Involuntary Disappearances	594
	3B3 Special Rapporteur on Freedom of Opinion and Expression	598
	3B4 Special Rapporteur on Torture	601
	3B5 Special Rapporteur on Violence Against Women	603
Appendix 3C	Guiding Principles on Internal Displacement	605
Appendix 3D	Principles on the Detention of Asylum-Seekers and Immigrants of the Working Group on Arbitrary Detention	619
Appendix 4A	Requirements for Complaints to the African Commission on Human and Peoples' Rights	623
Appendix 4B	Useful Addresses	625
Appendix 5A	Requirements for Complaints to the European Court of Human Rights	629
Appendix 6A	Sample IACHR Complaint Form	631
Appendix 6B	States Parties to the Organization of American States Charter	635
Appendix 7A	Contact Information (International Criminal Tribunals)	637

Bibliography of Cited International Instruments — 639

Index — 647

About The Procedural Aspects of International Law Institute — 663

Procedural Aspects of International Law Monograph Series — 663

Other PAIL Institute Publications — 665

Acknowledgments

The genesis of this Guide was with Anne Bayefsky, the Director of the Refugee Studies Program at York University, who perceived the need for a specialized manual on human rights mechanisms for the benefit of refugees, asylum-seekers, and internally displaced persons. The Mellon Foundation provided generous funding to assist the project to its completion.

The contributors benefited greatly from a Consultation on International Complaints Mechanisms held at Queen Elizabeth House in Oxford in July 2000, with the assistance of the Refugee Studies Centre. The tireless efforts of Diane Atkinson-Sanford made this Consultation possible. The substantial assistance of Margaret Hauser of the Refugee Studies Centre and from Erika Fortuny, Emily Headings, and Sherilyn Holcombe at the University of Washington is gratefully acknowledged. A number of distinguished experts took time to critique the draft chapters and to offer their valuable advice on the concept and structure of the Guide. The experts participating in the Consultation are listed in Appendix 1-B.

The production of this Guide would not have been possible without the sustained efforts of Sherilyn Holcombe and Perveen Ali, who spent countless hours in the editing process. Assistance with technical editing was also received from Anne Fitzpatrick.

Burns Weston provided valuable editorial guidance on behalf of the Procedural Aspects of International Law Institute. Appreciation is extended also to Christina D. Carmichael, a third-year law student at The University of Iowa and research assistant to Professor Weston, who helped with the proofing and cite-checking of the footnotes.

Finally, I would like to express my deep appreciation to my son Devin and to Yacine Aounallah whose love and support have sustained me during the editing process.

July 2001
Seattle, Washington

Editor's Foreword

Refugees, asylum-seekers, and internally displaced persons typically suffer serious human rights violations. The two characteristics of being a human rights victim and of being forcibly displaced are interrelated in a complex fashion. This Guide situates the forcibly displaced within the international human rights regime, with two aims in mind.

First, the contributors provide detailed maps for navigating the multiple and overlapping international mechanisms that offer redress for human rights violations committed against refugees, asylum-seekers, an internally displaced persons. While these mechanisms are highly relevant to the forcibly displaced, they have not often been invoked by those whose plight is the focus of this Guide. The chapters provide a wealth of procedural guidance as well as a comprehensive analysis of the relevant jurisprudence. The contributors possess substantial expertise regarding the mechanisms they explain, and their chapters are enhanced by their practical knowledge as well as their scholarly acuity. The forcibly displaced and their advocates may draw upon these materials to present complaints or to engage in other types of advocacy. The appendices (whose numbering denotes relevance to specific chapters) offer useful supplementary information and model forms. In this respect, the Guide serves as a specialized companion to Hurst Hannum's GUIDE TO INTERNATIONAL HUMAN RIGHTS PRACTICE (3d ed. 1999), also a publication of the Procedural Aspects of International Law Institute.

Second, this Guide explores the specific human rights concerns of the forcibly displaced with two other sets of readers in mind. Just as refugees, asylum-seekers, and internally displaced persons have not often turned to the international mechanisms, the experts who operate the mechanisms have not often considered the particular interests and experiences of the forcibly displaced. The scenarios presented in Chapter 1 and the analysis of specific international instruments and interpretive jurisprudence in the following chapters are designed to assist the international bodies to provide enhanced protection for refugees, asylum-seekers, and internally displaced persons. Scholars and others interested in the interrelationships between refugee law and human rights law will benefit from the analysis of the international instruments and jurisprudence. The contributors offer candid appraisals of the merits and deficiencies of the various bodies, which will be of interest to those concerned with international organizations and the future of the international human rights regime.

Contributors

Kelly Askin is a Fellow at the Carr Center for Human Rights Policy at Harvard University. Previously she was Acting Executive Director of the War Crimes Research Office of the Washington College of Law at American University in Washington, D.C. She serves as a Legal Adviser and Consultant for the Serious Crimes Division and Sex Crimes Unit of the United Nations Transitional Administration in East Timor and for the International Criminal Tribunal for the former Yugoslavia. She is the author of WAR CRIMES AGAINST WOMEN: PROSECUTION IN INTERNATIONAL WAR CRIMES TRIBUNALS (1997) and co-editor of WOMEN AND INTERNATIONAL HUMAN RIGHTS LAW (3 VOLS. 1999–2001).

Diane Atkinson-Sanford is a Visiting Scholar at the University of Washington and organized the Consultation on the International Complaints Mechanisms Available to Refugees and Internally Displaced Persons in July 2000 at Queen Elizabeth House, Oxford. She was educated at Oxford University and New York University.

Anne Bayefsky is Professor in the Political Sciences Department at York University in Canada and Director of a study on the United Nations Human Rights Treaty System, sponsored by the United Nations High Commissioner for Human Rights and the Ford Foundation. Formerly, she was Director of the Centre for Refugee Studies at York University. Her books include THE UN HUMAN RIGHTS TREATY SYSTEM: UNIVERSALITY AT THE CROSSROADS (2001) and THE UN HUMAN RIGHTS TREATY SYSTEM IN THE 21ST CENTURY (2000). She is co-editor of HUMAN RIGHTS AND FORCED DISPLACEMENT (2000) and Editor-in-Chief of a book series on Refugees and Human Rights for Martinus Nijhoff Publishers. She has published numerous articles on international human rights, the United Nations, international law, jurisprudence, and the constitutional law of Canada.

Marcus Cox is a practitioner in the field of post-conflict reconstruction, and a specialist in the rights of refugees and displaced persons and the question of residential property rights. He has been a legal adviser to the Commission for Real Property Claims and the Office of the High Representative in Bosnia and Herzegovina, as well as a consultant to the UN mission in Kosovo. He is currently the director of the Bosnia project of the European Stability Initiative, a research institute based in Berlin and examining the impact of international programs in South Eastern Europe. He has a Ph.D. in international law from Cambridge University. He has published articles on refugee law and internally displaced persons.

Stephanie Farrior is Professor of Law at Pennsylvania State University, Dickinson School of Law, and has taught at Oxford University and New York University. She has been a Visiting Researcher at Harvard Law School and a Visiting Scholar at Georgetown University Law Center. She formerly served as Legal Director of Amnesty International in London. She is the author of many articles on international human rights law and women's rights. She served as legal expert on human rights missions to Yemen, India, Malawi, and Pakistan, and is active in human rights organizations, including the Center for Justice and Accountability and Human Rights Watch.

Joan Fitzpatrick is Jeffrey & Susan Brotman Professor of Law at the University of Washington School of Law. She is the author of HUMAN RIGHTS IN CRISIS: THE INTERNATIONAL SYSTEM FOR PROTECTING RIGHTS DURING STATES OF EMERGENCY (1994), co-author of INTERNATIONAL HUMAN RIGHTS: LAW, POLICY AND PROCESS (3RD ED. 2001), and co-editor of HUMAN RIGHTS AND FORCED DISPLACEMENT (2000) and several other books. She has published numerous articles on international human rights and refugee law, and has served as a consultant to the United Nations High Commissioner for Refugees. She serves on the Board of Editors of the AMERICAN JOURNAL OF INTERNATIONAL LAW and the Advisory Council and Editorial Board of the Procedural Aspects of International Law Institute.

Camille Giffard is a Member of the Human Rights Centre at the University of Essex and a Ph.D. candidate at the University of Bristol. She has carried out research on customary humanitarian law for the International Committee of the Red Cross, worked as a special assistant to the UN Special Rapporteur on Torture at the Office of the High Commissioner for Human Rights in Geneva, and has taught postgraduate human rights courses. She is the author of THE TORTURE REPORTING HANDBOOK, a joint project of the Foreign and Commonwealth Office of the United Kingdom and the Human Rights Centre, University of Essex.

Karen Hanrahan is engaged in the private practice of law in Washington, D.C., specialized in international finance. She received a J.D. from the University of Washington School of Law and an M.A. in International Politics from American University. She has worked with non-governmental organizations in the field of conflict resolution in the Middle East, Turkey, and North Africa.

Christopher Harland, a Canadian lawyer, is the Head of the Human Rights and Rule of Law Department at the Office of the High Representative in Bosnia and Herzegovina (OHR). The OHR is the lead agency responsible for the co-ordination of civilian implementation of the Dayton Peace Agreement. He is involved in issues such as labor law reform, educational reform, property law, liaison with NGOs, and relations with the International Criminal Tribunal for the former Yugoslavia. He has worked with the United Nations in Central Africa and in Geneva on human rights matters.

Meagan Hrle is a human rights lawyer currently working for the United Nations High Commissioner for Refugees in Bosnia and Herzegovina. Previously, she worked for the Organization for Security and Cooperation in Europe. She received a J.D. from the University of Washington School of Law.

Andrew Langham is engaged in the private practice of law in New York City. He received a J.D. from the University of Washington School of Law. He has written about asylum law in Australia.

Beth Lyon is Assistant Professor and Director of the Farmworker Legal Aid Clinic at the Villanova University School of Law. Formerly she was a Practitioner-in-Residence at the Washington College of Law at American University in Washington, D.C., where she worked on immigration and asylum issues and the Inter-American human rights system; and an attorney with the Lawyers Committee for Human Rights. Her scholarship concerns immigration, asylum, and poverty alleviation. She received a masters degree from the School of Foreign Service and a J.D. from the Law Center at Georgetown University.

Chidi Anselm Odinkalu is Senior Legal Officer for the Africa and the Liberty and Security of Persons programs at Interights (the International Centre for the Legal Protection of Human Rights) in London. He is a Solicitor and Advocate of the Supreme Court of Nigeria. He previously served as a Human Rights Advisor for the UN Observer Mission in Sierra Leone. He serves on the boards of several human rights organizations in Africa and formerly edited the JOURNAL OF HUMAN RIGHTS LAW AND PRACTICE. He is the author of many articles on refugee law and human rights in Africa, and has litigated cases before African regional human rights bodies.

Soren Rottman is engaged in the private practice of law in Seattle, Washington. He received a J.D. from the University of Washington School of Law. He has served as an intern at the Border Association for Refugees from Central America and at the Organization of American States.

Åsa Rydberg is Associate Legal Officer at the International Criminal Tribunal for the former Yugoslavia in The Hague, where she formerly served in the Registry Legal Advisory Section. She received a Masters in Law from Uppsala University in Sweden. She has published articles concerning international criminal law.

Monette Zard is an Associate at the Migration Policy Institute in Washington, D.C. Formerly, she was Ford Foundation Visiting Research Fellow at the Refugee Studies Centre at Oxford University and Senior Coordinator of the International Refugee Program at the Lawyers Committee for Human Rights in New York, where she focused on refugee protection issues in East and West Africa. She worked as a consultant for the Human Rights Watch/Arms Project in Southern Lebanon and with the United Nations High Commissioner for Refugees in the bureau covering Central and South West Africa, the Middle East, and North Africa. She has a law degree from Cambridge University and an M.A. in International Relations from the School of Advanced International Studies at Johns Hopkins University.

Table of Abbreviations

AEC	African Economic Community
BCEAO	Banque Centrale des Etats de l'Afrique de l'Ouest
BOAD	Banque Ouest Africaine de Developpement
CARICOM	Caribbean Community and Common Market
CAT	Committee Against Torture
CEDAW	Committee on the Elimination of Discrimination Against Women
CEDAW OP	Optional Protocol to the Convention on the Elimination of All Forms of Discrimination Against Women
CERD	Committee on the Elimination of Racial Discrimination
CESCR	Committee on Economic, Social and Cultural Rights
CEJIL	Center for Justice and International Law
CID	cruel, inhuman and degrading (treatment or punishment)
CIREFCA	International Conference on Central American Refugees
CPT	European Committee for the Prevention of Torture and Inhuman or Degrading Treatment or Punishment
CRC	Committee on the Rights of the Child
CRM	Conflict Resolution Mechanism (of the Organization of African Unity)
CRPC	Commission for Real Property Claims of Displaced Persons and Refugees
CSW	Commission on the Status of Women
DAW	Division for the Advancement of Women
DESA	Department of Economic and Social Affairs (of the United Nations)
DEVAW	Declaration on the Elimination of Violence Against Women

DRC	Democratic Republic of the Congo
EAC	East African Community
ECHR	European Convention for the Protection of Human Rights and Fundamental Freedoms
ECJ	European Court of Justice
ECOMOG	Economic Community of West African States Monitoring Group
ECOSOC	Economic and Social Council
ECOWAS	Economic Community of West African States
EU	European Union
EUCFR	Charter of Fundamental Rights of the European Union
EWS	Early Warning System
GA	General Assembly
GATT	General Agreement on Tariffs and Trade
HRC	Human Rights Committee
IACHR	Inter-American Commission on Human Rights
IASC	Inter-Agency Standing Committee
ICC	International Criminal Court
ICCPR	International Covenant on Civil and Political Rights
ICESCR	International Covenant on Economic, Social and Cultural Rights
ICTR	International Criminal Tribunal for Rwanda
ICTY	International Criminal Tribunal for the former Yugoslavia
IDP	internally displaced person
IGAD	Inter-Governmental Authority on Development
IGO	inter-governmental organization
ILO	International Labor Organization
IOM	International Organization for Migration
ISDSC	Inter-State Defence and Security Committee (of the Southern African Development Community)
NATO	North Atlantic Treaty Organization
NGO	non-governmental organization
OAS	Organization of American States
OAU	Organization of African Unity
OCHA	Office for the Coordinator of Humanitarian Affairs
ODIHR	Office for Democratic Institutions and Human Rights (of the Organization for Security and Cooperation in Europe)
OHCHR	Office of the High Commissioner for Human Rights
OP	Optional Protocol to the International Covenant on Civil and Political Rights

OPDS	Organ on Politics, Defence and Security (of the Southern African Development Community)
OSCE	Organization for Security and Cooperation in Europe
OTP	Office of the Prosecutor (of the International Criminal Tribunals for the former Yugoslavia and for Rwanda)
PKK	Kurdish Workers Party
SADC	Southern African Development Community
SR	Special Rapporteur
SRSG	Special Representative of the Secretary-General
TEU	Treaty of the European Union
UEMOA	L'Union Economique et Monetaire de l'Afrique de l'Ouest
UN	United Nations
UNHCR	United Nations High Commissioner for Refugees
UNICEF	United Nations Children's Fund
UNTAET	United Nations Transitional Administration for East Timor
USCR	United States Committee for Refugees
VWS	Victims and Witnesses Section (of the Office of the Prosecutor for the International Criminal Tribunals for the former Yugoslavia and for Rwanda)
WG	Working Group
WGAD	Working Group on Arbitrary Detention
WGEID	Working Group on Enforced and Involuntary Disappearances

Chapter 1
The Human Rights of Refugees, Asylum-Seekers, and Internally Displaced Persons: A Basic Introduction

Joan Fitzpatrick

1. Introduction

The forcibly displaced are persons in grave need of international protection, whether they have crossed an international border or are dislocated within their own country. Unfortunately, their access to the international human rights regime is not assured. The purpose of this Guide is to increase that access, by explaining in clear, critical detail the mechanisms that may assist refugees, asylum-seekers, and internally displaced persons (IDPs) to prevent or redress violations of their fundamental human rights. Human rights violations occur before displacement, during flight, and after the victim has found refuge or has returned. All of these situations are addressed in this Guide. The following chapters describe the mechanisms, substantive rights, and remedies provided by the United Nations and regional bodies of relevance to the forcibly displaced. The authors are persons having direct familiarity with the mechanisms they profile, and they address advocacy techniques from a broad perspective.

Many forcibly displaced persons find vital protection under refugee treaties. However, these instruments do not reach all in need. Refugee protection is sometimes viewed as the province of the United Nations High Commissioner for Refugees (UNHCR), and to consist primarily of the prohibition against refoulement (forced return) to persecution. We do not discount the value of protection under refugee treaties and national laws implementing these standards. However, we believe that human rights norms are equally important to forced migrants, and that their advocates should become more familiar with the mechanisms for the international protection of human rights.

Refugees, asylum-seekers, and IDPs require protection against a wide array of human rights violations—they are at risk of losing everything from their lives to their livestock. The United Nations and regional organizations provide important complementary human rights protection to the forcibly displaced, and this Guide offers a pathway into what may at first appear a maze of procedures and institutions.

In recent years, awareness has grown that three formerly distinct legal regimes—human rights law, refugee law, and humanitarian law—must converge substantively and procedurally, to provide more effective redress to victims of forced displacement. As internal wars proliferate and ethnic cleansing assumes a prominent role in military and political strategy, the need to marshal international resources for victims of forced displacement becomes ever more imperative.

Refugees, asylum-seekers, and IDPs, just like the non-displaced, are entitled to the full scope of human rights protection under ratified treaties and customary law. For the sake of brevity and utility, we place primary emphasis on those human rights that are especially imperiled by displacement. This Guide presents a comprehensive explication of the existing jurisprudence on the human rights of those who have been forcibly displaced, as well as precedents that are relevant by analogy. We focus on mechanisms that can be directly invoked by refugees, asylum-seekers, and IDPs. However, we also describe opportunities for advocacy concerning widespread forced displacement and longer-term strategies for improving protection and for reducing risks of displacement.

Thus, in the discussion of human rights treaties within the United Nations system (Chapter 2), we concentrate upon individual complaints mechanisms rather than the review of state reports or inter-state complaints. However, we glean important normative guidance from treaty body report reviews and general comments on treaty interpretation to describe how advocates may use those processes to advance awareness of the rights of the displaced.

With respect to the Charter-based human rights mechanisms of the United Nations (Chapter 3), we concentrate upon those that can be put into operation by the filing of an individual or group complaint. Thus, we do not examine in detail those mechanisms scrutinizing the general situation of human rights in a specific state or analyzing a human rights issue in the abstract. However, we do profile certain Charter-based investigatory initiatives that do not accommodate individual complaints, of which the work of the Secretary-General's Representative on Internal Displacement is the most significant. Our choice of mechanisms to stress is derived from our sense of their relative importance and accessibility to refugees, asylum-seekers, and IDPs.

Our examination of regional human rights systems in Africa, Europe, and the Americas (Chapters 4, 5 and 6) similarly emphasizes procedures that may be initiated or accessed by individuals and their advocates. For example, we stress the Inter-American mechanisms that can be initiated by victims and their representatives, rather than the on-site visits and reports on particular states that are undertaken by the Inter-American Commission on Human Rights (IACHR). However, such reports are of value to refugees, asylum-seekers, and IDPs, since the IACHR's findings may support allegations in individual complaints (whether to the IACHR or to another body) and they may contain interpretive guidance concerning regional norms. The jurisprudence of regional bodies is of interest for refugees, asylum-seekers, and IDPs from outside these regions, because the interpretation of regional treaties can influence understanding of other human rights instruments. These chapters also describe important structural innovations to which broader, long-term advocacy should be addressed.

We also examine in Chapter 7 international criminal tribunals as a source of redress, although victims are unable to initiate prosecutions in the international courts that presently exist or are planned. The forced displacement of civilians, often targeted because of discrimination and hostility based on their identity, is closely linked with many contemporary armed conflicts. Thus, we conclude that international prosecutions are of special relevance to refugees, asylum-seekers, and IDPs and that they should be advised how to induce international authorities to investigate and prosecute their cases. Further, they should have a clear understanding of the important victim and witness protection measures that have been adopted.

We include a case study on the institutions established in Bosnia-Herzegovina, which deal with many complaints related to forced displacement. We believe lessons learned from the work of these bodies may assist the international community in improving response to the plight of refugees, asylum-seekers, and IDPs, especially once mass repatriation commences or when the international community has assumed the task of governing during a transition period. Chapter 8 also explores the possibilities of replicating or improving on the Bosnian model in other post-conflict situations.

2. Who Are Refugees, Asylum-Seekers, and Internally Displaced Persons?

We take a comprehensive approach to forced displacement in this Guide, and attempt to provide assistance for a broad range of victims to access a variety of procedures and institutions. We do not limit our concern to "Convention" refugees, who are defined in the 1951 Convention relating to the Status of Refugees and its 1967 Protocol (in Article 1A(2)) as follows:[1]

> [Any person who] owing to a well-founded fear of being persecuted for reasons of race, religion, nationality, membership of a particular social group or political opinion, is outside the country of his nationality and is unable or, owing to such fear, is unwilling to avail himself of the protection of that country; or who, not having a nationality and being outside the country of his former habitual residence as a result of such events, is unable or, owing to such fear, is unwilling to return to it.

Refugee law is implemented in a manner that differs significantly from international human rights law. No international tribunal exists to adjudicate claims that refugees' rights under the 1951 Convention and 1967 Protocol have been violated. Refugees and asylum-seekers must depend upon national authorities in the state of refuge for protection. Because they have crossed an international border and thus have lost the direct protection of their own sovereign, they can make a special claim on the state of refuge. The United Nations High Commissioner for Refugees (UNHCR) plays a pivotal role in the refugee regime, but UNHCR's functions differ in many respects from those of the human rights bodies we describe in this Guide. UNHCR provides protection and assistance to refugees (both before and after they have been officially recognized) and in some states participates in the determination of refugee status. UNHCR has also taken on an increasing role in providing assistance to IDPs, some of whom are repatriated refugees or failed asylum-seekers.[2] UNHCR also advises states on compliance with the 1951 Convention and 1967 Protocol, and publicly criticizes states that violate their obligations. The Executive Committee of the High Commissioner's Programme also provides important interpretive guidance through its Conclusions.[3] We do not examine the inter-

---

[1] See Bibliography of Cited International Instruments for full citations to these and other international instruments mentioned in this chapter..

[2] UNHCR, *Internally Displaced Persons: The Role of the United Nations High Commissioner for Refugees*, U.N. Doc. EC/SO/SC/INF.2 (2000).

[3] These Conclusions can be found in UNHCR, *Conclusions on the International Protection of Refugees adopted by the Executive Committee of the UNHCR Programme* (1995). More recent Conclusions can be accessed on the UNHCR website, at <www.unhcr.ch>.

national refugee regime in detail in this Guide, but instead focus on human rights bodies that may also assist refugees, asylum-seekers, and IDPs.

The definition of a refugee was broadened in the 1969 Organization of African Unity Convention on the Specific Aspects of Refugee Problems in Africa and the 1984 Cartagena Declaration, adopted at a colloquium in Colombia, to include victims of armed conflict and violence who have been forced to cross a border in order to seek safety. In practice, UNHCR protects and assists many such victims. Moreover, some states have created forms of temporary protection or humanitarian leave to remain for asylum-seekers at grave risk to life or liberty, but unable to establish a well-founded fear of persecution. Refugees within this broader definition are within the scope of our concerns. Indeed, the non-refoulement provisions of human rights treaties are of particular value to such persons, especially in states that narrowly interpret the 1951 Convention refugee definition.

The internally displaced also have a compelling need for international human rights protection. UNHCR's role in protecting IDPs has grown, but the concept of state sovereignty still poses a daunting barrier to assuring their safety and fundamental rights. IDPs remain under the formal protection of their own state, even though officials of that state may have deliberately caused their displacement. Where the state has violated human rights treaties or customary law in its treatment of IDPs, it is subject to international scrutiny and cannot invoke its sovereignty as a shield.

However, in this Guide we are candid about the limits of the human rights system, the paucity of available resources, and the difficulties many victims experience in obtaining international protection. For example, treaties bind only ratifying states, and ratification may be subject to reservations, or the state may choose not to accept optional individual complaints mechanisms. We strive to provide a practical guide to refugees, asylum-seekers, and IDPs on both the value and the flaws of these mechanisms.

Much important theoretical work has been done in recent years to define the rights of IDPs and to improve their protection. Of special relevance are the studies, reports, and Guiding Principles presented by the Secretary-General's Representative to the United Nations Commission on Human Rights.[4] Scholars have also contributed to the

---

[4] *Internally Displaced Persons, Report of the Representative of the Secretary-General, Mr. Francis Deng,* U.N. Doc. E/CN.4/1995/50 (1995); *Internally Displaced Persons, Report of the Representative of the Secretary-General, Mr. Francis Deng, Compilation and Analysis of legal norms,* U.N. Doc. E/CN.4/1996/52/Add.2 (1995); *Report of the*

analysis of the plight of IDPs and have identified legal gaps and practical obstacles.[5] Protection of IDPs falls squarely within the international human rights regime, as no separate refugee-like legal system exists to protect them. The Guiding Principles particularize general human rights principles to the specific situation of the internally displaced.

There has been extensive debate over the definition of IDPs and whether they should enjoy a special protection regime distinct from other victims of human rights who remain within their own states.[6] We do not attempt to resolve these issues but seek to provide a comprehensive guide to the human rights system for all forcibly displaced persons. Those persons and their advocates may select the mechanism that appears best suited to redress their specific concerns, depending upon the causes and consequences of their displacement, and the pertinence of the remedies offered by the body whose authority is invoked.

International humanitarian law is also significant because of the link between displacement and armed conflict. In this Guide, we examine in detail only one aspect of its enforcement—prosecution of war crimes and crimes against humanity in international criminal tribunals. National courts are increasingly important instruments for the prosecution of and imposition of civil liability on perpetrators of gross human rights violations triggering mass displacement, but we do not elaborate on these national measures in this Guide.

3. Identifying Rights at Risk and Framing a Human Rights Claim

Forced displacement is often the result of human rights violations; flight itself can involve additional harms; and, after a person has stopped

---

Representative of the Secretary-General, Mr. Francis Deng, Addendum: Compilation and Analysis of Legal Norms, Part II: Legal Aspects Relating to the Protection Against Arbitrary Displacement, U.N. Doc. E/CN.4/1998/53/Add.1 (1998); *Internally Displaced Persons, Report of the Representative of the Secretary-General, Mr. Francis Deng,* U.N. Doc. E/CN.4/1998/53/Add.2 (1998) (containing the Guiding Principles on Internal Displacement).

[5] ROBERTA COHEN AND FRANCIS M. DENG, MASSES IN FLIGHT: THE GLOBAL CRISIS OF INTERNAL DISPLACEMENT (1998); WALTER KÄLIN, GUIDING PRINCIPLES ON INTERNAL DISPLACEMENT: ANNOTATIONS (2000); Nils Geissler, *The International Protection of Internally Displaced Persons,* 11 INT'L J. REFUGEE L. 451 (1999). Maria Stavropoulou, who worked closely with the Secretary-General's Representative, has described in detail the meandering course of concern with forced displacement in UN human rights bodies in *Displacement and Human Rights: Reflections on UN Practice,* 20 HUM. RTS. Q. 515 (1998).

[6] Geissler, *supra* note 5, at 452–458.

fleeing, he or she may face additional deprivations. Detailed examination of the specific rights that refugees, asylum-seekers, and IDPs can claim is included in each chapter.

This introduction provides a sketch of the rights potentially most relevant to refugees, asylum-seekers, and IDPs, to provide a basic road map to victims and their advocates. To help illustrate how rights are protected under these mechanisms, some of the chapters use six scenarios that illustrate typical problems of forced migrants, and analyze whether a particular human rights mechanism can redress these harms. In these scenarios, we try to indicate how deprivations of civil and political rights are interlinked with violations of economic, social, and cultural rights. Certain mechanisms address only a subset of these rights, and an advocate may find it necessary to invoke several different mechanisms to gain full redress for the victim, or to make the hard choice to seek relief from only one body.[7] We try to distinguish mech-

> **Scenario 1:** Chen has been imprisoned, tortured, and involuntarily expatriated by her government, in retaliation for her religious activities. Several of her family members have been killed by security forces, and her home and personal property were seized. She has managed to cross the border and has been granted refugee status under the 1951 Convention relating to the Status of Refugees. However, the asylum state has denied her request that her two children be permitted to join her. She has had several frightening and violent encounters with the local police who suspect that her presence is illegal. Because of hostility in the local community to persons of her race, she has suffered discrimination in housing and employment.

> **Scenario 2:** Ibrahim has suffered detention without charge or trial and torture in his state of origin because of his activities with an opposition political party. He has fled from his country and is an asylum-seeker. He has been denied employment, health care, and social support in the asylum state, while his status is being determined. He was attacked by hostile members of the local community, while the police refused to come to his aid. When he and a group of other asylum-seekers attempted to conduct a rally in the city square to protest this pattern of violence, they were forced to leave and their banners were destroyed by the police. Recently, Ibrahim was detained pursuant to a new policy on mandatory detention for asylum-seekers. In his interview with refugee status determination officials, he was informed that his claim would be denied

---

[7] *See* Laurence R. Helfer, *Forum Shopping for Human Rights*, 148 U. PENN. L. REV. 285 (1999).

> **Scenario 2:** (continued)
> because he can safely relocate to a different province in his state of origin. However, Ibrahim fears that the security forces will locate him and subject him to renewed torture.

> **Scenario 3:** Maria was forced from her home by security forces who suspected her of aiding an insurgent group. She was beaten and raped and her identity documents were seized. Her oldest son was killed during the eviction. She and her younger children are living in an abandoned warehouse, where they lack adequate food, medical care, and education. Having been evicted from their farmland, they lack any means of employment. They are unable to cross the border to find safety. Without identity documents, Maria is unable to obtain justice from the national courts and she is deprived of political rights. The family is under constant threat both by state security forces and the insurgents because they are loyal to neither side.

> **Scenario 4:** Assume that Chen is part of a mass influx, and that she receives only temporary protection rather than refugee status in the asylum state. This requires her to live in a reception center and forbids her from seeking employment for a period of three years.

> **Scenario 5:** Assume that Ibrahim is part of a mass influx fleeing by boat and that he is intercepted in international waters and returned to his country without consideration of his claim to refugee status.

> **Scenario 6:** Assume that Maria is part of a mass internal displacement. Her 14-year-old son has been forcibly recruited into the military.

anisms that are designed to deal with serious crises involving numerous victims, from situations in which an individual is targeted and seeks reparations or other specific relief.

3.1 The Right to Life and to Physical Integrity

Refugees, asylum-seekers, and IDPs are often at grave risk of losing their lives; many have fled life-threatening danger. Following their displacement, they may be subject to attack, severe health damage, and deprivation of basic subsistence needs. Many of the treaties and declarations profiled in this Guide include guarantees of the right to life, as does international customary law. Some mechanisms, such the Special Rapporteur on Summary and Arbitrary Executions of the UN Commission on Human Rights, focus explicitly upon the right to life. Prosecutions for war crimes and crimes against humanity draw upon norms of humanitarian law intended to protect civilian lives during armed conflict. The prohibition of genocide is also of special relevance, because genocidal violence contributes so greatly to mass displacement.

Certain human rights treaties also protect victims from forced return to a country where they would be at grave risk of potentially life-threatening torture (for example, Article 3 of the 1950 European Convention for the Protection of Human Rights and Fundamental Freedoms and Article 3 of the 1984 Convention Against Torture and Other Cruel, Inhuman or Degrading Treatment or Punishment). Some mechanisms focus upon specific groups of persons whose lives may be imperiled for reasons of identity, such as the Committee on the Elimination of All Forms of Discrimination Against Women, the Special Rapporteur on Violence Against Women, and the Committee on the Rights of the Child.

Refugees, asylum-seekers, and IDPs are often subjected to torture in their states of origin. International and regional instruments prohibit torture and cruel, inhuman, or degrading (CID) treatment or punishment. Some mechanisms specialize in the prohibition of torture, including the Committee Against Torture and the Special Rapporteur on Torture. Rape is now widely recognized as a form of torture and can be the subject of complaints under treaties, several different mechanisms of the UN Commission on Human Rights, and in international criminal prosecutions. Refugee women and children are often exposed to grave risks of rape and other forms of sexual abuse because of their vulnerable situation.

Refugees, asylum-seekers, and IDPs who are detained following their displacement may challenge the conditions of their confinement under the prohibitions of cruel, inhuman, or degrading treatment. The prohibition on torture and CID, like the right to life, is among the non-derogable provisions of human rights law, meaning that it is not subject to suspension even during times of emergency or armed conflict.

3.2 Equality and Non-Discrimination

Refugees are often targeted because they possess an identity that their persecutor will not tolerate. They are victims of prohibited discrimination and may wish to assert their equality rights by invoking the mechanisms profiled in this Guide. Certain bodies focus on non-discrimination, including the Committee on the Elimination of Discrimination Against Women and the Committee on the Elimination of Racial Discrimination. Article 24 of the 1989 Convention on the Rights of the Child provides that states have a special obligation to protect children because of their minority. General human rights treaties, such as the 1969 American Convention on Human Rights and the 1966 International Covenant on Civil and Political Rights, contain important prohibitions on discrimination. Non-discrimination norms are also a recognized part of customary international law.

The displacement of refugees, asylum-seekers, and IDPs can expose them to a risk of discrimination. The right to equality is not absolute, and states may draw distinctions that are reasonable and proportionate to a legitimate state objective. Non-citizens (such as refugees and asylum-seekers) may experience disparate treatment, compared to citizens of the state of refuge, especially with respect to political rights. However, such distinctions can be challenged if arbitrary or disproportionate. Similarly, if IDPs are subjected to disparate treatment within their own state because of their identity or their displacement, they may also invoke non-discrimination provisions to question such treatment.

3.3 Personal Liberty

The prohibition on arbitrary detention, although derogable and subject to limitation, is often of special relevance to refugees, asylum-seekers, and IDPs. Refugees may be confined to closed camps that expose them to human rights violations by governments and armed political groups. Detention of asylum-seekers may be challenged under many of the treaties discussed in this Guide, and it may also be raised before such bodies as the Working Group on Arbitrary Detention of the UN Commission on Human Rights. IDPs may be forced into closed camps by authorities in their state, in violation of the prohibitions on arbitrary detention and freedom of movement.

Refugees, asylum-seekers, and IDPs may also suffer severe deprivations of the right to personal liberty as a result of hostage taking and seizure as human shields during warfare. Non-derogable anti-slavery provisions address the plight of certain refugees, asylum-seekers, and IDPs, including those subjected to contemporary forms of slavery such as forced labor for the military, sex trafficking, or forced prostitution. In addition, forced recruitment into the military is an important human rights issue, especially with respect to children. Both treaty and thematic mechanisms address these issues.

3.4 Other Civil and Political Rights

A wide range of other civil and political rights is of importance to refugees, asylum-seekers, and IDPs. Because they are often politically disfavored, IDPs and repatriated refugees or asylum-seekers may be unable to vote or to participate in the political process.[8] The freedom of expression and association of refugees and asylum-seekers may have been impaired prior to flight, especially when they are members of opposition political parties or disfavored organizations. IDPs may continue to suffer similar violations because of their inability to flee. Freedom of religion may be denied because of intolerance. Even in states of refuge, prejudice against the identity and beliefs of refugees and asylum-seekers may subject them to human rights violations that restrict their ability to express themselves politically, to engage in religious practices, or to associate with others who share their opinions.

3.5 Freedom of Movement

The link between forced displacement and deprivations of freedom of movement is obvious but complex. The essence of freedom of movement is the right to choose one's own residence and to determine where and when one wishes to travel. Freedom of movement rights are subject to reasonable and proportionate limitations to serve a legitimate state interest. Permissible limitations are specified in the various instruments.

An aspect of freedom of movement is the right to seek asylum, which is guaranteed by the 1948 Universal Declaration of Human Rights and certain treaties. This right is threatened by practices such as visa requirements, carrier sanctions, the closing of borders, forced return of asylum-seekers, and confinement in internal "safe zones" which do not deserve that title.

Important non-refoulement norms are included in certain treaties, for example those that prohibit torture. A prohibition by a human rights body on deportation to torture or cruel, inhuman, or degrading treatment or punishment may function as a type of *de facto* asylum, even for those who do not qualify for refugee status.

The right to leave any country and the right to return to one's own country are guaranteed in some human rights treaties, for example the 1966 International Covenant on Civil and Political Rights. The

---

[8] Refugees in a state of asylum generally do not enjoy these political rights, because in many states citizenship is a prerequisite for exercising them. Such restrictions are not ordinarily considered a violation of human rights.

right to leave is of special significance for IDPs who cannot find safety within their own state, and likewise for asylum-seekers. The right to return is of particular value to refugees who wish to repatriate, but whose state of origin rejects or has expatriated them.

Within a state, lawfully present refugees, asylum-seekers, and IDPs have a right to determine their own residence (for example under Article 12(1) of the 1966 International Covenant on Civil and Political Rights), subject to reasonable limitations. The Representative of the Secretary-General on Internal Displacement submitted a detailed report on the right not to be forcibly displaced within the territory of one's own state in 1998.[9] Mechanisms dealing with freedom of movement issues might be invoked to assert such rights.

International humanitarian law addresses the right of civilians not to be forcibly removed from their homes except for reasons of military necessity and only if they are moved to a situation in which their needs are met (for example, in Article 17 of 1977 Protocol II Additional to the Geneva Conventions). Indigenous persons are often at risk of forced displacement and may have close ties to their lands. Their right not to be displaced, except as an exceptional measure, is guaranteed in the International Labor Organization's 1991 Convention concerning Indigenous and Tribal Peoples in Independent Countries, ILO Convention No. 169.

It is less clear that refugees, asylum-seekers, and IDPs have a categorical right to return to their own homes.[10] Many refugees and IDPs suffer permanent dislocation, especially where populations have been divided on ethnic grounds. Some states have repatriated refugees and asylum-seekers even though they are unable to obtain safe access to their former homes, on the basis that they have an internal flight alternative and thus are not in need of international protection. The consequence is that returned refugees and asylum-seekers join the ranks of the internally displaced. A right to compensation for the loss of one's home is of potential significance to such persons, and Chapter 8, describing redress mechanisms in Bosnia-Herzegovina, examines initiatives to provide such compensation.

The opposite situation, forced return to an unsafe home, also implicates human rights norms, though these are more implicit than explicit in the existing instruments. The non-refoulement provisions

---

[9] *See* U.N. Doc. E/CN.4/1998/53/Add.1, *supra* note 4.

[10] *See* Marcus Cox, *The Right to Return Home: International Intervention and Ethnic Cleansing in Bosnia and Herzegovina*, 47 INT'L & COMP. L.Q. 599 (1998); Eric Rosand, *The Right to Return Under International Law Following Mass Displacement: The Bosnia Precedent?*, 19 MICH. J. INT'L L. 1091 (1998).

of human rights treaties such as the 1984 Torture Convention prohibit forced transboundary movement of asylum-seekers who face a substantial risk of such mistreatment. For IDPs, the right to life provisions and the norms against torture and other cruel, inhuman, and degrading treatment or punishment, as well as freedom of movement provisions, can be read to prohibit forced return to unsafe areas within one's own state.

Some of the instruments discussed in this Guide prohibit mass expulsion of non-citizens.[11] Arbitrary and discriminatory expulsions are a particular concern to refugees and asylum-seekers.

3.6 The Right to Family Life

Forced displacement may result in separation of family members, either because of a chaotic situation or because an endangered person must flee persecution or violence, leaving other family members behind. The right to family life is protected under many of the instruments described in this Guide, including the 1966 International Covenant on Civil and Political Rights, the 1950 European Convention, the 1969 American Convention, the 1981 African Charter on Human and Peoples' Rights, and the 1989 Convention on the Rights of the Child. Especially within the European system, the right of foreigners to avoid deportation in order to protect family unity and, to a lesser extent, their right to enter a state for purposes of family reunification have been the subject of a number of cases.[12] Advocates may cite this European practice before other bodies by analogy and seek a similar interpretation of other treaties protecting the family.

International humanitarian law also addresses the needs of separated family members, with provisions on evacuation of children and the identification and protection of orphaned or unaccompanied children. Tracing activities are an aspect of protection of civilians during armed conflict, which is an important function of the International Committee of the Red Cross.

Another dimension of the right to family life is the prohibition on interference with private life and the home, which is addressed in a number of the treaties we examine. Particularly during periods of ethnic cleansing, the invasion of homes by security forces frequently occurs.

---

[11] JEAN-MARIE HENCKAERTS, MASS EXPULSION IN MODERN INTERNATIONAL LAW AND PRACTICE (1995).

[12] *See* Hélène Lambert, *The European Court of Human Rights and the Rights of Refugees and other Persons in Need of Protection to Family Reunion*, 11 INT'L J. REFUGEE L. 427 (1999).

3.7 Social and Economic Rights

Refugees, asylum-seekers, and IDPs face dire situations in which they lack access to sufficient food, clothing, shelter, health care, education, employment, and social support. These deprivations may be addressed in several different ways. The 1966 International Covenant on Economic, Social and Cultural Rights has been interpreted to impose minimum core obligations on ratifying states with regard to all of these needs. However, no individual complaints mechanism yet exists under this treaty. The right to life, however, also has a positive dimension requiring states to take measures to protect life. A number of the treaties, as well as customary law, include right to life provisions.

Where refugees, asylum-seekers, and IDPs are subject to differential denial of access to the means of satisfying their basic needs, non-discrimination norms can be invoked. Some treaties only prohibit discrimination in the enjoyment of rights that they specifically guarantee, while others include a more general proscription against discrimination. Treaties concerning race and gender discrimination and the protection of children may be suitable vehicles for raising discrimination claims on behalf of minority, female, or child refugees, asylum-seekers, and IDPs, because they often guarantee subsistence rights. Moreover, international humanitarian law protects civilians from deliberate starvation as a method of warfare. The special vulnerability of children deprived of proper care is addressed not only in the 1989 Convention on the Rights of the Child but also in more general instruments such as the 1966 International Covenant on Civil and Political Rights.

3.8 The Need for Documents

The seizure of the personal identification documents during the ethnic cleansing in Kosovo illustrates how refugees, asylum-seekers, and IDPs frequently suffer in this regard. While a right to identity documents is often not explicitly addressed in the treaties we describe, it may be asserted indirectly under certain other provisions. The seizure of documents may violate non-discrimination norms, because the victims may suffer the deprivation of fundamental political rights (for example, the rights to vote and to possess a nationality) as well as basic social rights (for example, the rights to education and health care). The right to recognition as a person before the law, another non-derogable right, is closely related to the right to possess necessary identity papers.

The right to family life may also be impaired if parents are unable to register children at birth, or if the lack of a passport prevents family reunification. The rights of the child include guarantees of identity and nationality. The loss of passports may impair freedom of movement, while the loss of ordinary identity documents may expose a person to harsh law enforcement, arbitrary detention, and denial of the right to work.

3.9 Property Rights

Depictions of refugees, asylum-seekers, and IDPs typically are of persons who carry only their most precious pieces of personal property, and sometimes no more than the clothes on their back. For those who have fled, the right to return often signifies the restoration of homes and land. Many are unable to recover their property, because the political and ethnic landscape has shifted during conflict and persecution, or their property was looted or destroyed.

The right to property is not well developed in international human rights law, compared to other rights such as the prohibition on torture. Some regional instruments (for example the 1950 European Convention and the 1948 American Declaration on the Rights and Duties of Man) do protect this right, as does the 1948 Universal Declaration of Human Rights. Treaties addressing race and gender bias forbid discrimination in the enjoyment of property rights for reasons of identity. A right to compensation is developing within international human rights law, but is not yet fully protected.[13] In recognition that deprivation of property is a severe problem for refugees, asylum-seekers, and IDPs, mechanisms have been established in Bosnia-Herzegovina to provide compensation, as noted in Chapter 8. These bodies may provide a valuable precedent for dealing with this aspect of forced displacement.

4. A Basic Primer on the Nature of International Human Rights Law and the Varied Functions of Enforcement Bodies

Advocates must frequently make strategic choices regarding which mechanisms to invoke on behalf of victims. To do so, they must understand differences among the sources of international human rights law and variations in the authority of the bodies that possess enforcement authority.

---

[13] *See Study concerning the right to restitution, compensation and rehabilitation for victims of gross violations of human rights and fundamental freedoms: final report by Mr. Theo Van Boven,* U.N. Doc. E/CN.4/Sub.2/1993/8 (1993).

4.1 The Nature of International Human Rights Law

In general, international law consists of treaties and customary law. However, in the human rights field, certain so-called "soft law" instruments have also had a substantial influence, and they are frequently cited by human rights bodies. "Soft law" can be found in declarations adopted by bodies such as the United Nations General Assembly, bodies of principles, and conclusions adopted at international conferences. For example, the 1948 Universal Declaration of Human Rights, adopted by the General Assembly in 1948, is frequently cited in the decisions and reports of many of the bodies profiled in this Guide. Moreover, such soft law instruments may be evidence that the norm asserted has become a part of customary international law.

4.1.1 Treaties

The law of treaties is complex, and this capsule summary is intended only as a basic initiation. Many terms are used in the titles of treaties—convention, covenant, pact, protocol, etc. These variations do not have any particular significance with respect to the relative weight of the instrument in question.

Perhaps the most important aspect of treaties for the purposes of this Guide is that they bind only states that have ratified, acceded, or succeeded to them.[14] Differing processes exist by which states accept treaty obligations, and national law will set out the necessary procedure.

Sometimes states are willing to accept only a portion of the obligations imposed by a treaty. International law permits states, under certain circumstances, to attach reservations to their acceptance of a treaty's terms. This is a very common and rather controversial practice with respect to human rights treaties. Advocates seeking to file a complaint under a treaty must determine whether the article they wish to invoke applies to the state in question, by first ascertaining whether the state has ratified and then determining if that state has attached a reservation to the article in question. Not all reservations are valid, however. In particular, those that defeat the "object and purpose" of the treaty are void. This is one of the most complex areas of treaty doctrine, and advocates should be warned that mounting an attack on an apparently void reservation would require fairly sophisticated legal

---

[14] Ratification involves signing a treaty and subsequently accepting it according to the constitutional provisions of the state. Accession involves acceptance of the treaty (pursuant to the constitutional requirements of national law) without formal signing. Succession involves the process by which reconfigured states or new regimes are bound by previously accepted treaty obligations.

argumentation. However, some treaty bodies, including the Human Rights Committee and the European Court of Human Rights, have pronounced certain reservations invalid.

Certain treaty obligations are non-derogable, which means that they cannot be suspended even in times of an emergency that threatens the life of the nation. Crises that produce mass forced displacement will sometimes meet that definition. Thus, advocates should take special note of the derogable or non-derogable character of any right they seek to enforce.

Many treaty rights, including such basic rights as freedom of expression, are subject to limitations defined in the specific article. These limitations must be legitimate and proportional. Thus, when asserting a right that is subject to limitations, the advocate must frame an argument that the state's action against refugees, asylum-seekers, or IDPs was not permissible under the specific limitations clause.

Just as treaty obligations can be assumed by states, they can also be renounced. There is a growing trend among states that have been found in violation of human rights treaties to try to renounce the treaty entirely or to withdraw their acceptance of an optional complaints mechanism. If the renunciation does not conform to the treaty's terms, the treaty body may nevertheless grant relief to the complainant. In such circumstances, the state's compliance with the decision may be unlikely.

A major flaw in many of the mechanisms described in this Guide is their lack of binding legal obligation. With a few exceptions (the European Court of Human Rights and the Inter-American Court of Human Rights) judgments or decisions are not technically legally binding on states. International criminal tribunals have the unusual power to adopt judgments that may result in a convicted individual's incarceration, and they may order states to take certain actions, for example to render suspects for trial.

States have both a legal and moral obligation to conform to international human rights law. But no effective system for enforcing many decisions and recommendations yet exists. The human rights system has historically relied primarily on the "mobilization of shame" to secure compliance. States do sometimes respond positively to the non-binding views of human rights bodies (both treaty bodies and those established under the charters of international organizations), to prove their legitimacy to various internal and external audiences (the voting public, other states, international financial institutions, the Security Council, private aid agencies, the media, potential tourists, etc.).

We focus in this Guide on the technical aspects of accessing human rights mechanisms in a particular case involving refugees, asylum-seekers, or IDPs. Advocates with an enduring involvement in the protection of the forcibly displaced should consider a long-term strategy of lobbying violator states to ratify the relevant treaties. All advocates must consider a strategy, when they receive a favorable decision from a human rights body, for inducing the state to comply. Abstract victories are not without value in the mobilization of shame. However, protection and redress for the victim are of paramount importance.

The ensuing chapters will explain in detail the various barriers that victims face in receiving a decision on their claim. Treaties establish various "admissibility" requirements that can be quite complex. Unless the victim complies with all of these requirements, the claim will not proceed and no relief will be obtained.

4.1.2 Customary Law

The process by which customary law is made differs substantially from treaty drafting and ratification. Customary law develops in an evolutionary manner. A customary norm emerges when state practice becomes widespread and consistent and states conform to the rule out of a sense of legal obligation. An advocate seeking to claim a right under customary law must prove that a legal rule actually exists.

In the practice of the Charter-based bodies we examine, customary norms figure largely in their analysis. Such bodies also frequently rely on the "soft law" of declarations, resolutions, and bodies of principles, some of which express binding customary law.

The international criminal tribunals are somewhat different, in that they operate under statutes adopted by the United Nations Security Council or by participating states. However, in defining the crimes punishable by these tribunals, customary human rights law and humanitarian law have been very influential.

Human rights treaties sometimes include provisions that permit the treaty body to take into account the respondent state's other obligations under international law, including customary law.

4.2 Differing Mandates and Powers of Human Rights Mechanisms

The chapters of this Guide describe mechanisms that vary substantially in their substantive and procedural capacities. The treaty bodies derive their mandate from the treaty they enforce. Thus, it is important to examine with care the treaty provisions that define their substantive and enforcement capacities. Many individual complaints mechanisms are optional, which is also true of treaty mechanisms for systematic violations or inter-state complaints. Some bodies have the capacity to issue interpretive guidelines, in the form of advisory opinions or general comments. These bodies may rely on this interpretive precedent when deciding the merits of an individual complaint. Additionally, human rights bodies may make reference to concluding observations they have issued in the context of the review of state reports when deciding individual complaints. Some human rights mechanisms, notably the Inter-American Commission on Human Rights (IACHR), both implement a treaty and possess other powers under the charter of their founding organization. When considering an individual complaint, such a body may draw upon findings and legal interpretations that it has made in the context of a general study of the human rights situation in a particular state. The IACHR also implements the 1948 American Declaration on the Rights and Duties of Man, with respect to OAS member states that have not ratified the 1969 American Convention, and it seeks consistency between interpretations of analogous articles of the Declaration and the American Convention.

The international criminal tribunals so far established derive their authority from the UN Security Council. Thus, their statutes and rules of procedure and evidence must be consulted to determine their authority. They do not condemn states; they either convict a suspect, acquit that person, or dismiss the indictment. They also possess the authority to order reparations.

The Charter-based bodies of the United Nations are generally established by resolution of the United Nations Commission on Human Rights. The scope of their authority is defined in these resolutions, and it differs widely among the thematic mechanisms. The mandate of a particular rapporteur or working group is frequently altered at subsequent sessions of the Commission when the mandate is renewed. Thus, it is important to examine the most recent resolution of the Commission concerning the mechanism in question.

The rapporteurs and working groups of the Commission usually perform several different functions. Some may consider individual communications. The urgent action procedure that some thematic mechanisms implement is of special significance for endangered refugees, asylum-seekers, and IDPs. The capacity to make an on-site visit is typical, but such visits occur only with the consent of the investigated state. Reports are issued following these visits, and they contain useful information for advocates who wish to frame an individual communication to that or another mechanism. Annual reports often include valuable interpretations of the rights these mechanisms were established to protect and to promote.

The mechanisms established in Bosnia-Herzegovina, as described in Chapter 8, represent an interesting new paradigm. They are nation-specific but possess an internationalized aspect. Such mixed national-international bodies are a growing trend, as indicated by negotiations to establish mixed criminal tribunals in Cambodia and Sierra Leone, states that have experienced massive refugee flows and internal displacement as a result of persecution and armed conflict.

Increasingly, the United Nations has assumed primary governing authority in regions where serious human rights violations, resulting in massive forced displacement, have occurred. The UN authorities in Kosovo and East Timor face serious challenges in their effort to establish national institutions to guarantee basic human rights protections for persons of all ethnic, religious, and political identities.

Finally, the role of national institutions in the enforcement of international human rights should not go unnoted, although we do not include a chapter on the incorporation of international law into national law, nor do we survey national remedies.[15] National remedies are significant for at least two reasons. First, one of the common admissibility barriers to international bodies is a requirement that the victim first exhaust domestic (national) remedies. This admissibility requirement is analyzed in the relevant chapters of this manual. Second, victims should ideally be able to obtain protection and redress close to home, in the tribunals and agencies of the state that has violated their rights. The international mechanisms we profile in this Guide exist because that goal has not yet been achieved.

5. Conclusion

This Guide seeks to open underutilized mechanisms for the protection of human rights to advocates for refugees, asylum-seekers, and internally displaced persons. We provide a general discussion of the structure and practice of the seven sets of mechanisms that we have selected as most relevant and promising, because this information is necessary for effective advocacy. At the same time, we particularize our analysis of these bodies to the needs of those who have been forcibly displaced.

Appendix 1A offers information on other manuals that may be of use to advocates for refugees, asylum-seekers, and internally displaced persons. Appendix 1B lists the experts who participated in a consultation in July 2000 on a draft version of this Guide. Appendix 1-C suggests how the Guiding Principles on Internal Displacement can assist

---

[15] The role of national judicial authorities is addressed in Joan Fitzpatrick, *The Role of Domestic Courts in Enforcing International Human Rights Law, in* GUIDE TO INTERNATIONAL HUMAN RIGHTS PRACTICE (HURST HANNUM ED., 3d ed., 1999).

human rights bodies to interpret general human rights norms in a manner appropriate to the specific deprivations experienced by those forcibly displaced. Appendix 1-D lists the states that are parties to the most relevant treaties examined in this Guide.

Bibliography

Books

AMNESTY INTERNATIONAL & THE INTERNATIONAL SERVICE FOR HUMAN RIGHTS, THE UN AND REFUGEES' HUMAN RIGHTS (1997).

COHEN, ROBERTA & FRANCIS M. DENG, MASSES IN FLIGHT: THE GLOBAL CRISIS OF INTERNAL DISPLACEMENT (1998).

GUIDE TO INTERNATIONAL HUMAN RIGHTS PRACTICE (HURST HANNUM ED., 3d ed. 1999).

HENCKAERTS, JEAN-MARIE, MASS EXPULSION IN MODERN INTERNATIONAL LAW AND PRACTICE (1995).

KÄLIN, WALTER, AMERICAN SOCIETY OF INTERNATIONAL LAW & THE BROOKINGS INSTITUTION, GUIDING PRINCIPLES ON INTERNAL DISPLACEMENT (2000).

UNITED NATIONS HIGH COMMISSIONER FOR REFUGEES, CONCLUSIONS ON THE INTERNATIONAL PROTECTION OF REFUGEES ADOPTED BY THE EXECUTIVE COMMITTEE OF THE UNHCR PROGRAMME (1995).

Chapters

Fitzpatrick, Joan, *The Role of Domestic Courts in Enforcing International Human Rights Law*, in GUIDE TO INTERNATIONAL HUMAN RIGHTS PRACTICE 247 (HURST HANNUM ED., 3d ed. 1999).

Journal Articles

Cox, Marcus, *The Right to Return Home: International Intervention and Ethnic Cleansing in Bosnia and Herzegovina*, 47 INT'L & COMP. L.Q. 599 (1998).

Geissler, Nils, *The International Protection of Internally Displaced Persons*, 11 INT'L. J. REFUGEE L. 451 (1999).

Helfer, Laurence R., *Forum Shopping for Human Rights*, 148 U. PENN. L.R. 285 (1999).

Lambert, Hélène, *The European Court of Human Rights and the Right of Refugees and Other Persons in Need of Protection to Family Reunion*, 11 INT'L. J. REFUGEE L. 427 (1999).

Rosand, Eric, *The Right to Return Under International Law Following Mass Displacement: The Bosnia Precedent?*, 19 MICH. J. INT'L L. 1091 (1998).

Stavropoulou, Maria, *Displacement and Human Rights: Reflections on UN Practice*, 20 HUM. RTS. Q. 515 (1998).

UN Documents

Internally Displaced Persons, Report of the Representative of the Secretary-General, Mr. Francis Deng, U.N. Doc. E/CN.4/1995/50 (1995).

Internally Displaced Persons, Report of the Representative of the Secretary-General, Mr. Francis Deng, Compilation and Analysis of legal norms, U.N. Doc. E/CN.4/1996/52/Add.2 (1995).

Internally Displaced Persons—Report of the Representative of the Secretary-General, Mr. Francis Deng, U.N. Doc. E/CN.4/1998/53/Add.2 (1998).

Report of the Representative of the Secretary-General, Mr. Francis Deng, Addendum: Compilation and Analysis of Legal Norms, Part II: Legal Aspects Relating to the Protection Against Arbitrary Displacement, U.N. Doc. E/CN.4/1998/53/Add.1 (1998).

Study concerning the right to restitution, compensation and rehabilitation for victims of gross violations of human rights and fundamental freedoms: final report submitted by Mr. Theo Van Boven, U.N. Doc. E/CN.4/Sub.2/ 1993/8 (1993).

UNITED NATIONS HIGH COMMISSIONER FOR HUMAN RIGHTS, INTERNALLY DISPLACED PERSONS: COMPILATION AND ANALYSIS OF LEGAL NORMS, U.N. Sales No. E.97.XIV.2 (1998).

United Nations High Commissioner for Refugees, Internally Displaced Persons: The Role of the United Nations High Commissioner for Refugees, U.N. Doc. EC/SO/SC/INF.2 (2000).

Internet Souces

United Nations High Commissioner for Refugees, at <http://www.unhcr.ch>.

Chapter 2
Protection Under the Complaint Procedures of the United Nations Treaty Bodies

Anne Bayefsky
Stephanie Farrior
Karen Hanrahan
Andrew Langham

1. Brief Overview of Individual Complaints Under International Human Rights Treaties

International human rights treaties set forth a number of rights relevant to the lives of refugees, asylum-seekers, and internally displaced persons. Yet, forced migrants rarely seek protection under these mechanisms. This chapter will explain the steps that must be taken to access human rights bodies, the rights they implement, and the likelihood that forced migrants will gain concrete protection for their rights. For each of these treaties a committee of independent experts exists to monitor compliance by ratifying states. One procedure by which compliance is monitored is the reporting mechanism, under which states must submit periodic reports to the relevant committee indicating what measures they have taken to implement the treaty provisions. The committee reviews the state's report, poses questions to the government concerned, and issues comments, conclusions, and recommendations, which are public and may be used by advocates in urging the state to comply.

To help provide protection to individuals who suffer from human rights violations, four human rights treaties provide an individual complaint mechanism, either through an optional protocol to the treaty or in the treaty itself: the 1966 International Covenant on Civil and Political Rights (ICCPR);[1] the 1984 Convention Against Torture and Other Cruel,

---

[1] *See* Bibliography of Cited International Instruments for full citations to this and other international instruments mentioned in this chapter.

Inhuman or Degrading Treatment or Punishment (Torture Convention);[2] the 1965 International Convention on the Elimination of All Forms of Racial Discrimination (Racial Discrimination Convention);[3] and the 1979 Convention on the Elimination of All Forms of Discrimination Against Women (Women's Convention),[4] whose 1999 Optional Protocol (CEDAW OP)[5] entered into force in December 2000.

If the state in question has given its consent to use of the relevant individual complaint mechanism, a refugee, asylum-seeker, or an internally displaced person (IDP) who has suffered a human rights abuse in violation of one of these treaties may seek redress by submitting a complaint to the independent committee of experts established by the treaty to monitor state compliance. Upon considering the complaint, the committee may issue its views as to whether the complainant's rights under the treaty have been violated. If it finds a violation, the committee informs the state party and indicates that to be in compliance with the treaty a remedy should be provided. However, the committees do not have authority to compel compliance. It is important to note that the complaint mechanism is not for use against individual perpetrators of human rights violations, and it does not result in a finding of responsibility on the part of individuals. Instead, the purpose of the mechanism is to establish whether the petitioner's rights were violated by the state against which the complaint is lodged.

Each of these treaties contains a number of substantive rights that are relevant to refugees, asylum-seekers, and IDPs, though none of them contains a right to asylum. Of the four treaties, the ICCPR contains the widest range of protected rights, ranging from the right to liberty and security of the person, to a fair hearing before expulsion, to freedom from arbitrary detention, and to the right to be treated with humanity and respect for human dignity when being detained. In the Torture Convention, the provision most frequently applied to refugees and asylum-seekers is the prohibition against returning a person to a state where that person would be in danger of being subjected to torture. The Racial Discrimination Convention provides a number of substantive rights relevant to refugees, asylum-seekers, and IDPs, including rights to work, housing, education, and equality before the law without distinction as to race, color, or national or ethnic origin. The Optional Protocol to the Women's Convention provides a promising

---

[2] *Id.*
[3] *Id.*
[4] *Id.*
[5] *Id.*

forum for female forced migrants seeking redress for human rights violations grounded in sex discrimination.

Among the four UN human rights treaties that have an individual complaint procedure there is a certain amount of overlap regarding the substantive rights protected. For example, protection against cruel, inhuman, or degrading treatment or punishment is included in both the ICCPR and the Torture Convention. The right to equality before the law is declared in the ICCPR, the Racial Discrimination Convention and the Women's Convention. Because of the substantive overlap and because all of the treaties, except the Racial Discrimination Convention, impose a requirement that the same complaint cannot be pending before another international investigatory or settlement procedure, or in some cases has never been considered by another international procedure, it is necessary to consider which committee is the most appropriate mechanism for a particular complaint.

Section 2 of this chapter sets forth the procedural requirements—called "admissibility" requirements—for having a complaint considered by each of the treaty bodies. A treaty body will not examine a petition unless it meets each of these requirements.

Section 3 of this chapter sets out the substantive provisions of each of the treaties most relevant to refugees, asylum-seekers, and IDPs, along with the jurisprudence developed by the treaty-monitoring bodies on the various rights. After setting out and discussing the relevant human rights in each treaty, this part presents a strategic advocacy section that discusses, among other things, the availability of interim measures that may be taken while an individual complaint is awaiting consideration by a treaty body, confidentiality issues, remedies, and legal aid. Section 3 ends with a brief overview of rights and jurisprudence under two additional treaties that, although lacking an individual complaint mechanism, do contain rights of great relevance to refugees, asylum-seekers, and IDPs: the 1989 Convention on the Rights of the Child[6] and the 1966 International Covenant on Economic, Social and Cultural Rights.[7]

Section 4 discusses the strengths and weaknesses of the individual complaints mechanisms under the UN human rights treaties, and Section 5 briefly describes other advocacy possibilities available under those treaties in addition to individual complaints.

---

[6] *Id.*
[7] *Id.*

2. Admissibility Criteria for Individual Complaints

For a human rights treaty body to examine an individual complaint (a "communication") two requirements must be fulfilled: the state in question has formally consented to the procedure and the complaint meets a number of set criteria. These criteria determine whether the committee will deem the complaint "admissible" so as to proceed to an examination of the alleged violation of the petitioner's rights. Two treaty bodies, the Committee Against Torture (CAT) and the Human Rights Committee (HRC), tend to make a simultaneous determination of admissibility and the merits. For all the treaty bodies, it is vitally important to meet every aspect of the admissibility criteria in order to ensure the committee's examination of the merits of a petition. Communications should also be as fully documented as possible, since the written record is often the only source of information the treaty body has regarding the allegations.

What follows is an outline of the criteria for admissibility; the Rules of Procedure for each treaty body should be checked for a complete review of the requirements.[8] Though there are some differences in the admissibility criteria of the four individual complaint mechanisms, the basics of many of the criteria are the same. As for jurisprudence on the criteria, the Human Rights Committee has the most developed body of jurisprudence, and the Committee Against Torture has somewhat less, while Committee on the Elimination of Racial Discrimination (CERD) has little, as it has rendered only 14 decisions in total (ten on cases deemed admissible; four cases deemed inadmissible). There is no jurisprudence to date under the 1999 Optional Protocol to the Women's Convention.

2.1 Jurisdiction Ratione Personae—Eligible Complaints

2.1.1 Who Can Bring a Complaint?

All four of the UN treaty mechanisms require that to bring a complaint one must personally be the victim of a violation of one or more of the rights set out in the treaty. The individual need not be a national of the state against which the complaint is being lodged, but must have been subject to the state's jurisdiction when the events giving rise to the complaint took place (on this latter point, see Section 2.1.2, *infra*).

---

[8] For the *Human Rights Committee Revised Rules of Procedure, see* U.N. Doc. CCPR/C/3/Rev.5 (1997); for the *CAT Rules of Procedure, see* U.N. Doc. CAT/C/3/Rev.3 (1998); for the *CERD Rules of Procedure, see* U.N. Doc. CERD/C/35/Rev.3 (1989); for the *CEDAW Rules of Procedure, see* U.N. Doc. CEDAW/C/ROP (2001).

Each of these treaties allows the actual filing of the complaint by someone acting on behalf of the individual (a lawyer, or, in very limited circumstances, a person who is closely associated with the victim is permitted to communicate on behalf of the victim where the victim is unable to act). "Groups of individuals" who are victims may file under the procedures for two of the treaties—the Racial Discrimination Convention and the Women's Convention—but several individuals have submitted claims together under the Optional Protocol to the ICCPR[9] (First Optional Protocol), without encountering admissibility problems on that ground.

1966 International Covenant on Civil and Political Rights (Optional Protocol, Article 1)

To be a "victim" of a violation of the ICCPR one must be actually and personally affected by the violation.[10] In addition, the complainant must have personal standing. Entities such as organizations, associations, and political parties cannot claim to be a victim of a violation of rights in the ICCPR. Individual members of the organization may submit a communication so long as they have been personally affected by a breach of the Covenant.

---

[9] *See* Bibliography of Cited International Instruments.

[10] A classic example illustrating the concept of "victim" under the Optional Protocol is the *Mauritian Women Case*, in which 20 Mauritian women submitted a communication claiming that their rights were violated by legislation on immigration and deportation under which alien husbands of Mauritian women lost their residence status in Mauritius and were required to apply for a residence permit, whereas the new law did not affect the residence status of alien wives of Mauritian men. *Shirin Aumeeruddy-Cziffra and Nineteen Other Mauritian Women v. Mauritius,* Communication 35/1978, *views adopted on* 9 April 1981, U.N. Doc. A/36/40, at 134. They claimed the legislation constituted discrimination on the basis of sex against Mauritian women, and violated the right to found a family and a home and to be guaranteed equal protection of the courts of law, in violation of *ICCPR* Articles 2, 3, 4, 17, 23, 24, and 26. The Human Rights Committee declared that of the 20 complainants, only the three married petitioners were "victims" of a violation of their rights because they were "actually affected by these laws" by virtue of the precarious and uncertain residence status of their husbands, and the possibility of deportation without judicial review at any time. The Committee determined that the 17 unmarried petitioners, however, could not claim to be "victims " of a breach of the Covenant, because there was no evidence that any of them was actually facing a personal risk of being affected in the enjoyment of her rights by the legislation.

To be considered a victim of a violation, one's own rights must have been violated. Family members of the disappeared have been considered victims in their own right of a violation of the prohibition of torture because of the psychological torture experienced due to the disappearance.[11]

The risk of injury is sufficient to make one a victim if an act or omission by the state that will adversely affect the person's enjoyment of his or her rights is "imminent, for example on the basis of existing law and/or judicial or administrative decision or practice."[12] The risk must be more than theoretical.

The HRC may not rule in the abstract whether legislation or a constitutional interpretation is valid or contravenes the ICCPR. The Committee is authorized only to determine whether an individual has suffered a violation of the treaty. Thus, the individual complainant must show that he or she has been directly affected by the legislation in a manner that contravenes the ICCPR.

If the victim is unable to submit the communication—for example, Maria's son in Scenario Six who had been forcibly recruited—the victim's representative (such as his mother) may submit it.[13] The representative (which may include a nongovernmental organization) acting on behalf of victims "must show that they have real authorization from the victims (or their immediate family) to act on their behalf, that there were circumstances which prevented counsel from receiving such authorization, or that given the close relationship in the past between counsel and the alleged victim it is fair to assume that the victim did indeed authorize counsel to proceed with a communication to the Human Rights Committee."[14]

1984 Torture Convention (Article 22)

Only an individual who claims to be a victim of a violation of the Convention may submit a communication. Relatives of the disappeared

---

[11] *Quinteros v. Uruguay*, Communication No. 107/1981, *views adopted on* 21 July 1983, U.N. GAOR, 38th Sess., Supp. No. 40, U.N. Doc. A/38/40 at 224, ¶ 14 (mother's right to freedom from torture violated because of the psychological torture she endured when her daughter was "disappeared" and the government would give her no information as to her daughter's fate or whereabouts).

[12] *E.W. et al. v. the Netherlands*, Communication No. 429/1990, *decision on admissibility adopted on* 8 April 1993, U.N. GAOR, 48th Sess., Supp. No. 40, U.N. Doc. A/48/40, vol. II at 203, ¶ 6.4; U.N. Doc. CCPR/C/60/D/429/1990.

[13] HRC Rule of Procedure 90. The scenarios are set out in Chapter 1 at 7-8.

[14] *Y. v. Australia*, Communication No. 772/1997, *decision adopted on* 17 July 2000, U.N. Doc. A/55/40, vol. II at 199.

are deemed to be direct victims of torture by virtue of the mental suffering to which they are subjected. Dependents of a torture victim who dies as a result of the torture are entitled to compensation (Article 14(1)), and a state party's failure to fulfill this obligation could make them victims of a violation of the Torture Convention. For example, Chen in Scenario One and Maria in Scenario Three have both had family members killed by security forces. If those deaths involved torture, this CAT rule would apply.

The risk of being subjected to torture may give rise to a communication to the CAT, if the return to another state violates the state party's obligation under Article 3 of the Torture Convention not to return a person to another state where there are substantial grounds for believing that he or she would be personally in danger of being subjected to torture.[15]

If the victim is unable to submit the communication, a relative, a designated representative, or other person acting on behalf of the victim—including an NGO—may submit the communication, but that person must justify acting on the victim's behalf. Failure to provide sufficient justification has led the CAT to reject a communication.

1965 Racial Discrimination Convention (Article 14(1))

As indicated above, not only individuals but also groups of individuals within the jurisdiction of a state party to the Convention may submit a communication to CERD. Organizations do not fall within the term "groups of individuals."

The CERD Rules of Procedure provide that, in "exceptional circumstances," a third person may file the complaint on behalf of the victim(s) if they are unable to file it themselves and the author of the communication justifies his or her acting on the victim's behalf.[16]

1979 Women's Convention (Optional Protocol, Article 2)

Communications may be filed by or on behalf of individuals or groups of individuals under the jurisdiction of a state party to the Convention who claim to be victims of a violation of the Convention. The CEDAW OP specifies that if a communication is submitted "on behalf of" alleged victims, it must be with their consent unless the author can justify acting on their behalf without such consent.

---

[15] For discussion of the jurisprudence on Article 3 of CAT, see *infra* Section 3.2.1.

[16] *CERD Rule of Procedure* 91(b).

30 Human Rights Protection for Displaced Persons

2.1.2 Against Whom May a Complaint Be Filed?

Under all four complaint procedures, a communication may be filed only against states (a) that have consented to the individual complaint procedure and (b) to whose jurisdiction the individual is subject.

The individual complaint procedures are based on a state's consent to use of that procedure. A complaint may be filed against a state that has accepted the individual petition procedure by ratifying the treaty establishing the complaint mechanism or making a declaration under the treaty provision establishing the mechanism. It is against the state that a complaint is filed, not against the particular person or persons who acted or failed to act.

It is important to check whether the state in question has entered a reservation to the substantive right(s) alleged to have been violated. If it has, then no complaint may be lodged, unless the right falls within the group of non-derogable rights in the treaty, rights from which no state party may derogate even in a time of emergency.[17] The very large number of reservations to the 1979 Women's Convention is likely to pose a challenge to bringing complaints under that treaty.

1966 International Covenant on Civil and Political Rights

The state must have ratified both the ICCPR and its First Optional Protocol[18] and the victim must have been subject to the state's jurisdiction when the events giving rise to the complaint occurred.

The victim's presence in the state at the time of the violation is sufficient to establish the state's jurisdiction, even if the victim has since moved to another state.[19] Where a state commits the violation against its own national but outside the state's territory, the victim is still subject to the jurisdiction of the state and thus may bring a complaint against that state. In addition, acts by officials of the state that violate a person's rights outside the territory of the state have been deemed to fall within the territory and jurisdiction requirements, as for example when security forces of a state kidnap and mistreat someone in

---

17   The ICCPR, the only treaty among those addressed in this chapter to include a derogation clause, lists its non-derogable rights and other restrictions on derogation in Article 4.

18   As of March 28, 2001, 98 of the 148 states parties to the ICCPR had ratified the First Optional Protocol.

19   *See for example, Quinteros v. Uruguay*, Communication No. 107/1981, *views adopted on* 21 July 1983, U.N. GAOR, 38th Sess., Supp. No. 40, U.N. Doc. A/38/40 at 216 (petitioner submitted a claim against Uruguay after she had moved to Sweden but was a resident of Uruguay when the violations occurred).

another state,[20] or when Ibrahim (Scenario Five) was intercepted on the high seas.

1984 Torture Convention

The state must have both ratified the Torture Convention and made a declaration under Article 22 accepting the individual complaint procedure, and the complainant must have been subject to the state's jurisdiction.

1965 Racial Discrimination Convention

The state must have both ratified the Racial Discrimination Convention and made a declaration under Article 14 accepting the individual complaint procedure, and the complainant must have been subject to the state's jurisdiction. Regarding this consent, however, it is important to check whether the state has qualified its declaration to provide that it accepts the competence of CERD to consider a communication only if the same matter is not being, or has not been considered, by another procedure of international investigation or settlement, for example by another treaty body (see section 2.7 on concurrent jurisdiction, *infra*).

1979 Women's Convention

The state must have ratified both the Women's Convention and its 1999 Optional Protocol, and the complainant must be under the jurisdiction of that state.

2.2 Jurisdiction Ratione Materiae—What Must the Complaint Concern?

All four of the mechanisms require the complaint to allege a violation of the treaty involved. Both action and inaction on the part of the state may give rise to a complaint. Advocates should be sure to check whether the state has entered a reservation to the provision setting forth the substantive right alleged to have been violated; if a valid reservation has been made, that right may not be the basis of a complaint.

---

[20] *See López Burgos v. Uruguay*, Communication No. 52/1979, U.N. GAOR, 36th Sess., Supp. No. 40, U.N. Doc. A/36/40 at 176.

1966 International Covenant on Civil and Political Rights

In applying the rule that the complaint must allege a violation of a right or rights set forth in the ICCPR, the Committee has determined that the very existence of a law can constitute a violation of a person's rights even if that law has not been enforced against the applicant, if enforcement would constitute a violation.[21]

The failure to act may constitute a violation as well as an act; the substantive articles are read in conjunction with the obligation of states parties in Article 2 to "ensure" the rights in the ICCPR as in the example in which Ibrahim (Scenario Two) was attacked by racist elements and the police failed to come to his assistance. For example, having received information on the extent of trafficking of women into Macau for the purpose of prostitution, the Human Rights Committee said it was "extremely concerned at the inaction by the authorities in preventing and penalizing exploitation of these women and that, in particular, immigration and police officials are not taking effective measures to protect these women and to impose sanctions on those who are exploiting women through prostitution in violation of Article 8 of the Covenant."[22] Although these remarks appear in the context of reviewing a periodic report, they demonstrate the potential for the finding of a violation of rights that could be the subject of an individual complaint in a state that has ratified the First Optional Protocol to the ICCPR.

The failure to enforce laws protecting human rights may also violate the rights of individuals under the ICCPR. The Human Rights Committee, noting the persistence of trafficking in women and prostitution in Macau, stated that, although the Penal Code prohibits organized crime (the main perpetrator of this abuse), the Committee was very concerned about the authorities' failure to take action to protect the victims and recommended action to stamp out trafficking.[23]

1984 Torture Convention

The complaint must allege a violation of the Torture Convention. This may result from action or inaction by the state official. An act of torture constitutes a violation when committed directly by a state agent,

---

[21] See *Toonen v. Australia*, in which the HRC determined that the threat of enforcement of a law criminalizing homosexual acts in and of itself violated the applicant's rights, even though the statute had not been enforced for years. *Nicholas Toonen v. Australia*, Communication No. 488/1992, *views adopted on* 31 March 1994, U.N. Doc. A/49/40, vol. II at 226.

[22] *Concluding Observations of the Human Rights Committee: Portugal (Macau)*, U.N. Doc. CCPR/C/79/Add.77 at para. 13 (5 May 1997).

[23] *Id.*

or when torture takes place "at the instigation of or with the consent or acquiescence of a public official or other person acting in an official capacity." Thus, the failure on the part of a public official to act to prevent torture may be the subject of a complaint. The failure to investigate when there are reasonable grounds to believe an act of torture has been committed (Article 12), the failure to have a complaint of torture promptly and impartially examined (Article 13), and the failure to ensure the right to compensation (Article 14) may also be violations of the Convention.[24]

1965 Racial Discrimination Convention

The complaint must allege a violation of a right or rights set forth in the Convention. Both acts and the failure to act may constitute a violation. CERD has found a violation, for example, when the state did not adequately fulfill its obligation "actively to prosecute cases of alleged discrimination" or conduct a complete and diligent investigation of complaints of racial discrimination in the areas covered in Article 5. Such inaction is contrary to the obligation to provide the individual with effective protection and remedies within the meaning of Article 6.[25]

1979 Women's Convention

The complaint must allege a violation of a right or rights set forth in the Women's Convention. The failure of the state to act to protect against abuse by private actors may violate the Women's Convention and thus be the subject of a communication under the 1999 Optional Protocol.[26]

2.3 Jurisdiction Ratione Temporis—When Must the Alleged Violation Have Occurred?

In general, the treaty bodies will not consider a complaint based on events that took place before the state's consent to the individual complaint procedure entered into force. Note that for complaints of

---

[24] *See* discussion of CAT's comments in this regard in reviewing states parties' periodic reports, *infra* section 3.2.1.

[25] *For example, L.K. v. The Netherlands*, Communication No. 4/1991, *opinion adopted on* 16 March 1993, U.N. GAOR 48th Sess., Supp. No. 18, U.N. Doc. A/48/18 (1993) at 135, ¶¶ 6.3–6.7.

[26] *See* discussion of jurisprudence on substantive rights in the Women's Convention, *infra* Section 3.4.

violations of the 1966 ICCPR and the 1979 Women's Convention, this means the entry into force of the ratification of the relevant Optional Protocol, if subsequent to the state's ratification of the covenant or convention. Each treaty contains a provision indicating when the ratification takes effect for that state, designating a specified period of time after the deposit of the instrument of ratification of the treaty.[27] The applicable period is given below for each treaty.

1966 International Covenant on Civil and Political Rights (First Optional Protocol)

The Covenant enters into force for a given state three months after deposit of the state's instrument of ratification. Although the Human Rights Committee will not consider a complaint if the events giving rise to the complaint took place prior to that entry into force, if the violation is considered to have "continuing effects" after that date, the Committee has stated that it will consider the communication. A violation is deemed to have continuing effects if there is an "affirmation, after the entry into force of the Protocol, by act or by clear implication, of the previous violations of the State party."[28]

1984 Torture Convention

The Convention enters into force on the 30th day after the date of the deposit of the state's instrument of ratification. Thus, the events that give rise to the communication must have occurred at least 30 days after the entry into force for the state in question.

---

[27] The formal completion of ratification takes place when what is called the "instrument of ratification" is deposited with the authority specified in the treaty for such purposes. For each of the treaties discussed in this chapter, the depositary is the Secretary-General of the United Nations.

[28] *Simunek et al. v. the Czech Republic*, Communication No. 516/1992, *views adopted on* 19 July 1995, U.N. GAOR 50th Sess., Supp. No. 40, U.N. Doc. A/50/40, vol. II at 89; U.N. Doc. CCPR/C/54/D/516/1992 (1995) (a prison sentence was not deemed to be the "continuing effect" of an alleged violation of the right to a fair trial, thereby rendering inadmissible a communication in which the trial took place before the First Optional Protocol entered info force in the state concerned). The Committee viewed the sentence as a consequence of the trial but said that consequence must itself constitute a violation of the ICCPR for purposes of admissibility. *See also, J.K. v. Canada*, Communication No. 174/1984, *decision on admissibility adopted on* 7 May 1984, U.N. Doc. A/40/40 at 215.

Protection Under Complaint Procedures of UN Treaty Bodies 35

1965 Racial Discrimination Convention

The Convention enters into force on the 30th day after the date of the deposit of the state's instrument of ratification. Thus, the events that give rise to the communication must have occurred at least 30 days after the entry into force for the state in question.

1979 Women's Convention (1999 Optional Protocol)

The 1999 Optional Protocol to the Women's Convention enters into force three months after the date of deposit of the state's instrument of ratification. The facts that are the subject of a communication must have occurred after the entry into force of the CEDAW OP for the state party concerned "unless those facts continued after that date" (Article 4(2)(v)).

2.4 Jurisdiction Rationae Loci—Where Must the Violation Have Occurred?

For all four mechanisms, the complainant must be subject to the jurisdiction of the state in question for a communication to be admissible.[29] If the events giving rise to the communication took place within the territory of the state party concerned, this requirement is met. However, events that take place outside the territory of the state may still give rise to a complaint if perpetrated by state agents.

1966 International Covenant on Civil and Political Rights

The Human Rights Committee has stated that the reference to "individuals subject to [the state party's] jurisdiction" in the First Optional Protocol "is not to the place where the violation occurred, but rather to the relationship between the individual and the State in violation" of the rights in the ICCPR "wherever they occurred."[30] The HRC applied this in one case, for example, to determine that it had jurisdiction where Uruguayan security forces kidnapped and mistreated the victim in Argentina.

In a series of passport cases, the Human Rights Committee has rejected the argument that the individual is not "subject to" the state

---

[29] The Racial Discrimination Convention uses the term "within" the jurisdiction of the state; the others use "subject to" the jurisdiction.

[30] *López Burgos v. Uruguay*, Communication No. 52/1979, U.N. GAOR, 36th Sess., Supp. No. 40, U.N. Doc. A/36/40 at 182, ¶ 12.2.

party's jurisdiction by virtue of being outside the territory of the state at the time of application, since the issuance of a passport "is clearly within the jurisdiction" of the state authorities.[31] Finding that a passport is a means of enabling an individual to exercise the right under ICCPR Article 12(2) "to leave any country, including his own," the HRC noted that the obligation runs to the state of nationality, thereby demonstrating that the "subject to the jurisdiction" clause is not limited to those within the state's territory.[32]

2.5 Must Domestic Remedies Have Been Exhausted?

The treaty bodies will not consider a communication unless the petitioner has exhausted "all available domestic remedies."[33] This requirement does not preclude admissibility of the communication, however, if the remedies would be ineffective, unavailable, or unreasonably prolonged. During a forced migration crisis, this may be the case because judicial and administrative processes may be severely disrupted. To demonstrate the exhaustion of remedies, the communication should be accompanied by a copy of judgments of the relevant tribunal or official or other body, where they exist. An assertion in a communication that domestic remedies are ineffective, unavailable, or unreasonably prolonged should be accompanied by material or information providing clear support for this assertion. If a treaty body finds that domestic remedies have not been exhausted with respect to one claim in a communication, it may still examine another claim in the same communication with respect to which domestic remedies have been exhausted.

1966 International Covenant on Civil and Political Rights

The First Optional Protocol specifies that the exhaustion of remedies rule does not apply where the application of remedies is "unreasonably prolonged." In addition, the jurisprudence of the Committee

---

[31] *See, for example., Lichtenstein v. Uruguay*, Communication No. 77/1980, *views adopted on* 31 March 1983, U.N. Doc. A/38/40 at 166. For cites to more passport cases, *see* DOMINIC MCGOLDRICK, THE HUMAN RIGHTS COMMITTEE: ITS ROLE IN THE DEVELOPMENT OF THE INTERNATIONAL COVENANT ON CIVIL AND POLITICAL RIGHTS 178–79 (1994).

[32] *Id.*

[33] *OP*, art. 2, 5.2(b); *Torture Convention*, art. 22.5(b); *Racial Discrimination Convention*, art. 14.7(a); *CEDAW OP*, art. 4(1).

establishes that the exhaustion of remedies rule applies only to the extent such remedies are available and effective.[34]

The burden is on complainants to show that they have exhausted all domestic remedies or that domestic remedies are ineffective, unavailable, or unreasonably prolonged. Doubts alone regarding the effectiveness of a remedy, without more, will be insufficient.[35] If the author makes what the Committee considers to be a plausible argument that domestic remedies are not available or effective, it then falls to the state party to give "details of the remedies which it submitted had been available to the author in the circumstances of his case, together with evidence that there would be a reasonable prospect that such remedies would be effective."[36] A general description by the state of the remedies available, without reference to the remedies provided or available in the particular case, is not sufficient to counter a petitioner's claim. The Committee has a history of considering carefully whether a remedy would or would not be effective.

Failure to avail oneself of existing remedies by failing to follow available procedures, for example by missing the filing deadline for an appeal, does not make the domestic remedy "unavailable" within the meaning of the exception to the exhaustion rule,[37] unless there is a reasonable explanation, such as ambiguity in the procedures due to conflicting deadlines.[38]

The argument that no remedy was available has been accepted, for example, where there were special security laws in place thereby rendering the remedy inapplicable *de jure*,[39] and where the state failed to make a decision on an appeal within a reasonable amount of time, thereby rendering the remedy unavailable *de facto*.[40]

---

[34] For more details on the jurisprudence regarding the exhaustion of remedies rule and its exceptions, *see for example* McGoldrick, *supra* note 31, at 187–197.

[35] *See for example, Triboulet v. France,* Communication No. 661/1995, *decision on admissibility adopted on* 29 July 1997, U.N. GAOR, 52nd Sess., Supp. No. 40, U.N. Doc. A/52/40, vol. II at 326, ¶ 6.4; U.N. Doc. CCPR/C/60/D/661/1995.

[36] *Torres Ramírez v. Uruguay,* Communication No. 4/1977, U.N. GAOR, 35th Sess., Supp. No. 40, U.N. Doc. A/35/40 at 122–123, ¶¶ 5 and 9(a).

[37] *See, for example, N.S. v. Canada,* cited in McGoldrick, *supra* note 31, at 242, n.724.

[38] *For example, J.R.T. and W.G. Party v. Canada,* Communication No. 104/1981, *decision on admissibility adopted on* 6 April 1983, U.N. Doc. A/38/40 at 231 (declared inadmissible on other grounds).

[39] *See Santullo (Valcada) v. Uruguay,* U.N. Doc. A/35/40, at 107, and additional cases cited in McGoldrick, *supra* note 31, at 191–192.

[40] *Id.*

In criminal cases, the failure or refusal by the state to permit legal assistance, or to provide it if necessary, may give rise to a claim that a domestic remedy was unavailable, given the requirement in Article 14 of the ICCPR on fair trial guarantees.[41]

Pursuit of a remedy may be deemed futile due to the doctrine of precedent.[42] The HRC has stated, "The local remedies rule does not require resort to appeals that objectively have no prospect of success."[43]

The HRC has concluded the pursuit of domestic remedies would be "unreasonably prolonged" in a case where the domestic appeal process took over four years,[44] and in another case in which the high court had dismissed the case six years earlier but still had not issued a written judgment,[45] but not in one where the delay of six and a half years was caused by the author himself.[46]

1984 Torture Convention

The exhaustion of remedies rule does not preclude admissibility of the communication where the application of the remedies is "unreasonably prolonged or is unlikely to bring effective relief to the person who is the victim of the violation" of the Torture Convention (Article 22(5)(b)). If the author of the communication argues the latter, it is incumbent on the state party to provide sufficient details about the proceedings that would be available in order to make the remedy effective.

The CAT examines closely claims of unavailability or futility of domestic remedies. In *D. v. France*,[47] the CAT found a communication inadmissible despite the author's claim that he was unable to file an appeal with the Conseil d'État because only a lawyer may file appeals and he was not provided with legal aid.[48] He also asserted that he was unable to request cancellation before the administrative court of his

---

[41] *See*, MCGOLDRICK, *supra* note 31, at 193.
[42] *See, for example., Pratt and Morgan v. Jamaica*, Communication Nos. 210/1986 and 225/1987, *views adopted on* 6 April 1989, U.N. Doc. A/44/40 at 226, ¶ 9.3.
[43] *Id.*
[44] *Hammel v. Madagascar*, U.N. Doc. A/42/40 at 130.
[45] *Lenford Hamilton. v. Jamaica*, U.N. Doc. A/49/40 (1994).
[46] *H.S. v. France*, U.N. Doc. A/41/40 at 169.
[47] *D. v. France*, Communication No. 45/1996, *decision on admissibility adopted on* 10 November 1997, U.N. Doc. A/53/44 at 120.
[48] The complainant's denial of asylum had been upheld on appeal by the French Commission de Recours des Réfugiés (Commission of Appeal in Refugee Matters). Once that Commission rejects an appeal, the individual is summoned

summons to leave the country because, he claimed, he never received the summons and was informed of it by the police only after the 24-hour time limit for appeal had expired, an assertion the state argued was unlikely to be the case. The CAT declared the communication inadmissible because the author had not exhausted all available remedies, stating that "[t]he reasons given by the author do not show that such appeals were unlikely to succeed."[49]

In a communication prompted by a deportation order in the same country, the CAT determined that an appeal against the deportation order "would not have been effective or even possible, since it would not have had a suspensive effect and the deportation measure was enforced immediately following notification thereof, leaving the person concerned no time to seek a remedy."[50] Accordingly, the communication was not deemed inadmissible for failure to exhaust domestic remedies.

1965 Racial Discrimination Convention

The exhaustion of remedies rule does not apply where the application of the remedies is "unreasonably prolonged" (Racial Discrimination Convention, Article 14(7)(a)), "unreasonably lengthy or would be unlikely to bring effective relief." (Rule of Procedure 91). If the state party in question disputes the contention of the author of a communication that all available domestic remedies have been exhausted, the state party is required to give details of the effective remedies it claims are still available to the alleged victim in the particular circumstances of the case (Rule 108(7)).

The CERD has been fairly strict in the face of claims of futility of pursuing a domestic remedy. In *D.S. v. Sweden*,[51] a job appointment case, the CERD was not persuaded by the author's argument that she did not avail herself of possible remedies because she thought they

---

to leave within a month of notification of the decision. The individual is entitled to submit an application for judicial review of the Commission's decision with the Conseil d'État, and to request cancellation of the summons to leave before the administrative court. *Id.*

[49] *Id.* at 122.

[50] *Josu Arkauz Arana v. France*, Communication No. 63/1997, *decision adopted on* 9 November 1999, U.N. Doc. A/55/44 at 83, ¶ 6.1; U.N. Doc. CAT/C/23/D/63/1997.

[51] *D.S. v. Sweden*, Communication No. 9/1997, *decision on admissibility adopted on* 17 August 1998, U.N. Doc. CERD/C/390 (compilation of opinions and decisions adopted by the Committee under Article 14 of the Convention) at 102.

would be futile and because of alleged previous negative experiences with both avenues potentially available to her. It was necessary to pursue these remedies, including a complaint before a District Court, even though in a previous job appointment case which she did bring to that court, the court decided that it had no competence to examine decisions on job appointments and dismissed her case as well as her legal aid request. "Mere doubts about the effectiveness of such remedies, or the belief that the resort to them may incur costs, do not absolve a complainant from pursuing them."[52]

In a case in which the author of the communication had not appealed a Federal Court's decision to the High Court of Australia, the CERD considered that, even if this possibility were still open to the author, in light of the length of the appeal process, the circumstances of the case justified the conclusion that the application of domestic remedies had been unreasonably prolonged.[53] The communication was therefore not deemed inadmissible for failure to exhaust domestic remedies.

When the failure to exhaust remedies was the fault of the applicant's lawyer, the CERD has considered the communication inadmissible on the ground that the failure to exhaust cannot be attributed to the state party,[54] at least where the lawyer is privately retained and not supplied by the state.[55] This was so even in a case in which the CERD indicated that the claim of a violation of Article 6 had merit, but found the communication inadmissible because "the author did not provide

---

[52] *Id.* at 107.

[53] *B.M.S. v. Australia*, Communication No. 8/1996, *opinion adopted on* 12 March 1999, U.N. Doc. CERD/C/390 at 51, ¶ 6.2.

[54] In *Barbaro v. Australia*, the CERD concluded that the author had failed to exhaust domestic remedies that were both available and effective, since he could have sought judicial review of the decision, even though the author had not been informed of the availability of this remedy. The CERD noted that the author was legally represented during the hearing and that it was incumbent upon his legal representative to inform him of possible avenues of appeal after the commission's decision. "That the author was not informed of potential judicial remedies by the judicial authorities of South Australia did not absolve him from seeking to pursue avenues of judicial redress; nor can the impossibility to do so now, after expiration of statutory deadlines for the filing of appeals, be attributed to the State party." *Barbaro v. Australia*, Communication No. 7/1995, *decision on admissibility adopted on* 14 August 1997, U.N. Doc. CERD/C/390 at 101, ¶ 10.4.

[55] *C.P. v. Denmark*, Communication No. 5/1994, *decision on admissibility adopted* 15 March 1995, UN Doc. CERD/C/390 at 157–158, ¶ 6.2 (5 June 2000) (compilation of opinions and decisions adopted by the Committee under Article 14 of the Convention).

prima facie evidence that the judicial authorities were tainted by racially discriminatory considerations and since it was the author's own responsibility to pursue the domestic remedies."[56]

1979 Women's Convention

The exhaustion of remedies rule applies "unless the application of such remedies is unreasonably prolonged or unlikely to bring effective relief." (CEDAW OP, Article 4(1)).

2.6 Are There Any Time Limits for Bringing a Complaint?

Three of the four UN treaty mechanisms provide no time limit for bringing a complaint once domestic remedies have been exhausted: the First Optional Protocol to the 1966 ICCPR, the 1984 Torture Convention, and the 1999 Optional Protocol to the Women's Convention. Under the 1965 Racial Discrimination Convention, individual complaints must be submitted within six months after all available domestic remedies have been exhausted, "except in the case of duly verified exceptional circumstances."[57]

2.7 Concurrent and Successive Jurisdiction

If the matter is being or has been considered by another international body, may the treaty body still consider it? Under the 1984 Torture Convention and the 1999 Optional Protocol to the Women's Convention, a communication is not admissible if the same matter has been, or is being, examined under another procedure of international investigation or settlement.[58] The First Optional Protocol to the 1966 ICCPR precludes only simultaneous examination,[59] not subsequent examination. The 1965 Racial Discrimination Convention is silent on the issue.[60]

---

[56] *Id.*

[57] *CERD Rule of Procedure* 91.

[58] *CEDAW OP*, art. 4(2)(a); *Torture Convention*, art. 22(5)(a).

[59] The communication is inadmissible unless "the same matter is not being examined" under another international complaint procedure. *Optional Protocol to ICCPR*, art. 5(2)(a).

[60] *CERD Rule of Procedure* 84(1)(g) authorizes the U.N. Secretary-General to inquire of the petitioner on the CERD's behalf "the extent to which the same matter is being examined under another procedure of international investigation or settlement," but no rule renders the communication inadmissible if such examination is in fact taking place.

1966 International Covenant on Civil and Political Rights

Since only the simultaneous examination of a case by another international body is precluded, the Human Rights Committee may consider cases that have been examined elsewhere once that other examination is no longer pending. Because of this, some states have made a reservation upon ratification of the First Optional Protocol precluding consideration of the same matter if it has been addressed by another international body.[61] On the basis of such reservations, the HRC has declared inadmissible cases that have been examined by the European Commission on Human Rights, whereas it has considered admissible a number of cases submitted to it that had already been examined by the European Commission that were filed against states that had not made such a reservation.[62]

The rule against concurrent jurisdiction applies only if "the same matter" is being examined by another international body. The phrase "the same matter" refers to "identical parties, to the complaints advanced and facts adduced in support of them."[63] However, a two-line reference to someone in a case before the Inter-American Commission on Human Rights that listed hundreds of other persons similarly situated was not considered to place the "same matter" before the Human Rights Committee.[64]

The Human Rights Committee has determined that the "same matter" clause applies only to other individual petition procedures. Thus, the inclusion of the facts of a case in a communication to the Commission on Human Rights under the resolution 1503 procedure as being part of a pattern of gross human rights violations (see, *infra*, Chapter 3 on the UN Charter-based mechanisms) would not preclude the HRC from examining the case, as the Commission examines "situations" and the HRC examines individual cases. The HRC has so far taken a similar view of cases handled by the U.N. Special Rapporteurs and Working Groups (although not without objection by some states). Similarly, mention of the case in material submitted to the HRC under the state periodic reporting procedure does not mean the "same matter" is before the HRC in an individual petition under the First Optional Protocol.

---

[61] These states include Denmark, France, Germany, Iceland, Ireland, Italy, Luxembourg, Malta, Norway, Poland, Romania, the Russian Federation, Slovenia, Spain, and Sweden, as well as Austria whose reservation refers specifically to the procedure established under 1950 European Convention on Human Rights.

[62] *Id.*

[63] *V.Ø. v. Norway*, Communication No. 168/1984, *decision on admissibility adopted on* 17 July 1985, U.N. Doc. A/40/40 at 235, ¶ 4.4.

[64] *Sequeira v. Uruguay*, U.N. Doc. A/35/40 at 127, ¶ 9.

With regard to cases against states parties that have made reservations to subsequent jurisdiction, the HRC has determined that if another international body has declared a petition to be inadmissible and therefore has not addressed the merits of the claim, the same matter has nonetheless "been considered" by that other body, thereby rendering the communication inadmissible.[65]

The HRC has taken a restrictive approach where the facts are the same, but the treaty provisions of the ICCPR and the other treaty being invoked in the concurrent case are somewhat different, and therefore provide arguably different rights.[66] However, in a recent case that appears to mark a divergence from its previous jurisprudence, the HRC determined a communication to be admissible even though the same facts were before another international body, where the communication alleged the violation of a right in the ICCPR that was not protected under the other treaty.[67]

1965 Racial Discrimination Convention

Because the Racial Discrimination Convention is silent on the issue of concurrent and subsequent jurisdiction, some states parties have made reservations with their Article 14 declarations, specifying that the CERD may not consider a communication unless it has ascertained that the same matter has not been, and is not being, examined under another procedure of international investigation or settlement.[68]

2.8   Other Admissibility Criteria

2.8.1   Anonymity

All four UN human rights treaty complaint procedures provide that anonymous communications shall be inadmissible.[69]

---

[65] *See, for example., A.M. v. Denmark*, Communication No. 26/121, *decision on admissibility adopted* on 23 July 1982, U.N. Doc. A/37/40 at 212.

[66] *See, for example., V.O. v. Norway*, Communication. No. 168/1984.

[67] *Casanovas v. France*, Communication No. 441/1990, *views adopted* on 19 July 1994, U.N. Doc. A/49/40 at 131; U.N. Doc. CCPR/C/51/D/441/1990 (1994). For a detailed discussion of cases addressing the "same matter" issue, see Lawrence Helfer, *Forum Shopping for Human Rights*, 148 U. PA. L. REV. 285 (1999) at nn. 71–116 and accompanying text.

[68] Denmark, Finland, Iceland, Italy, Norway, and Sweden.

[69] *OP to ICCPR*, art. 3; *Torture Convention*, art. 22(2); *Racial Discrimination Convention*, art. 14.6(a); *CEDAW OP*, art. 3.

2.8.2 Abuse of the Right to Submit a Communication

Three of the UN human rights treaty complaint procedures provide that a communication shall be considered inadmissible when the treaty body considers it an abuse of the right to submit a communication: the First Optional Protocol to the 1966 ICCPR, the 1984 Torture Convention and the 1999 Optional Protocol to the Women's Convention.[70] The 1965 Racial Discrimination Convention is silent on the matter. Examples of the abuse of right clause would be where there is virtually nothing in the facts or in the law to support the claim in a communication, or where the petitioner submits a communication substantially similar to one already declared inadmissible by that body, with no new facts or circumstances added to support the claim. It is very rare for a communication to be deemed inadmissible on this ground.

2.8.3 Incompatibility with the Provisions of the Treaty—Manifestly Ill-Founded Complaint

The 1984 Torture Convention and First Optional Protocol to the 1966 ICCPR provide that a communication shall be inadmissible if it is "incompatible" with the provisions of the treaty,[71] and the 1999 Optional Protocol to the Women's Convention provides for inadmissibility if the communication is "manifestly ill-founded."[72] The 1965 Racial Discrimination Convention is silent on this issue. In general, if a communication does not meet the requirements of admissibility *ratione personae, materiae, temporis,* and *loci,* it is considered to be "incompatible" with the provisions of the treaty.

2.9 Checklist for Submissions

Communications under all the complaint mechanisms should include the following basic information:

(1) Full name, date and place of birth, address (or address for purposes of correspondence), and nationality of the victim; complaints may not be anonymous;

(2) If filed by a representative, the representative's full name, date and place of birth, address, nationality; a statement of

---

[70] *OP to ICCPR,* art. 3; *Torture Convention,* art. 22(2); *CEDAW OP,* art. 4(2)(d).
[71] *OP to ICCPR,* art. 3; *Torture Convention,* art. 22(2).
[72] *CEDAW OP,* art. 4(2)(c).

the representative's relationship to the victim (accompanied by supporting documentation), and of the reasons for acting on behalf of the victim;

(3) The state party against whom the complaint is being made;

(4) A list of the rights in the relevant treaty alleged to have been violated, with reference to specific articles;

(5) Steps taken to exhaust domestic remedies, or a statement of why such remedies would be inadequate, ineffective, or unreasonably prolonged;

(6) For all but communications to the CERD, a statement that the same matter is not being considered by another international body;

(7) A statement supporting the allegations, including as much factual detail as possible regarding events—in chronological order and with specific dates wherever possible; parties, including names and other information about any officials involved; detailed descriptions of any locations, rooms, buildings, or other sites if relevant; names and addresses of witnesses or others with knowledge relevant to the complaint; and any other pertinent information.

(8) As extensive documentation as possible should accompany the communication, including affidavits of witnesses, medical reports, the text of any relevant laws or regulations, press reports, and copies of any decisions of national courts, tribunals, and authorities;

(9) If the author wishes information in the communication to be kept confidential, including from the state concerned (for example, the author's address), a statement to this effect.

3. Substantive Rights and Significant Jurisprudence

3.1 Protection Under the 1966 International Covenant on Civil and Political Rights

Individual refugees, asylum-seekers, and IDPs may file complaints with the Human Rights Committee alleging that their rights under the 1966 International Covenant on Civil and Political Rights have been violated if the state in question has ratified both the ICCPR and its First Optional Protocol. As of March 28, 2001, 98 of the 148 parties to the ICCPR had ratified the First Optional Protocol.[73] Most of the rights

---

[73] For a list of states parties to the *First Optional Protocol, see* website of the Office of the High Commissioner for Human Rights, at <http://www.unhchr.ch>.

listed in the ICCPR protect refugees, asylum-seekers, and IDPs, but some are more relevant to their protection and welfare than others.

Although the ICCPR is not specifically directed at economic and social rights, two provisions provide recourse in the event of a deprivation of those rights: Article 24 on the protection of the child and Article 26 on equal protection of the law. These articles may be invoked in the protection of the rights to food, clothing, shelter, health care, education, and social support.

> **Rights at a Glance:**
> Rights of most relevance to refugees, asylum-seekers, and IDPs include:
> - The right to life (Article 6);
> - The right to freedom from torture and cruel, inhuman, and degrading treatment (Article 7), which encompasses a right not to be returned to a country where there is a risk of torture;
> - The right to liberty and security (Article 9);
> - The right not to be subjected to arbitrary arrest or detention (Article 9);
> - The right to be treated with humanity and dignity when detained (Article 10);
> - The right to liberty of movement and freedom to choose one's residence (Article 12);
> - The right to leave one's own country (Article 12);
> - Freedom from arbitrary expulsion (Article 13), which could be invoked regarding unfair asylum procedures and unfair hearings before expulsion;
> - The right to recognition as a person before the law (Article 16), which can be particularly relevant if the state has confiscated identification papers;
> - The right to non-interference with family (Article 17), which could be invoked when refugee families are split;
> - Special protection for minors (Article 24);
> - Equal protection of the law (Article 26), which may be invoked along with Article 13 in the case of arbitrary expulsion, and is also relevant when the police do not protect refugees of particular ethnic origin from racist attacks; and
> - For ethnic, religious, and linguistic minorities, enjoyment of their own culture, religion, and language (Article 27).

It should also be emphasized that in addition to the above, refugees, asylum-seekers, and IDPs have the right to non-discriminatory application of the guarantees of the ICCPR (Article 2) and the right to equal protection of domestic law (Article 26). Also important, but perhaps less directly invoked by refugees, asylum-seekers, and IDPs, are the rights regarding arrest and fair trial (Articles 9, 10, and 14), peaceful assembly (Article 21), freedom of thought, conscience, and religion (Article 18), and freedom of association (Article 22).

Because states parties have an obligation under the ICCPR to "ensure" the rights in the Covenant to all within their territory or jurisdiction (Article 2), states must take steps not only against abuses committed directly by state authorities, but also those committed by private individuals.[74] Accordingly, in reviewing state parties' reports, the HRC has considered a failure to take sufficient measures to protect individuals from dangers, such as attacks by racist groups, to be a violation of the ICCPR.

Article 4 of the ICCPR permits states to derogate from some of their obligations but only under very limited circumstances. There must exist a "public emergency which threatens the life of the nation and the existence of which is officially proclaimed." These measures may only be taken to the extent strictly required by the exigencies of the situation, only if they are not inconsistent with the state's other obligations under international law, and only if they are not discriminatory. In Scenario Three, Maria has been forcibly displaced, violating her freedom of movement. The state must show this measure was strictly required.[75] Those rights from which states may never derogate include the right to life; the prohibition of torture and cruel, inhuman, and degrading treatment; the right to recognition as a person before the law; freedom of thought, conscience, and religion; and non-discrimination.[76] Although the conflict and disaster situations that often lead to refugee flows and displaced populations could justify restrictions on certain human rights, they do not necessarily constitute the kind of genuine public emergency that would permit a state to derogate from guaranteed rights under the ICCPR.

To seek guidance in formulating a communication (the term used for an individual complaint) and in assessing the likelihood of success, advocates for forced migrants can look to the jurisprudence of the

---

[74] *See, for example*, HRC, *General Comment No. 20 (Article 7)* in HRI/GEN/1/Rev.4 at 108, on the obligation of states to act against torture and ill treatment whether committed by public authorities or private individuals. *See also, ICCPR*, Article 8 on the prohibition of slavery and the slave trade, which are most often engaged in by private actors rather than state officials.

[75] Francis M. Deng, *Guiding Principles on Internal Displacement, Report of the Representative of the Secretary-General, Mr. Francis Deng*, U.N. Doc. E/CN.4/1998/53/Add.2 (1998) (suggesting a very high threshold for such forced displacement of civilians, even during armed conflict).

[76] *ICCPR*, art. 4(1), (2).

48   *Human Rights Protection for Displaced Persons*

Human Rights Committee. Because the HRC has heard few individual cases to which refugees, asylum-seekers, or IDPs were parties, many of the rights of the ICCPR have not yet been tested in the context of these victims. The jurisprudence outlined below comes not only from the HRC's views on previous individual complaints, but also its General Comments (the committee's authoritative interpretations of the treaty's provisions), and the "concluding observations" that the HRC makes after reviewing state periodic reports. The following summary of jurisprudence is selective; authors of communications may wish to examine all of the relevant ICCPR articles and views before petitioning the HRC.

3.1.1   The Right to Life and Physical Integrity

Internally displaced persons and refugees in flight are frequently at risk of acts of violence, including killings, torture, rape, forcible disappearance, and even genocide. These acts are addressed in a number of articles in the ICCPR.

Right to Life

Article 6 of the ICCPR declares that everyone has the right to life, that this right is to be protected by law, and that no one shall be arbitrarily deprived of life. The state may not derogate from the right to life even in a time of public emergency (Article 4).

Duty Not to Take Life

Article 6(1) states that no one shall be arbitrarily deprived of life. Death that results from torture constitutes a violation of Article 6, as well as death resulting from disappearance. With respect to the death penalty, Article 6 does not prohibit it, but allows it to be imposed only for the "most serious crimes" and to be carried out only pursuant to a final judgement of a competent court. The HRC has examined closely the laws and practices of states that impose the death penalty and has concluded in some instances that they result in the arbitrary deprivation of life in violation of the state's obligations under Article 6.

Positive Obligation to Protect Life

According to the HRC, the obligation of the state to respect and ensure the right to life entails responsibility to take positive measures to protect this right. States must take affirmative steps to prevent arbitrary killing by criminal elements, security forces, and state authorities.[77] This is relevant, for example, where the internally displaced are preyed upon by paramilitary groups or by private criminal gangs who kill in their efforts to control, punish, or intimidate.

Failure to take appropriate measures to prevent a disappearance and to investigate the responsibility for the subsequent killing has been found to constitute a violation of Article 6.[78] Forcibly displaced persons are too frequently victims of massacres and buried in secret graves. The state's failure to investigate their killing violates Article 6.

The right to life provision is also relevant to conditions in refugee camps. The clause has been interpreted to require states to take positive measures to reduce infant mortality and to eliminate malnutrition and epidemics.[79] In the HRC's 1996 concluding observations on Gabon's state report, it expressed particular concern over the appalling conditions in refugee centers and detention camps, particularly those conditions that have caused refugees to die.[80]

The right to life article also has relevance in deportation and refoulement cases. Although the HRC has stated that the death penalty does not *per se* violate Article 6, it has shown a willingness to find a violation of the right to life where sending an individual to a country will foreseeably and necessarily result in the death penalty.[81] The 1998 concluding observations to Tanzania's state report suggest that Article 6 means that no refugee may be returned to another state unless it is certain that, once there, that person will not be executed.[82] However, the HRC has found no violation of Article 6 where the authors were to be deported for committing serious crimes and failed to substantiate their

---

[77] HRC, *General Comment No. 6 (Article 6)* (Sixteenth session, 1982) in HRI/GEN/1/Rev.4 at 85, ¶ 3.

[78] *See, for example,* U.N. Doc. A/43/40 at 190.

[79] HRC, *General Comment No. 6 (Article 6)* (Sixteenth session, 1982) in HRI/GEN/1/Rev.4 at 85–86, ¶ 5.

[80] HRC, *Concluding Observations on the Initial Report of Gabon, adopted on* 6 November 1996, U.N. Doc. A/52/40 at 25, ¶ 132; U.N. Doc. CCPR/C/79/Add.71. *See also, Report of the Human Rights Committee,* A/52/40 (1997) at 80, ¶ 486. States should also take specific and effective measures to prevent the disappearance of individuals and establish effective facilities and procedures to investigate cases of missing persons and enforced disappearances.

[81] *See, generally, A.R.J. v. Australia,* Communication No. 692/1996, *views adopted on* 28 July 1997, 52nd Sess., Supp. No. 40, U.N. Doc. A/52/40, vol. II at 205; U.N. Doc. CCPR/C/60/D/692/1996 (Committee found no Article 6 violation in this case).

[82] HRC, *Concluding Observations on the Third Periodic Report of Tanzania, adopted on* 30 July 1998, U.N. Doc. A/53/40, ¶ 401; U.N. Doc. CCPR/C/79/Add.97 at ¶ 17 (18 Aug. 1998).

claims that the crime was punishable by death in the receiving country.[83] The individual must prove that the crime charged carries a death penalty in the law of the receiving country or, where this is not the case, that other individuals in similar situations have been sentenced to death.

The right to life provision is also relevant to procedures used in detaining unsuccessful asylum seekers who are to be deported. For example, the HRC expressed concern about the risk to life posed by the procedure used by Belgium in the repatriation of some asylum seekers of placing a cushion on the face of the individual to overcome resistance. A Nigerian national had died as a result of this procedure.[84]

Prohibition Against Torture and Cruel, Inhuman, and Degrading Treatment

Article 7 of the ICCPR requires states to protect individuals from torture and cruel, inhuman, and degrading treatment or punishment. Torture is defined to include both mental and physical suffering,[85] and applies to both official and private acts of torture and ill-treatment. Unlike the 1984 Torture Convention, the ICCPR contains no requirement that the torture be for a particular purpose to fall within the prohibition; it is enough that what is inflicted on an individual reach a certain level of severe pain and suffering to constitute torture. When Maria was raped by security forces (Scenario 3), this would amount to torture under Article 7.

---

[83] *See for example, T. v. Australia*, Communication No. 706/1996, *views adopted on* 4 November 1997, U.N. Doc. A/53/40, vol. II at 191–192, ¶¶ 8.4–8.5; U.N. Doc. CCPR/C/60/D/706/1996 (Committee found no Article 6 violation where Australia deported the complainant to Malaysia, where he may face the death penalty, after having served a drug-related sentence of imprisonment in Australia); *A.R.J. v. Australia*, Communication No. 692/1996, *views adopted on* 28 July 1997, 52nd Sess., Supp. No. 40, U.N. Doc. A/52/40, vol. II at 214–215, ¶¶ 6.12–6.13; U.N. Doc. CCPR/C/60/D/692/1996 (Committee found no Article 6 violation where Australia deported the complainant to Iran where he claimed he may face the death penalty for a drug-related crime committed in Australia and where Australia proved he would not necessarily face the death penalty).

[84] The HRC said this person's death illustrated the need for Belgium to "reexamine the whole procedure of forcible deportations." The HRC asked Belgium to report on the results of investigations into the death and on any criminal or disciplinary proceedings. *Concluding Observations, Belgium*, U.N. Doc. CCPR/C/79/Add.99 at ¶ 16 (19 Nov. 1998).

[85] *See General Comment No. 20 (Article 7)* (Forty-fourth session, 1992) in HRI/GEN/1/Rev.4 at 108, ¶ 5.

Refugees, asylum-seekers, and internally displaced persons may be entitled to request positive measures by authorities against unlawful acts by both state and non-state actors. The HRC has indicated that states have the duty to protect all individuals, without discrimination, through legislative or other measures from torture and cruel, inhuman, and degrading treatment or punishment inflicted by individuals acting in their official, unofficial, or private capacities.[86] States must not only prohibit such treatment but must take legislative, administrative, judicial, and other measures in any territory under their jurisdiction to prevent and punish treatment that violates Article 7. Thus, for example, a state violates Article 7 when it fails to take sufficient measures to protect women refugees, asylum-seekers, or IDPs from rape.

The HRC has stated that states must not expose individuals to the danger of torture or cruel, inhuman, or degrading treatment by returning them to another country through expulsion or refoulement.[87] For example, the HRC urged Tanzania to return no refugee to another state unless the government was "certain" that once there, he or she would not be subject to torture or other form of inhuman treatment.[88] However, the HRC will only find a violation if the torture or ill treatment or punishment is a "necessary and foreseeable" consequence of deportation.[89] For example, in *A.R.J. v. Australia* the HRC found that the state would not violate Article 7 by deporting the author to Iran. There, the author claimed that deportation to Iran (where the sentence for his crime was twenty to seventy-four lashes) would expose him to cruel and inhuman treatment.[90] Australia prevailed by showing that

---

[86] *Id.* at 108, ¶ 2.

[87] *See for example, A.R.J. v. Australia*, Communication No. 692/1996, *views adopted on* 28 July 1997, 52nd Sess., Supp. No. 40, A/52/40 at 205; in *Report of the Human Rights Committee, vol.II*, U.N. Doc. CCPR/C/60/D/692/1996; *General Comment No. 20 (Article 7)* (Forty-fourth session, 1992) in HRI/GEN/1/Rev.4 at 109, ¶ 9.

[88] *Concluding Observations on the Third Periodic Report of Tanzania, adopted on* 30 July 1998, A/53/40 at ¶ 401; U.N. Doc. CCPR/C/79/Add.97 at ¶ 17 (18 Aug. 1998).

[89] The Committee found no violation in two cases because the prohibited treatment would not be a necessary and foreseeable consequence of deportation. *See, A.R.J. v. Australia*, Communication No. 692/1996, *views adopted on* 28 July 1997, 52nd Sess., Supp. No. 40, U.N. Doc. A/52/40, vol. II at 215, ¶ 6.14; U.N. Doc. CCPR/C/60/D/692/1996; and *T. v. Australia*, Communication No. 706/1996, *views adopted on* 4 November 1997, U.N. Doc. A/53/40, vol. II at 191–192, ¶ 8.4; U.N. Doc. CCPR/C/60/D/706/1996.

[90] *A.R.J. v. Australia*, Communication No. 692/1996, *views adopted on* 28 July 1997, 52nd Sess., Supp. No. 40, U.N. Doc. A/52/40, vol. II at 205; U.N. Doc. CCPR/C/60/D/692/1996.

there was no evidence of Iran's intention to prosecute the author and that previous individuals deported to Iran for similar reasons were not prosecuted.

Article 7 could also provide a basis for a complaint for the cruel or degrading treatment inflicted on a woman or girl who is trafficked or exploited for prostitution.[91] Even if these practices are not engaged in directly by the state, states parties have responsibility under the ICCPR if they fail to take adequate measures to ensure the rights in the Covenant to people in their territory or jurisdiction, including the Article 7 right not to be subjected to cruel, inhuman, or degrading treatment.

3.1.2   Equality and Non-Discrimination

The equality and non-discrimination provisions in the ICCPR may also protect refugees, asylum-seekers, and IDPs. Articles 2 and 3 establish the obligation of states to ensure to all individuals the rights recognized in the ICCPR, and to ensure the equal right of men and women to these rights. Article 26 provides for equal protection of the law, and is not limited to the rights enumerated in the ICCPR. It is broader than Article 2 and the corresponding article in the 1950 European Convention on Human Rights (ECHR), which limits protection against discrimination to those rights set out in the ECHR (see Chapter Five, and discussion of the broader principle that will apply under ECHR Protocol 12).

Non-Discrimination

Article 2, paragraph 1 obligates each state to respect and to ensure the rights in the ICCPR to all persons subject to its jurisdiction without distinctions such as race, color, sex, language, religion, political or other opinion, national or social origin, property, birth, or other status. The HRC has interpreted the term "discrimination" to imply any distinction, exclusion, restriction, or preference based on any of the grounds listed above that has the purpose or effect of nullifying or impairing the recognition, enjoyment, or exercise by all persons, on an equal footing, of all rights and freedoms.[92] However, the ICCPR's non-discrimination provisions do not necessarily require that all peo-

---

[91]   *See infra* section 3.4.1.
[92]   HRC, *General Comment No. 18 (Non-discrimination)* (Thirty-seventh session, 1989) in HRI/GEN/1/Rev.4 at 104–105, ¶ 7.

ple be treated identically in every instance.[93] Disparate treatment is permissible if the criteria for differentiation are reasonable and objective and if the aim is to achieve a purpose that is legitimate under the ICCPR.[94]

It is not only the nationals of the state concerned whose rights must be protected without discrimination; states parties are obliged to guarantee the rights in the ICCPR to all persons who are in the state's territory or subject to the state's jurisdiction, which would of course include refugees and asylum-seekers. A state violates the ICCPR, for example, if it takes steps to protect its nationals from violent crime but does not protect refugees who are of a different ethnic background. Depending on the facts, the claim could allege a violation of the state's obligation to ensure, without discrimination on the basis of race or ethnic origin (Article 2), the right to security of the person (Article 9), and to freedom from inhuman and degrading treatment (Article 7).

Displaced persons may seek protection under the ICCPR from discrimination based on grounds commonly related to situations of displacement such as race, religion, national or social origin, and lack of property. In addition, displaced persons may be protected against discrimination based on "other status," which is to be interpreted broadly.[95] The fact of being a refugee, asylum-seeker, or IDP qualifies as an "other status" if that status is the basis for the distinction. The complaint could also allege a violation of a substantive right in the ICCPR in conjunction with the Article 2 obligation to ensure the right without discrimination.

Equal Enjoyment of Rights by Men and Women

Article 3 of the Covenant requires states to provide to men and women equally the enjoyment of all the rights of the ICCPR. In 2000, the HRC issued a detailed General Comment on Article 3. Among other things, Article 3 requires states to adopt protective and positive measures that ensure the equal and effective empowerment of women without restriction or derogation.[96] To fulfill Article 3, states must, for example, protect women from rape, abduction, and other forms of gender-based violence, during internal and international conflicts as well

---

[93] *Id.* at 104–105, ¶ 8.

[94] *Id.* at 106, ¶ 13.

[95] *Internally Displaced Persons, Report of the Representative of the Secretary-General, Mr. Francis Deng*, submitted pursuant to Commission on Human Rights Resolution 1995/57, U.N. Doc. E/CN.4/1996/52/Add.2 (1995), ¶ 52.

[96] *See generally* HRC, *General Comment No. 28 (Equality of rights between men and women: article 3)* (29 March 2000), CCPR/C/21/Rev.1/Add.10 (unedited version).

as in peacetime.[97] Furthermore, they must take steps to prevent and protect women against the gender-specific practices and laws that violate ICCPR rights, such as female genital mutilation, forced marriage, polygamy, clothing restrictions, domestic violence, interference with reproductive freedom, unequal divorce requirements, and discrimination against unmarried women, which may cause women to seek asylum.[98] The HRC has yet to be apply these standards in the individual complaint context.

Equality Before the Law and Equal Protection of the Law

Article 26 provides that all persons are equal before the law and are entitled to equal protection of the law without discrimination based on the same grounds enumerated in Article 2. While the scope of protection of Articles 2 and 3 is limited to rights protected by the ICCPR, the scope of Article 26 prohibits discrimination in law or in fact in any field regulated and protected by public authorities.[99] Thus, when a state adopts any type of domestic legislation, it must comply with Article 26.

However, as with the Article 3 equal rights provision, differentiations will be permissible where they are based on reasonable and objective criteria. For example, a law that provides restitution to those who suffered under one regime but not to those who suffered under the previous regime is not *prima facie* discriminatory.[100]

States of Emergency and the Non-Discrimination Requirement

Although states may legitimately derogate from some of their ICCPR obligations in an emergency (Article 4), any such measures may not involve discrimination solely on the ground of race, color, sex, language, religion, or social origin. The test for derogation will always be strict when emergency measures involve discriminatory intentions or consequences. Accordingly, if the state invokes Article 4 as justification to derogate from its ICCPR obligations during a state of emergency by forcibly displacing people, the HRC may strictly scrutinize whether the forced displacement disproportionately and unnecessarily affects a par-

---

[97] *Id.* at ¶ 8.

[98] *Id.*

[99] HRC, *General Comment No. 18 (Non-discrimination)* (Thirty-seventh session, 1989) in HRI/GEN/1/Rev.4 at 104–105, ¶ 12.

[100] *Drobek v. Slovakia*, Communication No. 643/1995, *decision on admissibility adopted on* 14 July 1997, U.N. GAOR, 52nd Sess., Supp. No. 40, U.N. Doc. A/52/40, vol.II at 302, ¶ 6.5; U.N. Doc. CCPR/C/60/D/643/1995.

ticular ethnic group. This might be applied in the individual complaint context either through Article 26 or possibly Article 27.

Rights of Racial, Ethnic, and Linguistic Minorities

Article 27 of the ICCPR protects the right of "racial, ethnic and linguistic minorities" to enjoy their own culture, religion, and language. This article is distinct from, and in addition to, all other rights under the ICCPR.

Article 27 protects individuals, whether or not they are citizens or permanent residents of the state party, who belong to a group and who share a common culture, religion, and/or language. Those who have gained asylum may not be excluded from the affected minority[101] and thereby be precluded from claiming rights under Article 27. The existence of a minority in a given state party must be determined by objective criteria and not by a decision of that state party.[102] So, when Chen (Scenario One) is forbidden to practice her religion in the asylum state, she has suffered a violation of this right.

IDPs may be subjected to restrictions on their rights to practice their religion and to speak their language. If they are a racial, ethnic, or linguistic minority, individuals who have been deprived of these rights may have a claim under Article 27.

The HRC has recognized that culture manifests itself in many forms and may require protection of a particular use of land and resources.[103] Depending on the country situation, this aspect of Article 27 may be relevant to IDPs. Further, the HRC has stipulated that economic activities may be protected by Article 27 if they are an essential element of the culture of a minority.[104] Measures that have a limited impact on a minority's way of life and livelihood do not necessarily violate Article 27.[105] The enjoyment of these rights may require positive legal measures to ensure effective participation of minorities in decisions that affect them.[106] Again, however, the HRC's individual complaint mechanism is yet to be tested in these circumstances.

---

[101] HRC, *Concluding Observations on the Fourth Periodic Report of Germany*, *adopted on* 7 November 1996, U.N. Doc. A/52/40 at ¶ 183.

[102] HRC, *General Comment No. 23 (Article 27)* (Fiftieth session, 1994) in HRI/GEN/1/Rev.4 at 116, ¶ 5.2.

[103] *See generally, Kitok v. Sweden*, Communication No. 197/1985, *views adopted on* 27 July 1988, U.N. GAOR, 43rd Sess., Supp. No. 40, U.N. Doc. A/43/40 at 221.

[104] *Report of the Human Rights Committee*, U.N. GAOR, 52nd Sess., Supp. No. 40, U.N. Doc. A/52/40 at 87, ¶ 516.

[105] *Id.*

[106] HRC, *General Comment No. 23 (Article 27)* (Fiftieth session, 1994) in HRI/GEN/1/Rev.4 at 117, ¶ 7.

3.1.3 Personal Liberty

Arbitrary Arrest or Detention

Article 9 of the Covenant contains a number of provisions to protect against arbitrary arrest and detention. It states that no one may be subjected to arbitrary arrest or detention, any arrested person must be informed at the time of the arrest of the reasons and charges, anyone arrested on a criminal charge must be brought promptly before a judge who will decide the validity of the detention, and a state must compensate improperly detained individuals where it has breached this article.

Article 9 applies to all types of detention whether in criminal cases or not; the HRC has specified that this includes preventive detention[107] and detention in the course of immigration control. The Article 9 guarantee of security of the person also applies to non-detention situations in which an individual is subject to harassment, intimidation, and threats.[108] A detention is "arbitrary" within the meaning of Article 9 not only if it is "against the law." The Committee has said the term "must be interpreted more broadly to include elements of inappropriateness, injustice, lack of predictability and due process of law."[109]

The detention of displaced persons in a closed camp would be permissible under Article 9 only if imposed according to grounds and procedures established by law and not for an arbitrary reason, and if court control of the detention is available.

The HRC has rejected the claim that detention of asylum seekers is *per se* arbitrary. However, individual detentions may be found to be arbitrary. Each claim of arbitrary detention must be evaluated on its facts, and even detention that is initially permissible should not continue beyond the justification for the detention. Illegal entry, for example, may require initial detention for investigation and protection against flight, but should not continue when those needs or risks are no longer present. Accordingly, where a refugee claimant from Cambodia was detained for five years after arriving illegally in Australia, the HRC found that Australia violated Article 9 because it could not justify the pro-

---

[107] HRC, *General Comment No. 8 (Article 9)* (Sixteenth session, 1982) in HRI/GEN/1/Rev.4 at 89, ¶ 4.

[108] *See for example, Oló Bahamonde v. Equatorial Guinea*, Communication No. 468/199, *views adopted on* 20 October 1993, U.N. GAOR, 49th Sess., Supp. No. 40, U.N. Doc. A/49/40, vol. II at 187, ¶ 9.2 (finding a violation of the Article 9 guarantee of security of the person for threats to a non-detained person).

[109] *Mukong v. Cameroon*, Communication No. 458/1991, *views adopted on* 21 July 1994, U.N. GAOR, 49th Sess., Supp. No. 40, U.N. Doc. A/49/40, vol. II at 181, ¶ 9.8.

longed detention.[110] With respect to determining when a detention changes from being lawful to being arbitrary, the HRC has stated that five to eight months detention of asylum seekers may be arbitrary unless the detention is subject to judicial review that results in the release of the person if no lawful purpose is served.[111]

The HRC has also expressed concern over the practice of holding indefinitely those excludable aliens who cannot be deported or extradited.[112]

Rights upon Detention on Criminal Charge

When someone is detained on criminal charges, Article 9 requires that the individual be informed of the charges against him or her. For the right to be meaningful, this could entail providing an interpreter. Where an individual does not speak the language of the arresting authorities, the HRC has stated in one case that the state did not violate Article 9 merely because it did not provide translation of the charges,[113] but in that case the HRC emphasized that the charges were so obvious, translation was not necessary. That approach would not likely apply where the charges are less obvious.

The mere fact that the accused is a foreigner is not a valid justification for automatically detaining the person pending trial.[114]

Treatment of Detainees

Where individuals are deprived of their liberty, Article 10 of the Covenant requires that the state treat them with humanity and respect

---

[110] *A. v. Australia*, Communication No. 560/1993, *views adopted on* 3 April 1997, U.N. GAOR, 52nd Sess., Supp. No. 40, U.N. Doc. A/52/40, vol. II at 143, ¶¶ 9.2–9.4; CCPR/C/59/D/560/1993.

[111] HRC, *Concluding Observations on the Third Periodic Report of Belgium, adopted on* 2 November 1998, U.N. Doc. A/54/40 at ¶ 84; U.N. Doc. CCPR/C/79/Add.99.

[112] HRC, *Concluding Observations on the Initial Report of the United States, adopted on* 6 April 1995, A/50/40 at 56, ¶ 9.2; U.N. Doc. CCPR/C/79/Add.50.

[113] *Griffin v. Spain*, Communication No. 493/1992, *views adopted on* 4 April 1995, U.N. GAOR, 50th Sess., Supp. No. 40, U.N. Doc. A/50/40, vol. II at 56, ¶ 9.2; U.N. Doc. CCPR/C/53/D/493/1992.

[114] *Hill v. Spain*, Communication No. 526/1993, *views adopted on* 2 April 1997, U.N. GAOR, 52nd Sess., Supp. No. 40, U.N. Doc. A/52/40, vol. II at 17, ¶ 12.3 (finding, in a case where the applicants were foreigners who had been refused bail, that in the absence of any justification for their lengthy pre-trial detention, there was a violation of art. 9(3)).

for their human dignity. Article 10 applies to those in detention camps, prisons, correctional institutions, or any other institution or establishment where individuals are held.[115]

Article 10 is relevant to such practices as detaining asylum-seekers together with prisoners, by virtue of its requirement that accused persons be kept separate from convicted persons. The principle underlying this clause applies to the detention of those not accused of criminal wrongdoing. When Finland detained asylum-seekers in public prisons, for example, the HRC recommended in the context of reviewing the state report that the government establish separate areas for asylum-seekers.[116]

The Article 10 requirement that those in detention be treated with humanity and with respect for their dignity complements the Article 7 prohibition on cruel, inhuman, and degrading treatment or punishment. The HRC has explained that Article 10 requires that detained individuals may not be subjected to any hardship or constraint other than that resulting from the deprivation of liberty.[117] The HRC has also pointed out that the standards for appropriate treatment can be found in relevant United Nations documents, such as the Standard Minimum Rules for the Treatment of Prisoners, the Body of Principles for the Protection of All Persons under Any Form of Detention or Imprisonment, and the Code of Conduct for Law Enforcement Officials.[118] The humane treatment of those deprived of their liberty may not be dependent on the material resources available in the state party.[119] Moreover, Article 10 must be applied without distinction as to race, color, sex, language, religion, political or other opinion, national or social origin, property, birth, or other status.[120]

An example of the application of Article 10 to conditions in detention of asylum-seekers appears in the HRC review of a periodic report of the United Kingdom, in which the Committee expressed its concern about conditions relation to Vietnamese asylum-seekers in Hong Kong.[121]

---

[115] HRC, *General Comment No. 21 (Article 10)* (Forty-fourth session, 1982) in HRI/GEN/1/Rev.4 at 110, ¶ 2.

[116] HRC, *Concluding Observations on the Fourth Periodic Report of Finland*, adopted on 6 April 1998, U.N. Doc. A/53/40 at ¶ 270; U.N. Doc. CCPR/C/79/Add.97.

[117] HRC, *General Comment No. 2, supra* note 115 at 110, ¶ 3.

[118] *Id.* at 110, ¶ 5.

[119] *Id.* at 110, ¶ 4.

[120] *Id.*

[121] HRC, *Concluding Observations on the Fourth Periodic Report of the United Kingdom of Great Britain and Northern Ireland (Hong Kong)*, adopted on 1 November 1995, A/51/40 at 15, ¶ 63.

3.1.4 Right to a Fair Trial and Due Process of Law

Article 14 provides individuals with extensive rights to fair trial both in the determination of a "criminal charge" and of a person's "rights and obligations in a suit at law." The due process guarantees in this detailed article do not apply to asylum hearings or extradition proceedings; they apply only to criminal proceedings and to lawsuits.

Article 14 provides for the equality of all persons before the courts and tribunals; the right to a fair and public hearing by a competent, independent, and impartial tribunal established by law and the presumption of innocence. In paragraph 3 it provides a number of important guarantees in the determination of criminal charges, including the right to have the free assistance of an interpreter if the individual cannot understand or speak the language used in court, and the right to have legal assistance, including the assignment of free legal assistance where the accused has insufficient means.

Individuals facing deportation after committing a crime in one country may assert that deportation will result in a violation of their Article 14 procedural rights.[122] They must convince the HRC that the violation of their Article 14 rights in the receiving country would be "the necessary and foreseeable consequence" of deportation to that country.[123] However, where the receiving country has in place tribunals to examine the author's case and provisions for review of conviction and sentencing in the event of a prosecution in that country, the HRC is unlikely to find deportation to violate Article 14. In one case the HRC impliedly suggested that a breach of Article 14 may result if a case is made out that fair trial procedures are not in place in the receiving country.[124]

The HRC has also determined that a retrial in the receiving country of someone deported after being tried and convicted of committing a crime in the sending country does not violate the Article 14(7) prohibition of double jeopardy.[125]

---

[122] *See for example, A.R.J. v. Australia*, Communication No. 692/1996, *views adopted on* 28 July 1997, 52nd Sess., Supp. No. 40, A/52/40, vol. II at 214–215, ¶¶ 6.6, 6.10, 6.15; U.N. Doc. CCPR/C/60/D/692/1996.

[123] *Id.* at 215, ¶ 6.14

[124] *Id.* at 214–215, ¶¶ 6.10 and 6.15.

[125] *Id.* at 213, ¶ 6.4 ("article 14, paragraph 7, of the Covenant does not guarantee *ne bis in idem* with respect to the national jurisdictions of two or more states").

60   Human Rights Protection for Displaced Persons

3.1.5   Right to Vote and Participate in the Political Process

Article 25 guarantees the right and the opportunity "to take part in the conduct of public affairs" as well as to vote, to be elected, and to have access to public service in one's country. In contrast with the other rights in the ICCPR, which are held by all persons in the territory or jurisdiction of the state party, Article 25 guarantees the rights of "every citizen" to political participation. It is important that it specifies that every citizen shall have these rights "without any of the distinctions mentioned in article 2." Thus, no distinction in the enjoyment of these rights is permitted on the basis of, for example, national origin, birth, or other status. The HRC has stated that distinctions between citizens by birth and citizens through naturalization "may raise questions of compatibility with Article 25."[126]

Internally displaced persons, such as Maria in Scenario Three, may face particular difficulties in realizing the right to vote. The HRC has indicated to states parties that "[p]ositive measures should be taken to overcome specific difficulties, such as . . . impediments to freedom of movement which prevent persons entitled to vote from exercising their rights effectively."[127] If a state takes no such measures, it may be seen as having failed in its obligation to ensure Article 25 rights. Furthermore, states must ensure that persons are able to exercise their right to vote without undue influence or coercion, which might inhibit the free expression of the elector's will. Article 25 ensures the independent formation of opinion, and protects against violence or the threat of violence, compulsion, inducement, or manipulation. The failure to protect against coercion or threats may constitute a violation of Article 25.

3.1.6   Freedom of Religion

Article 18 of the Covenant provides for the right to freedom of thought, conscience, and religion. This right is far-reaching and encompasses freedom of thought in all matters, personal conviction, and religion or belief, whether manifested individually or in community with others.[128] Chen clearly suffered a serious violation of this right by her state of origin, in Scenario One. Although states may not derogate from

---

[126] HRC, *General Comment 25 (Article 25)* (Fifty-seventh session, 1996) in HRI/GEN/1/Rev.4 at 125, ¶ 3.

[127] *Id.* at 127, ¶ 12.

[128] HRC, *General Comment No. 22 (Article 18)* (Forty-eighth session) in HRI/GEN/1/Rev.4 at 112, ¶ 1.

this provision, even during times of public emergency, they may limit the right if the restriction meets two requirements: it must be prescribed by law, and be necessary to protect public safety, order, health or morals, or the fundamental rights and freedoms of others.[129] This limitation on the exercise of religion is also relevant to the right of minorities in Article 27 to practice their religion.

The freedom to manifest religion in observance, practice, or worship includes the right to build places of worship, use ritual formulae and objects, display symbols, and observe holidays and days of rest, restrict diet, wear distinctive clothing, participate in rituals associated with certain stages of life, and use a particular language.[130] Individuals may also set up schools and other institutions to teach their religion or beliefs. The HRC has stated that aliens (such as Chen) enjoy this right to the same extent as non-aliens.[131]

3.1.7 Freedom of Expression

Article 19 guarantees the right to freedom of expression. This right includes not only "freedom to impart information and ideas of all kinds," but also freedom to "seek" and "receive" information and ideas. The HRC has stipulated that states must ensure that aliens enjoy freedom of expression to the same extent as non-aliens.[132] Thus, the suppression of Ibrahim's demonstration in Scenario Five violated his rights under Article 19.

Article 19, paragraph 3 emphasizes that freedom of expression carries with it special duties and responsibilities and that, as a consequence, certain restrictions are permitted in order to protect individuals or a community. However, these restrictions must meet two requirements: they must be provided by law, and be necessary for respect of the rights and reputations of others or for the protection of national security, public order, public health, or morals.

The HRC examines very closely any claim by the state that restriction of someone's freedom of expression is justified on the above grounds. In one case, for example, where the state claimed a legitimate objective of safeguarding and strengthening national unity under difficult circumstances, the HRC found a violation of Article 19, noting

---

[129]   *Id.*

[130]   *Id.* at 113, ¶ 4.

[131]   HRC, *General Comment No. 15 (The position of aliens under the Covenant)* (Twenty-seventh session, 1986) in HRI/GEN/1/Rev.4 at 98, ¶ 7.

[132]   *Id.*

that such unity cannot be achieved by attempting to "muzzle advocacy of multi-party democracy, democratic tenets and human rights."[133]

Freedom "from" Expression—Protection from Incitement to National, Racial, or Religious Hatred

Article 20, paragraph 2 requires states to prohibit by law "any advocacy of national, racial or religious hatred that constitutes incitement to discrimination, hostility or violence." Given the hateful vitriol to which refugees and asylum-seekers are subjected in some countries, this article may be invoked in a claim seeking state protection from such hate propaganda.

The HRC has stated that for Article 20 to become fully effective, states must enact laws "making it clear that . . . advocacy as described [in Article 20 is] contrary to public policy and providing for an appropriate sanction in case of violation." The HRC has stated its opinion that Article 20 is "fully compatible with the right of freedom of expression as contained in Article 19, the exercise of which carries with it special duties and responsibilities." In rejecting an individual complaint brought by a Canadian complaining that the government had violated his right to freedom of expression when it cut off his telephone service, which he used to disseminate derogatory messages about Jews, the HRC noted that the opinions that the petitioner sought to disseminate "clearly constitute the advocacy of racial or religious hatred which Canada has an obligation under article 20(2) to prohibit."[134]

3.1.8 Freedom of Association

Freedom of association is protected under Article 22. Although the main aim of this article is to protect the right to form and join trade unions, it is not explicitly restricted to that activity. Aliens enjoy the same right to freedom of association as non-aliens.[135]

---

[133] *Mukong v. Cameroon*, Communication No. 458/1991, *views adopted on* 21 July 1994, U.N. GAOR, 49th Sess., Supp. No. 40, U.N. Doc. A/49/40, vol. II at 181, ¶ 9.7.

[134] Human Rights Committee, *Advocacy of Racial Hatred and Admissibility of a Communication: Case of Taylor v. Canada [communication No. R. 24/104 (1981)*, *reprinted in* 4 HUM. RTS. L. J. 194 (1983).

[135] HRC, *General Comment No. 15 (The position of aliens under the Covenant)* (Twenty-seventh session, 1986) in HRI/GEN/1/Rev.4 at 98, ¶ 7.

3.1.9 Freedom of Movement

One of the ICCPR articles most relevant to refugees, asylum-seekers, and IDPs is Article 12, which addresses freedom of movement, choice of residence, and the rights to leave and to return to one's own country. It guarantees:

- To "everyone lawfully within the territory of a state" the right to liberty of movement and freedom to choose residence within that territory (¶ 1);
- To "everyone" the right to leave "any country, including his own"(¶ 2) and the right not to be arbitrarily deprived of the right to enter one's "own country"(¶ 4).

Paragraphs 1 and 2 are subject to restrictions under paragraph 3, which requires that such restrictions be (a) provided by law; (b) consistent with other rights recognized in the ICCPR; and (c) necessary to protect national security, public order, public health or morals, or the rights and freedoms of others.

The Article 12 right to reside in a place of one's choice within the territory includes protection against all forms of forced internal displacement.[136] It also prohibits states from preventing individuals from entering or remaining in a defined part of the territory.[137]

Freedom of Movement and Residence—A Right of Those Lawfully Within a State

Article 12, paragraph 1 includes the right to liberty of movement and freedom to choose one's residence when one is lawfully within the territory of the state. Whereas citizens are presumably lawfully within the territory of the state, the lawfulness of an alien's status is subject to domestic law, which may limit an alien's ability to enter the state's territory.[138] The HRC has stated that an alien who entered the state illegally, but whose status has been regularized, must be considered to be lawfully within the state's territory.[139]

Those lawfully within the state must be able to move around in the entire territory and establish themselves in a place of their choice.

---

[136] HRC, *General Comment No. 27 (Article 12: Freedom of Movement)* (Sixty-seventh session, 1999) in HRI/GEN/1/Rev.4 at 132, ¶ 7.

[137] *Id.*

[138] *Id.* at 131, ¶ 4.

[139] *Celepli v. Sweden*, Communication No. 456/1991, *views adopted on* 18 July 1994, 49th Sess., Supp. No. 40, U.N. Doc. A/49/40, vol. II, 165, at 169–170, ¶ 9.2.

The enjoyment of this right cannot depend on the purpose or reason for the person wanting to move or to stay in a place.[140]

The state must ensure that Article 12 rights are protected from interference not only by public authorities but also by private individuals.[141] This requirement obligates the state to ensure that the freedom of movement of women is not limited by law or by a woman's relatives.[142] The Committee has stated that measures requiring women to have the consent or the escort of a male person in order to move about or leave a country constitute a violation of Article 12.[143]

Once a person is lawfully within the state, the state must justify any restrictions it places on freedom of movement and on the right to leave, as well as any difference in treatment in this regard between aliens and nationals or between different groups of aliens.[144] Article 12(3) provides that any restrictions upon freedom of movement, as well as on the right to leave a country, are permissible only if they meet three requirements: the restrictions must be provided by law; necessary to protect national security, public order, public health or morals, or the rights and freedoms of others; and consistent with all other rights in the ICCPR, including the principles of equality and non-discrimination. Furthermore, the restrictions must be proportional in the sense that they are appropriate to achieve their protective function, the least intrusive instrument to achieve the result, and proportionate to the interest being protected.[145]

Significantly, the HRC has expressed concern over the many legal and administrative barriers that unnecessarily restrict individuals' freedom of movement[146] and may well find a violation where these barriers are not lifted.

Prohibition on Expulsion from One's Own Country

Under Article 13 of the Covenant, states may expel an alien lawfully within the territory only pursuant to a decision reached in accor-

---

[140] HRC, *General Comment No. 27 (Article 12: Freedom of Movement)* (Sixty-seventh session, 1999) in HRI/GEN/1/Rev.4 at 131, ¶ 5.

[141] *Id.* at ¶ 6.

[142] *Id.*

[143] *Id.* at 134, ¶ 18.

[144] HRC, *General Comment No. 15 (The position of aliens under the Covenant)* (twenty-seventh session, 1986) in HRI/GEN/1/Rev.4 at 98, ¶ 8.

[145] HRC, *General Comment No. 27 (Article 12: Freedom of Movement)* (Sixty-seventh session, 1999) in HRI/GEN/1/Rev.4 at 133, ¶¶ 13, 14 and 15.

[146] *Id.* at 133–134, ¶ 17 ("the Committee has criticized [states'] provisions

dance with law. This provision is aimed at preventing arbitrary expulsions, and applies to all procedures that are aimed at the obligatory departure of aliens, whether described in national law as expulsions or otherwise.[147] Although illegal entrants and aliens who have stayed longer than the law or their permits allow are not protected under Article 13, if the legality of their entry or stay is in dispute, any decision on this point leading to expulsion or deportation should be taken in accordance with Article 13 as well as with the Article 26 requirement of equality before the law.[148]

In the event of a decision to expel, the alien has a right under Article 13 to present reasons against expulsion and to have the case reviewed by a competent authority. For this right to be effective, an alien "must be given full facilities for pursuing [t]his remedy against expulsion."[149] Article 13 allows the state to depart from the review procedure only when required for "compelling reasons of national security."

An example of a state practice that the HRC has found to raise questions under Article 13 is that of relinquishing an expulsion decision to the executive branch of government. In reviewing the periodic report of Sweden, for example, the Committee expressed concern that "the Board of Immigration and the Aliens Appeals Board may in certain cases yield their jurisdiction to the Government, resulting in decisions for expulsion or denial of immigration or asylum status without the affected individuals having been given an appropriate hearing."[150] The HRC recommended that the government review its asylum procedures to limit the possibility of detention and to ensure that a competent authority reviews each case.

Collective or Mass Expulsions

Collective or mass expulsions are not permissible under the Covenant even if national law or decisions permit them. This is evident in the requirement of Article 13 that each alien receives a decision in

---

requiring individuals to apply for permission to change their residence or to seek the approval of the local authorities of the place of destination, as well as delays in processing such written applications.")

[147] HRC, *General Comment No. 15 (The position of aliens under the Covenant)* (Twenty-seventh session, 1986) in HRI/GEN/1/Rev.4 at 98, at ¶ 9.

[148] *Id.*

[149] *Id.* at 98, ¶ 10.

[150] *Concluding Observations on the Fourth Periodic Report of Sweden, adopted on* 1 November 1995, U.N. Doc. A/51/40 at 88, ¶ 18.

his or her case and has full facilities for having his or her expulsion decision reviewed. Additional authority for the prohibition of mass expulsions as well as of forced transfers to other countries lies in Article 12, paragraph 4 (prohibition on arbitrary deprivation of right to enter one's own country), which the HRC has stated implicitly prohibits mass expulsions and transfers.[151]

Article 13 also prohibits states from discriminating between different categories of aliens when making decisions regarding expulsion.[152] In addition, female aliens must be entitled to have their case reviewed and to submit reasons against expulsion that are based on gender-specific violations.

Freedom to Leave One's Country

Perhaps the most important issue for refugees, asylum-seekers, and IDPs addressed in Article 12 of the Covenant is the freedom to leave any country, including one's own. This right, provided in paragraph 2 of Article 12, imposes on the state of nationality the obligation of issuing travel documents, including a passport, even if the individual is residing in another state.[153] The individual has the right to travel abroad, emigrate, and choose the destination state.[154] Because paragraph 2 does not require that the individual be lawfully within the territory, an alien being legally expelled from the state has the right to choose the state of destination, subject to the agreement of that state.[155] Ultimately, the state has the obligation of revising its administrative procedures so they do not unjustifiably restrict the right to leave the individual's own country.

The HRC has criticized at least two states for policies that affected refugees' right to leave other countries. For example, the HRC expressed concern in light of Article 12(2) over France's practice of not allowing refugees to disembark at French ports because it restricted the refugees' ability to leave their own country and prevented them from having their individual claims heard.[156] For similar reasons, the Committee criti-

---

[151] HRC, *General Comment No. 27 (Article 12: Freedom of Movement)* (Sixty-seventh session, 1999) in HRI/GEN/1/Rev.4 at 134, ¶ 19.

[152] HRC, *General Comment No. 15 (The position of aliens under the Covenant)* (Twenty-seventh session, 1986) in HRI/GEN/1/Rev.4 at 98, ¶ 10.

[153] HRC, *General Comment No. 27 (Article 12: Freedom of Movement)* (Sixty-seventh session, 1999) in HRI/GEN/1/Rev.4 at 132, ¶ 9.

[154] *Id.* at 132, ¶ 8.

[155] *Id.; see also,* HRC, *General Comment No. 15 (The position of aliens under the Covenant)* (Twenty-seventh session, 1986) in HRI/GEN/1/Rev.4 at 98, ¶ 9.

[156] HRC, *Concluding Observations on the Third Periodic Report of France, adopted*

cized Austria's sanctions against passenger carriers that carry refugees.[157]

States must also free women from obstacles that may prevent them from traveling, such as a cultural practice or legal requirement that a woman obtain her husband's or other party's consent in order to receive a passport or other travel document.[158]

Right to Return to One's Own Country

Article 12, paragraph 4 establishes the right not to be arbitrarily deprived of the right to enter one's own country. Paragraph 4 includes the right to return after having left one's own country, important for those refugees seeking voluntary repatriation.[159] In its 1992 concluding observations on Burundi's state report, the HRC commended the government's implementation of a policy of voluntary repatriation, resettlement, and social and occupational reintegration of Burundian refugees.[160]

The right in Article 12(4) encompasses the right of individuals to come to their country for the first time if they were born outside the country.[161] It has also been interpreted to imply the right to remain in one's own country.[162]

Whether or not the right to enter one's own country applies to aliens entering a country not of their nationality depends upon the interpretation of the scope of the phrase "his own country."[163] The HRC has interpreted the scope of this phrase to be broader than the concept of "country of nationality" and therefore does not limit it to nation-

---

on 31 July 1997, U.N. Doc. A/52/40 at 64, ¶ 407; U.N. Doc. CCPR/C/79/Add.80.

[157] HRC, *Concluding Observations on the Third Periodic Report of Austria, adopted on* 5 November 1998, U.N. Doc. A/54/40 at 43, ¶ 188; UN Doc. CCPR/C/79/Add.103 (9 November 1998).

[158] HRC, *General Comment No. 28 (Equality of rights between men and women: article 3)* (29 March 2000), CCPR/C/21/Rev.1/Add.10 (unedited version) at ¶ 16.

[159] HRC, *General Comment No. 27 (Article 12: Freedom of Movement)* (Sixty-seventh session, 1999) in HRI/GEN/1/Rev.4 at 134, ¶ 19.

[160] HRC, *Concluding Observations on the Initial Report of Burundi, adopted on* 5 November 1992, U.N. Doc. A/48/40 at ¶ 77; U.N. Doc. CCPR/C/79/Add.9.

[161] HRC, *General Comment No. 27 (Article 12: Freedom of Movement)* (Sixty-seventh session, 1999) in HRI/GEN/1/Rev.4 at 134, ¶ 19.

[162] *Id.*

[163] *See, Stewart v. Canada*, Communication No. 538/1993, *views adopted on* 1 November 1996, 52nd Sess., Supp. No. 40, U.N. Doc. A/52/40, vol. II at 58, ¶ 12.4; U.N. Doc. CCPR/C/60/D/538/1993 (1997).

ality acquired at birth or by conferral.[164] It includes an individual whose special ties or relation to a state render the individual more than a mere alien.[165] For example, the phrase may include nationals stripped of their nationality, individuals whose country of nationality has been incorporated into another state, or individuals whose nationality has been arbitrarily denied.[166] The phrase may also permit inclusion of stateless persons arbitrarily deprived of the right to acquire the nationality of the country in which they have resided for a long time.[167]

Freedom to Enter Another Country

The Covenant does not recognize a right to enter another country. Instead, it is for each state to determine whom to admit.[168]

The Right to Asylum

The ICCPR does not include a right to asylum or a right to seek asylum. The HRC has found inadmissible *ratione materiae* an individual complaint on the ground that the ICCPR does not protect a right to asylum.[169]

3.1.10 The Right to Family and Private Life

The ICCPR provides individuals with rights to family and privacy in two articles. Article 17 protects individuals against arbitrary or unlawful interference with privacy, family, home, or correspondence, and attacks on an individual's honor or reputation. Article 23 provides certain rights with respect to the family.

Duty Not to Interfere with Family or Private Life

Refugees, asylum-seekers, and IDPs frequently lose their homes and family members. Forced displacement and detention frequently separate families, as do other forms of state action or inaction that lead

---

[164] *Id.*; HRC, *General Comment No. 27 (Article 12: Freedom of Movement)* (Sixty-seventh session, 1999) in HRI/GEN/1/Rev.4 at 134, ¶ 20.

[165] *Id.*

[166] *Id.*

[167] *Id.*

[168] HRC, *General Comment No. 15 (The position of aliens under the Covenant)* (Twenty-seventh session, 1986) in HRI/GEN/1/Rev.4 at 97, ¶ 5.

[169] *See, V.M.R.B. v. Canada*, U.N. GAOR, 43rd Sess., Supp. No. 40, U.N. Doc. A/43/40 at 262, ¶ 6.3 (in which the HRC declared inadmissible *ratione materiae* a communication because "a right of asylum is not protected by the Covenant.").

to internal displacement. Furthermore, deportation or rejection of asylum claims may force one family member to leave the country while the rest of the family stays behind. The state has an obligation to guarantee the right of everyone—including refugees and IDPs—to family and home against arbitrary and unlawful interference by both state authorities and natural or legal persons.[170]

The HRC has stated that the term "family" must be given a broad interpretation so as to include all those comprising the family as understood in the society in question.[171] In addition, the term "unlawful" means that no interference may take place except where provided by law, and any authorized interference must comply with the provisions, aims, and objectives of the ICCPR.[172] The term "arbitrary interference" may extend even to those interferences permitted by the law if they do not comply with other ICCPR provisions and objectives.[173]

Right to Family Reunification

Article 23 of the ICCPR provides that the family is entitled to protection by society and the state. The right to found a family implies the right to live together. In its General Comment on Article 23, the HRC has said that the possibility to live together implies the adoption by states of measures "to ensure the unity or reunification of families, particularly when their members are separated for political, economic or similar reasons."[174] Thus Chen in Scenario One, as a recognized refugee, could allege that the refusal to permit her to reunify with her children violates Article 23. The HRC has recommended, for example, that Denmark improve its regulations regarding reunification of refugee families in order to meet its obligations under Article 23.[175]

---

[170] HRC, *General Comment No. 16 (Article 17)* (Thirty-second session, 1988) in HRI/GEN/1/Rev.4 at 99, ¶ 1.

[171] *Hopu and Bessart v. France*, Communication No. 549/1993, *views adopted on* 29 July 1997, U.N. GAOR, 52nd Sess., Supp. No. 40, U.N. Doc. A/52/40, vol. II at 79, ¶ 10.3; in *Report of the Human Rights Committee.* (Committee found a violation where the authors protested against the building of a hotel complex on their ancestral burial grounds where they claimed family members were buried).

[172] HRC, *General Comment No. 16 (Article 17)* (Thirty-second session, 1988) in HRI/GEN/1/Rev.4 at 99, ¶ 3.

[173] *Id.* at 99, ¶ 4.

[174] HRC, *General Comment No. 19 (Article 23)* (Thirty-ninth session, 1990) in HRI/GEN/1/Rev.4 at 107, ¶ 5.

[175] HRC, *Concluding Observations on the Third Periodic Report of Denmark, adopted on* 6 November 1996, U.N. Doc. A/52/40 at 15–16, ¶ 73; U.N. Doc. CCPR/C/79/Add.68.

3.1.11 Right to a Nationality

Article 24, paragraph 3 sets forth a right that is relevant to those in flight, settled refugees, and IDPs: it requires states to protect the right of every child to acquire a nationality. Although this provision does not obligate states to give their nationality to every child born in their territory,[176] it does obligate them to devise and adopt measures, both internally and in cooperation with other states, to ensure that every child has a nationality when he or she is born.[177] Furthermore, states may not discriminate in their internal law against children based on the alien or stateless status of their parents.[178]

The right to a nationality may also be relevant to the right in Article 12(4) not to be arbitrarily deprived of the right to enter one's own country, and to the rights to freedom of movement and residence.

3.1.12 Recognition as a Person Before the Law

Article 16 sets forth the right to be recognized everywhere as a person before the law. Where refugees, asylum-seekers, and IDPs lose access to their personal papers and documentation, or have been unable to properly register a birth or death, they may invoke their right to be recognized everywhere as a person before the law. The HRC illustrated the relevance of this article to refugees, asylum-seekers, and IDPs when it expressed concern over the large number of unregistered births to undocumented refugees in Ecuador. Because this problem prevented children from claiming Ecuadorian nationality, to which they had a right under Ecuadorian law, the HRC recommended that the government adopt measures to assume the automatic nationality of refugee babies.[179]

The right to recognition as a person before the law is also relevant to Article 12 (on the right to enter one's own country) and the rights of the child set out in Article 24, in particular those relating to registration of birth and to having a nationality.

---

[176] HRC, *General Comment No. 17 (Article 24)* (Thirty-fifth session, 1989) in HRI/GEN/1/Rev.4 at 103, ¶ 8.
[177] *Id.*
[178] *Id.*
[179] HRC, *Concluding Observations on the Fourth Periodic Report of Ecuador, adopted on* 27 July 1998, U.N. Doc. A/53/40, ¶ 291; U.N. Doc. CCPR/C/79/Add.92.

3.1.13 Prohibition of Trafficking of Women and Girls and Exploitation of Prostitution

Displaced women and girls and those who are in flight are often preyed upon by traffickers and others who seek to exploit them for prostitution. The harsh economic conditions in which these women and girls find themselves make them particularly vulnerable to being forced into prostitution. Although, unlike the Women's Convention,[180] the ICCPR does not contain an article specifically addressing trafficking and exploitation of prostitution, these practices violate several provisions in the ICCPR: the right to life (Article 6); the right to be free from cruel, inhuman, and degrading treatment (Article 7); the right not to be subjected to slavery (Article 8); the right to personal liberty and security (Article 9); freedom of movement (Article 12); and equal protection of the law (Article 26). The Human Rights Committee has expressed concern about trafficking of women in reviewing a number of states' reports. In its examination of Peru's report in 1992, for example, HRC members requested information "concerning child prostitution and trafficking in women and children."[181] In its review of the report of Spain, the HRC asked "what authorities had done to put an end to the practice of traffic in women along the border with Portugal."[182] In commenting on the extent of trafficking of women for prostitution in Macau, the Human Rights Committee said it was "extremely concerned . . . in particular, [that] immigration and police officials are not taking effective measures to protect these women and to impose sanctions on those who are exploiting women through prostitution in violation of article 8 of the Covenant."[183]

Article 8 of the ICCPR, which prohibits slavery and the slave trade, might also form the basis of a complaint to the HRC, since these practices have long been considered by the United Nations to encompass trafficking in persons and exploitation of prostitution.[184] Failure by a

---

[180] *See infra* section 3.4.1.

[181] HRC, *Concluding Observations on the Second Periodic Report of Peru, adopted on* 21 July 1992, U.N. Doc. A/47/40 at 76, ¶ 320.

[182] HRC, *Concluding Observations on the Third Periodic Report of Spain, adopted on* 30 October 1990, U.N. Doc. A/46/40 at 38, ¶ 153.

[183] HRC, *Concluding Observations: Portugal (Macau)*, U.N. Doc. CCPR/C/79/Add.77 (5 May 1997).

[184] *See, for example,* the mandate of the U.N. Working Group on Contemporary Forms of Slavery to review developments in the field of the slave trade "in all their practices and manifestations, including the slavery-like practice of . . . the traffic in persons and the exploitation of the prostitution of others. . . ." ECOSOC Decision 16 (LVI), 56th Sess., Supp. No. 1 at 25, U.N. Doc. E/55/44

state to take sufficient measures to ensure protection against these practices violates the state's obligation under Article 8.

Article 7 could also provide a basis for a complaint of cruel or degrading treatment to which women and girls are subjected when trafficked or exploited for prostitution.[185] Even if these practices are not engaged in directly by the state, states parties have responsibility under the ICCPR to take adequate measures to ensure the protection of the rights in the Covenant to people in their territory or jurisdiction, including the Article 7 right not to be subjected to cruel, inhuman, or degrading treatment.

3.1.14 Economic and Social Rights of the Child

Article 24 of the ICCPR recognizes the right of every child to receive protection from his or her family, from society, and from the state. States must adopt special measures to protect children in their territory and within their jurisdiction.[186] The HRC has specified that these measures of protection must be non-discriminatory, particularly as between children who are nationals and those who are aliens.[187]

Although these measures of protection are aimed primarily at ensuring that children enjoy fully the rights in the ICCPR, they may also be economic, social, and cultural. The HRC has stated that pursuant to Article 24, states should take "every possible economic and social measure . . . to reduce infant mortality and to eradicate malnutrition among children and to prevent them from being subjected to acts of violence and cruel and inhuman treatment or from being exploited by means of forced labor or prostitution, or by their use in the illicit trafficking of narcotic drugs, or by any other means."[188] Article 24 also encompasses the right of children to be provided with "a level of education that will enable them to enjoy the rights recognized in the Covenant, particularly the right to freedom of opinion and expression."[189] Refugees, asylum-seekers, and IDPs, such as Maria in Scenario Three, may invoke this article where children are deprived of, or denied

---

(1974). The main theme of the Working Group's 1991 session was the prevention of trafficking and of the exploitation of prostitution. See U.N. Doc. E/CN.4/Sub.2/AC.2/1991/5/Add.1 (1991).

[185] *See infra* section 3.4.1.
[186] HRC, *General Comment No. 17 (Article 24)* (Thirty-fifth session, 1989) in HRI/GEN/1/Rev.4 at 103 ¶ 1.
[187] *Id.* at 103 ¶ 5.
[188] *Id.* at 103 ¶ 3.
[189] *Id.*

safe access to, subsistence needs such as food, water, housing, clothing, health care, and sanitation, as well as education.

It is under Article 24 that the Human Rights Committee has drawn the attention of states parties to the need to ensure that children do not take a direct part in armed conflicts.[190]

3.1.15 Economic and Social Rights Through Equality Before the Law and Equal Protection of the Law

Another article in the ICCPR that may be invoked to protect economic and social rights is Article 26, which stipulates that the law shall guarantee to all persons equal protection against discrimination on any ground such as race, color, sex, language, religion, national origin, or other status. Article 26 prohibits discrimination in law or in fact in any field that is regulated and protected by public authorities. Importantly, it is not limited to ICCPR rights.[191] Whenever a state adopts domestic legislation, it must comply with Article 26 and ensure that the legislation and its implementation are non-discriminatory. This also extends coverage of the ICCPR beyond a limited list of civil and political rights.

The HRC, applying Article 26 in assessing an individual complaint, has determined that where refugees or asylum-seekers have left their countries and the state has confiscated their property, any law enacted to provide for restitution may not exclude non-residents and non-citizens.[192] In that case, Article 26 was invoked successfully in a claim for property. The authors had left their country for political reasons and their property was confiscated by the Communist Government. The Committee found a violation of Article 26 when the state enacted a law in 1991 that provided for restitution for the confiscations but excluded non-residents and non-citizens from the remedy.

3.2 Protection Under the 1984 Convention Against Torture and Other Cruel, Inhuman or Degrading Treatment or Punishment

Although torture is prohibited under the ICCPR, the Convention against Torture and Other Cruel, Inhuman or Degrading Treatment or Punishment sets out in more detail specific steps that states should

---

[190] *Id.*

[191] HRC, *General Comment No. 18 (Non-discrimination)* (Thirty-seventh session, 1989) in HRI/GEN/1/Rev.4 at 104–105, ¶ 12.

[192] *Simunek et al. v. the Czech Republic*, Communication No. 516/1992, *views adopted on* 19 July 1995, U.N. GAOR, 50th Sess., Supp. No. 40, U.N. Doc. A/50/40, vol. II at 96, ¶ 11.6; U.N. Doc. CCPR/C/54/D/516/1992.

take to protect and enforce the right to be free from torture. The Torture Convention therefore may be of particular use to refugees, asylum-seekers, and internally displaced persons who have been victims of torture. The body that monitors whether states are complying with the Torture Convention is the Committee against Torture (CAT).

The Torture Convention establishes two complaint procedures that are relevant in theory to protecting refugees, asylum-seekers, and IDPs: an individual complaint procedure (Article 22) and an investigation procedure (Article 20).[193]

Rights at a Glance:
Provisions of most relevance to refugees, asylum-seekers, and IDPs include:
- The prohibition on expulsion, refoulement, or extradition to a state where there are substantial grounds for believing the person would be in danger of being subjected to torture (Article 3);
- The obligation of the state to ensure a prompt and impartial investigation where there is reasonable ground to believe an act of torture has been committed (Article 12);
- The right of anyone who has been tortured to complain to competent authorities and have the case promptly and impartially examined (Article 13);
- The obligation of the state to ensure that the complainant and witnesses are protected against ill-treatment or intimidation as a consequence of the complaint (Article 13);
- The right of torture victims to redress and to adequate compensation, including the means for as full rehabilitation as possible; if the victim dies as a result of the torture, the dependents are entitled to compensation (Article 14);
- The prohibition on the use as evidence of any statement made as a result of torture (Article 15)

An act of torture within the meaning of the Torture Convention consists of several elements: intent, a certain level of severity of pain, a particular purpose, and some degree of official involvement or acquiescence. Article 1 defines "torture" as:

- the intentional infliction
- of "severe pain or suffering, whether physical or mental"
- for such purposes as
  — obtaining from the individual or a third person information or a confession

---

[193] Regarding the inquiry procedure, *see infra* section 6.3.

- punishing the individual
- intimidating or coercing the individual or a third person
- "[a]ny reason based on discrimination of any kind"
• when inflicted or instigated by someone acting in an official capacity, or with the consent or acquiescence of such a person.

Acts that fall within this definition include rape in custody. In addition, members of the family of a person who has been disappeared are also considered to experience torture, because of the severe mental suffering they experience because of the disappearance.

It should be noted that the torture addressed by the Torture Convention is somewhat more limited than that covered in the ICCPR. "Torture" as covered by the Torture Convention must be inflicted for certain purposes such as obtaining a confession or punishing someone, and must be committed at the instigation of a public official or with official consent or acquiescence (Article 1), whereas the ICCPR simply requires states to ensure protection against torture, without reference to any purposes or perpetrators. It may therefore be preferable in some cases to address a complaint to the HRC, rather than the CAT, in order to invoke the broader scope of the ICCPR.

The body of jurisprudence that has emerged from the CAT's consideration of individual communications provides a foundation from which to draft complaints relating to refugees, asylum-seekers, and IDPs.[194] The most frequently invoked provision of the Torture Convention is Article 3, which prohibits expulsion, refoulement, or extradition to a state where the person would face a risk of torture. The vast majority of CAT's jurisprudence on individual complaints arises from Article 3 and refoulement issues. Of the 32 individual complaints considered on the merits by CAT between 1994 and 1999, 28 involved asylum-seekers and others facing deportation, of which 13 resulted in favorable opinions.

---

[194] The jurisprudence of the Human Rights Committee regarding Article 7 of the *ICCPR* (prohibition of torture) may also be persuasive before CAT. See Siân Lewis-Anthony, *Treaty-Based Procedures for Making Human Rights Complaints within the U.N. System, in* GUIDE TO INTERNATIONAL HUMAN RIGHTS PRACTICE 53 (HURST HANNUM ED., 3rd ed. 1999). Lewis-Anthony argues that the Torture Convention admonition in Article 17(2) on the usefulness of selecting members to CAT who are also members of the HRC should be interpreted as intending that CAT should also draw on the jurisprudence of HRC.

3.2.1 The Right to Physical and Mental Integrity—Prohibition Against Torture

The purpose of the Torture Convention is to protect the right to physical and mental integrity, including the right to life, by setting out specific obligations relating to the prohibition of torture and other cruel, inhuman, and degrading treatment.

Prohibition on Expulsion, Refoulement, and Extradition Where There Is Risk of Torture

Article 3 of the Torture Convention prohibits the expulsion, refoulement, or extradition of an individual to a state where there are "substantial grounds for believing" that the person would be in danger of being subjected to torture. Although the existence in the state concerned of "a consistent pattern of gross, flagrant or mass violations of human rights" may be relevant in assessing the risk of torture, a determination of danger of torture in the individual case is required. CAT must establish "whether the individual concerned would be personally at risk of being subjected to torture in the country to which he or she would return."[195] Ibrahim (Scenario Two), as a failed asylum-seeker with a fear of torture, should seek relief under Article 3 of CAT if the asylum state accepts the complaint mechanism.

The detailed General Comment that CAT has issued on the implementation of Article 3 in the context of individual complaints notes that although the risk of torture must "go beyond mere theory or suspicion," the risk does not have to be "highly probable." Information that the CAT lists in the General Comment as being pertinent in assessing the risk of torture includes:

- Whether in the state concerned there is a "consistent pattern of gross, flagrant or mass violations of human rights" (as mentioned in Article 3(2) of the Convention);
- Whether the individual has been tortured or maltreated by or with the consent or acquiescence of someone acting in an official capacity, and, if so, whether this was in the recent past;
- Whether there is medical or other independent evidence to support the claim of past torture or maltreatment, and whether the torture has had after-effects;
- Whether the situation in the state referred to above has

---

[195] *A. v. The Netherlands*, Communication No. 91/1997; *views adopted on* 13 November 1998, U.N. Doc. A/54/44, ¶ 6.3.

changed, and whether the internal situation in respect of human rights has altered;
- Whether the individual has engaged in political or other activity within or outside the state concerned which would appear to make him/her particularly vulnerable to the risk of torture if sent there;
- Whether there is any evidence as to the credibility of the individual; and
- Whether there are factual inconsistencies in the individual's claim, and if so, whether they are relevant.

Given the frequency with which Article 3 is invoked in communications under the Torture Convention, numerous examples exist to illustrate when the CAT has and has not determined that there are "substantial grounds to believe" there is a risk of torture. In a communication filed against Sweden, for example, the CAT determined that where the author was a known political activist who had a past history of being tortured and who suffered from post-traumatic stress disorder, substantial grounds existed to believe that the author would be in danger of being subject to torture if returned to Iran.[196] In another case, by contrast, the CAT found the complainants' fears of torture to be unsubstantiated where, although the complainants had in the past been detained and tortured for being affiliated with a political opposition group, that group was now part of the alliance forming the government.[197]

---

[196] *Ali Falakaflaki v. Sweden*, Communication No. 89/1997, *views adopted on* 8 May 1998, U.N. Doc. A/53/44 at 105, ¶¶ 6.5 and 6.7. *See also, A. v. The Netherlands, supra* note 200, ¶¶ 6.7 and 6.8 (substantial grounds existed where the complainant had a past history of torture and detention, had assisted a member of an illegal political group, *Al-Nahda*, and had deserted from the Army); *Orhan Ayas v. Sweden*, Communication No. 97/1998, *views adopted on* 12 November 1998, U.N. Doc. A/54/44, ¶¶ 6.5 and 6.6 (substantial grounds existed where the complainant was affiliated with the opposition group the "Kurdish Workers' party" and had a history of being subjected to detention and torture); *Tala v. Sweden*, Communication No. 43/1996, *views adopted on* 15 November 1996, U.N. Doc. A/52/44 at 62, ¶ 10.3 and 10.5 (substantial grounds existed where complainant affiliated with the political organization the *People's Mujahedin Organization* and had a history of being subjected to detention and torture in Iran); *Alan v. Switzerland*, Communication No. 21/1995, *views adopted on* 8 May 1996, U.N. Doc. A/51/44 at 74–75, ¶ 11.4 (substantial grounds determined where the complainant was a Kurd who had a history of detention and torture and had fled Turkey because the police were looking for him).

[197] *X., Y. and Z. v. Sweden*, Communication No. 61/1996, *views adopted on* 6 May 1998, U.N. Doc. A/53/44 at 81, ¶ 11.3 (where although complainants were

When certain factors exist, such as an inconsistent story or a long period of time between the past history of torture and the present, the CAT is unlikely to find substantial grounds for believing that the person would be in danger of being subject to torture. In *N.P. v. Australia*, the CAT noted that although complete accuracy is seldom expected from victims of torture, the information available did not show substantial grounds when "important inconsistencies" existed in the complainant's story.[198] In *E.A. v. Switzerland*, the CAT found no violation of Article 3 where the incidents of torture dated back to the early 1980s and no evidence was provided to substantiate that the authorities were still looking for the complainant.[199]

A risk of being detained, without an accompanying threat of torture, is also insufficient to make out a claim under Article 3.[200]

Credibility issues will not automatically cause the CAT to reject a communication. In *Khan v. Canada*,[201] Canada claimed that the applicant's credibility was in doubt because it was only after his application for refugee status was rejected that he submitted medical evidence that he had been tortured. The CAT said this was not uncommon behavior for torture victims, and determined that Canada should not expel the applicant to Pakistan, noting the evidence that torture was widely practiced against dissidents there.

In another case involving the credibility of the applicant, *Mutumbo v. Switzerland*, the CAT stated that "even if there are doubts about the facts adduced by the author, [the state] must ensure that [the person's] security is not endangered."[202] In reaching its conclusion that Switzerland was obligated not to return a national of former Zaire to his country, the CAT took into consideration those statements in the author's communication that were not disputed by Switzerland, which included the fact that the person had deserted from the army, left the country in a

---

formerly detained and tortured for being affiliated with a political opposition group, the *people's Revolutionary Party*, that group now formed part of the alliance forming the government of the Democratic Republic of the Congo, and therefore the complainant's fears were unsubstantiated).

[198] *N.P. v. Australia*, Communication No. 106/1998, *views adopted on* 6 May 1999, U.N. Doc. A/54/44, ¶ 6.6; *see also*, *X. v. Switzerland*, Communication No. 27/1995, *views adopted on* 28 April 1997, U.N. Doc. A/52/44 at 70, ¶ 11.4.

[199] *E.A. v. Switzerland*, Communication No. 28/1995, *views adopted on* 10 November 1997, U.N. Doc. A/53/44 at 59, ¶¶ 11.4 and 11.6.

[200] *I.A.O. v. Sweden*, Communication No. 65/1997, *views adopted on* 6 May 1998, U.N. Doc. A/53/44 at 90–91, ¶ 14.5.

[201] *Khan v. Canada*, Communication No. 15/1994, *views adopted on* 15 November 1994, U.N. Doc. A/50/44 at 46.

[202] *Mutumbo v. Switzerland*, Communication No. 13/1993, *views adopted on* 27 April 1994, U.N. Doc. A/49/44 at 51, ¶ 9.2.

clandestine manner, and made statements in his asylum application that could be considered defamatory.[203]

As mentioned above, in addition to the complainant's specific circumstances, the CAT will also consider the general human rights circumstances of the state concerned, including patterns of gross, flagrant, or mass violations of human rights, per Article 3(2). In *Mutumbo v. Switzerland* for example, the CAT reached its views on the risk of torture in part because of the conclusions of other UN human rights bodies, including the Commission on Human Rights, that there was a consistent pattern of gross, flagrant, or mass violations of human rights in former Zaire.

The CAT has specified in its General Comment on Article 3 that the term "gross, flagrant or mass human rights violations" refers only to violations committed by, or at the instigation of, or with the consent or acquiescence of, a public official or other person acting in an official capacity, and it has applied this principle in a case where it found no violation of the Torture Convention because it determined the risk of torture would be inflicted by a non-governmental entity, without the consent or acquiescence of the government.[204]

Significantly, the CAT has determined that where a state lacks a central government and is instead comprised of a number of warring factions, such as in Somalia, the members of those factions can fall within the phrase "public officials or other persons acting in an official capacity."[205] Accordingly, the CAT will find a violation of Article 3 if a state sends someone to face a risk of torture by such factions.

Although the general human rights situation may be relevant in determining a risk of torture, it is not necessarily so, and thus it is not necessary for the author of a communication to establish that the state generally engages in human rights violations. Just as a person may lawfully be returned to a country known to engage in human rights violations when the individual has failed to demonstrate that he or she would personally face a danger of torture, a person must not be returned to a country where, despite the absence of general human rights violations, the applicant does face a personal danger of torture.[206]

---

[203] *Id.* at 52, ¶ 9.4.

[204] *G.R.B. v. Sweden*, Communication No. 83/1997, *views adopted on* 15 May 1998, U.N. Doc. A/53/44 at 98, ¶ 6.5.

[205] *Sadiq Shek Elmi v. Australia*, Communication No. 120/1998; *views adopted on* 14 May 1999, U.N. Doc. A/54/44 at ¶ 6.5.

[206] J. HERMAN BURGERS AND HANS DANELIUS, THE UNITED NATIONS CONVENTION AGAINST TORTURE: A HANDBOOK ON THE CONVENTION AGAINST TORTURE AND OTHER CRUEL, INHUMAN, OR DEGRADING TREATMENT OR PUNISHMENT 128 (1988).

The CAT has applied the prohibition in Article 3 against sending a person to "another state" to face a risk of torture to include a prohibition on sending a person to a third country where there is a risk that the person would be expelled from that third country to another state where a risk of torture exists. Accordingly, for example, the CAT found Sweden in violation of Article 3 when Swedish authorities ordered the complainant's expulsion to Jordan.[207] Although the Swedish authorities were not attempting to return the complainant to Iraq, where substantial grounds existed for believing he would be in danger of being subjected to torture, his expulsion to Jordan presented a risk that he would then be returned to Iraq. Similarly, the CAT noted in another case that the state party had an obligation to refrain from forcibly returning the complainant to Turkey, as well as to any other country where he ran a real risk of being expelled or returned to Turkey.[208]

It is important for advocates to know that even if the author of the communication may be ineligible for refugee status by virtue of Article 1(F) of the 1951 Refugee Convention,[209] the Torture Convention prohibits states parties from sending the person to a country to face a risk of torture. The CAT applied this principle in *Tapia Paez v. Sweden*, in which the author was a Peruvian who had been active in Sendero Luminoso. Declaring that returning the author to Peru would constitute a violation of Article 3 of the Convention, the CAT stated that "the test of article 3 of the Convention [i]s absolute and . . . the nature of the activities in which the person concerned engaged could not be a material consideration when making a decision under article 3."[210]

Rights to Investigation of Torture Complaint and to Redress and Compensation

A state party to the Torture Convention must ensure a "prompt and impartial" investigation whenever there is reasonable ground to believe that an act of torture has taken place in its jurisdiction (Article 12). In addition, states must ensure the right of an alleged torture victim to complain to the state's competent authorities and to have the

---

[207] *Avedes Hamayak Korban v. Sweden*, Communication No. 88/1997, *views adopted on* 16 November 1998, U.N. Doc. A/54/44 at 45.

[208] *Halil Haydin v. Sweden*, Communication No. 101/1997, *views adopted on* 20 November 1998, U.N. Doc. A/54/44 at 67.

[209] For the full citation, see the Bibliography of Cited International Instruments.

[210] *Tapia Paez v. Sweden*, Communication No. 39/1996, *views adopted on* 28 April 1997, U.N. Doc. A/52/44 at 94, ¶ 14.5.

case promptly and impartially examined (Article 13). States must also ensure protection of the complainant and witnesses from ill treatment or intimidation. Furthermore, states must ensure that victims of torture obtain redress and have a right to adequate compensation, which includes the means for as full rehabilitation as possible. If the victim dies from the torture, his or her dependants are entitled to compensation (Article 14).

Delay by a state in commencing an investigation has led the CAT to find a violation of the Torture Convention. In *Halimi Bedzibi v. Austria*, the CAT found a violation of Article 12 when government officials waited 15 months before investigating the complainant's allegations of torture.[211] In *Encarnación Blanco Abad v. Spain*, the CAT found violations of both Articles 12 and 13 based on excessive delay in starting an investigation and the domestic court's refusal to hear the complainant's evidence.[212] In that case, the CAT found that a 19-day delay between the court's initial notification of the possibility that the complainant had been subjected to torture and the date that the preliminary investigation was initiated constituted a violation of Article 12's prompt investigation requirement.[213] The CAT further noted that the formal filing of a complaint is not required to trigger the responsibility to conduct a torture investigation.[214] Rather, if the victim simply brings the facts to the attention of an authority of the state, the state "is obliged to consider it as a tacit but unequivocal expression of the victim's wish that the facts should be promptly and impartially investigated."[215] The CAT has also found violations of Article 13 for failure to conduct the investigation promptly, as well as for violations of the impartiality requirement.[216]

Article 14 requires redress for torture victims as well as compensation, with compensation due the victims' family if torture results in death. The members of the family of a person who has been disappeared may be direct complainants for the mental torture they experience caused by the disappearance.

---

[211] *Halimi-Nedzibi v. Austria*, Communication No. 8/1991, *views adopted on* 18 November 1993, U.N. Doc. A/49/44 at 45, ¶ 13.5.
[212] *Encarnación Blanco Abad v. Spain*, Communication No. 59/1996, *views adopted on* 14 May 1998, U.N. Doc. A/53/44 at 73–74, ¶¶ 8.5 and 8.7.
[213] *Id.* at 73, ¶¶ 8.4 and 8.5.
[214] *Id.* at 73, ¶ 8.6.
[215] *Id.*
[216] *Id.* at 73–74, ¶¶ 8.7 and 8.8.

Training of Officials

The Torture Convention contains additional measures that, although they do not directly give rise to individual claims, are relevant to the protection of refugees, asylum-seekers, and IDPs and may therefore be usefully raised in assessing the extent to which a state is in compliance with its obligations under the Torture Convention. One such provision is the requirement in Article 10 that states parties provide training on the prohibition against torture to law enforcement, medical personnel, and other persons who may be involved with people subject to any form of detention. The need for specialized training is keen due to the particular needs of refugees and asylum-seekers who have experienced torture, fled their country and who are likely to be culturally different from the officials they encounter. The CAT has made note of this in reviewing states' reports. For example, the CAT noted with satisfaction Finland's efforts to provide law enforcement and other personnel with educational programs relating to refugees.[217] In contrast, after reviewing other state reports, the CAT has commented on the need to provide education programs regarding refugee issues to law enforcement and medical personnel where such programs do not exist. After examining Jordan's initial report in 1995, the CAT commented that educational programs targeted at police and security forces, as well as medical personnel, should be started as a matter of urgency.[218]

3.2.2 Equality and Non-Discrimination

The important norm of non-discrimination appears in Article 1 of the Torture Convention, which defines the acts of torture that come within the coverage of the treaty. For purposes of the Torture Convention, "torture" is an act intentionally inflicting severe pain or suffering on a person for certain purposes such as obtaining information or a confession or in order to punish the person, "or for any reason based on discrimination of any kind," if done by or with the consent or acquiescence of a public official. Thus, an individual complaint could be filed if an official acquiesced in the torture of someone even if the

---

[217] CAT, *Concluding Observations on the Third Periodic Report of Finland*, adopted on 12 November 1999, U.N. Doc. A/55/44 at 13, ¶ 53 (g); *see also*, CAT, *Summary Record of the First Part of the 395th Meeting: Austria*, held on 15 November 1999, U.N. Doc. CAT/C/SR.395 at ¶ 21.

[218] CAT, *Concluding Observations on the Initial Report of Jordan*, adopted on 26 July 1995, U.N. Doc. A/50/44 at 25, ¶ 179; *see also*, Brian Gorlick, *The Convention and the Committee against Torture: A Complementary Protection Regime for Refugees*, 11 INT'L J. REFUGEE L. 493 (1999).

act was not done for such purposes as obtaining information, if it could be established that it was inflicted for any reason based on the victim's race, ethnic origin, sex, language, or religion.

3.2.3 Personal Liberty

Detention of Refugees

When detention of refugees is required, the CAT has repeatedly commented on the need to detain them in a facility other than a general prison, and if they are held in a prison, that refugees not be held together with the general prison population. This position arises from dual considerations relating (1) to the less favorable conditions found in prisons, including endemic violence and inhuman or degrading treatment, and (2) the importance of disassociating, in the public's mind, refugees from criminal populations. In examining Finland's third report in 1999, for example, the CAT commented with satisfaction that legal measures had been taken to accommodate asylum-seekers in places other than prisons.[219] In contrast, after examining the reports of the United Kingdom and Austria, the CAT voiced concern at the failure to detain refugees in facilities separate from general prisons.[220]

3.2.4 Right to a Fair Trial and Due Process of Law

A basic fair trial right is provided in Article 15, under which states parties must ensure that any statement made as a result of torture shall not be invoked as evidence in a proceeding. The only exception is that in a proceeding against someone accused of torture, such a statement may be introduced as evidence that the statement was made.

3.2.5 Freedom of Movement

Prohibition on Expulsion from One's Own Country

Article 3 of the Torture Convention covers expulsion from one's own country, to the extent that no one may be expelled or extradited to another state where there are substantial grounds for believing the person would be in danger of being subjected to torture. For the

---

[219] CAT, *Concluding Observations: Finland, supra* note 217 at 13, ¶ 53(h).

[220] *See,* CAT, *Concluding Observations on the Third Periodic Report of the United Kingdom of Great Britain and Northern Ireland, adopted on* 17 November 1998, U.N. Doc. A/54/44 at ¶ 76(b); *see also,* CAT, *Summary Record: Austria, supra* note 217 at ¶ 20.

84 *Human Rights Protection for Displaced Persons*

jurisprudence on Article 3, see section 3.2.1.1, *supra*, on the prohibition of refoulement.

The Right to Asylum

Although the CAT does make determinations on refoulement under Article 3, it is not authorized to determine whether the claimant was entitled to asylum under the national laws of a country, or whether the individual was entitled to the protection of the 1951 Refugee Convention. The authority of the CAT in this context is limited to determining whether there would be or has been a violation of Article 3 of the Torture Convention if the person is returned to a particular state.

The CAT has, however, addressed procedures for processing asylum claims. In reviewing states parties' periodic reports, the CAT has on occasion found it relevant to address a country's process used to determine refugee status. For example, the CAT recommended to one state after reviewing its report that procedures for dealing with and deciding asylum applications should occur in a formal hearing. To provide a formal hearing would allow an opportunity to present relevant evidence and to provide other protections associated with due process of the law.[221] In contrast, the CAT has commended another state for having an in-country right of appeal for all refused asylum-seekers.[222]

3.3 Protection Under the 1965 Convention on the Elimination of All Forms of Racial Discrimination

The 1965 International Convention on the Elimination of All Forms of Racial Discrimination sets forth both substantive rights regarding racial discrimination and a series of specific steps for states to eliminate such discrimination. The body that monitors state compliance with the Racial Discrimination Convention is the Committee on the Elimination of Racial Discrimination (CERD).

Given the racial and ethnic discrimination that refugees and asylum-seekers often face in a range of areas covered by the Racial Discrimination Convention, including housing, employment, and police protection from attacks, the Convention has significant relevance in their lives. The CERD has often indicated to states parties that they

---

[221] CAT, *Concluding Observations on the Initial Report of Venezuela, adopted on* 5 May 1999, A/54/44 at ¶ 147.

[222] CAT, *Concluding Observations on the Second Periodic Report of the United Kingdom of Great Britain and Northern Ireland, adopted on* 9 July 1996, U.N. Doc. CAT A/51/44 at 12, ¶ 60(a).

should include in their periodic reports information on laws and policies that affect non-citizens. The CERD has also issued a General Recommendation on refugees and displaced persons.[223]

"Racial discrimination" includes discrimination on the basis of "race, color, descent, or national or ethnic origin" (Article 1, paragraph 1). The Racial Discrimination Convention specifies that it does not apply to exclusions or restrictions on rights "between citizens and non-citizens" (paragraph 2). Nonetheless, the Racial Discrimination Convention protections are fully applicable if the discrimination a person faces is on the basis of race or ethnic origin rather than alienage.

The Racial Discrimination Convention defines "discrimination" to include exclusions or restrictions that have the "purpose or effect" of nullifying or impairing the enjoyment or exercise of human rights on a basis of equality (Article 1). Unlike some state legislation, the Racial Discrimination Convention does not require that the discrimination in question be "solely" on the basis of race. In recognition of the fact that some human rights violations are prompted by a confluence of discriminatory attitudes, the CERD has issued a General Recommendation on race and gender.[224]

---

[223] CERD, *General Recommendation XXII: Article 5 and refugees and displaced persons* (Forty-ninth session, 1996) in HRI/GEN/1Rev.4 at 150. This general recommendation was prompted by what the CERD notes in the preamble as "foreign military, non-military and/or ethnic conflicts [that] have resulted in massive flows of refugees and the displacement of persons on the basis of ethnic criteria in many parts of the world." After reiterating the obligation of states under Article 5 of the Racial Discrimination Convention to eliminate racial discrimination in the enjoyment of civil, political, economic, social, and cultural rights and freedoms, the General Recommendation then sets out several areas for emphasis in this respect.

- States parties are obliged to ensure that the return of such refugees and displaced persons is voluntary and to observe the principle of non-refoulement and non-expulsion of refugees.
- All such refugees and displaced persons have, after their return to their homes of origin, the right to have restored to them property of which they were deprived in the course of the conflict and to be compensated appropriately for any such property that cannot be restored to them. Any commitments or statements relating to such property made under duress are null and void.
- All such refugees and displaced persons have, after their return to their homes of origin, the right to participate fully and equally in public affairs at all levels and to have equal access to public services and to receive rehabilitation assistance.

[224] CERD, *General Recommendation XXV Gender-Related Dimensions of Racial Discrimination* (fifty-sixth session, 2000), U.N. Doc. A/55/18 at 152.

Though the individual complaint mechanism under the CERD has been rarely used, and a large number of states have failed to accept this mechanism, the Racial Discrimination Convention contains numerous rights of relevance to refugees, asylum-seekers, and IDPs that may be invoked in a complaint.

> **Rights at a Glance:**
> Provisions of most relevance to refugees, asylum-seekers, and IDPs include:
> **Article 4**: Protection from racist propaganda and incitement to hatred.
> **Article 5**: The right to freedom from racial discrimination and to equality before the law:
> - The right to equal treatment before tribunals and other justice organs (para (a));
> - The right to security of the person and protection by the state against violence and bodily harm, "whether inflicted by government officials or by any individual, group or institution" (para (b));
> - The right to vote and participate in elections and in the conduct of public affairs (para (c));
> - The right to freedom of movement and residence within the state (subpara (d)(i));
> - The right to leave any country including one's own, and to return to one's country (subpara (d)(ii));
> - The right to nationality (subpara (d)(iii));
> - The right to marriage and choice of spouse (subpara (d)(iv)), which would include equal protection against forced marriage;
> - The right to own property (subpara (d)(v));
> - The right to freedom of thought and religion (subpara (d)(vii));
> - The right to freedom of opinion and expression (subpara (d)(viii));
> - The right to freedom of assembly and association (subpara (d)(ix));
> - The right to work and to equal pay for equal work, and to just and favorable conditions of work (subpara (e)(i));
> - The right to housing (subpara (e)(iii));
> - The right to public health, medical care and social services (subpara (e)(iv));
> - The right to education (subpara (e)(v));
> - The right of access to places open to the public (para (f));
>
> **Article 6**: Right to a remedy against acts of racial discrimination that violate the above rights, and to seek reparation for any damage suffered as a result of such discrimination.

The few cases that have been considered by the CERD under the individual complaint mechanism have not dealt specifically with refugees, asylum-seekers, or IDPs, but several have addressed issues very relevant in the lives of forced migrants, who often face racial or ethnic discrimination. Additional guidance on the interpretation and application of the Racial Discrimination Convention appears in the CERD's examination of states parties' reports.

3.3.1 The Right to Life and Physical Integrity

Right to Life

Although the right to life is not explicitly mentioned in the Racial Discrimination Convention, it is encompassed in the obligation of states in Article 5(b) to guarantee the right of everyone the full enjoyment of the right to "security of the person and protection by the state against violence or bodily harm, whether inflicted by government officials or by any individual, group or institution." The failure of the state to protect the right to life because of racial discrimination could be the basis for an individual complaint, invoking Article 5(b).

Although there is no duty imposed by the Racial Discrimination Convention not to take life, states parties are under an obligation under Article 5 to guarantee equality before the law. So if a state party should choose to impose the death penalty, for example, it must ensure that there is no racial or ethnic bias in the process.

Prohibition Against Torture and Cruel, Inhuman, or Degrading Treatment or Punishment

Although torture and inhuman or degrading treatment or punishment are not explicitly mentioned in the Racial Discrimination Convention, they are implicitly included by virtue of the Article 5(b) guarantee of the right to protection by the state against violence or bodily harm, whether inflicted by government officials or by any individual, group, or institution.

In addition, the CERD's *General Recommendation XXII on refugees and displaced persons* stipulates that states parties "are obliged . . . to observe the principle of non-refoulement."[225]

Protection from Racist Propaganda and Incitement to Hatred

The right to life and the right to security of the person are indirectly addressed in Article 4 of the Racial Discrimination Convention, which requires states to declare an offence punishable by law, among

---

[225] *Supra* note at 223, at 151, ¶ 2(b).

other things, all acts of violence or incitement to such acts against a racial or ethnic group. This article is of great relevance to asylum applicants as well as settled refugees who are the target of racist propaganda.

3.3.2 Equality and Non-Discrimination

It goes without saying that the entire Racial Discrimination Convention addresses the subject of equality and non-discrimination. In addition to the areas of non-discrimination discussed under other headings in this section, it is important to note that failure on the part of the state to investigate complaints of racial discrimination may amount to a violation of both Articles 4 and 5. Article 4 requires states parties "actively to prosecute cases of alleged discrimination."[226] Article 5 requires a complete and diligent investigation of complaints of racial discrimination in the areas covered in that provision.

In *L.K. v. The Netherlands*, the CERD found a violation of the Racial Discrimination Convention because the police investigation of a complaint alleging that racially discriminatory remarks amounted to incitement to acts of violence was inadequate.[227] The complainant had alleged that such remarks were in violation of laws that made racial discrimination a criminal act. The CERD declared that the police had a duty to investigate the complaint with due diligence.[228] Further, the CERD commented that the enactment of laws making racial discrimination a criminal act did not in itself represent full compliance with the Racial Discrimination Convention, but that enforcement of those laws is also required.[229]

Right to a Remedy for Humiliation Due to Racial or Ethnic Background

The CERD has recognized a right to a remedy where the discrimination has not resulted in any physical damage but has caused humiliation or similar suffering.[230] In *B.J. v. Denmark*, the CERD noted that "[b]eing refused access to a place of service intended for the use

---

[226] *Yilmaz-Dogan v. Netherlands*, Communication No. 1/1984, *opinion adopted on* 10 August 1988, U.N. Doc. CERD/C/390 at 7, ¶ 9.4.

[227] *L.K. v. The Netherlands*, Communication No. 4/1991, *opinion adopted on* 16 March 1993, U.N. Doc. CERD/C/390 at 29, ¶ 6.3.

[228] *Id.* at 30, ¶ 6.6.

[229] *Id.* at 29–30, ¶¶ 6.4 and 6.5.

[230] *B.J. v. Denmark*, Communication No. 17/1999, *opinion adopted on* 17 March 2000, UN Doc. CERD/C/390 at 82–83, ¶ 6.2.

of the general public solely on the ground of a person's national or ethnic background is a humiliating experience which, in the opinion of the Committee, may merit economic compensation and cannot always be adequately repaired or satisfied by merely imposing a criminal sanction on the perpetrator."[231]

3.3.3 Personal Liberty

The Article 5(a) obligation of states to guarantee equal treatment before its tribunals and all other organs administering justice would entail an obligation to ensure there is no racial discrimination when the state exercises its authority to deprive someone of his or her liberty. A violation of this requirement could give rise to an individual complaint.

3.3.4 Right to a Fair Trial and Due Process of Law

Article 5(a) guarantees the right to equal treatment before the tribunals and all other organs administering justice. Discrimination on the basis of race in failing to observe trial and due process guarantees could give rise to an individual complaint to the CERD.

3.3.5 Right to Vote and Participate in the Political Process

Under Article 5(a), states guarantee to everyone on a basis of non-discrimination political rights, including the right to vote and stand for election, and to take part in government and in the conduct of public affairs. In its *General Recommendation XXII on refugees and displaced persons*, the CERD stated that "refugees and displaced persons have, after their return to their homes of origin, the right to participate fully and equally in public affairs at all levels and to have equal access to public services and to receive rehabilitation assistance."

3.3.6 Freedom of Religion

Under Article 5(d)(vii), states parties are to guarantee without racial discrimination the right to freedom of religion.

3.3.7 Freedom of Expression

Under Article 5(d)(viii), states parties are to guarantee without racial discrimination the right to freedom of expression.

---

[231] *Id.* at 83, ¶ 6.3.

3.3.8 Freedom of Association

Under Article 5(d)(ix), states parties are to guarantee without racial discrimination the right to freedom of association.

3.3.9 Freedom of Movement

Article 5(i) guarantees the right without racial discrimination "to freedom of movement and residence within the border of the state." When Croatia refused to allow 30,000 refugees to leave appalling camp conditions, the CERD expressed concern at such a restriction on movement.[232]

Under *General Recommendation XXII on refugees and displaced persons*, states parties are obliged to ensure that the return of refugees and displaced persons is voluntary.

Freedom of movement is also related to Article 5(f) in its guarantee of access to any place or service intended for the general public, such as transport, hotels, restaurants, cafés, theaters, and parks. This right can be particularly relevant to refugees and asylum-seekers facing racial or ethnic discrimination in the asylum state.

Prohibition on Expulsion from One's Own Country

Under *General Recommendation XXII on refugees and displaced persons*, states parties are obliged to observe the principle against mass expulsion of refugees.

Freedom to Leave One's Own Country

Article 5(d)(ii) guarantees the right of everyone, without racial discrimination, to leave any country including one's own.

Right to Return to One's Own Country

The same clause that guarantees the right to leave also guarantees the right to return to one's own country (Article 5(d)(ii)). In addition, the CERD has stated in its *General Recommendation XXII on refugees and displaced persons* that all refugees and displaced persons have the right freely to return to their homes of origin under conditions of safety.

---

[232] CERD, *Concluding Observations on the Periodic Report of Croatia, adopted on* 16 March 1995, U.N. Doc. A/50/18 at 40, ¶ 169.

Freedom to Enter Another Country

This is not addressed explicitly in the Racial Discrimination Convention. As with other areas, though, states parties are obligated to eliminate racial discrimination "in all its forms" (Articles 2 and 5), so any state laws, policies, and practices regarding entry into the country must be without racial discrimination.

The Right to Asylum

The Racial Discrimination Convention does not guarantee the right to asylum or to seek asylum. However, asylum procedures have been the subject of comment by the CERD in reviewing some states' reports. In commenting on Germany's report in 1993, for example, the CERD recommended that the government "consider reviewing certain restrictive provisions recently adopted with regard to asylum seekers, to ensure that they did not result in any discrimination in effect on the grounds of ethnic origin."[233] In reviewing the report of France in 1994, the CERD expressed concern that its laws on immigration and asylum "could have racially discriminatory consequences, particularly with the imposition of limitations on the right of appeal against expulsion orders and the preventive detention of foreigners at points of entry for excessively long periods."[234]

3.3.10 Right to Family and Private Life

The right of everyone to marriage and choice of spouse must be guaranteed on the basis of non-discrimination, under Article 5(d)(iv). This right is violated, for example, when the state does not intervene to protect refugee women of certain ethnic backgrounds from forced marriage, the effect of which is that women of do not enjoy the same right as others to freely choose their spouse.

3.3.11 Right to a Nationality

Among the other civil rights to be guaranteed without racial discrimination is the right to a nationality, in Article 5(d)(iii).

---

[233] CERD, *Concluding Observations on the Eleventh and Twelfth Periodic Reports of Germany, adopted on* 18 August 1993, U.N. Doc. A/48/18 at 86, ¶ 448.

[234] CERD, *Concluding Observations on the Ninth, Tenth and Eleventh Periodic Reports of France, adopted on* 18 March 1994, U.N. Doc. A/49/18 at 25, ¶ 144.

3.3.12 Right to Shelter/Housing

States must guarantee the right of everyone, without racial discrimination, the right to housing, under Article 5(e)(iii). A state violates this right when it fails, for example, to restore to returning refugees, asylum-seekers, or IDPs real property of which they were deprived during the course of an ethnic conflict.

3.3.13 Right to Health Care

States must guarantee the right of everyone, without racial discrimination, to public health and medical services, under Article 5(e)(iv).

3.3.14 Right to Education

States must guarantee the right of everyone, without racial discrimination, to education and training, under Article 5(e)(v). Refugees may face discrimination in the asylum state in the area of education because of their race or ethnicity.

3.3.15 Right to Work

Article 5(e)(i) obliges states to guarantee to everyone, without racial discrimination, the right to work, to free choice of employment, to just and favorable work conditions, and to equal pay for equal work.

The CERD has expressed concern over proposed legislation that would prohibit employers from employing persons in the process of appealing a decision that rejected their petition to remain.[235]

Those with permission to remain, including those with refugee status, may face racial or ethnic discrimination in the workplace. The CERD is very clear on the obligation of the state to investigate adequately allegations of employment discrimination. In *Yilmaz-Dogan v. The Netherlands*, the CERD found a violation of Article 5 because the state had not adequately protected the petitioner's right to work under Article 5(e)(i). The petitioner, a Turkish national, had been dismissed from work because she became pregnant. In submitting to a cantonal tribunal a special request to terminate her employment, the employer had made an explicit distinction between Dutch women and "our for-

---

[235] CERD, *Concluding Observations on the Thirteenth Periodic Report of the United Kingdom of Great Britain and Northern Ireland, adopted on* 14 March 1996, U.N. Doc. A/51/18 at 37–38, ¶ 235.

eign women workers."[236] The CERD found a violation because the Dutch court reviewing her claim had failed to take into account all the circumstances in the case, and, in particular, had never addressed the alleged discrimination in the employer's letter.

3.3.16 Right to Social Support

Article 5(e)(iv) obliges states to guarantee the right of everyone, without racial discrimination, to social security and social services.

In reviewing states parties' reports the CERD has commented on the denial or restrictions of government services to refugees and IDPs. For example, after examining a United Kingdom report in 1996, the CERD expressed concern at proposed legislation that would deny a number of social services to persons who had been granted permission to remain in the United Kingdom permanently, but who had not been naturalized as British citizens.[237] The CERD expressed similar concern after considering Croatia's state report in 1995, in relation to government imposed restrictions that had resulted in refugees failing, or having great difficulty and extreme delay in obtaining, the necessary documentation to allow them access to essential social and humanitarian services. In fact, these restrictions were so harsh and the benefits so critical to the refugees, that a number of refugees were forced to return to Bosnia and Herzegovina.[238]

3.3.17 Property Rights

According to Article 17 of the Universal Declaration of Human Rights, states must guarantee to everyone, without discrimination, "the right to own property alone as well as in association with others." In its *General Recommendation XXII on refugees and displaced persons,* CERD states that all refugees and displaced persons "have, after their return to their

---

[236] The employer's submission stated: "When a Netherlands girl marries and has a baby, she stops working. Our foreign women workers, on the other hand, take the child to neighbors or family and at the slightest set-back disappear on sick-leave under the terms of the Sickness Acct. They repeat that endlessly. Since we do our utmost to avoid going under, we cannot afford such goings on." *Yilmaz-Dogan v. Netherlands,* Communication No. 1/1984, *opinion adopted on* 10 August 1988, U.N. Doc. CERD/C/390 at 3, ¶ 2.2.

[237] CERD, *Concluding Observations on the Thirteenth Periodic Report of the United Kingdom of Great Britain and Northern Ireland, adopted on* 14 March 1996, U.N. Doc. A/51/18 at 37–38, ¶ 235.

[238] CERD, *Concluding Observations on the Periodic Report of Croatia, adopted on* 16 March 1995, U.N. Doc. A/50/18 at 40, ¶ 169.

homes of origin, the right to have restored to them property of which they were deprived in the course of the conflict and to be compensated appropriately for any such property that cannot be restored to them. Any commitments or statements relating to such property made under duress are null and void."[239]

3.3.18 Additional Issues

Although they do not involve rights that might be directly invoked in a complaint, there are additional statements of the CERD of relevance to the application of the Racial Discrimination Convention to refugees, asylum-seekers, and IDPs. For example, the CERD has consistently urged states parties to develop training programs for law enforcement officials to teach them how to avoid committing human rights violations, such as arbitrary arrests, detention, and disappearances of stateless refugees and foreigners.[240] In addition, the CERD has welcomed legislative measures aimed at protecting refugees, such as legislation by Cyprus designed to protect the rights of refugees and displaced persons regardless of their ethnic origin.[241] The CERD has also voiced its approval of legislation broadening the definition of a refugee.[242]

Also of importance is the obligation of states parties not only to legislate but also to educate, so as to eliminate the root causes of racial discrimination. Article 7 requires states to take measures in the fields of "teaching, education, culture and information" to combat "prejudices which lead to racial discrimination" and to promote "understanding, tolerance and friendship" among racial and ethnic groups.[243]

---

[239] CERD, *General Recommendation XXII: Article 5 and refugees and displaced persons* (Forty-ninth session, 1996) in HRI/GEN/1Rev.4 at 151, ¶ 2(c).

[240] CERD, *Concluding Observations on the Twelfth, Thirteenth, Fourteenth and Fifteenth Periodic Reports of the Syrian Arab Republic, adopted on* 19 March 1999, U.N. Doc. A/54/18 at 24, ¶ 181; U.N. Doc. CERD/C/304/Add.70.

[241] CERD, *Concluding Observations on the Fourteenth Periodic Report of Cyprus, adopted on* 12 August 1998, U.N. Doc. A/53/18 at 63, ¶ 333; U.N. Doc. CERD/C/304/Add.56.

[242] CERD, *Concluding Observations on the Twelfth Periodic Report of Sweden, adopted on* 20 August 1997, U.N. Doc A/52/18 at 66, ¶ 496.

[243] For information on the steps that the CERD has suggested states should take to fulfill their obligations under this article, *see* Stephanie Farrior, *The Neglected Pillar: The 'Teaching Tolerance' Provision of the International Convention on the Elimination of All Forms of Racial Discrimination*, 12 ILSA J. INT'L L. 291 (1999).

3.4 Protection Under the 1979 Convention on the Elimination of All Forms of Discrimination Against Women and the 1999 Optional Protocol

The 1979 Convention on the Elimination of All Forms of Discrimination against Women sets out specific steps that states are to take to eliminate discrimination against women in political, public, and civic life; in economic and social life; in the fields of education, employment, and health care; and in matters relating to marriage and family relations. The body that monitors state compliance with these treaty obligations is the Committee on the Elimination of Discrimination against Women (CEDAW).

The 1999 Optional Protocol has considerable potential as a forum for refugee, asylum-seeker, and IDP women whose rights under the Women's Convention have been violated.[244] It establishes two mechanisms: (a) an individual complaint procedure, under which individuals may file complaints with the CEDAW alleging a violation of their rights under the Women's Convention, and (b) an inquiry procedure, under which the CEDAW may initiate its own investigation when it receives information indicating "grave or systematic" violations of the rights in the Women's Convention. Comments made by the CEDAW in the course of examining state reports and in General Recommendations are indicative of its interpretation of the provisions of the Women's Convention, and possible application to future individual cases.

It should be borne in mind that a significant number of states parties to the Women's Convention have reservations that purport to impede the substantive application of the Convention to their state. A complainant must therefore be aware of these substantive reservations, and be prepared to challenge their legitimacy. This would entail, for example, arguing that the reservation was incompatible with the object and purpose of the Women's Convention, and thus should not prevent the application of the right to the individual victim.

3.4.1 Definition of Discrimination Against Women

The Women's Convention prohibits discrimination against women in the legal, political, economic, social, and cultural spheres. Article 1 defines the term "discrimination against women" as distinctions or restrictions made on the basis of sex which have the "effect or purpose" of impairing or nullifying the enjoyment or exercise of human rights

---

[244] The *Optional Protocol* came into force in December 2000 for those states that have ratified it.

by women, irrespective of their marital status, on the basis of equality of men and women. This extends to discrimination by both public authorities and private individuals. Though the Women's Convention does not contain an article specifically addressing violence against women, the general prohibition on sex discrimination has been interpreted to encompass a prohibition of violence against women, since such violence violates so many fundamental rights.[245]

> **Rights at a Glance:**
> Provisions of most relevance to refugees, asylum-seekers, and IDPs include: States parties are to:
> - ensure that public authorities refrain from any act or practice of discrimination against women (Article 2(d));
> - eliminate discrimination against women by any person, organization, or enterprise (Article 2(e));
> - ensure the exercise and enjoyment of fundamental rights on a basis of equality with men, via measures including legislation (Article 3), interpreted to include:
>   - the right to life,
>   - the right to physical integrity (including protection from sexual violence, torture, and other violence);
> - suppress traffic in women and exploitation of prostitution of women (Article 6);
> - ensure equality before the law (Article 15);
>
> and to eliminate discrimination against women in:
>
> - political and public life including the right to vote and hold public office (Article 7);
> - acquiring, changing, or retaining their nationality (Article 9);
> - education (Article 10);
> - employment (Article 11);
> - health care, including access to family planning (Article 12);
> - economic life, including family benefits and bank loans (Article 13);
> - marriage and family relations (Article 16).

---

[245] *See generally*, CEDAW, *General Recommendation No. 19: Violence Against Women* (Eleventh Session, 1992) in HRI/GEN/1/Rev.4 at 166–172.

3.4.2 The Right to Life and Physical Integrity

Violence Against Women

Although no article explicitly mentions violence against women, the CEDAW has clearly stated that states parties must take measures to eliminate violence because it falls squarely within the definition of discrimination in the Women's Convention, and because violence "seriously inhibits women's ability to enjoy rights and freedoms on a basis of equality with men." The definition of violence against women includes acts that inflict physical, mental, or sexual suffering; threats of such acts; coercion; and other deprivations of liberty, whether committed by a private person or by a public official. The CEDAW has called on states to take measures to prevent and punish gender-based violence and to support victims of such acts.[246]

An example of the application of these principles to refugee and displaced women appears in the review by the CEDAW of the report of the Democratic Republic of Congo. The CEDAW expressed grave concern over violence against refugee and displaced women in that state and recommended that the government adopt specific measures, including legislation, to protect women from such acts.[247] The CEDAW further recommended that the government provide psychological support and socio-economic integration opportunities to refugee and displaced women.[248]

The CEDAW also expressed grave concern over the widespread violence against refugee and displaced women in its 1994 concluding observations on state reports from Yugoslavia and Bosnia and Herzegovina. The Committee called on the Bosnian government to do all it could to prevent rape and protect women's human rights.[249]

The CEDAW also recommended in 1994 that the Armenian government encourage public discussion of violence against women; initiate legislation; train judges, security forces, and health care professionals to identify and eliminate manifestations of violence; and ensure that

---

[246] *Id.* at 172, ¶ 24(t).

[247] CEDAW, *Concluding Observations on the Initial, Second and Third Periodic Reports of the Democratic Republic of the Congo, adopted on* 1 February 2000, U.N. Doc. A/55/38 (Part I) at 25, ¶ 218; U.N. Doc. CEDAW/C/2000/I/CRP.3/Add.6/Rev.1.

[248] *Id.*

[249] CEDAW, *Concluding Observations on Report of the Federal Republic of Yugoslavia (Serbia and Montenegro), adopted on* 2 February 1994, U.N. GAOR, 49th Session, Supplement No. 38, U.N. Doc. A/49/38 at 133; *Concluding Observations on the Report of Bosnia and Herzegovina, adopted on* 1 February 1994, U.N. GAOR, 49th Session, Supplement No. 38, U.N. Doc. A/49/38 at 133, ¶ 757.

refugee and displaced victims of such violence have access to health and psychological services.[250]

Protection of the right to life may also be found in the requirement in Article 3 that states ensure women the enjoyment of rights and freedoms on a basis of equality with men. In reviewing the report of Congo, for example, the CEDAW urged the state to take immediate steps to protect the physical integrity of refugee and displaced women.[251] Failure on the part of a state to take measures to deal with violence against refugee or internally displaced women could form the basis of an individual complaint to the CEDAW of a violation of Article 3.

Traffic in Women and Exploitation of Prostitution

Article 6 requires states to take all appropriate measures to suppress traffic in women and exploitation of prostitution of women. The right to life of women exploited for prostitution, and their right to security of their person, is often in jeopardy. A state's failure to take adequate steps to protect against trafficking and exploitation of prostitution could form the basis of an individual complaint to the CEDAW.[252]

Displaced women are frequently coerced into providing sexual acts in return for food, shelter, security, documentation, or other forms of assistance.[253] Prostitution is also common, particularly in situations where it is one of the only forms of economic support.[254] Because their status may be unlawful, the CEDAW's *General Recommendation 19 on violence against women* notes that trafficked women and those forced into prostitution tend to be marginalized and thus are particularly vulnerable to violence and in need of increased legal protection.

---

[250] CEDAW, *Concluding Observations on the Initial Report of Armenia, adopted on* 14 July 1997, U.N. Doc. A/52/38/Rev.1 (Part II) at 81, ¶ 6.4.

[251] CEDAW, *Concluding Observations on the Report of Zaire, adopted on* 16 January 1997, U.N. GAOR, 52nd Sess., Supp. No. 38, U.N. Doc. A/52/38/Rev.1 at 50, ¶ 350.

[252] Although the Women's Convention does not define specific measures that would be "appropriate" under Article 6, Article 2 of the treaty sets out a general framework of steps that states parties must undertake to implement all the rights in the Convention. The CEDAW has issued an analysis of Article 2 elaborating on these steps. *Analysis of Article 2 of the Convention*, CEDAW, 14th Sess., Agenda Item 7, U.N. Doc. CEDAW/C/1995/4 (1994).

[253] Francis M. Deng, *Internally Displaced Persons, Report of the Representative of the Secretary-General*, submitted pursuant to Commission on Human Rights Resolution 1995/57, U.N. Doc. E/CN.4/1996/52/Add.2 at ¶ 125 (1995).

[254] *Id.* at ¶ 132.

In implementing Article 6, states must address the conditions that cause female prostitution, such as underdevelopment, poverty, drug abuse, illiteracy, and lack of training, education, and employment opportunities.[255] States should also provide women with alternatives to prostitution by creating opportunities through rehabilitation, job training, and job-referral services.[256] States that tolerate exploitation of girls and women, including any slave-like practices, are in clear violation of their obligations.[257]

In its 1998 concluding observations to Azerbaijan's state report, the CEDAW expressed concern over the government's failure to address the needs of refugee women and recommended that it provide them with information to protect them from traffickers and others who seek to exploit women for prostitution.[258] The 1999 Optional Protocol now challenges the CEDAW to translate and apply such concerns to the consideration and determination of individual cases.

3.4.3 Equality and Non-Discrimination

Measures to Ensure Equal Enjoyment of Rights

Because women refugees are so often deprived of their rights because they are women, Article 3, the equal rights provision, is of particular importance. This Article obligates states parties to take action in political, social, economic, and cultural fields to promote the advancement and full development of women on a basis of equality with men. Failure to take appropriate measures to fulfill this obligation could provide the substance of an individual complaint to the CEDAW or of a suggestion that the CEDAW undertake an inquiry under the 1999 Optional Protocol.

In the context of Article 3, the CEDAW has expressed particular concern over the failure of several states to take appropriate measures to protect and provide support for refugee populations, as seen in its

---

[255] *Fact Sheet No. 22.* See <http://www.unhchr.ch/html/menu6/2/fs22.htm>. CEDAW, *General Recommendation No. 19: Violence Against Women* (Eleventh Session, 1992) in HRI/GEN/1/Rev.4 at 168–169, ¶¶ 14 and 15, notes that "[p]overty and unemployment increase opportunities for trafficking in women," and "force many [females] into prostitution."

[256] *Fact Sheet No. 22.* See <http://www.unhchr.ch/html/menu6/2/fs22.htm>.

[257] *Id.*

[258] CEDAW, *Concluding Observations on the Initial Report of Azerbaijan, adopted on* 14 May 1998, U.N. GAOR, 53rd Sess., Supp. 38, U.N. Doc. A/53/38 at 10, ¶ 75.

concluding comments on state reports from the Congo[259] and Peru[260] (see also concluding comments on Tanzania[261] and Rwanda[262]). In the case of the Congo, the CEDAW urged the government to take immediate effective measures to protect the physical and moral integrity of refugee and displaced women. The CEDAW expressed concern at the Congo's lack of understanding of the relationship between discrimination and violence against women, particularly in conflict situations. The CEDAW also recommended that the government take steps to consider the living conditions of these women in order to provide further information on the consequences of armed conflict in its forthcoming report.[263]

In the case of Tanzania, the CEDAW requested additional information on the measures the state was taking to protect women refugees. In its recommendations to Peru in 1995, the CEDAW called for more effective measures to hasten the reintegration of displaced and refugee women into society. The CEDAW also expressed grave concern for the repatriation and resettlement of refugees, the majority of whom were women and children. The CEDAW 's concerns and recommendations on these and other state reports reflect its recognition of refugee and displaced women as particularly vulnerable populations in need of protection of all of the applicable substantive rights in the Women's Convention. Again, the 1999 Optional Protocol will require the CEDAW, when faced with a complaint, to translate its concerns into findings of violations of the rights of individual refugees or displaced girls and women.

Equality Before the Law

Article 15 requires states parties to ensure women's equality with men in legal and civil matters. States must repeal or amend any laws or

---

[259] CEDAW, *Concluding Observations on the Report of Zaire, adopted on* 16 January 1997, U.N. GAOR, 52nd Sess., Supp. No. 38, U.N. Doc. A/52/38/Rev.1 at 46, ¶ 350.

[260] CEDAW, *Concluding Observations on the Second Periodic Report of Peru, adopted on* 27 January 1995, U.N. GAOR, 50th Sess., Supp. No. 38, U.N. Doc. A/50/38 at 87, ¶ 448.

[261] CEDAW, *Concluding Observations on the Second and Third Periodic Reports of the United Republic of Tanzania, adopted on* 1 July 1998, U.N. Doc. A/53/38/Rev.1 at 68, ¶ 24.

[262] CEDAW, *Concluding Observations on the Report of Rwanda, adopted on* 31 January 1996, U.N. Doc. A/51/38 at 37–38, ¶¶ 317 and 331.

[263] CEDAW, *Concluding Observations on the Report of Zaire, adopted on* 16 January 1997, U.N. GAOR, 52nd Sess., Supp. No. 38, U.N. Doc. A/52/38/Rev.1 at 46, ¶¶ 350, 351.

instruments that have the effect of restricting women's legal capacity, including property and inheritance laws and contract laws. The CEDAW invoked these obligations in its 1997 concluding observations on Denmark's state report, when it expressed concern over the inadequacy of culturally- and gender-sensitive programs for refugee women to enable them to benefit from the legal and social services available in Denmark.[264]

3.4.4 Rights to Fair Trial and Due Process

Given the requirement in Article 3 that women be guaranteed the exercise and enjoyment of human rights and fundamental freedoms on a basis of equality with men, and the right to equality before the law in Article 15, states must ensure that trial procedures and due process protections be guaranteed to women without discrimination.

3.4.5 Right to Vote and Participate in the Political Process

Article 7 requires states parties to eliminate discrimination in political and public life. They are to ensure to women, on equal terms with men, the right to vote, to stand for election, to participate in the formulation of public policy, and to hold public office. The CEDAW has noted that restrictions on freedom of movement are a factor impeding women's exercise of the right to vote and otherwise participate in the political process.[265]

The exclusion of women IDPs from public fora for decision-making regarding the displaced population is a frequent and serious problem and could give rise to an individual complaint under the 1999 Optional Protocol, so long as the complainant can allege that she was the individual victim of such a violation.

3.4.6 Freedom of Religion

Although freedom of religion is not explicitly mentioned in the Women's Convention, it is guaranteed to women on a basis of equality with men by virtue of the Article 3 guarantee of equality in the enjoyment and exercise of human rights and fundamental freedoms.

---

[264] CEDAW, *Concluding Observations on the Third Periodic Report of Denmark*, adopted on 24 January 1997, U.N. GAOR, 52nd Sess., Supp. No. 38, U.N. Doc. A/52/38/Rev.1 at 36, ¶ 263.

[265] CEDAW, *General Recommendation No.23 (Political and public life)* (Forty-ninth session, 1997) in HRI/GEN/1/Rev.4 at 188, ¶ 20(d).

With regard to religious beliefs or practices that hinder the equal enjoyment by women of human rights, it should be noted that Article 5(a) requires state parties to "modify the social and cultural patterns of conduct of men and women" to eliminate "customary and other practices . . . based on the idea of inferiority or superiority of either of the sexes."

3.4.7 Freedom of Expression

As with the other rights not explicitly mentioned in the Women's Convention, this right is guaranteed on a basis of equality with men by virtue of Article 3.

3.4.8 Freedom of Association

As with the other rights not explicitly mentioned in the Women's Convention, this right is guaranteed on a basis of equality with men by virtue of Article 3.

3.4.9 Freedom of Movement

Article 15(4) requires equality in rights with regard to the law relating to the "movement of persons and the freedom to choose [one's] residence and domicile." Under this provision, a law that makes a woman's domicile dependent upon her husband's would be considered discriminatory, as would a law that operated to restrict the right of a woman to choose where she lives or travels. The rights to leave and enter one's country and to travel must be guaranteed on a basis of equality with men, per Article 3.

As for a right to asylum, it is not mentioned in the Women's Convention, but if a state has laws regarding asylum, they must be in substance and application without discrimination on the basis of sex.

3.4.10 The Right to Family and Private Life

Article 16 requires the elimination of discrimination against women in all matters relating to marriage and family relations. It does not address arbitrary interference with family or private life per se, but, as with other rights, states parties must guarantee against such interference without discrimination on the basis of sex.

Article 16 also requires states parties to ensure equality of men and women in matters relating to their children. States that discriminate against women regarding the nationality of their children, for example, violate this article. Article 16 also guarantees equality in rights during marriage and upon divorce.

Article 16(b) guarantees the right "freely to choose a spouse and to enter into marriage only with their free and full consent." The failure of states to stop the practice of forced marriage violates this article. If a state stands by and does nothing, for example, to protect girl and women refugees who are forced into marriage by their families, saying it is a traditional cultural practice,[266] such state inaction could form the basis of an individual complaint under the 1999 Optional Protocol.

3.4.11 Rights Regarding Nationality

The nationality rights set out in Article 9 are frequently of concern to refugee women. This article requires states to guarantee equality of men and women with regard to acquiring, changing or retaining their nationality and conferring it upon their spouse and children. For example, states may not permit foreign wives of male nationals to acquire their husband's nationality if they prohibit foreign husbands of female nationals from doing the same. The result would be that female nationals marrying foreign men may be forced to move to their husband's country of origin. This article also stipulates that nationality may not be passed down to children solely through the father.

The CEDAW has explained that the Women's Convention aims to prevent the loss of women's nationality because, as it noted in its *General Recommendation 21 on equality in marriage and family relations:* "Nationality is critical to full participation in society . . . . Without status as nationals or citizens, women are deprived of the right to vote or to stand for public office and may be denied access to public benefits and a choice of residence. Nationality should be capable of change by an adult woman and should not be arbitrarily removed because of marriage or dissolution of marriage or because her husband or father changes his nationality."[267]

---

[266] This is also an example of a violation resulting from the intersection of race and gender discrimination. For more on this subject, *see* CERD, *General Recommendation XXV(Gender Related Dimensions of Racial Discrimination)* (Fifty-sixth session, 2000), U.N. Doc. A/55/18 at 152.

[267] CEDAW, *General Recommendation 21 (Equality in marriage and family relations)* (Thirteenth session, 1994) in HRI/GEN/1/Rev.4 at 174, ¶ 6.

3.4.12 Rights to Food, Clothing, and Shelter

Although the Convention does not explicitly mention these rights, Article 3 provides that women are to be guaranteed the exercise and enjoyment of human rights—including those in the social, economic, and cultural fields—on a basis of equality with men.

3.4.13 Access to Health Care

Article 12 requires states to eliminate discrimination against women in the field of health care in order to ensure access on a basis of equality of men and women. The right of equal access to health care includes those services related to family planning. States must also ensure to women appropriate services in connection with pregnancy and the postnatal period. These services, as well as adequate nutrition during pregnancy and lactation, must be provided free where necessary.

States must remove any legal and social barriers that may operate to prevent or discourage women from making full use of available health care services.[268] This would include barriers such as poverty, illiteracy, and physical isolation. The CEDAW has also noted the obligation of states to avoid discrimination against women in national strategies for the prevention and control of acquired immunodeficiency syndrome (AIDS)[269] and against disabled women.[270]

The CEDAW has commented that special attention should be given to the health needs and rights of women belonging to vulnerable and disadvantaged groups, such as refugee and internally displaced women.[271] In addition to the health problems faced by refugee and dis-

---

[268] CEDAW, *General Recommendation No. 24: Article 12 of the Convention on the Elimination of All Forms of Discrimination Against Women—Women and Health* (Twentieth session, 1999) in HRI/GEN/1/Rev.4 at 199–201, ¶¶ 19–23 and 31(b).

[269] *See* CEDAW, *General Recommendation No. 15: Avoidance of discrimination against women in national strategies for the prevention and control of acquired immunodeficiency syndrome (AIDS)* (Ninth session, 1990) in HRI/GEN/1/Rev. 4 at 163–164 (states are required to increase education about AIDS to women, incorporate the special needs and problems of women into AIDS programs, ensure the active participation of women in primary health care, and report to the CEDAW on the situation of women as it relates to AIDS).

[270] CEDAW, *General Recommendation No. 18: Disabled Women* (Tenth session, 1991) in HRI/GEN/1/Rev.4 at 166 (states must report on special measures they take to ensure disabled women have equal access to education, employment, health services, social security, and social and cultural life.).

[271] CEDAW, *General Recommendation No. 24: Article 12 of the Convention on the Elimination of All Forms of Discrimination Against Women—Women and Health* (Twentieth session, 1999) in HRI/GEN/1/Rev.4 at 195, ¶ 6.

placed men, refugee and displaced women suffer from inadequate health care for pregnancy, menstruation, gynecological illnesses, and health problems faced predominantly by women. Because decision-makers are frequently men, women's health issues are often overlooked.

The CEDAW has emphasized that women in especially difficult circumstances, such as those trapped in situations of armed conflict and women refugees, should be ensured the provision of adequate protection and health services, including trauma treatment and counseling.[272]

Also relevant to health care is the right in Article 16 "to decide freely and responsibly on the number and spacing of their children, and to have access to the information, education and means" to be able to exercise this right.

In the context of Article 12 the CEDAW has addressed a concern that has been a reason for women's flight from persecution—female circumcision. The CEDAW has condemned this practice as discriminatory and seriously harmful to the health of women.[273] States are to take appropriate measures to eradicate the practice of female circumcision. This should include increased public education about the harmful effects of this practice, and the encouragement of community leaders to influence attitudes towards the eradication of the practice.[274] National health policies must also include strategies aimed at eradicating female circumcision and assistance, where appropriate, from United Nations organs.[275]

3.4.14 Right to Education

Article 10 guarantees equal rights in education, broadly defined to include pre-school, general, technical, professional, and adult education; access to scholarships and sports; information on family planning; and career and vocational training. Article 10 requires states to take appropriate measures to ensure that women and girls have equal access to equivalent conditions for career and vocational training and to the same curricula, examinations, teachers, and quality of education (paragraph b). Furthermore, states are required to eliminate stereotyped concepts of the roles of men and women in the education system and in textbooks (paragraph c).

---

[272] *Id.* at 198, ¶ 16.
[273] CEDAW, *General Recommendation No. 14: Female circumcision* (Ninth session, 1990) in HRI/GEN/1/Rev.4 at 161–163.
[274] *Id.* at 162, ¶ (a).
[275] *Id.* at 162 ¶¶ (b) and (c).

Refugee and displaced women and girls are often excluded from the educational opportunities that men and boys enjoy and that provide a basis for self-sufficiency. These girls and women may also need specialized education because most have lost their sources of income and livelihood.[276] Such training may concern survival skills, job skills, leadership, and conflict resolution.[277] Failure on the part of a state to ensure equal access to education may form the basis of an individual complaint under the 1999 Optional Protocol.

3.4.15 Employment Rights

Article 11 of the Women's Convention guarantees women equal rights with men in employment. These rights include:

(1) the right to work as an inalienable right of all human beings;
(2) the right to the same employment opportunities;
(3) the equal right to free choice of profession, promotion, job security, benefits, and vocational training;
(4) the right to equal remuneration and equal treatment for work of equal value;[278]
(5) the right to social security and paid leave; and
(6) the right to protection of health and safety in work conditions.

Furthermore, Article 11 prohibits discrimination against women in employment on the grounds of marriage or maternity.

The opportunity for employment activities constitutes a principal need of internally displaced people, particularly where they have been forced to abandon their sources of economic livelihood.[279]

---

[276] Francis M. Deng, *Internally Displaced Persons, Report of the Representative of the Secretary-General*, submitted pursuant to Commission on Human Rights Resolution 1995/57, U.N. Doc. E/CN.4/1996/52/Add.2, ¶ 328.

[277] *Id.* at ¶ 333.

[278] The Committee has issued brief additional comments on equal remuneration in CEDAW, *General Recommendation No. 13: Equal Remuneration for work of equal value* (Eighth session, 1989) in HRI/GEN/1/Rev.4 at 160–161.

[279] Francis M. Deng, *Internally Displaced Persons, Report of the Representative of the Secretary-General*, submitted pursuant to Commission on Human Rights Resolution 1995/57, Doc. E/CN.4/1996/52/Add.2 at 81 (1995). UNHCR has recognized the need to provide all refugee girls and women with effective and equitable access to skills training and wage-earning opportunities. Office of the United Nations High Commissioner for Refugees, *UNHCR Guidelines on the Protection of Refugee Women* at ¶¶ 111–120 (1991); *Refugee Women, 1999 Global*

3.4.16 Equal Rights in Economic Life

Of serious concern to both refugee women and internally displaced women is the extent to which they are discriminated against in economic life. Article 13 requires states to eliminate discrimination against women in economic life. This includes the obligation to ensure that women have the right to bank loans and other forms of financial credit on a basis of equality with men (paragraph b). States that distribute aid or make available economic opportunities to men rather than to men and women violate Article 13. Article 13 has great potential to assist women refugees, asylum-seekers, and IDPs under the 1999 Optional Protocol.

3.4.17 Property Rights

Restrictions on property rights can seriously limit a woman's ability to provide for herself and her dependants, and to obtain shelter. Article 16(1)(h) provides that states must ensure to women equal rights with men in the ownership, acquisition, management, administration, enjoyment, and disposition of property. Article 15(2) of the Women's Convention requires states parties to accord women equal rights with men to administer property.

3.5 Additional Relevant Articles in the Women's Convention

3.5.1 Temporary Measures to Accelerate Equality

Special measures such as quotas and affirmative action that are aimed at accelerating *de facto* equality between men and women are not considered discriminatory under the Women's Convention, according to Article 4. The CEDAW has recommended that states make more use of temporary measures that offer women preferential treatment in order to advance their integration into the education system, the economy, politics, and employment.[280] In its concluding observations to Azerbaijan's state report, for example, the CEDAW expressed concern that the government had not utilized temporary special measures to accelerate *de facto* equality, particularly in regard to assistance for displaced and refugee women.[281]

Appeal & Programme Overview, December 1998, online at <http://www.unhcr.ch/fdrs/ga99/women.htm>.

[280] CEDAW, *General Recommendation No. 5: Temporary Special Measures* (Seventh session, 1998) in HRI/GEN/1/Rev.4 at 155–156.

[281] CEDAW, *Concluding Observations on the Initial Report of Azerbaijan, adopted on* 14 May 1998, U.N. GAOR, 53rd Sess., Supp. 38, U.N. Doc. A/53/38 at 9, ¶ 62.

3.5.2 Obligation to Modify Social and Cultural Patterns of Conduct

Article 5 requires states to "modify the social, cultural and traditional patterns of conduct" so as to eliminate "prejudices and customary and all other practices which are based on the idea of inferiority or superiority of either of the sexes or on stereotyped roles for men and women." Accordingly, states must take steps to eliminate discrimination in the private sphere, particularly within the family.[282]

3.6 Other Relevant International Human Rights Treaties

Two additional human rights treaties merit mention even though they do not have individual complaint procedures: the 1989 Convention on the Rights of the Child and the 1966 International Covenant on Economic, Social and Cultural Rights. Although the bodies that monitor state party compliance with these treaties do not have authority to consider individual complaints alleging a violation, the reporting mechanism may serve as a way to bring concerns to the attention of the treaty bodies and to the governments concerned. In addition, the provisions of these two treaties may serve to inform the interpretation of related articles in the treaties that do have individual complaint mechanisms.

3.6.1 1989 Convention on the Rights of the Child

The 1989 Convention on the Rights of the Child sets out a series of civil, political, economic, social, and cultural rights of children, many of which are relevant to child refugees, asylum-seekers, and IDPs. The monitoring body of this treaty is the Committee on the Rights of the Child (CRC). UNHCR relies heavily on the Children's Convention in dealing with refugee children's issues. Similarly, the CRC makes reference to the 1951 Refugee Convention in its concluding observations on state reports.

The term "child" is defined as those under age 18. It is notable that although the CRC is not empowered to receive individual complaints, it is specifically authorized to request information relating to state reports from the United Nations Children's Fund (UNICEF), other UN agencies, and "other competent bodies" (Article 45). In practice, the CRC

---

[282] For elaboration on this point, *see, Fact Sheet No. 22*, at <http://www.unhchr.ch/html/menu6/2/fs22.htm>. If suggesting to the CEDAW that it undertake an inquiry into grave or systematic violations of the Women's Convention being experienced by refugee or IDP women, it may be relevant and useful to cite Article 5 and set out information about the cultural or social context in which the violations are grounded.

has also made requests from NGOs for information on state reports.

Child refugees and asylum-seekers are specifically addressed in Article 22, which requires states parties to take appropriate measures to ensure that a child who is a refugee or who is seeking refugee status, whether accompanied or unaccompanied by parent or guardian, "receive[s] appropriate protection and humanitarian assistance in the enjoyment of the applicable rights set forth in the Convention and in other international human rights or humanitarian instruments" to which the state is a party. Also of relevance is the non-discrimination clause, Article 2, which requires states parties to ensure the rights in the Children's Convention to each child in their jurisdiction "without discrimination of any kind," including "race, color, sex., language, religion, . . . national ethnic or social origin."

Rights at a Glance:
Rights of relevance to refugees, asylum-seekers, and IDPs include:
- The right to life (Article 6);
- Registration immediately after birth, and the right to a nationality (Article 7);
- The right of the child to preserve his or her identity, including nationality, name, and family relations (Article 8);
- The state obligation to ensure that a child is not separated from his or her parents against their will (Article 9), in accordance with which "applications by a child or his or her parents to enter or leave a State Party for the purpose of family reunification shall be dealt with . . . in a positive, humane and expeditious manner" (Article 10);
- The right to protection from arbitrary interference with his or her family (Article 16), which may be relevant in family reunification determinations as well;
- Health rights (Article 24), including the right of access to health care, and the obligation of states to take all effective measures to abolish "traditional practices prejudicial to the health of children," which has been interpreted to include female circumcision;
- The rights to education (Article 28) and social security (Article 25);
- The right to protection from sexual exploitation (Article 34);
- The obligation of states to ensure that detention of a child be used only as a measure of last resort and for the shortest appropriate period of time (Article 37), which has led the CRC to ask a state in reviewing its periodic report "What measures have been taken to avoid asylum-seeking children being kept in custody while awaiting deportation?"[283]
- The obligation of states to respect rules of international humanitarian law in armed conflicts that are relevant to the child (Article 38).

---

[283] *CRC, 8th Sess.* (January 1995) (reviewing report of Denmark).

In addition to the above rights, the Children's Convention has two additional protocols, adopted in 2000, that have relevance to child refugees, asylum-seekers, and IDPs: one on child soldiers[284] and one on the sale of children and child prostitution.[285]

3.6.2 1966 International Covenant on Economic, Social and Cultural Rights

The 1966 International Covenant on Economic, Social and Cultural Rights (ICESCR) contains numerous rights of relevance to the lives of refugees, asylum-seekers, and IDPs. UNHCR has found the ICESCR to be relevant, for example, in the area of property rights. The ICESCR provides that the obligation of a state party is to take steps, "to the maximum of its available resources, with a view to achieving progressively" the rights in the ICESCR (Article 2, paragraph 1). However, regardless of what resources a state has, it must guarantee the rights in the ICESCR without discrimination on the basis of race, color, sex, language, religion, or national or social origin (Article 2, paragraph 2). Indeed it is often in the context of discrimination that states have come under scrutiny in relation to their treatment of refugees and asylum-seekers.

The body that monitors state compliance with the ICESCR is the Committee on Economic, Social and Cultural Rights (CESCR). In reviewing state reports, the CESCR has often read one of the substantive rights

---

Rights at a Glance:
Rights in the ICESCR relevant to refugees, asylum-seekers, and IDPs include:
- The rights to work (Article 6), which is relevant when, for example, someone is denied a job due to discrimination on the basis of race, religion, or ethnicity;
- The right to just conditions of work as well as equal remuneration for equal work (Article 7);
- The right to social security (Article 9);
- Protection and assistance to the family (Article 10), which can be relevant in family reunification matters;
- The right to an adequate standard of living, including adequate food, clothing, and housing (Article 11);
- The right to adequate health care (Article 12); and
- The right to education (Article 13).

---

[284] *See* Bibliography of Cited International Instruments.
[285] *Id.*

listed above in conjunction with the non-discrimination requirement in Article 2 to ask states about policies that may discriminate against refugees and asylum-seekers. In the context of the right to housing, for example, the CESCR strongly urged Belgium "to fully ensure that persons belonging to ethnic minorities, refugees and asylum seekers are fully protected from any acts or laws which in any way result in discriminatory treatment within the housing sector."[286]

With respect to IDPs, the CESCR has, for example, expressed concern about the sizeable number of internally displaced persons in the Sudan, "many of whom are women and abandoned children, who have migrated from the war zones in the South to the North, where they live in abject poverty and without adequate shelter or employment."[287] In its Suggestions and Recommendations, the CESCR urged Sudan "to address the root causes of the problem of internally displaced persons," and to cooperate with organizations working in this field in order to provide measures to ensure "the basic needs of this group, such as adequate basic shelter, employment, food and health care, and the continuation of education for the children."[288]

4. Additional Considerations

In addition to considering issues regarding admissibility and substantive rights, advocates may wish to consider four additional areas in determining whether to pursue an individual complaint under one of the UN human rights treaties: the availability of interim measures (called "provisional measures" in some of the other human rights mechanisms), remedies, confidentiality, and legal aid.

4.1 Interim Measures

Given the length of time that can pass between submission of a complaint to a treaty body and a decision on the merits,[289] the availability of interim measures in urgent cases can be important.[290] A grant

---

[286] U.N. Doc. E/C.12/1994/7 (1994) at ¶ 14.

[287] *Concluding Observations of the Committee on Economic, Social and Cultural Rights: Sudan*, UN Doc. E/C.12/1/Add.48 at ¶ 24 (September 1, 2000).

[288] *Id.* at ¶ 35.

[289] HRC: between two and five years; CAT: about one year, though can take longer; CERD: usually one to three years.

[290] The term "interim measures" is used in the UN human rights treaty procedures rather than "provisional measures," which is the more common term in several other fora.

of interim measures may result, for example, in an individual's being given medical treatment, or not being deported, tortured, or executed.

All four treaties' procedures provide that the treaty body may request under certain circumstances that the state take interim measures. The HRC, the CAT, and the CEDAW may request the state party to take interim measures at any time after the receipt of the communication; the CERD rules restrict this procedure to communications already determined to be admissible for examination on the merits. Under all four mechanisms, when it requests the state to take interim measures the treaty body also informs the state that the request does not prejudge its final views on the merits of the communication.

It is rare for the Human Rights Committee to exercise its option to request interim measures; it has requested them most often in death penalty cases in which individuals awaiting execution have alleged violation of the right to a fair trial, though it has also done so in withholding of expulsion and in deportation cases. Interim measures are frequently sought from the CAT, and granted, in deportation cases. To date there is no experience by the CERD or the CEDAW with requests for interim measures.

1966 International Covenant on Civil and Political Rights—Optional Protocol

The Human Rights Committee may, after receipt of a communication and before adopting views in the case, request a state party to take interim measures in order to avoid "irreparable damage" to the victim of the alleged violations.[291] In an interim measures request, the state is asked to refrain from taking particular steps until the HRC has decided on the admissibility and merits of the communication.

Although the most common request for interim measures is to prevent executions, the Human Rights Committee has called on states to withhold expulsion or deportation of individuals from a state until it has ruled on the communication.[292] For example, in *O.E. v. S.*, the

---

[291] *HRC Rule of Procedure* 86. The request may be made by the HRC or the Special Rapporteur on New Communications (a member of the HRC). The Special Rapporteur is designated to receive communications between sessions of the HRC. *See*, terms of reference for the Special Rapporteur, GAOR, 46th Session, Supplement No. 40, U.N. Doc. A/45/40; in *Report of the Human Rights Committee*, at 218 (1991).

[292] *See O.E. v. S.*, Selected Decisions I at p. 5; *ARJ v. Australia*, 52nd Sess., Supp. No. 40, U.N. Doc. A/52/40; in *Report of the Human Rights Committee, vol.II*, U.N. Doc. CCPR/C/60/D/692/1996 (1997).

Committee requested that S. not expel O.E., who sought refuge in S., pending further consideration by the HRC.[293] In *A.R.J. v. Australia*, the HRC requested that the state refrain from any action that might result in the forced deportation of the author to Iran where the author claimed he would face the death penalty.[294]

In a case in which the individual had already been deported from Canada to Italy, the HRC turned down a request that it ask the state to take interim measures because the case did not meet the "irreparable damage" requirement.[295] In that case, the HRC determined that the author's deportation to Italy could not be considered to constitute "irreparable damage" because if the HRC were to conclude that the deportation was contrary to the ICCPR, the state party would be under an obligation to allow him to re-enter Canada, thereby placing him in the position he was prior to deportation.

The health of the victim may also cause the HRC to request interim measures in the form of a medical examination and report to the Committee.[296] The HRC has also requested that states take interim measures of protection where a particular way of life and culture is threatened.[297]

1984 Torture Convention

Under the CAT Rules of Procedure, once a communication is received the CAT may "inform the State party . . . of the desirability" of taking interim measures in order to avoid "possible irreparable damage" to the individual.[298] This provision is often invoked in the case of persons seeking to prevent their imminent expulsion by a state party. States are not legally bound to comply with a request for interim measures. Although some states have not complied with the CAT's request,[299] most states have done so.

---

[293] *Id.*.

[294] GAOR, 52nd Session, Supplement No. 40 (A/52/40); in *Report of the Human Rights Committee, vol.II*, U.N. Doc. CCPR/C/60/D/692/1996 (1997).

[295] *Canepa v. Canada*, UN Doc. CCPR/C/59/D/558/1993 (20 June 1997).

[296] *Altesor v. Uruguay*, Communication No. R.2/10, *views adopted on* 29 March 1982, GAOR, 37th Sess., Supp. No. 40, U.N. Doc. A/37/40 at 123–124, ¶ 4(c).

[297] *See for example, Ominayak, Chief of the Lubicon Lake Band v. Canada*, Communication No. 167/1984, *views adopted on* 26 March 1990, GAOR, 45th Session, Supp. No.40, U.N. Doc. A/45/40 at 10, ¶ 14; *Sara et al. v. Finland*, Communication No. 431/1990, *revised decision on admissibility adopted on* 23 March 1994, 49th Sess., Supp. No. 40, U.N. Doc. A/49/40, vol. II at 262, ¶ 5.6.

[298] *CAT Rule of Procedure* 108(9).

[299] *See, for example, Cecilia Rosana Núñez Chipana v. Venezuela*, Communication

1965 Racial Discrimination Convention

After a communication has been declared admissible, the CERD may request that the state concerned take interim measures to avoid "possible irreparable damage" to the person claiming to be a victim of a violation.[300] Although this provision closely mirrors similar provisions in the other treaties' rules, it provides for interim measures only after a decision on admissibility has been made, rather than after receipt of the communication, as provided by the other three treaties' procedures.

1979 Women's Convention—1999 Optional Protocol

Article 5 of the 1999 Optional Protocol provides that, after a communication is received, the CEDAW may, before it reaches a determination on the merits, transmit to the state party "for its urgent consideration" a request that it take interim measures as necessary to avoid "possible irreparable damage" to the victim or victims of the alleged violation.

4.2 Remedies

In general, upon examining a communication, a UN human rights treaty body will announce its "views," that is, whether it concludes that the petitioner's rights have been violated. The treaty body is not limited to determining whether or not there has been a violation. If it does find a violation, the treaty body transmits this conclusion to the parties and may recommend or suggest specific steps for the state party to take. The treaty bodies' views are their expert opinion concerning the interpretation of the treaty and its application to the individual case. The Human Rights Committee has said that ratification of the First Optional Protocol to the ICCPR requires states to provide a remedy when it finds a violation of the ICCPR. While the ICCPR itself does not render the views legally binding, it is arguable that the years of HRC practice, without objection from virtually all participating states parties, mean that ratification should be considered a commitment to provide a remedy in response to the HRC's finding of a violation. In some instances the state concerned has, as a result of the views of the treaty body, changed its legislation or policy, released a detainee, or provided compensation

---

No. 110/1998, *views adopted on* 10 November 1998, U.N. Doc. A/54/44 at ¶ 8 (the CAT expressed deep concern that Venezuela did not accede to the request for interim measures to refrain from expelling or extraditing the alleged victim while the CAT considered the communication).

[300] *CERD Rule of Procedure* 94(3).

to the individual whose rights were violated. It is not uncommon, however, for states to ignore the treaty body's recommendations.[301] For this reason, advocates who wish a binding judgment should consider pursuing a case before a regional human rights court, if one is available. Indeed, many individuals in Europe choose to pursue their case in the European system instead of through one of the UN mechanisms, since it may result in a binding judgment of the European Court of Human Rights.

1966 International Covenant on Civil and Political Rights—Optional Protocol

If the Human Rights Committee determines that a communication shows that the petitioner's rights under the ICCPR were violated, it conveys this to the parties and proceeds to ask the state concerned to take appropriate steps to remedy the violation. These recommendations have ranged from the general (for example, to provide immediate and effective remedies to the victims, or to change legislation so as to give effect to the provisions of the ICCPR) to the more specific (for example to give the individual permission to leave the country;[302] to release the individual immediately, to investigate the allegations of torture, to bring to justice those responsible, to provide compensation to the individual for the torture, to ensure that similar violations do not occur in the future,[303] and to return property to the victim).[304]

---

[301] Non-compliance by states parties with the Human Rights Committee's views was such that the HRC established in 1991 a Special Rapporteur for Follow-Up of Views to monitor what action states have taken to "give effect" to the committee's views. For the Special Rapporteur's detailed report on follow-up activities on cases from 1991–1998, *see, Human Rights Committee, Annual Report*, U.N. Doc. A/53/40, at Ch. VIII (1998). The Special Rapporteur's mandate has been interpreted to allow on-site missions, so long as the state has consented, but thus far only one such visit has taken place (to Jamaica), in part because of funding constraints.

[302] *For example, López Burgos v. Uruguay*, Communication No. 52/1979, U.N. GAOR, 36th Sess., Supp. No. 40, U.N. Doc. A/36/40; in *Report of the Human Rights Committee*, 176 (1981); U.N. Doc. CCPR/C/OP/1 (1984) at 88, U.N. Doc. CCPR/C/OP/1 (1985).

[303] *See, for example,* the set of recommendations made with respect to numerous communications in *Annual Report of Human Rights Committee*, U.N. Doc. A/49/40 (1994).

[304] *For example, Ex-Philibert v. Zaire*, Communication No. 90/1981, *views adopted on* 21 July 1983, U.N. Doc. A/38/40 at 197.

1984 Torture Convention

If the CAT issues a finding that expulsion or return of the author to a given country would constitute a violation of Article 3, it also declares that the state party has an obligation to refrain from returning the applicant to that country. The CAT sometimes adds that there is also an obligation to refrain from sending the individual to any other country where the individual runs a real risk of being expelled or returned to the country where torture is feared. If the individual has already been returned to a country in circumstances the CAT believes violated Article 3, the CAT's comments are limited to a finding of the violation; no additional measure is recommended.

In cases in which the CAT has found a violation of other provisions of the Torture Convention, such as the obligation to investigate allegations of torture under Article 12, or to ensure that a case alleging torture is investigated promptly and impartially under Article 13, the CAT has included a generally worded request that the state party ensure that similar violations do not occur in the future.

1965 Racial Discrimination Convention

If the CERD issues a finding of a violation of the Racial Discrimination Convention, it will also issue a generally worded recommendation to the state concerned. In a case involving deprivation of the right to work, for example, it asked the state to "use its good offices to secure alternative employment for her and/or to provide her with such other relief as may be considered equitable."[305] In a case in which it found that the state had failed to provide adequate protection against threats of racist violence, the CERD recommended that the state review its policy and procedures concerning the decision to prosecute in cases of alleged racial discrimination, provide the applicant with relief commensurate with the moral damage he has suffered, and in its next report to the CERD, inform the Committee about any action it had taken with respect to the recommendations.[306] In another case, upon finding a violation the CERD recommended to the state party "to ensure that the police and the public prosecutors properly investigate accusations and complaints related to acts of racial discrimination which should be pun-

---

[305] *A. Yilmaz-Dogan v. The Netherlands*, Communication No. 1/1984, UN Doc. CERD/C/390, at 7 (5 June 2000) (compilation of opinions and decisions adopted by the Committee under article 14 of the Convention).

[306] *L.K. v. The Netherlands*, Communication No. 4/1991, UN Doc. CERD/C/390, at 30 (5 June 2000) (compilation of opinions and decisions adopted by the Committee under article 14 of the Convention).

ishable by law according to article 4 of the Convention."[307]

Significantly, the CERD has recommended certain measures to the state even in some cases in which it has determined that the subject of the complaint technically falls outside its competence,[308] or that the facts as established do not disclose a violation of the Racial Discrimination Convention.[309] The CERD makes these recommendations pursuant to Article 14(7)(b) of the Racial Discrimination Convention, under which it is to forward to the petitioner and the state party concerned its suggestions and recommendation. The clause is not explicitly limited to cases in which the CERD finds a violation of the Racial Discrimination Convention.

1979 Women's Convention—1999 Optional Protocol

The 1999 Optional Protocol to Women's Convention provides that, after examining a communication, the CEDAW transmits to the parties its views on the communication along with its recommendations, if any.[310] The state is to "give due consideration" to the CEDAW's views and recommendations, and submit within six months a written response, including any action taken to comply.

---

[307] *Kashif v. Ahmad*, Communication No. 16/1999, UN Doc. CERD/C/390, at 76 (5 June 2000) (compilation of opinions and decisions adopted by the Committee under article 14 of the Convention).

[308] *For example. Narrainen v. Norway*, Communication No. 3/1991, U.N. Doc. CERD/C/390, at 23 (5 June 2000) (compilation of opinions and decisions adopted by the Committee under article 14 of the Convention), in which CERD noted it was not its function to interpret the state party's rules on criminal procedure concerning the disqualification of jurors on account of racial bias, or to decide as to whether the juror had to be disqualified on that basis ("The Committee recommends to the State party that every effort should be made to prevent any form of racial bias from entering into judicial proceedings which might result in adversely affecting the administration of justice on the basis of equality and non-discrimination. Consequently, the Committee recommends that in criminal cases like the one it has examined, due attention be given to the impartiality of juries, in line with the principles underlying article 5(a) of the Convention.").

[309] *For example., Z U.B.S. v. Australia*, Communication No. 6/1995, U.N. Doc. CERD/C/390 at 47 (5 June 2000) ("The Committee suggests that the State party simplify the procedures to deal with complaints of racial discrimination, in particular those in which more than one recourse measure is available, and avoid any delay in the consideration of such complaints.").

[310] *CEDAW OP*, art. 7(3).

118 Human Rights Protection for Displaced Persons

4.3 Confidentiality

The procedures regarding confidentiality vary somewhat among the four complaint mechanisms. When a communication is submitted to the HRC and the CAT, the treaty body brings it to the attention of the state party concerned; the identity of the author is disclosed to the state, though the complainant's identity may remain confidential (even after a decision on the merits) should the Committee, Working Group, or Special Rapporteur on new Communications so decide.[311] The CERD will not reveal the identity of the author without that person's express authorization.[312] The CEDAW will bring a communication to the attention of the state party concerned only if the individual or individuals consent to the disclosure of their identity to that state.

1966 Covenant on Civil and Political Rights

When a communication is submitted to the Human Rights Committee, the HRC brings it to the attention of the state party concerned. The state party is informed of the identity of the author so that it may reply to the allegations, but the HRC may decide to keep the complainant's identity confidential if the complainant so requests. The HRC examines communications in closed session, and all documents relating to the consideration of a communication are confidential. However, the author and the state may make public any submissions or information bearing on the proceedings[313] unless otherwise requested by the HRC.[314] The identity of the author remains confidential when the HRC publishes its decisions on inadmissibility. It may continue to remain confidential following the decision on the merits if the HRC so decides.

1984 Torture Convention

When a communication is submitted to the Committee against Torture, the CAT brings it to the attention of the state party concerned. The identity of the author is disclosed to the state so that the state may reply to the allegations, but all meetings of the CAT concerning the individual communication are closed.[315] The text of the CAT's decisions declaring communications inadmissible under Article 22 of the

---

[311] *HRC Rule of Procedure* 96(4).
[312] *CERD Rule of Procedure* 94(1).
[313] *HRC Rule of Procedure* 96(2) and (3).
[314] *HRC Rule of Procedure* 96(3).
[315] *CAT Rule of Procedure* 101(1).

Torture Convention are made public without disclosing the identity of the author of the communication, but identifying the state party concerned. The identity of the author is disclosed to the public only if a violation is determined to have occurred, and may remain confidential if the CAT so decides. In order to ensure the confidentiality of particularly sensitive documents and information, it is advised that the individual complaint clearly state which parts of the communication are confidential.

1965 Racial Discrimination Convention

The CERD will not reveal the identity of the complainant "unless he has given his express consent."[316] Meetings during which the CERD examines communications are closed.

1979 Women's Convention

When a communication is submitted to the CEDAW the Committee will bring it confidentially to the attention of the state party, provided that the complainant consents to the disclosure of her identity to the state concerned.[317] The CEDAW will examine the submissions in closed meetings.[318] The 1999 Optional Protocol also contains a provision explicitly requiring states to "take all appropriate steps to ensure that those who communicate with the Committee are not subjected to ill-treatment or intimidation."[319]

4.4 Legal Aid

None of the UN human rights individual complaint mechanisms provides for legal aid to assist those who may wish to submit a complaint.

5. Strengths and Weaknesses of the UN Treaty Mechanisms for Individual Complaints

The UN treaty mechanisms for individual complaints can provide valuable but limited protection for refugees, asylum-seekers, and internally displaced persons. The individual petitions filed with the treaty

---

[316] *CERD Rule of Procedure* 94; *see also, Racial Discrimination Convention,* art.14(6)(a).
[317] *CEDAW OP*, art. 6(1).
[318] *CEDAW OP*, art. 7.
[319] *CEDAW OP*, art. 11.

bodies have directly helped some individuals. Though state compliance with the treaty bodies' views on individual cases is weak, an official pronouncement that the petitioner's rights have been violated carries significance in a number of ways even without a formal enforcement system. If one seeks a legally binding judgment one should look elsewhere. If, however, such an avenue is not available, the UN treaty mechanisms are worth considering. Some of the benefits and drawbacks of pursuing a claim under the individual complaint mechanism of a UN treaty body are set out below.

5.1   Finding of a Violation by an International Body

An individual complaint submitted to a UN human rights treaty body can result in an official finding that the petitioner's rights were indeed violated. Given the lack of a forum in some states for individuals to seek vindication of their rights, the availability of a petition procedure under the UN treaties can be particularly important.

5.2   Publicity

By shining an international spotlight on an individual case, the UN individual complaint mechanisms have the potential to bring redress in that case and to pressure the government to desist from similar human rights violations. That spotlight shines at several intervals. First, when a communication is filed the treaty body seeks the state party's response, thereby bringing to the state's attention the fact that an independent international body is aware of the allegations in the case. Second, if the committee determines there has been a violation it transmits its views including recommendations to the state party, again calling attention to the case. In addition, the treaty bodies submit to the UN General Assembly an annual report that includes their views on the cases taken up that year. The sessions in which the treaty bodies examine individual communications are not public, which serves to dim the international spotlight somewhat. Their findings, however, are public.

5.3   Moral Vindication

Even if the state does not follow the recommendations of the treaty body, the finding by a UN human rights body that the individual's rights have been violated can provide important moral support to individual petitioners, their families, and colleagues.

5.4 Role for Individuals

It is highly significant that a procedure exists in which an individual may challenge a state, given what is otherwise a very state-centered framework of international law. Though the role for individuals is a limited one—they are not invited to provide oral testimony,[320] and the committee considers communications in closed meetings—the complaint mechanisms provide individuals with access to a forum to register a complaint against the state and to have it heard by an independent body.

5.5 May Prevent Expulsion or Deportation

Both the CAT and the HRC procedures have been used successfully in preventing expulsion of an individual to face a substantial risk of torture. Though the recommendations of these committees on individual petitions are not legally binding, states usually comply with their request for urgent interim measures in these cases. Though neither the CERD nor the CEDAW procedures have not yet been used to seek prevention of deportation, they have the potential to be so used.

Given the increasingly restrictive interpretations of the 1951 Refugee Convention by domestic institutions, more asylum-seekers may need to turn to alternative bars to refoulement, such as that in Article 3 of the 1984 Torture Convention.

5.6 Limits on Availability of Mechanism

The individual complaint mechanism under any of the UN human rights treaties is available only if the state in question has both ratified the treaty and consented to use of the complaint mechanism under that treaty. This limits the availability of these procedures considerably. As the figures below show, some of the complaint procedures have a low rate of acceptance.[321] That of the Racial Discrimination Convention is particularly low, and that of the Torture Convention—so important because of the Article 3 provision on non-refoulement—is only marginally higher.

---

[320] Both the Torture Convention and the Racial Discrimination Convention provide that the committee may invite the presence of the petitioner or his representative and the presence of representatives of the state party concerned in order to provide additional information or to answer questions on the merits of the communication. *CAT Rule of Procedure* 110; *CERD Rule of Procedure* 94(5). To date this has not happened.

[321] Acceptances as of 28 March 2001.

Civil and Political Rights Covenant: 98 of the 148 states parties
Torture Convention: 43 of the 123 states parties
Racial Discrimination Convention: 29 of the 157 states parties
Women's Convention: 17 of the 167 states parties (plus 49 signatories)[322]

As noted above, the availability of the UN treaty mechanisms may be further limited by reservations made by some states to substantive rights in the treaty. This problem is particularly acute in the context of the Women's Convention.

5.7 Lengthy Time Between Filing and Decision

The length of time it takes from the date of submission of a communication to a decision by the treaty body can be considerable. In the HRC, it takes between two and five years; in the CAT, about one to one-and-a-half years, though it can take longer; and in the CERD, usually one to three years. Though the new procedure under the CEDAW has not yet begun, similar delays are likely. Interim measures are available but will not be sought of the state by the treaty body unless there is a risk of "irreparable harm," which does not apply in many cases.

The delays are due in part to various procedures for consulting with the state and the complainant, as well as the fact that each committee meets in session for only a limited number of weeks per year.[323] During these sessions the committee examines not only individual communications but also several states parties' reports (see *infra* at section 6.2). As the number of individual communications increases,[324] delays are likely to increase unless additional resources are provided.

---

[322] A "signature" by the state indicates intent to ratify. Each state has its own procedures for completing the ratification process after signing a treaty.

[323] Excluding pre-sessional meetings, HRC: three times a year for three weeks each; CAT: twice a year for 2–3 weeks each; CERD: twice a year for 3–4 weeks each; CEDAW: twice a year for three weeks each.

[324] The number of decisions (final views, admissible, inadmissible or discontinued) taken annually by the CAT on individual cases has risen from 3 in 1990, to 11 in 1995, to 24 in 2000. As of the 2000 Annual Report, the CAT had registered 163 communications in total; *Report of the Committee Against Torture*, U.N. Doc. A/55/44.

5.8 The Issue of the Binding Nature of Opinions

A treaty body is not a court. Its views are not rendered legally binding by the treaty, although treaty body practice suggests a degree of obligation to provide a remedy in response to a finding of a violation. At the same time, there is no formal enforcement system, and it is fairly common for the state to ignore the treaty body's views.

Despite their weaknesses, the UN treaty mechanisms for individual complaints have brought positive results for some petitioners, and have brought about some legislative and policy changes. Even in cases where the state does not comply with the recommendations of the treaty body, the views of the treaty bodies on individual complaints serve to emphasize accountability on the part of the state for human rights violations in specific cases.

6. Other Advocacy Possibilities

A number of avenues for advocacy exist under the major UN human rights treaties in addition to the individual complaint mechanisms. All of these treaties contain a reporting and monitoring procedure. In addition, all the treaty bodies issue authoritative interpretations of the provisions of the treaty monitored by that body that can be a valuable resource for advocates. Two of the treaties authorize an inquiry by the treaty body into reports of violations: the 1984 Torture Convention and the 1999 Optional Protocol to the Women's Convention. Three of the treaties establish a procedure whereby a state may bring a complaint alleging that another state is not in compliance with the treaty: the 1966 International Covenant on Civil and Political Rights, the 1984 Torture Convention, the 1965 Racial Discrimination Convention.[325] There is a role for NGOs and other advocates in all these procedures, though some warrant more attention than others.

---

[325] *ICCPR*, art. 41; *Torture Convention*, art. 21; *Racial Discrimination Convention*, art.11. State-to-State complaints: The ICCPR and the Torture Convention's interstate complaint procedures are optional; they may be used only if both the filing state and the state filed against have made a declaration recognizing the competence of the relevant treaty body to consider such communications. In contrast, parties to the Racial Discrimination Convention consent to an interstate complaint procedure by virtue of their ratification of the convention. To date none of these three interstate complaint procedures has been used.

6.1 State Reporting Procedure

Each of the major UN human rights treaties establishes a reporting and monitoring procedure under which the state party periodically submits to the treaty body a report on measures it has taken to implement the treaty. The treaty body then examines these reports, meets in session to pose questions of government representatives, and issues comments on the information in the report and recommendations to the state concerned that are published by the UN.

The states parties' reports as well as the treaty bodies' conclusions, observations, and recommendations can be very useful sources in preparing asylum claims. Documents generated by the reporting procedure are available on the UN's human rights website: <www.unhchr.ch>. This site also provides information on when each treaty body will be meeting and where (New York or Geneva) and which states' reports it will be examining in its upcoming sessions. The site also provides the treaty body's conclusions, observations, and recommendations, normally copies of the states parties' reports, and in some cases the summary records of the treaty bodies' sessions with government representatives.

This process provides a number of opportunities for NGOs and other advocates to use in efforts to protect the rights of refugees, asylum-seekers, and IDPs. Advocates can try to engage state representatives in a dialogue on the issues in the process of drafting the state report. Advocates may also send information to the treaty body on the situation in a state party, so that the state's report is not the sole source of information the body has before it. Information about an individual case can be helpful to the committee members, since states are generally not forthcoming in reporting on human rights violations in their territory. The information sent may take the form of a shadow report to the committee on the state's implementation—or lack thereof—of one or more articles of the treaty. Usually, although some of the committees (notably the CRC) have suggestions for NGO submissions, there is no prescribed format for such reports to follow, though it is helpful to the committee if information is presented as relevant to a specific article of the treaty. Specific questions for the committee members to pose to government representatives when they meet in session may also be useful. Information should be sent to a treaty body well before it meets to review a state's report in order to give sufficient time to committee members to review it. This is often prior to the session preceding the active dialogue with the state party in order to be considered at the time. Four of six of the committees frame the "list of questions" to be posed to states parties.

NGOs may also request a meeting to brief the committee or individual members before the committee takes up the state's report with government representatives. Before, during, and after the session, one can contact the press to share one's information and be available for follow-up questions or statements.

Advocates can also publicize within the state being examined both the state's report and the advocates' own report or own information, as well as the comments and recommendations of the treaty body once issued. The comments and recommendations can also be used by NGOs within the state in pressuring the government for change, and to hold it to the obligations it undertook in satisfying the treaty.

The state reporting process can spotlight the human rights situation in a given country. It provides advocates with recommendations by an expert body to the state on areas of concern. A major limiting factor is that many states fail to submit their reports, and some of the committees will not consider a country in the absence of a report.

Since neither the 1989 Convention on the Rights of the Child nor the 1966 International Covenant on Economic, Social and Cultural Rights has an individual complaint mechanism yet,[326] advocates should consider using the reporting mechanism under both treaties for calling the attention of the relevant treaty body to cases and situations violating treaty rights.

6.2 General Comments and Recommendations of the Treaty Bodies

Each of the treaty bodies issues "general comments" or "general recommendations," which provide interpretations of various provisions of the treaty they monitor. Though not legally binding on states parties, general comments are generally considered to be authoritative and can be a valuable resource regarding the specific content of rights and procedures in the treaty.

Issued in order to guide states in implementing their obligations under the treaty, general comments address issues only in the abstract, without reference to specific countries or cases. Some general comments focus on a particular article, as for example the Human Rights Committee *General Comment on Article 7 of the ICCPR regarding the obligation of states to act against torture and ill-treatment*. Other general comments address subjects that may involve several treaty provisions, such as the CERD *General Recommendation XXII on Refugees and Displaced Persons*.

Given the importance of treaty interpretation, it can be useful for NGOs and other advocates to attempt to share their expertise and

---

[326] Discussions are underway to develop individual complaint procedures under both these treaties, but it is unclear if and when such a procedure will be in place for either treaty.

experience with the treaty bodies during the drafting of general comments, thereby helping to shape an understanding of the meaning of certain norms. On this basis they may urge a particular interpretation on a treaty body during drafting. Advocates may also suggest to a treaty body the need for a general comment on a particular treaty provision or issue, providing the body with background information to support the suggestion.[327]

6.3 Inquiry Procedure

Two international human rights treaties authorize the relevant treaty body to undertake an inquiry into alleged violations. The CAT may initiate an inquiry upon information that torture is being "systematically practiced" in a state party, whereas the CEDAW procedure in the Optional Protocol may be triggered by information that "grave or systematic violations" of the rights in the Women's Convention are taking place. The Torture Convention and the CEDAW Optional Protocol contain an opt-out clause under which the state party may declare that it does not recognize the competence of the committee with regard to the inquiry procedure.

Advocates may wish to consider submitting cases and other information on alleged violations to the CAT or the CEDAW with a view to prompting an inquiry by the treaty body in order to bring attention not to just one case, but to the situation demonstrated by the existence of many such cases. Though the CAT has completed and published only two inquiries to date, there is reason to believe that the CEDAW will make greater use of the inquiry procedure available under its Optional Protocol.

6.3.1 Torture Convention

The Committee against Torture may initiate a confidential inquiry by one or more of its members if it receives reliable information indicating that torture is being "systematically practiced" in a state party's territory. The inquiry may include an on-site visit if the state consents to it. Anyone, including non-governmental organizations, may submit information that alerts the CAT to the possible occurrence of systematic torture. A state party can avoid inquiries under this procedure, however, by making a declaration under Article 28 that it does not recognize the authority of the CAT to undertake this investigatory procedure.

---

[327] Advocates may wish, for example, to approach the treaty bodies about making reference to the various Guiding Principles on Internal Displacement to guide interpretation of a number of human rights relevant to IDPs.

The CAT has interpreted "systematic practice" to be when "the torture cases reported have not occurred fortuitously in a particular place or at a particular time, but are seen to be habitual, widespread and deliberate in at least a considerable part" of the state."[328] The government does not have to intend to engage in a systematic practice of torture.[329] Instead, the systematic practice of torture "may be the consequence of factors which the Government has difficulty in controlling" and may indicate a discrepancy between policy and implementation of that policy.[330]

Although the inquiry is confidential, the CAT may decide to include a summary account of the results of the inquiry in its annual report to the UN General Assembly. Since 1985, when the Torture Convention entered into force, only two inquiries have been concluded and published, one on Turkey and one on Egypt. Numerous procedural regulations of the CAT, including its reluctance to release inquiry results in a timely fashion, have contributed to the inefficient use of the inquiry procedure, as has the lack of cooperation by states. These drawbacks may suggest to some advocates that their efforts are best placed elsewhere.

6.3.2 Women's Convention

The 1999 Optional Protocol to the Women's Convention authorizes the CEDAW to initiate a confidential investigation by one or more of its members when it has received reliable information of "grave or systematic violations" by a state party of rights in the Convention. The use of "or" rather than "and" in this clause is important, for the CEDAW does not have to determine whether the information it has received indicates that violations are "systematic" to proceed to an inquiry, so long as it determines that the violations are "grave." As with the procedure under the Torture Convention, the treaty body is authorized to visit the territory of the state to conduct an investigation, but only so long as the state consents. States parties may opt out of the inquiry procedure under Article 10 of the Optional Protocol.

This inquiry procedure has the potential to be a valuable avenue for vindicating the rights of women and girl refugees, asylum-seekers, and IDPs. The procedure allows for inquiry into the situation in a state without being tied to the five-year schedule for examination of reports.

---

[328] CAT, *Summary account of the proceedings concerning the inquiry on Turkey*, U.N. Doc. A/48/44/Add.1 at 7–8, ¶ 39.
[329] *Id.*
[330] *Id.*

In addition, NGOs or other advocates may use the procedure to call attention to cases for which it is difficult to submit an individual complaint. Given the mass nature of some of the violations to which forcibly displaced women are subjected, advocates may transmit information to the CEDAW on grave violations or systematic violations with a view to prompting an inquiry under this procedure.

Bibliography

Books

McGoldrick, Dominic, The Human Rights Committee: Its Role in the Development of the International Covenant on Civil and Political Rights (1994).

Chapters

Lewis-Anthony, Siân, *Treaty-Based Procedures for Making Human Rights Complaints within the U.N. System, in* Guide to International Human Rights Practice 53 (Hurst Hannum ed., 3rd ed. 1999).

Articles

Farrior, Stephanie, *The Neglected Pillar: The 'Teaching Tolerance' Provision of the International Convention on the Elimination of All Forms of Racial Discrimination*, 12 ILSA J. Int'l & Comp. L. 291 (1999).

Gorlick, Brian, *The Convention and the Committee against Torture: A Complementary Protection Regime for Refugees*, 11 Int'l J. Refugee L. 493 (1999).

Helfer, Lawrence, *Forum Shopping For Human Rights*, 148 U. Pa. L. Rev. 285 (1999).

U.N. Documents

CAT:

Activities of the Committee against Torture pursuant to article 20 of the Convention against Torture and other Cruel, Inhuman or Degrading Treatment or Punishment, U.N. Doc. A/48/44/Add.1 (1993).

Committee Against Torture Annual Report, U.N. Doc. A/52/44 (1997).

Committee Against Torture Annual Report, Communication No. 45/1996, U.N. Doc. A/53/44 (1998).

Committee Against Torture, Rules of Procedure, U.N. Doc. CAT/C/3/Rev.3 (1998).

Concluding Observations of the Committee against Torture: Finland, U.N. Doc. CAT/C/23/3 (1999).
Concluding Observations of the Committee against Torture: Jordan, U.N. Doc. CAT A/50/44 (1995).
Concluding Observations of the Committee against Torture: United Kingdom of Great Britain and Northern Island, U.N. Doc. CAT A/51/44 (1996).
Concluding Observations of the Committee against Torture: United Kingdom of Great Britain and Northern Ireland, U.N. Doc. CAT A/54/44 (1998).
Concluding Observations of the Committee against Torture: Venezuela, U.N. Doc. A/54/44 (1999).
Summary Record of the First Part of the 395th Meeting: Austria, U.N. Doc. CAT/C/SR.395 (1999).

CEDAW:

CEDAW, *Analysis of Article 2 of the Convention*, U.N. Doc. CEDAW/C/1995/4 (1994).
CEDAW, *General Recommendation No. 5*, U.N. Doc. HRI/GEN/1/Rev.4 (1988).
CEDAW, *General Recommendation No. 14*, U.N. Doc. HRI/GEN/1/Rev.4 (1990).
CEDAW, *General Recommendation No. 15*, U.N. Doc. HRI/GEN/1/Rev. 4 (1990).
CEDAW, *General Recommendation No. 18*, U.N. Doc. HRI/GEN/1/Rev.4 (1991).
CEDAW, *General Recommendation No. 19*, U.N. Doc. HRI/GEN/1/Rev.4 (1992).
CEDAW, *General Recommendation No. 21*, U.N. Doc. HRI/GEN/1/Rev.4 (1994).
CEDAW, *General Recommendation No. 23*, U.N. Doc. HRI/GEN/1/Rev.4 (1997).
CEDAW, General Recommendation No. 24, U.N. Doc. HRI/GEN/1/Rev.4 (1999).
Concluding Observations, U.N. Doc. A/52/38, *reprinted in Report of the Committee on the Elimination of Discrimination Against Women* (1997).
Concluding Observations, U.N. Doc.A/53/38, *reprinted in Report of the Committee on the Elimination of Discrimination Against Women* (1998).
Concluding Observations, Armenia, U.N. Doc. A/49/40 *reprinted in Report of the Committee on the Elimination of Discrimination Against Women* (1994).
Concluding Observations, Bosnia and Herzegovina, U.N. Doc .A/49/38, *reprinted in Report of the Committee on the Elimination of Discrimination Against Women* (1994).

Concluding Observations, Democratic Republic of the Congo, U.N. Doc. CEDAW/C/2000/I/CRP.3/Add.6/Rev.1 (2000).
Concluding Observations, Federal Republic of Yugoslavia, U.N. Doc. A/49/38, reprinted in *Report of the Committee on the Elimination of Discrimination Against Women* (1994).
Concluding Observations, Peru, U.N. Doc. A/50/38, *reprinted in Report of the Committee on the Elimination of Discrimination against Women* (1995).
Concluding Observations, Rwanda, U.N. Doc. A/51/38, *reprinted in Report of the Committee on the Elimination of Discrimination against Women* (1996).
Consideration of State Reports, U.N. Doc. A/53/38, *reprinted in Report of the Committee on the Elimination of Discrimination Against Women* (1988).
Report of the Committee on the Elimination of Discrimination Against Women, U.N. Doc. A/52/38/Rev.1 (1997).
Report of the Committee on the Elimination of Discrimination Against Women, U.N. Doc. A/53/38/Rev.1 (1998).

CERD:

CERD, General Recommendation 22, U.N. Doc. A/51/18 (1996).
CERD, General Recommendation 25, U.N. Doc. A/55/18, Annex V (2000).
CERD Report, U.N. Doc. A/48/18 (1993).
CERD Report, U.N. Doc. A/49/18 (1994).
Concluding Observations of the Committee on the Elimination of Racial Discrimination: Croatia, U.N. Doc. A/50/18 (1995).
Concluding Observations of the Committee on the Elimination of All Forms of Racial Discrimination: Cyprus, U.N. Doc. CERD/C/304/Add.56 (1999).
Concluding Observations of the Committee on the Elimination of Racial Discrimination: Syrian Arab Republic, U.N. Doc. CERD/C/304/Add.70 (1999).
Concluding Observations of the Committee on the Elimination of Racial Discrimination: the United Kingdom of Great Britain and Northern Ireland, U.N. Doc. CERD/C/304/Add.9 (1996).
International Convention on the Elimination of Racial Discrimination, Rules of Procedure, U.N. Doc. CERD/C/35/Rev.3 (1989).

CESCR:

Concluding Observations of the Committee on Economic, Social and Cultural Rights, U.N. Doc. E/C.12/1994/7 (1994).

Concluding Observations of the Committee on Economic, Social and Cultural Rights: Sudan, U.N. Doc. E/C.12/1/Add.48 (2000).

HRC:

Annual Report of Human Rights Committee, U.N. Doc. A/49/40 (1994).
Annual Report of the Human Rights Committee, U.N. Doc. A/51/40 (1996).
Annual Report of the Human Rights Committee, U.N. Doc. A/53/40 (1998).
Concluding Observations, Belgium, U.N. Doc. CCPR/C/79/Add.99 (1998).
Concluding Observations, Burundi, Doc. CCPR/C/79/Add.9 (1992).
Concluding Observations, Denmark, U.N. Doc. CCPR/C/79/Add.68 (1996).
Concluding Observations, Ecuador, U.N. Doc. CCPR/C/79/Add.92 (1998).
Concluding Observations, France, U.N. Doc. CCPR/C/79/Add.80 (1997).
Concluding Observations, Gabon, U.N. Doc. CCPR/C/79/Add.71 (1996).
Concluding Observations, Germany, U.N. Doc. CCPR/C/79/Add.73 (1996).
Concluding Observations, Tanzania, U.N. Doc. CCPR/C/79/Add.97 (1998).
Concluding Observations, United Kingdom, U.N. Doc. CCPR/C/79/Add.57 (1995).
Concluding Observations, United States, U.N. Doc. CCPR/C/79/Add.50 (1995).
Concluding Observations, Austria, U.N. Doc. CCPR/C/79/Add.103 (1998).
Report of the Human Rights Committee, U.N. Doc. A/38/40 (1983).
Report of the Human Rights Committee, U.N. Doc. A/45/40 (1991).
Report of the Human Rights Committee, U.N. Doc. A/52/40, U.N. Doc. CCPR/C/60/D/692/1996 (1997).

Other:

Deng, Francis, *Internally Displaced Persons, Report of the Representative of the Secretary-General,* U.N. Doc. E/CN.4/1996/52/Add.2 (1995).
Office of the United Nations High Commissioner for Refugees, *UNHCR Guidelines on the Protection of Refugee Women* (1991).

Cases

A. v. Australia, U.N. Doc. A/52/40, *in* Report of the Human Rights Committee, vol.II, U.N. Doc. CCPR/C/59/D/560/1993 (1997).
A. v. The Netherlands, Communication No. 91/1997, *in* Report of the Committee against Torture 1998, at Annex III, U.N. Doc. A/54/44 (1999).
A.M. v. Denmark, Communication No. 26/121, U.N. Doc. A/37/40 (1982).

ARJ v. Australia, U.N. Doc. A/52/40, *in* Report of the Human Rights Committee, vol.II, U.N. Doc. CCPR/C/60/D/692/1996 (1997).
Encarnación Blanco Abad v. Spain, Communication No. 59/1996, *in* Report of the Committee against Torture 1998, U.N. Doc.A/53/44 (1998).
Alan v. Switzerland, Communication No. 21/1995, *in* Report of the Committee against Torture 1995–1996, U.N. Doc.A/51/44 (1996).
Altesor v. Uruguay, GAOR, 37th Sess., Supp. No. 40, U.N. Doc. A/37/40, *in* Report of the Human Rights Committee (1982).
Josu Arkauz Arana v. France, Communication No. 63/1997, U.N. Doc. CAT/C/23/D/63/1997 (2000).
Shirin Aumeeruddy-Cziffra and Nineteen Other Mauritian Women v. Mauritius, U.N. Doc. A/36/40 (1981).
Orhan Ayas v. Sweden, Communication No. 97/1998, *in* Report of the Committee against Torture 1998, U.N. Doc.A/53/44 (1998).
B.J. v. Denmark, Communication No. 17/1999, *in* Compilation of opinions and decisions adopted under article 14 of the Convention, U.N. Doc. CERD/C/390 (2000).
B.M.S. v. Australia, Communication No. 8/1996, *in* Compilation of opinions and decisions adopted under article 14 of the Convention, U.N. Doc. CERD/C/390 (2000).
Angel N. Olo Bahamonde v. Equatorial Guinea, Communication No. 468/199, U.N. GAOR, 49th Sess., Supp. No. 40, U.N. Doc. A/49/40, *in* Report of the Human Rights Committee (1994).
Barbaro v. Australia, Communication No. 7/1995, *in* Compilation of opinions and decisions adopted under article 14 of the Convention, U.N. Doc. CERD/C/390 (2000).
Lopez Burgos v. Uruguay, Communication No. 52/1079, U.N. GAOR, 36th Sess., Supp. No. 40, U.N. Doc. A/36/40, *in* Report of the Human Rights Committee (1981).
Lopez Burgos v. Uruguay, Communication No. 52/1079, U.N. Doc. CCPR/C/OP/1 (1985).
C.P. v. Denmark, Communication No. 5/1994, *decision on admissibility adopted* March 15, 1995, *in* Compilation of opinions and decisions adopted under article 14 of the Convention, U.N. Doc. CERD/C/390 (2000).
Canepa v. Canada, U.N. Doc. CCPR/C/59/D/558/1993 (1997).
Casanovas v. France, U.N. GAOR, Hum. Rts. Comm., 51st Sess., Annex, U.N. Doc. CCPR/C/51/D/441/1990 (1994).
Celepli v. Sweden, Communication No. 456/1991, 49th Sess., Supp. No. 40, U.N. Doc. A/49/40, *in* Report of the Human Rights Committee (1997).
Cecilia Rosana Núñez Chipana v. Venezuela, Communication No. 110/1998 *in* Report of the Committee against Torture 1999, U.N. Doc. A/54/44 (1999).

D.S. v. Sweden, Communication No. 9/1997, *in* Compilation of opinions and decisions adopted under article 14 of the Convention, U.N. Doc. CERD/C/390 (2000).
Drobek v. Slovakia, U.N. GAOR, 52nd Sess., Supp. No. 40, U.N. Doc. A/52/40, vol.II, CCPR/C/60/D643/1995 (1995).
E.A. v. Switzerland, Communication No. 28/1995, *in* Report of the Committee against Torture 1998, U.N. Doc.A/53/44 (1998).
E.W. et al. v. the Netherlands, U.N. GAOR, 48th Sess., Supp. No. 40, U.N. Doc. A/48/40, *in* Report of the Human Rights Committee, vol. II, U.N. Doc. CCPR/C/60/D/429/1990 (1990)
Ex-Philibert v. Zaire, U.N. Doc. A/38/40 (1983).
Sadiq Shek Elmi v. Australia, Communication No. 120/199, *in* Report of the Committee Against Torture 1999, U.N. Doc. A/54/44 (1999).
Ali Falakaflaki v. Sweden, Communication No. 89/1997, *in* Report of the Committee Against Torture 1998, U.N. Doc.A/53/44 (1998).
G.R.B. v. Sweden, Communication No. 83/1997, *in* Report of the Committee Against Torture 1998, U.N. Doc.A/53/44 (1998).
Griffin v. Spain, 50th Sess., Supp. No. 40, U.N. Doc. A/50/40, in Report of the Human Rights Committee, vol.II, U.N. Doc. CCPR/C/53/D/493/1992 (1994).
H.S. v. France, U.N. Doc. A/41/40.
Ziad Ben Ahmed Habassi v. Denmark, Communication No. 10/1997, *in* Report of the Committee on the Elimination of Racial Discrimination, U.N. GAOR 54th Sess., Supp. No. 18, U.N. Doc. A/54/18 (1999).
Lenford Hamilton. v. Jamaica, U.N. Doc. A/49/40 (1994).
Hammel v. Madagascar, U.N. Doc. A/42/40 (1987).
Halil Haydin v. Sweden, Communication No. 101/1997, *in* Report of the Committee Against Torture 1999, U.N. Doc. A/54/44 (1999).
Hertzenberg and Others v. Finland, U.N. Doc. A/37/40 (1982).
Hopu and Bessart v. France, U.N. GAOR, 52nd Sess., Supp. No. 40, U.N. Doc. A/52/40, *in* Report of the Human Rights Committee, annex VII (1997).
Hill v. Spain, U.N. GAOR, 52nd Sess., Supp. No. 40, U.N. Doc. A/52/40, *in* Report of the Human Rights Committee, annex VII (1997).
I.A.O. v. Sweden, Communication No. 65/1997, *in* Report of the Committee against Torture 1998, U.N. Doc.A/53/44 (1998).
J.K. v. Canada, U.N. Doc. A/40/40 (1985).
J.R.T. and Western Guard Party v. Canada, U.N. Doc. A/38/40 (1983).
Kashif v. Ahmad, Communication No. 16/1999, *in* Compilation of opinions and decisions adopted under article 14 of the Convention, U.N. Doc. CERD/C/390 (2000).
Khan v. Canada, Communication No. 15/1994, U.N. Doc. CAT/C/13/D/15/1994 (1994).

Kitok v. Sweden, U.N. GAOR, 45th Sess., Supp. No. 40, U.N. Doc. A/45/40, in Report of the Human Rights Committee, annex VII (1990).

Avedes Hamayak Korban v. Sweden, Communication No. 88/1997, *in* Report of the Committee against Torture 1999, U.N. Doc. A/54/44 (1999).

L.K. v. The Netherlands, Communication No. 4/1991, *Report of the Committee on the Elimination of Racial Discrimination*, U.N. GAOR 48th Sess., Supp. No. 18, U.N. Doc. A/48/18 (1993).

L.K. v. The Netherlands, Communication No. 4/1991, *in* Compilation of opinions and decisions adopted under article 14 of the Convention, U.N. Doc. CERD/C/390 (2000).

Lichtensztein v. Uruguay, U.N. Doc. A/38/40 (1983).

M.A. v. Italy, U.N. Doc. A/38/40 (1983).

Colin Mc Donald and Mr. Nicholas Poynder on behalf of Mr. Y v. Australia, Communication No 772/1997, U.N. Doc. CCPR/C/69/D/772/1997 (2000).

Albert W. Mukong v. Cameroon, Communication No. 458/1991, U.N. GAOR, 49th Sess., Supp. No. 40, U.N. Doc. A/49/40, in Report of the Human Rights Committee, vol.II (1994).

Mutumbo v. Switzerland, Communication No. 13/1993, U.N. Doc. A/49/44, *in* Report of the Committee Against Torture 1993–1994, U.N. Doc. A/49/44 (1994).

N.P. v. Australia, Communication No. 106/1998, *in* Report of the Committee Against Torture 1999, U.N. Doc. A/54/44 (1999).

Narrainen v. Norway, Communication No. 3/1991, *in* Compilation of opinions and decisions adopted under article 14 of the Convention, U.N. Doc. CERD/C/390 (2000).

Halimi Nedzibi v. Austria, Communication No. 8/1991, *in* Report of the Committee Against Torture 1993–1994, U.N. Doc. A/49/44 (1994).

Ominayak, Chief of the Lubicon Lake Band v. Canada. U.N. GAOR, 45th Sess., Supp. No.40, U.N. Doc. A/45/40, *in* Report of the Human Rights Committee (1990).

Pratt and Morgan v. Jamaica, U.N. Doc. A/44/40 (1987).

Quinteros v. Uruguay, U.N. GAOR, 38th Sess., Supp. No. 40, U.N. Doc. A/38/40, *in* Report of the Human Rights Committee (1983).

Ramirez v. Uruguay, Case No. 4/1977, U.N. Doc. A/35/40 (1980).

Santullo (Valcada) v. Uruguay, U.N. Doc. A/35/40 (1980).

Sara et al. v. Finland, 49th Sess., Supp. No. 40, U.N. Doc. A/49/40, *in* Report of the Human Rights Committee, vol.II (1994).

Sequeira v. Uruguay, U.N. Doc. A/35/40 (1980).

Simunek et al. v. the Czech Republic, U.N. GAOR 50th Sess., Supp. No. 40

U.N. Doc. A/50/40, *in* Report of the Human Rights Committee, vol.II, U.N. Doc. CCPR/C/54/D/516/1992 (1995).

Stewart v. Canada, 52nd Sess., Supp. No. 40, U.N. Doc. A/52/40, *in* Report of the Human Rights Committee, vol.II, U.N. Doc. CCPR/C/60/D/538/1993 (1997).

T. v. Australia, U.N. GAOR, 52nd Sess., Supp. No. 40, U.N. Doc. A/52/40, *in* Report of the Human Rights Committee, vol.II, U.N. Doc. CCPR/C/60/D/706/1996 (1997).

Tala v. Sweden, Communication No. 43/1996, *in* Report of the Committee Against Torture, U.N. Doc. A/52/44 (1997).

Nicholas Toonen v. Australia, Communication No. 488/1992, *views adopted* at 50th Sess., March 31, 1994.

Triboulet v. France, U.N. GAOR, 52nd Sess., Supp. No. 40 U.N. Doc. A/52/40, *in Report of the Human Rights Committee, vol.II*, U.N. Doc. CCPR/C/60/D/661/1995.

V.M. v. Norway, Communication. No. 168/1984.

V.M.R.B. v. Canada, U.N. GAOR, 43rd Sess., Supp. No. 40, U.N. Doc. A/43/40, *in* Report of the Human Rights Committee (1988).

V.O. v. Norway, U.N. Doc. A/40/40 (1985).

X. v. Switzerland, Communication No. 27/1995, *in* Report of the Committee Against Torture 1997, U.N. Doc. A/52/44 (1997).

X., Y. and Z. v. Sweden, Communication No. 61/1996, *in* Report of the Committee Against Torture 1998, U.N. Doc.A/53/44 (1998).

Yilmaz-Dogan v. Netherlands, Communication No. 1/1984, in *Report of CERD*, Annex IV, (Op. adopted on 10 Aug. 1988), U.N. GAOR, 43d Sess., Supp. No. 18, U.N. Doc. A/43/18 (1988).

A. Yilmaz-Dogan v. The Netherlands, Communication No. 1/1984, *in* Compilation of opinions and decisions adopted under article 14 of the Convention, U.N. Doc. CERD/C/390 (2000).

Z.U.B.S. v. Australia, Communication No. 6/1995, *in* Compilation of opinions and decisions adopted under article 14 of the Convention, U.N. Doc. CERD/C/390 (2000).

Internet Sources

United Nations High Commissioner for Human Rights, *Fact Sheet No. 22: Discrimination against Women,* at <http://www.unhchr.ch/html/menu6/2/fs22.htm>.

Chapter 3
The United Nations Charter-Based Mechanisms

Camille Giffard
Meagan Hrle

1. Introduction

The United Nations Charter-based mechanisms are unique among the mechanisms described in this manual because they can examine information relative to any state that is a member of the United Nations (UN). In practice, this means that they can deal with complaints concerning virtually any state in the world. Their drawback is that they are not judicial in nature, and so have limited enforcement powers—they rely on political influence to achieve concrete results. Nonetheless, their value should not be underestimated. When no other avenues exist for an individual whose rights have been violated, perhaps because the state concerned has not signed on to any human rights treaties, access to the Charter-based mechanisms is still possible. Even where other options are available, the combination of public embarrassment and political pressure inherent in the Charter-based mechanisms can prove extremely persuasive.

This chapter[1] will explain exactly what is meant by Charter-based mechanisms, how they may be used, and why they are important

---

[1] The authors would like to thank all those persons who have provided assistance with this chapter. In particular, they would like to thank Martine Anstett, Jan Bauer, Jean-Nicolas Beuze, Connie de la Vega, Pablo Espiñella, Fatouh Houel, Miguel De la Lama, Rafael Miranda, Erin Mooney, Jennifer Philpot, Christina Saunders, Markus Schmidt, Anne Slowgrove, Eleanor Solo, Charlotte Stahl, and Henrik Stenman. Some parts of certain passages in Section 4 and Section 5 have previously appeared in actual or modified form in CAMILLE GIFFARD, THE TORTURE REPORTING HANDBOOK: HOW TO DOCUMENT AND RESPOND TO ALLEGATIONS OF TORTURE WITH IN THE INTERNATIONAL SYSTEM FOR THE PROTECTION OF HUMAN RIGHTS (2000). The authors are grateful to the Human Rights Centre of the University of Essex for their kind permission to reproduce these passages.

resources for refugees, asylum-seekers, and internally displaced persons and their representatives. The objective is to enable readers with little or no previous knowledge to pursue these modes of action as easily and effectively as possible by establishing detailed guidelines on use, accompanied by explanations of the most important aspects of each mechanism.

2. Setting the Context

2.1 Context in Which the Charter-Based Mechanisms Function

The United Nations has created two types of human rights institutions, treaty-based and Charter-based. Treaty-based mechanisms are grounded on a state's ratification of individual treaties, and these are fully discussed in Chapter 2. Charter-based mechanisms were created on the authority of the UN Charter and apply to all UN member states. The Charter was adopted in 1945 and is the founding document of the United Nations. Article 55 sets out that the UN shall promote "universal respect for . . . human rights . . . without discrimination." Article 56 provides that all members shall pledge "joint and separate action . . . for the achievement of the purposes set forth in Article 55." The Charter is binding on all members of the United Nations, and creates a political community where all members are accountable to one another.[2]

The UN Charter creates and governs the powers of the principal organs of the UN, in particular the General Assembly, the Security Council, ECOSOC, and the Secretariat. These principal UN bodies are responsible for the creation of the Charter-based mechanisms and are themselves of relevance to advocates. What follows in this section is a brief summary of each body's basic functions and role. This section is intended to be your "road map," providing a context for the Charter-based mechanisms and highlighting the interrelationships among the UN organs. Section 2.2 will identify how these organs may be exploited by refugees, asylum-seekers, and internally displaced persons and their advocates.

General Assembly: The General Assembly (GA) is the primary source of international declarations and conventions. Because all UN members are entitled to vote, it is the most representative decision-making body of the UN. The General Assembly has six main committees; the Third Committee on Social, Humanitarian, and Cultural Issues addresses

---

[2] Patrick James Flood, The Effectiveness of UN Human Rights Institutions 6 (1998).

human rights violations. Like the Commission on Human Rights, described below, the General Assembly may debate thematic issues and country-specific issues, and pass resolutions accordingly, although these are non-binding. In theory, the General Assembly has a supervisory and priority-setting mandate, although more often than not the General Assembly takes its cues from, or follows up on, work initiated by the Commission on Human Rights.[3] The General Assembly regularly reviews reports from several of the human rights treaty bodies and considers several hundred resolutions each year. The General Assembly can be criticized for falling into patterns of fairly ineffective activity.[4] It normally meets once a year from September through December in New York.

Advocates can approach governmental representatives in the Third Committee to attempt to influence resolutions. However, because the GA usually follows the Commission's lead on issues, advocates with limited resources may be better off focusing their efforts on the Commission and Sub-Commission.

Security Council: The Security Council is the primary UN organ. It is composed of five permanent members and ten non-permanent members. The Security Council is mandated to maintain or restore international peace and security, in furtherance of which it may employ humanitarian aid, economic sanctions, and/or military intervention. A Security Council resolution is the highest form of UN authority. The Security Council has established *ad hoc* war crimes tribunals to address human rights violations in the former Yugoslavia and in Rwanda, which are discussed in Chapter 7.[5]

Economic and Social Council: The Economic and Social Council (ECOSOC) was established by the Charter. Under the authority of the General Assembly, it is the principal organ for promoting economic and social progress and development; finding solutions to international economic, social, health, and related problems; and fostering universal respect for and observance of human rights and fundamental freedoms.[6] The ECOSOC has 54 members who are elected for three-year terms by the General Assembly. Generally, the ECOSOC meets once a year for a five- to six-week substantive session, alternating between Geneva and New

---

[3] John Quinn, *The General Assembly into the 1990s, in* THE UNITED NATIONS AND HUMAN RIGHTS: A CRITICAL APPRAISAL 55, 79 (Philip Alston ed., 1992).

[4] *Id.* at 96.

[5] FRANK NEWMAN AND DAVID WEISSBRODT, INTERNATIONAL HUMAN RIGHTS: LAW, POLICY AND PROCESS (2D ED. 1996).

[6] *Overview of UN Organs,* at <www.un.org/overview/organs/ecosoc.html>.

York, and once a year for an organizational session in New York. The year-round work of the ECOSOC is carried out by its subsidiary bodies, such as the Commission on Human Rights and the Commission on the Status of Women, which report back to the ECOSOC.[7]

The Commission on Human Rights: The Commission on Human Rights (Commission), one of the subsidiary bodies of ECOSOC, is at present composed of 53 governmental members elected by the ECOSOC. The UN Charter gives the Commission the power to make recommendations to further human rights and fundamental freedoms for all.[8] The Commission meets annually in Geneva for six weeks in the spring. During these meetings, governmental representatives make statements and vote on proposed resolutions and decisions. In certain circumstances, the Commission can call a special session if agreed to by the majority of its members. These special sessions typically last only a day or two—just long enough to provide a response to the crisis situation.

The Commission is the primary body responsible for monitoring the implementation and violations of international human rights standards, recommending new standards, and providing technical and advisory services to countries in need of assistance. The Commission is authorized to pass resolutions, consider country situations under the confidential procedure of ECOSOC Resolution 1503, establish country rapporteurs under the authority of ECOSOC Resolution 1235 to monitor the human rights situation in any given country, and establish thematic review mechanisms to monitor the state of one particular human rights issue throughout the world.[9]

The Commission has become the foremost UN human rights institution, although it is not without its drawbacks and deficiencies. Any advocate who has worked with the Commission can comment on the bilateral attacks that can occur and the unwillingness to address human rights issues that are deemed too sensitive. The work of the Commission is highly politicized, as governmental representatives are reluctant to criticize their own country and foreign policy often dictates their actions more than human rights issues.[10] Adding to that, the Commission works

---

[7] PENNY PARKER AND DAVID WEISSBRODT, MINNESOTA ADVOCATES FOR HUMAN RIGHTS, ORIENTATION MANUAL: THE UN COMMISSION ON HUMAN RIGHTS, ITS SUB-COMMISSION AND RELATED PROCEDURES 2 (1993).

[8] FLOOD, *supra* note 2, at 39.

[9] PARKER & WEISSBRODT, *supra* note 7, at 2.

[10] AMNESTY INTERNATIONAL AND INTERNATIONAL SERVICE FOR HUMAN RIGHTS, THE UN AND REFUGEES' HUMAN RIGHTS: A MANUAL ON HOW UN HUMAN RIGHTS MECHANISMS CAN PROTECT THE RIGHTS OF REFUGEES 18 (1997).

largely by consensus, which slows down the process and often prevents strong censure of certain situations.[11]

The Commission has created a number of special country-specific and thematic procedures. Some of these include individual complaint procedures and will be discussed in depth later in this chapter. The special procedures provide the Commission with facts, analysis, and recommendations on specific situations and countries. The Commission and Sub-Commission also draw upon reports from the various treaty bodies and input from non-governmental organizations (NGOs).

Commission on the Status of Women: The Commission on the Status of Women (CSW), like the Commission on Human Rights, is a functional commission of the ECOSOC consisting of 45 governmental representatives elected by the ECOSOC. The CSW prepares studies, reports and recommendations to promote women's rights in political, economic, civil, social, and educational spheres. The CSW primarily serves to monitor programs and provide follow-up to world conferences. It also makes recommendations to the Secretary-General of the UN regarding the increased participation of women in the UN system and the implementation and coordination of UN programs to advance the rights of women.[12] The CSW holds annual sessions in which NGOs participate. The CSW is serviced by the Division for the Advancement of Women (DAW).[13]

Sub-Commission on the Promotion and Protection of Human Rights: The Sub-Commission on the Promotion and Protection of Human Rights (formerly known as the Sub-Commission on the Prevention of Discrimination and the Protection of Minorities) consists of 26 members who serve in their individual capacities and not as governmental representatives. The Commission elects members of the Sub Commission for four-year terms.[14] The Sub-Commission is unique in its role as a "think tank" for the UN's primary policy-making body, the Commission. The Sub-Commission functions as a forum where new ideas and trends are identified, debated, and formulated into proposals for action.[15]

---

[12] Sandra Coliver, *UN Machineries on Women's Rights: How Might they Help Women Whose Rights are Being Violated, in* NEW DIRECTIONS IN HUMAN RIGHTS 25, 29 (ELLEN LUTZ ET AL. EDS., 1989).

[13] *See* <www.un.org/womenwatch/daw/csw> for more information.

[14] *Organization of Work. Methods of Work of the Sub-Commission. Enhancing the Effectiveness of the Sub-Commission. Note by the Chairman,* U.N. Doc. E/CN.4/Sub.2/1998/38 (13 August 1998).

[15] *Report of the Sub-Commission on the Prevention of Discrimination and Protection*

The Sub-Commission's mandate is to undertake comprehensive studies that contribute to the work of the human rights bodies, draw the attention of the Commission to situations that are not already under review but that appear to reveal gross and systematic violations of human rights, and support its working groups. The Sub-Commission encourages NGO participation in its activities; the thematic working groups, in particular, provide a platform for NGO participation.[16] Many NGOs attend the annual Sub-Commission meeting, which lasts for three weeks every August.[17] Currently, the role and working methods of the Sub-Commission are under review.[18]

Secretariat: The UN Charter created the Secretariat as the principal support service for the organization, including the support and implementation of the human rights programs developed by other UN organs.[19] The head of the Secretariat is the Secretary-General, established by Article 97 of the UN Charter as the chief "administrative officer of the organization."[20] The Secretary-General is appointed by the General Assembly on the recommendation of the Security Council for a five-year, renewable term. The current Secretary-General, Kofi Annan, took office on January 1, 1997.

---

of Minorities on its fiftieth session. Report of Mr. El-Hadji Guissé, Chairman of the Sub-Commission at its fiftieth session, prepared in accordance with paragraphs 9(d) and 11 of Commission on Human Rights resolution 1998/28, U.N. Doc. E/CN.4/1999/84 (30 December 1998).

[16] The thematic working groups that are open to NGO participation are the Working Group on Contemporary Forms of Slavery, Working Group on Indigenous Peoples, and Working Group on Minorities.

[17] The length of the Sub-Commission session was reduced from four to three weeks with effect from its 52nd Session in August 2000. *See Rationalization of the Work of the Commission. Report of the Inter-Sessional Open-Ended Working Group on Enhancing the Effectiveness of the Mechanisms of the Commission on Human Rights*, U.N. Doc. E/CN.4/2000/112 ¶ 56 (16 February 2000) approved by *Enhancing the Effectiveness of the Mechanisms of the Commission on Human Rights*, U.N. Doc. E/CN.4/DEC/2000/109 (27 April 2000)[hereinafter *Report on Enhancing the Effectiveness of the Mechanisms of the Commission on Human Rights February 2000, and Report on Enhancing the Effectiveness of the Mechanisms of the Commission on Human Rights April 2000 respectively*].

[18] *See Report on Enhancing the Effectiveness of the Mechanisms of the Commission on Human Rights February 2000, supra* note 17, ¶¶ 42–46 approved by *Report on Enhancing the Effectiveness of the Mechanisms of the Commission on Human Rights April 2000, supra* note 17, ¶ 1 for proposed changes.

[19] Theo C. Van Boven, *The Role of the United Nations Secretariat, in* THE UNITED NATIONS AND HUMAN RIGHTS, *supra* note 3, at 549, 562.

[20] *Id.* at 549.

Office of the High Commissioner for Human Rights: The Office of the High Commissioner for Human Rights (OHCHR) (formerly known as the UN Centre for Human Rights) is a branch of the Secretariat that provides support for all UN human rights activities. The High Commissioner for Human Rights, currently Mary Robinson, has direct authority over the resources and work of the OHCHR. Located in Geneva, the staff is composed of international civil servants who are drawn from all regions of the world and are to carry out their work impartially. The staff service most of the Charter-based bodies, such as the Commission, Sub-Commission, and Special Rapporteurs, and, in fact, make many of the preliminary decisions regarding the workings of those bodies. Decisions such as what information is credible, what information needs corroboration, which governments should be contacted or visited, and so on, may be made by the staff, pending review by the mechanisms.[21] The staff can be an invaluable resource. Advocates ought to become familiar with the relevant staff persons and utilize their expertise when particularly needed.

2.2 Why Are Charter-Based Mechanisms Relevant to Refugees, Asylum-Seekers, and Internally Displaced Persons?

The UN Charter organs discussed previously are all political organs, representing a community of states bound by the precepts contained in the UN Charter. These organs have the ability to focus on a range of human rights issues and are bodies where, in theory, all states are actual or potential respondents. The Charter-based mechanisms, created by and operating in the context of the UN Charter organs, are significant and useful tools for several reasons. First, they apply to all UN member states, not just to those states that have agreed to a particular treaty, as is the case for the treaty-based mechanisms. Second, they generally do not require the exhaustion of domestic remedies (except for the resolution 1503 procedure), which is a great benefit when countries attempt to frustrate intervention by delaying domestic procedures. Third, the Charter-based mechanisms may have great political influence on countries, and the negative publicity generated from these procedures may prompt countries to address the problem. Fourth, Charter-based mechanisms may be used to make system-wide changes and address serious human rights violations. For example, the creation of a new Special Rapporteur of the Commission on Human Rights may highlight a worldwide problem and seek solutions through an array of tactics.

---

[21] FLOOD, *supra* note 2, at 44.

The UN Charter organs and their mechanisms may be used in two principal ways: as individual complaint procedures and as advocacy tools. These two approaches should be seen as complementary rather than mutually exclusive.

2.2.1 As Individual Complaint Mechanisms

The UN Charter organs have created a range of mechanisms that establish individual complaint procedures for examining human rights abuses. With the exception of the individual complaint procedure within the Commission on the Status of Women, these function entirely within the auspices of the Commission on Human Rights. The Commission's special procedures that include an individual complaint mechanism or that are relevant to refugees, asylum-seekers, and internally displaced persons in other ways, will be examined in detail.

2.2.2 As Advocacy Tools

With respect to advocacy, the Commission and its Sub-Commission serve as legitimate fora in which to rally for change and bring human rights violations to the attention of the international community. Advocacy tactics undertaken at the Commission and Sub-Commission may influence the formation and adoption of standards and encourage action around a particular human rights violation or an international response to a crisis. In general, these bodies do not operate quickly and have typically failed to provide a rapid response to crisis situations. Consequently, advocates should always bear in mind that advocacy efforts require a long-term commitment, particularly at the Commission and Sub-Commission. Although the focus of this chapter will be on the individual complaint procedures, advocacy aspects will be addressed in Section 7.

3. How Do the Charter-Based Mechanisms Work and What Can You Achieve by Using Them?

The kind of procedures described in this chapter are unlike many of the others considered in this Guide because they are not, strictly speaking, individual complaint procedures—that is, they were not created specifically to provide remedies for individuals. Instead, their function is to monitor respect for human rights throughout the world and report on it, often publicly. They do this by receiving and gathering information from states and third parties in order to report on situations, either at the state level or world-wide, as well as by carrying out fact-finding visits to states. They do not have the power to make legally binding decisions or to award reparations to individuals. Rather, they rely on the weighty political influence of the Commission on Human Rights for the enforcement of their recommendations.

In practice, however, their activities can have significant impact on individual victims, particularly as some of the mechanisms have procedures for receiving information concerning individual cases, in the context of their more general monitoring activities. Even those that have not specifically established procedures concerning individual cases may take action in ways that result in improvements in a country, and consequently for the individuals in that country. They may even take exceptional action in individual cases. Thus, it is important to be aware that even where a mechanism or procedure does not formally address individual grievances, providing the mechanism with information concerning individual cases can still be extremely valuable.

While a few of the procedures focus on issues of direct relevance to displaced persons, they are the exception. Most of the procedures discussed in this chapter are intended to monitor a range of human rights that are not exclusive to the categories of persons dealt with in this Guide. Human rights violations are often among the root causes of displacement. Indeed, they very often represent grounds for seeking asylum. It is important for those seeking redress for displaced persons not to focus exclusively on their status as displaced persons, but to remember that the full range of human rights procedures is available to them as it is to any other category of persons. In recognition of this, the Commission on Human Rights has requested that the special procedures pay particular attention to information concerning refugees and displaced persons in carrying out their mandates.[22]

3.1 What Are the Special Procedures of the Commission on Human Rights?

As previously noted, the two principal bodies responsible for questions relating to human rights within the UN system are the Commission on Human Rights and the Sub-Commission on the Promotion and Protection of Human Rights. One of the ways in which they carry out their tasks is to create and supervise subsidiary procedures to assist them by carrying out studies, drafting, and engaging in monitoring.

---

[22] *See, e.g., Internally-Displaced Persons*, U.N. Doc. E/CN.4/RES/2000/53 (25 April 2000) and *Human Rights and Mass Exoduses*, U.N. Doc. E/CN.4/RES/2000/55 (25 April 2000).

The special procedures of the UN Commission on Human Rights are set up to monitor either specific subject areas on a world-wide scale, or particular countries in relation to the full range of human rights. They are most commonly known as *Special Rapporteurs* or *Working Groups*, but other names include *Independent Experts* and *Special Representatives*. They are created by resolution in response to situations that are considered to be of sufficient concern to require an in-depth study. Their mandates are reviewed periodically, and it is possible for a particular special procedure to be discontinued or a new one created from one year to the next. The procedures report publicly to the Commission on Human Rights each year, and some also report to the UN General Assembly. They depend on these political bodies for any enforcement.

3.2 How Do the Special Procedures Work?

The general task of the special procedures is to present to the Commission on Human Rights as accurate a picture as possible of a wide range of human rights issues throughout the world and to develop methods of addressing them. In order to do this, they rely on information received and sought from a variety of sources, including NGOs, inter-governmental organizations (IGOs), individuals, and governments themselves. Their principal methods of work are to:

- Engage governments in *dialogue* about credible allegations brought to their attention, usually by way of standard communications in non-urgent cases, and urgent appeals where a serious violation is believed to be imminent or ongoing.
- Carry out *fact-finding* visits.
- *Analyze* practice and patterns.
- *Research* themes and develop standards.

The following descriptions of these working methods apply generally to the special procedures unless noted otherwise in Section 5.2 of this chapter, which outlines each procedure in detail.

Dialogue: Dialogue with a government can begin in one of two ways. If allegations are received that are believed to be credible, they may be transmitted to a government either as an urgent appeal or as a standard communication, although not all of the procedures described have established a formal urgent appeal procedure.

The urgent appeal procedure is designed to respond swiftly to information that an individual or group of persons may be at risk of human rights violations, particularly those that are life-threatening in nature. This includes a situation where an individual is about to be deported to a country where he or she may be at risk of torture, summary execution, or disappearance. The urgent appeal procedure is used to *prevent* the occurrence of such incidents and is therefore used only where information is very recent. It is a non-accusatory procedure, which means that it merely asks the government to take steps to ensure that the violations do not materialize, without adopting any position on whether or not the fear might be justified.

Standard communications are transmitted to governments on a periodic basis and usually contain allegations concerning individual cases (individual allegations) and those concerning general trends, patterns, and special factors relevant to the mandate of the procedure in question (general allegations).

Standard communications are intended to give the government named in the allegations an opportunity to comment on them. Depending on the response received from the government, further enquiries or recommendations may be made. Replies received from governments will usually be forwarded to the source for comment, although not all of the procedures have the resources to do this systematically. Some of the procedures require that the source respond within a certain period of time, after which the governmental reply is presumed to have been accepted. If relevant new information is submitted by the source or if the special procedure deems that further information is required from the government, it may decide to re-transmit a case to the government. Cases that are communicated to governments are normally summarized in the annual report to the Commission on Human Rights, although the way in which they are presented may vary from one procedure to another.

Fact-finding: Many of the special procedures also carry out fact-finding visits to obtain first-hand information. They do not have an automatic right to visit a country, but must first obtain an invitation from the government to carry out a visit. During the visit, meetings take place with government officials, NGO representatives, and alleged victims; locations relevant to the mandate are sought out. The objective is to obtain a good sense of the actual situation on the ground. Following the visit, a report is usually produced in which the conclusions reached about the scope of the problem, or the lack of it, are presented and recommendations are made about any measures that could be taken to improve the situation. Countries are also asked to provide information on the steps taken to implement the recommendations.

Analysis: The special procedures normally include a section in both their annual report and their visit reports that addresses a theme or situation from an analytical point of view, assessing the scope of the problem, identifying patterns and particular areas of concern, and making recommendations for ways of tackling the problem. This analysis is often based on, but is distinct from, consideration of the allegations themselves.

Research: Research-based procedures are usually tasked with the study of human rights issues that have not yet been fully developed or addressed. Often, the objective is to develop standards that should apply in relation to a particular subject, such as the principles adopted by the Special Representative of the Secretary-General on IDPs. Some research mandates are for a fixed period, others are open-ended. The working methods are generally quite flexible, and require the seeking out of information in a more active way than with complaint-based mandates.

3.3 What Can You Achieve by Submitting Information in the Context of the Special Procedures?

The special procedures are essentially of two types—those that base their activities mainly on individual cases, and those that engage primarily in research. What you can achieve depends to a great extent on the type of mandate of any particular procedure, but the following consideration applies in all cases: any conclusions adopted by a special procedure, whether relating to an individual case or to a general theme, are only recommendations. This means that there are no legal means to enforce them, and if a state wishes to ignore them there is little the special procedures themselves can do. Nonetheless, not many states are immune to public condemnation, and the publicity of the findings and recommendations creates pressure for states to cooperate. Moreover, where there is sufficient political will among the members of the Commission on Human Rights, a resolution can be adopted condemning a state's human rights record.

A procedure that takes up individual cases may, following dialogue with the government, make recommendations in an individual case or group of cases, including recommending investigation of allegations and prosecution of perpetrators. Urgent appeals are taken seriously by many governments, if only to discourage any further scrutiny of their activities. Any cases in which action has been taken are made public in the procedure's annual report to the Commission on Human Rights.

Those special procedures that have urgent appeal procedures may use them to intervene in cases where an individual is about to be deported to a country where he or she is believed to be at risk of serious human rights violations, particularly torture, summary execution, and disappearance. In such cases, they may request that the decision to deport be reconsidered or, if an individual must be deported, that he or she be deported to a third country where there is no risk. As a minimum, they will seek assurances from the country in question that the person will not be subject to human rights violations if he or she is returned.

Except where they form an inherent part of the mandate (e.g., the Special Rapporteur on Violence Against Women), the special procedures are not normally able to take action in cases concerning the activities of non-state actors. This is because they work from the premise that the state is responsible for human rights violations within its borders. Under human rights law, however, states do have an obligation to take measures to prevent such violations or investigate them when they occur. For example, where there is a pattern of abuses by non-state actors that appear to be tolerated by the government, this may be raised in a communication to the government. One example of this might be state tolerance of the practice of "honor killings," where women are killed by members of their family on grounds of bringing dishonor upon them.[23] Submitting information concerning the activities of non-state actors can also be relevant where governments attempt to avoid responsibility for violations by claiming that they were perpetrated by non-state actors. Keeping the special procedures informed of the actual activities of non-state actors can help them to judge when such assertions are likely to be untrue.

Research-based procedures will not normally act in individual cases, although some may do so in exceptional cases. Their primary function is generally to contribute to the development of standards or to assess the scope of a problem. Submitting information to such a procedure is vital if progress is to be made in addressing new and developing human rights issues, many of which are extremely relevant to refugees, asylum-seekers, and internally displaced persons.

---

[23] *See, e.g., Integration of the Human Rights of Women and the Gender Perspective: Violence Against Women. Report of the Special Rapporteur on Violence Against Women, its Causes And Consequences, Ms. Radhika Coomaraswamy submitted in accordance with Commission on Human Rights resolution 1995/85*, U.N. Doc. E/CN.4/1999/68 ¶ 18 (10 March 1999); *Civil and Political Rights, Including Questions of: Disappearances and Summary Executions. Extrajudicial, Summary or Arbitrary Executions. Report of the Special Rapporteur, Ms. Asma Jahangir, submitted pursuant to Commission on Human Rights resolution 1999/35*, U.N. Doc. E/CN.4/2000/3 ¶¶ 78–84 (25 January 2000) [hereinafter *2000 Report of the SR on Extrajudicial, Summary or Arbitrary Executions*].

4. What Mechanisms Are Available and How Can You Identify Which Ones May Apply in Your Case?

The range of special procedures available is very wide. The first step in submitting a communication is to identify which procedures might be able to address your case. This means knowing which procedures are available and what kind of information each of those procedures is willing to consider. More detailed descriptions of each individual mandate may be found in Section 5.2, but at this stage the objective is more basic: how to match the facts of your case to the general subject matter of a mandate.

4.1 Available Mechanisms

Procedure	Type of Facts Considered	Mandate Focus	Section
THEMATIC PROCEDURES:			
WG on Arbitrary Detention	The WG examines cases in which detention is **arbitrary**. This means detention that (1) is not based on law (including where the detention is longer than the period allowed by law; in such a case, the detention starts out lawful but becomes unlawful once the lawful period has expired); (2) is a response to the exercise of fundamental rights, such as freedom of expression (e.g., the arrest of a journalist for writing an article criticizing the government); or (3) was ordered after an unfair trial in which did due process guarantees were not respected (e.g., where the person detained did not have access to a lawyer or was not allowed to present a defense). Cases will not normally be examined after the individual has already been released, unless they raise a question of principle.	Cases	5.2.1(1)

KEY: SR = Special Rapporteur; SRSG = Special Representative of the Secretary General; WG = Working Group

UN Charter-Based Mechanisms   151

	The detention of an asylum-seeker may be considered arbitrary if it does not respect the principles developed by the WG.		
WG on Enforced and Involuntary Disappearances	Cases where individuals are arrested, detained, or abducted against their will by persons acting on behalf of or with the support or consent of the government. What makes a disappearance different from detention is that those who carry out the detention or abduction do not acknowledge that they have done so, or refuse to give information about what has happened to the person.	Cases	5.2.1(2)
SR on Extra-Judicial, Arbitrary or Summary Executions	An execution or killing falls into this category when it is not ordered by a judge in proper application of the law. The SR can take action in cases where the following result from the actions of state officials or groups cooperating with or tolerated by the government: (1) the death penalty, where there has been an unfair trial, a person has not been allowed to appeal, or involving a minor, a mentally retarded or insane person, a pregnant woman or a recent mother; (2) death threats or imminent risk of extra-judicial execution; (3) deaths in custody owing to torture, neglect, use of force, or life-threatening conditions of detention; (4) deaths resulting from unnecessary or disproportionate use of force (e.g., where a policeman shoots dead an unarmed protester marching peacefully in the street); (5) deaths in violation of international humanitarian law (e.g., where soldiers deliberately target	Cases	5.2.1(3)

KEY: SR = Special Rapporteur; SRSG = Special Representative of the Secretary General; WG = Working Group

	civilians); (6) expulsion to a country where there is a risk to life; (7) genocide; (8) a breach of the obligation to investigate, bring perpetrators to justice, and provide adequate compensation. A state can be held responsible not only for the death itself, but also for failing to investigate it properly. Remember that action can be taken not only where these results have already occurred, but also where there is a **significant risk** that they may occur.		
SR on Torture	Any information relating to the torture or ill-treatment of persons by or with the consent of state officials. This includes cases where ill-treatment has not yet occurred but the person is believed to be at risk. It also includes cases where the state fails to investigate an allegation of torture. The more details are available of the treatment involved, the more likely the case is to fall within the mandate.	Cases	5.2.1(4)
SR on the Independence of Judges and Lawyers	Information can be received about judges, lawyers and court officials of all kinds, including jurors. The SR is essentially concerned with the independence and proper functioning of the justice system.	Cases	5.2.1(5)
SR on Freedom of Expression	The SR's areas of interest include: persons exercising or promoting the exercise of the right to freedom of expression, including professionals in the field of information; political opposition parties and trade union activists; the media (print and broadcast), including any threats to	Cases; some research	5.2.1(6)

KEY: SR = Special Rapporteur; SRSG = Special Representative of the Secretary General; WG = Working Group

	their independence; publishers and performers in other media; human rights defenders; obstacles to women's right to be heard; obstacles to access to information.		
SR on Religious Intolerance	All official activities interfering with a person's ability to hold or express a religion or belief. This might include discriminatory treatment of persons of a particular religion, making unlawful the holding of religious services of a particular type, or the persecution of individuals on account of their beliefs.	Cases; some research	5.2.1(7)
SR on Violence Against Women	The SR examines cases of violence against women **on account of** their gender—the facts should establish that the woman involved was targeted **because of** her gender. A special feature of this mandate is that it looks at violence not only by state officials, but also where it is condoned by the state in the community and within the family.	Cases; some research	5.2.1(8)
SR on Racism	The full title of this SR is the SR on contemporary forms of racism, racial discrimination, xenophobia and related intolerance. The SR on Racism considers cases involving measures targeted against foreigners, migrants, or persons of a particular race or ethnic group, including acts of racism and violence carried out by private individuals.	Cases; some research	5.2.1(9)
SR on the Sale of Children	The full title of this SR is the SR on the sale of children, child prostitution and child pornography. Information should concern persons under the age of 18 who are in such a situation,	Research; some cases	5.2.1(10)

KEY: SR = Special Rapporteur; SRSG = Special Representative of the Secretary General; WG = Working Group

	or activities facilitating or promoting such situations, such as publications promoting sex with children or pornographic films.		
SRSG on Children in Armed Conflict	Information can concern any situation involving children in the context of an armed conflict.	Research	5.2.1(11)
SRSG on Internally-Displaced Persons	The SRSG is mandated to study situations involving groups of persons displaced within their own country who have been obliged to leave their normal place of residence (generally as a result of an armed conflict, a situation of general violence, or a natural or other disaster) and who have not crossed an international border. The information should relate to groups of displaced persons or individuals belonging to such groups.	Research; some cases	5.2.1(12)
SR on the Human Rights of Migrants	Information should concern the human rights of migrants, including those who are lawfully in a country and those who are undocumented or otherwise in an irregular situation. It can relate to both groups and individuals falling into this category.	Not yet determined	5.2.1(13)
SR on Adequate Housing	Information should concern situations where the quality of housing negatively affects an individual's or group's standard of living.	Not yet determined	5.2.1(14)
SRSG on the Situation of Human Rights Defenders	Information should concern the situation of persons acting to promote and protect human rights. This could include NGO activists, lawyers taking cases against the state alleging human rights violations, medical personnel examining persons who have been tortured, etc.	Not yet determined	5.2.1(14)

KEY: SR = Special Rapporteur; SRSG = Special Representative of the Secretary General; WG = Working Group

SR on the Right to Food	Information should concern the ability of individuals or groups to feed themselves sufficiently to ensure their survival.	Not yet determined	5.2.1.14
COUNTRY-SPECIFIC PROCEDURES:			
Relating to (as of 2000) Afghanistan, Burundi, Cambodia, Cyprus, Democratic Republic of Congo, East Timor, Equatorial Guinea, Former Yugoslavia, Haiti, Iran, Iraq, Myanmar, Occupied Arab Territories, Rwanda, Somalia, and Sudan	Country-specific mandates cover all potential aspects of human rights within a country, so information concerning refugees, asylum-seekers, and internally displaced persons in the country in question will always be relevant. The mandates are most likely to focus on situations involving large-scale violations, however.	Variable	5.2.2

KEY: SR = Special Rapporteur; SRSG = Special Representative of the Secretary General; WG = Working Group

The extent to which the different procedures take action jointly varies from one procedure to another—some are very active when it comes to joint interventions, others prefer to work independently. The important point to note is that the different mechanisms are not mutually exclusive and may make either joint or separate interventions in connection with the same allegation.

In general, where the facts of an allegation appear to reveal several possible human rights abuses, you should try to send it to all the relevant special procedures or indicate on your letter to which special procedures you would like it distributed. Action by more than one rapporteur or working group will often carry more weight and is likely to influence a state even more than where only one procedure expresses concern.

An example of an allegation that could be distributed to more than one procedure would be the violent arrest and detention of a female journalist by state officials on account of her journalistic activities, including rape and beating with truncheons at the time of arrest. Depending on the degree of detail available and the particular circumstances, this could potentially motivate action by the Special Rapporteurs on Torture, Violence Against Women, and Freedom of Expression, as well as the Working Group on Arbitrary Detention. If the arrest and detention took place in a country for which there is a Special Rapporteur—e.g., Myanmar (Burma), Equatorial Guinea, or Iran—that SR should also receive the information.

4.2 Identifying Applicable Mechanisms: Case Studies

> **Scenario 1: Chen**
> (See Chapter 1 for complete facts)
> In order to identify the procedures to which Chen might be able to submit her case, the first step is to work through the facts in order to identify each distinct human rights violation to which she or her family may have been subjected. Once this is done, it will be easier to match each violation to a procedure.
>
> 1. Chen has been imprisoned.
> 2. Chen has been tortured.
> 3. Chen was expatriated against her will and stripped of her identity documents.
> 4. The motive for each of these three events was her religious activities.
> 5. Several family members have been killed.
> 6. Chen's home and personal property have been seized.
> 7. Chen's children are not being allowed to join her in the asylum state.
> 8. Chen is being intimidated by the local police in the asylum state.
> 9. Chen is suffering discrimination in employment, housing, and education due to hostility in the local community.
>
> Taking each of these separately, do they raise any issues that can be examined by the special procedures?
> Some preliminary points:
> - Points 1–6 relate to events in Chen's state of origin and any complaint arising from those facts should be made in relation to that state. On the facts, all the actions complained of appear to have been carried out by the state.

Scenario 1: Chen (continued)
- Points 7–9 relate to events in the asylum state and any complaint arising from those facts should be made in relation to that state. On the facts, Points 7 and 8 appear to relate to official actions, while Point 9 relates to the actions of the local community (non-state actors).

Points 1–2:
Would the imprisonment fall under the mandate of the WG on Arbitrary Detention? In principle, the subject matter would do so, as the detention occurred in response to Chen's religious activities (the exercise of a fundamental right). However, Chen is no longer in detention, which removes the incident from the WG's competence. The only possibility would be to argue that the case raises a question of principle—for example, that Chen was arrested under a law which allows the arrest of persons on account of their religious activities, and that her arrest is one of a large number of arrests based on this law.

Would the torture fall under the mandate of the SR on Torture? In principle yes, but any action taken by the Special Rapporteur would depend on the specific treatment suffered.

Would the imprisonment and torture fall under any other mandate? As the events appear to be in direct response to Chen's exercise of her religious activities, the case would seem to fall within the mandate of the SR on Religious Intolerance. Also, as Chen is a woman, her case could be submitted to the SR on Violence Against Women, particularly if her torture involved a gender-based form of torture, such as rape.

It may be worth seeking additional information from Chen, particularly about the way in which she was placed in detention. If she was imprisoned as a result of an unfair trial, the case could raise issues of relevance to the SR on the Independence of Judges and Lawyers. If Chen was taking part in a public demonstration with others of her religion at the time of her arrest, or if one of her religious activities was to publish a religious newspaper, the case might also be of interest to the SR on Freedom of Expression. If Chen belongs to an ethnic minority whose religion is distinct from that of the national majority, such that religious discrimination may in practice amount to racial discrimination, it might be possible to argue that this falls within the domain of the SR on Racism.

Point 3:
This would not in itself appear to fall within the competence of any of the existing special procedures (though it certainly raises issues under other mechanisms dealt with in this manual). However, as the motive for the actions is religious, again this would be relevant to the SR on Religious Intolerance.

> **Scenario 1: Chen** (continued)
>
> Point 5:
> The facts strongly suggest that the killings occurred arbitrarily at the hands of state agents. They should therefore fall within the mandate of the SR on Executions. If the motive for the killings is also religious or racial, as with Chen herself, those facts could also be relevant to the SRs on Religious Intolerance and/or Racism as at Points 1–2 above.
>
> Point 6:
> The same considerations apply as for Point 3.
>
> Point 7:
> Again, this does not fall clearly within any special procedures mandate, but would raise issues under other mechanisms dealt with in this manual.
>
> Point 8:
> Depending on the nature of the intimidation and violence, this could amount to ill-treatment on the part of the asylum state police, thus possibly falling within the mandate of the SR on Torture. It could also be of potential relevance to the SR on Racism if Chen is being targeted because of her foreign appearance.
>
> Point 9:
> The discrimination Chen is suffering would appear to be of concern to the SR on Racism. Although the actions are those of the local community, the SR does examine the actions of private persons. In addition, the asylum state may be facilitating such actions through its legislation or by adopting a tolerant attitude to such behavior. Potentially, if the mandate is developed in this direction, the SR on the Right to Adequate Housing might be interested if the situation leads to Chen being unable to house herself.
>
> In summary, Chen's case raises issues under a number of mandates. When submitting the facts of the case to these mandates, the complete set of facts should be submitted to each mandate so that they can understand the context in which everything has occurred.

> **Scenario 2: Ibrahim**
> (See Chapter 1 for complete facts)
> Following the same procedure as when analyzing Chen's case, what are the potential violations?
>
> 1. Ibrahim has been detained without charge or trial.
> 2. Ibrahim has been tortured.

Scenario 2: Ibrahim (continued)
3. The motive for these events was his activities with an opposition political party.
4. He is being denied employment, housing, health care, education, and social support in the state in which he is seeking asylum.
5. He has been harassed and beaten by the police of the state in which he is seeking asylum.
6. He has been attacked by the local community while the police refused to assist him.
7. He has been detained under a policy of mandatory detention of asylum-seekers.
8. He has been told that he will be returned to his state of origin, where he fears he will be tortured.
9. He wishes to be reunited with his children in the state in which he is seeking asylum.

Preliminary points:
- Points 1–3 relate to Ibrahim's state of origin and any complaint arising from those facts should be made against that state. On the facts, the actions appear to have been carried out by the state.
- Points 4–9 relate to the state in which Ibrahim is seeking asylum and complaints arising from those facts should be made against that state. Points 3–4 and 6–8 relate to state actions, while Point 5 relates to actions of the local community with the tolerance of officials.

Points 1–3:
These events are similar to those that happened to Chen above, and similar reasoning applies. Ibrahim's detention was arbitrary because it was not ordered following a trial. Again, however, he is no longer in detention, so the case would only be relevant to the WG on Arbitrary Detention if it could be presented as a question of principle. In addition, instead of being motivated by religious activities they are motivated by political opposition activity, and therefore fall within the mandate of the SR on Freedom of Expression rather than that of the SR on Religious Intolerance. Of course, the SR on Violence Against Women would also not be competent in this case as it does not concern a woman. In Ibrahim's case, it is expressly stated that his imprisonment occurred without a trial, which may bring the case within the mandate of the SR on the Independence of Judges and Lawyers.

Point 4:
Unlike Chen's case, the facts suggest that Ibrahim is being denied housing, employment and other forms of support not as a result of discrimination within the local community, but through state policy toward asylum-seekers. This

Scenario 2: Ibrahim (continued)

does not in principle raise issues under any of the existing mandates unless it can be argued to be racially motivated (SR on Racism), but it would raise issues under other mechanisms contained in this manual. It may also be of relevance to the SR on Adequate Housing if the mandate is developed to take an interest in such matters.

Point 5:
This corresponds to Point 8 in Chen's case.

Point 6:
Although Ibrahim has been attacked by private individuals, the attack appears to have occurred with the tolerance of the state officials. This means that the events may fall within the mandate of both the SR on Torture and the SR on Racism, because a state's obligation is not only not to actively engage in such activities itself, but also not to tolerate them where it is in a position to prevent them.

Point 7:
It is unclear from the facts if Ibrahim is currently in detention or if he has already been released. If he is still in detention, his case may fall within the mandate of the WG on Arbitrary Detention, particularly as the WG has developed a list of guarantees that should be respected regarding the detention of asylum-seekers.

Point 8:
If Ibrahim fears that he will be tortured if he is returned to his state of origin, he can submit his case to the SR on Torture, who may be able to send an urgent appeal requesting the asylum state not to deport him without at least seeking assurances from the destination state that he will not be tortured. Some of the other mechanisms in this manual may be more effective in this domain, particularly the Committee Against Torture (see Chapter 2), but urgent appeals by the special procedures can also have positive results.

Point 9:
This corresponds to Point 7 in Chen's case and the same considerations apply.

As with Chen, Ibrahim's case raises issues under a number of mandates.

Scenario 3: Maria

(See Chapter 1 for complete facts)
Following the same procedure as when analyzing Chen's case, what are the potential violations?

1. Maria has been forced from her home and farm by security forces on suspicion of assisting an insurgent group.

Scenario 3: Maria (continued)
2. She was beaten and raped.
3. Her identity documents were seized.
4. Her oldest son was killed during the eviction.
5. She and her children are living in an abandoned warehouse without adequate food, shelter, medical care, education, or means of employment.
6. Maria cannot partake in the political process as she has no identity documents.
7. Maria cannot seek redress in the courts as she has no identity documents.
8. Maria and her family are under constant threat from both sides in the conflict.

Preliminary points:

- Maria and her family are internally displaced as they have not crossed an international border.
- All the actions complained of appear on the facts to have been carried out by official forces. There is, however, an ongoing threat from the insurgent (non-state) forces.
- The events described appear to be taking place in the context of a non-international armed conflict.

Points 1–8:
The situation as a whole falls within the mandate of the SRSG on Internally Displaced Persons (IDPs), whose mandate is concerned with the situation of those involuntarily displaced within their own state. Furthermore, the situation of Maria's children would fall within the mandate of the SRSG on Children in Armed Conflict if there is indeed an ongoing internal conflict. In addition, the facts raise a number of more specific issues.

Point 2:
The rape and beating of Maria by the security forces appear to fall within the competence of the SRs on Torture and Violence Against Women.

Points 3, 6 and 7:
The seizing of the identity documents does not in itself raise issues under the special procedures except insofar as it is a measure applied against IDPs (SRSG on IDPs). However, the consequent restrictions on access to justice for Maria probably do fall within the mandate of the SR on the Independence of Judges and Lawyers. Her inability to partake in the political process is not a matter for the existing special procedures, again with the exception of the SRSG on IDPs, but it does raise issues under other mechanisms contained in this Guide.

Point 4:
In principle, the killing of Maria's eldest son during the eviction could fall within the mandate of the SR on Executions, but more precise facts would need to

> **Scenario 3: Maria** (continued)
>
> be provided. It is not out of the question, for example, that the eldest son was a fighter for the insurgent group, fighting to defend the farm at the time of the eviction, and thus a legitimate target for the security forces. At the very least, this is what the state is likely to argue, so it would be useful to possess sufficient facts about the incident to be able to rebut this.
>
> Point 5:
> The lack of food, shelter, medical care, education, and employment, apart from falling within the mandate of the SRSG on IDPs, could potentially be relevant to the new mandates on Adequate Housing and the Right to Food.
>
> Point 8:
> Depending on the nature and seriousness of the threat to Maria and her family by the security forces and the insurgents, it may be relevant to seek urgent appeals from all or any of the SRs on Torture, on Executions, and on Violence Against Women. The SRSG on IDPs may also be in a position to intervene. Although the SRs on Torture and Executions focus on the activities of state officials, the SR on Violence Against Women is prepared to examine the actions of non-state actors and could address the threat by both the official and non-state actors.

> **Scenarios 4, 5, and 6**
> (See Chapter 1 for complete facts)
> Each of these scenarios is a variation on the previous cases of Chen, Ibrahim, and Maria. In each, focus is transferred from the individual to the group of which the individual is a part. Presenting patterns of violation or individual cases as examples of large-scale violations or official policies can be very effective. Many of the special procedures, while taking up individual cases, will be quicker to express concern in cases of large-scale violations. Some, such as the SRSG on IDPs and the SRSG on Children in Armed Conflict, act almost exclusively in such cases. Country-specific mandates also focus on patterns of violations against identifiable groups. Addressing large-scale violations in the context of a group or category of persons is often more effective for initiating long-term change in official policy than a series of individual cases. Where an individual whose rights have been violated is part of a greater group whose rights are being violated in the same way in pursuance of an official policy, thought should be given to presenting the case not only from the individual perspective but also from the group perspective. The special procedures are well-suited to receiving information concerning group grievances because their point of departure is to report on a general thematic or country situation rather than to resolve individual cases.

Remember to check if a country-specific mandate exists for the country under consideration.

5. Once You Have Identified the Available Mechanisms, How Do You Go About Using Them?

The procedures discussed below have many characteristics in common, and many comments are equally applicable to each of them. These common aspects will therefore be addressed first, before proceeding to a presentation of the mechanisms themselves.

5.1 Common Aspects

5.1.1 Practical Considerations

With a few exceptions noted below, the United Nations human rights mechanisms are all based at and run from the Office of the High Commissioner for Human Rights (OHCHR) at the UN Office in Geneva. The OHCHR staff are overworked and subject to serious budgetary constraints, facts which have important implications for those wishing to submit information to any of the procedures operating from the Office.

Languages: The UN has six official languages (English, French, Spanish, Russian, Chinese, and Arabic), but only three working languages (English, French, and Spanish). In practice, the most widely understood language within the OHCHR is English. Limited resources mean that translation is not always a priority, particularly if there is no indication of the value of a communication. If you wish your communication to receive the best consideration possible, you should attempt to submit it in a working language. This does not mean that you must translate every supporting document, but it does mean that your cover letter should be in one of these languages and that it should clearly indicate the content of each of the attached documents. If you cannot do this, you should at least make sure that a short summary is provided in a working language indicating the essential elements of the information or complaint. You should set out clearly:

(1) to whom the communication is addressed (e.g., Special Rapporteur on Torture);
(2) who you are (e.g., NGO working with asylum-seekers);
(3) which country the allegation is about;
(4) the purpose or content of your information and if urgent action is required (e.g., "Mrs. Y to be deported to country

X where likely to be tortured; was severely tortured eight months ago before leaving country (including electric shocks and severe beatings resulting in a fractured skull—medical certificate enclosed) and brother still in the country recently arrested and questioned about the applicant's whereabouts; deportation due on [date]—URGENT").

Submitting information to more than one procedure: If you want your communication to be sent to more than one procedure at the OHCHR, the most reliable approach is for you to send a copy to each procedure yourself, as it can sometimes happen that information is not passed on from one procedure to another within the OHCHR. You will also usually need to emphasize different points for the different procedures.

If you do not have the resources to send more than one copy, you should mark very clearly who you wish to receive the information, in order to guarantee that it is distributed to all of the procedures you have chosen. This will be particularly relevant where you want the information to be sent to several Special Rapporteurs. Some organizations that submit information to the OHCHR on a regular basis have prepared a standard form listing all the available procedures, and mark the ones they would like to contact in any particular case.

Knowing if your submission has been acted upon: None of the special procedures has the resources to acknowledge receipt of every piece of information. You will usually only receive correspondence from the special procedures if a reply has been received from the relevant government regarding your allegation. The most reliable way of knowing if your submission has been acted upon is to read the next annual report of the procedure in question; if action was taken, this will be specified in the report. Note, however, that the cut-off date for inclusion of information in the reports is approximately October. Action taken in response to allegations received after completion of the report would not be made public until the following year.

Following up your written submission: You should aim to strike a balance between drawing attention to your case and being over-solicitous, which can be detrimental. The large volume of work facing the OHCHR staff means that an extra communication or a visit can help to make your case stand out, but it also means that over-persistence can be greeted with a shortage of patience. A phone call to draw attention to a written submission that has recently been received can have positive effects. Phoning every day to find out if any action has been taken will not. Phone calls that are not accompanied by written submissions should be avoided at all costs—they provide the staff member with no opportunity to assess your identity or credibility, and facilitate errors and misunderstandings.

5.1.2 General Characteristics of a Communication

The mechanisms described in this chapter are swamped with information from a multitude of sources, much of which is of dubious quality or lacks the precise detail to be useful. There are a number of guidelines you can follow to help your communication stand out and inspire confidence. These relate to form, style and content.

Form

The communication should be no longer than it really needs to be. If it exceeds 8 or 10 pages, it should be accompanied by a summary of the essential points so that it is easy for the staff member to see if it is useful. Extensive materials in which an allegation is deeply buried and needs to be extracted makes the international bodies' work more difficult, as do large amounts of general information with little precise detail. Many organizations send what amount to books—these are unlikely to be read, whereas a one-page summary will be.

You should not assume any specialized knowledge on the part of the staff receiving the communication. Terms that seem familiar to you may not be widely understood outside your country. Always use simple language and explain specialized terms. In particular, avoid the use of abbreviations and acronyms unless you explain them.

Where you are not able to submit your entire communication in a working language, you should provide at least a summary of the content in one of those languages.

The response you obtain to your submission will depend very much on the impression produced by your organization, its reliability, and your motives in sending the information. It is important to create a good reputation for yourself and your organization so that over time you will become a trusted source. If you have not previously introduced yourself, you can start by explaining your mandate; the easiest way is to include a copy of your statutes or of an annual report that gives a good indication of your activities. If you are affiliated with an international NGO, you should say so—this will provide an easy way of checking out your credentials. Make sure to explain not only your activities, but also your purpose and objectives. If you are a politically oriented organization, say so—this will help to place your information in context and also show that you have nothing to hide. Explain your methods of work: How is your information collected? Is it first-hand information or has it been obtained by word of mouth or from press reports? The aim is to include any information that will help the mechanism form an accurate impression of your organization and the quality of your information.

Style

Always make sure that your presentation of the information is balanced. An objective, balanced view of a situation will make your communication more credible and show that you are interested in presenting the real situation and not just one perspective. While it is normal for information to appear somewhat one-sided if it is trying to establish a pattern of violation, it is important to present it in an objective context. Explain the background carefully, so that the information cannot be perceived as having been taken out of context.

Avoid using political language or making political statements. The human rights officers are concerned with potential human rights violations, and communications that are obviously politically motivated will not be considered.

Using sensational language or dramatic descriptions is likely to be detrimental to your submission. The international mechanisms receive many communications that are full of sensational claims and contain no facts or substance. A balanced, informative communication supported by examples will stand out from the rest of the many unsupported allegations and will receive far more attention.

Content

The most common complaint made by staff at the OHCHR about the information it receives is that it is too vague. You should provide sufficient information for an international body to be able to reach its own conclusions about whether a violation of human rights has occurred—this means that you should be as precise as possible while at the same time remaining concise.

When preparing a submission, the following general guidelines should be borne in mind with respect to the *minimum amount of detail* that must be provided. In addition, you should follow any specific guidelines relating to the particular procedure in question.

The guiding principle must be that in order for action to be taken, the information should be precise enough to make it possible for the government to investigate the allegation if it is communicated to it. As a minimum, therefore:

- The alleged victim or victims must be clearly identifiable.
- The perpetrators of the violation must be clearly identifiable. As a minimum, where it is not possible to identify the perpetrators by name, there must be a demonstrable link between the alleged perpetrator(s) and the state, e.g., it must be established that the perpetrators belonged to an institution representing the state, such as the police, the army, a branch of government, or even a paramilitary group.
- There should be a detailed description of the circumstances in which the alleged violation occurred. This should include at least the date and location of the incident(s), and a clear description of what actually happened and how.
- The person or organization submitting the information must be clearly identified. Anonymous communications are not accepted.

Unless otherwise noted in relation to a specific mechanism, the identity of the source of information is never revealed, either to the government concerned or to the public. However, if there are details in an allegation that are confidential, this should always be clearly marked in the submission. In general, if the name of a victim is to be kept confidential, this means that it will not be possible to submit the individual allegation to the government (as it would not be possible for the government to investigate the case without that information), but the procedure in question may still be able to use the information (leaving out the name) when transmitting general allegations about a particular practice or pattern.

Where it is available, supporting evidence can be valuable. This could include any petitions or complaints made to the authorities; any domestic judicial and administrative decisions in the case, including details of any penalties awarded against the perpetrator(s), decisions of the prosecutor not to prosecute or otherwise pursue a case, and/or decisions of incompetence to examine a case; victim statements; witness statements; medical reports or certificates, including both physical and psychological assessments, if they exist; autopsy reports; photographs; media reports; and general information, such as NGO reports, indicating that the particular type of human rights violation alleged is practiced in the country in question. Always send copies of the documents, *not the originals*, as they will not be returned to you. Official documents can generally be submitted in their original language, but you should indicate what their relevance is. If possible, provide a short summary in a working language of, for example, the result of the judgment or of the injuries recorded in the medical certificate.

If you wish to use your information to establish a pattern, it is not enough to list a few individual cases or make unsupported statements alleging widespread human rights violations in a country. You should use as many *concrete examples* as possible and *analyze* the individual allegations in order to identify *patterns*. One way to present your findings is to, first, summarize all of the patterns you have identified; next, take each proposition one by one and explain it in general terms; finally, after each proposition, provide as many examples as possible to support your statement.

5.1.3 Submitting Information in Cases of Imminent Deportation

Those special procedures that have urgent appeal procedures may use them to intervene in cases where an individual is about to be deported to a country where he or she is believed to be at risk of serious human rights violations, particularly torture, summary execution, and disappearance. In such cases, they may request that the decision to deport be reconsidered or, if an individual must be deported, that he or she be deported to a third country where there is no risk. As a minimum, they will seek assurances from the country in question that the person will not be subject to human rights violations if returned. When submitting information in such a case you should:

- Try to avoid a last-minute intervention if at all possible. It can sometimes take time to contact the correct authorities, and urgent appeals have sometimes arrived too late. It may also be necessary to seek further information from you or other sources. If you believe that a scheduled decision is likely to conclude in favor of deportation and that no further appeal will be available, you should warn the relevant procedure in advance, so that it is already aware of the situation and familiar with the facts. Even in cases where deportation is truly imminent, however, an urgent appeal can still sometimes succeed.
- Provide as many details as possible about the circumstances of the imminent deportation, such as the precise date it is due to be implemented and the airport of departure and flight number, if available.
- Provide detailed information about the domestic remedies used (judicial or administrative decisions, including appeals) in order to establish if the imminent decision is in fact a final one, or if further means are available to delay the deportation without resorting to an urgent appeal. A refusal to grant refugee status

does not necessarily mean that an individual will be deported or that the individual will be deported to his or her country of origin.
* Establish that the individual is at risk. The special procedures will not act in every case of scheduled deportation; on the contrary, the facts must be compelling in order for them to take action in such cases. It must be shown that the risk is ongoing, not merely based on events that happened in the distant past, and that the individual is personally at risk (i.e., it would not be sufficient to state that human rights violations occur in the country in question; rather it must be shown that there is a risk to the specific person being returned). Factors that might help to show this include previous incidents of arbitrary detention, torture, or ill treatment of the person; membership, particularly in a leadership capacity, of a group that is specifically targeted; or the harassment or torture of family members remaining in the country.

5.2 The Special Procedures of the Commission on Human Rights

5.2.1 Thematic Procedures

(1) Working Group on Arbitrary Detention

Basic Facts About: The Working Group on Arbitrary Detention			
Origin:	How was it created?	By resolution 1991/42 of the UNCHR	
	When was it created?	1991	
Working Methods:	Dialogue:	Yes	Fact-finding:	Yes
	— Standard communications	Yes	Analysis:	Yes
	— Urgent appeals	Yes	Research:	No

What does the mandate of the Working Group cover? The mandate of the Working Group on Arbitrary Detention (WGAD) is to "investigate cases of deprivation of liberty imposed arbitrarily" in violation of the relevant international instruments applicable in the particular country concerned.[24]

---

[24] AMNESTY INTERNATIONAL AND THE LAW SOCIETY, THE UNITED NATIONS THEMATIC MECHANISMS, AN OVERVIEW OF THEIR WORK 21 (1999). *See* <http://www.amnesty.org/ailib/aipub/2000/IOR/I4002000.htm> for the July 2000 UN Human Rights Thematic Mechanisms report.

The WGAD has created three broad categories of cases, and is only competent to consider a case if it falls into one of these categories.

Category I: Cases in which it is impossible to invoke any legal basis for justifying the detention or arrest (for example, when an individual continues to be held after the completion of his or her sentence).

Category II: Cases of deprivation of freedom resulting from the exercise of certain fundamental freedoms guaranteed in the 1948 Universal Declaration of Human Rights, specifically in Articles 7,13,14,18, 19, 20, and 21, and for states party to the 1966 International Covenant on Civil and Political Rights, Articles 12, 18, 19, 21, 22, 25, 26, and 27.

Category III: Cases where the non-observance of international standards concerning the right to a fair trial, such as contained in the Universal Declaration of Human Rights, is so flagrant that the deprivation of freedom may be considered arbitrary.

In principle, every situation of arbitrary deprivation of liberty could fall into one of the above categories. The WGAD has outlined one exception where they would not consider the case even if it fell squarely into one of the three categories. This exception is when (a) a "final decision" has been taken in the case and (b) the final decision was taken by domestic courts and (c) the final decision taken by the domestic courts conforms to domestic laws and relevant international standards. Also, situations of armed conflict and instances where non-state actors detain individuals do not fall within the competence of the WGAD.[25]

What law or standards does the Working Group rely on or interpret? The WGAD primarily relies on the 1948 Universal Declaration of Human Rights, Article 9 ("No one shall be subjected to arbitrary arrest, detention, or exile") and the 1966 International Covenant on Civil and Political Rights, Article 9 (1) ("No one shall be subjected to arbitrary arrest or detention") to support its mandate. Other international instruments that may apply include:

---

[25] *Question of the Human Rights of All Persons Subject to Any Form of Detention or Imprisonment. Report of the Working Group on Arbitrary Detention,* U.N. Doc. E/CN.4/1998/44 Annex 1 (19 December 1997) [hereinafter *1997 Report of the Working Group on Arbitrary Detention*].

- 1988 Body of Principles for the Protection of All Persons Under Any Form of Detention or Imprisonment
- 1955 Standard Minimum Rules for the Treatment of Prisoners
- 1990 UN Rules for the Protection of Juveniles Deprived of their Liberty
- 1985 UN Standard Minimum Rules for the Administration of Juvenile Justice (the Beijing Rules)[26]

Has the WGAD addressed issues specific to refugees, asylum-seekers, and internally displaced persons? While the WGAD has not yet specifically considered issues relating to the arbitrary detention of refugees or IDPs, it has addressed the situation of asylum-seekers. In 1997, the Commission called upon the WGAD to respond to the issue of asylum-seekers being held in prolonged administrative detention. As a result, the WGAD has developed principles to determine if custody is arbitrary or not (reproduced in Appendix 3D). These principles set forth the state's duties vis-à-vis detaining asylum-seekers or any alien seeking entry. Custody refers to any deprivation of liberty that occurs while the authorities review the individual's asylum application, and in the event of denial, the period preceding his or her expulsion. The WGAD has also developed principles governing the administrative detention of asylum-seekers and immigrants[27] and has provided a detailed list of pre-trial and post-trial practices that it considers to constitute arbitrary detention.[28]

Example:
In 1998 WGAD visited Romania and the United Kingdom to specifically examine asylum policies, and the ensuing reports contain strong conclusions and recommendations to governments.[29]

---

[26] *See* Bibliography of Cited International Instruments for full citations to these and other international instruments mentioned in this chapter.

[27] *Civil and Political Rights, Including Questions of: Torture and Detention. Report of the Working Group on Arbitrary Detention*, U.N. Doc. E/CN.4/2000/4 Annex II (28 December 1999).

[28] *The Right to Development. Report of the Secretary-General submitted in accordance with Commission on Human Rights resolution 1998/72*, U.N. Doc. E/CN.4/1999/20 (28 December 1998).

[29] The report on Romania can be found in *Civil and Political Rights Including Questions of: Torture and Detention. Report of the Working Group on Arbitrary Detention. Addendum. Visit to Romania*, U.N. Doc. E/CN.4/1999/63/Add. 4 (16 December 1998); for the United Kingdom in *Civil and Political Rights Including Questions of: Torture and Detention. Report of the Working Group on Arbitrary Detention. Addendum. Report on the Visit of the Working Group to the United Kingdom on the issue of Immigrants and Asylum-seekers*, U.N. Doc. E/CN.4/1999/63/Add.3 (18 December 1998).

Are there any specific points to note regarding the working methods of the WGAD, and what can be achieved by submitting information to it? When the WGAD deems a detention arbitrary, it renders an "opinion" to make recommendations to the government concerned. The opinion always references the category of arbitrary detention the case falls into; if the WGAD deems that it is not a case of arbitrary detention, the opinion will note this. If the WGAD needs additional information from the government or source, it may keep the case pending.

The WGAD is increasingly being used by asylum-seekers and immigrants seeking redress for unnecessary detention. In 1999, the WGAD issued approximately five opinions on administrative detention of asylum-seekers; other cases are pending. Asylum-seekers in custody generally fall into Category II, as Article 14 of the Universal Declaration of Human Rights sets forth the right to seek and enjoy asylum in other countries. However, where asylum-seekers are detained in countries party to the First Optional Protocol of the 1966 International Covenant on Civil and Political Rights, this avenue is better suited and has more pull (see Chapter 2 for details on this procedure). Where the WGAD receives information concerning such a country, it will normally contact the source and ask it to make a choice between the Human Rights Committee and the WGAD. For asylum-seekers from countries not detained in First Optional Protocol countries, the WGAD procedure is appropriate.

What motivates the WGAD to take action? A staff member at the OHCHR screens all of the complaints received. Action is then taken according to the criteria of urgency and, to some extent, the geographical balance in registration of complaints.

Urgent appeals are used for cases where the WGAD has received sufficiently reliable information that the detention is arbitrary and the person's life or health may be in danger, as well as other cases that warrant it. Factors relevant to urgent actions include the urgency of the situation, whether the detention is incommunicado, who ordered the detention, and the country's human rights record in general.

Urgent appeals are made on purely humanitarian grounds and do not preclude the WGAD from later rendering an official opinion as to whether the deprivation was arbitrary or not.[30]

The WGAD is developing a follow-up procedure for recommendations contained in reports on country visits; however, there is no follow up procedure for opinions adopted or urgent appeals sent. The

---

[30] *See* <www.unhcr.ch/html/menu2/7/b/mardintro.htm.>.

only other measure the WGAD may take is to send an additional urgent appeal on the same case if the authorities fail to respond.

What should your communication contain? The WGAD has developed a model questionnaire (reproduced in Appendix 3B1), which it encourages applicants to use. Any communication must contain as many details as possible about an arrest, detention, or any other form of deprivation of liberty. Ideally, each person detained should form a separate submission identifying the person's family name, first name, any other identifying information, and legal status.

If the model questionnaire is not used, each submission should as a minimum contain the following:

- date and place of arrest or detention or of any other form of deprivation of liberty and the identity of those presumed to have carried them out, together with any other information that will shed light on the circumstances in which the person was deprived of liberty
- reasons given by authority for the arrest and/or deprivation of liberty
- legislation applied in the case
- action taken, including investigatory action or the exercise of internal remedies, in terms of approaches to administrative and judicial authorities, particularly for verification of the measure of deprivation of liberty; steps at the international or regional levels, as appropriate; and the results of such action or the reasons why such measures were ineffective or were not taken
- an account of the reasons why the deprivation of liberty is deemed arbitrary[31]

Miscellaneous practical information The WGAD meets at least three times a year and is composed of five independent experts. The opinions are published in its annual report submitted to the Commission on Human Rights. The opinions are the result of consensus, and where consensus cannot be reached, the view of the majority is adopted.[32]

---

[31] *1997 Report of the Working Group on Arbitrary Detention, supra* note 25.
[32] *Id.*

(2)   Working Group on Enforced and Involuntary Disappearances

Basic Facts About: The Working Group on Enforced and Involuntary Displacemetn				
Origin:	How was it created?		By resolution 20(XXXVI) of the UNCHR	
	When was it created?		1991	
Working Methods:	Dialogue: — Standard communications — Urgent appeals	Yes Yes Yes	Fact-finding: Analysis: Research:	Yes Yes No

What does the mandate of the Working Group on Enforced and Involuntary Disappearances cover? The Working Group on Enforced and Involuntary Disappearances (WGEID) is mandated to examine questions of enforced or involuntary disappearances, to assist families by helping them establish the fate and whereabouts of their missing relatives, and to monitor states' compliance with their obligations under the Declaration on the Protection of All Persons from Enforced or Involuntary Disappearances.[33]

According to the General Assembly resolution adopting the Declaration, an enforced disappearance takes place where:

> Persons are arrested, detained or abducted against their will or otherwise deprived of their liberty by a) officials of different branches or levels of government, or b) organized groups or private individuals acting on behalf of, or with the support (direct or indirect), consent or acquiescence of a government; followed by a refusal to disclose the fate or whereabouts of the persons concerned or a refusal to acknowledge the deprivation of their liberty, which places such persons outside the protection of the law.[34]

What law or standards does the WGEID rely on or interpret? The WGEID relies on the 1966 International Covenant on Civil and Political Rights and the 1992 Declaration on the Protection of All Persons from Enforced Disappearance.

---

[33]   *Question of the Human Rights of All Persons Subjected to Any Form of Detention or Imprisonment. Question of Enforced or Involuntary Disappearances. Report of the Working Group on Enforced or Involuntary Disappearances*, U.N. Doc. E/CN.4/1998/43, at 4 (12 January 1998) [hereinafter *1998 WGEID Report*].

[34]   *Declaration on the Protection of All Persons from Enforced Disappearance*, G.A. Res. 47/133, U.N. GAOR, 47th Sess., U.N. Doc. A/RES/47/33 (18 December 1992).

Has the WGEID addressed issues specific to refugees, asylum-seekers, and internally displaced persons? The WGEID has not specifically addressed such issues. The UN Declaration on Disappearances provides in Article 8 that no person shall be refouled (sent back) to a country where there are substantial grounds to believe that the person is at risk of being disappeared. Potentially, therefore, the WGEID could take up cases of such possible refoulement of asylum-seekers, including in an urgent appeal, but this has until now never been invoked. In addition, it is worth noting that a significant number of cases of alleged disappearances reported to the WGEID later turn out to relate to persons who have in fact become displaced.

Examples:

2000: During its visit to Sri Lanka, the WGEID noted that internally displaced Tamils living in informal shelters were at risk of disappearance, particularly during cordon and search operations.[35]

2000: The WGEID expressed concern that the Colombian government failed to protect internally displaced persons seeking to return to their place of origin from attacks by paramilitary groups.[36]

1999: The WGEID expressed concern at the disappearance of Rwandan refugees in the Democratic Republic of Congo.[37]

1998: The WGEID took up the case of Afghan refugees abducted from Pakistan with the alleged acquiescence of the Pakistani authorities.[38]

1997: The WGEID took up the case of an Ethiopian refugee allegedly arrested in a refugee camp in Djibouti by members of the Djibouti police and handed over to the Ethiopian authorities.[39]

---

[35] *Civil and Political Rights, Including Questions of: Disappearnces and Summary Executions. Report of the Working Group on Enforced or Involuntary Disappearnces. Addendum. Report on the Visit to Sri Lanka by a member of the Working Group on Enforced or Involuntary Disappearances (25–29 October 1999)*, U.N. Doc. E/CN.4/2000/64/Add.1 ¶ 2 (21 December 1999).

[36] *Id.* ¶ 36.

[37] *Civil and Political Rights, Including Questions of: Disappearances and Summary Executions. Report of the Working Group on Enforced or Involuntary Disappearances*, U.N. Doc. E/CN.4/1999/62 ¶¶ 96–97 (28 December 1998).

[38] *1998 WGEID Report, supra* note 33, ¶ 290.

[39] *Question of the Human Rights of All Persons Subjected to Any Form of Detention*

Are there any specific points to note regarding the working methods of the WGEID, and what can be achieved by submitting information to it? Unlike most other special procedures, the WGEID adopts formal decisions in individual cases. A case is not normally considered "clarified" until the whereabouts of the disappeared person have been found. This can include cases where the person is found to have died or is officially declared to be presumed dead by the competent authorities of the country. Where it considers that it can no longer play a useful role, the WGEID may decide to discontinue the case, for example where the source is no longer in existence or when the family no longer wishes to pursue the case. In order to address the possibility that a decision to withdraw a case may stem from intimidation, the WGEID writes to the family concerned in order to ask them to confirm that they do indeed wish to withdraw the case. In such instances, the case is not considered clarified as such, but rather withdrawn from consideration.

The principal result of communicating information to the WGEID, therefore, is to prompt the government to investigate an individual case with the objective of identifying the whereabouts of the disappeared person. Even where a case is not clarified, it is brought to public attention in the annual report.

What motivates the WGEID to take action? The communication must concern a clearly identifiable individual or individuals alleged to have disappeared.

The WGEID accepts information that is submitted directly or indirectly by the family or friends of the disappeared person. This means that information may be submitted by representatives of the family, including an NGO, but any representative must be able to show that he or she is in touch with the family and thus in a position to follow up the whereabouts of the person with the family.

The urgent action procedure is initiated in cases that allegedly occurred within the three months preceding the receipt of a complaint.

What should your communication contain? A communication to the WGEID must contain the following elements:[40]

---

or Imprisonment. Question of Enforced or Involuntary Disappearances. Report of the Working Group on Enforced or Involuntary Disappearances, U.N. Doc. E/CN.4/1997/34 ¶ 148 (13 December 1996).

[40] *Explanatory Note for the Submission of Information on Enforced or Involuntary Disappearances of Persons*, <www.unhchr.ch/html/menu2/7/b/disappea/explanote.htm>.

- full name of the missing person and any relevant identification information, such as national identity document number, photograph, etc.
- year, month, day of the disappearance
- place of arrest or abduction, or where the missing person was last seen
- name of parties believed to have carried out the arrest or abduction
- steps taken to determine the fate or whereabouts of the missing person
- identity of the person or organization submitting the report (name and address will be kept confidential upon request)

Ideal communications should use the WGEID suggested format, contain as many details as possible, and include attachments where relevant: a picture of the disappeared, copies of any actions taken (such as habeas corpus), and/or copies of witness statements. Only copies of original documents should be sent, as they will not be returned.

Miscellaneous practical information. The WGEID usually meets three times a year.

Any replies received from a government will be communicated to the source of the information. If this is not the family of the disappeared, the source will be expected to stay in contact with the family in order to be able to pass on the information, as it is communicated exclusively for the information of the family. If the source wishes to comment on the information, it should do so within six months.

(3) Special Rapporteur on Extra-Judicial, Arbitrary or Summary Executions

Basic Facts About: The Special Rapporteur on Extra-Judicial, Arbitrary or Summary Executions			
Origin:	How was it created?	By resolution 1982/29 of the UNCHR	
	When was it created?	1982	
Working Methods:	Dialogue:	Yes	Fact-finding:	Yes
	— Standard communications	Yes	Analysis:	Yes
	— Urgent appeals	Yes	Research:	No

What does the mandate of the Special Rapporteur cover? The Special Rapporteur on Extra-Judicial, Arbitrary or Summary Executions (SR on Executions) is mandated to examine situations of extra-judicial, summary, or arbitrary executions. This encompasses all human rights violations that constitute violations of the right to life as established by the international human rights instruments governing the mandate.

The following violations are included in the mandate of the SR on Executions:[41]

- expulsion, refoulement, or return of persons to a country or place where their lives are in danger
- the death penalty, where there has been an unfair trial, there has been a breach of a right to appeal or seek pardon, or it involves a minor, the mentally retarded, an insane person, a pregnant woman, or a recent mother
- death threats or imminent risk of extra-judicial execution
- deaths in custody
- deaths due to excessive use of force by law enforcement officials
- deaths due to attacks by security forces, paramilitary groups, or private forces cooperating with or tolerated by the government
- violations of the right to life during armed conflict, especially of the civilian population, contrary to humanitarian law
- genocide
- failure of the government to investigate violations of the right to life and bring to justice the responsible parties
- failure of the government to provide adequate compensation to victims or families of victims for violations of the right to life

What law or standards does the Special Rapporteur rely on or interpret? The Special Rapporteur on Executions relies on the following:

- 1948 Universal Declaration of Human Rights, Article 3, and 1966 International Covenant on Civil and Political Rights, Article 6, which both recognize the inherent right of every person to life
- 1989 Convention on the Rights of the Child, Article 6, which specifically extends state responsibility to protect the right to life of children under age 18

---

[41] *2000 Report of the SR on Extrajudicial, Summary or Arbitrary Executions, supra* note 23. *See also* <www.unhchr.ch/html/menu2/7/b/execut/exe_mand.htm>.

- 1948 Universal Declaration of Human Rights, Article 2, and 1966 International Covenant on Civil and Political Rights, Articles 2 and 26, which set forth that everyone is entitled to protection of the right of life without discrimination or distinction of any kind, and that all persons shall have equal access to a remedy

In addition to these international instruments, the SR on Executions relies on a number of other treaties, resolutions, conventions, and declarations. One of the most important of these is the Principles on the Effective Prevention and Investigation of Extra-legal, Arbitrary and Summary Executions, adopted in 1989 by the ECOSOC.[42]

Has the Special Rapporteur addressed issues specific to refugees, asylum-seekers, and internally displaced persons? The SR on Executions is particularly concerned about the rights of refugees and internally displaced persons. In her 2000 report, the SR on Executions highlighted the violations of the right to life that internally displaced persons have experienced in the context of internal conflict, such as in East Timor in 1999, and the continuing reports of killings of refugees and IDPs in Rwanda. The SR on Executions has identified violations of the right to life faced by refugees and IDPs as among the few issues requiring her special attention.[43]

In her 2000 report, the SR on Executions calls on governments that have not yet ratified the 1951 Convention and 1967 Protocol relating to the Status of Refugees to do so immediately. She requests that governments refrain from expelling individuals when their right to life is not guaranteed. Also, return or refoulement of IDPs or refugees to places or countries where their right to life is not guaranteed is strictly forbidden.[44]

> **Examples:**
> 1999: The SR on Executions sent an urgent action on behalf of the entire population of Grozny, Chechnya. Also, she sent a joint urgent appeal with the SR on Torture to Uzbekistan regarding the alleged forcible repatriation from Russia of an Uzbek national who might face the death penalty in Uzbekistan.[45]

---

[42] *Effective Prevention and Investigation of Extra-legal, Arbitrary and Summary Executions,* U.N. Doc. E/RES/1989/65 (24 May 1989).

[43] *2000 Report of the SR on Extrajudicial, Summary or Arbitrary Executions, supra* note 23, ¶ 43.

[44] *Id.,* ¶ 106.

[45] *Civil and Political Rights, Including Questions of: Disappearances and Summary*

180   Human Rights Protection for Displaced Persons

> **Examples:** (continued)
> 1998: The SR on Executions transmitted an urgent appeal to the Government of Kazakhstan on behalf of three Uighur nationals from China who were being threatened with extradition to China, where they would allegedly face torture and execution.[46]
> 1998: The SR on Executions communicated with the respective governments on behalf of 70 displaced families in Colombia who have received death threats from paramilitary groups, 64 Rwandan refugees in the Congo who were reportedly killed while returning home, and 45 Karen-minority individuals who were forcibly relocated to Myanmar.[47]
> 1993: The SR on Executions addressed an urgent appeal to the United States regarding the forcible repatriation of Haitian migrants intercepted at sea, calling on the US to refrain from forcibly returning Haitian nationals in all cases where their lives and physical integrity would be in danger.[48]

Are there any specific points to note regarding the working methods of the Special Rapporteur, and what can be achieved by submitting information to him or her?
When transmitting an urgent appeal, the SR on Executions requests the competent authorities to conduct a full and impartial investigation to determine the cause and circumstances of the case and to bring those responsible for the violations to justice.

In cases of a less urgent nature, the SR on Executions informs the government of the allegations and requests that the government provide the following information:[49]

Executions. Extrajudicial, Summary or Arbitrary Executions. Report of the Special Rapporteur, Ms. Asma Jahangir, submitted pursuant to Commission on Human Rights resolution 1999/35. Addendum. Summary of cases transmitted to Governments and replies received, U.N. Doc. E/CN.4/2000/3/Add.1 ¶ 385 (Russian Federation); ¶ 484 (Uzbekistan) (2 February 2000).

[46] *Civil and Political Rights, Including Questions of : Disappearances and Summary Executions. Extrajudicial, Summary or Arbitrary Executions. Report of the Special Rapporteur, Ms. Asma Jahangir, submitted pursuant to Commission on Human Rights resolution 1998/68*, U.N. Doc. E/CN.4/1999/39 ¶ 28 (6 January 1999).

[47] *Id.*, ¶ 39.

[48] *Question of the Violation of Human Rights and Fundamental Freedoms, In Any Part of the World, with particular reference to Colonial and Other Dependent Countries and Territories: Extrajudicial, Summary or Arbitrary Executions. Report by the Special Rapporteur, Mr. Bacre Waly Ndiaye, submitted pursuant to Commission on Human Rights resolution 1993/71*, U.N. Doc. E/CN.4/1994/7 ¶ 621 (7 December 1993).

[49] *Question of the Violation of Human Rights and Fundamental Freedoms In Any Part of the World, with particular reference to Colonial and Other Dependent Countries*

- whether the allegations are factually accurate
- any factual circumstances that should be considered in assessing the allegations
- the cause of death as indicated on the death certificate and the results of the autopsy, if one had been performed, and the identity of the responsible person or agency
- the court or other body charged with the investigation of the allegations or the prosecution of those responsible
- the identity of the person(s), group(s), or unit responsible for the killing, as well as the identity of any military, police, paramilitary, civil defense, or similar body to which those responsible belong
- the decision on a complaint, the grounds for the decision, and any disciplinary or criminal sanctions imposed, and information as to whether the measures imposed were final
- the status of any investigation or legal action not yet completed
- the nature and amount of compensation provided to the family of the victim
- if the investigation or prosecution has not yet been completed, the reasons why this is the case
- any other information the government deems relevant to the case

What motivates the Special Rapporteur to take action? In principle, the SR on Executions will always act on communications unless there are significant indications that the information is not reliable. Receiving similar information from multiple sources is considered a particularly compelling factor when deciding to take action.

Urgent appeals are transmitted where there are grounds to believe that a person or group of persons is at risk of arbitrary deprivation of life.

What should your communication contain? You should include at the minimum the following information:

- information regarding the incident: date; place; description of how the incident occurred
- in cases of imminent violations of the right to life, the reasons why the person's life is feared to be at risk

---

and Territories. Extrajudicial, Summary or Arbitrary Executions. Report by the Special Rapporteur, Mr. Bacre Waly Ndiaye, submitted pursuant to Commission On Human Rights resolution 1992/72, U.N. Doc. E/CN.4/1993/46 ¶ 79 (23 December 1992).

182   Human Rights Protection for Displaced Persons

- information regarding the victims of the incident: the number of victims; if known, and each victim's name, age, sex, profession, and/or activities if related to the (imminent) violation of their right to life
- information regarding the source of the allegations: the name and full address of the individual or organization submitting the allegations to the SR on Executions

If available, the following information is also helpful to the SR on Executions:[50]

- additional information regarding the victims of the incident, such as place of residence or origin
- additional information regarding the alleged perpetrators: names, the unit or service to which they belong, and their rank or functions
- information regarding steps taken by the victims or their families. In particular, if any complaints were filed it should be noted who filed the complaint and before which body. If no complaint was filed, explain why not
- information regarding the steps taken by the authorities to investigate the alleged violation of the right to life and/or measures adopted to protect the persons under threat and to prevent future incidents. If complaints were filed, describe the action taken by the relevant body upon receipt of the complaint. Also describe the progress and status of the investigation, if one has been undertaken. If the investigation is completed in an unsatisfactory manner, describe why this is so

(4)   Special Rapporteur on Torture

Basic Facts About: The Special Rapporteur on Torture				
Origin:	How was it created?		By resolution 1982/33 of the UNCHR	
	When was it created?		1982	
Working Methods:	Dialogue: — Standard communications — Urgent appeals	Yes Yes Yes	Fact-finding: Analysis: Research:	Yes Yes No

---

[50]   *Information needed for Special Rapporteur to take action*, <www.unhchr.ch/html/menu2/7/b/execut/exe_info.htm>.

What does the mandate of the Special Rapporteur cover? The Special Rapporteur on Torture was created to "examine questions relevant to torture" and to report on "the occurrence and extent of its practice." In recent years, the SR on Torture has also been requested by the CHR to pay particular attention to the torture of specific groups of persons, namely women and children. Information sent to the SR on Torture should relate to the actual or risk of torture or ill treatment of persons by state officials.

The SR on Torture does not normally examine cases relating to conditions of detention as such unless these are considered to amount to torture or ill treatment. For example, the SR would not normally consider a case alleging that the inmates of a particular prison are given poor food and inadequate clothing, and are kept four to a cell designed for two persons. However, if the same inmates are developing starvation-related medical conditions, or are kept naked in freezing temperatures, or if the cells are so overcrowded that it is not possible to sit down, then the case may fall within the mandate. A particularly extreme example of such conditions may be found in the SR on Torture's report on his visit to the Russian Federation in 1994.[51]

What law or standards does the Special Rapporteur rely on or interpret? The SR on Torture relies on the following:

- 1984 Torture Convention
- 1966 International Covenant on Civil and Political Rights, Articles 7 and 10
- 1948 Universal Declaration on Human Rights, Article 5
- 1975 Declaration Against Torture
- 1955 Standard Minimum Rules on the Treatment of Prisoners
- 1949 Geneva Conventions on the Protection of Victims of Armed Conflict and their 1977 Additional Protocols

According to Article 1 of the 1984 Torture Convention, torture may be defined as:

> any act by which severe pain or suffering, whether physical or mental, is intentionally inflicted on a person for such purposes as obtaining from him or a third person information

---

[51] *Question of the Human Rights of All Persons Subjected to Any Form of Detention or Imprisonment, In Particular: Torture and Other Cruel, Inhuman or Degrading Treatment or Punishment. Report of the Special Rapporteur, Mr. Nigel S. Rodley, submitted pursuant to Commission On Human Rights Resolution 1994/37. Addendum. Visit by the Special Rapporteur to the Russian Federation,* U.N. Doc. E/CN.4/1995/34/Add.1 (16 November 1994).

or a confession, punishing him for an act he or a third person has committed or is suspected of having committed, or intimidating or coercing him or a third person, or for any reason based on discrimination of any kind, when such pain or suffering is inflicted by or at the instigation of or with the consent or acquiescence of a public official or other person acting in an official capacity. It does not include pain or suffering arising only from, inherent in or incidental to lawful sanctions.

Specifically with regard to deportation cases, the SR on Torture refers to the 1948 Universal Declaration of Human Rights, the 1966 International Covenant on Civil and Political Rights, Article 3 of the 1984 Torture Convention, and the Human Rights Committee General Comment 20 on Article 7, including cases involving non-parties, on the basis that they are part of the overall customary obligation not to engage in or facilitate torture.

Has the Special Rapporteur addressed issues specific to refugees, asylum-seekers, and internally displaced persons? The SR on Torture has intervened by sending urgent appeals in cases where asylum-seekers were about to be deported to countries where they were believed to be at risk of torture. Such interventions have been relatively infrequent (two or three times a year initially, now about five to ten appeals per year), possibly due to the fact that many cases of this nature concern countries that are parties to the 1984 Torture Convention and have accepted the individual complaint mechanism, thus encouraging legal representatives to apply to the Committee Against Torture for provisional measures, rather than to the SR on Torture. Similarly, where a case concerns a complaint against a state party to the European Convention on Human Rights and the complaint has been lodged within that system, the SR on Torture generally considers that the European Court of Human Rights is better placed to intervene. Despite this relative caution, however, urgent appeals in such cases can have impressive effects—in one case, an individual who was already on a plane in the process of being deported was brought back. Whether this was in response to the SR on Torture's urgent appeal cannot be proven with certainty, but it is likely to have played a role.

Deportation cases aside, it is not common for individuals to apply to the mechanism specifically in relation to their capacity as refugees or IDPs, although reports are sometimes received relating to ill-treatment in the context of displacement caused by conflict. In this context, the SR on Torture is increasingly intervening in cases concerning IDPs (e.g., ill treatment during displacement or in camps, detention of IDPs considered at risk of ill treatment, ill treatment or detention of humanitarian personnel working with IDPs). Information is sometimes received from or about refugees, but generally in relation to ill treatment suffered in their home country prior to leaving it. In such cases, although the ill treatment may have been a factor in the decision to seek refugee status abroad, the application is treated as an individual allegation of torture in the regular fashion—no specific considerations apply on account of the refugee status.

> **Example:**
> 1997: An urgent appeal was transmitted in connection with the imminent deportation of a Turkish Kurd from Sweden. The man had allegedly been previously arrested and tortured prior to fleeing Turkey, and was said to be suffering from post-traumatic shock disorder.[52]

What motivates the Special Rapporteur to take action? Information sent to the SR on Torture should relate to the torture or ill treatment of persons by state officials, or the risk thereof. In particular, the communication should contain a detailed description of the alleged ill treatment. If the communication merely asserts that someone was tortured and does not explain what is meant by the term "torture" and describe what happened, then no action will be taken. The information must be sufficient for the SR on Torture to make his own assessment of whether torture has occurred.

Urgent appeals are sent in response to credible information indicating that a person or group of persons is at risk of torture at the hands of state officials. This could be either a risk of an initial incident of torture or of continuing torture of an individual who remains in custody. Factors that might contribute to establishing such a risk could include: the person is kept incommunicado or his or her detention is unacknowledged; the fact that this same person was tortured when arrested on a previous occasion; knowledge that persons arrested by this particular branch of the police are often tortured; or information that members of a particular group to which this person belongs are often

---

[52] *Question of the Human Rights of all Persons Subjected to Any Form of Detention or Imprisonment, In Particular: Torture and Other Cruel, Inhuman or Degrading Treatment or Punishment. Report of the Special Rapporteur, Mr. Nigel S. Rodley, submitted pursuant to Commission on Human Rights resolution 1997/38. Addendum. Summary of cases transmitted to Governments and replies recieved,* U.N. Doc. E/CN.4/1998/38/Add.1 ¶ 473 (24 December 1997).

tortured when arrested. The SR on Torture gives particular weight to incommunicado detention, as he considers such conditions to very significantly facilitate the occurrence of torture.

What should your communication contain? The SR on Torture has developed a model questionnaire (reproduced in Appendix 3B4). If this is not used, and to assist in filling out the questionnaire, you should include and consider the following elements:

- *Identity of the victim:* This should include both first and last names unless it is the local custom to have only one name. If the name is very common, other identifying details should be given, such as address or place of residence, age, sex, or profession. Such details are always valuable and should be given if known. Most of the mechanisms cannot take action on behalf of an unidentified individual. The only exception where names might not be required would be where a clearly identifiable group is involved (say, a group of 50 students arrested after demonstrating outside the mayor's office of City X on 19 November 1999). Still, names should always be included if available.
- *Date of the incident:* This should be as precise as possible and include both the date of apprehension by the state officials and of any incident(s) of torture, if these dates are different. Dates are important as they help to understand the sequence of events. If you know the time of day (either the exact time or whether the incident took place in the morning or evening), this can also be helpful.
- *Place of the incident:* This should include the name of the town, village, or local district, and the name of the state or region, where applicable. Make sure that you include the place of any incident of torture or other ill treatment, which may mean more than one place if there have been several incidents, as well as the place of arrest if this is different.
- *Alleged perpetrator(s):* Keep in mind that the perpetrator(s) must have a connection with the state. Information should include the name and rank of the perpetrator if known; at the least, you should identify the branch of the security forces or military involved, or the police station with which the perpetrator is associated. It is often possible to identify the group involved by the uniform worn. In an area where apprehensions by plainclothes police or military are known to be common, it may not

be necessary to name the perpetrators, as it will be possible to draw a strong inference from the surrounding circumstances.
- *Details of treatment:* Avoid using the term "torture" or "tortured" without describing the treatment involved. Not every incident of unpleasant treatment will be serious enough to constitute torture in legal terms, even though you may feel very strongly about it. The best approach is to describe the treatment in as much detail as possible. In this way, the international body will be able to determine for itself whether torture in the legal sense has taken place. Where the torture was physical, the details should include descriptions of the *treatment* involved, any *instruments* used, the *parts of the body* to which the treatment was applied, and any *injuries* suffered. For example, instead of saying "Mr. X was beaten," which could mean just about anything, it is much more informative to say "Mr. X was severely beaten in the face and head with a metal bar, resulting in a fractured skull and a perforated eardrum." Where the torture was psychological, you should describe what it *consisted of,* how the victim *felt* while it was going on and subsequently, and details of any way in which the victim's behavior or mental state has been *affected* by the treatment (e.g., if he is suffering from nightmares or paranoia).

While there is a minimum amount of detail that should be present, there is really no maximum to the amount of relevant details that can be included. What does relevant mean? Basically, it means anything that helps the SR on Torture understand what happened and decide whether a state is respecting its obligations. As states have obligations to investigate and remedy incidents of torture, this includes information about what happened after the incident. Details that might be relevant and should be included if known include:

- age and profession of the victim and whether the person is male or female (it can sometimes be difficult for someone unfamiliar with the local language to determine this)
- identity card number
- address or place of residence
- race or ethnic group
- any injuries or long-term effects suffered
- whether the victim was granted access to a lawyer and/or doctor during his detention
- whether the victim made a complaint about the incident of torture

- if a complaint was made, what the state authorities have done in response. Has there been an investigation or prosecution? If there has been a prosecution, was any penalty imposed?

If you would like the Special Rapporteur to use the urgent appeal procedure, you should follow the guidelines mentioned above as much as possible and, in addition, bear in mind that:

- where torture has not yet occurred, the relevant date, time, and location will generally be those of the taking into custody.
- you must show that there is a risk that torture may occur. This means that you need to emphasize the factors that show that this risk exists: e.g., the incommunicado or unacknowledged nature of the person's detention; the fact that this same person was tortured when arrested on a previous occasion; knowledge that persons arrested by this particular branch of the police are usually tortured; or knowledge that members of a particular group to which this person belongs are often tortured when arrested.

(5) Special Rapporteur on Independence of Judges and Lawyers

Basic Facts About: The Special Rapporteur on the Independence of Judges and Lawyers

Origin:	How was it created?	By resolution 1994/41 of the UNCHR	
	When was it created?	1994	
Working Methods:	Dialogue:	Yes	Fact-finding:	Yes
	— Standard communications	Yes	Analysis:	Yes
	— Urgent appeals	Yes	Research:	No

What does the mandate of the Special Rapporteur cover? The mandate of the Special Rapporteur on the Independence of Judges and Lawyers is concerned with the independence and impartiality of the various components of legal systems: the judiciary, lawyers, and court officials. The SR on the Independence of Judges and Lawyers does this by (1) following up on communications received and reporting on his conclusions, (2) monitoring attacks on the independence of the judiciary and related officials as well as progress in rendering technical assistance, and (3) conducting studies and writing proposals aimed at enhancing the independence of the judiciary and lawyers.

In terms of the categories of legal personnel and officials falling within the mandate, the SR on the Independence of Judges and Lawyers has indicated that his interpretation of the mandate is a broad one. He addresses all cases concerning the activities of the judiciary at all levels, including special tribunals, and those of jurors, assessors, and lawyers of all types, irrespective of whether these are professionals or lay persons, whether they are standard or ad hoc appointments, and whether their qualifications are formal in nature or otherwise. Interferences with the activities of these persons might include individual measures (reprisals for the performance of professional functions; professional sanctions, including dismissal; arbitrary arrest and detention; or attacks on their physical integrity) or they might be carried out through systemic measures such as legislation.[53]

What law or standards does the Special Rapporteur rely on or interpret? The Special Rapporteur applies general principles of both natural and positive law, as well as customary obligations. The principal norms of general application upon which he relies are Articles 7, 8, 10, and 11 of the 1948 Universal Declaration on Human Rights and Articles 2, 14, and 26 of the 1966 International Covenant on Civil and Political Rights. Other conventions are also relied on as appropriate. His main terms of reference, however, are the three soft law instruments adopted specifically in relation to legal professionals and officials:

- 1985 Basic Principles on the Independence of the Judiciary
- 1990 Basic Principles on the Role of Lawyers
- 1990 Guidelines on the Role of Prosecutors[54]

Has the Special Rapporteur addressed issues specific to refugees, asylum-seekers, and internally displaced persons? In laying out the legal framework for his mandate, the SR on the Independence of Judges and Lawyers specifically referred to Article 16 of the 1951 Convention relating to the Status

---

[53] *Question of the Human Rights of All Persons Subjected to Any Form of Detention or Imprisonment, In Particular: (a) Torture and Other Cruel, Inhuman or Degrading Treatment or Punishment; (b) Status of the Convention Against Torture and Other Cruel, Inhuman or Degrading Treatment or Punishment; (c) Question of Enforced or Involuntary Disappearances; (d) Question of a Draft Optional Protocol to the Convention Against Torture and Other Cruel, Inhuman or Degrading Treatment or Punishment. Independence and Impartiality of the Judiciary, Jurors and Assessors and the Independence of Lawyers. Report of the Special Rapporteur, Mr. Param Cumaraswamy, submitted in accordance with Commission On Human Rights resolution 1994/41*, U.N. Doc. E/CN.4/1995/39 ¶¶ 63–65 (6 February 1995).

[54] *Id.*, ¶¶ 32–52.

of Refugees, and Article 16 of the 1954 Convention relating to the Status of Stateless Persons. Both of these articles provide that refugees and stateless persons shall have access to the courts, and shall enjoy the same access to courts, including legal assistance, as exercised by nationals. The SR on the Independence of Judges and Lawyers noted that the reference to "courts" implies the standard conditions of independence and impartiality.[55]

> **Examples:**
> 1998: The Special Rapporteur sent an urgent appeal on behalf of a Somali national in Australia who was believed to be at risk of torture or execution if returned to his country of origin. The case fell within the mandate because the man had been transferred from an Immigration Detention Centre in Melbourne to one in Western Australia. His legal representatives remained in Melbourne and, as a result of the high cost of phone calls, his access to his legal representatives was restricted. The man was subsequently returned to Melbourne and provided with free phone calls to his legal representatives.[56]
> 1997: Following his visit to Colombia, the Special Rapporteur reported that persons displaced as a result of the armed conflict had difficulties with access to justice, particularly in connection with seeking judicial decisions concerning the violation of fundamental rights due to their displacement and poor living conditions.[57]

Are there any specific points to note regarding the working methods of the Special Rapporteur, and what can be achieved by submitting information to him or her? For the SR on the Independence of Judges and Lawyers to consider a case clarified, a satisfactory response must be received from the government in question. In order to be considered "satisfactory," a response must demonstrate respect for the independence of the judiciary and the legal profession in practice. Merely citing principles from

---

[55] *Id.*, ¶ 49.

[56] *Civil and Political Rights, Including the Questions of: Independence of the Judiciary, Administration of Justice, Impunity. Report of the Special Rapporteur on the Independence of Judges and Lawyers, Mr. Param Cumaraswamy*, submitted in accordance with Commission resolution 1999/31, U.N. Doc. E/CN.4/2000/61 ¶ 43–45 (21 February 2000).

[57] *Question of the Human Rights of All Persons Subjected to Any Form of Detention or Imprisonment. Report of the Special Rapporteur on the Independence of Judges and Lawyers, Mr. Param Cumaraswamy. Addendum. Report on the Mission of the Special Rapporteur to Columbia*, U.N. Doc. E/CN.4/1998/39/Add.2 ¶¶ 29–30 (30 March 1998).

the constitution of the state involved is not a satisfactory response because it does not demonstrate how the state is actively applying those principles.[58]

What motivates the Special Rapporteur to take action? Action is initiated by the receipt of prima facie credible information. The credibility of the source will be assessed on the basis of the degree of detail presented about the victim and the alleged facts, the existence of corroborative sources, the consistency of the allegation, and the legal framework of the state concerned.

The SR on the Independence of Judges and Lawyers will use an urgent action to governments for cases that involve particularly grave allegations of violations, such as threats to the life of the alleged victim.[59]

What should your communication contain? You should follow the general guidelines in Section 5.1.2 for preparing a communication. You should clearly establish that the information relates to the categories of persons and institutions falling within the mandate.

(6)   Special Rapporteur on Freedom of Expression

Basic Facts About: The Special Rapporteur on Freedom of Expression			
Origin:	How was it created?		By resolution 1993/45 of the UNCHR
	When was it created?		1993
Working Methods:	Dialogue:	Yes	Fact-finding:	Yes
	— Standard communications	Yes	Analysis:	Yes
	— Urgent appeals	Yes	Research:	Yes

What does the mandate of the Special Rapporteur cover? The mandate of the Special Rapporteur on Freedom of Expression concerns the promotion and protection of the right to freedom of opinion and expression, including the right to seek, receive, and impart information. The SR on Freedom of Expression is involved with both individual cases and with consideration of laws and practices relating to these rights.[60]

---

[58]   *Question of the Human Rights of all Persons Subjected to Any Form of Detention or Imprisonment. Note by the Secretary-General,* U.N. Doc. E/CN.4/1995/30 ¶¶ 80–81 (1 February 1995).
[59]   *Id.* ¶¶ 74–76.
[60]   *Civil and Political Rights, Including the Question of: Freedom of Expression.*

In particular, the SR on Freedom of Expression seeks information regarding:[61]

- detention, discrimination, threats or use of violence, and harassment, including persecution and intimidation, directed at persons seeking to exercise or promote the exercise of the right to freedom of opinion and expression, including professionals in the field of information
- activities of political opposition and trade union activists, both groups and individuals
- actions against the media (print and broadcast) or impediments to their independent operation
- actions against publishers and performers in other media
- activities of human rights defenders
- women's human rights, within the context of obstacles, including laws and practices, that impede the rights of women to express their views and be heard, participate in the decision-making process, have equal standing before the law, and seek and receive information on matters of particular relevance to them, such as family planning and violence against women
- obstacles to access information at the local, regional, and national levels on projects and initiatives proposed by the government to advance the right to development; obstacles to the decision making process; or obstacles to access information on other subjects such as environmental and health impact studies, national budgets, social spending, trade policies, etc.

What law or standards does the Special Rapporteur rely on or interpret? The Special Rapporteur on Freedom of Expression relies on:

- 1948 Universal Declaration of Human Rights Article 19 (freedom of opinion and expression)
- 1966 International Covenant on Civil and Political Rights Articles 19 (freedom of opinon and expression) and 20 (pro-

---

Report of the Special Rapporteur on the Protection and Promotion of the Right to Freedom of Opinion and Expression, Mr. Abid Hussain, U.N. Doc. E/CN.4/1999/64, Annex: How to bring information before the Special Rapporteur on the promotion and protection of the right to freedom of opinion and expression (29 January 1999) [hereinafter *How to Bring Information Before the SR on Freedom of Expression*].

[61] *Id.*

hibition on incitement to discrimination, hostility, violence, and propoganda for war)

Has the Special Rapporteur addressed issues specific to refugees, asylum-seekers, and internally displaced persons? The SR on Freedom of Expression has not specifically addressed these categories of persons in defining the scope of his mandate, but he has occasionally come across relevant cases of concern.

> **Examples:**
> 1999: During his visit to Ireland, the Special Rapporteur examined issues relating to the Irish Travelers and the growing numbers of refugees and migrants, in particular their under-representation and the role of the media in contributing to the intensification of prejudices against them. He welcomed positive measures to promote and guarantee the right to freedom of opinion and expression of refugees and minorities, particularly the efforts of the Irish media to adopt a more constructive and tolerant approach in portraying them than has been the case in the recent past.[62]
>
> 1999: During his visit to Tunisia, the Special Rapporteur noted and condemned the harassment and ill treatment of wives and other relatives of those in opposition who are in exile.[63]

What motivates the Special Rapporteur to take action? Action may be initiated by the receipt of prima facie credible and reliable information.

The SR on Freedom of Expression will use an urgent action to governments for cases that are life threatening in nature, or other situations where the particular circumstances require urgent attention.

What should your communication contain? The following minimum information must be provided:[64]

---

[62] *Civil and Political Rights, Including the Question of: Freedom of Expression Report of the Special Rapporteur on the Promotion and Protection of the Right to Freedom of Opinion and Expression, Mr. Abid Hussain, submitted in accordance with Commission resolution 1999/36. Addendum. Report on the mission to Ireland,* U.N. Doc. E/CN.4/2000/63/Add.2 ¶¶ 64, 69, 78 (10 January 2000).

[63] *Civil and Political Rights, Including the Question of: Freedom of Expression. Report of the Special Rapporteur on the Promotion and Protection of the Right to Freedom of Opinion and Expression, Mr. Abid Hussain, submitted in accordance with Commission resolution 1999/36. Report on the Mission to Tunisia,.* U.N. Doc. E/CN.4/2000/63/Add.4 ¶ 79 (23 February 2000).

[64] *How to Bring Information Before the SR on Freedom of Expression, supra* note 60.

- *If the allegation is regarding a person or persons:* provide as detailed a description as possible, including name, age, gender, ethnic background (if relevant), profession, views or affiliations, past or present participation in political, social, ethnic, or labor group/activity, and any other information on other specific activities relating to the alleged incident.
- *If the allegation is regarding a medium of communication:* provide as detailed a description as possible, including date, location, and circumstances of the event; nature of medium affected (e.g., newspaper, independent radio), including circulation and frequency of publication or broadcasting; and political orientation of the medium (if relevant).
- *Provide information regarding the alleged perpetrators:* name, governmental affiliation (e.g., military, police), and reasons why they are considered responsible. For non-state actors, description of how they related to the government (e.g., cooperation with or support by governmental security forces). If applicable, describe governmental encouragement or tolerance of activities of non-state actors, whether groups or individuals, including threats or use of violence and harassment against individuals exercising their right to freedom of opinion and expression, including the right to seek, receive, and impart information.
- *Provide information related to state actions:*
    - If the incident involves restrictions on a medium (censorship, closure of news organ, banning of book, etc.), provide the full identity of the authority involved, the legal statute invoked, and the steps taken to seek a domestic remedy.
    - If the incident involves arrest of an individual or individuals, the identity of the authority involved, legal statute invoked, location of detention if known, information on provision of access to legal counsel and family members, and steps taken to seek a domestic remedy or clarification of the person's situation or status.
- *Provide information on the source of the communication:* including name and full address, telephone and Fax numbers, and e-mail address, if possible.

(7) Special Rapporteur on Religious Intolerance

Basic Facts About: The Special Rapporteur on Religious Intolerance				
Origin:	How was it created?		By resolution 1986/20 of the UNCHR	
	When was it created?		1986	
Working Methods:	Dialogue:	Yes	Fact-finding:	Yes
	— Standard communications	Yes	Analysis:	Yes
	— Urgent appeals	Yes	Research:	Yes

What does the mandate of the Special Rapporteur cover? The mandate of the Special Rapporteur on Religious Intolerance is to examine incidents and governmental action in all parts of the world that are inconsistent with the provisions of the 1981 Declaration on the Elimination of All Forms of Intolerance and Discrimination Based on Religion or Belief, and to make recommendations to remedy these situations.

In analyzing the communications received, the SR on Religious Intolerance summarizes the violations into seven categories:

- violations of the principles of non-discrimination in matters of religion and belief
- violations of the principle of tolerance in matters of religious and belief
- violations of freedom of thought, conscience, and religion or belief
- violations of the freedom to manifest one's religion or belief
- violations of the freedom to dispose of religious property
- violations of physical integrity and health of persons
- violations affecting women[65]

What law or standards does the Special Rapporteur rely on or interpret? The SR on Religious Intolerance relies on the 1981 Declaration on the Elimination of All Forms of Intolerance and of Discrimination Based on Religion or Belief.

Has the Special Rapporteur addressed issues specific to refugees, asylum-seekers, and internally displaced persons? The SR on Religious Intolerance has not

---

[65] *Civil and Political Rights, Including Religious Intolerance. Report submitted by Mr. Abdelfattah Amor, Special Rapporteur, in accordance with Commission on Human Rights resolution 1998/18*, U.N. Doc. E/CN.4/1999/58 ¶¶ 104–114 (11 January 1999) [hereinafter *Report of the SR on Religious Intolerance*].

196   *Human Rights Protection for Displaced Persons*

specifically addressed these categories of persons in defining the scope of his mandate, but he has occasionally come across relevant cases.

> **Examples:**
>
> 1998: Following his visit to the United States, the SR on Religious Intolerance noted with concern a tendency in the media to stir up hatred against Muslims, in particular by equating them with extremists and terrorists. As a consequence, he considered that, because of their perceived association with terrorists, Arabs and Muslims were most likely to be affected by legislation to allow the deportation of non-citizens on grounds of suspicion of links to terrorist organizations abroad, as well as legislation making it more difficult to secure political asylum.[66]
>
> 1998: The SR on Religious Intolerance reported an alleged practice of intolerance and discrimination against Muslim religious minorities in certain parts of Myanmar, in particular through the admission of refugees at the Thai border only on condition that they convert to Buddhism.[67]

Are there any specific points to note regarding the working methods of the Special Rapporteur, and what can be achieved by submitting information to him or her? The SR on Religious Intolerance requests that governments respond within two months for an ordinary communication and two weeks for an urgent action. It should be noted that the SR on Religious Intolerance sends very few urgent appeals. For example, out of 93 communications transmitted during the period covered by the 2000 report, only two were urgent appeals.[68]

The SR on Religious Intolerance also conducts studies on religious intolerance. Currently being researched are (a) the status of women with regard to religion, (b) proselytism, freedom of religion, and poverty, and (c) new sects, new religious movements, and communities of religion and belief.[69] With regard to preventative measures, the SR on Religious Intolerance is analyzing curricula and textbooks in primary and secondary schools, and plans to convene an international conference on the topic in 2001.[70]

---

[66] *Civil and Political Rights, Including Religious Intolerance. Report submitted by Mr. Abdelfattah Amor, Special Rapporteur, in accordance with Commission on Human Rights resolution 1998/18. Addendum. Visit to the United States of America*, U.N. Doc. E/CN.4/1999/58/Add.1 ¶¶ 36–38 (9 December 1998).

[67] *Report of the SR on Religious Intolerance, supra* note 65, ¶¶ 81–82.

[68] *Civil and Political Rights, Including Religious Intolerance. Report submitted by Mr. Abdelfattah Amor, Special Rapporteur, in accordance with Commission on Human Rights resolution 1999/39*, U.N. Doc. E/CN.4/2000/65 (15 February 2000).

[69] *Id.*, ¶ 113.

[70] *Id.*, ¶ 114.

The SR on Religious Intolerance is creating an international compendium of national enactments relating to freedom of religion and belief, which is expected to be made public on the Internet.[71]

What motivates the Special Rapporteur to take action? Action may be initiated by the receipt of credible information falling within the mandate.

What should your communication contain? You should refer to the general guidelines in Section 5.2.1 for the submission of a communication. You must establish that any violations and facts alleged have a religious dimension.

(8) Special Rapporteur on Violence Against Women

Basic Facts About: The Special Rapporteur on Violence Against Women			
Origin:	How was it created?	By resolution 1994/45 of the UNCHR	
	When was it created?	1986	
Working Methods:	Dialogue:	Yes	Fact-finding:	Yes
	— Standard communications	Yes	Analysis:	Yes
	— Urgent appeals	Yes	Research:	Yes

What does the mandate of the Special Rapporteur cover? The Special Rapporteur on Violence Against Women is mandated to "seek and receive information on violence against women, its causes and consequences," respond effectively to such information, and to recommend appropriate measures to halt its occurrence.[72]

The violation must be gender-specific, that is, violence or threats of violence directed against women on account of their gender. The definition of gender-based violence used by the SR on Violence Against Women is taken from the 1993 Declaration on the Elimination of Violence Against Women (DEVAW), adopted by the GA in its Resolution 48/104 of December 1993. According to Article 2, violence against women encompasses, but is not limited to, physical, sexual, and psychological violence, which:

---

[71] *Id.*, ¶ 112.
[72] *Question of Integrating the Rights of Women into the Human Rights Mechanisms of the United Nations and the Elimination of Violence Against Women*, U.N. Doc. E/CN.4/RES/1994/45 (4 March 1994).

- occurs in the family, including battering, sexual abuse of female children in the household, dowry-related violence, marital rape, female genital mutilation and other traditional practices harmful to women, non-spousal violence, and violence related to exploitation;
- occurs in the community, including rape, sexual abuse, sexual harassment and intimidation at work, in educational institutions, and elsewhere, trafficking in women, and forced prostitution; or
- is perpetrated or condoned by the state, including during times of armed conflict.

Unlike other Special Procedures, the Special Rapporteur encourages submissions in respect to non-state actors, on the basis that states have a duty to act with due diligence to prevent, investigate, and punish all violations of human rights, whether they occur in public or private.

What law or standards does the Special Rapporteur rely on or interpret? The SR on Violence Against Women relies on the 1979 Convention on the Elimination of Discrimination Against Women and the 1993 Declaration on the Elimination of Violence Against Women (DEVAW).

The Women's Convention is the most extensive instrument dealing exclusively with the rights of women. Although the instrument does not deal explicitly with violence against women except in the areas of trafficking and prostitution (Article 6), many of its anti-discrimination clauses provide for the protection of women from violence. It is supplemented by General Recommendation No.19 of the Committee for the Elimination of Discrimination Against Women, which addresses the issue of gender-based violence.

DEVAW deals exclusively with violence against women and is a comprehensive statement of international standards on the subject. Although the document is not legally binding, it sets out international norms that states have recognized as being fundamental in the struggle to eliminate all forms of violence against women.

State responsibility for the violation of women's human rights by private actors is anticipated by customary international law. The "due diligence" standard has been generally accepted as a measure of evaluating a state's responsibility for violation of human rights by private actors. This emerging trend is reflected in both the Women's Convention and DEVAW. Article 4(c) of DEVAW proclaims that states should "exercise due diligence to prevent, investigate and, in accordance with national legislation, punish acts of violence against women, whether those acts are perpetrated by the State or by private persons." This emergence of state responsibility for violence in society plays a crucial role in efforts to eradicate gender-based violence.

Many international legal instruments that deal with human rights include in their provisions the protection of women from violence. The SR on Violence Against Women uses other relevant international instruments and evolving norms, depending on the specific case or issue.

Has the Special Rapporteur addressed issues specific to refugees, asylum-seekers, and internally displaced persons? In 1998, the SR on Violence Against Women highlighted the plight of refugee and internally displaced women, and the suffering that they may face on account of their gender. The risks to which they are exposed were considered in two ways: the persecution that they fear or have suffered and that has caused them to leave their homes, and the risk of ensuing violence they face after having become refugees or internally displaced. Gender-based violence has been widely documented and includes, among other things, the use of systematic rape during armed conflict, harmful traditional practices affecting the health of women, especially female genital mutilation, the risk of being killed or persecuted by one's family for "crimes against honor," and the failure of authorities to protect women from domestic violence and rape. The SR on Violence Against Women notes with approval that states and international organizations are increasingly recognizing gender-based violence as a legitimate ground for granting refugee status. For example, the threat of female genital mutilation constitutes persecution under the Canadian "Gender Guidelines for Asylum Adjudications."[73]

Again in her 1998 report, the SR on Violence Against Women supported the recommendations made by the Expert Group Meeting on Gender-Based Persecution in Toronto (9–12 December 1997), convened by the United Nations Division for the Advancement of Women in cooperation with the Centre for Refugee Studies at York University. Among the recommendations adopted were the following:

- That severe discrimination and harassment may constitute persecution. Severe restrictions on women's enjoyment of their

---

[73] *Further Promotion and Encouragement of Human Rights and Fundamental Freedoms, Including the Question of the Programme and Methods of Work of the Commission. Alternative Approaches and Ways and Means within the United Nations System for Improving the Effective Enjoyment of Human Rights and Fundamental Freedoms. Report of the Special Rapporteur on Violence Against Women, its Causes and Consequences, Ms. Radhika Coomaraswamy, submitted in accordance with Commission resolution 1997/44*, U.N. Doc. E/CN.4/1998/54 (26 January 1998).

human rights, including with respect to education, employment, and freedom of movement, such as forced seclusion, meet the definition of persecution for the purposes of the 1951 Refugee Convention in those cases where women experience such restrictions as a profound violation of their dignity, autonomy, and status as human beings. In addition, the penalties imposed on women for violating social mores, which do not amount to violations of human rights, may be disproportionate and, in such circumstances, social mores and the threat of penalty for their transgression will amount to persecution. Such ill treatment may thus give rise to compelling reasons for non-return.

- That persecution as a result of (1) expressed or imputed feminism, (2) failure to conform to conventional gender roles, (3) activities during armed conflict, or (4) imputed opinion resulting from her relationship to family members should all be regarded as persecution on the grounds of political opinion for the purposes of the 1951 Refugee Convention.
- That where a woman's gender is a significant reason for persecution, her fear of persecution should be recognized as being on account of her membership of a particular social group (namely, "women") under the 1951 Refugee Convention. The claimant should, however, not need to prove that all other women have a well-founded fear of persecution or, conversely, that she would be singled out from among other women.

> **Examples:**
> 1999: An urgent appeal was sent on behalf of a Ukrainian national in Australia facing deportation, requesting that Australia not deport her until her physical security could be ensured in the Ukraine. She had been trafficked from the Ukraine for prostitution by a gang and feared that her life would be at risk if returned. She applied for refugee status on the basis of belonging to a particular social group of persons facing a "real chance of becoming victims of mafia gangs or criminal groups operating in her country of origin."[74]

---

[74] *Integration of the Human Rights of Women and the Gender Perspective. Violence Against Women. Report of the Special Rapporteur on Violence Against Women, its Causes and Consequences, Ms. Radhika Coomaraswamy. Submitted in accordance with Commission resolution 1997/44. Addendum. Communications to and from Governments*, U.N. Doc. E/CN.4/2000/68/Add.1 ¶ 4 (27 January 2000) [hereinafter *2000 Communications of the SR on Violence Against Women*].

> **Examples:** (continued)
> 1998: The SR on Violence Against Women reported a case involving the assault of a group of members of a women's organization working with returned refugees and displaced persons in Guatemala. They were reported to have been beaten and their personal possessions stolen. They had also allegedly received death threats urging them to renounce their work on behalf of returned refugee women.[75]

Are there any specific points to note regarding the working methods of the Special Rapporteur, and what can be achieved by submitting information to him or her? The SR on Violence Against Women has understood her mandate to contain two components. The first consists of setting out the elements of the problem, the international standards, and a general survey of incidents and issues as they relate to the many problem areas. The second component consists of identifying and investigating factual situations, as well as allegations that may be forwarded to the SR on Violence Against Women by concerned parties. The SR on Violence Against Women reports on particular topics of concern to draw attention to and prevent violence against women. Past reports have covered such issues as domestic violence, trafficking and forced prostitution, and women in armed conflict, among others.

What motivates the Special Rapporteur to take action? The claim must involve violence or threat of violence directed at a woman specifically on account of her gender. The decision as to what form the action will take depends on the content of the submission. It may involve an individual complaint, pattern of abuse, general submission, etc.

The urgent action procedure is used when the case involves an imminent threat, or fear of threat, to the right to personal security or the life of a woman.

What should your communication contain? The SR on Violence Against Women has produced a standard reporting form (reproduced in Appendix 3B5), indicating the type of information that would be helpful to the SR.[76]

---

[75] *Integration of the Human Rights of Women and the Gender Perspective. Violence Against Women. Report of the Special Rapporteur on Violence Against Women, its Causes and Consequences, Ms. Radhika Coomaraswamy. Addendum. Communications to and from Governments*, U.N. Doc. E/CN.4/1999/68/Add.1 ¶ 5 (11 January 1999).

[76] *2000 Communications of the SR on Violence Against Women, supra* note 74, Annex: Confidential violence against women information form.

In order to hold governments accountable, the Special Rapporteur must be able to link the specific violation to the government, either by documenting that a government actor or agent perpetrated the violation, by showing that the government has not exercised due diligence in preventing, investigating, or prosecuting violence against women, or by showing that the government has created an atmosphere within which the violence was a likely or inevitable outcome. The latter might include showing how the government has failed to provide social or legal remedies, support mechanisms, or training to relevant state institutions. The Special Rapporteur maintains an archive of information, which she relies on when drafting her reports, preparing for her field investigations, and responding to allegations.

What has proved most helpful to the reporting function of the Special Rapporteur is documentation that illustrates or documents a particular violation or violations. It is useful if the document places such violations within relevant social, cultural, political, economic, or legal contexts. This is necessary to demonstrate how and why the government and/or, if relevant, a non-state actor is responsible.

The Special Rapporteur also welcomes other forms of submissions such as articles of a theoretical or conceptual nature, conference reports, research results, etc. When lengthy research reports of a general or specific nature are submitted, an executive summary highlighting the most significant aspects of the report (particularly those that demonstrate the points discussed above) helps facilitate the Special Rapporteur's use of the material in her work.

Miscellaneous practical information. The SR on Violence Against Women will present a follow-up report to the Commission on Human Rights at the end of her 9-year term (in 2003), intended to provide a systematic review of states' compliance with their international obligations with respect to violence against women. The SR on Violence Against Women will request governments to provide her with a written account and copies of the measures taken since 1994 to bring state policy and practice into compliance with her recommendations.

Since the SR on Violence Against Women's work is ongoing, deadlines determine when and how the information will be used, rather than whether it will be used. Reports presented during the Commission for Human Rights sessions in March and April of each year must be submitted by the SR by the end of the preceding year. Thus, the SR asks that documentation intended for the current year's report be submitted by the end of September.

(9) Special Rapporteur on Contemporary Forms of Racism, Racial Discrimination, Xenophobia and Related Intolerance

Basic Facts About: The Special Rapporteur on Contemporary Forms of Racism, Racial Discrimination, Xenophobia and Ralated Intolerance					
Origin:	How was it created?		By resolution 1993/20 of the UNCHR		
	When was it created?		1986		
Working Methods:	Dialogue:	Yes	Fact-finding:		Yes
	— Standard communications	Yes	Analysis:		Yes
	— Urgent appeals	Yes	Research:		Yes

What does the mandate of the Special Rapporteur cover? The mandate of the Special Rapporteur on Racism includes "racism, racial discrimination, xenophobia and related intolerance" and thus encompasses a broad range of situations. However, the Commission has requested that the SR on Racism focus on situations of racism and xenophobia in developed countries, and in particular on the situation of migrant workers and other vulnerable groups. He also notes that racism and racial discrimination can occur both through institutionalized governmental policy and through other indirect forms.[77]

The SR on Racism does transmit allegations of racism and violence perpetrated by non-state actors.

What law or standards does the Special Rapporteur rely on or interpret? The SR on Racism relies on the:

- 1948 Universal Declaration of Human Rights, Article 2
- 1966 International Covenant on Civil and Political Rights, Article 2
- 1966 International Covenant on Economic, Social and Cultural Rights, Article 2

---

[77] *Implementation of the Programme of Action for the Second Decade to Combat Racism and Racial Discrimination. Report by Mr. Maurice Glele-Ahanhanzo, Special Rapporteur on Contemporary Forms of Racism, Racial Discrimination, Xenophobia and Related Intolerance, submitted pursuant to Commission on Human Rights resolution 1993/20*, U.N. Doc. E/CN.4/1994/66 ¶¶ 13–17 (2 February 1994) [hereinafter *Implementation of the Programme of Action for the Second Decade to Combat Racism and Racial Discrimination*].

- 1992 Declaration of the Rights of Persons Belonging to National or Ethnic, Religious and Linguistic Minorities
- 1990 Convention on the Protection of the Rights of All Migrant Workers and Members of their Families.

Has the Special Rapporteur addressed issues specific to refugees, asylum-seekers, and internally displaced persons? In assessing the national legal framework, the SR on Racism may examine the country's asylum laws, as in the case of France. The 2000 report details allegations of racism and xenophobia received from many immigrants and governmental replies to these allegations. In particular, the SR on Racism received allegations of mistreatment and abuse from the Roma in Germany, and immigrants from Africa in Spain. The SR on Racism also notes that the governments of countries that he visited have taken measures to implement many of his recommendations. For example, France has revised its immigration and asylum policies, and South Africa has initiated a campaign to end xenophobia.[78]

> **Example:**
> The SR on Racism has specifically focused on racism experienced by immigrants, Roma, and migrant workers, which may also be of relevance to refugees, asylum-seekers, and internally displaced persons. For example, the SR has received many reports of racism and xenophobia from immigrants in Spain, who may also be refugees or asylum-seekers in some cases.[79]

Are there any specific points to note regarding the working methods of the Special Rapporteur, and what can be achieved by submitting information to him or her? The SR on Racism has interpreted his mandate as consisting of two methodological aspects: a factual one, and a theoretical and conceptual one. Although the SR considers it desirable to study cases in order to carry out the factual aspect of his mandate, much emphasis is placed

---

[78] *Racism, Racial Discrimination, Xenophobia and All Forms of Discrimination. Report by Mr. Maurice Glèlè-Ahanhanzo, Special Rapporteur on Contemporary Forms of Racism, Racial Discrimination, Xenophobia and Related Intolerance, submitted pursuant to Commission on Human Rights resolution 1999/78*, U.N. Doc. E/CN.4/2000/16 ¶¶ 154–165 (10 February 2000). See also *Racism, Racial Discrimination, Xenophobia and All Forms of Discrimination. Report by Mr. Maurice Glèlè-Ahanhanzo, Special Rapporteur on Contemporary Forms of Racism, Racial Discrimination, Xenophobia and Related Intolerance, submitted pursuant to Commission on Human Rights resolution 1997/73*, U.N. Doc. E/CN.4/1998/79 ¶¶ 46–48 (14 January 1998), for similar information.

[79] *Id.*

on the conceptual development of the mandate, particularly through analysis of the relevant phenomena and their underlying causes.[80] Cases and examples often appear to be used selectively to illustrate global and system-wide problems and patterns relevant to the mandate rather than in their own right.

What should your communication contain? The allegation that an incident was racist or xenophobic should be supported with factual evidence such as. relevant statistics, a racial slur used in the incident, or the authorities' pattern of treating immigrants in a similar manner.

Miscellaneous practical information. The Special Rapporteur often names sources in his annual reports. Although this is unlikely to be done without the consent of the source, it is advisable to state clearly in your communication whether you wish the identity of the source to be kept confidential.

(10) Special Rapporteur on the Sale of Children

Basic Facts About: The Special Rapporteur on Sale of Children, Child Prostitution and Child Pornography			
Origin:	How was it created?	By resolution 1990/68 of the UNCHR	
	When was it created?	1986	
Working Methods:	Dialogue:	Yes	Fact-finding:	Yes
	— Standard communications	Yes	Analysis:	Yes
	— Urgent appeals	Yes	Research:	Yes

What does the mandate of the Special Rapporteur cover? Information falling within the mandate should concern a child under 18 and a situation of sale, prostitution, or pornography. However, the SR on the Sale of Children might also take action against publications, films, or Internet downloads that might in some way promote sex with children (for example, the use on the Internet "pseudo" children—adult faces morphed onto children's bodies, or vice versa).

---

[80] *Implementation of the Programme of Action for the Second Decade to Combat Racism and Racial Discrimination, supra* note 77, ¶¶ 35–45.

What law or standards does the Special Rapporteur rely on or interpret? The SR on the Sale of Children relies on the 1989 Convention on the Rights of the Child, as well as soft law and evolving principles on such issues as definitions as to what constitutes child pornography. Appeals may also be made on moral grounds, for example where sexual exploitation is concerned.

Has the Special Rapporteur addressed issues specific to refugees, asylum-seekers, and internally displaced persons? The SR on the Sale of Children has done so when directly confronted with these concerns in the context of the mandate.

> **Example:**
> 1998: The SR on the Sale of Children found on a visit to Belgium and Netherlands that one particularly vulnerable group are minor girls who find themselves in prostitution and who are pseudo or genuine asylum-seekers. These girls are often tricked into leaving their home countries by members of trafficking networks, who then take them to or through Belgium. The girls claim to be from a country other than their actual country of origin (e.g., at the time, Albanians were pretending to be Kosovars), declare themselves as asylum-seekers, and are given a temporary residency permit while their cases are investigated. This permit allows them to work, and prostitution is not illegal. Proving their ages is also difficult. In this context, the SR on the Sale of Children recommended that the government create a reception center/safe house (**not** a detention facility) where young asylum-seekers could be housed.[81]

Are there any specific points to note regarding the working methods of the Special Rapporteur, and what can be achieved by submitting information to him or her? This mandate receives few individual communications, which has consequently made it difficult to develop clear methods of work. Most of the work is carried out through analysis and investigative country missions.

Although there is no formal complaint procedure, the SR on the Sale of Children may still be able to intervene upon receipt of information relating to individual cases, particularly urgent information.

---

[81] *Rights of the Child. Report of the Special Rapporteur on the Sale of Children, Child Prostitution and Child Pornography, Ms. Ofelia Calcetas-Santos. Addendum. Report on the Mission of the Special Rapporteur to Belgium and the Netherlands on the Issue of Commercial Sexual Exploitation of Children (30 November–4 December 1998)*, U.N. Doc. E/CN.4/2000/73/Add.1 ¶¶ 18–27 (22 December 1999).

What motivates the Special Rapporteur to take action? There are no clear criteria. In practice, it most often depends upon the source of the information.

What should your communication contain? Authors of communications should ensure that the information falls within the mandate, that is, that it concerns a child under 18 in a situation of sale, prostitution, or pornography. An example of the kind of information that would not fall within the mandate is that relating to custody battles between estranged couples.

(11) Special Representative of the Secretary-General on Children in Armed Conflict

Basic Facts About: The Special Representative of the Secretary-General on Children in Armed Conflict				
Origin:	How was it created?		Appointed by the Secretary-General pursuamt to GA Resolution 51/77	
	When was it created?		1997	
Working Methods:	Dialogue: — Standard communications — Urgent appeals	Yes Yes Yes	Fact-finding: Analysis: Research:	Yes Yes Yes

What does the mandate of the Special Rapporteur cover? The Special Representative of the Secretary-General (SRSG) is mandated to study the phenomenon of armed conflict and children. As stated in one of his first reports, his task is to "combine normative, political and humanitarian strategies in efforts to promote prevention, protection and rehabilitation for the benefit of children."[82] His mandate recommends that he (1) assess progress achieved, steps taken, and difficulties encountered in strengthening the protection of children in situations of armed conflict; (2) raise awareness and promote the collection of information about the plight of children affected by armed conflict and encourage the development of networking; (3) work closely with the Committee on the Rights of the Child and other relevant IGOs and NGOs; and

---

[82] *Rights of the Child. Children in Armed Conflict. Interim Report of the Special Representative of the Secretary-General, Mr. Olara A. Otunnu, Submitted pursuant to General Assembly res. 52/107*, U.N. Doc. E/CN.4/1998/119 ¶ 19 (12 March 1998).

(4) encourage and facilitate international cooperation to ensure respect for the rights of children in these situations.[83]

What law or standards does the Special Rapporteur rely on or interpret? This mandate relies on a wide range of treaty and soft law:

- 1989 Convention on the Rights of the Child
- 1949 Geneva Conventions on the Protection of Victims of Armed Conflict and their 1977 Additional Protocols
- 1990 African Charter on the Rights and Welfare of the Child
- Security Council Resolutions, such as Resolution 1261

Has the Special Rapporteur addressed issues specific to refugees, asylum-seekers, and internally displaced persons? A focus of the work of the SRSG on Children in Armed Conflict is to mobilize efforts concerning the return and reintegration of displaced and refugee children. The SRSG has consistently spoken out on behalf of refugee and internally displaced children and has called for the international community to develop a more systematic response and framework for providing protection and practical support to IDPs, the vast majority of whom are women and children. The SRSG on Children in Armed Conflict is particularly vocal in supporting the mandate of the Special Representative of the Secretary-General on IDPs and in promoting the Guiding Principles on Internal Displacement. In his most recent report, the SRSG on Children in Armed Conflict has launched an "era of application" of international norms, and hopes to encourage the international community to focus on ensuring the application and respect for international human rights norms.

Security Council Resolution 1261 (1999), among other things, calls on governments to address the needs of children during peace processes, requests the UN to train all personnel involved with peacekeeping in the protection and rights of children, calls for an end to the recruitment and use of child soldiers, calls for their demobilization and rehabilitation, and calls on parties in armed conflict to abide by concrete commitments made to ensure the safety of children, such as unhindered access to humanitarian assistance.[84] The SRSG on Children in Armed Conflict has described the resolution as a "landmark in the campaign for children affected by armed conflict and a powerful new

---

[83] *The Rights of the Child*, G.A. Res. 51/77, U.N. GAOR. 51th Sess., U.N. Doc. A/RES/51/77 (20 Febeuary 1997).

[84] *Security Council Resolution 1261(1999) on the Children and Armed Conflict*, U.N. SCOR, 4037th mtg., U.N. Doc. S/Res/1261 (25 August 1999).

weapon in the campaign against the brutalising of children."[85]

Prior to the establishment of the current SRSG on Children in Armed Conflict, the Secretary-General appointed an independent expert, Graça Machel, whose groundbreaking report *Impact of Armed Conflict on Children*, also referred to as the Machel Report, sets the framework for the subsequent work of the SRSG. In this report, Machel discusses the unique issues that refugee and internally displaced children face and sets forth specific recommendations regarding this population. These recommendations include (1) immediate adoption of procedures to protect unaccompanied children in emergency situations; (2) whenever possible, finding extended family members to care for unaccompanied children, rather than in institutions; and (3) creating practical protection measures in refugee camps to prevent sexual violence, discrimination in the distribution of relief materials, and the risk of recruitment into the armed forces.[86]

Are there any specific points to note regarding the working methods of the Special Rapporteur and what can be achieved by submitting information to him or her?
The SRSG on Children in Armed Conflict works in three primary modalities: through public advocacy for children, by engaging in political and humanitarian diplomacy, and by mobilizing a coordinated response to address post-conflict needs with other UN agencies, programs, bodies, and mechanisms, as well as with NGOs.[87]

There is no urgent action procedure and the SRSG on Children in Armed Conflict has not so far acted in any systematic way on individual cases, although he may attempt to intervene on behalf of groups of children, particularly during his country missions and in discussions with high-level government officials.

Examples of cases in which the SRSG on Children in Armed Conflict has intervened include the following:

- During his visit to Uganda, the government pledged to assist with the ongoing efforts to release the children who were abducted from northern Uganda by Ugandan rebel groups. During 1998, two groups of children were released and

---

[85] See <www.un.org/special-rep/children-armed-conflict/scr1216OnePage Ver.htm.>.

[86] *Promotion and Protection of the Rights of Children. Impact of Armed Conflict on Children. Note by the Secretary-General,* U.N. Doc. A/51/306 ¶ 90 (26 August 1996).

[87] *Rights of the Child. Children in Armed Conflict. Interim Report of the Special Representative of the Secretary-General, Mr. Olara A. Otunnu, Submitted pursuant to General Assembly resolution 52/107,* U.N. Doc. E/CN.4/1998/119 ¶ 20 (12 March 1998).

210   Human Rights Protection for Displaced Persons

repatriated to Uganda with the cooperation of the Government of the Sudan.[88]
- On his visit to Columbia, the SRSG on Children in Armed Conflict urged the government to address the needs of displaced communities in terms of health, education, sanitary conditions, shelter, water, registration, and economic opportunities. He also asked the government to ensure their physical protection and security during displacement and to secure the conditions for the return to their homes.[89]

What should your communication contain? You should refer to the general guidelines in Section 5.1.2 setting out the minimum content of a communication.

Miscellaneous practical information. The Special Representative's web site, which provides useful information and more details about his work, can be found at <www.un.org/special-rep/children-armed-conflict>.

The SRSG on Children in Armed Conflict has an office in New York and is also represented at the OHCHR, which can result in lack of coordination between the two offices. Although information can be received by both offices in connection with this mandate, the OHCHR staff members are most familiar with the process of individual communications and may perhaps be persuaded in the future to take action in such cases.

(12) Special Representative of the Secretary-General on Internally Displaced Persons

Basic Facts About: The Special Representative of the Secretary-General on Internally-Displaced Persons				
Origin:	How was it created?		Appointed by the Secretary-General pursuamt to GA Resolution 1992/73 of the UNCHR	
	When was it created?		1997	
Working Methods:	Dialogue:	Yes	Fact-finding:	Yes
	— Standard communications	No	Analysis:	Yes
	— Urgent appeals	No	Research:	Yes

---

[88]   *Rights of the Child. Additional report of the Special Representative of the Secretary-General for Children and Armed Conflict, Mr. Olara Otunnu, submitted in accordance with General Assembly resolution 53/128,* U.N. Doc. E/CN.4/2000/71 ¶ 23 (9 February 2000).

[89]   *Id.,* ¶ 65

What does the mandate of the Special Representative cover? The Secretary-General first appointed Francis M. Deng to be the Special Representative on Internally Displaced Persons in 1992. The Special Representative of the Secretary-General (SRSG) is requested to study the causes of displacement, the needs of those displaced, and ways to strengthen protection, assistance, and solutions for the internally displaced. He accomplishes this through dialogue with governments, regional organizations, IGOs, and NGOs, and by taking into account specific situations.[90]

What law or standards does the Special Representative rely on or interpret? The Special Representative on IDPs relies on the Guiding Principles on Internal Displacement.[91]

Has the SRSG addressed issues specific to refugees, asylum-seekers, and internally displaced persons? As evidenced from the title of the mandate, the SRSG on IDPs focuses exclusively on internally displaced persons. The SRSG has defined an internally displaced person or persons as those "who have been forced or obliged to flee or leave their homes or places of habitual residence, in particular as a result of or in order to avoid the effects of armed conflict, situations of generalised violence, violations

---

[90] *Specific Groups and Individuals: Mass Exoduses and Displaced Persons. Internally Displaced Persons. Report of the Representative of the Secretary-General, Mr. Francis M. Deng, submitted pursuant to Commission on Human Right resolution 1999/47*, U.N. Doc. E/CN.4/2000/83 (26 January 2000) [hereinafter *2000 Report of the SRSG on IDPs*].

[91] The Guiding Principles are contained in *Further Promotion and Encouragement of Human Rights and Fundamental Freedoms, Including the Question of the Programme and Methods of Work of the Commission Human Rights, Mass Exoduses and Displaced Persons. Report of the Representative of the Secretary-General, Mr. Francis Deng, submitted pursuant to Commission resolution 1997/39. Addendum. Guiding Principles on Internal Displacement*, U.N. Doc. E/CN.4/1998/53/Add.2 (11 February 1998) [hereinafter *Guiding Principles on Internal Dispacement*]. They are available in Arabic, Chinese, English, French, Russian, Spanish, on the web at <www.reliefweb.int/library>. Unofficial translations are available in Portugese (booklet published by OCHA—NY), Tamil (booklet published by OCHA—Sri Lanka), Sinhala (booklet published by OCHA—Sri Lanka), Georgian (booklet published by OCHA—Georgia), Dari (booklet published by OCHA—Afghanistan), Pashtu (booklet published by OCHA—Afghanistan), Azerbaijani (by UNHCR Baku), Burmese (booklet published by local NGO), Sgaw Karen (booklet published by local NGO), Armenian (forthcoming late 2000). Contact Erin Mooney, the staff person at OHCHR who services the SRSG, to obtain copies of the unofficial translations, Tel: 41-22-927-9280. The Guiding Principles are reproduced in Appendix 3-D.

of human rights or natural or human-made disasters, and who have not crossed an internationally recognised border."[92]

The SRSG on IDPs was first asked to examine the extent to which existing international law addressed the needs of the internally displaced. The result was a two-part compilation and analysis, entitled *Compilation of Norms Relevant to Internally Displaced Persons*. The first part of the compilation and analysis[93] examined the relevant provision of international human rights law, international humanitarian law, and refugee law by analogy, protecting individuals once they have been displaced. The second part[94] examined the legal aspects of the right to not be arbitrarily displaced. On the basis of this compilation and analysis, the Commission called upon the SRSG on IDPs to develop a comprehensive normative framework of protection and assistance for internally displaced persons. Pursuant to this request, the SRSG, together with a team of experts in international law, drafted a set of guiding principals relating to internally displaced persons.[95] The Guiding Principles on Internal Displacement represent a formidable accomplishment and the first normative framework that IDPs and their advocates can call upon.

The Guiding Principles, thirty in all, seek to unify in one document relevant principles of international human rights and humanitarian law, clarify any grey areas, and fill in any gaps that may exist with regard to the protection of the internally displaced. The Guiding Principles address three aspects of internal displacement: a preventative phase, or the right not to be displaced; access to protection and assistance while internally displaced; and durable solutions through safe return and reintegration, or alternative settlement. Among other

---

[92] *Id.* ¶ 2.

[93] *Further Promotion and Encouragement of Human Rights and Fundamental Freedoms, Including the Question of the Programme and Methods of Work of the Commission: Human Rights, Mass Exoduses and Displaced Persons. Internally Displaced Persons. Report of the Representative of the Secretary-General, Mr. Francis M. Deng, submitted pursuant to Commission On Human Rights resolution 1995/57. Compilation and Analysis of Legal Norms*, U.N. Doc. E/CN.4/1996/52/Add.2 (5 December 1995).

[94] *Further Promotion and Encouragement of Human Rights and Fundamental Freedoms, Including the Question of the Programme and Methods of Work of the Commission: Human Rights, Mass Exoduses and Displaced Persons. Internally Displaced Persons. Report of the Representative of the Secretary-General, Mr. Francis M. Deng, submitted pursuant to Commission on Human Rights resolution 1995/39. Addendum. Compilation and Analysis of Legal Norms, Part II: Legal Aspects Relating to the Protection against Arbitrary Displacement*, U.N. Doc. E/CN.4/1998/53/Add.1 (11 February 1998).

[95] *Guiding Principles on Internal Displacement*, supra note 91. The sources of international law from which the Guiding Principles are drawn are elaborated in WALTER KÄLIN, GUIDING PRINCIPLES ON INTERNAL DISPLACEMENT: ANNOTATIONS (2000).

things, the Guiding Principles define who the internally displaced are, restate the large body of law already in existence applicable to the internally displaced, and outline the responsibilities of states. The Guiding Principles make clear that the internally displaced have the right to leave their country, seek asylum, and be protected from forcible return.[96]

The SRSG on IDPs uses the Guiding Principles as the basis for monitoring situations of displacement and as a common framework to dialogue with and mobilize governments, IGOs, and NGOs to address situations of internal displacement. The Guiding Principles are intended to serve as an authoritative statement that should provide practical guidance, aid in prevention, and serve as a public policy education tool, as well as raise public consciousness about the plight of the displaced.[97]

In a relatively short time, the Guiding Principles have become an important tool for the protection of the internally displaced. The Commission on Human Rights, the General Assembly, the Economic and Social Council, and all other relevant UN agencies have responded positively to the Guiding Principles and encouraged their dissemination and application. The Inter-Agency Standing Committee (IASC), comprised of NGOs and the major UN humanitarian, human rights, and development agencies, is actively promoting and disseminating the Guiding Principals. Regional organizations, such as the Organization of African Unity (OAU), the Inter-American Commission on Human Rights (IACHR), and the Organization for Security and Cooperation in Europe (OSCE), are also working to promote the Guiding Principles. Non-governmental organizations, such as Amnesty International and the Norwegian Refugee Council, also actively promote and apply the Guiding Principles in their work.[98]

As of yet, the Guiding Principles have no enforcement mechanism and are not in themselves legally binding. While governments are free to ignore them, the SRSG has noted that the Principles are increasingly being treated as binding customary law, partly because they are based on "hard" law.[99]

---

[96] Francis Deng, *Flocks without Shepherds: The International Dilemma of Internal Displacement*, <www. nrc.no/global_idp_survey/rights_have_no_borders/deng. htm.>.

[97] *Id.*

[98] *Specific Groups and Individuals: Mass Exodus and Displaced Persons. Internally Displaced Persons. Report of the Representative of the Secretary-General Mr. Francis M. Deng, submitted pursuant to Commission of Human Rights resolution 1998/50*, U.N. Doc. E/CN.4/1999/79 ¶¶ 13–24 (25 January 1999) [hereinafter *1998 Report of the SRSG on IDPs*].

[99] Interview with Francis Deng, SRSG on IDPs, REFUGEES MAGAZINE, Issue 117, 1999, <www.unhcr.ch/pubs/rm117/rm11703.htm.>.

Are there any specific points to note regarding the working methods of the Special Rapporteur, and what can be achieved by submitting information to him or her? The work of the SRSG on IDPs can be distilled into three areas: to establish a normative framework, to create an institutional framework, and to conduct country visits. The Guiding Principles represent a major step in the establishment of a normative framework. In the future, the SRSG would like the international community to establish a monitoring framework to accompany the Guiding Principles.

Regarding the institutional framework, the SRSG on IDPs identified the lack of a lead organization for internally displaced persons as a major obstacle to be remedied. In 1997, the Secretary-General placed the Emergency Relief Coordinator within the Office for the Coordination of Humanitarian Affairs (OCHA) in charge of ensuring that protection and assistance to IDPs is properly addressed and coordinated by the international community. The Emergency Relief Coordinator chairs the Inter-Agency Standing Committee (IASC) and its Working Group. The IASC Working Group is the main interagency forum for consultation on all matters relating to IDPs and supports the work of the Emergency Relief Coordinator. The SRSG has forged a strong cooperative relationship with these bodies.[100]

The SRSG on IDPs falls into that category of special procedures that does not possess a formal individual complaint mechanism. However, the SRSG does receive communications, most often concerning groups of internally displaced persons at risk. The SRSG regards communications as a catalyst for further investigation of a situation. Thus a communication received from an NGO may provide the launching point for the SRSG to conduct further research and develop an appropriate response to the situation as a whole.

The SRSG has recently begun issuing "statements of concern" as another means of focusing attention on the plight of the internally displaced. In 1999, the SRSG issued statements of concern regarding internally displaced persons in Kosovo, East Timor, and Chechnya. In the case of East Timor, in fact, the SRSG issued a joint urgent appeal with the Special Rapporteur on Extra-judicial, Summary or Arbitrary Executions, the Special Rapporteur on Torture, and the Working Group on Arbitrary Detention. The urgent appeal highlighted specific provisions of the Guiding Principles and urged the government to take steps to ensure the protection of the right not to be internally displaced.[101]

The SRSG on IDPs has identified country missions as the operational pillar of his mandate. The SRSG conducts, on average, two coun-

---

[100] *1998 Report of the SRSG on IDPs, supra* note 98, ¶¶ 37–39.
[101] *2000 Report of the SRSG on IDPs, supra* note 90, ¶¶ 61–65.

try missions a year.[102] Country missions allow the SRSG to assess the extent to which the protection, assistance, and development needs of the internally displaced are being met in specific situations, and to engage in solution-oriented dialogue with the government and relevant non-governmental organizations. Following each mission, the SRSG publishes a report that includes recommendations to the government and international community. These missions have generally resulted in positive steps being taken to improve the situation of the internally displaced.[103] For example, in response to the SRSG's recommendations to the Government of Azerbaijan, the president issued a decree setting forth the government's new strategies to address their massive situation of internal displacement. The new policies specifically incorporated two important recommendations advocated by the SRSG.[104] Ideally, the SRSG would prefer to conduct follow-up country visits, but owing to budget constraints the SRSG has only done this for Colombia and Burundi. The SRSG requests to be informed of any developments and progress following his visits.

What motivates the Special Representative to take action? There are no clear-cut indicators as to when the SRSG on IDPs will take action. As discussed earlier, communications generally provide the impetus for the SRSG to investigate further.

What should your communication contain? Communications must concern the situation of internally displaced persons, as defined by the SRSG,[105] or persons at risk of becoming internally displaced. The communication should reference precisely which articles of the Guiding Principles are in question or being violated.

The same general guidelines regarding communications apply to the SRSG (see Section 4.1.3). Any communication should contain information that is as detailed as possible. In addition, a one to two page executive summary will help ensure that your communication is properly reviewed.

If the purpose of the communication is to encourage the SRSG on IDPs to conduct a mission to a particular country, this should be

---

[102] As of January 2000, the Special Representative had undertaken 14 country visits to Azerbaijan, Burundi, Colombia (twice), El Salvador, Mozambique, Peru, the Russian Federation, Rwanda, Somalia, Sri Lanka, the Sudan, Tajikistan, and the former Yugoslavia, *2000 Report of the SRSG on IDPs, supra* note 90, ¶ 48.

[103] Deng, *supra* note 96.

[104] *2000 Report of the SRSG on IDPs, supra* note 90, ¶ 53.

[105] *Guiding Principles on Internal Displacement, supra* note 91 ¶ 2.

clearly stated. Advocates might consider working with other national and international NGOs to submit documentation to the SRSG describing why the country concerned should be visited. Although the SRSG must take into account a host of factors, including budgetary constraints that generally limit visits to two a year, the SRSG values non-governmental input as to which countries should be visited.

Miscellaneous practical information. The SRSG on IDPs has long advocated the creation of a mechanism to systematically collect, receive, and disseminate information on internal displacement. This project came to fruition in December 1999 with the launching of the Global IDP Database (<www.idpproject.org>). The objectives of the database are:

- To offer central access to information regarding internally displaced persons and to support the mandates of the SRSG, the Inter-Agency Standing Committee, and the Emergency Response Coordinator by providing up-to-date accurate information on internal displacement;
- To assist humanitarian organizations in field operations and to become a major NGO focal point for advocacy and information on the protection and assistance needs of the internally displaced; and
- To assist in assessing the impact of the Guiding Principles by monitoring situations of internal displacement world-wide.[106]

The following resources may be useful for advocates who wish to utilize the Guiding Principles:

- *Guiding Principles on Internal Displacement* in English, French, Spanish, Russian, and Arabic, UN Office for the Coordination of Humanitarian Affairs, available at <www.reliefweb.int/ library> and at <www.ohchr.ch>
- *Handbook for Applying the Guiding Principles on Internal Displacement,* by Susan Forbes Martin, The Brookings Institution Project on Internal Displacement, Office for the Coordination of Humanitarian Affairs, United Nations, New York, November 1999, available at <www.reliefweb.int/library>
- *Manual on Field Practice in Internal Displacement: Examples from UN Agencies and Partner Organizations of Field-based Initiatives Supporting Internally Displaced Persons,* Inter-Agency Standing

---

[106] *2000 Report of the SRSG on IDPs, supra* note 90, ¶ 43.

Committee Policy Paper Series No. 1, Office for the Coordination of Humanitarian Affairs, United Nations, New York, November 1999, available at <www.reliefweb.int/library>
- *The Guiding Principles on Internal Displacement: Annotations*, by Walter Kälin, jointly published by the American Society of International Law and the Brookings Institution Project on Internal Displacement. This volume consists of the Annotations of the Guiding Principles that explain the legal basis for the Guiding Principles, and the two compilations of legal norms that were the two initial studies leading to the development of the Guiding Principles. To obtain a copy of the Annotations, please contact the American Society of International Law in Washington, DC, at 202-939-6000.

The Brookings Institution's Project on Internal Displacement also has a number of resources on their web site, <http://www.brook.edu/fp/projects/idp/idp.htm> or by contacting them at 202-797-6000 in Washington, D.C.

The SRSG on IDPs has also released a series of "Profiles in Displacement," each relating to a particular country based largely on his country visits. These are available on the OHCHR web site in English, French, and Spanish, unless otherwise stated, for the following countries: Azerbaijan (1/25/99), Mozambique (2/24/97), Tajikistan (10/24/96), Peru (4/01/96), Rwanda (2/16/95), Burundi (11/28/94), Colombia (10/03/94) and follow-up mission (1/11/00), and Sri Lanka (French and Spanish only) (1/25/94).

(13) Special Rapporteur on the Human Rights of Migrants

Basic Facts About: The Special Rapporteur on the Human Rights of Migrants			
Origin:	How was it created?	By resolution 1999/44 of the UNCHR	
	When was it created?	1999	
Working Methods:	Dialogue:	Yes	Fact-finding:	Yes
	— Standard communications	Not Clear	Analysis:	Yes
			Research:	Yes
	— Urgent appeals	Not Clear		

What does the mandate of the Special Rapporteur cover? Gabriela Rodriguez Pizarro was appointed Special Rapporteur on the Human Rights of Migrants in 1999. Her mandate includes examining ways and means to overcome violations of the human rights of migrants, including undocumented migrants and those in an irregular situation; to request and receive information from all relevant sources, including migrants themselves; to promote the application of the relevant norms and standards; and to make recommendations to eliminate human rights violations experienced by migrants.[107]

What law or standards does the Special Rapporteur rely on or interpret? One of the obstacles identified by the Special Rapporteur is the absence or non-acceptance of international human rights standards supporting the rights of migrant workers. The 1990 International Convention on the Protection of the Rights of All Migrant Workers and Members of Their Families has not entered into force because not enough countries have ratified it. Thus, at the time of this writing, the SR is still developing what laws and standards will govern her work. In the meantime, it should be emphasized that advocates can freely interpret articles in the 1948 Universal Declaration of Human Rights, the 1966 International Covenant on Civil and Political Rights, and the International Labor Organization (ILO) Conventions as applying to the rights of migrants.

The Special Rapporteur envisions that a major part of her work will be to encourage the ratification of the Convention on Migrant Workers and create standards applicable at the local, national, and international levels.

Has the Special Rapporteur addressed issues specific to refugees, asylum-seekers, and internally displaced persons? The SR focuses on migrants and does not address issues related to refugees, asylum-seekers, and internally displaced persons. In her first report, the SR discussed at length issues regarding the definition of a migrant. The draft definition from that report is as follows:

> (a) Persons who are outside the territory of the state of which they are nationals or citizens, are not subject to its legal protection, and are in the territory of another state;

---

[107] *Specific Groups and Individual Migrant Workers. Human Rights of Migrants. Report of the Special Rapporteur, Ms. Gabriela Rodríguez Pizarro*, submitted pursuant to Commission on Human Rights resolution 1999/44, U.N. Doc. E/CN.4/2000/82 ¶¶ 1–2 (6 January 2000).

(b) Persons who do not enjoy the general legal recognition of rights which is inherent in the granting by the host state of the status of refugee, permanent resident, or naturalized person or of similar status; and

(c) Persons who do not enjoy general legal protection of their fundamental rights by virtue of diplomatic agreements, visas, or other agreements.[108]

Are there any specific points to note regarding the working methods of the Special Rapporteur, and what can be achieved by submitting information to him or her? Again, due to the relative newness of this mechanism, it is not clear how the SR on the Human Rights of Migrants will respond to communications.

The SR on the Human Rights of Migrants has identified a plan of action for her three-year term. This involves addressing the legal framework for migrants, surveying regional instruments, creating a program to end discrimination against migrants, participating in the World Conference against Racism, and campaigning for the ratification of the 1990 International Convention of the Rights of All Migrant Workers and Members of Their Families, as well as other international human rights instruments.[109]

What should your communication contain? You should follow the general guidelines for communications as explained in Section 5.1.2.

(14) New Mandates of Potential Relevance to Refugees, Asylum-Seekers, and Internally Displaced Persons

At its 56th Session in March/April 2000, the Commission on Human Rights created a number of new mandates that are of potential relevance to refugees, asylum-seekers, and internally displaced persons. Although they have not yet adopted their working methods or attempted to define the scope of their mandates, their progress and development should be watched with interest. The new mandates are the following:

Special Rapporteur on Adequate Housing. The Special Rapporteur on Adequate Housing was created by Resolution 2000/9, and is mandated to examine the theme of adequate housing as a component of the right to an adequate standard of living. The SR is requested to "report on

---

[108] *Id.,* ¶ 36.
[109] *Id.,* ¶¶ 16–20.

the status of the realization of these rights which are relevant to the mandate in accordance with the provisions of the relevant instrument, and on developments relating to these rights, including on laws, policies, and good practices most beneficial to their enjoyment and difficulties and obstacles encountered domestically and internationally."

Special Representative of the Secretary-General on the Situation of Human Rights Defenders. This Special Representative was recommended by Resolution 2000/61, to be approved by the ECOSOC, and is mandated to "report on the situation of human rights defenders in all parts of the world and on possible means to enhance their protection in compliance with the [1998] Declaration on the Right and Responsibility of Individuals, Groups and Organs of Society to Promote and Protect Universally Recognized Human Rights and Fundamental Freedoms." The main activities of the SR will be:

- to seek, receive, examine, and respond to information on the situation and the rights of anyone, acting individually or in association with others, to promote and protect human rights;
- to establish cooperation and conduct dialogue with governments and other interested actors on the promotion and effective implementation of the Declaration;
- to recommend effective strategies to better protect human rights defenders and follow up on these recommendations.

Special Rapporteur on the Right to Food. The Special Rapporteur on the Right to Food was created by Resolution 2000/10. The mandate is to be accomplished by:

- seeking, receiving, and responding to information on all aspects of the realization of the right to food, including the urgent necessity of eradicating hunger;
- establishing cooperation with governments, intergovernmental organizations, and non-governmental organizations on the promotion and effective implementation of the right to food, and to make appropriate recommendations on the realization thereof;
- identifying emerging issues relating to the right to food worldwide.

5.2.2 Country-Specific Procedures

In addition to thematic rapporteurs and working groups, the Commission on Human Rights also appoints country-specific rapporteurs (or *independent experts* or *special representatives*) whose task is to report on the full range of human rights in the specific country for which they are responsible. In general, such rapporteurs will be appointed in relation to countries that have particularly serious human rights situations, including those caused by war or internal conflict. The singling out of a country for such scrutiny is inevitably a politically sensitive matter, however, and there must be sufficient agreement among states at the Commission on Human Rights for a country-specific rapporteur to be created.

Like thematic rapporteurs, the objective of country-specific rapporteurs is to paint an accurate picture of a situation. However, instead of a world-wide portrait of a specific phenomenon, a country-specific report should be a far more comprehensive examination of the human rights situation in a single country. At the time of writing, country-specific mandates existed in relation to Afghanistan, Burundi, Cambodia, Cyprus, Democratic Republic of Congo, East Timor, Equatorial Guinea, Former Yugoslavia, Haiti, Iran, Iraq, Myanmar, Occupied Arab Territories, Rwanda, Somalia, and Sudan.

The country-specific rapporteurs adopt working methods similar to those of the thematic rapporteurs. How much emphasis they place on individual allegations varies from one mechanism to another, however. Most place the greatest importance on fact-finding visits, which allow them to examine situations close up. Not all country rapporteurs are able to obtain such cooperation from the relevant country, however, and in such cases they become more dependent on other sources of information, including individual allegations.

Some country-specific rapporteurs send urgent appeals, though not all are willing to send them jointly with other thematic rapporteurs. Many also transmit standard communications. Others, however, view their task as being to facilitate technical cooperation activities, and prefer to adopt a more diplomatic approach rather than engage in contentious allegations and finger-pointing. It is fair to say that the degree of activity emanating from a country-specific rapporteur depends largely on the mandate holder.

Although not all country-specific rapporteurs are willing to take action in individual cases, all as a minimum consider allegations of value for gaining information on the situation in the country for which they are responsible. As a country-specific mandate is a wide one covering all potential aspects of human rights within a country, it will always be relevant to submit information concerning refugees, asylum-seekers, and internally displaced persons in the country in question.

When submitting information to a country-specific Special Rapporteur, you should follow the general guidelines in Section 5.1.2 on preparing your submission.

6. How Effective Are the Mechanisms?

Faced with the wide range of procedures encompassed by the category of Charter-based mechanisms, how should one go about assessing the relative merit of each mechanism, as well as making a choice between them or between Charter-based mechanisms and other types of complaint procedures described in this Guide? In order to evaluate their utility, the mechanisms must be assessed both from a mechanism-based perspective (how effective the mechanisms are in their own right) and from an objective-based standpoint (how effective the mechanisms are at achieving the likely objectives of potential users).

6.1 Thematic Procedures

As noted earlier, thematic mandates may be broadly divided into two types: traditional and research-based. The mandates sometimes referred to as traditional mandates are those whose principal methods of work involve the transmission of individual communications, including urgent appeals. Falling squarely into this category are the Working Groups on Arbitrary Detention and Enforced or Involuntary Disappearances and the Special Rapporteurs on Torture, Executions, and the Independence of the Judiciary. Also in this category, but with a more noticeable focus on research and conceptual development, are the Special Rapporteurs on Freedom of Expression, Religious Intolerance, Violence Against Women, and Racism.

Research-based mandates may send the occasional individual communication, but tend to do so on an illustrative basis. They focus instead on researching and developing the scope of the mandate and on standard setting. Mandates that fall into this category include the Special Rapporteurs on Migrants and the Sale of Children and the Special Representatives of the Secretary-General on Children in Armed Conflict and Internally Displaced Persons.

At the time of writing, it is difficult to predict which category the three new mandates created in 2000 will fall into, but it is probable that the Special Rapporteurs on Adequate Housing and the Right to Food will tend toward research-based mandates, while the Special Representative on Human Rights Defenders will receive a significant number of individual communications.

In general terms, the utility of each type of mandate depends on the objectives desired. Traditional mandates are clearly more oriented toward providing an individual remedy than are research-based mandates. Provided the information received falls within the mandate and appears credible, it will be transmitted to the government concerned, which will be asked to answer the allegations. At a minimum, any information communicated to the government in this way will be reproduced in the annual report, along with any response from the government. Seeing the government's actions made public can provide a measure of satisfaction for victims. More concrete remedies can range from recommending prosecution of perpetrators or compensation of victims, to requesting a review of a deportation order or the seeking of assurances from the country to which an individual is due to be returned. It should be borne in mind, however, that those recommendations are not binding and states may choose to ignore them.

Research-based mandates are not designed to provide these types of remedies, though they can do so on the few occasions when individual cases are taken up with governments. Instead, they can be used to develop protection from potential future violations by contributing to the elaboration of standards. They can also be used to draw attention to serious general situations of concern to the mandate.

Both traditional and research-based mandates carry out fact-finding visits. The impetus for seeking such visits is often provided by receipt of a large volume of communications concerning a country, whether formally requesting a fact-finding visit or not. Visits are often the most effective arm of the mandates, providing an opportunity to make concrete recommendations that may actually lead to system-wide improvements. Responses from governments vary widely, however, and while some will devote large amounts of energy to implementing these recommendations, others appear merely to pay them lip service, then dispose of them in a deep and dark drawer. A further limitation of the visit system is of course the need for an invitation from the state before a visit can be carried out. This allows the most persistent offenders to escape close scrutiny.

Both types of mandates are effective in their own right. Ultimately, the effectiveness of an individual mandate will depend on the nature and approach of the mandate-holder and his or her staff members. Some are tireless in the pursuance of their mandate aims, others can be disappointingly inert. The value of comments on individual mandate-holders will be limited in time, particularly in view of the recent decision to set a maximum term for each individual, including members of Working Groups.[110] Nonetheless, some general points are worth

---

[110] *Chairperson's Statement, Statement by the Chairperson on behalf of the Commission on Human Rights (55th session) Geneva, 22 March–30 April 1999. Review of Mechanisms*, U.N. Doc. OHCHR/STM/99/5 ¶ 7(ii) (28 April 1999); *Report on Enhancing the Effectiveness of the Mechanisms of the Commission on Human Rights February 2000, supra* note 17 ¶ 4(ii), approved by *Report on Enhancing the*

noting about the current status of certain mandates.

The Special Rapporteurs on Torture and Executions and the Working Groups on Arbitrary Detention and Enforced and Involuntary Disappearances have always been notably active mandates, carrying out intensive case-based work. The Working Groups may to some extent be hindered by the more cumbersome and formal nature of their machinery, but overall these mechanisms have proved relatively effective. In recent years, they have become somewhat overburdened by the quantity of information they receive and a certain amount of backlog has begun to accrue, particularly with the Working Group on Enforced and Involuntary Disappearances. It is probably fair to say that these are the mechanisms that carry the most weight at the Commission, although they have to some extent had to make way for newer and more "fashionable" mandates, such as Violence Against Women, as far as the allocation of resources is concerned. From a substantive point of view, these mandates are very relevant to refugees, asylum-seekers, and internally displaced persons because they have taken action in many individual cases concerning these categories of persons. They are especially significant for asylum-seekers because they are able to intervene in cases of imminent deportation to a country where an individual is at risk of serious human rights violations.

The Special Rapporteurs on the Independence of Judges and Lawyers, Freedom of Expression, Religious Intolerance, Violence Against Women, and Racism are all in the process of development. Of these, the mandate on Violence Against Women is by far the most active and perhaps the most relevant, particularly given the Special Rapporteur's interest in refugee and displaced women. Least active in terms of individual cases are the mandates on Religious Intolerance and Racism, especially with respect to urgent appeals, which are resorted to extremely sparingly. It is worth using these mandates creatively, however. Although their subject matter may seem less pertinent, they can still be useful to refugees, asylum-seekers, and internally displaced persons where the issues in a case fall within the relevant mandate. Examples of cases in which these mandates have acted can be found in the mandate-specific sections earlier in this chapter.

The mandates on Migrants, the Sale of Children, Children in Armed Conflict, and Internally Displaced Persons are the least active of all the mandates in terms of individual cases, which are taken up on a strictly exceptional basis. This does not, however, mean that such working methods will not be further developed in the years to come.

Effectiveness of the Mechanisms of the Commission on Human Rights April 2000, supra note 17 ¶ 1.

Already, the Special Representative of the Secretary-General on IDPs has begun to intervene more frequently in specific cases.

Although the working methods of these mandates are the least user-friendly when it comes to individual cases, they are noticeably relevant to refugees, asylum-seekers, and internally displaced persons in terms of subject matter, and can consequently have an impact in practice. This is particularly true of the Special Representative of the Secretary-General on Internally Displaced Persons. While the SRSG's Guiding Principles, the basis for all his work, are not enforceable, they do represent the first serious attempt at devising consistent standards for the benefit of IDPs. In particular, the Principles may be used for domestic and international advocacy activities. For example, the specificity of the Guiding Principles may assist UN and regional treaty bodies to interpret general human rights norms in a manner appropriate to the situation of the internally displaced. Moreover, in response to serious situations of internal displacement, the SRSG can exercise a fair amount of political clout in bilateral meetings with other governments and with the Inter-Agency Standing Committee (IASC). Governments have generally responded favorably to the SRSG's recommendations following a country visit.

The Special Rapporteur on Migrants is of potential significance for refugees, asylum-seekers, and internally displaced persons. At the time of writing, it is too early to assess the effectiveness of this rapporteur. For now, advocates should not expect any results from submissions. However, by attempting to engage the Special Rapporteur to respond to individual cases, advocates may be able to encourage her to adopt proactive working methods, including forwarding communications to the government concerned, sending urgent appeals, and generally responding to individual complaints. This was the intention of the advocacy groups who called for the establishment of this rapporteur, although it remains to be seen if she will fulfill this role.

In conclusion, thematic mandates are as effective as their working methods permit them to be. Those that engage in the transmission of individual cases can in practice provide remedies for individuals, although they do not have the enforcement powers to support their recommendations. Research-based mandates cannot generally provide this form of tangible outcome, or choose not to, but their importance should nonetheless not be underestimated. It is with them that the responsibility lies for the protection of their particular area of human rights in the future, and it is crucial that their work reflect actual situations and problems.

6.2 Country-Specific Procedures

As with thematic mandates, the effectiveness of country mandates depends largely on the mandate-holder. While their working methods vary from one Special Rapporteur to the next, they will resemble those of the thematic mechanisms. The central issue in assessing an individual mandate is the extent to which the rapporteur in question is willing to challenge the authorities of the country for which he or she is responsible, or, conversely, the extent to which he or she is willing to compromise the disclosure of violations in return for technical and other forms of cooperation. Unlike most thematic mechanisms, because a country-specific rapporteur concentrates his activities on a single country, it is possible to build up a relationship with the authorities concerned. This can lead to an unwillingness to rock the boat. Some rapporteurs consider the transmission of individual communications to be detrimental to achieving cooperation, and refuse to send them. In other cases, however, cooperation is never secured and the rapporteur is not even allowed to visit the country in person. Advocates who wish to obtain a sense of the approach of a particular country-specific rapporteur should consult previous annual reports if these are available, as the tone of the report should quickly make this obvious. Country desk officers at the OHCHR and in the field offices should also be able to provide an indication of the working methods an individual country rapporteur has adopted.

6.3 Concluding Note

Charter-based mechanisms vary in effectiveness according to their objectives and working methods. They provide a good resource for those who seek to take action with regard to countries that have not accepted the individual complaint procedures outlined in the human rights treaty bodies discussed in Chapters 2, 4, 5, and 6. They also represent a reliable option for those who do not wish to engage in the treaty bodies' formal and lengthy judicial-style procedures, or who merely wish to ensure that the international community is kept informed of developments in a country or region. In general, however, those who particularly seek a potent and enforceable individual remedy in relation to a country that has accepted a relevant individual complaint procedure under one of the human rights treaties should be encouraged to pursue that avenue. The overarching characteristic of the Charter-based mechanisms is that they are ultimately dependent on the unpredictable force of political will for their effectiveness.

7. Other Advocacy Possibilities in the Context of the UN Charter Organs

Relevant possibilities for action in the context of the UN Charter organs are not limited to the Special Procedures of the Commission on Human Rights. However, because they are not designed to address individual complaints, these other courses of action cannot really be described as complaint mechanisms in the same way as many of the Special Procedures can be. In addition to presenting a small number of additional mechanisms, this section will provide an overview of advocacy and lobbying strategies that may be of use. It would be misleading to suggest that any of the mechanisms described in this chapter can or should be viewed entirely outside the inherently political context of the UN Charter organs, and it is important to consider the potential for longer-term or systemic change that can be promoted alongside individual complaints.

7.1 Additional Mechanisms

7.1.1 1503 Procedure

What is the 1503 Procedure? The 1503 Procedure was created in 1970 and takes its name from the number of the Commission on Human Rights resolution that created it. Its purpose is to examine complaints of gross violations of human rights in a country in order to identify patterns of violation. It is not the responsibility of a special body, but is implemented instead by the Sub-Commission on the Promotion and Protection of Human Rights and the Commission on Human Rights. The most notable characteristic of the procedure is that it is confidential and those who submit information are not informed of the outcome.

How does the 1503 Procedure work?

Basic Chronology of 1503 Procedure	
A communication is received. ⇓	⇓
IF ELIGIBLE for consideration (e.g., is not being considered under a public procedure of the Commission on Human Rights), the complaint is transmitted to the government in question, which is asked to comment.	IF INELIGIBLE, the complaint goes no further.

⇓

August/September: Examination of complaints and replies by a five-member Working Group of the Sub-Commission (WG on Communications). Communications that "appear to reveal a consistent pattern" of violations are transmitted to the Commission Working Group on Situations.	⇒ If it does not appear to reveal a consistent pattern of violations, it is either dropped or kept pending until the following year.

⇓

February/March: Consideration of the complaints and replies by the WG on Situations prior to the Commission session. Its task is to produce recommendations to the Commission on a course of action.	⇒ If it does not appear to reveal a "situation," it is either dropped or kept pending until the following year.

⇓

March/April: During its session, the Commission on Human Rights considers the situations referred to it in private meetings, with the exception that governments are invited to be present for consideration of their "situation."

⇓

The countries discussed are named, as are those who have been dropped. This means that, by process of elimination, there is public notice of those states that have been kept under consideration. A situation can sometimes be made public and become the subject of open discussion in the Commission.

How is the 1503 Procedure relevant to refugees, asylum-seekers, and internally displaced persons? Because the 1503 Procedure is confidential, individual cases examined in the context of the wider country situation are not known to the public, making it difficult to analyze relevant practice. Nonetheless, the following should be borne in mind by refugees, asylum-seekers, and internally displaced persons who wish to make use of the procedure:

The 1503 Procedure is designed to address situations of gross violations of human rights. This may include violations of the rights of persons who then become displaced as a result of the violations or of displaced persons on account of their status as displaced persons. For such cases to fall within the scope of the 1503 Procedure, they should amount to a "situation" and not merely an isolated incident.

If information is received by the 1503 Procedure that the Commission thinks would be better dealt with elsewhere, the information will usually be forwarded to the appropriate authorities. Complaints from recognized refugees will normally be sent to UNHCR, while those concerning IDPs will be forwarded to the Special Representative of the Secretary-General on Internally Displaced Persons. Individual cases from asylum-seekers are normally better suited to consideration under a treaty-based or thematic procedure. However, where individual cases may potentially amount to a "situation" concerning asylum-seekers, they could be examined under the 1503 Procedure.

What should your communication contain? A communication to the 1503 Procedure *must*:

- Be *addressed to the UN* or any of its bodies or staff members. In other words, it does not specifically need to be addressed to the 1503 Procedure, but must at least be requesting action by the UN.

A communication to the 1503 Procedure must not:

- Be *anonymous*. The name will be deleted before the communication is transmitted to the state unless the writer has no objection to his or her name being divulged.
- Contain *abusive language.*
- Be *merely politically motivated* or an opportunity to express propaganda; it should be the expression of a genuine grievance.

The 1503 Procedure is designed to identify and follow up on "situations which appear to reveal a consistent pattern of gross and reliably attested violations of human rights." This means that the following considerations should be taken into account when preparing a communication under 1503:

- Explain why you think there has been a violation and why you think the facts reveal a consistent pattern of gross violations. The objective of the communication is to draw attention to a situation, rather than to an individual case, and should help to establish a pattern of violations. This means that it is very helpful for individual cases to be compiled into one document rather than submitted one by one. Although an individual case combined with others can initiate consideration of a "situation," it will rarely be sufficient on its own.
- The evidence should relate to gross violations of human rights.
- The evidence should be consistent over time and among different sources of information.
- The evidence of violation must be reliable. This means that you should avoid contradictions, provide as much supporting evidence as possible to support your allegations, and avoid vagueness.
- Explain whether any domestic remedies have been sought and the result, including copies of court judgments if relevant. If no domestic remedies have been sought, reasons should be given for this.
- Include any suggestions you might have for an appropriate course of action, such as the appointment of a Special Rapporteur, or an investigation, or simply action by the UN to end the violations.

Miscellaneous practical information. The name of the author of the communication will be deleted for transmission to the government unless the author has no objection to his or her name being divulged. The confidentiality of the procedure means that no case under consideration is ever made public.

As the procedure is confidential, you will not receive any feedback about the content of your submission or of any action taken. You will, however, receive an acknowledgement that the submission has been dealt with under the procedure.

If you want your communication to be considered at the next session of the Sub-Commission Working Group in late August/early September, you should make sure that it reaches the OHCHR by early May. Otherwise it will not be considered until the following August.

The 1503 Procedure accepts communications by email, which the Committee Against Torture and the Human Rights Committee do not.

You should note that:

Complaints will not be accepted if they concern a state:	**Complaints will be accepted if they concern a state:**
That is being considered under a public procedure of the Commission on Human Rights. That has accepted the right of individual petition under the ICCPR, the CAT, or the CERD, where the complaint relates to an individual violation of a right that is protected under one of those instruments.	That has accepted the right of individual petition under the ICCPR, the CAT, or the CERD, but the complaint relates to general information about the state rather than an individual complaint.

How effective is the 1503 Procedure? In concrete terms, the 1503 Procedure can be fairly described as somewhat toothless, at least from the perspective of an individual seeking redress. It was designed to focus on situations of gross violations of human rights and not to address individual grievances. Even in this area, its effectiveness is handicapped by its confidential nature. However, the practice, which the Commission on Human Rights has developed, of announcing the names of the states under consideration and indicating the ones that have been dropped from consideration, goes some way toward improving this. It means at least that the fact that a state is under consideration becomes public knowledge and lets it be known that a serious situation of gross violations exists.

Within the constraints of the confidential procedure, however, a state *can* be made to account for and respond to individual allegations. As an incidental result of the procedure, the mere transmission of a complaint to a government may motivate it to investigate and rectify the situation complained of, or may prompt it to suspend or terminate a practice, in order to discourage referral of the complaint to the Working Group on Communications. For those complaints and replies that do make their way to the Commission, that body identifies issues of concern during its consideration of "situations" and might ask the states in question to make improvements. It might request answers to specific questions. The Commission has the power to initiate a study or to set up an ad hoc investigatory body with the express consent of the government concerned. Over the years, however, it has developed its own ways of dealing with serious cases by appointing an independent expert who carries out field missions and submits a confidential report to the Commission at its next session. In exceptionally serious cases, the Commission on Human Rights may choose to transfer the situation to a public procedure. This may include the appointment of a Special Rapporteur.

The 1503 Procedure would be of most use to refugees, asylum-seekers, and internally displaced persons where large numbers of violations are taking place against these categories of persons, which might be considered to amount to a situation of gross violations of human rights. In such cases, it is preferable to submit a compendium of cases demonstrating the alleged pattern rather than send individual cases, which, in themselves, would not suffice to motivate action under the 1503 Procedure. Complaints from recognized refugees would however normally be referred to UNHCR, and information concerning IDPs often forwarded to the SRSG on IDPs, largely because of the likelihood such complaints would be likely to obtain a more useful response from those actors.

7.1.2 Sub-Commission on the Promotion and Protection of Human Rights

How is the Sub-Commission relevant to refugees, asylum-seekers, and internally displaced persons? The Sub-Commission does not implement any specific individual complaint procedures. It does, however, require its members to carry out studies and prepare working papers and reports on specific themes. Some of these can be of significant relevance to refugees, asylum-seekers, and internally displaced persons. In the same way that it is important to provide information to the research-based mandates of the Commission on Human Rights, advocates should be aware of the progress of the studies undertaken by the Sub-Commission and, when relevant, submit information. Studies begun at the Sub-Commission level can provide the impetus for the appointment of a Special Rapporteur at a later stage if the work reveals important issues and problems that need to be addressed.

A complete list of studies ongoing at any particular time can be found annexed to the current report of the Sub-Commission to the Commission on Human Rights. Studies in progress at the time of writing include:

- the concept and practice of affirmative action
- traditional practices affecting the health of women and the girl child
- systematic rape, sexual slavery, and slavery-like practices during armed conflict, including internal armed conflict
- indigenous people and their relationship to land

- human rights and terrorism
- the right to education
- the right to drinking water supply and sanitation services
- review of international standards on slavery
- human rights problems and protections of the Roma
- observance of human rights by states not parties to UN human rights conventions
- globalization and its impact on the enjoyment of human rights
- the adverse consequences on human rights of economic sanctions
- implementation of the Guidelines on HIV and AIDS
- the rights of non-citizens
- reservations to human rights treaties

Anyone who wishes to provide information of relevance to a study may do so by intervening at the Sub-Commission when the particular study is being examined, subject to the rules on access to the UN bodies explained in Section 3.3. Written information can also be submitted at any time to the OHCHR staff members responsible for servicing the Sub-Commission, with a request to forward the information to the Sub-Commission member tasked with carrying out the study. You should clearly indicate the study to which you think the information is relevant. This is important because, in contrast to research activities carried out by the Special Procedures of the Commission on Human Rights, Sub-Commission studies are usually carried out by the members themselves or their personal researchers rather than by the OHCHR staff members.

The contact details are the same as for a standard OHCHR communication, but you should make sure to address your communication clearly to: "Sub-Commission on the Promotion and Protection of Human Rights—Study on [insert the appropriate title]."

Can anything be achieved by contributing to Sub-Commission studies? Sub-Commission studies are not "effective" in any immediately identifiable way. They can, however, help to identify issues of concern and develop standards. Perhaps their most tangible result is their potential for contributing to the creation of a Special Rapporteur of the Commission on Human Rights. Although sending information for these studies could not be said to be a priority where resources are limited, advocates should as a minimum remain aware of the subject matter and progress of ongoing studies. Where a study of direct relevance to refugees, asylum-seekers, and internally displaced persons is being carried out, advocates can

234　Human Rights Protection for Displaced Persons

play a valuable role in ensuring that the study reflects the actual issues in practice.

7.1.3　Commission on the Status of Women

The individual complaint procedure. The individual complaint procedure of the Commission on the Status of Women (CSW) is distinct from all other complaint procedures because the identified goal of examining communications is to "inform [the Commission] of patterns of violations of women's rights so it can recommend the adoption of appropriate policy measures."[111] The CSW has not been empowered, nor has it attempted, to engage in fact-finding, to offer remedies for individuals, or to force states to comply with recommendations. Thus, refugees, asylum-seekers, and displaced persons seeking an individualized response would not benefit from submitting information to the CSW. The CSW solicits information regarding women's human rights violations to aid its policy development, and not to provide any response or redress or response in individual cases.[112] However, the individual complaint mechanism of the CSW may be a useful tool as one prong of a larger campaign to draw attention to a particular issue.

Working method. With regard to the types of cases the CSW considers, the content of a communication must refer to women's issues only, "that is, injustices or discriminatory acts or practices against women."[113] Advocates should submit a communication in a similar fashion as for the Special Rapporteur on Violence Against Women. The CSW usually contacts governments regarding communications, but governmental replies are not included in the annual reports. The CSW is not very accessible for advocates and, after submitting information, advocates will often not receive any further information regarding the communication.

The CSW created a Working Group to review communications. The report of the Working Group is published annually and generally notes how many communications were considered and issues statements of concern regarding any number of human rights violations. For exam-

---

[111] *Monitoring the Implementation of the Nairobi Forward-Looking Strategies for the Advancement of Women. Examining Existing Mechanisms for Communications on the Status of Women. Report of the Secretary-General,* U.N. Doc. E/CN.6/1991/10 ¶ 83 (9 November 1990).

[112] Laura Reanda, *The Commission on the Status of Women, in* THE UNITED NATIONS AND HUMAN RIGHTS, *supra* note 3, at 265, 274.

[113] *See* <www.un.org/womenwatch/daw/csw97.htm.>.

ple, in the 1999 report the Working Group expressed concern regarding internally displaced persons being subject to confiscation of property, torture and floggings, harassment, and forcible evictions in conflict situations.[114]

The Division for the Advancement of Women, the body that supports the Commission's work, is increasingly cooperating with the special procedures of the Commission on Human Rights, and in particular with the Special Rapporteur on Violence Against Women and the Special Rapporteur on the Human Rights of Migrants. The CSW has begun to forward information gained from communications to these bodies. The Division is also working with the human rights treaty bodies to ensure that a gender perspective is integrated into all of their work.[115]

The Division is based in New York, not at the OHCHR. Contact details for those who wish to use the individual complaint procedure are:

UN Division for the Advancement of Women
2 United Nations Plaza, Rm. DC2-1220
New York, NY 10017
USA
Tel.: 212-963-5086 / Fax: 212-963-3463
E-mail: *daw@un.org* / web site: <www.un.org/womenwatch/daw/csw>

Effectiveness. As noted previously, although the CSW has established an individual complaint procedure, its objective is not to provide individual remedies but rather to use the information from the complaints it receives to assist its policy development. This complaint procedure would be of most relevance to refugees, asylum-seekers, and internally displaced persons who wish to contribute to the development of policies relating to women who belong to such categories.

7.2 Advocacy and Lobbying: Influencing the UN Charter Organs at the Decision-Making Level

A section on advocacy strategies and lobbying may at first glance appear anomalous in a guide emphasizing individual complaint mechanisms. It is, however, a reflection of the nature of the Charter-based mechanisms. In practice, it is lobbying and advocacy campaigns that

---

[114] *Commission on the Status of Women. Report on the Forty-Third Session (1–12 March and 1 April 1999)*, U.N. Doc. E/CN.6/1999/10, at ch. IV, ¶ 4 (1999).

[115] *Joint Work Plan of the Division for the Advancement of Women and the Office of the United Nations High Commissioner for Human Rights. Report of the Secretary-General*, U.N. Doc. E/CN.6/2000/8 ¶¶ 14–15 (31 January 2000).

often prove most successful in obtaining results. Even where individual complaints are submitted to the mechanisms, they are often more likely to succeed if they are accompanied by lobbying to draw attention to their content and gravity. Lobbying at the UN may be fairly described as a complex maze. Knowing how to negotiate this maze is the first step toward achieving results.

7.2.1 Where Does an Advocacy Campaign Begin?

Historically, the Commission and its Sub-Commission are the prime UN Charter organs for NGO participation because they have been the most flexible and welcoming regarding NGOs. This section will focus on these two bodies exclusively, although advocates should not overlook other venues that may prove useful, such as the Commission on the Status of Women, the General Assembly, and world conferences. This section is not intended to be the definitive guide on how to engage in advocacy at the Commission and Sub-Commission. Rather, it is a broad overview of the process. Many other resources exist regarding advocacy at the UN that should be consulted as well.[116] Also, refugees, asylum-seekers, and internally displaced persons and their advocates should seek out training on how to effectively use UN human rights machinery. National and international NGOs often sponsor such training sessions, subject to budgetary constraints.[117]

---

[116] See *Orientation Manual: the U.N. Commission on Human Rights, its Sub-Commission, and Related Procedures*, see *supra* note 7, available from Minnesota Advocates for Human Rights, Minneapolis, Minnesota and the International Service for Human Rights, Geneva; *Human Rights Defender's Manual*, see *infra* note 120, available from Diplomacy Training Program, Ltd., University of New South Whales, Kensington, Australia, and WOMEN, LAW AND DEVELOPMENT AND HUMAN RIGHTS WATCH WOMEN'S RIGHTS PROJECT, WOMEN'S HUMAN RIGHTS STEP BY STEP: A PRACTICAL GUIDE TO USING INTERNATIONAL HUMAN RIGHTS LAW AND MECHANISMS TO DEFEND WOMEN'S HUMAN RIGHTS (MARGARET A. SCHULER & DOROTHY Q. THOMAS EDS., 1997), available from Women, Law and Development International, Washington, D.C.

[117] More funding for hands on advocacy training programs is needed to effectively meet the needs of non-governmental organizations seeking to access UN mechanisms. As no comprehensive listing of the training programs available exists, the major national human rights organizations in your country or region would likely be the most knowledgeable regarding training programs offered.

Create a Strategy

A crucial part of any lobbying campaign is the creation of a concrete strategy. This can begin by finding a clear answer to the question "What do we want to achieve by going to the UN?" Advocacy efforts are generally not conducive to obtaining specific relief in an individual case or in any other case that requires a quick fix. Advocacy before the Commission and Sub-Commission around issues relevant to this manual may take the form of highlighting asylum policies in particular countries that violate international human rights standards, calling for a way to make the *Guiding Principles on Internal Displacement* enforceable, or drawing attention to situations of large-scale displacement of persons.[118]

Advocacy efforts before the Commission and Sub-Commission require a long-term strategy that acknowledges that these bodies are fora for negotiations, where consensus is the guiding principle and politics may influence outcomes more than pressing human rights violations.[119] Success requires a commitment to a continuing process, building relationships with other NGOs and governments, an understanding of the political landscape and how to negotiate it, accurate documentation, and solid knowledge of the workings of these bodies and the relevant human rights instruments and international law related to one's advocacy efforts.[120]

Build Relationships

The second important step in advocacy is to identify one's allies. This is particularly true with regard to issues involving refugees, asylum-seekers, and displaced persons. In addition to bolstering the legitimacy of the lobbying campaign, working with other NGOs may provide "how-to" guidance on negotiating unfamiliar territory in Geneva. Some NGOs have significant experience in working with the Commission and Sub-Commission and can be invaluable resources for NGOs with less familiarity with the workings of these UN bodies. In particular, the International Service for Human Rights, a Geneva-based NGO, guides and assists other NGOs.[121] Also, the International Service for Human

---

[118] *See generally*, Maria Stavropoulou, *Displacement and Human Rights: Reflections on UN Practice*, 20 HUM. RTS. Q. 515 (1998).

[119] AMNESTY INTERNATIONAL AND INTERNATIONAL SERVICE FOR HUMAN RIGHTS, *supra* note 10, at 18.

[120] JOHN SCOTT-MURPHY, HUMAN RIGHTS DEFENDER'S MANUAL, ch. 8, p. 1 (1994).

[121] International Service for Human Rights, P.O Box 16-CH 1211, Geneva 20, Switzerland, Tel: 41-22-733-5123, Fax: 41-22-733-0826.

Rights and the Minnesota Advocates for Human Rights have jointly published the *Orientation Manual: The UN Commission on Human Rights, its Sub-Commission, and related procedures*, which is a detailed guide for advocacy work before the Commission and Sub-Commission. This document can be obtained by contacting either of these organizations.[122]

To use the Charter-based bodies effectively requires a tremendous amount of preparation and year-round work in order to cultivate relationships with the relevant foreign offices, Special Rapporteurs, and other NGOs. Foreign offices (many countries have offices in Geneva) or government foreign affairs departments are key players in the annual work of the Commission and Sub-Commission; they should be lobbied accordingly. Depending on your strategy, you may need to be in contact with foreign desk officers regarding their government's position on a resolution or to seek support for a particular resolution or issue. Most often, these offices must be approached with a short and concise lobbying document that sets forth the problem, the specific human rights violation, what the Commission is being asked do, and the legal authority for that action. The document should include an executive summary and an outline that condenses the information. Merely sending your organization's annual report will not suffice as a lobbying tactic. Strategic phone calls and letters should follow the submission of any document.

Relationships should also be cultivated with the relevant thematic and country-specific Special Rapporteurs, who could be a key part of your success in achieving your lobbying goals. It is crucial to establish a relationship with the staff who service the rapporteur, keep them abreast of the issue, and let them know how you would like the rapporteur to respond. During the Commission session itself, rapporteurs often schedule informal brown-bag lunches to discuss their work; in recent years, the number of advocates in attendance has dwindled to an astonishingly paltry number.[123] Outside of the Commission, rapporteurs can also be lobbied in much the same fashion as you would lobby governmental representatives.

---

[122] Minnesota Advocates for Human Rights, 400 Second Ave. So., Suite 1050, Minneapolis, MN, 55402, USA, Tel: 612-341-3302, Fax: 612-341-2971, *hrights@mnadvocates.org*; International Service for Human Rights, 1 rue de Varembe, PO Box 16, 1211 Geneva 20, CIC, Switzerland, Tel: 41-22-733-5123, Fax: 41-22-733-0826.

[123] Jan Bauer, *Report on the 55th Session of the UN Commission on Human Rights, For the Record: The UN Human Rights System*, <www.hri.ca/uninfo.unchr99/report2.shtml.>.

Finally, cultivating relationships with other NGOs will greatly increase your effectiveness and legitimacy in the eyes of the international community, which will result in greater success in the achievement of your advocacy goals.[124]

Lobby

NGO participation is a two-way street because Commission and Sub-Commission members have grown to rely on NGO input for accurate information regarding human rights abuses in various parts of the world. In fact, NGOs with reputations for accuracy are often sought out for such information. NGOs, in turn, have the opportunity to greatly influence the workings of the Commission and Sub-Commission.[125] NGOs may participate formally (by making oral or written interventions [statements]), or informally (through any number of lobbying tactics). Informal lobbying may take place in meeting rooms outside the formal Commission session, in the corridors prior to and following the sessions, over lunch, etc. State representatives support resolutions on the basis of their own government's political interests, alliances with other states, and the strength of public opinion, particularly in their own country. Strong lobbying can make a difference with regard to the text of a resolution, whether the agenda item is dropped or carried over to the next year, or in the establishment of a special mechanism.

7.2.2 What Are the Potential Results of Advocacy Efforts?

The results of a lobbying strategy before the Commission and/or Sub-Commission may result in any of the following tangible outcomes.

Resolutions

The Commission and Sub-Commission are empowered to adopt resolutions on country-specific situations and on thematic topics. Resolutions may note with concern, condemn, and/or request a future report or monitoring of the situation. Country-specific resolutions draw attention to human rights violations, call for change in order to prevent future violations, and follow up on the government's implementation of

---

[124] Thanks to Jan Bauer for her input on these issues. She attends and documents each Commission session and her detailed reports can be found in *For the Record: The UN Human Rights System*, available through Human Rights Internet as hard copies or on the web at: <www.hri.ca/fortherecord1998/intro/htm.>.

[125] PARKER AND WEISSBRODT, *supra* note 7, at 21.

any previous requests and/or recommendations that were made. NGOs may involve themselves by drafting a resolution and finding a state representative willing to support it, or by providing input or a critique of resolutions that are being debated.

A resolution may be helpful for several reasons. First, it may provide the political impetus for further action by other UN or international bodies. For example, a resolution at the Sub-Commission level may prompt the Commission to devote more attention or resources to the situation, perhaps through the appointment of a Special Rapporteur. In a related vein, resolutions may call for other UN organs to further study or investigate the situation, which builds up an official documentary record that may eventually prompt action. Second, resolutions represent the opinion of a formally constituted UN body, which may be used by NGOs as one component of an overall campaign.[126]

Unfortunately, resolutions increasingly contain less substantive text and more technical references, such as to previous resolutions, which decreases their potency as advocacy tools. Resolutions drafters should be encouraged to include substantive text that directly reflects the work, conclusions, and recommendations generated through the special procedures.[127]

Appointment of a Special Rapporteur

Only the Commission has the authority to appoint a country-specific or thematic Special Rapporteur, although the Sub-Commission's recommendations in this domain are extremely influential. The recent appointment of the Special Rapporteur on the Human Rights of Migrants was the result of a sustained campaign by a number of NGOs. The establishment of a rapporteur is one of the most concrete and substantial mechanisms for censuring a country or drawing attention to a global human rights violation.

Chairperson and Country Statements

Short of a resolution, the Chairperson of the Commission can issue a statement, which often happens with more politically sensitive cases where some state representatives on the Commission object to the proposed resolution. The Chairperson's statements tend to be

---

[126] Nigel S. Rodley, *United Nations Non-Treaty Procedures for Dealing with Human Rights Violations, in* GUIDE TO INTERNATIONAL HUMAN RIGHTS PROTECTION 61, 63 (HURST HANNUM ED., 3d ed. 1999).

[127] Bauer, *supra* note 123.

watered down and fail to reflect the gravity of the human rights abuses in the country concerned. Sometimes, a statement may be issued in return for a positive commitment from the state concerned. For example, in 1998, a Chairperson's statement on the human rights situation in East Timor made reference to an invitation by the Indonesian government to the Working Group on Arbitrary Detention to visit East Timor.[128] Also, although rare, the representative from the country concerned could make a statement regarding measures the country will take to combat the human rights concerns raised during the Commission's session.[129]

Advisory Services

The Commission can place countries on its Advisory Services Program, which includes support/technical services in such areas as national plans of action, constitutions, elections, the judiciary and legal profession, internal conflict resolution, etc. In theory, this means that the country has made some progress toward implementing human rights but needs some special assistance. In practice, however, this is often used even when the country's human rights record has not significantly improved.[130] Advisory Services can only be developed effectively with the consent and cooperation of the state concerned. At the time of writing, countries receiving Advisory Services included Somalia, Cambodia, Haiti, and Chad.[131] Advisory Services are considered under Item 19 of the Commission's agenda.

What Is Consultative Status?

NGOs regularly participate in UN activities and advocate on behalf of the individuals they serve. From the outset, it should be noted that any individual or organization may access the Charter-based mechanisms

---

[128] *Statement by the Chairperson of the Commission Concerning the Human Rights Situation in East Timor*, U.N. Doc. OHCHR/STM/98/3 (1998).

[129] AMNESTY INTERNATIONAL, 1997 UN COMMISSION OH HUMAN RIGHTS—50 YEARS OLD 6 (1997).

[130] MURPHY, *supra* note 120, at ch. 8, p.5.

[131] *See Organization of Work. Work Methods of the Sub-Commission*, U.N. Doc. E/CN.4/Sub.2/1999/3, Annex 2 (28 May 1999). In an effort to avoid duplication of work between the Commission and Sub-Commission, the Secretariat has adopted the practice of providing, prior to the Sub-Commission session, a list of countries under consideration by the Commission, including under the agenda item entitled 'Advisory services and technical cooperation in the field of human rights.' This list is then published as a Sub-Commission document.

(details regarding those mechanisms are set forth in Section 4 of this chapter). Also, any individual may lobby state representatives on an individual basis, outside the formal setting of the Commission or Sub-Commission. As discussed earlier, lobbying foreign desk officers is a key component of an advocacy strategy and does not require any special UN status.[132] This section concerns NGOs that wish to engage in advocacy activities at the Commission, its Sub-Commission, or other UN bodies. NGO participation is premised on a reciprocal relationship whereby the UN benefits from expert information and advice from NGOs with expertise in particular areas and NGOs are able to bring their concerns to an international arena.

The UN has established a somewhat complex process whereby NGOs must first obtain consultative status before accessing the UN bodies. Specifically, NGO participation is governed by Article 71 of the Charter and ECOSOC Resolution 1996/31. NGOs must apply for consultative status at the Committee on NGOs, which implements these resolutions and approves applications. Among other things required to gain consultative status, organizations are required to demonstrate that their mandate is relevant to the work of the ECOSOC, that they operate with a democratic decision-making structure, and that they have officially been in existence for at least two years. Complete requirements are contained in ECOSOC Resolution 1996/31.

How to Gain Consultative Status

To begin the process, organizations must send a written letter of intent to apply for consultative status to the Non-Governmental Organizations Section (NGO Section) of the Division for ECOSOC Support and Co-ordination in the Department of Economic and Social Affairs (DESA). The letter should be on the organization's letterhead and signed by its director or president.[133] After the NGO Section receives the letter, the application package and background materials are mailed to the organization. Applications received *prior to June 1* are considered during the following year by the Committee on NGOs and the ECOSOC. For example, an application received prior to June 1, 2000, will not receive consultative status until the fall of 2001. The Committee on

---

[132] Although it should be noted that even foreign desk officers are more likely to be influenced by individuals who are associated with a NGO having consultative status.

[133] The letter must be addressed to: NGO Section/DESA, UN Room DC1-1480, New York, NY 10017, USA, Fax: 212-963-4116. *See* <http://www.un.org/esa/coordination/ngo/ngo.htm> for more information.

NGOs would review the application during the spring of 2001 and notify the organization in writing as to the Committee on NGO's decision. However, consultative status is not official until the ECOSOC approves the Committee on NGOs' decision, which usually occurs in August or September, at which time the organization will receive a letter granting them consultative status. The NGO Section has valuable information and advice, including guidelines for the completion of an application for NGOs seeking consultative status. These can be found on their web site or by contacting the office directly.[134]

What Are the Consultative Status Categories?

NGOs may apply for one of three categories of consultative status: General, Special, or Roster. General Category (formerly known as Category I) status is for organizations "concerned with most of the activities of the ECOSOC and its subsidiary bodies."[135] These organizations are typically large international NGOs with a broad geographical reach. Special Category (formerly known as Category II) is granted to organizations that have a special competence or expertise in only a few fields of activities covered by the ECOSOC. Roster status is granted to NGOs that "can make occasional and useful contributions to the work of ECOSOC or its subsidiary bodies."[136] Each status category has its own set of privileges and obligations, although the General and Special categories have many common. Roster status allows for the least degree of participation. General, Special, and Roster status NGOs may all designate UN representatives, be invited to participate in UN conferences, and attend meetings of the ECOSOC and its subsidiary bodies (such

---

[134] *See* <www.un.org/esa/coordination/ngo> for more information, or contact NGO Section/DESA, UN Room DC1-1480, New York, NY 10017, USA; Tel. 212-963-9248; Fax: 212-963-8652.

[135] *Consultative Relationship between the United Nations and Non-Governmental Organizations. Arrangements for Consultation with Non-Governmental Organizations. Part I. Principles to be Applied in the Establishment of Consultative Relations. Part II. Principles Governing the Nature of Consultative Arrangements. Part III. Establishment of Consultative Relationships. Part IV. Consultation with the Council. Part V. Consultation with Commissions and other Subsidiary Organs of the Council. Part VI. Consultations with Ad Hoc Committees of the Council. Part VII. Participation of Non-Governmental Organizations in International Conferences Convened by the United Nations and their Preparatory Process. Part VIII. Suspension and Withdrawal of Consultative Status. Part IX. Council Committee on Non-Governmental Organizations. Part X. Consultation with the Secretariat. Part XI. Secretariat Support,* U.N. Doc. E/RES/1996/31 ¶ 22 (25 July 1996).

[136] *Id.,* ¶ 24.

as the Commission and Sub-Commission). Also, General and Special status NGOs have the right to circulate statements and make oral interventions at ECOSOC meetings and subsidiary body meetings. General and Special status NGOs must meet the "quadrennial reporting requirement," which requires that every four years the NGO submit a report detailing its activities in support of the UN.[137]

7.2.3 How Can NGOs Intervene in the Commission and Sub-Commission?

Normally, the secretariat of the Commission sends an informational letter with details about the Commission and Sub-Commission to all NGOs with consultative status approximately eight to ten weeks prior to the annual Commission session. The secretariat also schedules an information briefing for NGOs, IGOs, and governments before the Commission session opens to provide clarification regarding the procedures and answer any questions. NGOs should contact the secretariat to find out when the information briefing will be held prior to the annual session.

In addition to consultative status, persons attending the Commission or Sub-Commission must be accredited. This must be done every year, even if the same representatives are attending. This involves sending a letter to the NGO Liaison Officer at the United Nations.[138] The letter should formally identify and designate the individual as representing the organization and should be signed by one of its principal officers, ideally the head of the organization. NGOs will not receive any response to their request for accreditation, so representatives should also carry copies of these letters with them on their first day at the UN to ensure that they receive their badges for entry.[139]

Agenda

The Commission's lengthy agenda, which remains largely the same from year to year, dictates what topics will be addressed.[140] NGOs are

---

[137] UN web site faq sheet, *Consultative Relationship Between the ECOSOC and NGOs*, at <www.un.org/esa/coordination/ngo/faq/htm>.

[138] The letter should be addressed to the NGO Liaison Officer at the United Nations, Palais des Nations, Room 153, 1211 Geneva 10, Switzerland; or via Fax: 41-22-917-0583. The NGO Liaison Officer can be reached at 41-22-917-2126.

[139] PARKER AND WEISSBRODT, *supra* note 7, at 25–26.

[140] The agenda was modified in 1999 and the new agenda was used for the first time at the 2000 session.

not allowed to intervene under some agenda items, such as "adoption of the agenda" or "organization of the work of the session."[141] The agenda gives no real indication of the relative importance of the agenda items. Some items consist of token resolutions that change little from year to year, while on others it may be conducive for NGOs to negotiate and provide input toward a potential resolution.[142] For example, the consideration of individual countries under Item 19, "Advisory Services," generally implies that the country is facing less grave human rights violations than countries considered under Item 9, "Question of the violation of human rights and fundamental freedoms in any part of the world." NGOs that are not certain where to intervene should consult with more experienced NGOs or contact the OHCHR for advice.

The annotated agendas are an extremely useful tool for all who participate in the sessions of the Commission and Sub-Commission. The annotated agendas give the background to each item and sub-item, including references to past resolutions and decisions, and should be studied to determine how best to intervene.[143] The annotated agendas of the forthcoming sessions of the Commission and Sub-Commission are available at the Office of the High Commissioner's web site, <www.unhchr.ch>. Agenda items that may be appropriate for refugees, asylum-seekers, and internally displaced persons include Item 14, "Specific Groups and Individuals," which includes sub-items (a) on migrant workers and (c) on mass exoduses and displaced persons; Item 9, "Question of the violation of human rights and fundamental freedoms in any part of the world;" Item 11, "Civil and Political Rights," which includes sub-items (a) on torture and detention and (b) on disappearances and summary executions; or Item 13, "Rights of the Child."

1235 Procedure

Resolution 1235, adopted in 1967, gives the Commission and Sub-Commission authority to debate specific country situations and adopt resolutions or make conduct thorough studies. The formal procedure set forth in this resolution has greatly evolved into very loose parameters that allow these two bodies to discuss virtually any country-specific situation.[144] Since its inception, more than 25 country-specific procedures have been established as a result, and the Commission has adopted a number of resolutions and decisions specifically condemning state

---

[141] RODLEY, *supra* note 126, at 74.
[142] ALSTON, *supra* note 11, at 196.
[143] RODLEY, *supra* note 126, at 75.
[144] ALSTON, *supra* note 11, at 155.

practices.[145] A public debate via the 1235 Procedure is helpful where advocates want the situation made public as soon as possible and where public action and continuous monitoring are required. Sometimes mere public discussion prompts governments to take constructive measures to avoid the risk of a resolution or the initiation of a special procedure.[146]

Working Groups

Both the Commission and Sub-Commission have working groups where individuals and NGOs may effectively participate. However, few of these working groups address substantive refugee, asylee, or IDP issues. The Sub-Commission's working groups include Detention, Indigenous Populations, Contemporary Forms of Slavery, and Minorities. Advocates may participate in these working groups, with the exception of the Working Group on Detention, which is not open to the public, and should consult the calendar of meetings on the OHCHR web site to find out the session dates.

The Commission working groups that are of relevance to refugees, asylum-seekers, and internally displaced persons—the Working Group on Arbitrary Detention and the Working Group on Enforced or Involuntary Disappearances—have already been discussed in detail. The Commission also has a number of drafting working groups where NGOs with significant backgrounds in the area of concern may provide input. These include working groups on the Optional Protocol to the 1984 Torture Convention; the Optional Protocol to the 1989 Convention on the Rights of the Child, related to children in armed conflict; and the Optional Protocol to the 1989 Convention on the Rights of the Child, related to the sale of children.

How Can NGOs Make Formal Interventions?

Written statements. General status NGOs may submit written statements that do not exceed 2,000 words, while Special status NGOs are limited

---

[145] Special Procedures launched under the 1235 Procedure include: Afghanistan, Bolivia, Bosnia and Herzegovina, Burundi, Chila, Cuba, Cyprus, Democratic Kampuchea, Democratic Republic of the Congo, East Timor, El Salvador, Equatorial Guinea, Federal Republic of Yugoslavia, Guatemala, Haiti, Iran, Iraq, Kosovo, Myanmar, Nicaragua, Occupied Kuwait, Occupied Territories, Poland, Republic of Croatia, Romania, Rwanda, Sierra Leone, Sudan. *Organization of Work. Work Methods of the Sub-Commission, supra* note 131, Annex I.

[146] ALSTON, *supra* note 11, at 161.

to 500 words. Statements must be submitted in one of the UN's official languages at least six weeks in advance of the meeting. For the Commission, this means that statements should be submitted by December 31 of the year preceding the session. The Secretariat can only ensure circulation of written statements that are received prior to the established deadline. If at all possible, the Secretariat prefers to receive the statements in the three working languages of the UN (English, French, and Spanish).

Oral statements. General and Special status NGOs may make oral interventions at the meetings of ECOSOC subsidiary bodies, which include the Commission and Sub-Commission. Oral statements should be used sparingly, while joint statements with other NGOs proposing concrete initiatives to tackle a widespread human rights problem are encouraged.

Procedure. To make an oral statement, one must sign up on the speaker's list kept by the conference officer before the Chair announces that the speaker's list for that particular agenda item is closed. The conference officer is usually at a table to the side and below the podium in the front of the room. The speaker's list grows quickly on popular agenda items, so it is best to sign up as soon as possible. It is also a good idea to check how many speakers are before you as you sign up. After signing up, you should make every effort to remain in the room, as it is never certain when you will be called. NGOs generally speak after members and observer governments, although sometimes NGOs will speak first if the members and governments wish to organize their strategies. If the representative is not in the room when called upon, the opportunity for intervention may be lost.

Representatives should have 30 to 40 copies of their statement ready for distribution. Shortly before the intervention (usually an hour or two), the Secretariat will request copies for the translators and press release staff. Other governments or NGOs may also want copies after the speech is delivered.

Presentation and timing issues. The statement must be delivered in a measured and slow voice so as to ensure proper simultaneous translation and the greatest impact. Also, it is recommended that another member of your delegation listen to the translation and cue the presenter when he or she is speaking too quickly. The time limits for oral interventions by NGOs are always subject to change. At the present time, the time limit is five minutes for a single intervention under normal agenda items, but this should always be confirmed. Also, the Chair may shorten the time given for NGO interventions, so NGOs should be prepared to modify their statements accordingly. In that case, you may wish to state that you will be giving a shortened version of your presentation but would like to distribute a copy of your full written statement to the members of the Commission.[147]

Cooperation with other NGOs. As mentioned previously, working with other NGOs is crucial to effectively influence the work of the Commission. With regard to oral interventions, NGOs should attempt to work together as much as possible. This means that if other NGOs will be speaking on the same or similar topic, it is advisable to meet to ensure that the presentations are not repetitive and to explore the possibility of making joint statements.

Miscellaneous Information

Conference rooms and lounge. Accredited NGO representatives may reserve a conference room to have meetings on pertinent topics during Commission and Sub-Commission sessions. NGOs should contact the Secretariat to reserve these rooms. These meetings will then be announced on a notice board placed outside of conference room XVII for this purpose. An NGO lounge on the ground floor is available for NGO representatives throughout the session.

Bibliography

Books

AMNESTY INTERNATIONAL, 1997 UN COMMISSION ON HUMAN RIGHTS—50 YEARS OLD (1997).

AMNESTY INTERNATIONAL & INTERNATIONAL SERVICE FOR HUMAN RIGHTS, THE UN AND REFUGEES' HUMAN RIGHTS: A MANUAL ON HOW UN HUMAN RIGHTS MECHANISMS CAN PROTECT THE RIGHTS OF REFUGEES (1997).

AMNESTY INTERNATIONAL & THE LAW SOCIETY, THE UNITED NATIONS THEMATIC MECHANISMS, AN OVERVIEW OF THEIR WORK (1999).

FLOOD, PATRICK JAMES, THE EFFECTIVENESS OF UN HUMAN RIGHTS INSTITUTIONS (1998).

GIFFORD, CAMILLE, THE TORTURE REPORTING HANDBOOK: HOW TO DOCUMENT AND RESPOND TO ALLEGATIONS OF TORTURE WITHIN THE INTERNATIONAL SYSTEM FOR THE PROTECTION OF HUMAN RIGHTS (2000).

NEWMAN, FRANK & DAVID WEISSBRODT, INTERNATIONAL HUMAN RIGHTS: LAW, POLICY AND PROCESS (2d ed. 1996).

---

[147] MURPHY, *supra* note 120, at ch. 8, p.15.

PARKER, PENNY & DAVID WEISSBRODT, MINNESOTA ADVOCATES FOR HUMAN RIGHTS, ORIENTATION MANUAL: THE UN COMMISSION ON HUMAN RIGHTS, ITS SUB-COMMISSION AND RELATED PROCEDURES (1993).
SCOTT-MURPHY, JOHN, HUMAN RIGHTS DEFENDER'S MANUAL (1994).
WOMEN, LAW & DEVELOPMENT & HUMAN RIGHTS WATCH WOMEN'S RIGHTS PROJECT, WOMEN'S HUMAN RIGHTS STEP BY STEP: A PRACTICAL GUIDE TO USING INTERNATIONAL HUMAN RIGHTS LAW AND MECHANISMS TO DEFEND WOMEN'S HUMAN RIGHTS (Margaret A. Schuler & Dorothy Q. Thomas eds., 1997).

Chapters

Alston, Phillip, *The Commission on Human Rights*, in THE UNITED NATIONS AND HUMAN RIGHTS: A CRITICAL APPRAISAL 126 (PHILLIP ALSTON ED., 1992).

Coliver, Sandra, *UN Machineries on Women's Rights: How Might they Help Women Whose Rights are Being Violated*, in NEW DIRECTIONS IN HUMAN RIGHTS 25 (ELLEN LUTZ ET AL. EDS., 1989).

Quinn, John, *The General Assembly into the 1990s*, in THE UNITED NATIONS AND HUMAN RIGHTS: A CRITICAL APPRAISAL 55 (PHILLIP ALSTON ED., 1992).

Reanda, Laura, *The Commission on the Status of Women*, in THE UNITED NATIONS AND HUMAN RIGHTS: A CRITICAL APPRAISAL 265 (PHILLIP ALSTON ED., 1992).

Rodley, Nigel S., *United Nations Non-Treaty Procedures for Dealing with Human Rights Violations*, in GUIDE TO INTERNATIONAL HUMAN RIGHTS PRACTICE 61 (HURST HANNUM ED., 3d ed., 1999).

Van Boven, Theo C., *The Role of the United Nations Secretariat*, in THE UNITED NATIONS AND HUMAN RIGHTS, THE UNITED NATIONS AND HUMAN RIGHTS: A CRITICAL APPRAISAL 549 (PHILLIP ALSTON ED., 1992).

Articles

Stavropoulou, Maria, *Displacement and Human Rights: Reflections on UN Practice*, 20 HUM. RTS. Q. 515 (1998).

UN Documents

Chairperson's Statement, Statement by the Chairperson on behalf of the Commission on Human Rights (55th session) Geneva, 22 March–30 April 1999. Review of Mechanisms, U.N. Doc. OHCHR/STM/99/5 (1999).

Civil and Political Rights, Including Questions of: Disappearnces and Summary Executions. Report of the Working Group on Enforced or Involuntary Disappearnces. Addendum. Report on the Visit to Sri Lanka by a member of the Working Group on Enforced or Involuntary Disappearances (25–29 October 1999), U.N. Doc. E/CN.4/2000/64/Add.1 (1999).

Civil and Political Rights, Including Questions of: Disappearances and Summary Executions. Report of the Working Group on Enforced or Involuntary Disappearances, U.N. Doc. E/CN.4/1999/62 (1998).

Civil and Political Rights, Including Questions of: Disappearances and Summary Executions. Extrajudicial, Summary or Arbitrary Executions. Report of the Special Rapporteur, Ms. Asma Jahangir, submitted pursuant to Commission on Human Rights resolution 1999/35, U.N. Doc. E/CN.4/2000/3 (2000).

Civil and Political Rights, Including Questions of: Disappearances and Summary Executions. Extrajudicial, Summary or Arbitrary Executions. Report of the Special Rapporteur, Ms. Asma Jahangir, submitted pursuant to Commission on Human Rights resolution 1999/35. Addendum. Summary of cases transmitted to Governments and replies received, U.N. Doc. E/CN.4/2000/3/Add.1 (2000).

Civil and Political Rights, Including Questions of: Disappearances and Summary Executions. Extrajudicial, Summary or Arbitrary Executions. Report of the Special Rapporteur, Ms. Asma Jahangir, submitted pursuant to Commission on Human Rights resolution 1998/68, U.N. Doc. E/CN.4/1999/39 (1999).

Civil and Political Rights, Including Questions of: Torture and Detention. Report of the Working Group on Arbitrary Detention, U.N. Doc. E/CN.4/2000/4 (1999).

Civil and Political Rights Including Questions of: Torture and Detention. Report of the Working Group on Arbitrary Detention. Addendum. Visit to Romania, U.N. Doc. E/CN.4/1999/63/Add. 4 (1998).

Civil and Political Rights Including Questions of: Torture and Detention. Report of the Working Group on Arbitrary Detention. Addendum. Report on the Visit of the Working Group to the United Kingdom on the issue of Immigrants and Asylum Seekers, U.N. Doc. E/CN.4/1999/63/Add.3 (1998).

Civil and Political Rights, Including the Questions of: Independence of the Judiciary, Administration of Justice, Impunity. Report of the Special Rapporteur on the Independence of Judges and Lawyers, Mr. Padam Cumaraswamy, submitted in accordance with Commission resolution 1999/31, U.N. Doc. E/CN.4/2000/61 (2000).

Civil and Political Rights, Including the Question of: Freedom of Expression. Report of the Special Rapporteur on the Protection and Promotion of the Right to Freedom of Opinion and Expression, Mr. Abid Hussain, U.N. Doc. E/CN.4/1999/64 (1999).

Civil and Political Rights, Including the Question of: Freedom of Expression Report of the Special Rapporteur on the Promotion and Protection of the Right to Freedom of Opinion and Expression, Mr. Abid Hussain, submitted in accordance with Commission resolution 1999/36. Addendum. Report on the mission to Ireland, U.N. Doc. E/CN.4/2000/63/Add.2 (2000).

Civil and Political Rights, Including the Question of: Freedom of Expression. Report of the Special Rapporteur on the Promotion and Protection of the Right to Freedom of Opinion and Expression, Mr. Abid Hussain, submitted in accordance with Commission resolution 1999/36. Report on the Mission to Tunisia,. U.N. Doc. E/CN.4/2000/63/Add.4 (2000).

Civil and Political Rights, Including Religious Intolerance. Report submitted by Mr. Abdelfattah Amor, Special Rapporteur, in accordance with Commission on Human Rights resolution 1998/18, U.N. Doc. E/CN.4/1999/58 (1999).

Civil and Political Rights, Including Religious Intolerance. Report submitted by Mr. Abdelfattah Amor, Special Rapporteur, in accordance with Commission on Human Rights resolution 1998/18. Addendum. Visit to the United States of America, U.N. Doc. E/CN.4/1999/58/Add.1 (1998).

Civil and Political Rights, Including Religious Intolerance. Report submitted by Mr. Abdelfattah Amor, Special Rapporteur, in accordance with Commission on Human Rights resolution 1999/39, U.N. Doc. E/CN.4/2000/65 (2000).

Commission on the Status of Women. Report on the Forty-Third Session (1–12 March and 1 April 1999), U.N. Doc. E/CN.6/1999/10 (1999).

Consultative Relationship between the United Nations and Non-Governmental Organizations. Arrangements for Consultation with Non-Governmental Organizations. Part I. Principles to be Applied in the Establishment of Consultative Relations. Part II. Principles Governing the Nature of Consultative Arrangements. Part III. Establishment of Consultative Relationships. Part IV. Consultation with the Council. Part V. Consultation with Commissions and other Subsidiary Organs of the Council. Part VI. Consultations with Ad Hoc Committees of the Council. Part VII. Participation of Non-Governmental Organizations in International Conferences Convened by the United Nations and their Preparatory Process. Part VIII. Suspension and Withdrawal of Consultative Status. Part IX. Council Committee on Non-Governmental Organizations. Part X. Consultation with the Secretariat. Part XI. Secretariat Support, U.N. Doc. E/RES/1996/31 (1996).

Declaration on the Protection of All Persons from Enforced Disappearance, U.N. Doc. A/RES/47/33 (1992).

Effective Prevention and Investigation of Extra-legal, Arbitrary and Summary Executions, U.N. Doc. E/RES/1989/65 (1989).

Enhancing the Effectiveness of the Mechanisms of the Commission on Human Rights, U.N. Doc. E/CN.4/DEC/2000/109 (2000).

Further Promotion and Encouragement of Human Rights and Fundamental Freedoms, Including the Question of the Programme and Methods of Work of the Commission. Alternative Approaches and Ways and Means within the United Nations System for Improving the Effective Enjoyment of Human Rights and Fundamental Freedoms. Report of the Special Rapporteur on Violence Against Women, its Causes and Consequences, Ms. Radhika Coomaraswamy, submitted in accordance with Commission resolution 1997/44, U.N. Doc. E/CN.4/1998/54 (1998).

Further Promotion and Encouragement of Human Rights and Fundamental Freedoms, Including the Question of the Programme and Methods of Work of the Commission Human Rights, Mass Exoduses and Displaced Persons. Report of the Representative of the Secretary-General, Mr. Francis Deng, submitted pursuant to Commission resolution 1997/39. Addendum. Guiding Principles on Internal Displacement, U.N. Doc. E/CN.4/1998/53/Add.2 (1998).

Further Promotion and Encouragement of Human Rights and Fundamental Freedoms, Including the Question of the Programme and Methods of Work of the Commission: Human Rights, Mass Exoduses and Displaced Persons. Internally Displaced Persons. Report of the Representative of the Secretary-General, Mr. Francis M. Deng, submitted pursuant to Commission On Human Rights resolution 1995/57. Compilation and Analysis of Legal Norms, U.N. Doc. E/CN.4/1996/52/Add.2 (1995).

Further Promotion and Encouragement of Human Rights and Fundamental Freedoms, Including the Question of the Programme and Methods of Work of the Commission: Human Rights, Mass Exoduses and Displaced Persons. Internally Displaced Persons. Report of the Representative of the Secretary-General, Mr. Francis M. Deng, submitted pursuant to Commission on Human Rights resolution 1995/39. Addendum. Compilation and Analysis of Legal Norms, Part II: Legal Aspects Relating to the Protection against Arbitrary Displacement, U.N. Doc. E/CN.4/1998/53/Add.1 (1998).

Human Rights and Mass Exoduses, U.N. Doc. E/CN.4/RES/2000/55 (2000).

Implementation of the Programme of Action for the Second Decade to Combat Racism and Racial Discrimination. Report by Mr. Maurice Glele-Ahanhanzo, Special Rapporteur on Contemporary Forms of Racism, Racial Discrimination, Xenophobia and Related Intolerance, submitted pursuant to Commission on Human Rights resolution 1993/20, U.N. Doc. E/CN.4/1994/66 (1994).

Integration of the Human Rights of Women and the Gender Perspective: Violence Against Women. Report of the Special Rapporteur on Violence Against Women, its Causes And Consequences, Ms. Radhika Coomaraswamy submitted in accordance with Commission on Human Rights resolution 1995/85, U.N. Doc. E/CN.4/1999/68 (1999).

Integration of the Human Rights of Women and the Gender Perspective. Violence Against Women. Report of the Special Rapporteur on Violence Against Women, its Causes and Consequences, Ms. Radhika Coomaraswamy. Submitted in accordance with Commission resolution 1997/44. Addendum. Communications to and from Governments, U.N. Doc. E/CN.4/2000/68/Add.1 (2000).

Integration of the Human Rights of Women and the Gender Perspective. Violence Against Women. Report of the Special Rapporteur on Violence Against Women, its Causes and Consequences, Ms. Radhika Coomaraswamy. Addendum. Communications to and from Governments, U.N. Doc. E/CN.4/1999/68/Add.1 (1999).

Internally Displaced Persons, U.N. Doc. E/CN.4/RES/2000/53 (2000).

Joint Work Plan of the Division for the Advancement of Women and the Office of the United Nations High Commissioner for Human Rights. Report of the Secretary-General, U.N. Doc. E/CN.6/2000/8 (2000).

Monitoring the Implementation of the Nairobi Forward-Looking Strategies for the Advancement of Women. Examining Existing Mechanisms for Communications on the Status of Women. Report of the Secretary-General, U.N. Doc. E/CN.6/1991/10 (1990).

Organization of Work. Work Methods of the Sub-Commission, U.N. Doc. E/CN.4/Sub.2/1999/3, Annex 2 (1999).

Organization of Work. Methods of Work of the Sub-Commission. Enhancing the Effectiveness of the Sub-Commission. Note by the Chairman, U.N. Doc. E/CN.4/Sub.2/1998/38 (1998).

Promotion and Protection of the Rights of Children. Impact of Armed Conflict on Children. Note by the Secretary-General, U.N. Doc. A/51/306 (1996).

Question of the Human Rights of All Persons Subjected to Any Form of Detention or Imprisonment. Question of Enforced or Involuntary Disappearances. Report of the Working Group on Enforced or Involuntary Disappearances, U.N. Doc. E/CN.4/1998/43 (1998).

Question of the Human Rights of All Persons Subject to Any Form of Detention or Imprisonment. Report of the Working Group on Arbitrary Detention, U.N. Doc. E/CN.4/1998/44 Annex 1 (1997).

Question of the Human Rights of All Persons Subjected to Any Form of Detention or Imprisonment. Question of Enforced or Involuntary Disappearances. Report of the Working Group on Enforced or Involuntary Disappearances, U.N. Doc. E/CN.4/1997/34 (1996).

Question of the Violation of Human Rights and Fundamental Freedoms, In Any Part of the World, with particular reference to Colonial and Other Dependent Countries and Territories: Extrajudicial, Summary or Arbitrary Executions. Report by the Special Rapporteur, Mr. Bacre Waly Ndiaye, submitted pursuant to Commission on Human Rights resolution 1993/71, U.N. Doc. E/CN.4/1994/7 (1993).

Question of the Violation of Human Rights and Fundamental Freedoms In Any Part of the World, with particular reference to Colonial and Other Dependent Countries and Territories. Extrajudicial, Summary or Arbitrary Executions. Report by the Special Rapporteur, Mr. Bacre Waly Ndiaye, submitted pursuant to Commission On Human Rights resolution 1992/72, U.N. Doc. E/CN.4/1993/46 (1992).

Question of the Human Rights of All Persons Subjected to Any Form of Detention or Imprisonment, In Particular: Torture and Other Cruel, Inhuman or Degrading Treatment or Punishment. Report of the Special Rapporteur, Mr. Nigel S. Rodley, submitted pursuant to Commission On Human Rights Resolution 1994/37. Addendum. Visit by the Special Rapporteur to the Russian Federation, U.N. Doc. E/CN.4/1995/34/Add.1 (1994).

Question of the Human Rights of all Persons Subjected to Any Form of Detention or Imprisonment, In Particular: Torture and Other Cruel, Inhuman or Degrading Treatment or Punishment. Report of the Special Rapporteur, Mr. Nigel S. Rodley, submitted pursuant to Commission on Human Rights resolution 1997/38. Addendum. Summary of cases transmitted to Governments and replies recieved, U.N. Doc.E/CN.4/1998/38/Add.1 (1997).

Question of the Human Rights of All Persons Subjected to Any Form of Detention or Imprisonment, In Particular: (a) Torture and Other Cruel, Inhuman or Degrading Treatment or Punishment; (b) Status of the Convention Against Torture and Other Cruel, Inhuman or Degrading Treatment or Punishment; (c) Question of Enforced or Involuntary Disappearances; (d) Question of a Draft Optional Protocol to the Convention Against Torture and Other Cruel, Inhuman or Degrading Treatment or Punishment. Independence and Impartiality of the Judiciary, Jurors and Assessors and the Independence of Lawyers. Report of the Special Rapporteur, Mr. Param Cumaraswamy, submitted in accordance with Commission On Human Rights resolution 1994/41, U.N. Doc. E/CN.4/1995/39 (1995).

Question of the Human Rights of All Persons Subjected to Any Form of Detention or Imprisonment. Report of the Special Rapporteur on the Independence of Judges and Lawyers, Mr. Param Cumaraswamy. Addendum. Report on the Mission of the Special Rapporteur to Columbia, U.N. Doc. E/CN.4/1998/39/Add.2 (1998).

Question of the Human Rights of all Persons Subjected to Any Form of Detention or Imprisonment. Note by the Secretary-General, U.N. Doc. E/CN.4/1995/30 (1995).

Question of Integrating the Rights of Women into the Human Rights Mechanisms of the United Nations and the Elimination of Violence Against Women, U.N. Doc. E/CN.4/RES/1994/45 (1994).

Racism, Racial Discrimination, Xenophobia and All Forms of Discrimination. Report by Mr. Maurice Glèlè-Ahanhanzo, Special Rapporteur on Contemporary Forms of Racism, Racial Discrimination, Xenophobia and

Related Intolerance, submitted pursuant to Commission on Human Rights resolution 1999/78, U.N. Doc. E/CN.4/2000/16 (2000).

Racism, Racial Discrimination, Xenophobia and All Forms of Discrimination. Report by Mr. Maurice Glèlè-Ahanhanzo, Special Rapporteur on Contemporary Forms of Racism, Racial Discrimination, Xenophobia and Related Intolerance, submitted pursuant to Commission on Human Rights resolution 1997/73, U.N. Doc. E/CN.4/1998/79 (1998).

Rationalization of the Work of the Commission. Report of the Inter-Sessional Open-Ended Working Group on Enhancing the Effectiveness of the Mechanisms of the Commission on Human Rights, U.N. Doc. E/CN.4/2000/112 (2000)

Report of the Sub-Commission on the Prevention of Discrimination and Protection of Minorities on its fiftieth session. Report of Mr. El-Hadji Guissé, Chairman of the Sub-Commission at its fiftieth session, prepared in accordance with paragraphs 9(d) and 11 of Commission on Human Rights resolution 1998/28, U.N. Doc. E/CN.4/1999/84 (1998).

The Right to Development. Report of the Secretary-General submitted in accordance with Commission on Human Rights resolution 1998/72, U.N. Doc. E/CN.4/1999/20 (1998).

Rights of the Child. Report of the Special Rapporteur on the Sale of Children, Child Prostitution and Child Pornography, Ms. Ofelia Calcetas-Santos. Addendum. Report on the Mission of the Special Rapporteur to Belgium and the Netherlands on the Issue of Commercial Sexual Exploitation of Children (30 November–4 December 1998), U.N. Doc. E/CN.4/2000/73/Add.1 (1999).

Rights of the Child. Children in Armed Conflict. Interim Report of the Special Representative of the Secretary-General, Mr. Olara A. Otunnu, Submitted pursuant to General Assembly resolution 52/107, U.N. Doc. E/CN.4/1998/119 (1998).

The Rights of the Child, G.A. Res. 51/77, U.N. GAOR, 51st Sess., U.N. Doc. A/RES/51/77 (1997).

Rights of the Child. Children in Armed Conflict. Interim Report of the Special Representative of the Secretary-General, Mr. Olara A. Otunnu, Submitted pursuant to General Assembly resolution 52/107, U.N. Doc. E/CN.4/1998/119 (1998).

Rights of the Child. Additional report of the Special Representative of the Secretary-General for Children and Armed Conflict, Mr. Olara Otunnu, submitted in accordance with General Assembly resolution 53/128, U.N. Doc. E/CN.4/2000/71 (2000).

Security Council Resolution 1261(1999) on the Children and Armed Conflict, U.N. SCOR, 4037th mtg., U.N. Doc. S/Res/1261 (1999).

Specific Groups and Individuals: Mass Exodus and Displaced Persons. Internally Displaced Persons. Report of the Representative of the Secretary-General

Mr. Francis M. Deng, submitted pursuant to Commission of Human Rights resolution 1998/50, U.N. Doc. E/CN.4/1999/79 (1999).

Specific Groups and Individual Migrant Workers. Human Rights of Migrants. Report of the Special Rapporteur, Ms. Gabriela Rodríguez Pizzaro, submitted pursuant to Commission on Human Rights resolution 1999/44, U.N. Doc. E/CN.4/2000/82 1–2 (2000).

Specific Groups and Individuals: Mass Exoduses and Displaced Persons. Internally Displaced Persons. Report of the Representative of the Secretary-General, Mr. Francis M. Deng, submitted pursuant to Commission on Human Right resolution 1999/47, U.N. Doc. E/CN.4/2000/83 (2000).

Statement by the Chairperson of the Commission Concerning the Human Rights Situation in East Timor, U.N. Doc. OHCHR/STM/98/3 (1998).

Work of the Sub-Commission on the Promotion and Protection of Human Rights, U.N. Doc E/CN.4/RES/2000/83 (2000).

NGO Reports

Amnesty International, *Human Rights Thematic Mechanisms 2000*, AI INDEX: IOR 40/020/2000 (2000), at <http://www.web.amnesty.org/ai.nsf/index/IOR400202000>.

Internet Sources

Division for the Advancement of Women, *Commission on the Status of Women*, at <http://www.un.org/womenwatch/daw/csw>.

Human Rights Internet, *Introduction 1998*, FOR THE RECORD: THE UN HUMAN RIGHTS SYSTEM, Volume 1, 1998, at <http://www.hri.ca>.

Human Rights Internet, *Overview 1999*, FOR THE RECORD: THE UN HUMAN RIGHTS SYSTEM, Volume 1, 1999, at <http://www.hri.ca>.

Interview with Francis Deng, SRSG on IDPs, REFUGEES MAGAZINE, Issue 117, 1999, at <http://www.unhcr.ch/pubs/rm117/rm11703.htm>.

Special Representative of the Secretary-General for Children and Armed Conflict, at <http://www.un.org/special-rep/children-armed-conflict>.

United Nations, Economic and Social Council, *NGO related frequently asked questions*, at <http://www.un.org/esa/coordination/ngo/faq/htm>.

United Nations High Commissioner for Human Rights, *Explanatory Note for the Submission of Information on Enforced or Involuntary Disappearances of Persons*, at <http://www.unhchr.ch/html/menu2/7/b/disappea/explanote.htm>.

United Nations High Commissioner for Human Rights, *Special Rapporteur for Extrajudicial, Summary and Arbitrary Executions: Information needed for Special Rapporteur to take action,* at <http://www.unhchr.ch/html/menu2/7/b/execut/exe_info.htm>.

United Nations High Commissioner for Human Rights, *Special Rapporteur for Extrajudicial, Summary and Arbitrary Executions: Mandate,* at <http://www.unhchr.ch/html/menu2/7/b/execut/exe_mand.htm>.

Chapter 4
African Regional Mechanisms That Can Be Utilized on Behalf of the Forcibly Displaced

Chidi Anselm Odinkalu
Monette Zard

1. Introduction

The scale and complexity of the refugee problem facing Africa today is enormous. Africa is host to some 3.5 million refugees, as well as 1.7 million internally displaced persons and 0.9 million returnees.[1] In 1969, when the OAU adopted the Convention Governing the Specific Aspects of Refugee Problems in Africa,[2] there were just 700,000 refugees in Africa. The proliferation of conflict and the scale of the resulting human displacement, combined with the perception on the part of African States that there has been a lack of attention by the international community to sharing their burden, have increasingly eroded a once generous tradition of hospitality towards refugees. In a climate in which support for basic principles of international protection is under threat and where abiding by one's obligations under international refugee law is increasingly being seen as optional, it becomes abundantly clear that traditional approaches to refugee protection are in need of supplementation. Greater attention to burden-sharing is a must as are political initiatives to tackle the root causes of displacement.

However, it is also important that advocates look for ways in which to reassert the legal and binding nature of international law in this area. To date, it is remarkable that both the major instruments for the protection of refugees—the 1951 UN Refugee Convention and the 1969

---

[1] *UNHCR News, Country Updates, Africa Fact Sheet* (May 2000), available at <http://www.unhcr.ch/news/cupdates/0005afri.htm>.

[2] *See* Bibliography of Cited International Instruments for full citations to this and other international instruments mentioned in this chapter.

OAU Convention—are without adequate supervisory mechanisms to ensure their effective implementation. Whilst the IDP Guiding Principles[3] are merely a restatement of existing legal norms, these norms are also in need of judicial reinforcement. In the search for new approaches and strategies to use on behalf of refugees, asylum-seekers, and internally displaced persons, an advocate would be well advised to have regard to mechanisms which are currently evolving on the regional and sub-regional level in Africa. The last two decades have witnessed a veritable explosion of regional and sub-regional mechanisms on the continent that offer themselves up to advocates and legal practitioners to develop and exploit on behalf of those who are forcible displaced. Many, indeed most are still in their infancy and thus it may not be possible to outline a wealth of jurisprudence as a guide for lawyers to follow. However, the field is dynamic and rapidly developing and advocates with initiative can capitalize on the opportunities that this presents.

The 1969 OAU Convention Governing the Specific Aspects of Refugee Problems in Africa marked an important step forward in strengthening the protection for those forcibly displaced on the continent. At the time of its adoption, African States were struggling to cope with mass influxes of refugees precipitated by the struggle against colonial occupation and wars of national liberation. This situation highlighted the limitations of the individualized, persecution-based definition of refugees contained in the 1951 UN Refugee Convention. Whilst the OAU Convention retained the individual definition for determining refugee status in Article I.A(1), it also introduced a new expanded definition of who is a refugee: Article I.A(2) of the OAU Convention provides that:

> The term "refugee" shall also apply to every person who, owing to external aggression, occupation, foreign domination or events seriously disturbing public order in either part or the whole of his country of origin or nationality, is compelled to leave his habitual place of residence in order to seek refuge in another place outside his country of origin or nationality.

In practice both individual and group determination processes exist side by side in the African system. Large groups of refugees fleeing war or generalized violence are granted status on the basis of their nationality or ethnicity, whilst individual applicants, usually in urban

---

[3] *Internally Displaced Persons, Report of the Representative of the Secretary-General, Mr. Francis Deng,* U.N. Doc. E/CN.4/1998/53/Add.2 (1998).

areas, are required to undergo individual status determination procedures. Similarly, the OAU Convention should be seen as complementary to and applied in conjunction with the 1951 UN Refugee Convention. Both systems should operate in the context of broader human rights law and in particular the 1981 African Charter of Human and People's Rights.

The OAU Convention is progressive in a number of ways. It strengthens the principle of non-refoulement by including a prohibition on rejection at the frontier (Article II(3)); it urges member states to receive refugees (Article II(1)); it refers to a spirit of African solidarity in relation to burden-sharing (Article II(4)); it characterizes asylum as a peaceful and humanitarian act that should not be regarded by the state of origin as unfriendly (Article II(2)); and it specifically prohibits repatriation against the will of the refugee (Article V).

The issues and hurdles facing refugees in Africa are numerous. Refugees in urban areas encounter familiar problems with respect to ensuring a fair and expeditious determination of their status through national asylum procedures (where these exist). Inadequate documentation, detention, as well as a host of social and economic rights questions confront the individual asylum-seeker and refugee. In mass influxes, freedom of movement can be an issue, with host governments often limiting assistance and recognition of status to certain areas or zones. Moreover, the rights of refugees to express themselves freely are by no means assured. Although Articles 9 and 10 of the 1981 African Charter on Human and People's Rights provide for the rights to freedom of expression and assembly, the 1969 OAU Convention in Article III establishes explicit prohibitions on "subversive activities" by refugees against any member states of the OAU. In particular, states parties undertake to prohibit refugees from any activity likely to cause tension between member states and in particular, by use of arms, through *the press or by radio*"[4] (emphasis added).

What follows is an overview of mechanisms currently evolving in Africa that have the potential to provide real solutions to the plight of both the individual refugee and to groups of refugees. In particular, the chapter will highlight the important steps made by the African Commission in elaborating upon the substantive rights contained in the 1981 African Charter on Human and People's Rights, for the benefit of those forcibly displaced. Whilst the focus is primarily on judicial fora, the chapter also looks at other mechanisms, in particular the evolving conflict resolution mechanisms of the OAU and of regional integration mechanisms in Africa, such as the Inter-Governmental Authority

---

[4] *Id.* at art. III, ¶¶ 1 and 2.

on Development (IGAD) that have the potential to offer up a remedy for those forcibly displaced.

2. African Regional Mechanisms

2.1 The Organization of African Unity (OAU)

The Organization of African Unity (OAU) was established in May 1963 under a Charter with treaty status adopted by the then newly independent African states.[5] Among its objectives, the Charter mandates the African States in the OAU "to coordinate and intensify their cooperation and efforts to achieve a better life for the peoples of Africa"[6] and "promote international cooperation, having due regard to the Charter of the United Nations and the [1948] Universal Declaration of Human Rights."[7] Among the principal institutions of the OAU, the Charter establishes the Assembly of Heads of State and Government as the "supreme organ of the Organization."[8] Other principal institutions include the Council of Ministers and the Secretariat-General, which is responsible for the operations of the OAU. In addition to servicing the operations of the Charter institutions, the Secretariat also supports the operations of implementing bodies for treaties adopted or established by or among OAU member states.[9] Under the auspices of the OAU, a number of mechanisms have developed that may provide a remedy to those forcibly displaced.

---

[5] *Charter of the Organization of African Unity (OAU)*, 479 U.N.T.S. 39, *entered into force* Sept. 13, 1963, reprinted *in* 2 I.L.M. 766 (1963).
[6] *Id*, at art. II(1)(b).
[7] *Id.* at art. II(1)(e).
[8] *Id.* at art. VII(1) & VIII.
[9] The OAU only adopted rules on consultative arrangements with NGOs in 1993. Under these rules, there are two forms of consultative arrangements—Observer Status and a more specialized Co-operation Agreement. Only African NGOs may seek Observer Status with the OAU, unlike the more specialized Co-operation Agreement which may also be concluded with non-African NGOs. In order to qualify for Observer Status, an NGO would have to show that their objectives and activities conform with the fundamental principles and objectives of the OAU, as elaborated in the Charter; that they are an African organization, registered and head-quartered in Africa and that their membership is composed of a majority of Africans. They must also demonstrate that they have a secure financial basis and that the majority of their funding comes from African sources. *Critere d'Octroi du Statut d'Observateur aupres de l'OUA tels qu'amendes Par la 29 eme session Ordinaire des Chefs d'Etat et de Gouvernement*, art. 1(a)–(c), AHG/192(XXIX). NGOs wishing to apply for Observer Status must submit a written request to the Secretary General at least 6 months before the next meeting of

2.1.1 The 1981 African Charter on Human and Peoples' Rights

Of the existing international and regional treaties for the protection of human rights, the 1981 African Charter on Human and Peoples' Rights[10] contains perhaps the most far reaching normative framework for the protection of refugees. Apart from Articles 12(4) and 13 of the Charter, applicable respectively to non-nationals and citizens, the subject of the rights guaranteed in the Charter is a gender-neutral "individual." Theoretically, therefore, the Charter provisions are applicable to refugees through all stages of displacement, including flight, status determination, asylum, and return or voluntary repatriation.

With respect to the internally displaced, the African Commission on Human and Peoples' Rights[11] has held that Article 23(1) of the Charter (which provides that "all peoples shall have the right to national and international peace and security") included "the responsibility for protection" of nationals.[12] In Communication 74/92, *Commission Nationale des Droits de l'Homme et des Libertés v. Chad*,[13] the Commission suggested that Article 23(1) included a duty on states to provide security and stability to the inhabitants of their territories. Where, however, internal displacement results from a failure of the authority and institutions of a state party to the Charter, there are unlikely to exist national

---

the Council of Ministers and include their Charter and rules and regulations, a current membership list, sources of funding, their last account balance and a memorandum of the organization's activities, past and present. These materials should be submitted in one of the languages of the OAU and in sufficient quantities that they can be circulated to all member states. *Id.* at art. 2(a), 2(b), 5. In addition, the application must include a statement of support from at least 5 member states of the OAU, including at least one based at the Organization's headquarters. Decisions on Observer Status or consultative arrangements are taken by the Assembly of Heads of State and Governments, by consensus. *Id.* at art. 6. There are currently about 60 organizations with Observer status. Observers are able to attend in a purely observer capacity, both public and private meetings of the OAU, have access to OAU documentation [which is not of a confidential nature] and where authorized by the President they can participate in the debate or make a presentation on a topic of concern to them. *Id.* at arts. 4, 5.

[10] Hereinafter called "the African Charter" or "the Charter."

[11] Hereinafter called "the African Commission" or "the Commission."

[12] *Malawi African Association & Others v. Mauritania*, Communication 54/91, ¶ 138 (1999) (hereinafter called "the *Mauritania cases*").

[13] *Commission Nationale des Droits de l'Homme et des Libertés v. Chad*, Communication 74/92, ¶ 22 (1995).

processes and institutions capable of implementing Charter obligations to protect the individual. Depending on the causes of internal displacement, there may thus be practical—but not normative—difficulties in extending the protection of Charter provisions to IDPs. This does not, however, render the Charter or international law generally irrelevant to such situations.[14]

The general foundation for the protection of the human rights of refugees under the Charter is in the guarantees of equal protection of the law,[15] life,[16] human dignity, including the prohibition of all forms of torture, cruel, inhuman and degrading treatment,[17] personal liberty,[18] and fair trial and due process.[19] These norms appertain to all human beings in all situations prior to, during, and after displacement. The Commission has consistently held that "contrary to other human rights instruments, the African Charter does not allow for derogation from obligations due to emergency situations. Thus, even a situation of . . . war . . . cannot be cited as justification for the violation by the State or its authority to violate the African Charter."[20] In implementing the rights contained in it, moreover, the Charter enjoins states parties "to secure the rights protected in the Charter to all persons within their jurisdiction, nationals or non-nationals."[21]

General Rights of Refugees as Human Persons

Under the Charter, refugees should not be subjected to summary, arbitrary, or extra-judicial executions.[22] The African Commission has held that forced nudity, electricity burns, and sexual assaults constitute together and separately, violations of Article 5 of the Charter.[23] Although

---

[14] *Cf., Elmi v. Australia*, Committee against Torture, 22nd session, U.N. Doc. CAT/C/22/D/120/1998 (25 May 1999), at <http://unbisnet.un.org/webpacbin/wgbroker?1106184915075418274+1+scan+select+1+0>.

[15] *Id.* at art. 3(2).

[16] *Id.* at art. 4.

[17] *Id.* at art. 5.

[18] *Id.* at art. 6.

[19] *Id.* at art. 7.

[20] *Commission Nationale des Droits de l'Homme et des Libertés v. Chad*, Communication 74/92, ¶ 36 (1995); *The Mauritania Cases, supra* note 12 at ¶ 84.

[21] *Rencontre Africaine pour la Defense des Droits de l'Homme (RADDHO) v. Zambia*, Communication 71/92, ¶ 22 (1997).

[22] *Commission Nationale des Droits de l'Homme et des Libertés v. Chad, supra* note 20; *Organisation Mondiale Contre la Torture v. Rwanda*, Communication 27/89 (1996).

[23] *The Commission Nationale des Droits de l'Homme case, supra* note 20; *Krishna Achutan (on Behalf of Aleke Banda) v. Malaw*, Communication 64/92 (1994).

decided in the context of detention and similar forms of deprivation of liberty, this principle is equally applicable to the delineation of minimum standards applicable to refugees, particularly those in camps.

Article 5 of the Charter also obliges states parties to refrain from returning refugees to a place where they may be subject to torture, cruel, inhuman and degrading treatment. The state is obliged to comply strictly with due process norms before removing refugees or persons seeking protection as refugees.[24] The African Commission has thus held the due process guarantees in Article 7 of the African Charter to be applicable to the involuntary removal of a refugee from a host state.[25] The Commission has elaborated that the right of the individual in Article 7 includes a duty on the government to provide the structures to enable the right to be exercised.[26] This implies a duty on the government to extend legal assistance to refugees generally or at least in cases that potentially or actually affect their continued enjoyment of the protection that comes from being afforded refugee status. The Commission has not yet addressed the question of whether Article 7 of the Charter extends to status determination.

Persons who have been forcibly displaced, whether as refugees or IDPs, also enjoy the protection of the provisions of the Charter pertaining to economic, social, and cultural rights. In the absence of an express guarantee of a right to housing in the Charter, the Commission has based protection for housing-related rights on the Article 5 guarantee of human dignity, including the prohibition of torture, cruel, inhuman and degrading treatment. In Communication 93/97, *John K. Modise v. Botswana*,[27] the author was rendered stateless by the respondent state, which cancelled his Botswana nationality and deported him to South Africa for political reasons. South Africa in turn deported him to the then Homeland of Bophuthatswana, which in turn deported him back to Botswana. Unable to resolve the question of where to keep the author, the authorities of the respondent state made him homeless over a long period on a specially created strip of border territory with South Africa called "no-man's land." The Commission found that such enforced homelessness was inhuman and degrading treatment that offended "the dignity of human beings and thus violated article 5."[28] The

---

[24] *Organisation Mondiale Contre la Torture et al v. Rwanda*, supra note 22, at ¶ 34.
[25] *Id.*
[26] *Constitutional Rights Project (in respect of Zamani Lekwot & 6 Others) v. Nigeria*, Communication 87/93, (1994).
[27] *John K. Modise v. Botswana*, Communication 97/93 (1996) (hereinafter called "the *Modise case*").
[28] *Id.* at ¶ 32.

Commission has similarly found that forced eviction violates the right to property.[29] The implications of this case are: first, that involuntary or forced displacement is a violation of the right to respect for human dignity; second, that victims of such displacement, such as refugees and IDPs, are at a minimum entitled to shelter; and third, that the status of being forcibly displaced is not incompatible with the right to property.

The *Mauritania cases*[30] comprised five consolidated communications arising from developments in Mauritania between 1986–1992. Briefly, these communications alleged the existence in that state of slavery and analogous practices, and of institutionalized racial discrimination perpetrated by the ruling Beydane community against the more populous black community. Among other things, the cases alleged that black Mauritanians were enslaved, routinely evicted or displaced from their lands that were then confiscated by the government. The communication also alleged that some detainees had been starved to death, left to die in severe weather without blankets or clothing, and were deprived of medical attention. The Commission found that starving prisoners and depriving them of blankets, clothing, and health care violated Article 16 of the Charter.[31]

The obligation to protect the family is entrenched in Article 18 of the African Charter. This right is applicable to refugees, asylum-seekers, and IDPs alike, entailing an obligation to ensure family reunion where displacement results in the break up of the family unit.[32]

Rights During Flight: Asylum as a Human Right Under the African Charter

Article 12 of the Charter contains specific guarantees protecting freedom of movement and the human rights of refugees. It prohibits forced exile[33] and guarantees to every individual when persecuted, the right "to seek *and obtain* asylum."[34] To the extent that this provision includes a right to "obtain asylum," the African Charter is unique in creating an obligation on states parties to grant refugee protection through the asylum process. Implied in this provision, therefore, is an obligation on the states parties to the Charter to establish institutions and fair procedures for status determination. This entails an extension

---

[29] The *Mauritania cases, supra* note 12, at ¶¶ 125–128.
[30] The *Mauritania cases, supra* note 12.
[31] *Id.* at ¶ 122.
[32] *Amnesty International v. Zambia*, Communication 212/98 (1998).
[33] *African Charter*, art. 12(2).
[34] *Id.* at art. 12(3) (emphasis added).

of the due process guarantees in Article 7 of the Charter to status determination procedures. Fair procedures in this context would include extending legal assistance to refugees in status determination processes.[35] This conclusion is fortified by the provision of Article 26 that requires states parties to the Charter to "allow the establishment and improvement of appropriate national institutions entrusted with the promotion and protection of the rights and freedoms guaranteed by the present Charter."[36]

The Charter also prohibits the collective expulsion of foreign nationals,[37] including refugees.[38] Article 12 of the Draft Protocol to the African Charter on Women's Rights seeks to extend this protection to female refugees. It seeks to commit states parties to "take all appropriate measures to involve women . . . in the local, national, sub-regional and international structures for the establishment and management of camps for refugees and displaced persons and for humanitarian assistance and aid."[39]

2.1.2 The African Commission on Human and Peoples' Rights

Established under Article 30 of the African Charter on Human and Peoples Rights, the African Commission on Human and Peoples' Rights comprises eleven "persons of the highest reputation," nationals of states parties to the Charter "known for their high morality, integrity, impartiality and competence in the field of human and peoples' rights"[40] and functioning as independent experts in their private capacity. It is empowered to "promote human and peoples' rights and ensure their protection in Africa."[41]

The Commission's Mandate

The mandate of the Commission, elaborated in Article 45 of the Charter, includes promotional work through awareness-raising programs

---

[35] See *supra* note 26 and accompanying text.
[36] *Id.* at art. 26.
[37] *Id.* at art. 12(4)–(5).
[38] *OMCT v. Rwanda, supra* note 22.
[39] See Bibliography of Cited International Instruments, Draft Protocol to the African Charter on Women's Rights, art. 12(2). This protocol is still being negotiated and has not yet been adopted.
[40] *African Charter*, art. 31(1).
[41] *Id.* at art. 30.

such as conferences, seminars, and symposia;[42] standard-setting involving the formulation of "principles and rules aimed at solving legal problems relating to human and peoples' rights and fundamental freedoms upon which African Governments may base their legislations;"[43] protective work, including the consideration of cases and communications;[44] and advisory work, including the interpretation of the Charter "at the request of a State party, an institution of the OAU or an African organization recognized by the OAU."[45] Both states[46] and non-state entities may initiate cases and communications.[47] In addition, the Commission monitors states parties' compliance with Charter provisions by receiving and considering periodic reports submitted by the states.[48] The Commission also has special investigative powers with respect to emergency situations or "special cases which reveal the existence of a series of serious and massive violations" of Charter rights.[49] Every refugee-producing situation is not necessarily to be classified as an emergency under this provision without regard to all the circumstances associated with the displacement, including the number of people displaced. Thus, a situation resulting in mass displacement, exodus, or influx inescapably merits consideration as an emergency.

To implement its mandate, the Charter confers three ancillary powers on the Commission relating respectively to evidence and interpretation. It empowers the Commission to "resort to any method of investigation"[50] including hearing from "the Secretary General of the Organization of African Unity or any other person capable of enlightening it."[51] In relation to the protection of refugees, this provision would enable the Commission to call on expert, governmental, non-govern-

---

[42] *Id*, at art. 45(1)(a).
[43] *Id.* at art. 45(1)(b).
[44] *Id.* at art. 45(2), and Ch. III, art. 47–59.
[45] *Id.* at art. 45(3).
[46] *Id.* at art. 47–54. *Democratic Republic of the Congo v. Burundi, Rwanda and Uganda*, Communication 227/98, is the only inter-state Communication so far registered by the African Commission. This communication is still pending.
[47] *African Charter*, arts. 55–57.
[48] *Id.* at art. 62.
[49] *Id.* at art. 58 (1)–(3). For an analysis of Article 58 of the African Charter, *see* Chidi Anselm Odinkalu and Rafikiel Mdoe, *Article 58 of the African Charter on Human Rights: A Legal Analysis and Proposals for Implementation*, INTERIGHTS (1996); Rachel Murray, *Serious and Massive Violations under the African Charter on Human and Peoples' Rights: A Comparison with the Inter-American and European Mechanisms*, 17 NETH. Q. HUM. RTS. 109 (1999).
[50] *African Charter*, art. 46.
[51] *Id.*

mental or inter-governmental testimony or sources as it sees fit. Concerning its interpretive latitude, the Charter permits the Commission to "draw inspiration from international law on human and peoples' rights," including other international instruments to which African states are party.[52] International standards in the field of refugee protection would naturally be among the sources of inspiration open to the Commission under this provision. The Charter further authorizes the Commission to "take into consideration as subsidiary measures to determine the principles of law"[53] other general or special international conventions, customs generally accepted as law, general principles of law recognized by African states, legal precedents and doctrine,[54] as well as African practices consistent with international norms on human and peoples' rights.[55]

Procedure for Redressing Violations: Non-State Complaints

Non-state complaints or communications alleging violations of rights may be initiated by a communication addressed to the Secretariat of the African Commission, located in Banjul, The Gambia. To qualify for consideration, a communication must fulfill certain conditions for admissibility stipulated in Article 56 of the Charter. The most significant of these conditions pertain to:

The authors:[56]

Communications should indicate the name and contact addresses of the authors. The authors need not be victims, their families or persons necessarily authorized by either.[57] Nor do they need to be citizens, or residents of a state party to the Charter. Communications may be submitted by any person, whether individual or corporate. Authors of communications may request the Commission to preserve their anonymity with respect to the state against whom a complaint has been made.[58]

---

[52] *Id.* at art. 60.
[53] *Id.* at art. 61.
[54] This would include, for instance, the Conclusions of the Executive Committee of the UN High Commissioner for Refugees.
[55] *Id.*
[56] *African Charter*, art. 56(1).
[57] *World Organization Against Torture et al v. Zaire* (Merits), Communication 25/89 (1997), *reprinted in* 4 INT'L HUM. RTS. REP. 89, 92 (1997).
[58] *Id.*

The subject matter:[59]

The complaint must allege a violation of a right recognized by the Charter, but not necessarily with reference to the specific articles or provisions in pertaining to that right under the Charter. The Commission can only adjudicate with respect to violations occurring after the respondent state ratified or acceded to the Charter. Where the violations alleged began before the ratification, the complaint may nevertheless be admissible if they have substantially continued since then.[60]

Compatibility with the 1963 OAU Charter:[61]

Article 56(2) contains a stipulation with potentially far reaching implications for the protection of refugees by the African Commission. It requires that communications be compatible with the 1963 Charter of the OAU. The full import of this provision for the African Commission's mandate with respect to protecting the human rights of refugees is better understood with reference to relevant provisions of both the OAU Charter and the 1969 OAU Convention Governing the Specific Aspects of Refugee Problems in Africa. Among the fundamental principles of the OAU, the OAU Charter entrenches non-interference in the internal affairs of states, respect for the sovereignty and territorial integrity of each state, and unreserved condemnation of subversive activities on the part of a neighboring state or any other states.[62] These priorities are reflected in Article 3 of the 1969 OAU Refugee Convention which provides as follows:

(1) Every refugee has duties to the country in which he finds himself, which require in particular that he conforms to its laws and regulations as well as to measures for the maintenance of public order. He shall also abstain from any subversive activities against any member State of the OAU.

(2) Signatory States undertake to prohibit refugees residing in their respective territories from attacking any State member of the OAU by any activity likely to cause tension between member States, *and in particular, by use of arms, through the press or by radio.*[63]

---

[59] *African Charter*, art. 56(2).[60] *See* the decisions of the Commission in *Emgba Louis Mekongo v. Cameroon*, Communication 59/91 (1994); and *John K. Modise v. Botswana*, Communication 97/93 (1997).
[61] *African Charter*, art. 56(2).
[62] *OAU Charter*, art. III.
[63] (Emphasis added).

Article 3(2) of the OAU Refugee Convention entails an admittedly non-self-executing obligation requiring as it does the adoption of measures to implement the undertaking entered into by the states parties. The provision nevertheless creates too wide a latitude for interfering with the human rights in general and free expression and associated rights, in particular, of refugees or refugee communities. Theoretically, Article 56(2) of the African Charter could excuse the rejection of a communication alleging such violations on the ground that such a communication is incompatible with the OAU Charter. It is doubtful, however, that the Charter would seek to accord second class or no protection at all in this way to refugees.[64] The Commission will clearly have little difficulty in rejecting resort to arms as an exercise of a Charter-protected right. But the prohibition of legitimate free expression, association or assembly by refugees ostensibly permitted by Article 3(2) of the OAU Refugee Convention, constitutes *prima facie* violations of Articles 9–11 of the African Charter.

Exhaustion of local remedies:[65]

The Charter requires that authors should exhaust local remedies before resorting to the procedures of the African Commission "unless it is obvious that this procedure is unduly prolonged."[66] Availability of and access to domestic adjudication procedures, including the means to pursue and exhaust them, is implied in this provision as an exception to the requirement to exhaust domestic remedies. In its Advisory Opinion on Exceptions to the Exhaustion of Domestic Remedies, the Inter-American Court of Human Rights concluded that:

> if legal services are required either as a matter of law or as a matter of fact in order for a right guaranteed by the Convention to be recognized and a persons is unable to obtain such services because of his indigency, then that person would be exempted from the requirement to exhaust domestic remedies. The same would be true of cases requiring the payment of a filing fee. That is to say, if it is impossible

---

[64] In the only communication in which it relied on this requirement in the African Charter, the African Commission held that its obligation to respect the territorial integrity of OAU member states under the OAU Charter precluded it from considering a communication asserting a right to secession as inherent in the rights of peoples to self determination. *See Katangese Peoples' Congress v. Zaire*, Communication 75/92, reprinted in 3 INT'L HUM. RTS. REP. 136 (1996).

[65] *African Charter*, art. 56(5).

[66] *Id.*

for an indigent to deposit such a fee, he cannot be required to exhaust domestic remedies unless the state provides some alternative mechanism.[67]

Refugees face particular economic, social, and material hardships associated with the condition of displacement that make exhaustion of local remedies a particularly onerous condition to meet. Two developments in the case law of the Commission are relevant in this context.

First, the Commission has established that the requirement to exhaust domestic remedies is subject to three principles of availability, adequacy, and effectiveness, so that an author is not bound to exhaust remedies that are "neither adequate nor effective."[68] In Communication 71/92, *RADDHO v. Zambia*,[69] the Government of Zambia objected on the ground of non-exhaustion of domestic remedies to the admissibility a case filed by on behalf of several hundred West African nationals who had been expelled *en masse* by Zambia. In dismissing Zambia's objection and upholding the admissibility of the communication, the Commission reasoned that Article 56(5) of the Charter "does not mean, however, that complainants are required to exhaust any local remedy which is found to be, as a practical matter, unavailable or ineffective."[70] The Commission pointed out that the victims and their families were collectively deported without regard to possible judicial challenge to such conduct and concluded that the remedies referred to by the respondent state were as a practical matter unavailable.[71] These principles, in the jurisprudence of the Commission, extend to those cases where it is "impractical or undesirable" for a victim or applicant to approach domestic courts,[72] undoubtedly the predicament of most refugee populations.

---

[67] *Advisory Opinion on Exceptions to the Exhaustion of Domestic Remedies in Cases of Indigency or Inability to Obtain Legal Representation Because of a Generalized Fear Within the Legal Community*, Advisory Opinion OC-11/90 (August 10, 1990), reprinted in 12 HUM. RTS. L. J. 20, 22, ¶ 30 (1991) (hereinafter called, "*Advisory Opinion on Exceptions to Exhaustion of Domestic Remedies*").

[68] *Constitutional Rights Project (in respect of Zamani Lekwot & 6 Ors) v. Nigeria*, Communication 87/93 (1995); 8th ANNUAL ACTIVITY REPORT OF THE AFRICAN COMMISSION, AHG/201/XXXI, ANNEX VI, 16, 18, ¶ 6 (1995) (hereinafter "8TH ANNUAL ACTIVITY RPT."), reprinted in 3 INT'L HUM. RTS. REP. 137, 138 (1996) (hereinafter called, "*the Lekwot case*").

[69] *Rencontre Africaine pour THE AFRICAN COMMISSION ON HUMAN & PEOPLES' RIGHTS*, DOC.OS/(XXII), ANNEX X, Communication 71/92, (1997), reprinted in 6 INT'L HUM. RTS. REP. 825 (hereinafter called "*the RADDHO case*").

[70] *Id.* at ¶ 12.

[71] *Id.* at ¶ 15.

[72] *World Organization Against Torture et al v. Zaire*, Communications 25/89, ¶ 37 (1996).

These cases provide proof that the mere existence of domestic procedures without sufficient assurance of accessibility is not of itself sufficient to meet the standard of availability under Article 56(5). Unaffordability of domestic procedures would surely raise questions of access, and therefore of availability, adequacy, and effectiveness.

Second, the Commission has taken the view that the rule regarding exhaustion of domestic remedies is dispensed with in cases of serious and massive violations of human rights. Thus the Commission holds that it must read Article 56(5) in the light of its duty to

> ensure the protection of the human and peoples' rights. . . . The Commission cannot hold the requirement of exhaustion of local remedies to apply literally in cases where it is impractical or undesirable for the complainant to seize the domestic courts in the case of each individual complaint. This is the case where there are a large number of individual victims. Due to the seriousness of the human rights situation as well as the number of people involved, such remedies as might exist in the domestic courts are as a practical matter unavailable or, in the words of the Charter, 'unduly prolonged.'[73]

This exception clearly applies to preclude the need to exhaust domestic remedies in cases of mass displacement or influx. It also extends to situations of indiscriminate violations directed at or against refugee populations. The African Commission took this view in Communication 27/89 etc., *Organisation Mondiale Contre la Torture et al v. Rwanda*, involving the mass expulsion to Burundi by the then Rwandan government of BaTutsi Burundian refugees. The Commission held, on the question of admissibility, that "in view of the vast and varied scope of the violations alleged and the large number of individuals involved...remedies need not be exhausted."[74] On the merits, the Commission found multiple violations of the African Charter including the prohibition against torture, cruel, inhuman and degrading treatment, and due process and affirmed with regard to Article 12(3) of the Charter that "this provision should be read as including a general protection of all those who

---

[73] *Id.* at ¶¶ 56–57.

[74] *Organisation Mondiale Contre la Torture et al v. Rwanda*, supra note 22, at ¶ 17. *Cf.*, however, in *Mouvement des Refugies Mauritaniens au Senegal v. Senegal*, Communication 162/97, (1997), the Commission declined on grounds of nonexhaustion of domestic remedies to consider a communication initiated on behalf of Mauritanian refugees in Senegal who alleged wide ranging violations against Senegalese security forces.

are subject to persecution, that they may seek refuge in another State,"[75] while Article 12(4) effectively prohibits refoulement of refugees.

Other admissibility conditions:

Among other admissibility conditions, Article 56(3) of the Charter requires that communications "are not written in disparaging or insulting language directed against the state concerned and its institutions or to the Organization of African Unity." A communication alleging "government barbarisms" and calling the government of the respondent state a "regime of torturers" has been held inadmissible on this ground.[76] The Charter also precludes the admissibility of communications based exclusively on media reports.[77] Where the domestic remedies were attempted, the communication should be initiated with reasonable promptness after the exhaustion of local remedies.[78] The Commission will not receive a communication that is submitted while a "case with the same parties, alleging the same facts as that before the Commission"[79] has been settled or is pending before another international adjudicatory mechanism.[80] The fact that a matter has been brought to the attention of the High Commissioner for Refugees should not preclude its being considered by the Commission under this requirement.[81]

---

[75] *Organisation Mondiale Contre la Torture et al v. Rwanda*, supra note 22, at ¶ 30. It should be stressed that the right guaranteed in Article 12(3) of the African Charter is that to "seek and obtain asylum." *African Charter*, art. 12(3). The African Charter is unique in this respect in including an implicit obligation on the States parties to grant asylum once the circumstances stipulated in Article 12(3) are met.

[76] *Ligue Cameroonaise des Droits de l'Homme v. Cameroon*, Communication 65/92, (1997). This decision is proof that the purpose of Article 56(3) of the Charter is hard to fathom. *See African Charter*, art. 56(3). It potentially justifies the dismissal of communications for reasons that have nothing to do with the merits of allegations contained in them. For this reason, the authors suggest that this is a provision that the African Commission should be most reluctant to apply.

[77] *African Charter*, art. 56(4).

[78] *Id.* at art. 56(6).

[79] *Mpaka-Nsusu Andre Alphonse v. Zaire*, Communication 15/88 (Admissibility, 1993).

[80] *African Charter*, art. 56(7).

[81] *See* Chidi Anselm Odinkalu and Camilla Christensen, *The African Commission on Human and Peoples' Rights: The Development of Its Non-State Communications Procedures*, 20 HUM. RTS. Q. 235, 266–268 (1998).

Remedies

To prevent irreparable harm in the intermission between the institution of a communication and its conclusion, the Rules of Procedure of the Commission authorize it to indicate as it deems fit interim measures for adoption by any of the parties to the proceedings.[82] For instance, in a case concerning status determination or seeking protection against refoulement, the Commission can request a respondent or host state to ensure that the refugee is not expelled from its territory pending the determination of the merits. The consideration of a Communication ends if or when the Commission finds it inadmissible. If, however, the Commission finds the Communication admissible, it proceeds to consider it on the merits. The Commission usually notifies parties to such proceedings. Through hearing notices issued by its Secretariat, the Commission invites the parties to attend and present their arguments to the hearings by themselves or through counsel if they so choose. The Commission would normally issue a decision at the end of this process, which is made public after it has been transmitted to and adopted by the Assembly of Heads of State and Government of the OAU.

2.1.3 African Court of Human and Peoples' Rights

In June 1998, the OAU supplemented the mechanisms for the protection of human rights in the African Charter by adopting a Protocol, which creates an African Court on Human and Peoples' Rights.[83] This Protocol, yet to come into force,[84] is "to complement the protective mandate of the African Commission on Human and Peoples'

---

[82] *Rules of Procedure of the African Commission on Human and Peoples' Rights*, Rules 111(1), *adopted* Oct. 6, 1995, (made available through the Danish Centre for Human Rights), at <http://www1.umn.edu/humanrts/africa/ rules.htm>.

[83] *See 1998 Protocol to the African Charter on Human and Peoples' Rights on the Establishment of an African Court on Human and Peoples' Rights* (hereinafter called "African Court Protocol") *in* Bibliography of Cited International Instruments.

[84] The Protocol shall come into force 30 days after receipt by the Secretariat of the OAU of the 15th instrument of ratification. *See African Court Protocol*, art. 34(3). As of April 2001, 35 African countries had signed the Protocol, although only five—Burkina Faso, The Gambia, Mali, Senegal, and Uganda—have ratified it. *Organization of African Unity, List of Countries Which have Signed, Ratified/Acceded to the Protocol to the African Charter on Human and Peoples' Rights on the Establishment of an African Court on Human and Peoples' Rights (as at April 2001)*, CAB/LEG/66.5 (2001).

Rights."[85] In effect, the African Court will function as a kind of appellate or review body over decisions reached by the African Commission. The Protocol provides that the jurisdiction of the Court shall extend to cases initiated by:

(1) the African Commission;
(2) a state party in a case in which it was a complainant before the Commission;
(3) a state party in a case in which it was a respondent before the Commission;
(4) a state party whose citizen has been a victim of human rights violations;
(5) African inter-governmental organizations.[86]

The Protocol is silent on this, but it is safe to presume that communications can only be instituted against states parties thereto. In exceptional cases or situations of emergency, the Court may receive directly cases initiated by NGOs in Observer Status with the African Commission against a state that has made the declaration under Article 34(6) of the Protocol recognizing the competence of the Court to consider such communications.[87] This provision could apply to situations of mass displacement resulting in mass exodus or influx of refugees. The Court also has an advisory jurisdiction drafted in terms adapted from Article 45(3) of the African Charter.[88]

The requirements for admissibility of a case by the Court are similar to those before the Commission.[89] In practice, it is unlikely that the Court will reopen the admissibility of cases in respect of which the African Commission has reached a decision on the merits. In the absence of interlocutory procedures enabling parties to appeal against admissibility decisions pending the merits stage, the admissibility requirements in Article 6(2) of the African Court Protocol will in reality only be applicable to those exceptional cases that can be initiated by NGOs under Article 5(3) of the Protocol against states that have made the declaration required to trigger a case in terms of Article 34(6) of the Protocol.

The Court will consist of eleven judges selected by virtue of their being jurists of high moral character with recognized practical, judicial, or academic ability in the field of human and peoples' rights who

---

[85] *African Court Protocol*, art. 2.
[86] *Id.* at art. 5(1).
[87] *Id.* at art. 5(3), 34(6).
[88] *Id.* at art. 4.
[89] *African Charter*, art. 56(1)–(7); *African Court Protocol*, art. 6.

shall serve for a term of six years.[90] The quorum for a sitting of the Court shall be seven.[91] Unlike the Commission, which is served by the Secretariat of the OAU, the Court will have its own Registry with dedicated staff.[92] The functioning of the Court when it comes into force will be governed by the Protocol and Rules of Procedure to be adopted by the Court itself. The Protocol empowers the Court to provide legal assistance to litigants before it, if "the interests of justice so require,"[93] and to indicate interim measures in cases where such is needed to avoid "irreparable harm to persons."[94] The Court will sit and conduct its proceedings in public,[95] and shall deliver its decisions within ninety days of conclusion of its deliberations.[96] A judgment of the Court shall be binding on states parties who shall be obliged to guarantee its execution.[97]

2.1.4 The African Committee of Experts on the Rights and Welfare of the Child

The African Committee of Experts on the Rights and Welfare of the Child (hereinafter "the African Children's Committee") is established under Article XXXII of the 1990 African Charter on the Rights and Welfare of the Child (hereinafter "the OAU Children's Charter" or "the Children's Charter") that came into force in November 1999.[98] The OAU Children's Charter defines a child as "every human being below the age of 18 years."[99] Article XXIII of this Children's Charter addresses refugee children and requires states parties to:

---

[90] *African Court Protocol*, arts. 12, 14.
[91] *Id.* at art. 23.
[92] *Id.* at art 55.
[93] *Id.* at art. 10(2).
[94] *Id.* at art. 27(2).
[95] *Id.* at art. 10(1).
[96] *Id.* at art. 28.
[97] *Id.* at art. 30.
[98] *See* Bibliography of Cited International Instruments. The Committee was to be elected by the 36th Ordinary Session of the Assembly of Heads of State and Government of the OAU in Lomé, Togo, in July 2000. However, at the Lomé Summit, there were only seven nominees for the eleven positions on the Committee. The elections were therefore deferred to the 37th Summit in Lusaka, Zambia in June 2001. Should these elections take place in Lusaka, the Committee will be inaugurated in the last quarter of 2001.
[99] *Id.* at art. II.

Take all appropriate measures to ensure that a child who is seeking refugee status or who is considered a refugee in accordance with applicable international or domestic law shall, whether unaccompanied, or accompanied by parents, legal guardians or close relatives, receive appropriate protection and humanitarian assistance in the enjoyment of the rights set out in this Charter and other international human rights and humanitarian instruments to which the States are parties.[100]

Under the Children's Charter, states parties owe refugee children the dual obligations of protection and assistance, extending, in the case of unaccompanied children, to facilitating the tracing of the child's parents and reunification.[101]

The African Children's Committee is mandated to "promote and protect the rights and welfare of the child" in Africa.[102] It will comprise eleven members "of high moral standing, integrity, impartiality and competence in matters of the rights and welfare of the child,"[103] elected for non-renewable terms of five years by the Assembly of Heads of State and Government of the OAU. The quorum of the Committee shall be seven members.[104] The OAU Children's Charter empowers the Committee to promote and protect the rights in the Charter by formulating and laying down principles and rules on the rights and welfare of the child; cooperating with other African and international institutions working to advance the rights and welfare of the child; monitoring the implementation of the Children's Charter; interpreting the provisions of the Children's Charter at the request of the OAU, its institutions or member states or any other person or institution recognized by the OAU; and performing such other tasks as may be entrusted to it by the OAU, its principal institutions or the United Nations.[105]

The sources that the Committee may look to in interpreting the OAU Children's Charter include the 1981 African Charter on Human and Peoples' Rights, the 1963 Charter of the OAU, the 1948 Universal Declaration of Human Rights, the 1989 Convention on the Rights of the Child, and "other instruments adopted by the United Nations and by African countries in the field of human rights."[106]

---

[100] *Id.* at art. XXIII(1).
[101] *Id.* at art. XXIII(2); XXV(1)–(3).
[102] *Id.* at art. XXXII.
[103] *Id.* at art. XXXIII(1).
[104] *Id.* at art. XXXVIII(3).
[105] *Id.* at art. XLII.
[106] *Id.* at art. XLVI. These sources include the relevant international standards governing refugee law and protection.

The Committee's monitoring role shall be performed through the examination of state reports, which states parties are obliged to submit biennially from the date of the entry into force of the Children's Charter.[107] The Committee may also receive "from any person, group or non-governmental organization recognized by the Organization of African Unity, a member state, or the United Nations" a complaint relating to any matter covered by the OAU Children's Charter.[108] It shall draw up its own rules of procedure.[109] The Committee may resort to any appropriate method of investigation in fulfilling its functions and shall report every two years to the Assembly of Heads of State and Government of the OAU on measures taken by it to realize its mandate.[110]

2.2 The OAU Division for Refugees, Displaced Persons, and Humanitarian Assistance

Since its creation on May 25, 1963, the Organization of African Unity has articulated its commitment to the protection and assistance of refugees. A 1968 conference in Addis Ababa focused attention on the legal, economic, and social aspects of the refugee problem and the particular educational needs of refugees. This led to the establishment of the OAU Bureau for the Placement, Education and Training of Refugees and was followed a year later by the 1969 OAU Convention Governing the Specific Aspects of Refugee Problems in Africa. The Convention's introduction of a new expanded definition of refugee status was one of the more progressive pieces of legislation of its time. Initially independent of the OAU Secretariat, the Refugee Bureau was brought under the direct control of the Political Department in 1974. Over the years, it has been restructured and renamed a number of times and today it is known as the Division for Refugees, Displaced Persons, and Humanitarian Assistance.

Historically, the Bureau for the Placement, Education, and Training of Refugees focused primarily on the issue of resettlement and the provision of education and training to refugees. However, with Africa's escalating refugee problem, there has been a subtle change in emphasis and the last decade has seen the OAU focus more on addressing the "root causes" of the African refugee crisis.[111] The incorporation of

---

[107] *Id.* at art. XLIII.
[108] *Id.* at art. XLIV.
[109] *Id.* at art. XXXVIII.
[110] *Id.* at art. XLV.
[111] This change in emphasis coincided with the reorganization in 1991 of the Political Department of the OAU which led to the creation of a division exclusively concerned with conflict management among member states, which

"displaced persons" into the title of the Division suggests an increasing awareness of the need to address the problem of internal displacement on the continent—a problem that in scale and complexity surpasses even that of the refugee crisis in Africa.

As noted above, since 1974 the Division has been an integral part of the Political Department, a fact that has hampered its ability to play an active role in the protection arena. Its mandate, developed over several years of its existence, is to:

(1) seek educational and economic opportunities for refugees in host countries;
(2) act as an information conduit to the member states and the international community on the patterns, causes and consequences of refugee movements in Africa;
(3) equip refugees with the resources that would assist them in coping with their predicament and upon their eventual voluntary return to their countries of origin;
(4) mediate between host countries and refugees with respect to alleged violations of national legislation committed by refugees; and
(5) operate in association with the UNHCR, voluntary agencies, and member states to ensure the realization of the objectives enshrined in the OAU Convention.[112]

A direct role in relation to monitoring and supervising the implementation of the 1969 OAU Refugee Convention is noticeably absent and, although the Division has often asserted that protection is a part of its activities, "it is apparent that the Bureau merely pays lip-service to the question of protection."[113] Given the inherently politicized environment in which it operates, the Division is unable to issue public criticisms of member states' policies vis-à-vis the displaced and must instead urge or encourage states through quiet diplomacy to abide by their obligations under the 1969 OAU Refugee Convention. Such interventions do not appear to have had much of an effect over the years.

The Division functions in large part as the secretariat to the Commission on Refugees, which meets once a year and is composed

---

itself offers up new and interesting possibilities for advancing the rights of those displaced (see discussion below).

[112] LAWYERS COMMITTEE FOR HUMAN RIGHTS, AFRICAN EXODUS: REFUGEE CRISIS, HUMAN RIGHTS AND THE 1969 OAU CONVENTION 144 (1995). See <http://www.lchr.org/pubs/pubs.htm#AFRICA>.

[113] Id. at 158.

of the Ambassadors of OAU Member States based in Addis Ababa. The Commission, established in 1964 as a Commission of 10, is today a Commission of 20, and is the principal policy-making organ of the OAU on all matters relating to refugees in Africa. It submits its recommendations to the Council of Ministers, which in turn reports to the Assembly of Heads of State. The Commission performs a number of functions; of most interest to advocates perhaps it its ability to undertake missions to OAU member states and provide advice to governments regarding the management of their refugee populations as well as emergency financial assistance to this end. Moreover, the Commission has the capacity to take initiatives to shape the OAU's response to refugee issues as it did with the 1991 Khartoum Declaration on Africa's Refugee Crisis. However its sphere of action is also constrained by the principle of non-interference, which is enshrined in the OAU Charter, and the composition of the Commission, which is highly politicized.

An obstacle currently faced by the Division is its inability to attract sufficient funding to fulfill even its nominal functions. Its basic operating funds are provided through the Refugee Contingency Fund established by the Assembly of Heads of States at the beginning of the 1990–91 financial year, which sets the operating budget at 2% of the OAU's annual operating budget. This in turn, however, is dependent on member states meeting their financial obligations to the OAU, which is not always a given.

The Refugee Division, it must be said, does not inspire much confidence in its current form. It is chronically understaffed, under-funded, and constrained by politics in pursuing any kind of effective protection strategy. Nevertheless, it is important that NGOs and advocates do not sideline the Division in their advocacy efforts. A collective effort to focus attention on the Division can only encourage it to live up to even the limited role that it has carved out for itself. The Division has a part to play with respect to both individual refugees (in fulfilling its mediation function between host countries and refugees) as well as in issues that impact broader groups of refugees or displaced persons. For instance, the Division's role in seeking out educational and economic opportunities for refugees in host countries should lead it to questions regarding the enabling environment which exist for refugees in these countries and, in particular, the question of access to socio-economic rights, including the right to education.

Finally, advocates would do well to highlight and reinforce the rights context for the work of the Refugee Division. Indeed, given the close relationship that exists between human rights violations and the occurrence of forced displacement, advocates should encourage closer working links between the African Commission, the Commission of 20 and the Refugee Division, a call that has been echoed a number of times by the African Commission itself.

2.3 The OAU Mechanism for Conflict Prevention, Management, and Resolution

The creation of the OAU Mechanism for Conflict Prevention, Management, and Resolution marks an important milestone in the development of the organization. In 1990, the OAU took the unprecedented step of committing itself to work towards the speedy resolution of all conflicts in Africa, including those *within* States. This led in June 1993 to a Declaration on the Establishment of a Mechanism for Conflict Prevention, Management and Resolution, adopted at the Cairo Summit. The OAU reaffirmed its commitment to a Mechanism in 1997, in another Declaration of the Heads of State during their Summit in Harare, Zimbabwe.

Although it is tempting to view the creation of the Mechanism as a departure from the OAU's commitment to the principle of non-interference in the internal affairs of member states, the 1993 Cairo Declaration refers to sovereign equality, non-interference, and the necessity for consent and cooperation among parties to a conflict. An important limitation on the effectiveness of the Mechanism thus lies in the need for the consent of the State concerned before any report on that country is placed on the agenda of the Central Organ.

The Conflict Resolution Mechanism (CRM) has two objectives: to anticipate and prevent conflicts in Africa and to plan and implement peace-making/peace-building functions where conflicts are already in progress. The emphasis of the CRM, however, is primarily on anticipatory and preventive action. Tackling the root causes of conflict is thus recognized as infinitely more desirable than the more complex and expensive option of dealing with conflicts after they break out.[114] Herein lies an opening for advocates to bring human rights concerns to the attention of the Mechanism.

The Mechanism is structured around a Central Organ, based in Addis Ababa, which is responsible for the overall direction and co-ordination of the Mechanism's activities. The Central Organ is composed of member states that meet at the level of Heads of State, Ministers, and Ambassadors, annually, bi-annually, and monthly respectively.

The operation arms of the Mechanism are the good offices function of the OAU Secretary General and the Conflict Management

---

[114] *See* Amnesty International, *Organization of African Unity: Making Human Rights a Reality for Africans*, §4.2, Report IOR 63/01/98 (1998).

Division of the OAU Department of Political Affairs. As the chief executive of the Central Organ, the Secretary General is empowered to take all appropriate measures to prevent, manage, and resolve conflicts, in consultation with concerned parties and in coordination with relevant international and regional actors. Measures at the Secretary-General's disposal can range from the issuance of statements to authorizing fact-finding missions and dispatching special envoys.

The Conflict Management Division of the OAU Secretariat is responsible for gathering information, assessing conflict situations, and preparing reports on behalf of the Secretary General for consideration by the Central Organ and the Council of Ministers. It is composed of three sections: (1) the Conflict Prevention and Research Section, (2) the Conflict Resolution, Defense and Security section and (3) the Military Section. The Division has also set up an early warning system, to enable it to receive and exchange information with other intergovernmental bodies, NGOs and academic institutions. Information is gathered by Early Warning System (EWS) staff primarily through OAU field offices. Where appropriate, the EWS will serve to warn the Secretary General of potential areas of conflict and propose appropriate forms of intervention. Although this is an important mechanism through which to bring human rights concerns to the table, it is unfortunate that few NGOs are aware of its existence.[115]

3. Sub-Regional Mechanisms

3.1 The Economic Community of West African States (ECOWAS)

The Economic Community of West African States (ECOWAS) was founded by treaty on May 28, 1975, to advance regional economic integration in West Africa.[116] It comprises the 16 West African States of Benin Republic, Burkina Faso, Cape Verde, Côte d'Ivoire, Gambia, Ghana, Guinea, Guinea Bissau, Liberia, Mali, Mauritania,[117] Niger, Nigeria, Senegal, Sierra Leone, and Togo. The main organs of the organization are a Secretariat hosted by Nigeria, a Ministerial Council, and the Authority of Heads of States and Governments (the authority)— the highest policy and decision making organ of the Community— which meets at least once annually.

---

[115] *Id.* at 13.

[116] *1975 Treaty Establishing the Economic Community of West African States (ECOWAS), in* Bibliography of Cited International Instruments.

[117] Mauritania has recently indicated its intention to denounce the ECOWAS Treaty thereby vacating its membership of the Community effective from the beginning of 2001.

284 Human Rights Protection for Displaced Persons

At its creation, ECOWAS was mostly, if not exclusively, conceived as a regional zone of preference allowed under Article XXIV of the General Agreement on Tariffs and Trade (GATT). The Protocol Relating to Mutual Assistance in Defense[118] adopted in May 1981 added regional defense and security to the mandate of ECOWAS. This Protocols articulated a rather narrow concept of peace and security that was reactive instead of proactive, and failed to include social justice, human rights, and democratic governance in the concept of regional security. The Protocol on Mutual Assistance, therefore, merely envisaged the deployment of the regional security efforts in reaction to situations of unrest, conflict, or mass displacement.

In December 1989, an insurgency led by Charles Taylor, now President of Liberia, began in Liberia. On August 25, 1990, at the invitation of the then government of Liberia, ECOWAS deployed a plurinational cease-fire Monitoring Group (ECOMOG), comprising military contingents contributed by respective member States of ECOWAS, to restore peace in Liberia.[119] This deployment was to trigger a re-think of the narrow perception of ECOWAS and an expansion of its mandate to actively include human rights and, implicitly, refugees in the preservation of regional peace and security. On May 30, 1990, shortly after the outbreak of hostilities in Liberia but prior to the deployment ECOMOG in Liberia, the Authority decided, in the light of evolving regional security concerns, to establish a Committee of Eminent Persons to review the 1975 treaty.[120]

Upon conclusion of its work in June 1992, the Committee proposed a new draft treaty with significant amendments giving prominence to social justice, human rights, and new institutions, including a Community Court of Justice.[121] Among its conclusions and recommendations, the Committee urged ECOWAS, within a revised treaty, to "shift from its exclusive focus on government to government, to involving the people, NGOs and private sector"[122] and adopt "provisions estab-

---

[118] See Bibliography of Cited International Instruments.

[119] It would appear that the legal bases of the ECOMOG intervention in Liberia were the *Community Protocol on Non-Aggression*, April 22, 1978, and the *Protocol Relating to Mutual Assistance on Defence*, May 29, 1981. *See* BRUNO SIMMA ET AL., THE CHARTER OF THE UNITED NATIONS: A COMMENTARY 707 (1995).

[120] Authority of Heads of States and Government, Decision A/Dec. 10/5/90, May 30, 1990.

[121] Economic Community of West African States (ECOWAS), *Review of the ECOWAS Treaty: Final Report by the Committee of Eminent Persons*, (June 1992), (hereinafter referred to as "Final Report of the Committee of Eminent Persons").

[122] *Id.* at ¶ 25(ii)(a).

lishing organs such as the Parliament of the Community composed of representatives elected by the peoples of the Member states, and an Economic and Social Council (ECOSOC) comprising socio-professional groups drawn from all sections and categories of the population of the Member States."[123] The revised Treaty was adopted in Cotonou, Benin Republic, in July 1993[124] and, together with the protocols adopted before and after 1993 represents, with the several protocols adopted within the Community framework, the current constitutional framework for ECOWAS.

3.1.1 Aims and Objectives of the ECOWAS

The objectives of ECOWAS are contained in Article 3 of the revised treaty of 1993. As stated in Article 3(1) of the treaty:

> [T]he aims of the Community are to promote co-operation and integration leading to the establishment of an economic union in West Africa in order to raise the living standards of its peoples, and to maintain and enhance economic stability, foster relations among member states and contribute to the progress and development of the African continent.

To achieve this aim, the West African states parties to the treaty undertake through the Community to pursue a set of objectives including harmonization and co-ordination of national policies and the promotion and integration of programs, projects, and activities in, *inter alia*, transport, natural resources, food and agriculture, economic reform policies, human resources, education, information, culture, science, the environment, health, tourism, and legal matters.[125] The Community confers legal mandate for the implementation of the obligations under the treaty through protocols and decisions of Authority of Heads of States and Governments.

One of the most far-reaching consequences of the review of the 1975 ECOWAS Treaty was a recommendation for the adoption of Fundamental Principles by the Community. These Principles, now contained in Article 4 of the 1993 Treaty, include maintenance of regional peace, stability, and security through the promotion of good

---

[123] *Id.* at ¶ 27(b)(vii).
[124] *1993 Revised Treaty of the Economic Community of West African States*, in Bibliography of Cited International Instruments (hereinafter called "Revised ECOWAS Treaty").
[125] *Id.* at art. 3(2)(a)–(b).

neighborliness;[126] peaceful settlement of disputes among member states;[127] recognition, promotion, and protection of human and peoples' rights in accordance with the provisions of the 1981 African Charter on Human and Peoples' Rights;[128] accountability, economic and social justice, and popular participation in development;[129] and promotion and consolidation of a democratic system of governance in each member state.[130] Through these new provisions, the Community adverts to the root causes of refugee flows in West Africa. The standards of the 1981 African Charter on Human and Peoples' Rights are specifically adopted as the reference point for the human rights obligations under the ECOWAS Treaty, including the obligations under Article 12(3) of the Charter guaranteeing "the right, when persecuted, to seek and obtain asylum in other countries,"[131] as well as the prohibition of mass expulsion of non-nationals under the Charter.[132] It is arguable that, to the extent that the ECOWAS treaty is a supranational treaty instrument directly applicable as domestic law within its member states, this provision achieves domestication of the 1981 African Charter on Human and Peoples' Rights.[133]

---

[126] *Id.* at art. 4(e).
[127] *Id.* at art. 4(f).
[128] *Id.* at art. 4(g). All the ECOWAS member States are also party to the African Charter.
[129] *Id.* at art. 4(h).
[130] *Id.* at art. 4(j).
[131] *African Charter*, art.12(3).
[132] *Id.* at 12(5).
[133] In its report, the Committee of Eminent Persons recommended that ECOWAS should operate on the principle of supranationality. In the words of the Committee:

> It is proposed that the principle of supranationality should be introduced in the ECOWAS structure and operations. . . . [I]t is sufficient to provide that decisions of the Authority and regulations of the Council shall be binding on not only the institutions of the Community but on Member States as well.

See Final Report of the Committee of Eminent Persons, supra note 121 at ¶¶ 57–58 (1992). This recommendation was implemented in Article 9(4) of the Revised Treaty of 1993 which provides that "[d]ecisions of the Authority shall be binding on the Member States and institutions of the Community. . . ." subject to the judicial powers reserved to the proposed Community Court of Justice by Article 15 of the Treaty. *Revised ECOWAS Treaty*, arts. 9(4), 15.

3.1.2 Institutions of the Community

The Institutions of the Community as envisaged under the revised Treaty are:

(i) the Authority of Heads of State and Governments;
(ii) the Council of Ministers;
(iii) the Community Parliament;
(iv) the Economic and Social Council;
(v) the Community Court of Justice;
(vi) the Executive Secretariat;
(vii) the Fund for Co-operation, Compensation and Development;
(viii) Specialized Technical Commissions; and
(ix) any other institutions established by the Authority.[134]

Among the technical Commissions, there is one on Political, Judicial and Legal Affairs. A technical body on regional security and immigration now comprises a regular meeting of the Service Chiefs or representatives of the Service Chiefs of the member states of the Community. The Field Commander of ECOMOG whose present operational base is in Freetown, Sierra Leone regularly joins them in their meetings.

3.1.3 The ECOWAS, Human Rights, and Migration

Among the declared objectives of ECOWAS, the Community seeks to achieve the liberalization of cross-border trade and movement among its members involving, among other things, the removal of obstacles to the free movement of persons, goods, services and capital, and to the rights of residence and establishment.[135] ECOWAS citizens[136] therefore enjoy rights of free movement within the sub-region including rights of residence and establishment in member states. These rights exist to protect all Community nationals in the territory of a member state of the Community irrespective of whether or not they are refugees.

The 1979 Protocol Relating to Free Movement of Persons and the Right of Residence and Establishment,[137] adopted in May 1979 and

---

[134] *Revised ECOWAS Treaty*, art. 6(1)(a)–(I).
[135] *Id.* at art. 3(d)(i)–(iii).
[136] The concept of "Community Citizen" and how it is acquired and lost is the subject of *Protocol Relating to the Definition of Community Citizen*, adopted by ECOWAS. *See* Bibliography of Cited International Instruments.
[137] *See* Bibliography of Cited International Instruments.

since then supplemented by decisions of the Community institutions, outlines the rights of Community citizens and the responsibilities that are incidental to these rights. Briefly, in its present stage of implementation, Community Citizens are entitled to visa free travel to within the territories of ECOWAS States for up to ninety days. To facilitate the right of free movement of persons in the Community, ECOWAS established an ECOWAS Travel Certificate ("ECOWAS Travel Card") that is obtainable from the government of each member state.[138] The right of residence within the Community is also presently operational. Community nationals resident in a country other than their country of nationality are entitled to a special ECOWAS residence card.[139] The third phase is the right to establishment which places states within the Community under an obligation to accord Community Nationals national treatment on a non-discriminatory basis in the establishment of businesses and services.[140] This is not yet fully operational.

A code of conduct regulates the operation of the rights of migrants in the Community. This code of conduct enjoys treaty status having been adopted as one of the implementing protocols to the Treaty.[141] Among other things, this protocol imposes obligations on member states relating the treatment of intra-community migrants, including migration resulting from forcible displacement. In practice, this entails that ECOWAS citizens who are involuntarily displaced from their own countries may nevertheless be able to relocate to other ECOWAS countries. The only reason why a member state may close its borders to community migrants is "internal security" and, in such situations, the member state taking the decision is required to promptly notify both the Executive Secretariat and the member states of the Community.[142] Theoretically at least, it is not open to ECOWAS states to refuse to admit migrants, including refugees who are Community citizens. Once on the territory of another state in the Community, Community citizens, "shall have . . . under the same conditions as . . . nationals, freedom to pros-

---

[138] *Decision of the Authority of Heads of State and Government of the Economic Community of West African States Relating to the Establishment of ECOWAS Travel Certificate for Member States*, A/Dec.2/7/85, July 6, 1985.

[139] *Decision of the Authority of Heads of State and Government Establishing a Residence Card in ECOWAS Member States*, A/Dec. 2/5/90, May 30, 1990.

[140] *1990 Supplementary Protocol on the Implementation of the Third Phase (Right of Establishment) of the Protocol on Free Movement of Persons, Right of Residence and Establishment.* See Bibliography of Cited International Instruments.

[141] *1985 Supplementary Protocol on the Code of Conduct for the Implementation of the Protocol on Free Movement of Persons, the Right of Residence and Establishment.* See Bibliography of Cited International Instruments.

[142] *Id.* at art. 8(2).

ecute and defend their rights under any jurisdiction."[143] The right most positively affected in this context is the right to freedom from discrimination as these provisions accord national treatment to Community citizens irrespective of their country of origin or reason for migration.

3.1.4 The Community Court of Justice

The rights in the Treaty and the Protocols are designed to be implemented through a combination of political, administrative, and judicial means. In its report, the Committee of Eminent Persons summarized these implementing mechanisms as follows:

> [L]egal proceedings against member states should however be a weapon of last resort for obvious reasons. As a rule, the Community should seek accountability from member states through such subtle means as regular submission of status reports by member states on implementation of Community decisions and regulations. . . . The Executive Secretariat may also be authorized to invite status reports on implementation from member states on a regular basis and also to bring to the attention of Council or the Authority breaches of Community Laws by member States. Where, however, a Community citizen alleges a breach or denial of a right conferred on him by a Community legislation, a Treaty provision or a protocol, it should be possible for him to seek redress in the national court or the Community Court of Justice. This is particularly germane to the application of the Community's Protocol on Free Movement of Persons, Right of Residence and Establishment.[144]

The 1991 Protocol on the Community Court of Justice[145] has recently come into force, although the Court has yet to be formally inaugurated. This Court has jurisdiction to supervise the implementation of the treaty, interpreting its provisions, adjudicating disputes arising under it, and enforcing the rights of Community nationals under the treaty.[146] The Court shall comprise seven "independent" members

---

[143] *Id.* at art. 7(5).
[144] *Final Report of the Committee of Eminent Persons, supra* note 121 at 20–21, ¶¶ 62–63.
[145] *See* Bibliography of Cited International Instruments.
[146] *Id.* at art. 9.

elected by the Authority of Heads of State and Government of ECOWAS.[147]

Under Article 9 of the Protocol establishing the Community Court of Justice, standing to bring cases to the Court is restricted to governments only. The Committee of Eminent Persons recommended that this provision should be amended to extend standing to individuals and NGOs[148] but this amendment has not yet been adopted. However, a member state may, on behalf of its nationals, institute proceedings against another member state or Institution of the Community.[149] At first blush, this provision would seem suited to the protection of refugees under the ECOWAS Treaty. However, the state of origin is unlikely to be in a position to take legal action against another state in the Community hosting its nationals as refugees in a situation of mass displacement. And a refugee who flees because of fear of persecution is not exactly the most likely person to benefit from the assertion of this prerogative of diplomatic protection either. Unless standing requirements for the institution of proceedings before the Community Court of Justice are liberalized through an amendment of the protocol or liberal rules of intervention are introduced in the rules of procedure of the Court when they are adopted, the Community Court of Justice currently offers little scope as a forum for the protection of the rights of refugees and other displaced persons in West Africa. Moreover, in the absence of a specific jurisdictional clause, it is unclear whether the incorporation by reference in the revised ECOWAS Treaty of the 1981 African Charter of Human and Peoples' Rights is sufficient to confer jurisdiction on the dispute resolution mechanisms under the Charter to protect the rights of migrants (including refugees) under the ECOWAS Treaty. This subject is suitable for the advisory jurisdiction of the African Charter institutions as well as the ECOWAS Court of Justice.

3.2 L'Union Économique et Monétaire de l'Afrique de l'Ouest (UEMOA)

On January 10, 1994, a Treaty establishing the Union Économique et Monétaire de L'Afrique de l'Ouest or the West African Economic and Monetary Union was signed into being by seven countries—Benin, Burkina Faso, Côte d'Ivoire, Mali, Niger, Senegal and Togo.[150] The

---

[147] *Id.* at art. 3 (1)–(2).
[148] *Final Report of the Committee of Eminent Persons, supra* note 121.
[149] *Revised ECOWAS Treaty*, art. 9(3).
[150] *1994 Union Economique et Monetaire de L'Afrique de l'Ouest* (hereinafter referred to as "UEMOA Treaty"). *See* Bibliography of Cited International Instruments.

Treaty entered into force in January 1995 and in May 1997 Guinea-Bissau joined the Union as the eighth member.

3.2.1 Aims and Objectives of the UEMOA

UEMOA's objectives, spelled out in Articles 2–8 of the Treaty, are principally economic and market-oriented in nature. Building on the common currency shared by the member states, the Union seeks to create a common market based on the free movement of persons, goods, services, and capital and the attainment of rights of residence and establishment in member states. To that end, the Treaty envisions the harmonization of the monetary and fiscal policies of the individual member states and common actions and conceivably common policies in the following areas: human resources, transport and telecommunications, community-based land reclamation, environment, agriculture, mining, energy, and industry. In addition, the Treaty envisions the harmonization of legislation of the member states. Article 6 provides that acts of the organs of the Union taken in pursuance of these objectives supercede domestic legislation.

3.2.2 Institutions of the Union

The Union establishes the following institutions:

(i) Authority of Heads of State and Governments
(ii) Council of Ministers
(iii) Commission
(iv) Court of Justice
(v) Court of Accounts
(vi) Interparliamentary Committee
(vii) Consultative Bodies—the Regional Consular Board
(viii) Autonomous Specialized Bodies—the Banque Centrale des Etats de l'Afrique de l'Ouest (BCEAO) and a Banque Ouest Africaine de Développement (BOAD)

The institutions of the UEMOA are outlined in Article 16 of the Treaty. The supreme organ is the Authority of the Heads of State and Government, which is the principal policy-making body of the Union, meeting at least once a year.[151] Below it is the Council of Ministers, which meets at least twice a year and which is responsible for the implementation of the policies and directions defined by the Authority. The

---

[151] *Id.* at art. 17–19.

Council exercises the functions assigned to it by the Union Treaty and operates under the supervision of the Authority. It is empowered to enforce regulations, directives, and decisions passed by the Authority. It is also responsible for drawing up the Union budget. The executive arm of the Union is the Commission. Commissioners are citizens of member states and appointed by the Authority of Heads of States and Governments for a renewable period of 4 years. The Commission is delegated by the Council to give recommendations and opinions that it deems useful for the preservation of the Union and its development. It is also responsible for executing the budget of the Union. The Commission is empowered to seize the Court of Justice when member states refuse to abide by Community based law. It is based in Ouagadougou, Burkina Faso. In addition, the Treaty also provides for a Court of Justice and a Budget and Finance Tribunal[152] as well as an Inter-Parliamentary Committee which foreshadows a future UEMOA Parliament. Composed of 40 members, 5 from each Member country, it is based in Bamako, Mali.[153] Finally, the Treaty provides for a number of autonomous specialized organs—the *Banque Centrale des Etats de l'Afrique de l'Ouest* (BCEAO) and a *Banque Ouest Africaine de Développement* (BOAD)[154] as well as a consultative organ, the Regional Consular Board, and reserves the option of creating other such bodies in the future.[155]

3.2.3 The UEMOA, Human Rights, and Migration

Despite the market orientation of the Union, Article 3 of the Treaty reaffirms the commitment of member states of the UEMOA to respect for the 1948 Universal Declaration of Human Rights as well as the 1981 African Charter on Human and People's Rights. Article 91 of the UEMOA Treaty provides for freedom of movement and the right of establishment of all citizens of member states within the territory of the Union and prohibits discrimination on the basis of nationality. Article 93 further provides for the free movement of services and stipulates that citizens of an UEMOA member state have the right to seek employment on the territory of another member state, on the same basis and under the same conditions imposed on nationals of that state. However, it remains to be seen how widely states will interpret the exceptions which they are allowed to invoke on grounds of public order, public security, and public health, in order to exempt themselves from the

---

[152] *Id.* at art. 38–39.
[153] *Id.* at art. 35–37.
[154] *Id.* at art. 41.
[155] *Id.* at art. 40.

freedom of movement provisions.[156] In addition, Article 94 adds "reasons of general public interest" to the list of possible grounds on which states can derogate from the free movement of services provisions and those providing for the right of establishment. However, states will have to inform the Commission of any such derogations and the Commission will review these annually in a bid to progressively eliminate them.[157] All of these provisions will have important implications for refugees in the region. On the plus side, measures assuring the free movement of Community citizens can support the implementation of the principle of non-refoulement; moreover the strong non-discrimination provisions contained in Article 91 and Article 96 may go some way towards alleviating the problems that skilled or urban refugees encounter in exile. However, it is important that such provisions should be seen as complementary to rather than a replacement of the Refugee Conventions.

3.2.4 The Community Court of Justice

The Community Court of Justice came into being six months after the UEMOA Treaty entered into force.[158] A number of additional Protocols and regulations have since been passed in order to supplement the Treaty and to provide greater detail on the structure and functioning of the Court.[159] The Court is based in Ouagadougou, Burkina Faso.[160] The official language of the Court is French.[161]

Justices at the Court are to be appointed by the Assembly of Heads of State and Government, with due regard to their judicial competency and independence, for a renewable period of 6 years. Seven judges are to sit on the court and a quorum of three must be present for a case to be heard.[162] The judges in turn nominate a President who is to serve

---

[156] *Id.* at art. 91[1], 91[3][c], 92[3], 93, 94.
[157] *Id.* at art. 94, at ¶ 2.
[158] *Id.* at art. 109.
[159] *Protocole Additionnel Rélatif aux Organes de Contrôle de l' UEMOA*, Additional Protocol No. 1, (hereinafter, "Protocol No. 1"); *L'Acte Additionnel no 1/95 du Mars 1995 portant nominations des membres de la cour de justice; Règlement portant Règlement de Procedures de la Cour de Justice*, réglement No. 1/96/CM/UEMOA (hereinafter Réglement No. 1/96/CM)); *Règlement portant statut de greffier de la Cour de Justice de l'UEMOA*, reglement no. 2/96/CM/UEMOA; *Règlement portant définition des caractéristiques des costumes d'audience des membres de la Cour de Justice de l'UEMOA et du greffier de la Cour*, réglement no. 3/96/CM/UEMOA *Règlement administratif de la Cour e Justice no. 01/CJUE adopté par la Cour de Justice de l'UEMOA le 10 Décembre 1996.*
[160] *Réglement No. 1/96/CM, supra* note 159, at art. 16.
[161] *Id.* at art. 21.
[162] *Id.* at arts. 1, 17.

for a term of 3 years.[163] Decisions are to be made by majority[164] and its judgments are binding on all national judicial and administrative bodies.[165] The Court's sessions are to be open to the public.[166]

All parties before the Court must be represented by a lawyer registered with the Bar Association of one of the member states.[167] However, indigent parties will be financially assisted by the Court in order to secure the services of a lawyer.[168]

Jurisdictional Issues, Admissibility Requirements, and Standing

The Court has jurisdiction over all matters relating to the interpretation and application of the UEMOA Treaty, as well as the legality and interpretation of measures taken by the various organs of the Union. In addition, the Court adjudicates on disputes between the Union and its agents or employees.[169] It is the only body competent to rule on the liability of the Union to pay damages or to take appropriate measures to redress an injury caused by the Union or one of its agents in the course of their work. However, any action for damages must occur within three years of the injury.[170]

Under Article 15(2) of *Règlement* No. 1, the Court can hear petitions to evaluate the legality of any act by the Union and its organs.[171] This measure can be invoked against any regulations, directives, or decisions of the Union organs.

All legal and natural persons have standing to petition if they believe that they have been harmed by an action of the UEMOA. Potentially, this enables a very wide class of persons, including refugees and the internally displaced, to bring a case before the Court. Indeed, since there is neither a citizenship nor residency requirement, it is conceivable that refugees from even farther afield than the UEMOA countries can benefit from the provision. Unfortunately, however, the *Senegal Conseil d'État* appeared to limit this prospect when it ruled that six stu-

---

[163] *Id.* at prot. no. 1 arts. 2, 6.
[164] *Id.* at art. 20.
[165] *Id.* at prot. no. 1 arts. 13, 14.
[166] *Id.* at prot. no. 1 art. 3.
[167] *Id.* at art. 22.
[168] *Id.* at art. 65.
[169] *Id.* at prot. no. 1 arts. 1, 12. The Court will also hear disputes between the Union and its employees or agents. *Id.* at prot. no. 1 art. 16. *See also id.* at art. 15(4) (*"du recours du personnel de l'union"*).
[170] *Id.* at art. 15(5) (*"du recour en responsabilité"*).
[171] *Id.* (*"du recours en appréciation de légalité"*).

dents from Cameroon were unable to benefit from the non-discrimination provisions of Article 96 of the UEMOA Treaty because they were not citizens of a member state of the Union.[172] In addition, member states as well as the Committee and Commission can petition the Court to evaluate the legality of decisions, regulations, and directives of the UEMOA. However, proceedings must be initiated within two months of publication or notification of the act to the injured party, or failing that, within two months of the day that it came to the attention of the injured party.[173] Where a member state refuses to abide by community law, the Court can hear petitions for non-performance of a Treaty obligation,[174] which can be initiated by the Commission and individual member states. However, the offending member state must have been notified by the Commission and three months elapsed without steps being taken to rectify the problem before the claim can be admitted before the Court. If the Court finds the complaint to be well founded, it will issue a judgment that is binding on all member states and their domestic institutions. If the state continues to refuse to abide by the Court's decision, the Court can refer the matter to the Authority, which is empowered to impose sanctions on the state concerned under Article 74 of the UEMOA Treaty. Whilst it is unlikely that a member state will ever institute an action on behalf of refugees, useful jurisprudence may emerge through this vehicle on the scope of the freedom of movement provisions of the UEMOA Treaty.

Where a question arises before a national court pertaining to the interpretation of the Treaty and the legality of its actions, the national court can voluntarily request an advisory opinion from the Community Court on the matter. However, where a question regarding one of these issues comes before a national court of last instance, it is under an obligation to refer them to the Court.[175] In addition the Court is able to render advisory opinions at the request of the Commission on any matter that the Commission is considering. Finally, the Committee, Commission and any member state can request the advisory opinion of the Court on the compatibility of international instruments with the UEMOA Treaty.[176]

---

[172] *Prosper Guéna NITCHEN et autres vs. L'Université Cheikh Anta Diop de Dakar*, Arret No. 0076, (August 31, 1994).
[173] *Protocol I, supra* note 159, at art. 8.
[174] *Réglement No. 1/96/CM, "Du recours en mânquement," supra* note 159 at art. 15(1).
[175] *Id.* at art. 15(6) *("du recours préjudiciel")*.
[176] *Id.* at art. 15(7) *("des avis et des recommandations")*.

Procedure Before the UEMOA Court

A case can be initiated before the Court by lodging a petition before the President of the Court which contains the full name and address of the petitioner, the name and address of the lawyer acting on their behalf, the name of the defendant in the proceedings, the object of the complaint, the brief of the petitioner, as well as a summary of the grounds for the petition.[177] Where the petitioner is requesting that a particular act be quashed, it should include a copy of the act or legislation in question. The defendant must respond to the petition within a month. An oral hearing follows.[178] Judgments are rendered in public[179] and are binding from the day that they are pronounced.[180] Costs are borne by the loser, although the Court reserves to itself the discretion to order a winner to bear part of the costs of the suit.[181]

Interim Measures

Whilst an action brought before the Court does not have automatic suspensive effect, the Court can order that interim measures be taken on a matter of which it is currently seized.[182] The petitioner would have to request such measures of the Court and show their legal and factual basis and why they are needed. The matter is adjudicated upon by the President of the Court.[183]

Review

It is possible to petition the Court to review its decision within three months of judgment, on a written application by the party seeking the review.[184]

---

[177] *Id.* at art. 26.
[178] *Id.* at arts. 34–54. Articles 34–54 specify in detail the conduct of the hearing.
[179] *Id.* at arts. 55–58.
[180] *Id.* at art. 57.
[181] Costs are dealt with under arts. 60–64.
[182] *Protocol I, supra* note 159, at art. 18; *Règlement No. 1/96/CM, supra* note 159, at arts. 72–76.
[183] *Règlement No. 1/96/CM, supra* note 159, at art. 72.
[184] *Id.* at arts. 82–84.

3.3 The Inter-Governmental Authority on Development (IGAD)

The Inter-Gvernmental Authority on Development (IGAD) is the primary regional organization now active in the Horn of Africa. Its membership is made up of Djibouti, Eritrea, Ethiopia, Kenya, Somalia, Sudan, and Uganda; the organization has its seat in Djibouti. Established in 1986 as the Inter-Gvernmental Authority on Drought and Development, IGAD was originally created to coordinate the efforts of member states in controlling drought and desertification.[185] IGAD was conceived as an early warning mechanism that could alert member states and the international community to humanitarian emergencies in the region and coordinate responses to cope with these crises. However, its potential to act as a medium through which the region could tackle other political and socio-economic issues was highlighted by the Sudan Peace Process, chaired by Kenyan President Daniel Arap Moi, which brought IGAD into the limelight. It led the member countries, including Eritrea since 1993, to reconceive the objectives and structure of the organization so as to better equip it to address a wider array of regional issues.

To this end, a Special Summit of the Heads of State and Government of IGAD was held on April 18, 1995 to deliberate on the revitalization of IGAD and potential areas of common interest. The revitalization process, which was completed in November 1996, resulted in a revised Charter and designated three priority areas for the organization:

- Food security and environmental protection;
- Political and humanitarian affairs, including conflict prevention, mitigation, and resolution; and
- Regional economic cooperation.

3.3.1 The IGAD Institutions

The Authority is composed of an Assembly of Heads of State and Government that meets at least once a year and is the supreme decision-

---

[185] The founding members were Djibouti, Ethiopia, Kenya, Somalia, Sudan, and Uganda, all of whom shared the hardship brought on by drought. The seventh member, Eritrea, was admitted at the fourth summit of the Heads of State and Government held in Addis Ababa in September 1993. *Confidence and Security Building Measures: Intergovernmental Authority on Development (IGAD)*, Bureau of Political-Military Affairs, U.S. Department of State, Washington, DC, (June 26, 2000), at <http://www.state.gov/www/global/arms/bureau_pm/ csbm/fs_000626_igad.html>. See also the IGAD Homepage, at <http://www.igadregion.org>.

making organ of the Authority; in addition a "Council of Ministers" meets twice a year and reports to the Assembly well as oversees the work of the secretariat, a Committee of Ambassadors based permanently at the Headquarters of the organization and a Secretariat.[186]

3.3.2 The IGAD, Human Rights, and Migration

The IGAD Agreement commits member states to a number of bedrock principles including the "recognition, promotion and protection of human and people's rights in accordance with the provisions of the African Charter on Human and People's Rights."[187] But the IGAD Agreement does not establish a clear program or regional structure to accomplish these aims.

Its provisions on the question of refugees and displacement are minimal—under the Agreement, member states agree to facilitate the "repatriation and reintegration of refugees, returnees and displaced persons and demobilized soldiers in cooperation with relevant governmental and non-governmental organizations in accordance with the existing national, regional and international instruments."[188] Member states agree to "develop and expand cooperation and undertake to respect the fundamental and basic rights of the peoples of the region to benefit from emergency and other forms of humanitarian assistance.[189] By formulating *a fundamental and basic right* to emergency and humanitarian assistance, the IGAD agreement breaks new ground that moves away from the charitable characterization of humanitarian assistance and places it firmly in the domain of rights advocacy. This creates a new basis for regional advocacy for the human rights (especially the economic, social, and cultural rights) of refugees and IDPs. The agreement does envision the creation of an area of free movement for citizens of member states and a right of establishment of residence for nationals within the sub-region,"[190] although this has yet to take effect. Unlike its counterparts in East and West Africa, no regional court is envisioned by the IGAD Agreement.

The IGAD agreement contains no specific provisions on the human rights of women . However, in July 2000, a meeting of IGAD ministers responsible for women and gender affairs agreed to main-

---

[186] See *1996 Agreement Establishing the Intergovernmental Authority on Development (hereinafter IGAD)*, arts. 8–12, *in* Bibliography of Cited International Instruments.
[187] *IGAD*, at art. 6A(f).
[188] *Id.* at art. 13(s).
[189] *Id.* at art. 13(q).
[190] *Id.* at art. 13(o).

stream gender in regional policymaking and adopted a framework to facilitate the implementation of the recommendations of the Beijing Platform of Action in IGAD priority areas.

3.3.3 The IGAD Conflict Resolution Mechanism

A fruitful avenue to pursue, however, may be the conflict resolution mechanism envisioned by IGAD. Among its core objectives outlined in Article 7 are the promotion of peace and stability in the sub-region and the creation of mechanisms within the sub-region for the "prevention, management and resolution of inter and intra-State conflicts through dialogue."[191] Article 18A elaborates upon this and envisions the creation of a Conflict Resolution Mechanism, through which member states can consult and cooperate to ensure the peaceful settlement of differences and disputes. Such a mechanism is being developed under the auspices of IGAD's Division of Political and Humanitarian Affairs that promotes regional dialogue to prevent, manage, and resolve international and domestic conflicts. The future program will seek to institutionalize consultations and decision-making processes; create a conflict early warning mechanisms; and coordinate peace-building efforts. Whilst this process is still in its early stages it is likely that it will provide a forum that NGOs can access to highlight instances of human rights violations that may lead to forcible displacement either within IGAD states or among IGAD states.

The organization's $2 million dollar budget is met by assessed contributions from member states. Its operational budget is reliant on external aid, which comes primarily from the IGAD Partnership Forum members; established in 1997, the Forum is composed of donor states and multilateral development agencies.

3.4 The East African Community (EAC)

Cooperation within the East African region was formalized on November 30, 1999, when the Presidents of Kenya, Tanzania, and Uganda signed the Treaty for the Establishment of East African Community. The Treaty is successor to a previous attempt at regional integration two decades earlier, which faltered when an alliance among the three member states (also known as the East African Community) collapsed in 1977. The new Treaty envisions cooperation in almost every sphere including political, economic, social and cultural affairs, defense, legal and judicial matters and it lays the foundation for community that will

---

[191] *Id.* at art. 7(g).

be highly integrated on a number fronts. The Treaty outlines plans for a Customs Union, a Common Market that is to be followed by a Monetary Union, and ultimately a Political Federation.[192] For the refugee advocate, the new community will offer up a new judicial forum—an East African Court of Justice[193]—in which the rights of those displaced can be asserted.

3.4.1 The EAC Institutions

The East African Community is composed of three operating organs with a Heads of State Summit at its apex. The Summit meets once a year in order to assess the progress of regional cooperation. The Permanent Tripartite Commission, established on November 30, 1993, is in charge of operationalizing cooperation in the political, economic, social, cultural, and security spheres and proposing new ventures to the Summit. The Commission is headed by the member states' Ministers for Cooperation as well as Ministers with responsibility in the area being considered for cooperation. The Coordination Committee is composed of the Permanent Secretaries responsible for the Ministries covering agreed areas for cooperation. The Committee coordinates the work of the various Committees, Sub-committees, and working groups that have been established by the Tripartite Commission to give effect to integration in the various fields. The Coordination Committee adopts the recommendations of these sub-committees and in turn forwards them to the Commission for decision-making. Finally, the Secretariat is headed by an Executive Secretary, assisted by two deputy Executive Secretaries who are in charge of the Projects and Programs, and Finance and Administration departments respectively. The Secretariat is the principal executing organ of the Community.

3.4.2 The EAC, Human Rights, and Migration

Members of the Community undertake to abide by six fundamental principles including democracy, the rule of law, accountability, transparency, social justice, equal opportunities, gender equality, as well as the recognition, promotion, and protection of human and peoples rights in accordance with the provisions of the 1981 African Charter on Human and Peoples' Rights.[194] Like its counterpart in West Africa,

---

[192] *Treaty for the Establishment of East African Community*, art. 5(2), *in* Bibliography of Cited International Instruments.
[193] *Treaty for the Establishment of East African Community*, at ch. 8, art. 23.
[194] *Id.* at art. 6(d).

the treaty envisages the creation of a region in which there is free movement of people, goods, and services.[195] To this end an East African passport is already in circulation.

What of refugees, however? They unfortunately do not fare so well and are briefly referred to in the context of Article 124, which addresses the issue of "Regional Peace and Security, " and provides that the Partner States shall undertake to establish common mechanisms for the management of refugees. It is perhaps indicative of the mood in the region that the very next subsection of the treaty moves on to deal with enhanced cooperation to tackle cross-border crime. It is envisioned that the Community will adopt a Protocol on Refugees in the near future.

3.4.3 The EAC Community Court of Justice

On a more positive note, the Treaty also creates a new East African Court of Justice, which is to stand as an appellate court for all three countries. Article 27 stipulates that the Court shall have jurisdiction over both the interpretation and application of the Treaty as well as any other original, appellate, human rights and other jurisdiction that the Council may determine at some future date. It is anticipated that a Protocol will be adopted which will elaborate on the jurisdiction of the Court in more detail. Articles 28–30 of the Treaty examine the issue of standing before the court and provide that in addition to Partner States and the Secretary General, "*any person who is resident* in a Partner State may refer for determination by the Court, the legality of any Act, regulation, directive, decision or action of a Partner State or an institution of the Community on the grounds that such Act, regulation, directive, decision or action is unlawful or is an infringement of the Provisions of the Treaty." The requirement that a person merely be "resident" in a member country leaves open the possibility that refugees who are lawfully present in a member country, may qualify under this provision; those internally displaced certainly would have standing before a future Court. Whilst much remains uncertain with respect to the functioning of the Court, it would appear that it may provide a useful avenue through which to pursue issues of concern to the forcibly displaced.

---

[195] *Id.* at art. 104(1), ch. 17. ("Free Movement of Persons, Labour, Services, Right of Establishment and Residence").

3.5 The Southern African Development Community (SADC)

The Southern African Development Community, originally known as the Southern African Development Co-ordination Conference (SADCC), was formed in Lusaka, Zambia, on April 1, 1980, following the adoption of the "Lusaka Declaration—Southern Africa: Towards Economic Liberation," by the nine founding member States.[196] The Declaration and Treaty Establishing the Southern African Development Community (SADC) that has replaced the Co-ordination Conference was signed at the Summit of Heads of State or Government on August 17, 1992, in Windhoek, Namibia. Member States are Angola, Botswana, Democratic Republic of Congo (DRC), Lesotho, Malawi, Mauritius, Mozambique, Namibia, Seychelles, South Africa, Swaziland, Tanzania, Zambia, and Zimbabwe. Each member state has responsibility to co-ordinate a sector or sectors on behalf of the others.

3.5.1 Aims and Objectives of the SADC

The Treaty Establishing the Southern African Development Community (SADC Treaty) is a legally binding and all-encompassing framework by which countries of the region co-ordinate, harmonize and rationalize their policies and strategies for sustainable development in all areas of human activity.[197] The Treaty commits member states to fundamental principles of:

- sovereign equality of member states.
- solidarity, peace, and security.
- human rights, democracy, and rule of law.
- equity, balance, and mutual benefit.[198]

Member states are expected to demonstrate their commitment to act in accordance with these principles.[199] The Treaty also commits the SADC and governments of member states to "involve fully the people of the region, and non-governmental organizations in the process of

---

[196] These are Angola, Botswana, Lesotho, Malawi, Mozambique, Swaziland, Tanzania, Zambia and Zimbabwe. Currently the membership is at fourteen with the joining of The Democratic Republic of Congo (DRC), Mauritius, Namibia, Seychelles and South Africa. *Lusaka Declaration—Southern Africa: Towards Economic Liberation.*
[197] *See* art. 4, in Bibliography of Cited International Instruments.
[198] *Id.*
[199] *Id.*

regional integration."[200] This provision contains an implicit challenge to the SADC countries to ensure the protection of forcibly displaced persons within the sub-region if these persons are not to be excluded from the gains of regional integration. This challenge is yet to be actively taken up by the institutions of SADC or by its member states. Within the Executive Secretariat of the SADC in Gaborone, Botswana, the Community has established an NGO Liaison Unit but there remain no clear guidelines in relation to any mechanisms for human rights monitoring in general or specific measures affecting forcibly displaced persons or populations in particular. However, at its meeting in Windhoek, Namibia in August 2000, the Summit of Heads of State or Government of the SADC expressed concern for the first time that "many people have been displaced as a result of war, and have become refugees both in their countries and in neighboring states."[201] Although it stopped short of indicating or adopting any specific remedial measures, this high level expression of concern for the victims of forcible displacement in the region may be evidence of an advocacy opportunity to extend the promise of regional integration in Southern Africa for forcibly displaced persons.

3.5.2 Institutions of the SADC

The SADC Treaty establishes the following as the core institutions of the Community, namely: a summit of Heads of State or Government, Council of Ministers, Commissions, a Standing Committee of Officials, an Executive Secretariat and a (judicial) Tribunal.[202] In addition, at its Gaborone Summit in June 1996, the Community constituted a subsidiary Organ on Politics, Defence and Security (OPDS).[203] Operating at Summit, Ministerial and technical levels, the mandate of the OPDS extends to promoting and enhancing "the development of democratic institutions and practices within member States, and to encourage the observance of universal human rights as provided for in the Charters and Conventions of the OAU and the United Nations."[204]

---

[200] *Id.*, at art. 23.

[201] Final Communiqué issued by the Summit of Heads of State or Government of the SADC, Windhoek, Namibia, 7 August, 2000, at <http://www.gta.gov.zw/Presidential%20Speeches/2000SADCsummit.htm>

[202] *Id.* at art. 9.

[203] Established/formalized through a *communiqué* following the 28 June 1996 summit meeting in Gaberone.

[204] Amnesty International, *Southern Africa: Politicking and Human Rights in the Southern African Development Community*, 1997, 10.

3.5.3 The SADC, Human Rights, and Migration

The Preamble to the SADC Treaty calls attention to, *inter alia*, the need to ground popular participation in regional integration in the triple guarantee of democratic rights, observance of human rights and the rule of law.[205] The Treaty reaffirms these values as part of the foundational principles of the Community.[206] Member states undertake far-reaching obligations to eliminate discrimination on grounds of gender, religion, political opinion, race, ethnic origin, culture, or disability.[207] It bears noting that the list of prohibited grounds of discrimination under the SADC Treaty includes all of the Convention grounds for asylum. On migration, the SADC member states commit themselves to "develop policies aimed at the progressive elimination of obstacles to the free movement of capital and labour, goods and services, and of the people of the region generally."[208] The treaty contains no timetable for developing such policies or benchmarks against which the policies could be measured.

Two major shortcomings of the SADC Treaty include the omission of firm commitments on regional migration and the failure to establish any organs to protect the minimal human rights commitments contained in it. The establishment of the SADC Organ on Politics, Defence and Security (OPDS) in 1996 gave the organisation a framework for addressing through preventive action, the causes and incidents of forcible displacement in Southern Africa where, in the past, they had been reluctant to act.[209] The emphasis on preventive action implied an integrated policy orientation involving military as well as civilian departments of government. In reality, however, the OPDS functions mostly, if not exclusively, at the level of the Heads of State and the Inter-State Defence and Security Committee (ISDSC). Defense Ministers of the member states, in rotation, chair the latter with three sub-committees, respectively on defense, security, and intelligence. The composition and structure of the ISDSC precludes habitual participation in its work by any of the civilian departments of government with responsibility for social justice issues, especially, Foreign or Home Affairs, Justice, Legal or Parliamentary Affairs. Military, security, and intelligence concerns therefore currently dominate the OPDS. This situation

---

[205] SADC Treaty, Preamble, ¶ 7.
[206] *Id.* at art. 4(c).
[207] *Id.* at art. 6(b).
[208] *Id.* at art. 5(2)(d).
[209] Malan, Mark and Cilliers, Jakkie, *SADC Organ on Politics, Defence and Security: Future Development*, Occasional Paper No. 19, March Institute for Security Studies, Halfway House, South Africa, (1997).

is compounded by the fact that with a few exceptions within the region, governments are impervious to NGO advocacy pressure and often hostile to NGOs.[210]

Ironically, therefore, for a region in which much of the current leadership benefited in the recent past from the liberal asylum policies of other African countries in response to Apartheid, the policy orientation of the SADC states only takes account of forcible displacement in the context of regional security concerns. Victims of internal displacement are more likely to be seen as subversives to be avoided rather than as bearers of rights in need of protection. The absence of an effective policy on migration and forced displacement within the Organ reflects the neglect of this issue in the institutional priorities of the SADC. The current failure of the Organ to prioritise migration and forcible displacement mirrors an institutional neglect of the subject and wider questions of human rights and governance within the SADC. As a result, the human rights component of its mandate extending to the protection of forcibly displaced persons remains to be developed.

3.5.4 The SADC and Gender

Article 6(2) of the SADC Treaty prohibits discrimination by member states on several grounds, including gender. To date all SADC member states have ratified and acceded to the United Nations Convention on the Elimination of all Forms of Discrimination against Women (CEDAW).[211] The SADC Heads of State and Government at the Blantyre summit in 1997 issued and signed the Declaration on Gender and Development.[212] The Declaration recognizes gender equality as a fundamental human right and acknowledges that greater benefits would be achieved from closer regional co-operation and collective action in eliminating gender discrimination. In line with part B (vi) of the Declaration, SADC set up a Gender Unit within its Secretariat in June 1998. Among its terms of reference, this Unit is mandated to:

---

[210] *Id.*

[211] *Preamble to the SADC Declaration on Gender and Development. See* <http://www.sadc./sadc/gender/index.html>.

[212] For texts of all the relevant SDAC standards on gender, *see* SADC, *Gender and Development: A Declaration by Heads of State or Government of the Southern African Development Community (SADC) and The Prevention and Eradication of Violence against Women and Children, an Addendum to the 1997 Declaration on Gender and Development by SADC Heads of State or Government.*

(a) design and elaborate a policy and institutional framework for gender mainstreaming at national and regional levels within the SADC region;
(b) cultivate and promote a culture of gender equality in the SADC region, and respect for the human rights of women;
(c) promote equality between men and women in the sharing of power and ensure the achievement of not less than 30% representation in decision-making structures by the year 2005;
(d) facilitate the achievement of gender equality, and gender equity, in access to economic structures and control of resources in the SADC region; and
(e) highlight the impact of war and armed conflict on the social, economic, psychological, and emotional condition of women and children.

The mandate of the Gender Unit clearly extends to monitoring the interplay of gender relations before, during, and after forced displacement. In particular, the Unit has a role in monitoring the human rights and well-being of displaced persons generally and of displaced women and children in particular.

3.5.5 The SADC Tribunal

The SADC Treaty provides for a Tribunal, "to ensure adherence to and the proper interpretation of the provisions of this Treaty and subsidiary instruments and to adjudicate upon such disputes as may be referred to it."[213] In August 2000, at its meeting in Windhoek, Namibia, the SADC Summit of Heads of State or Government adopted the Protocol constituting the Tribunal and designating its methods of work.[214] The Protocol has yet to come into force.

Under this Protocol, the Tribunal would comprise ten persons "appointed from nationals of States who possess the qualification required for appointment to the highest judicial offices of their respec-

---

[213] SADC Treaty, art. 16(1).

[214] Final Communiqué issued by the Summit of Heads of State or Government of the SADC, Windhoek, Namibia, 7 August, 2000, *supra* note 201. *See* Protocol on Tribunal in the Southern African Development Community including the Rules of Procedure of the Southern African Development Community Tribunal, *in* Bibliography of Cited International Instruments (hereinafter SADC Tribunal Protocol).

tive States or who are jurists of recognized competence."[215] Five of the members of the Tribunal shall be designated as regular members while another five shall be alternate members to function when a regular member is unable or unfit to sit as a judge. The tenure of members of the court is for five years, renewable only once for the same length of time.[216] The quorum for a sitting of the Tribunal is three members but it may decide to constitute a full bench of five.[217] The jurisdiction of the Tribunal extends to:

(a) interpretation of the treaty;
(b) interpretation and application of protocols and subsidiary instruments adopted within the SADC, and acts and institutions of the Community; and
(c) all matters specifically provided for in any other agreements concluded among the states parties or within the Community conferring jurisdiction on the Tribunal.[218]

The Tribunal shall also have an advisory jurisdiction.[219] It can adjudicate between states and, subject to the exhaustion of domestic remedies, between natural or legal persons, including institutions of the Community, and states.[220] The jurisdiction of the Tribunal may thus foreseeably extend to the protection of human rights and forcible displacement should the Community develop a clearer legal framework for this purpose in future. In cases before the Tribunal, diplomatic agents and advisors will represent states and institutions of the Community.[221] Non-state entities, including individuals, will equally be able to designate their own agents or advisors[222] but, unless the Tribunal decides otherwise, parties will bear their own costs.[223] However, the Court may make rules concerning fees and legal aid.[224] This provision will be particularly useful for guaranteeing access to the Tribunal for forcibly displaced persons. "Should state, natural or legal person consider that" they have "an interest of a legal nature that may be affected

---

[215] SADC Tribunal Protocol, art. 3(1).
[216] *Id.* at art. 6(1).
[217] *Id.* at art. 3(3).
[218] *Id.* at art. 14.
[219] *Id.* at art. 16.
[220] *Id.* at art. 15.
[221] *Id.* at art. 27(1).
[222] *Id.* at art. 27(2).
[223] *Id.* at art. 29.
[224] *Id.* at art. 31.

by the subject matter of a dispute before the Tribunal," Article 30 of the Protocol entitles them to apply to intervene in the proceedings. Judgments of the Tribunal shall be binding and may be enforced in accordance with the domestic rules governing the registration and enforcement of foreign judgments.[225]

3.6 The African Economic Community (AEC)

On June 3, 1991, the Heads of State and Government of the OAU signed the Treaty establishing the African Economic Community (AEC) during the 27th Ordinary session of their Assembly held in Abuja. The Treaty entered into force on May 12, 1994, following ratification by the requisite two-thirds of member states. The membership of the AEC is in effect the same member states of the OAU. Steps are now being taken to implement the treaty and establish the structure and policy organs of the Community. The timeframe for the establishment of the Community spans over 34 years and is broken into six distinct stages. Whilst far off in the future, the structures created by the AEC will likely have profound implications for the protection of refugees and the displaced in Africa.

3.6.1 Objectives

The objective of the AEC is to promote the economic, social, and cultural development and integration of African economies, as well as the mobilization of the human and material resources of Africa. To that end, the member states of the AEC have undertaken to liberalize trade and to create Free Trade areas and Customs Unions at sub-regional and regional levels that will ultimately converge into an African Common market. Member states have committed themselves to the gradual removal of obstacles to the free movement of persons, goods, services, and capital and the attainment of the rights of residence and establishment in the Community by citizens of participating countries.

3.6.2 Institutions

The Treaty establishing the African Economic Community provides for a number of institutions including (a) the Economic and Social Commission;[226] (b) the Pan-African Parliament; (c) the Court

---

[225] *Id.* at art. 52(1).
[226] The Economic and Social Commission (ECOSOC) is a major organ of the community, the functions of which are spelled out in the *Treaty Establishing the African Economic Community*, art. 7.

of Justice; and (d) a number of specialized technical committees, including a Committee on Trade, Customs and Immigration Matters; a Committee on Monetary and Financial Affairs; a Committee on Industry, Science, Technology, Energy, Natural Resources and Environment; a Committee on Transport, Communication and Tourism; a Committee on Rural Economy and Agricultural Matters; a Committee on Health, Labor and Social Affairs; and a Committee on Education, Culture and Human Resources. The Secretariat of the AEC is the same as that of the OAU, which is being reorganized to meet the challenge of continental integration.

3.7 The African Union

In July 2000 in Lomé, Togo, the Summit of the Assembly of Heads of State and Government of the OAU adopted a new foundational treaty—the Constitutive Act of the African Union.[227] The new Treaty replaces the Charter of the OAU and makes far-reaching provisions integrating human rights into the core of the new Union. It revises the OAU's policy regarding state sovereignty and non-interference in domestic affairs, designates new institutions and supersedes any inconsistent provisions in the Treaty Establishing the African Economic Community.

The new Treaty integrates political, economic, and human rights priorities into the objectives of the Union. The Union will seek to promote peace, security, and stability; promote democratic principles and institutions, popular participation and good governance; promote and protect human and peoples' rights in accordance with the African Charter; and to raise the living standards of African peoples. Article 4(h) establishes a new right of the Union to intervene in a member state pursuant to a decision of the Assembly where certain grave circumstances exist, in particular war crimes, genocide, and crimes against humanity. Article 4(j) anticipates that states may request intervention by the Union to restore peace and security. Unfortunately, the new Treaty does not include any reference to the OAU Refugee Convention.

The organs of the Union include an Assembly (Heads of State and Government), an Executive Council, a Parliament, a Court of Justice, and a Commission, which shall replace the existing OAU Secretariat. The new Assembly and Council will replace the existing Assembly and Ministerial Council of the OAU. The functions of the new Assembly include giving directives to the Executive Council on the management of conflicts and other emergency situations. The new Executive Council

---

[227] The Constitutive Act of the African Union, adopted by the 36th Ordinary Session of the Assembly of Heads of State and Government, July 11, 2000, Lomé, Togo, OAU/CAB/LEG/23.15.

will coordinate environmental protection, humanitarian action, and response to disasters. These functions will require political and budgetary commitments by the Union for the protection of refugees and IDPs. The Court will be established by a Protocol.

The new Treaty came into force on May 26, 2001, one month following the deposit of the 36th instrument of ratification. A transitional period of one year (or longer, as determined by the Assembly) will result in the Union replacing the OAU.

4. Conclusion

In conclusion, the legal and political landscape of Africa is undergoing a profound change that is likely to offer up numerous new and interesting fora for advocates to utilize on behalf of those forcibly displaced. East and West Africa now have Community Courts of Justice in which the rights of those displaced can be asserted, the African Commission has considerable potential to build on the jurisprudence which it is already developing around the issue of forcible displacement, and an African Court of Human Rights is around the corner. The prospect of region-wide freedom of movement is also a positive development for the displaced and can serve as an important complement to the refugee treaties. However, we are still early on in the process of integration. There remain many uncertainties. For instance, it remains to be seen how compatible the different mandates of the sub-regional and regional organizations will be with one another. Advocates of refugee rights can contribute to working out synergies and compatibility by monitoring and seeking to use them to protect in defense of the human rights of refugees. More daunting perhaps is whether the states that are members of these various organizations will exhibit the necessary political commitment to put their national rivalries and disputes to one side and to invest in making a success of the enterprise. Even then, there will remain serious problems of funding and capacity. However, it is only through investing the necessary time and commitment to working with these mechanisms and exploring their potential that advocates can ensure the development of an effective regional system through which to vindicate the rights of those forcibly displaced.

Bibliography

Books

COHEN, ROBERTA & FRANCIS M. DENG, MASSES IN FLIGHT—THE GLOBAL CRISIS OF INTERNAL DISPLACEMENT (1998).

MURRAY, RACHEL, THE AFRICAN COMMISSION ON PEOPLE'S RIGHTS AND INTERNATIONAL LAW (2000).
NALDI, GINO J., THE ORGANIZATION OF AFRICAN UNITY—AN ANALYSIS OF ITS ROLE (2d. ed. 1999).
SIMMA, BRUNO, ET AL., THE CHARTER OF THE UNITED NATIONS: A COMMENTARY (1995).

Journal Articles

Murray, Rachel, *Serious and Massive Violations under the African Charter on Human and Peoples' Rights: A Comparison with the Inter-American and European Mechanisms*, 17 NETH. Q. HUM. RTS. 109 (1999).
Odinkalu, Chidi Anselm & Camilla Christensen, *The African Commission on Human and Peoples' Rights: The Development of Its Non-State Communications Procedures*, 20 HUM. RTS. Q. 235 (1998).
Odinkalu, Chidi Anselm & Rafikiel Mdoe, *Article 58 of the African Charter on Human Rights: A Legal Analysis and Proposals for Implementation*, INTERIGHTS (1996).
Organization of African Unity/United Nations High Commissioner for Refugees, *Commemorative Symposium on Refugees and Forced Population Movements in Africa, Addis Ababa, 8–10 September, 1994*, INT'L J. REFUGEE L. (1995).
Viljoen, Frans, *The Realization of Human Rights in Africa Through Sub-Regional Institutions*, 7 AFR. Y.B. INT'L L. 185 (1999).

IGO Documents

Confidence and Security Building Measures: Intergovernmental Authority on Development (IGAD), Bureau of Political-Military Affairs, U.S. Department of State, Washington, DC, (26 June 2000), available at <http://www.state.gov/www/global/arms/bureau_pm/csbm/fs_000626_igad.html>.
Criteria for Granting OAU Observer Status as Amended by the 29th Ordinary Session of the Assembly of Heads of State and Governments/Critere d'Octroi du Statut d'Observateur aupres de l'OUA tels qu'amendes Par la 29 eme session Ordinaire des Chefs d'Etat et de Gouvernement, AHG/192 (XXIX), Rev. 1 (1993).
Decision of the Authority of Heads of State and Government of the Economic Community of West African States Relating to the Establishment of ECOWAS Travel Certificate for Member States, A/Dec.2/7/85, July 6, 1985.
Decision of the Authority of Heads of State and Government Establishing a Residence Card in ECOWAS Member States, A/Dec. 2/5/90, May 30, 1990.

Declaration of the Assembly of Heads of State and Government on the Establishment Within the OAU of a Mechanism for Conflict Prevention, Management and Resolution, adopted at the twenty-ninth Ordinary Session in Cairo, Egypt, June 1993, available <http://www.oau-oua.org>.

Economic Community of West African States (ECOWAS), *Review of the ECOWAS Treaty: Final Report by the Committee of Eminent Persons* (June 1992).

Final Communiqué of the 2000 SADC Summit, Windhoek, Namibia, 7 August, 2000, available at <http://www.gta.gov.zw/Presidential%20Speeches/2000SADCsummit.htm> visited May 05 2001.

Gender and Development: A Declaration by Heads of State and Government of the Southern African Development Community and the Prevention and Eradication of Violence against Women and Children (1997/1998) <http://www.sadc./sadc/gender/index.html>.

Khartoum Declaration of the 8th Summit of Heads of States and Government, IGAD, issued at Khartoum on 23rd November, 2000.

Recommandation No 03/99/CM/UEMOA relative à mise en œuvre d'actions communes en matière de promotion et de renforcement du rôle de la femme dans l'Union Economique et Monétaire Ouest Africaine (UEMOA), 16 Bulletin Officiel de l'Union Economique et Monétaire Ouest Africaine 62.

Recommandation No 01/2000/CM/UEMOA relative à mise en œuvre dans l'Union d'actions communes en matiere de sante, 19 Bulletin Officiel de l'Union Economique et Monétaire Ouest Africaine 137.

Règlement portant définition des caractéristiques des costumes d'audience des membres de la Cour de Justice de l'UEMOA et du greffier de la Cour, règlement no. 3/96/CM/UEMOA.

Règlement portant Règlement de Procedures de la Cour de Justice, reglement No. 1/96/CM/UEMOA.

Règlement portant statut de greffier de la Cour de Justice de l'UEMOA, reglement no. 2/96/CM/UEMOA.

Rules of Procedure of the African Commission on Human and Peoples' Rights, Rules 111(1), *adopted* October 6, 1995, ACHPR/RP/XIX (made available through the Danish Centre for Human Rights), available at <http://www1.umn.edu/humanrts/africa/rules.htm>.

UNHCR News, Country Updates, Africa Fact Sheet (May 2000), available at <http://www.unhcr.ch/news/cupdates/0005afri.htm>.

NGO Reports

Abiodun Alao, *The Role Of African Regional And Sub-Regional Organizations In Conflict Prevention And Resolution*, Working Paper No. 23, New

Issues in Refugee Research series, UNHCR (July 2000), <http://www.unhcr.ch>.
Amnesty International, *Organization of African Unity: Making Human Rights a Reality for Africans*, Report IOR 63/01/98 (1998).
Lawyers Committee for Human Rights, African Exodus: Refugee Crisis, Human Rights And The 1969 OAU Convention (1995), <http://www.lchr.org/pubs/pubs.htm#AFRICA>.
Malan, Mark & Jakkie Cilliers, *SADC Organ on Politics, Defence and Security: Future Development*; Occasional Paper No 19, March Institute for Security Studies, Halfway House, South Africa, (1997).
Mouhamadou Moctar Mbacke, La Cour de Justice de L'union Economique et Monetaire Ouest-Africaine (Uemoa): Son Organisation, Ses Competences et Ses Regles de Procedure, Collection, Droit Communiautaire Africain, EDJA, [1999].

Cases

Krishna Achutan (on Behalf of Aleke Banda) v. Malaw, Communication 64/92 (1994).
Advisory Opinion on Exceptions to the Exhaustion of domestic Remedies in Cases of Indigency or Inability to Obtain Legal Representation Because of a Generalized Fear Within the Legal Community, Advisory Opinion OC-11/90 (August 10, 1990), *reprinted in* 12 HUM. RTS. L.J. 20 (1991).
Amnesty International v. Zambia, Communication 212/98 (1998).
Commission Nationale des Droits de l'Homme et des Libertés v. Chad, Communication 74/92 (1995).
Constitutional Rights Project (in respect of Zamani Lekwot & 6 Others) v. Nigeria, Communication 87/93 (1994).
Constitutional Rights Project (in respect of Zamani Lekwot & 6 Ors) v. Nigeria, Communication 87/93 (1995); 8th ANNUAL ACTIVTY REPORT OF THE AFRICAN COMMISSION, AHG/201/XXXI, ANNEX VI, 16, 18 (1995), *reprinted in* 3 INT'L HUM. RTS. REP. 137 (1996).
Democratic Republic of the Congo v. Burundi, Rwanda and Uganda, Communication 227/98.
Elmi v. Australia, Committee against Torture, 22nd session, U.N. Doc. CAT/C/22/D/120/1998 (25 May 1999), *available at* <http://unbisnet.un.org/webpac-bin/wgbroker?1106184915075418274+1+scan+select+1+0>.
Katangese Peoples' Congress v. Zaire, Communication 75/92, *reprinted in* 3 INT'L HUM. RTS. REP. 136.
Ligue Cameroonaise des Droits de l'Homme v. Cameroon, Communication 65/92, (1997).

Malawi African Association & Others v. Mauritania, Communication 54/91 (1999);
Emgba Louis Mekongo v. Cameroon, Communication 59/91 (1994)
John K. Modise v. Botswana, Communication 97/93 (1996).
John K. Modise v. Botswana, Communication 97/93 (1997).
Mouvement des Refugies Mauritaniens au Senegal v. Senegal, Communication 162/97, (1997).
Mpaka-Nsusu Andre Alphonse v. Zaire, Communication 15/88 (Admissibility, 1993).
Prosper Guéna NITCHEN et autres v. L'Université Cheikh Anta Diop de Dakar, Arret No. 0076, (August 31, 1994).
Organisation Mondiale Contre la Torture et al v. Rwanda, Communication 27/89 (1986).
Organisation Mondiale Contre la Torture et al v. Rwanda, Communication 27/89 (Merits 1996).
Rencontre Africaine pour THE AFRICAN COMMISSION ON HUMAN & PEOPLES' RIGHTS, DOC.OS/(XXII), ANNEX X, Communication 71/92, (1997), *reprinted in* 6 INT'L HUM. RTS. REP. 825.
Rencontre Africaine pour la Defense des Droits de l'Homme (RADDHO) v. Zambia, Communication 71/92 (1997).
World Organization Against Torture et al v. Zaire (Merits), Communication 25/89 (1997), *reprinted in* 4 INT'L HUM. RTS. REP. 89 (1997).

Internet Sources

Oloka-Onyango, Joseph, *Human Rights and Sustainable Development in Contemporary Africa: A New Dawn, or Retreating Horizons?* Human Development Report 2000 Background Paper, at <http://www.undp.org/hdro/oloka-Onyango2000.html>.

Chapter 5
European Human Rights Mechanisms

Diane Atkinson-Sanford

1. Introduction

It is only comparatively recently that European human rights mechanisms have been confronted with situations of mass displacement within Europe.[1] In recent years, major refugee flows have emanated from within Europe, as well as from more distant states.[2] Both refugees and asylum-seekers look to international human rights standards to prevent unduly long separation from their family during and after flight. They urgently need a means of ensuring that they can claim basic rights to food, shelter, employment, education for their children, the preservation of their beliefs and culture, and generally non-discriminatory treatment in the receiving state. Those granted refugee status need some guarantee that the international standards relating to that status are upheld. Asylum-seekers need to be protected against indefinite internment, from circumstances that prevent them from lodging an asylum application, and from negligent review of their application. Persons forced by persecution or armed conflict to leave their homes, but unable to flee across an international border, need more than their property restored to them, and more than the chance to flee. They need to be safe from threats to their life and liberty, to express their views and needs, to have access to shelter, food, education for their children, and medical care. During flight, they need to ensure that their

---

[1] The author would like to thank Nicholas Blake QC, Christina Cerna, Elizabeth Evatt and Prof. Eckart Klein for their comments and advice and Perveen Ali and Sherilyn Holcombe for their assistance.

[2] The six main refugee groups in Europe in 1999 came from Turkey, Kosovo, and the Roma communities in Central Europe, and from the non-European states of Iran, Afghanistan, and Somalia. European Council on Refugees and Exiles, Country Report, 1999 at <http://www.ecre.org/publications/countryrpt.html>.

family will not be separated and that their cultural and religious practices and beliefs can be maintained. Finally, IDPs need means of identification, a chance to leave their country, if necessary.

1.1 Avenues of Redress in Europe

The mechanisms examined in this chapter offer two main avenues of human rights protection for refugees, asylum-seekers, and IDPs: advocacy and activism. In Europe, the foremost mechanism allowing individual petition is the European Court of Human Rights, which is administered by the Council of Europe. The Court is discussed at length below in Sections 2 and 3 of this chapter. It is charged with the task of interpreting and applying the European Convention for the Protection of Human Rights and Fundamental Freedoms (hereinafter the European Convention or ECHR),[3] which has 41 states parties.

Other Council of Europe bodies and instruments, including the 1961 European Social Charter, the Committee for the Prevention of Torture and Inhuman or Degrading Treatment or Punishment (CPT), and the 1995 Framework Convention for the Protection of Minorities will be considered in Section 5. These agreements have no individual petition mechanism. In the case of the Social Charter, a collective complaints mechanism has been established.

The Organization for Security and Co-operation in Europe (OSCE) and the European Union (EU) will also be considered in light of the needs of refugees, asylum-seekers, and IDPs in Section 5. The former serves a very useful diplomatic and conflict resolution function, in addition to fact-finding and on-site reporting. The latter is in the process of harmonizing the immigration and asylum policies of its 15 member states,[4] thus having a significant impact on the groups addressed by this Guide in Europe. Both the OSCE and the EU offer opportunities for activism by means of lobbying.

1.2 A Note on the Charter of Fundamental Rights of the European Union

Two instruments protecting individual human rights now co-exist in Europe. The final draft of the European Union's Charter of Fundamental Rights was issued on October 2, 2000. The difference

---

[3] *See* Bibliography of Cited International Instruments for full citations to this and other international instruments mentioned in this chapter.

[4] Austria, Belgium, Denmark, Finland, France, Germany, Greece, Ireland, Italy, Luxembourg, the Netherlands, Portugal, Spain, Sweden, the United Kingdom.

between the reach of the European Convention and European Union Charter rights will be the number of States bound by their precepts, since the ECHR applies to 41 European states, whereas the Charter will at first apply to 15.

The Charter includes not just the rights protected by the ECHR, but a number of other provisions including a right of respect for the home,[5] to asylum,[6] to good administration,[7] and prohibitions against collective expulsions[8] and human trafficking.[9] The Charter also includes a number of economic and social rights absent from the European Convention, such as a right to education, which includes the possibility of receiving a "free compulsory education,"[10] and a number of workers' rights.[11]

It is as yet unclear what the legal effect of the Charter will be.[12] The Charter was the subject of a solemn declaration by the Council of the EU in December 2000. It is therefore not directly legally binding, but the European Court of Justice (ECJ), which is situated in Luxembourg and has the task of interpreting and applying EU law, will likely refer to it as guidelines for the 15 member states of the EU. If the Charter becomes legally binding in the longer term, individuals may be able to invoke its provisions in national courts, ask the ECJ for preliminary rulings on its applicability in a given case, or even petition the ECJ directly in limited circumstances.[13] What would happen in case of conflict between the ECJ and European Court of Human Rights in matters of interpretation of rights expressly protected in both systems is uncertain and will be discussed below in Section 4. Since, however, the rights enshrined in the Charter will certainly be of significance in European human rights protection, they will be discussed below in Section 3 in relation to the substantive jurisprudence of the European Court of Human Rights. For the immediate future, the force of the Charter will be determined through activism in the form of lobbying the EU Parliament.

---

[5] Charter of Fundamental Rights of the European Union (hereinafter EUCFR), art. 7.
[6] *Id.* art. 18.
[7] *Id.* art. 41. This right appears to require administrative agencies that deal with asylum applications to do so "impartially, fairly and within a reasonable time."
[8] *Id.* art. 19 §1.
[9] *Id.* art. 5 § 3.
[10] *Id.* art. 14.
[11] *Id.* chapter IV, arts. 24–33.
[12] This is discussed further in Section 4.
[13] *See* below at Section 4.6.

2. Advocacy

2.1 Individual Petition Mechanisms in Europe: The European Court of Human Rights

The first concern of an advocate, when considering bringing a case on behalf of refugees, asylum-seekers, and IDPs, is securing a fast and effective remedy for the particular injury suffered. Refugees and asylum-seekers are not assured of state representation in the international system, most having left their country in the first place due to government-sanctioned persecution (whether by action or inaction). IDPs are usually ignored by their country for the same reason, but do not even have the option of seeking protection from another state. Thus, three factors are vital for the effective protection of the rights of these vulnerable groups:

- The existence of a mechanism which allows for cases to be brought by *individuals or groups* against states ("individual petition");
- A mechanism empowered to grant remedies that will provide adequate redress for the injury suffered;
- A mechanism whose judgments are enforceable within a reasonable time frame. Time is often of the essence for the groups in question.

The ECHR is central to one of the foremost regional human rights mechanisms in the world. Under Article 34 of the ECHR, the Court has compulsory jurisdiction to accept individual petitions from persons whose ECHR rights have been violated by any one of the 41 High Contracting Parties (hereinafter "states").

2.2 Some Background on the ECHR and the Court

The ECHR was conceived as a means to implement the 1948 Universal Declaration on Human Rights within Europe. Section I of the ECHR lists the substantive rights and freedoms, in Articles 2–18. These are supplemented by Protocols 1, 4, 6, and 7. When ratifying the ECHR, many states lodged reservations with the Council to specific articles, which should be considered where relevant.

Until November 1998, two organs existed to adjudicate claims under the ECHR. These organs were the European Commission of Human Rights and the European Court of Human Rights (hereinafter "Commission" and "Court" respectively). The system functioned in a unique, innovative, and interesting way. The Commission was entrusted with determining the admissibility of cases to the Court, fact-finding where relevant, and all efforts to secure a friendly settlement. The Commission was comprised of a body of experts, as many as there were parties to the ECHR, but no more than one of each member nationality. Members were elected for six-year renewable terms by the Committee of Ministers and Parliamentary Assembly of the Council of Europe. For each case that came before it, the Commission would submit a report detailing its findings as to the facts and law in the case. That report was submitted to the Court if the case was to be referred there, and to the Committee of Ministers of the Council of Europe if not.

Largely due to the success of this mechanism, the volume of applications increased dramatically over time. It is estimated that 40,000 complaints have now come before the ECHR organs as a whole.[14] In order to get through the huge backlog of cases facing the Commission and Court, extensive debate was undertaken on the subject of reforming the ECHR's machinery. At that time, the average length of ECHR proceedings was six years. In a human rights context, that was judged to be simply too long. The result was the entry into force of Protocol 11 in November 1998. It abolished the Commission and brought into being a single European Court of Human Rights, to do the work of both bodies. Thus, the amended ECHR in Articles 19–51 sets out the Court's composition, competence and the basic format of proceedings before it. This section is supplemented by the Rules of the Court. The ECHR also deals with issues such as reservations, denunciation, and ratification in Articles 52–59.

2.2.1 Institutional Framework of the Court

The Court is composed of a number of judges equal to the number of High Contracting Parties (forty-one at the last count). Judges are elected by the Parliamentary Assembly and must hold either the highest qualification required for high judicial office in their home state or be jurists of recognized competence.[15] The ECHR contains strong guarantees relating to judicial impartiality. Judges do not serve at the pleasure of their home state, though practice is currently to have one judge from each High Contracting Party on the bench. Given the relatively recent entry into the system of countries from Central and Eastern Europe, and the increasingly high caseload from that area, it

---

[14] Kevin Boyle, *Europe: The Council of Europe, the OSCE, and the European Union*, in GUIDE TO INTERNATIONAL HUMAN RIGHTS PRACTICE 135, 149 (HURST HANNUM ED., 3d ed. 1999).

[15] Art. 21 ECHR.

is appropriate to have judges versed in varied legal systems on the bench. Judges are elected for renewable six-year terms but must resign at the age of seventy.

The new Court is divided into various groupings, depending on function. The election of the President of the Court, its officers, and the adoption of the Rules of the Court are carried out by the whole court, or *Plenary Court*. The initial admissibility of applications is determined by *committees* of three judges. Applications can only be refused by a unanimous vote in clear circumstances and that decision is conclusive. The Court is then divided into four sections, each with its own President and Vice-President. According to rule 25(2) of the Rules of the Court, the sections must be "geographically and gender balanced."[16] These sections are further divided into Chambers, each comprised of seven judges that decide on the admissibility of the case and also render judgment on the merits. They act as a combination of the old Commission and Court. These decisions are final unless the Chamber refers the case to the Grand Chamber, comprised of 17 judges, before it hands down its judgment, or unless a party to the dispute refers it to the Grand Chamber for rehearing. The criteria for such a referral are set out in rules 72 and 73 of the Court and are explained below. The Grand Chamber does have jurisdiction to give Advisory Opinions, but not at the request of individuals.

2.2.2 Checklist: Are You Ready and Willing to Bring a Case Before the Court?

Questions to Ask Yourself When Considering Making an Application to the Court:

Does the Court Offer What You Need? See below at Section 2.2.3.
- ✓ What kind of remedy are you looking for? Do you want the state to do something to protect you or affect the injury you suffered other than paying compensation?
- ✓ How urgently do you need a remedy?
  NOTE: The Court can arrange for legal representation and legal aid is available.

Is Your Application Admissible?—See below at Section 2
- ✓ Was the state that committed the alleged violation a party to the ECHR at the time the violation occurred?

---

[16] *See* Boyle, *supra* note 14.

- ✓ Are you a "victim" within the meaning of the ECHR?
- ✓ If you are bringing a case as part of a group, are all members of the group "victims" of a violation of the ECHR?
- ✓ If you are a non-governmental organization, are you a "private" organization? Is the substance of the complaint an act actually directed at the organization itself?
- ✓ Does the injury you suffered concern a violation of one of the rights protected by the ECHR or its protocols?
- ✓ Is the state a party (i.e., has it ratified) the protocol in question and has it lodged any reservations that limit its liability under the relevant article?
- ✓ Did the violation occur within the jurisdiction of that state for the purposes of the ECHR?
- ✓ Could you have made the same kind of arguments as you will under the ECHR before domestic courts? Have you done so?
- ✓ Have you otherwise exhausted domestic remedies?
- ✓ Are you making the application within six months of having exhausted domestic remedies?
- ✓ Will your application fail on other admissibility grounds?—Is it written in an inflammatory style?
- ✓ Is it anonymous?
- ✓ Have you submitted substantially the same application before?
- ✓ Is your application being examined by another international body?

2.2.3 Interpreting the Checklist: What Do These Considerations Mean?

The Court has two main remedies at its disposal. It can oversee the parties in negotiations towards a friendly settlement, without having to finally decide the claim, or, if it finds that a violation of the ECHR has occurred, it can award "just satisfaction" (compensation and costs) under Article 41.

2.2.4 Interim Measures

Note: Requests for interim measures must be made in writing, and as soon as possible after the final domestic decision has been handed down in the case. The Secretary of the Court needs time to process the request, and time may be of the essence.

Interim measures may be sought under rule 39. The rule provides that the Chamber dealing with the application, or its President, may, either at the request of the parties or of its own motion, indicate any interim measures it regards as necessary in the interests of the parties or for the proper conduct of proceedings. Interim measures ordered by the Court are not binding on the parties.[17] States parties do not, in general, ignore such requests of the Court, and there is a degree of diplomatic pressure involved, as the Committee of Ministers is given notice of the measures under rule 39(2). The Chamber may request any information from the parties on matters connected with the interim measures sought.

2.2.5 Friendly Settlement

> **Note:** It is important to note that the danger of irreversible damage in the absence of interim measures must be high. Interim measures are generally granted in an expulsion or extradition context only where a breach of Article 3 is alleged.[18] (See below at Section 3.1.2.)

> **Tip:** Apply to the Court to give the application priority under rule 41. Ordinarily, cases are heard in the order in which they are ready for examination. However, the Court has discretion to accord priority in a case of genuine emergency or urgency.[19] A request for urgent examination should be made in the form of a cover letter attached to the application, clearly delineating the reasons for expedited examination of the case.

The option of coming to a friendly settlement has always been a cornerstone of the ECHR machinery. Now that the jurisprudence of the Court is sufficiently well developed to allow the parties to predict the outcome of disputes, this will undoubtedly continue, particularly as the caseload of the Court increases.[20]

The parties can begin working with the Court to achieve a friendly settlement, under Article 38 § 1, as soon as an application has been declared admissible. The Court itself initiates the process by contacting both parties and inviting proposals from both sides as to the terms of a potential settlement. Either side can refuse to engage in negotia-

---

[17] *Cruz Varas and Others v. Sweden*, 201 Eur. Ct. H.R. (ser. A) § 98 (1991).
[18] DONNA GOMIEN ET AL., LAW AND PRACTICE OF THE EUROPEAN CONVENTION ON HUMAN RIGHTS AND THE EUROPEAN SOCIAL CHARTER 52 (1996).
[19] Boyle, *supra* note 14, at 146.
[20] LUKE CLEMENTS ET AL., EUROPEAN HUMAN RIGHTS: TAKING A CASE UNDER THE CONVENTION 75 (2d ed. 1999).

tions for a friendly settlement at any time, although the remedy is often a highly advantageous one. This is especially true of cases where urgent relief is needed, as it often is for asylum-seekers and refugees. If both parties agree to pursue a friendly settlement, Article 38 § 2 of the ECHR and rule 62 of the Rules of the Court require that all negotiations to that end are strictly confidential.

At first, the Court will pass proposals between the parties without much intervention. The Chamber seized of the application can also indicate a provisional view of the merits to the parties in order to facilitate agreement.[21] As the negotiations progress, the parties can request the Court to assist more actively in the settlement and act as a mediator, if necessary.[22]

If the parties do come to a friendly settlement, the Court, acting under Article 39 of the ECHR, will strike the case from its list. This is accomplished by means of a very brief decision, usually just including the names of the parties, main facts of the case and terms of the settlement.[23] That decision is published by the Council of Europe, as are all the judgments and orders of the Court.

Main advantages for refugees, asylum-seekers, and IDPs of opting for a friendly settlement over just satisfaction:
- Speed in urgent situations, such as determination of refugee status or prolonged detention;
- Often the state will offer significantly greater compensation than under a just satisfaction award;[24]
- Redress is not limited to compensation and costs (see below), but can include in principle any negotiated form of redress, such as being granted leave to remain in a ECHR country or have one's children enter that country for the purposes of family reunification;

In the scenarios detailed in Chapter 1, seeking a friendly settlement would be most advantageous for:

IBRAHIM (Scenario 2)
Advantages for Ibrahim of seeking a friendly settlement (as against the asylum state):
- It is open to the asylum state fairly quickly to grant Ibrahim asylum or leave to remain, in some complementary form, on humanitarian grounds;

---

[21] Paragraph 78 of the Explanatory Report of the Council of Europe to Protocol No. 11 (Council of Europe Publishing, May 1994).
[22] CLEMENTS, *supra* note 20, at 76.
[23] *Id.* at 76.
[24] *Id.* at 75.

- Ibrahim could still ask, as part of the terms of the friendly settlement, for pecuniary compensation as regards the discriminatory treatment he has suffered in employment, housing, social support, and education, and permission for his children to enter.
- Disadvantages for Ibrahim of seeking a friendly settlement:
- As regards his claim against the police, he may wish to have a judgment in hand stating that the police acted against him in violation of fundamental norms of human rights. It is theoretically possible to settle on some issues and continue to trial with the application in others, although the reality of reaching a friendly settlement means compromising some claims for others and using the threat of bringing those claims before the Court as bargaining leverage. The advantages, in the end, need to be considered on a case-by-case basis.

2.2.6 Just Satisfaction

Under Article 41 and rule 75 of the ECHR, the Court may require states, if they are found to be in violation of the ECHR to pay:

- Compensation
- Costs

Tip: If you fail to make a specific claim for just satisfaction under Article 41, the Court will not grant the award. The claim must be made **within 2 months of the Court's admissibility decision**.[25]

Note: If the applicant is indebted to the state in another matter, the Court may attach some of the costs awarded to that liability. Whether or not it will do so depends to some degree on the type of injury suffered. When making the compensation claim, it is worth asking the Court in its order to provide expressly that the sum cannot be paid directly to a third party to satisfy their claim against the applicant.[26]

---

[25] *Id.* at 79; rule 60. See most recently *Van Vlimmeren and Van Ilneerenbeck v. the Netherlands* (Eur. Ct. H.R. Sept. 29, 2000), at <http://www.dhcour.coe.fr/hudoc/ViewRoot.asp?Item=0&Action=Html&X=1108041737&Notice=0&Noticemode=&RelatedMode=0> (application for just satisfaction rejected as claim was submitted too late).

[26] CLEMENTS, *supra* note 20, at 94. Compare *Ringeisen (no 3) v. Austria*, 16 Eur. Ct. H.R. (ser. A) (1973), to *Philis v. Greece*, 209 Eur. Ct. H.R. (ser. A) (1991). The former, where no attachment was allowed, involved the physical liberty of the applicant, whereas the latter involved a contractual interest.

European Human Rights Mechanisms 325

The object of the Court's award is to restore the applicant to the position occupied before the violation took place. However, the compensation awarded by the Court is *always monetary*. The Court cannot require that the state perform a specific task, such as to refrain from deporting an individual.[27]

> **Note:** It is always up to the state to determine what measures it will take to comply with the Court's judgments. When the finding of a violation condemns a domestic policy or piece of legislation to repeated challenge by numerous victims before the Court, the state will often endeavor to change the policy or repeal the legislation.[28] States have also made agreements in expulsion and deportation cases to find the applicant a safe receiving country in lieu of paying compensation alone.[29] This is not, however, required by the ECHR.

In order to be awarded just satisfaction, the applicant must establish a causal link between the injury suffered and the violation, on the basis of which damages can be assessed.[30]

It is also open to the Court to hold that the finding of a violation in itself constitutes just satisfaction, and award a nominal amount of damages accordingly.[31] Such a holding, however, is most common in cases where the violation itself is considered relatively minor. The kinds of injuries suffered by refugees, asylum-seekers, and IDPs are almost never of that type.

Compensation includes:

- Pecuniary loss
- Non-pecuniary loss

---

[27] *Nasri v. France*, 320-B Eur. Ct. H.R. (ser. A) (1995).

[28] *Open Door and Dublin Well Woman v. Ireland*, 246-A Eur. Ct. H.R. (ser. A) (1992).

[29] *Moustaquim v. Belgium*, 193 Eur. Ct. H.R. (ser. A) (1991), *Soering v. United Kingdom*, 161 Eur. Ct. H.R. (ser. A) (1989) (Soering was accused of the murder of his girlfriend's parents in the United States. The United States sought his extradition from Britain to try him for capital murder. The Court ruled that for Britain to extradite him with such a "real risk" of living for years on death row amounted to a breach of Article 3. Britain did extradite him, but only on condition that the capital charge be dropped in favor of life imprisonment).

[30] This link has not been made out, for instance, in cases where the applicant has claimed the costs incurred during bankruptcy proceedings in a case of a violation of the right to a fair hearing under Article 6: *Hauschildt v. Switzerland*, 154 Eur. Ct. H.R. (ser. A) § 60 (1989), and GOMIEN, *supra* note 18, at 84.

[31] *Golder v. the United Kingdom*, 18 Eur. Ct. H.R. (ser. A) (1975).

- Aggravated damages
- Costs

Pecuniary Loss

This includes all quantifiable expenses actually incurred as a direct result of the violation. Hypothetical losses are not included.[32] Out-of-pocket expenses and the value of property destroyed or lost due to Government action are included.

> **Chen**—who in Scenario 1 is a refugee. She will claim compensation from her country of origin (as long as it is bound by the ECHR) for her home and personal property, and probably also the cost of flight.
> **Maria**—who in Scenario 3 is an internally displaced person. She will claim the cost of the house and property she was forced to leave behind when she fled. If she left her job also, she can claim lost earnings.

Non-Pecuniary Loss

This includes damages for pain, suffering, ill treatment, loss of a loved one, and prolonged detention. It applies to injuries, which are much harder to quantify in terms of money. Such injuries are at the heart of the violations raised by refugees, asylum-seekers, and internally displaced persons. The Court will often be guided in this respect by the state's own practice of awarding damages. This may seem intuitively unjust, but is the Court's best way of assessing damages a state would be likely to pay.[33]

> **Ibrahim**—Scenario 2—In his country of origin, will seek compensation for non-pecuniary loss (ill-treatment and pain and suffering) with regard to:
> - Loss of his home[34]
> - Detention without charge or trial

---

[32] CLEMENTS, *supra* note 20, at 81.

[33] In *Aydin v. Turkey*, 1997-VI Eur. Ct. H.R., the Court awarded 25,000 pounds sterling in damages to the applicant, who had been raped and tortured in violation of Article 3. In an analogous French Article 3 case, involving an instance of police brutality (*Tomasi v. France*, 214-A Eur. Ct. H.R. (ser. A) (1992)), the Court awarded 85,000 pounds sterling based on domestic awards of damages. CLEMENTS, *supra* note 20, at 84.

[34] As regards at least the eviction from their homes of *Chen, Ibrahim*, and

> - Torture
> - Being prevented from expressing his political views.
> - As an asylum seeker, he will claim compensation for non-pecuniary loss (ill-treatment and pain and suffering) in the asylum state with regard to:
> - Discrimination in access to employment, housing, health care, education, and social support
> - Harassment and assault by the police
> - Failure of the police to come to his aid when he was attacked by members of the local community.
>
> Many of the same grounds for compensation apply to **Chen** in Scenario 1.

Aggravated Damages

The Court has never made an express award of aggravated damages, but it has hinted in a deportation context that uncooperative behavior on the part of the state can be a factor in determining whether or not a serious violation (in that context, of Article 3) has occurred.[35] It seems clear that the Court is not open to awarding punitive or exemplary damages.[36]

Costs

If the applicant is successful in establishing that a violation has occurred, the Court will also award costs and expenses, as long as they

---

Maria, the Court may very well combine the awards of pecuniary and non-pecuniary damages, as these are cases where the two categories are inextricably linked. This would be argued on the basis of *López-Ostra v. Spain*, 303-C Eur. Ct. H.R. (ser. A) (1994), where the victim was forced to move due to the proximity to her home of a waste treatment plant, which damaged her health and that of her family by emitting noxious fumes. There the Court joined the two heads of damages. The sum awarded was quantified on an equitable basis. It is unclear whether or not the award was more advantageous than it would have been had non-pecuniary loss been measured separately by the Spanish national standard. See CLEMENTS, *supra* note 20, at 83.

[35] *Cruz Varas and Others v. Sweden*, 201 Eur. Ct. H.R. (ser. A) (1991) (in the context of a state's failure to comply with an interim measures order of the Court). CLEMENTS, *supra* note 20, at 84 (citing the Court, 'if a state "knowingly assumes the risk of being found to be in breach of Article 3 . . . any such finding would be have to be seen as aggravated by the failure to comply"'). *See also Akdivar v. Turkey*, 1996-IV, No. 15, 23 E.H.R.R. 150.

[36] See *Aydin v. Turkey*, 1997-VI 25 E.H.R.R. 251 (rape and torture in violation of Article 3, no award of punitive damages).

are reasonable as to quantum[37] and *actually and necessarily incurred* (i.e., *reasonable* costs that can all be accounted for in full). In general terms, the Court will be guided by a reasonable assessment of lawyers' fees and case-preparation costs in the domestic system of the accused state when awarding costs, so it is accordingly to these that you should refer in preparing your claim for costs to the Court.

> **Note:** Under rule 60, you must submit a **separate** written claim detailing and accounting specifically for all costs claimed. These will then be deducted from any legal aid awarded by the Court.[38]

> **Tip:** Once that claim is submitted, it will be forwarded to the respondent Government. If the applicant and Government can simply not agree on the amount, the assessment of a domestic Court Officer will be approved by the Court,[39] provided it is adjudged reliable and impartial.

Costs should include:[40]

- Domestic court costs if the applicant was responsible for paying them in whole or in part[41] (i.e., not costs covered by domestic legal aid)
- Lawyers' fees, including costs for time spent working on the case[42]
- Reasonable travel expenses for fact-finding and case preparation.

Costs will probably not include:

- Costs *unreasonably* incurred, such as an engaging an extra firm of lawyers when the original representation of the applicant was perfectly sufficient.[43]

---

[37] Assessed as a question of proportionality: *Young, James and Webster v. the United Kingdom*, 44 Eur. Ct. H.R. (ser. A) (1981).

[38] Boyle, *supra* note 14, at 151.

[39] *Young, James and Webster v. the United Kingdom*, *supra* note 37.

[40] *See generally*, *Sunday Times v. the United Kingdom (No.2)*, 217 Eur. Ct. H.R. (ser. A) (1991).

[41] CLEMENTS, *supra* note 20, at 94.

[42] There is no easy way to calculate what rate to charge per hour of work done. National systems lawyers' annual salaries can be used as a rough guide if divided into weekly or indeed hourly earnings. It is important to keep a detailed log of hours spent on the claim, telephone calls made and all other resource-expenses incurred.

[43] Compare *Castells v. Spain*, 236 Eur. Ct. H.R. (ser. A) (1992), to *Aydin v.*

- Travel expenses to Strasbourg, although it is worth detailing them in your claim. Without that, there is no chance of reimbursement at all.

It is interesting to note that the Court will award costs even where the applicant clearly could not have paid the lawyers himself.[44]

> **Note:** If your client cannot pay your fees himself, it is best to set out in writing the costs agreement between you and your client as evidence for the Court.[45]

The only exception to this rule is the case of a lawyer who has clearly represented that he is acting without expectation of remuneration in the first place.[46] In that case, he will not be able to claim costs back from the Court in the event of success.

> **Main advantages for refugees, asylum-seekers, and IDPs of opting for just satisfaction over a friendly settlement:**
> - Greater degree of scrutiny over any agreement reached by the parties: Once the Court has pronounced on the merits of the case, it is still open to the parties to agree on the amount of just satisfaction to be awarded. The Court, under rule 75(4), only strikes the case off the list if it adjudges that agreement to be "equitable." Although it could in theory object to the amount of a friendly settlement, no such instances are recorded.
> - Getting a judgment on the merits is the only way to challenge a piece of legislation or entire governmental policy, such as to affect not just the applicant, but others similarly situated.
> - The satisfaction of having a published judgment from an international tribunal in hand attesting to the injustice of the treatment of the applicant.

Turkey, supra note 36. In the former, the Court refused to reimburse the applicant for the cost of four lawyers, which it held to be excessive. It awarded representation costs on an equitable basis. However, the Court judges each case on its facts. In *Aydin*, the applicant claimed costs both for Turkish and British legal representation, when the latter was far more expensive than the former would have been. The Court found the amount to be reasonable and awarded it accordingly. CLEMENTS, *supra* note 20, at 92.

[44] CLEMENTS, *supra* note 20, at 93, citing *Pakelli v. Germany*, 64 Eur. Ct. H.R. (ser. A) (1983) where a lawyer submitted claim for costs out of time, having earlier assumed that Court would not award costs the client could not pay. The Court awarded costs anyway.

[45] CLEMENTS, *supra* note 20, at 93.

[46] *McCann and Others v. the United Kingdom*, 324 Eur. Ct. H.R. (ser. A) (1995).

- Time-limits for the payment of the award can be set by the Court and interest charged for awards not paid within the time-limit set.[47]
- Enforcement of the judgment is overseen by the Committee of Ministers of the Council of Europe under Article 46(2) of the ECHR.

In the scenarios detailed in Chapter 1, seeking a friendly settlement would be most advantageous for:

Maria (Scenario 6)
- Advantages for **Maria** of seeking an award of just satisfaction:
- If the internal displacement to which Maria was subject was part of a state-sponsored or tolerated policy of discrimination and persecution, the policy could be declared to be generally in violation of ECHR obligations, as potentially applicable to all those affected. The same applies to a policy of forcible recruitment of minors into the military, as regards Maria's 14-year-old son;
- Restoring Maria to her property will not necessarily do her any good in a situation where she fears private attacks and where the rule of law appears to have broken down (provided the property is still habitable);
- Given that the ECHR never allows for the imprisonment of specific actors upon the finding of a violation, there is no other remedy for one's son being murdered, having oneself suffered beatings, and having been raped other than a judgment against the perpetrators acknowledging the injuries and facts and being compensated by the state accordingly;

Disadvantages for **Maria** of seeking just satisfaction:
- Compensation will not restore Maria's identity documentation to her, get her son back from the army, nor help her escape the country permanently.

2.2.7 Other Considerations: Legal Aid

Chapter X of the Rules of the Court covers the granting of legal aid, which is paid out of Council of Europe funds. *Legal aid can be granted by the Court, either at the request of an applicant or on the motion of the President of a Chamber, any time after the written comments on admissibility are received from the respondent state or even after their time limit for the submission of those observations has expired.*

Legal aid is free and is means-determined (rule 92 (b)). The need is assessed after the applicant has filled in an application detailing income, capital assets, financial commitments, and dependants, which must be certified by the domestic authorities. The respondent government's comments on the grant are also requested.

---

[47] Rule 75 (3).

Legal aid covers fees, traveling expenses, living expenses, and other "out of pocket expenses." It also pays for representation by one, or if the issues or number of applicants so require, more representatives, whether they are practitioners or law professors.

On the whole, the legal aid fees granted do not cover all expenses, but do allow all the necessary preparation to be made for a case and allow the parties to travel to the Court and subsist while there.

> **Note:** There is no filing fee for lodging an application with the Court.

Under rule 96, the President of the Chamber has the power to revoke the grant of legal aid at any time, if he considers that the eligibility requirements under rule 92 are no longer satisfied.

2.2.8 Legal Representation

Prior to the Protocol 11 reforms, *pro se* representation was fully accepted before the Court. In principle, this is still the case, although, under rule 36, the President of the Chamber may direct that the applicant be represented by an advocate authorized to practice in any of the contracting states and resident in the territory of one of them, or by a person otherwise approved by the President of the Chamber. This will be done ordinarily when the case involves particularly serious and complex issues under the ECHR. The applicant may change representatives at any time.

> **Note:** The President of the Chamber also has the power to remove a representative for misconduct at any point during the proceedings. After such removal, the representative in question is prevented from assisting the applicant in any way with the remainder of his case.

2.2.9 Language Considerations

Officially, the languages of the Court are French and English. All stages of the application process can be carried out in either language. Once the admissibility stage of proceedings has passed, leaving the written pleadings and hearings to follow, all submissions must be in either of the official languages, subject to special permission being granted by the President of the Chamber, under rule 34(4)(a). Nevertheless, the representative responsible for pleading and the oral hearing must have knowledge of either of the official languages, for practicality purposes at least.

> **Note:** If leave is granted to use a language other than English or French, the requesting party bears the burden of interpreting and translation costs.[48]

> **Note:** Applicants should never be dissuaded from applying to the Court on language grounds. However, the process is much longer and more arduous if it involves constant interpretation and translation, and, given the problems inherent in ensuring that translations are accurate, it always places the applicant in a disadvantageous position.[49]

> **Tip:** It is recommended that an advocate with the requisite language skills be sought. This is most easily accomplished by seeking the help of a non-governmental organization (NGO).

2.2.10 Enforcing the Court's Judgments—Effectiveness of Remedies

Under Article 46, states that are parties to a case agree to abide by the final judgment of the Court.[50] Depending on their undertakings, states may be obliged to take action in any of three ways in order to comply with a judgment of the Court:

- Payment of Court-awarded compensation and costs.
- Individual measures designed to remedy the particular violation.[51]
- Remedying a domestic legal defect, which is the source of the violation.[52]

---

[48] There is no reason, however, why these should not be borne by legal aid where it is granted. Moreover, the President can direct the respondent state to provide a translation into the language of the applicant in order to facilitate proceedings. The Registrar is responsible for providing interpreting for witnesses and experts.

[49] Boyle, *supra* note 14, at 145.

[50] In practice, judgments tend to have repercussions that extend beyond the actual parties to the suit. Other states will tend to modify their behavior in order to avoid the same suits being brought against them.

[51] This might include ordering a retrial where the violation involved a serious breach of Article 6 of the ECHR, the right to a fair hearing.

[52] This might include repealing legislation or enacting new legislation. This can take a very long time, and there is no time limit imposed by the Committee on states to take these measures. Following the Court's decision in *Marckx v. Belgium*, 31 Eur. Ct. H.R. (ser. A) (1979), Belgium took eight years to change domestic laws that discriminated unfairly against illegitimate children.

Article 46 § 2 provides that execution of judgments is supervised by the Committee of Ministers (hereinafter "the Committee"), "the political arm of the ECHR."[53] The Committee is comprised of the Foreign Minister of each member state of the Council of Europe.[54] The Committee meets during most months of the year. Each decision of the Court is referred to the Committee session following it.

Before the Committee, a state is required to report on the steps that have been taken to comply with the Court's judgment. Beyond the payment of compensation and costs, it is for the state to determine the appropriate compliance measures.

> **Note:** The applicant has no standing before the Committee. However, the applicant can keep track, through telephone communication with the Secretariat, of the progress towards fulfillment of the judgment.

States are required to report to the Committee at least every six months on the steps being taken to comply with a particular decision.

> **Note:** Damages and costs must be paid within 3 months of their award. If that time is exceeded, the applicant's representative may make a claim for interest, through the Registrar, at the rate set by the Court.

When the Committee considers that a state is in full compliance with a judgment of the Court, it issues a resolution declaring the judgment satisfied.

> **Note:** When a state enters a derogation under Article 15 of the ECHR, the Committee's power to supervise the execution of the judgment affected by that derogation is terminated. The applicant must reapply to the Court to have the validity of the derogation itself evaluated in light of Article 15 of the ECHR.

---

[53] Boyle, *supra* note 14, at 152

[54] The Committee meets formally twice a year. At all other meetings, the Ministers are usually represented by deputies, who have the authority to act on their Minister's behalf.

2.3 Admissibility Criteria

2.3.1 Jurisdiction Ratione Personae—Who Is Liable and Who Can Be Sued?

Individual Victims

In order to bring a case before the Court, individuals must be *victims* within the meaning of the ECHR.

- *There must be an injury.* In its simplest terms, being a victim of a violation of a right guaranteed by the ECHR implies that the violation caused injury to the applicant.[55] The relevant type of injury obviously varies with the violation alleged.
- *The injury need not be ongoing.* If the facts and circumstances, which gave rise to the injury, do not continue up to the date of complaint, the applicant may still qualify as a victim. In the case of *López Ostra*,[56] the government contended that the applicant had ceased to be a victim, because she had moved away from the site of an unlicensed waste treatment plant, which, due to its proximity to her home and noxious effects, had negated her right to private life and respect for her home. The Court held that the fact that Mrs. López-Ostra moved house, in order to place the health of her family out of danger, did not affect the injury she suffered, given that the state had failed to take any measures to mitigate the injury and that no less extreme measure had been open to her. Applying this reasoning to the refugee and asylum-seeker, a state may argue that flight deprived it of its opportunity to remedy the violation. This matter has never come before the Court, but if flight occurred pursuant to the violation of a right protected by the ECHR, the reasoning of *López Ostra* appears appropriate.

Indirect Victims

Claims of a violation of an ECHR right leading directly to the death of the victim can be pursued by the victim's heirs, family, or those in a close relationship[57] to the victim. They are thus "victims" them-

---

[55] An applicant does not lose victim status if the national courts have provided some relief, but have not remedied the specific violation of the ECHR. *Lüdi v. Switzerland*, 238 Eur. CT. H.R. (ser. A) § 34 (1992).
[56] *López Ostra v. Spain, supra* note 34.
[57] *See* for example *Velikova v. Bulgaria* (E.C.H.R. May 18 2000), at <http://www.dhcour.coe.fr/hudoc/ViewRoot.asp?Item=0&Action=Html&X=1025023358

selves, in the eyes of the Court, in the sense that they have standing to bring the application.

> **Maria**—an IDP in Scenario 3, is a "victim" for ECHR purposes as regards the murder of her oldest son by security forces.

Where an applicant dies, his heirs may inherit the claim and become victims in his place or on their own behalf. To do this, they must have a sufficient legal interest.

> **Note:** There is no fixed rule for determining what constitutes a "sufficient legal interest."

In the *Deweer* case,[58] standing was accorded to the victim's heirs on the grounds that the right allegedly violated was part of the estate of the victim, and was therefore inherited by his heirs.

The Court's case law does give some indication of when the heir's interest is *insufficient* to render him a victim. A marked lack of interest in the proceedings must be shown by the heir, in order to forfeit his victim status. The case *of Macaluso v. Italy*,[59] which involved a challenge to the length of administrative proceedings, was struck out of the list on two grounds:

(1) Upon the applicant's death, his heir remained silent as to his intent to pursue the application, in spite of "several reminders" from the Registry of the Court over a seven-month period. By analogy to the Rules of the Court in force at the time (1991) governing the friendly settlement of disputes, the Court held that their silence constituted an implied arrangement which amounted to the end of the matter, and

(2) There was no reason of *ordre public* (public order or the good of the Council of Europe community as a whole) to hear the case, as a number of cases on the same subject were pending before the Court at the time.

&Notice=0&Noticemode=&RelatedMode=0>. (art. 2 case brought by domestic partner of 12 years) and *Paton v. United Kingdom*, No. 8416/78, 19 DR 211 (1980) (Commission allowed art. 2 case to be brought by father on behalf of fetus after termination of his wife's pregnancy).

[58] *Deweer v. Belgium*, 35 Eur. Ct. H.R. (ser. A) 19, § 37 (1980).

[59] *Macaluso v. Italy*, decision of Dec. 3, 1991, at <http://hudoc.echr.coe.int/Hudoc1doc\HEJUD\sift\269.txt>.

Deweer and *Macaluso* occupy two ends of the "interest spectrum." Between them, the content of the "sufficient legal interest" is unclear. To some extent, the nature of the claim itself will affect the Court's determination as to the interest of a third party in bringing the case.[60] Each claim to continue a complaint following the death of an applicant will be evaluated on its own facts and in light of its importance for *ordre public* in the Council of Europe.

> **Tip:** In making a claim to the Court on behalf of relatives of a deceased refugee, asylum-seeker, or IDP, mention should be made of the importance in public policy of the Court's examination of the particular claim.

Family members of victims have the right, not only to bring applications following the *death* of a relative, but also to do so *in their own right for the injury they suffered as a result of the ill-treatment of a relative*. In the case of *Mrs. W v. UK*,[61] a widow was considered to be an indirect victim of a terrorist assault that killed her husband and unmarried brother, and at the same time a direct victim of the ongoing situation in Northern Ireland with regard to her own security.[62]

In the case of *Çakici v. Turkey*,[63] the applicant claimed that the continuing disappearance of his brother amounted not only to inhuman and degrading treatment, a violation of the right to life under Article 2 and a violation of the right to liberty and security of the person with regard to his brother, but also to inhuman treatment under Article 3 in relation to himself and other members of his family. The Court laid down the following test to determine whether or not a family member could claim to be the indirect victim of the disappearance of a close relative:

---

[60] In *Macaluso*, the administrative proceedings being challenged for their length involved a claim to disability benefit by the deceased applicant. In the case of *X v. France*, Eur. Ct.H.R. (ser.A) 234-C (1992), in contrast, the Court allowed the surviving parents of a victim, who had contracted AIDS from blood transfusions administered to him in a public hospital, to take over his application. The administrative proceedings impugned before the Court were those he had instituted against the Minister for Health, Solidarity and Social Protection for negligent delay in implementing appropriate rules for the supply of blood products (§11).

[61] *Mrs. W. v. United Kingdom*, no. 9348/81, 32 DR 211 (1983).

[62] DAVID J. HARRIS, MICHAEL O'BOYLE AND COLIN WARBRICK, LAW OF THE EUROPEAN CONVENTION ON HUMAN RIGHTS 637 (1995).

[63] *Çakici v. Turkey* (E.C.H.R. July 1999), at <http://hudoc.echr.coe.int/hudoc/ViewRoot.asp?Item=0&Action=Html&X=518122224&Notice=0&Noticemode=&RelatedMode=0>.

> **Test:** Do special factors exist which make the applicant's suffering distinct from the emotional distress which is inevitably suffered by a close relative of a victim of a human rights abuse?
>
> Questions to ask:
> - What was the proximity of the family tie (is the relationship one of a parent-child?)?
> - What were the circumstances of the relationship?
> - Did the family member witness the abuse?
> - Was the family member involved in the attempt to obtain evidence about the disappeared person?
> - How was the family member treated by authorities in the course of that attempt?
> - What were the reactions and attitudes of the authorities when the disappearance was brought to their attention?[64]

Under the particular circumstances of the case, the Court held that Mr. Çakici did not qualify as an indirect victim of inhuman and degrading treatment himself, but did not contest that he properly brought before the Court the other claims on his brother's behalf.

> **Maria**—who, in Scenario 3, is an IDP. With regard to the death of her oldest son, Maria will make an application, not only alleging a breach of Article 2 of the ECHR, the right to life, but also a breach of Article 3, the prohibition against cruel, inhuman or degrading treatment and punishment, in her own right.

---

[64] *Id.* § 98:

[W]hether a family member is such a victim will depend on the existence of special factors which gives the suffering of the applicant a dimension and character distinct from the emotional distress which may be regarded as inevitably caused to relatives of a victim of a serious human rights violation. Relevant elements will include the proximity of the family tie—in that context, a certain weight will attach to the parent-child bond—the particular circumstances of the relationship, the extent to which the family member witnessed the events in question, the involvement of the family member in the attempts to obtain information about the disappeared person and the way in which the authorities responded to those enquiries. The Court would further emphasize that the essence of such a violation does not so much lie in the fact of the "disappearance" of the family member, but rather concerns the authorities' reactions and attitudes to the situation when it is brought to their attention. It is especially in respect of the latter that a relative may claim directly to be a victim of the authorities' conduct.

> Although the case is not one involving the disappearance of a relative, the test in Çakici can be applied by analogy. Maria falls within its "special factors" on the following grounds:
> - Her son was killed, thus severing the parent-child bond;
> - She witnessed the murder;
> - The murder occurred in the course of an eviction by government security forces, who beat and raped Maria.

> **Note:** It is important to note that the Commission has held that a claim of risk of inhuman treatment in the event of extradition could not be brought after the death of the applicant.[65]

> **Tip:** Procedurally, in order to bring a claim as an indirect victim, the name of the victim must be revealed and he must have given permission for the claim to be brought on his behalf to the extent possible.[66]

Risk of a Violation Once Deported or Extradited

As will be discussed below, there are certain circumstances in which the alleged injury need not actually yet have happened to render the applicant a victim. *Most significantly for the claims of refugees and asylum-seekers, the Court has extended its reach under Article 3, the prohibition against torture, inhuman and degrading treatment, to include extradition, expulsion, and deportation cases where substantial grounds can be shown to believe that the person being expelled would be subject to a real risk of treatment prohibited by Article 3 in the receiving State.*[67] This is discussed in detail in Section 3 of this chapter in connection with Article 3. As long as the applicant can allege that he is at such risk, he will be considered a victim, even though he has not yet suffered an injury.

> **Note:** The only limitation is that he refrains from bringing his case until the extradition or expulsion order is actually issued.[68]

---

[65] *Altun v. Federal Republic of Germany*, No. 10308/83, 36 DR 236 (1983)
[66] GOMIEN, *supra* note 18, at 46.
[67] *Soering v. the United Kingdom*, *supra* note 29.
[68] *Vijayanathan and Puspurajah v. France*, 241-B Eur. Ct. H.R. (ser. A) § 46 (1992).

The Court has also extended the right to family and private life protected by Article 8, in certain circumstances, to prevent families from being separated by the extradition or expulsion of a member. This will also be discussed in detail in Section 3.

Court Decisions Interpreting National Legislation

On a number of occasions, the Court has also allowed *discrete* groups of applicants to challenge domestic decisions interpreting national legislation, which have not yet actually affected them, but by their definition significantly affect their freedom to act, in contravention of rights protected by the ECHR. This seems to be acceptable in rare cases where the group affected is capable of identification and where the Court does not foresee repeated challenges of the same legislation. The Court has allowed a group of applicants including "women of child-bearing age" to challenge an Irish Supreme Court injunction against the distribution of information detailing legal abortion facilities outside the jurisdiction of Ireland, even though none of them were pregnant at the time.[69]

Potential Victims and Challenges to Domestic Legislation

Note: As a general principle, there is no standing before the Court to challenge a hypothetical situation or a piece of legislation in the abstract.

Where the application of a particular domestic law is brought before the Court as constituting a violation of the ECHR, the Court will not ordinarily question the interpretation of that law by the national court, unless it is a specific requirement of the ECHR that an act be "in accordance with the law." However, in certain circumstances the Court has allowed individuals to challenge legislation on the grounds of incompatibility with ECHR obligations, before it is actually enforced.

Note: The general threshold applicants must meet to challenge legislation is a showing that they run a risk of being directly affected by the impugned legislation once implemented.[70]

---

[69] *Dublin Well Woman, supra* note 28.
[70] HARRIS, *supra* note 62, at 635.

Cases of this kind have exclusively been allowed by the Court where the legislation in question enshrines a moral principle out of keeping with the general social attitudes and legislation prevailing among Council of Europe members. These cases have included challenges to legislation limiting the succession rights of children born outside marriage[71] and to legislation prohibiting homosexual acts in private.[72] In *Dudgeon*, the Court noted with regard to the legislation in issue:

> [a]s compared with the era when that legislation was enacted, there is a better understanding, and in consequence an increased tolerance, of homosexual behavior to the extent that in the great majority of member States of the Council of Europe it is no longer considered to be necessary or appropriate to treat homosexual practices of the kind now in question as in themselves a matter to which the sanctions of the criminal law should be applied; the Court cannot overlook the marked changes which have occurred in this regard in the domestic law of the member States.

Therefore, a discrete group of IDPs wishing to bring a claim challenging legislation by which they would specifically adversely affected if implemented, might qualify as victims for the purposes of Article 34.

The situation of refugees and asylum-seekers challenging legislation governing determination of their status is more complicated. *The causal nexus between the legislation and injury is all-important.* Even if there existed legislation providing for group asylum application review only, rather than the evaluation of each case individually, it would be very difficult to establish that the process in itself puts a particular applicant in danger of inhuman or degrading treatment.

Groups of Individuals and Non-Governmental Organizations (NGOs)

No *actio popularis* can be brought before the Court. Therefore, in order for groups of individuals to bring a claim jointly before the Court, they must each individually be victims in their own right. Under Article 34, NGOs do have standing to make applications to the Court. "Non-governmental organizations" include organizations ranging from com-

---

[71] *Johnston v. Ireland*, 112 Eur. Ct. H.R. (ser. A) (1986), and *Marckx v. Belgium*, 31 Eur. Ct. H.R. (ser. A) § 27 (1979).

[72] *Dudgeon v. the United Kingdom*, 45 Eur. Ct. H.R. (ser. A) § 41 (1981), and *Norris v. Ireland*, 142 Eur. Ct. H.R. (ser. A) §§ 28, 34 (1988).

munity churches to trade unions. In keeping with Article 34, the organization must be *private* in order to have standing to bring a claim. The Court will undertake *its own independent examination* of the public or private character of the applicant organization, rather than relying on the characterization of it proffered by the Government.[73]

In order to qualify as victims of a violation of the ECHR, the organization or its members must:

- show that they were affected in some way by the alleged breach, i.e. satisfy the ECHR definition of a "victim";
- be able to identify its members;
- provide evidence of its authority to represent its members;[74]
- show that the act complained of was directed towards the organization itself.[75]

Note: The ability of NGOs to bring claims before the Court could be extremely useful in religious persecution cases concerning internally displaced persons. **Chen**—who, in Scenario 4 is a refugee, fled her country of origin due to religious persecution. Her faith group, provided the above criteria for victim status are met, could bring a claim on behalf of its members against the country of origin for religious persecution and potentially also against the receiving state for discriminatory treatment of its members (as long as the treatment was sufficiently uniform and widespread that it could be identified as directed towards the group itself).

Note: NGOs play a significant role in the ECHR system through the submission of amicus curiae briefs under rule 61(2) and Article 36 § 2.

Loss of Victim Status

This concept does not refer to a case where the harm done by the alleged injury somehow abates, but rather to a situation where a national

---

[73] *The Holy Monasteries v. Greece*, Eur. Ct. H.R. (ser. A) 310-A (1994), in which the monasteries of Mt. Athos challenged the state's claim to the land on which their monasteries had been situated, in some cases, for centuries.

[74] *X and Church of Scientology v. Sweden*, No. 7805/77, Dec. 5.5.79, D.R. 16 p. 68 and Gomien, *supra* note 18 at 43. The ability of an organization to bring a claim on behalf of its members was not self-evident in the ECHR system. The extension was made by the Commission in a case allowing the Church of Scientology to sue on its members' behalf.

[75] *Swedish Engine Drivers Union v. Sweden*, Eur. Ct. H.R. (ser. A) 20 (1976).

court intervenes to make the injury moot, without actually addressing and remedying its substance. For example, in *Dalban v. Romania*,[76] the applicant alleged that his conviction for libel, originally by a county court in Romania, had violated his freedom of expression under Article 10 of the ECHR. The Supreme Court was seized of the case and quashed the conviction, but instead of pronouncing on the freedom of expression issue, held that Mr. Dalban had acted "in good faith" and based on official documents (§ 42). The Court, citing its earlier holding in *Amuur v. France*,[77] held that " a decision or measure favorable to the applicant is not in principle sufficient to deprive him of his status as a victim unless the national authorities have acknowledged, either expressly or in substance, and then afforded redress for, the breach of the Convention."[78]

Waiver of Rights Nullifying Victim Status

The Court has held that a person cannot waive his fundamental rights in such a way as to deprive himself of victim status should he suffer a violation of those rights.[79]

Against Whom Can a Claim Be Brought?

Broadly speaking, acts or omissions that violate the ECHR must have been committed by the state, its bodies, agents, security forces, or local government in order to be actionable. An individual cannot complain of a violation committed by private persons or organizations, except where the alleged violation concerns one of the categories of positive duties imposed on the states by the ECHR. In general, states have a positive duty to have a legal system in place, which guarantees the effective protection of the rights enshrined in the ECHR.[80] Specific duties actively to protect ECHR rights, beyond the mere existence of an effective legal system, arise in the context of the right to life (Article

---

[76] *Dalban v. Romania*, (E.C.H.R. 28 September, 1999), at <http://hudoc.echr.coe.int/hudoc/ViewRoot.asp?Item=0&Action=Html&X=518123315&Notice=0&Noticemode=&RelatedMode=0>.

[77] *Amuur v. France*, 22 E.H.R.R. 491 (1996).

[78] *Dalban, supra* note 76 *§44*, citing *Ahmed v. the United Kingdom*, 1996-III Eur. Ct. H.R. 846 § 36.

[79] Held in the context of detention in *De Wilde, Oomas and Versyp* ("Vagrancy" Cases), 12 Eur. Ct. H.R. (ser. A) 36 § 65 (1971).

[80] See *Ergi v. Turkey* E.C.H.R. July 1998, at <http://hudoc.echr.coe.int/hudoc/ViewRoot.asp?Item=0&Action=Html&X=518123525&Notice=0&Noticemode=&RelatedMode=0>.

2), the prohibition on torture and inhuman and degrading treatment (Article 3), the right to freedom of expression (Article 10), and, to some extent, the right to a family and private life (Article 8).

In practice, drawing the line between state action and private action is not a clear-cut exercise. In the past, the Court has employed the logic that the state cannot absolve itself from responsibility under the ECHR by delegating its duties to private entities. This allowed the Court to consider the right to education under Article 2 of Protocol 1 in a private school context,[81] and the conflict with Articles 4 (the prohibition against forced labor) and 14 (anti-discrimination provision) of a legal aid system whose administration had been conferred on the Bar Association.[82] The ECHR can thus, in principle, reach the acts of private corporations to whom various aspects of government have been contracted out.

Although the precise limitations of the rule are uncertain, private corporations whose actions are effectively controlled or imputable to the state can be reached by the Court's jurisdiction. In the case of *Young, James and Webster*, the Court found actions imputable to the state, which were taken against the applicants by private corporations, merely because they were permitted to do so by the domestic law in force. In that case, it was adjudged to be contrary to the freedoms of thought and association protected by Articles 9 and 11 respectively to allow the applicants to continue in their jobs only if they became members of trade unions.

> **Ibrahim**—who in Scenario 2 is an asylum seeker. Although Ibrahim cannot bring an application against the individuals in the community of the receiving state who attacked him, he could bring an application against the state for failing to enforce its criminal law effectively and protect his ECHR right to physical integrity.
>
> **Maria**—who, in Scenario 3, is an IDP. There is no doubt that, under the above analysis, Maria could bring an application against the state for the actions of the security forces in evicting her, murdering her oldest son, beating and raping her, and indeed for the constant threats of attack by them. The security forces, acting as the enforcement arm of the executive, are state agents.
>
> **Could Maria bring a case against the state for damage done to her, her family, and property by the insurgents?**
>
> Following the decision of the Court in **Ergi v. Turkey** (see below in the context of Article 2 ECHR in section 3.1.1.1), Maria could make an argument that,

---

[81] *Costello-Roberts v. the United Kingdom*, 247-C Eur. Ct. H.R. (ser. A) §§ 25, 28 (1993).

[82] *Van der Mussele v. Belgium*, 70 Eur. Ct. H.R. (ser. A) § 28–30 (1983).

> at least in the context of ongoing conflict between state security forces and insurgent groups, the state had a duty to protect her son from a violation of his right to life, Article 2 of the ECHR, as a civilian caught in the "crossfire."

2.3.2 Jurisdiction Ratione Materiae—What Must the Complaint Concern?

A Right Protected by the ECHR and Its Protocols

Article 34 of the ECHR, read with Article 1 of the ECHR, enshrines an obligation on the part of all states parties to secure to those within their respective jurisdictions the rights and freedoms guaranteed. The Court has often interpreted ECHR rights broadly, in light of the its recognition of the ECHR as a "living instrument." Applicants are encouraged to make new arguments, which extend the bounds of the enumerated rights.

> **Note:** When your application concerns a right protected by a protocol to the ECHR, **always** make sure that the state against whom the application is being lodged has ratified that protocol. Also, watch out for **reservations** to all ECHR rights. These limit the obligations of the state and must be addressed when determining the extent of the state's duty.

The Court has no jurisdiction over rights not protected by the ECHR and its protocols, such as the right to employment or to collective bargaining.

> **Note:** The ECHR and its protocols do not guarantee a right to asylum as such. Such a right cannot be raised before the Court.

Acts or Omissions Committed by a State or Its Agents

This has been discussed above in the context of jurisdiction *ratione personae*. It is important to remember that acts *and omissions* are actionable before the Court, such as a state's failure to enforce its criminal law effectively.

The Doctrine of Fourth Instance or Quatrième Instance

This doctrine requires that the Court shall never act as a final court of appeal from national courts, and cannot review the findings of fact or law made by domestic tribunals. The Court is the ultimate overseer of the interpretation and application of the ECHR.

2.3.3 Jurisdiction Ratione Temporis—When Must the Alleged Events Have Occurred?

No state can be challenged under the ECHR for any violation committed by it prior to the date upon which it ratified the ECHR or relevant protocol. This varies from state to state and must be consulted in relation to each instrument before an application is made.

In addition, subject to the exhaustion of domestic remedies criteria below, claims must be brought within a period of six months from the date of the final decision before the domestic authorities on the violation in issue.

Where an applicant has already been expelled, the Court will primarily analyze the facts known to the state *at the time of extradition* to see if they indicated a real risk of torture, inhuman or degrading treatment in violations of Article 3. This will be so even if the applicant *actually* suffered injury in violation of Article 3 upon expulsion.[83]

In contrast, in a case where the applicant has yet to be deported, the Court will examine the conditions in the receiving state *at the time when the Court hears the case*, and not when the actual deportation decision was made.[84]

Tip: The advantage cannot be stressed enough to an applicant facing deportation, extradition, or expulsion of applying for interim measures to stay the actual deportation, extradition, or expulsion until the Court has examined the risk of harm on return in light of the ECHR. The Court employs a different temporal standard in dealing with the same case depending on whether the applicant is still within the asylum state or has been repatriated.

EXAMPLE:
Ibrahim—Scenario 2
Ibrahim is an asylum-seeker likely to be denied asylum and relocated to a province of his country of origin, which he considers unsafe. Imagine that, at the time when his application is denied, the political situation in his country seemed to be settling, but that it erupts into conflict once more shortly after the decision is made. If he is ordered deported, but the Court is able to

---

[83] *Vilvarajah v. United Kingdom,* Eur. Ct. H.R. (ser. A) 215 (1991).
[84] *Chahal v. United Kingdom,* 23 E.H.R.R. 413 (1996).

> examine his case before he is repatriated, it will evaluate his risk of torture, inhuman or degrading treatment and punishment on return based on the facts at the time when the case is heard. If he is, however, repatriated, and suffers treatment in breach of Article 3, the Court will evaluate the deportation decision based on the facts at the time when the decision was made (i.e. the political situation had improved somewhat). In those circumstances, the decision to deport is more likely to be upheld as not in violation of Article 3 of the ECHR, and Ibrahim is more likely to have suffered injury and be trapped inside the country he originally fled.

2.3.4 Jurisdiction Ratione Loci—Where Must the Alleged Violation Have Occurred?

On the Territory of the Respondent State

It is important to note that refugees, asylum-seekers, and internally displaced persons are not excluded from bringing a claim by virtue of their nationality or statelessness. They must, however, satisfy the definition discussed above of a "victim" and otherwise meet the jurisdictional requirements of the Court. Indeed, Article 1 of the ECHR expressly requires that the High Contracting Parties secure "to *everyone*[85] within their jurisdiction the rights and freedoms defined in Section I of the ECHR." National "jurisdiction" under the ECHR system has been interpreted as extending even beyond acts committed within the territorial limits of the states parties. Moreover, Article 14 of the ECHR itself expressly prohibits discrimination on the grounds of "national or social origin, association with a national minority, property, birth or other status."[86]

Has the Mechanism Extended Jurisdiction to Cover Extraterritorial Acts and Under What Circumstances?

States' responsibilities under the ECHR are not limited to acts or omissions within their territory. In *Cyprus v. Turkey*,[87] the Court found that:

> the authorized agents of the state, including diplomatic or counselor agents and armed forces, not only remain under its jurisdiction when abroad but bring any other person or

---

[85] Emphasis added.
[86] Art. 14.
[87] *Cyprus v. Turkey*, 4 E.H.R.R. 282.

property within that jurisdiction . . . to the extent that they exercise authority over such persons or property. Insofar as, by their acts or omissions, they affect such persons or property, the responsibility of the state is engaged.

This is so even when the internationally recognized Government of the territory where the violation occurred is not the Government to whom the violation is attributed.[88] The Court has also held, in *Amuur v. France*,[89] that asylum-seekers in detention in the international zone of Orly Airport are on French territory for the purposes of the ECHR, as they are subject to French law there.

Finally, the ECHR also has indirect effects on the territory of non-Contracting Parties through the application of its rules restricting extradition and expulsion, as discussed at length below in Section 3.1.2.

2.3.5 Must Domestic Remedies Have Been Exhausted?[90]

> **Tip:** Even after the Protocol 11 reforms of 1998, cases take a long time to proceed through the ECHR machinery. Once a case is in the final stages of exhausting domestic remedies, it is worth making the application to the Court. The application puts the Registry on notice of the case and holds its place in the system. It also obviates the danger of the claim being timed out according to the six-month rule (see below). The application can be withdrawn if domestic remedies prove effective after all. **There is no filing fee.**

> **Note:** The most frequent cause of application failure is a ruling of inadmissibility based on failure to exhaust domestic remedies.

---

[88] In *Loizidou v. Turkey*, 310 Eur. Ct. H.R. (ser. A) (1995), for example, the applicant successfully upheld a claim that Turkish-controlled forces in Northern Cyprus had interfered with her enjoyment of her property, protected by Article 1 of Protocol 1 to the ECHR, despite the fact that the Government of Cyprus was still recognized to be Greek Cypriot. The Court drew upon arguments based on the international law of state responsibility. As this area is developed further by the International Law Commission, its content could affect further the territorial reach of the ECHR.

[89] *Amuur v. France, supra* note 77.

[90] The author is indebted, as regards this section, to Luke Clements, Nuala Mole and Alan Simmons, *supra* note 20, for their excellent treatment of exhaustion of domestic remedies. The author largely follows the same scheme.

The requirement that an applicant exhaust domestic remedies before applying to the Court is one of general international law. It is enshrined in Article 35 of the ECHR. The respondent state must be allowed a chance to remedy the violation domestically before it is addressed by an international tribunal such as the Court. The requirement that domestic remedies be exhausted also reflects the conceptual relationship between the Court and national tribunals. In *Akdivar v. Turkey*, the Court stated that "the machinery of protection established by the ECHR is subsidiary to the national systems safeguarding human rights."[91]

Which Remedies?

The applicant is only required to pursue those domestic remedies that would be effective and capable of addressing the harm suffered. In certain contexts, that will be administrative rather than judicial remedies, as in the case of review of an asylum application in many states. In terms of assessing whether or not a particular remedy exists, the relevant time is normally the time when the act giving rise to the claim occurs.[92]

Where the applicant faces a choice of remedies, the applicant is expected to choose the remedy, preferably the most likely to be effective. The Court does not hold that once an applicant has pursued that remedy to its logical conclusion, he must restart proceedings with a view to the granting of another remedy.[93] However, if more than one potentially effective remedy is available, the applicant will be required to have recourse to those remedies also.[94]

In deciding which available remedies are the most sensible and effective, the Court may have regard to the applicant's individual circumstances. The Court has given some indication that it will not be persuaded, for example,[95] by a professor of civil procedure, who opts for the cheaper and faster option of two procedures, which ultimately is ineffective as compared with a potentially more costly and time-consuming alternative. It is unlikely that the Court would be quite so strict with a layperson representing himself, but the base requirement remains that all procedures generally regarded as available and effective must be pursued.[96]

---

[91] *Akdivar v. Turkey, supra* note 35, and CLEMENTS, *supra* note 20, at 25 et seq.
[92] *Amuur v. France, supra* note 77.
[93] *Leander v. Sweden*, Commission phase, No. 92148/81, 1983.
[94] *Chappell v. United Kingdom*, 152 Eur. Ct. H.R. (ser. A) (1989).
[95] *Beis v. Greece*, 25 E.H.R.R. 335 (1997).
[96] CLEMENTS, *supra* note 20, at 32.

> **Tip:** Identifying available and effective remedies is not always self-evident, though the requirement is strictly applied. Legal advice on the matter should be solicited, in so far as possible, from the outset.

Burden of Proof

The burden of proof with regard to the exhaustion of domestic remedies shifts as follows:

1. Applicant details in his original application to the Court the steps taken to meet the exhaustion requirement;
2. The state must then prove that the steps taken fail to satisfy the exhaustion standard. It must show that:
   (a) *adequate* and *effective* remedies were available in domestic law;[97]
   (b) that the applicant had effective access to those remedies; and
   (c) that the applicant failed to exhaust them.
   If the state does not challenge the applicant's assertion that he has already exhausted domestic remedies, or fails to do so with sufficient clarity, it is deemed to have waived the right to object and is prohibited from so doing at the merits stage of the claim.
3. The applicant must show that the remedy set out by the state was neither adequate nor effective.

What Must You Show to Prove that Domestic Remedies Have Been Exhausted?

Broadly speaking, two avenues exist for the applicant to assert that he has met the exhaustion requirements:

- Show that the remedies in question were inadequate and ineffective;
- Show that access to those remedies was ineffective.

An adequate and effective remedy must address and remedy the violation *directly*. For example, an appeal without suspensive effect will not be regarded as effective to remedy a threat of expulsion, where the

---

[97] *Stran Greek Refineries & Straits Andreadis v. Greece*, Eur. Ct. H.R. (ser. A) (1994).

applicant asserts that he will be subject to a real risk of serious harm if expelled. Applicants are not expected to pursue final appeals that have no prospect of success.

> **Note:** The Court has, however, held that expellees, who have been notified of their impending expulsion but not yet served with the relevant orders, have not exhausted domestic remedies, even though the order could be served at any time and in spite of the fact that once served, the order must be challenged in writing within 24 hours.[98]

In theory, the "exhaustion" of domestic remedies connotes recourse to the final level of appeal available domestically. In countries with a written Constitution, that will be the Constitutional Court.[99] If the relevant appellate court has consistently refused to examine the interest of the applicant or held against that interest in past cases, then the European Court does not go so far as to require that an appeal be pursued where the applicant is likely to fail.[100] Where there is a large amount of precedent suggesting that the domestic tribunal will reject the appeal, that precedent will suffice as evidence of the appeal's futility. In the absence of a significant amount of precedent, an opinion of a *senior lawyer* as to the likely outcome of the proceedings is accepted by the Court.[101]

> **Tip:** The Court does place importance on the senior status of the consulting attorney. That attorney's opinion should be formal, concise, and should not give unnecessary detail as to their view of the outcome of the proceedings in Strasbourg.[102]

Where the applicant can illustrate that he has no effective recourse in the respondent state, because the breach of the ECHR of which he complains is part of a tolerated policy, he need not attempt that which is clearly futile. The existence of such a policy must be proven "beyond a reasonable doubt."

The Court will generally regard as ineffective discretionary nonjudicial remedies. Despite doubts as to "effectiveness" of a judicial review

---

[98] *Vijaynathan and Pushparajah v. France*, Eur. Ct. H.R. (ser. A) 241-B (1992).
[99] HARRIS, *supra* note 62, at 610.
[100] *Dublin Well Woman and Others v. Ireland supra* note 28, at § 47.
[101] CLEMENTS, *supra* note 20, at 27.
[102] *Id.*

procedure in the context of *challenging refusal to grant political asylum*[103] or an extradition order,[104] *recourse to judicial review must be had in order to exhaust domestic remedies.*

Generally, a procedural mistake made by the applicant or his lawyers in the course of domestic proceedings, which causes the failure of a particular domestic remedy, is not deemed to have satisfied the Court's exhaustion requirements.[105] The Court has allowed exemptions from the requirement where special circumstances exist, including honest lack of knowledge of an applicant of the existence of a remedy or misadvise from the applicant's lawyer as to the *existence* of a particular remedy.

> **Note:** Of particular significance for refugees, asylum-seekers, and IDPs is the Commission's holding in Kuijk v. Greece, which stated that a foreign detainee could not be expected to have recourse to complex legal remedies, the availability of which was conveyed to him without legal representation[106] and explained by a non-legal interpreter.

By extension, applicants must also be able to instigate proceedings for a particular remedy themselves, without having to rely on the intervention of a public official.

Generally, a *final* domestic decision to refuse legal aid on the grounds that a case has no chance of success will be sufficient for domestic remedies to have been exhausted.[107] Where legal aid is refused on financial grounds, and the applicant still cannot afford representation, he is required to represent himself, if possible, in order to exhaust domestic remedies.[108] The key issue as regards legal aid is that the applicant has raised the substantive issue in the case before national courts.

> **Note:** The respondent state cannot easily require that the applicant reapply for legal aid once refused, in order to have exhausted domestic remedies. Such an argument will only be effective if there is **clear evidence that a new application would likely receive different treatment.**[109]

---

[103] *M v. UK*, DR 57/136 (1986).
[104] *Soering v. United Kingdom, supra* note 29.
[105] *Cunningham v. U.K.*, DR 43/171.
[106] No., 14986/89 (1991). HARRIS, *supra* note 62, at 618.
[107] CLEMENTS, *supra* note 20, at 28.
[108] *Id.*
[109] *Id. Granger v. U.K.*, 174 Eur. Ct. H.R.(ser. A) (1990).

Where domestic proceedings cease to progress at all, and that delay in proceedings forms part of the substance of the complaint under Article 6 of the ECHR, the Court will deem domestic remedies exhausted.[110]

In order to give domestic courts the opportunity to remedy an alleged breach of the ECHR, the applicant must raise the substance of the injury, and in so far as possible, the applicable ECHR arguments before those courts. If, however, the violation is not directly addressed by domestic law, the applicant must invoke the ECHR itself before the domestic courts, to give them the optimal chance of putting right the injury.[111] Raising ECHR arguments has the best chance of success in states that have incorporated the ECHR into domestic law.

Once Domestic Remedies Have Been Exhausted, Is There a Time Limit Within Which an Application Must Be Brought?

The six-months rule, also set down in Article 35, is *nearly absolute* in its application. It requires that, to be accepted by the Court, the application be filed "within six months of the date on which the final decision . . . was taken." The Court will calculate the six months back from the date upon which it first received communication of the application.

> **Tip:** A useful safety measure is to contact the Registry indicating that the application is being pursued, subject to the outcome of local proceedings. That communication must be in writing and contain "basic details of the nature of the complaint,"[112] such as the object of the application, domestic decisions on the matter, and the ECHR issues involved. This puts the Registry on notice of the complaint and obviates the expiration of the six-month period. The Registry does not require that the application be formally registered at that time.[113]

If it is being contended that local remedies were ineffective and inadequate, then the relevant date for the running of the six months is the date of the occurrence that forms the subject of the claim. The six-months rule is not applicable where a challenge to the existence of legislation or a continuing violation, such as enforced disappearance, is concerned.[114]

---

[110] CLEMENTS, *supra* note 20, at 32.
[111] *Deweer, supra* note 58, at § 26.
[112] CLEMENTS, *supra* note 20, at 35.
[113] Boyle, *supra* note 14, at 143.
[114] *Id.*

> **Note:** The Court will not wait indefinitely for the completion of the application once the initial letter has been registered. The decision as to when to put the Court on notice of the complaint must be taken judiciously, with due regard to the number of remedies, which must still be pursued domestically. If a number of avenues have yet to be explored domestically, the applicant is best advised to wait before submitting the initial letter.

2.3.6 Other Admissibility Criteria

Anonymity

Under rule 45, an application will fail for *anonymity*. An applicant can request that his identity be kept from the general public, though not of course from the respondent Government.

Applications "Substantially the Same" as Previously Submitted Applications

The Court, under Article 35 § 2, will also reject a claim on admissibility grounds if the claim is "substantially" the same as a previous application involving the applicant, or if the same case is pending before another international judicial body, as long as the claim before the Court does not involve any new evidence.[115]

Manifestly Ill-Founded

Under Article 35, a *manifestly ill-founded* application will not succeed before the Court. This is an application which the Court judges at the admissibility stage has no chance of success on its merits.

Abuse of Process

Lastly, an application written in a politicized, abusive, hostile, and otherwise inappropriate way will be rejected for abuse of process. The Council of Europe has a press office to deal with publicity. Inflammatory remarks do not help to convey a case fairly to the Judges.

2.3.7 Submitting the Application to the Court

Once the above steps have been thought through and it is determined that the claim being considered is appropriate for consideration by the Court, the first step in making an application to the Court

---

[115] On the *non bis in idem* principle, *see id.* at 143.

is to send a letter containing the following information to the Registrar of the Court at:

> The Registrar
> European Court of Human Rights
> Council of Europe
> F-67075 STRASBOURG CEDEX
> FRANCE.

This letter must contain the following information:

(1) The applicant's name, date of birth, nationality, sex, occupation, and address;
(2) the name, occupation, and address of the applicant's representative;
(3) a brief summary of the complaints;
(4) an indication of the ECHR rights regarded to have been violated;
(5) a statement of the remedies already used;
(6) a list of the official decisions in the case, the date of each decision, the court or authority which took it, and a brief summary of the decision itself;
(7) A general indication of any claims made for just satisfaction under Article 41 of the ECHR.

Attached to the letter must be a copy of the decisions. These documents are not returnable. Originals MUST be kept in the applicant's or representative's possession or at least not sent to the Court in this preliminary letter. If anonymity is desired, that request should be made in the letter, along with a statement of the reasons justifying such a departure from the normal rule of public access to information before the Court. The President of the Chamber, under rule 47(3), has the discretion to authorize anonymity in "exceptional and duly justified cases."

2.3.8 Timeline for Making an Application to the Court

Registrar receives letter as detailed above.
Secretariat opens a file for the application.

⇓

Secretariat sends letter to applicant in order to ensure that all requisite information has been provided. All responses should still be addressed to the Registrar.

European Human Rights Mechanisms

The Registrar notifies the applicant if an obvious ground of inadmissibility exists. The Applicant is not, however, obliged to withdraw the application.

⇩

REGISTRATION
The complaint becomes an application and is assigned a case number.

⇩

Process of Determining Admissibility Begins.
Case is assigned to a Chamber.
Judge Rapporteur is appointed.

⇩

Judge Rapporteur, with assistance of Secretariat, prepares report on admissibility of application.

⇩   ⇩

Judge Rapporteur proposes dismissal. Case is referred to 3-Judge Committee.	Judge Rapporteur finds case not to be inadmissible. Case is referred directly to Chamber.
⇩	⇩
If Committee rejects application by unanimous vote, decision is forwarded to applicant. DECISION IS FINAL.	Application will be communicated to respondent Government for observations on admissibility. OPPORTUNITY FOR REACHING FRIENDLY SETTLEMENT BEGINS, as Government is on notice of complaint.

⇩

Government must respond with observations within **SIX WEEKS**. Court can request that Government address issues ranging from admissibility to facts and merits. Copy of Government's observations is forwarded to applicant.

> Applicant sends written response to Government's observations to the Registrar. The purpose of the pleading exchange is to reduce the areas of contention between the applicant and respondent Government.

⇩

> Judge Rapporteur drafts new admissibility report.

⇩ ⇩

> Judge Rapporteur proposes dismissal. Case is referred to 3-Judge Committee.

> Judge Rapporteur finds case not to be inadmissible. Case is referred directly to Chamber for oral hearings.

⇩ ⇩

> If Committee rejects application by unanimous vote, decision is forwarded to applicant. DECISION IS FINAL.

> Chamber holds public hearing in Strasbourg. Oral submissions are made by both parties. Oral hearings can be held separately on issues of admissibility and on the merits, but most often both issues are heard together.

⇩

> **ORAL HEARINGS**
> Copies of the statements of the representatives of both parties must be provided in advance. The Judges may question the parties and the parties are given a chance to make brief replies to one another's arguments.

⇩

> **DECISION ON ADMISSIBILITY**
> After the Chamber deliberates, it immediately informally announces its decision on admissibility to the parties, in order to allow a friendly settlement to be reached as soon as possible. The decision on admissibility is published.

⇓

FACT-FINDING HEARINGS

If the case is such as to require a fact-finding hearing (i.e., one where there has been no adjudication on the issues of fact in domestic courts, such as in the Turkish forced disappearance cases above, Article 2), the Court will undertake a fact-finding mission to the country in question, take witness statements, and perform on-site inspections there. Under Article 38 §1 §a of the ECHR, governments must provide "all necessary facilities" to enable the Court to carry out its fact-finding mission successfully.

⇓

FRIENDLY SETTLEMENTS

The facilitation of a friendly settlement between the parties is an integral part of the ECHR system. After an application is admitted, the ECHR demands that the Court "place itself at the disposal" of the Parties to that end. Efforts towards securing a friendly settlement are undertaken in tandem with the investigations of the Court on the merits of the application. Negotiations and all documentation concerning friendly settlements are confidential.

Any settlement reached must be approved by the Court as consistent with the goals of the ECHR and respect for human rights.

⇓   ⇓

| Friendly settlement is reached. Settlement in BINDING on both parties. CASE IS CLOSED. | Friendly settlement is not reached. |

⇓

Section of the Court determines whether, under Rule 73(1), the case involves "a serious question affecting the interpretation or application of the ECHR or the protocols thereto, or [a] serious issue of general importance."

⇓   ⇓

| If so, Section refers case to Grand Chamber to be heard on its merits. | If not, Section hears case on its merits. |

⇓ ⇓

ORAL HEARINGS ON THE MERITS

The format of the hearing before both the Section and the Grand Chamber is the same.

⇓

Both parties are usually invited to submit comprehensive written memorials, addressing their views on the law and facts of the application. Oral presentations should not amount to a rereading of the submitted memorial. Oral statements should address the key points of the matter only. Oral hearings usually last about 90 minutes,[116] though a hearing before the Grand Chamber may last longer.

⇓

JUDGMENT

The Court retires to deliberate. Judgments are announced publicly and are published in the Reports of the Decisions of the Court. Judgments of the Grand Chamber are binding on the parties. Judgments of a Section of the Court are also binding, but subject to a judgment issued by the Grand Chamber if the case is reheard (below).

⇓

REHEARING

If the case has been heard by a Section of the Court and was NOT referred by that Section to the Grand Chamber for examination of the merits, either party has the ability to refer the case to the Grand Chamber of the Court under Rule 73(1), as detailed above. The admissibility of the case for rehearing will be determined by a panel of five judges from the Grand Chamber. It is likely that the panel will only grant rehearing in very rare circumstances.

---

[116] Boyle, *supra* note 14, at 151. This chart is adapted from Boyle.

> **ENFORCEMENT OF JUDGMENTS**
> Supervision of the execution of judgments is carried out by the Committee of Ministers, "the political arm of the ECHR."[117] Proceedings before the Committee are confidential, though the representatives of the applicant may make submissions to the Committee regarding the applicant's view of the changes, which must necessarily be made, in law and practice, in order to execute the judgment effectively.
> Usually, damages and costs must be paid within 3 months of the judgment in which they are granted. If that time is exceeded, the applicant's representative may make a claim for interest, [through the Registrar], at the rate set by the Court.
> The applicant can keep track of the progress towards fulfillment of the judgment through telephone communication with the Secretariat.
> The Committee of Ministers issues resolutions, detailing when it considers that a State is in full compliance with a judgment of the Court.

3. ECHR Jurisprudence and Refugees, Asylum-Seekers, and IDPs

It has been stated before that the Court is among the most effective, if not the most effective, international human rights mechanisms in the world. Many of the parties to the ECHR have incorporated it into domestic law (most recently, the United Kingdom via the Human Rights Act) and most do give effect to the judgments of the Court without question. However, it is an international body, created by states, and originally envisaged mainly to be petitioned primarily by them, not individuals, along the lines of the International Court of Justice. Although the Court shows no hesitation ruling against states and although its pronouncements carry the force of law, it is worth noting the aspects of its operation that reveal the complex relationship between the Court and states parties.

The Court is still dependent on state co-operation for fact-finding and enforcement of judgments, though the latter is overseen by the Committee of Ministers, thus adding political weight to the process. There is heavy emphasis, even after the abolition of the Commission, on consultation with governments while cases are being processed, and the procedures governing friendly settlements still play a major role in

---

[117] *Id.* at 152.

the progress of a case through the ECHR system. These provisions make the operation of the Court not only a legal, but a political, reality, and thus much more effective for the protection of individuals. With the exception of just a few articles, including the right to life (Article 2) and the prohibition on torture, inhuman and degrading treatment and punishment (Article 3), most provisions of the ECHR are subject to derogation by states "in times of war or other public emergencies threatening the life of the nation" (Article 15 § 1). In addition, two of the substantive doctrines of the Court, the use of the concept of "proportionality" and the "margin of appreciation," are both employed to strike a balance between state acts in the interests of the community as a whole and violations of individual rights.

Where a state has declared a state of emergency or imposed martial law, this determination is reviewable by the Court; it will not *per se* take the state's declaration at face value.[118] The margin of appreciation is fairly broad, although the Court will assess the specific derogation measures in accordance with the standard set out in Article 15 § 1, namely that those measures be taken only when "strictly required by the exigencies of the situation."

In the *Greek Case*[119] the Court set out a list of factors to define an Article 15 emergency:

- actual or imminent,
- involving the whole nation;
- the organized life of the community threatened;
- crisis or danger exceptional, in that the normal restrictions permitted for the maintenance of public safety, health, and order are plainly inadequate.

Article 15 § 3 imposes procedural notification requirements. States need not notify the Secretary General of the Council of Europe of any intended derogation measures before they are taken, but must do so within a reasonable time in order to show respect for the "collective" enforcement of the human rights philosophy of the ECHR. *In Lawless v. the United Kingdom*,[120] a lapse of twelve days between the instigation of the measures and notification to the Secretary General was not excessive.

With regard to the concept of proportionality, the Court must constantly evaluate the treatment of an individual applicant by the state

---

[118] This competence was established by the Commission in the case of *Greece v. the United Kingdom*, no. 176/56, Dec. 2.6.56, Yearbook 2 p.174 (1976).
[119] *Greek Case*, Comm. Report 5.11.69, § 153.
[120] *Lawless v. the United Kingdom*, Eur. Ct. H.R. (ser. A) 3 (1961).

in the context of the wider interests of the community. Articles 8–11 (the right to a private and family life, the right to freedom of thought, conscience and religion, the right to freedom of expression and the right to freedom of association respectively) permit limitations for community interests. Restrictions or interferences with the protected right committed by the state must be justified as "necessary in a democratic society" for limited public interest-based purposes. In the case of *Handyside v. the United Kingdom*, A 24 § 49 (1976), the Court interpreted that necessity as one that is "proportionate to the legitimate aim pursued."

The Court has found the test of proportionality a useful one, and has applied it to other rights, which are not framed in terms of competing interests. The notion of proportionality is found in Article 15 of the ECHR, permitting derogations only to the extent that they are "strictly required by the exigencies of the situation." The test formulated by the Court for the prohibition of a discriminatory act or omission under Article 14 demands that there be "no reasonable relationship of proportionality between the means employed and the aims" sought to be achieved.[121] Indeed, in relation to Article 14, the degree of deference shown to states has led to criticism that the prohibition is too weak. A balancing test based on proportionality has also been read into the right to liberty and security of the person (Article 5) and the right to the enjoyment of one's possessions (Article 1 of Protocol No. 1).

The doctrine of the "margin of appreciation" takes proportionality one step further. The margin of appreciation is invoked by the Court, in assessing proportionality, to give deference in the balancing of interests to the expertise and specific needs of the state. The margin of appreciation is used by the Court where the state has "discretion when taking legislative, administrative or judicial action in the area of a ECHR right."[122] It has been described[123] as "the lubricant at the interface between individual rights and the public interest."

In the case of *Handyside*,[124] which involved a challenge to conviction for possession of obscene materials under Article 10, the Court judged that the restriction could be justified for the "protection of public morals." While recognizing that states did not have unrestricted power to ride roughshod over freedom of expression in the name of public morals, the Court held that, on account of states' "direct and

---

[121] *Belgian Lingusitics (No.1)*, Eur. Ct. H.R. (ser. A) 5 (1967). For further analysis *see* HARRIS, *supra* note 62, at 11.
[122] HARRIS, *supra* note 62, at 12.
[123] *Id.* at 14–15.
[124] *Handyside v. the United Kingdom*, Eur. Ct. H.R. (ser. A) 24 (1976).

continuous contact with the vital forces of their countries," domestic legislators were in a better position than international judges to determine the content of their countries' morals. It is worth noting, however, that the Court has taken quite the opposite stance in cases where the state party is the last outpost of a dated moral stance enshrined in legislation, which the Court has construed as prohibited by the ECHR.[125]

In sum, it cannot be ignored that the Court is a body created by states and subject to a degree of subsidiarity. Nevertheless, the Court has exercised no little courage and innovation. The importance to the individual of human rights is in their on-the-ground, domestic enforcement, and the Court's creative jurisprudence has allowed it to achieve considerable results.

3.1 The Right to Life and Physical Integrity

It is a truism to say that the right to life is the most fundamental of all the rights protected by the ECHR. That fundamental character is displayed by the fact that the right to life is expressly non-derogable in times of war or other public emergencies.[126] Additionally, because it is the right that encompasses all others, it is also the focus for claims of a positive obligation inhering in the member states to provide adequate food, shelter, medical care, healthy working conditions, and a healthy environment.[127] The ECHR itself does not include specific rights to this effect. These are usually regarded as the province of the European Social Charter, discussed below in Section 4, whose individual petition mechanism is much less developed. As a result, there may be reason to push the bounds of Article 2 in this way.

Broadly speaking, the ECHR jurisprudence on the right to life falls into two categories:

(1) The prohibition on the taking of life and
(2) the obligation to protect the right to life by law.[128]

---

[125] *Dudgeon v. the United Kingdom*, 45 Eur. Ct. H.R. (ser. A) (1981).
[126] Art. 15 § 1.
[127] HARRIS, *supra* note 62, at 40.
[128] Most often, the content of the right to life has been inferred from situations where it has been held not to have been breached, due to the successful invocation of one of the exceptions under article 2 § 2. The Commission has determined that those exceptions are "exhaustive and must be narrowly interpreted" (*Stewart v. UK*, No.20044/82, 39 DR 162 at 169 (1984)); HARRIS, *supra* note 62, at 44).

Where loss of life cannot be proved by the applicant to the Court's satisfaction, the advocate should look to Article 3 of the ECHR, the prohibition against torture, inhuman and degrading treatment or punishment. In the case of treatment that constitutes an interference with an individual's physical integrity, but does not rise to the level of inhuman or degrading treatment, the advocate should turn to Article 8 of the ECHR, the right to private life. The three articles work together to form a spectrum.

3.1.1 The Prohibition on the Taking of Life

> **Chen**—Scenario 1—Chen may have an Article 2 claim with regard to her family members who were killed.
> **Maria**—Scenario 3—Maria may have an Article 2 claim with regard to the murder of her oldest son by security forces during the eviction.

Life must have been taken by the state or its agents (police, soldiers), or in a situation where the state should have provided adequate protection against the taking of life by private individuals. Outside of the forced disappearances and death in custody context (below Section 3.1.1.3), the fact that life has indeed been taken is not usually in dispute. It is more common that the state will assert that the taking of life in question occurred in accordance with one of the exceptions in Article 2 § 2.[129]

"Use of Force Which Is Absolutely Necessary" and Exceptions to Article 2 Liability

As noted above, the right to life cannot be derogated from in times of war or other public emergency,[130] but Article 2 does envisage circumstances in which life may be taken. In three contexts, deprivation of life will not amount to a violation if it occurs by "use of force which is absolutely necessary." The contexts are: for purposes of defending someone from unlawful violence, in order to effect a lawful arrest or to prevent someone lawfully detained from escaping, or in an action lawfully taken to quell a riot or insurrection.[131]

---

[129] *Osman v. United Kingdom*, 1998 VIII Eur. Ct. H.R.
[130] Except for death caused by lawful acts of war, under art. 15 § 2.
[131] Art. 2 § 2.

In the *McCann*[132] case, the Court held that Article 2 § 2 would be inconsistent with the object and purpose of the ECHR if it were regarded as applying only to intentional killings. Article 2 § 2 thus prohibits the use of more force than is absolutely necessary even where death is caused unintentionally. The degree of force used is relevant.[133]

An "absolutely necessary" use of force was explained by the Court in *McCann*[134] and reiterated in *Ergi v. Turkey*:[135]

> The use of the term 'absolutely necessary' suggests that a stricter and more compelling test of necessity must be employed from that normally applicable when determining whether State action is 'necessary in a democratic society' under paragraph 2 of Articles 8 to 11 of the ECHR. In particular, the force used must be strictly proportionate to the achievement of the aims set out in sub-paragraphs 2 (a), (b) and (c) of article 2.

"Proportionality is to be assessed having regard to the nature of the aim pursued, the dangers to life and limb inherent in the situation and the risk that the force employed might result in the loss of life."[136]

Article 2 and State-Planned Operations and Offensives

Situations of planned operations where lethal force is considered absolutely necessary are extremely rare. Article 2 may be used to evaluate the planning and conduct of police and military operations with intended and incidental civilian casualties alike.[137]

In *Ergi v. Turkey*,[138] the applicant's sister was fatally shot in the head during an ambush by security forces of the PKK in her village, when she went to get something from the balcony. In finding that the

---

[132] McCann, *supra* note 46, at § 148.
[133] GOMIEN, *supra* note 18, at 99.
[134] McCann, *supra* note 46, at §§ 148–150.
[135] Ergi v. Turkey, *supra* note 80, at § 79.
[136] HARRIS, *supra* note 62, at 99.
[137] Soldiers or police officers who have been given limited information which reasonably leads them to the honest belief that lethal force is the only option to protect others and apprehend a suspect (such as in a terrorist context) may not have violated Article 2. In *McCann*, whilst condemning those who planned the operation in Gibraltar, the Court exonerated the actual soldiers who carried out the "shoot to kill" instructions on the grounds that they were honestly obeying superior orders. *Supra* note 46, at § 200.
[138] Ergi v. Turkey, *supra* note 80.

security forces had acted in violation of Article 2, the Court held that they had a duty to plan and conduct the operation in "such a way as to avoid or minimize, to the greatest extent possible, any risk to the lives of the villagers, including from the fire power of the PKK members caught in the ambush."[139] States have a positive duty "to take all feasible precautions in the choice of means and methods of a security operation mounted against an opposing group with a view to avoiding and, in any event, to minimizing, incidental loss of civilian life."[140]

Situations of internal and international conflict trigger internal displacement and flight across international boundaries. The steadily rising number of Kosovar and Kurdish refugees in Europe attests to the importance of interpreting Article 2 to cover situations of misdirected fire causing civilian casualties.

> **Note:** Liability will attach to the state under the ECHR even if the victim's death might have been the result of actions of a non-state party (e.g., terrorists), as long as that death occurred in the context of a government-planned operation.

The Right to Life and Forced Disappearances

Until comparatively recently, the Court had not had the opportunity to examine Article 2 cases,[141] as most of the jurisprudence was developed by the Commission in this area. Since 1995 however, the single biggest group of cases before the Court on the substance of Article 2 have concerned the southeastern region of Turkey, involving persons who have disappeared.

There is no article in the ECHR that speaks specifically to forced disappearances, though in practice they are prohibited by a combination of the right to life (Article 2), the prohibition against inhuman and degrading treatment (Article 3) and the right to liberty and security of the person (Article 5).

The standard applied by the Court to determine whether death has occurred after disappearance or in custody is the *"beyond reasonable doubt"* standard.[142] Until very recently, that standard had been applied very strictly. The Court has repeatedly held that:

---

[139] *Id.* at § 79.
[140] *Id.*
[141] The first one being *McCann and Others v. United Kingdom, supra* note 46.
[142] *Ireland v. United Kingdom*, 25 Eur. Ct. H.R. (ser. A) § 61 (1978).

While the attainment of the required evidentiary standard . . . may follow from the co-existence of sufficiently strong, clear and concordant inferences or unrebutted presumptions . . . their evidential value must be considered in light of the circumstances of the individual case and the seriousness and nature of the charge to which they give rise against the respondent State.[143]

The Court faces difficult determinations of fact and analyses of inferences to be drawn from conflicting accounts.

Death in Custody

Where a person is taken into custody and dies there, without any intervening event, the court presumes that the authorities were responsible for his death.[144] In the case of *Velikova v. Bulgaria*,[145] a man of Roma descent was taken into custody by the authorities on suspicion of cattle theft. There he died, in circumstances described by the autopsy to have involved a "deliberate beating" with a hard, blunt object. The Court held that "where an individual is taken into police custody in good health but is later found dead, it is incumbent upon the State to provide a plausible explanation of the events leading to his death, failing which the authorities must be held responsible under article 2 of the ECHR."[146] It went on to explain that the "beyond reasonable doubt" standard may be met where "events in the issue lie wholly, or in large part, within the exclusive knowledge of the authorities, as in the case of persons within their control or custody." In such a case, strong presumptions of fact will arise in respect of injuries and death occurring during that detention. Indeed, "the burden of proof may be regarded

---

[143] Quoting *Aydin v. Turkey, supra* note 33, and *Kaya v. Turkey*, Reports 1998-I Eur. Ct. H.R., where the Court held that the probative force of the inferences drawn by the applicant of the circumstances surrounding the shooting of his brother were "offset by the total absence of any direct oral account of the applicant's version of the events before the delegates" of the Commission sent there to find facts (*Kaya*, § 77).

[144] The test works the same way for the purposes of Article 3. *Selmouni v. France* (E.C.H.R. July 28, 1999), at <http://www.dhcour.coe.fr/hudoc/ViewRoot.asp?Item=0&Action=Html&X=1025023138&Notice=0&Noticemode=&RelatedMode=0>.

[145] *Velikova v. Bulgaria* (E.C.H.R., § 4, May 18, 2000), at <http://www.dhcour.coe.fr/hudoc/ViewRoot.asp?Item=0&Action=Html&X=1025023358&Notice=0&Noticemode=&RelatedMode=0>.

[146] *Id.* § 70, citing *Selmouni v. France, supra* note 144.

as resting on the authorities to provide a satisfactory and convincing explanation" (§ 70).

This same shift in the burden of proof was applied to the case of *Ismail Ertak v. Turkey*.[147] The case involved the disappearance of the applicant's son after he had been taken into custody on suspicion of terrorist activity. Multiple witnesses confirmed that he had been arrested, kept in a cell (corroborated by statements of other detainees), tortured to the point of showing no sign of life, and was last seen, unconscious, being dragged from his cell. In *Ertak*, the Government did nothing adequately to rebut the evidence of Ertak's death in custody. The Court there found that the evidence against the Government was "sufficient circumstantial evidence, based on concrete elements, on which it may be concluded beyond reasonable doubt" that the applicant died following his arrest and detention by the security forces.[148]

In general, it seems that the Court needs something more than two unverifiable and conflicting accounts of the circumstances which caused the death in question, in order to assign responsibility for the killing directly to the state. The Court appears to require evidence enabling the presumed perpetrators of the particular attack "to be identified with sufficient precision,"[149] although precisely what constitutes "sufficient precision" is currently unanswered.

Where the victim has disappeared, though not verifiably while in custody, the standard will also be more difficult to meet. In the case of *Kurt v. Turkey*,[150] the applicant's son had been missing for four and a half years and was last seen by her surrounded by soldiers and with visible signs of injury. The Court held the state could not be impugned

---

[147] *Ismail Ertak v. Turkey*, May 9, 2000, at <http://hudoc.echr.coe. int/ Hudoc1doc2\HEJUD\2000102\chamber%20judgment>.

[148] As laid down in *Çakici v. Turkey*, *supra* note 63, where evidence that applicant's brother was taken into custody was corroborated by a number of witnesses who had seen him there. He was not seen outside custody before the Government reported, that his identity card had been found on a dead terrorist after an assault. § 85.

[149] *Per* the Court concerning the fatal shooting of the applicant's uncle while walking down the street with his son. The applicant had previously been wounded in a street shooting shortly after being threatened by the authorities unless he closed down his newspaper kiosk, which sold a Kurdish newspaper. *Yasa v. Turkey*, 1998-VI Eur. Ct. H.R., at <http://hudoc.echr.coe.int/ hudoc/ ViewRoot.asp?Item=0&Action=Html&X=518132714&Notice=0&Noticemode=&R elatedMode=0>.

[150] *Kurt v. Turkey*, E.C.H.R. 1998 at <http://hudoc.echr.coe.int/ hudoc/ ViewRoot.asp?Item=0&Action=Html&X=518132821&Notice=0&Noticemode=&R elatedMode=0>.

"beyond a reasonable doubt" for his death. The Government alleged that he had left to join the Kurdish resistance movement, the PKK. In such a difficult case with so little in the way of concrete supporting evidence, the Court deferred to the Commission, who had acted as an independent fact-finding body in the case. The Court noted that "the Commission [had] properly assessed all the evidence before it, weighing in the balance the elements which supported the applicant's account and those which cast doubt on either its credibility or plausibility" (§ 96). Although the Court acknowledged the distinct problems with the accounts on both sides, it found no exceptional circumstances to depart from the Commission's findings. The Court specifically distinguished *Ertak* from *Kurt* on the grounds that in *Kurt* there was no evidence of the treatment or fate met by the applicant's son.

The Court has laid down some specific indications of the elements of proof needed to establish beyond a reasonable doubt that the applicant died in custody. In the case of *Timurtas v. Turkey*,[151] the applicant's son was taken into custody by the security forces, as confirmed by witnesses, and failed to reappear for six and half years. There was no evidence to suggest that he had actually died. The Court held that the victim's son must be presumed dead following an unacknowledged detention by the security forces. It distinguished this case from *Kurt* on the grounds that the length of the disappearance (six and a half years) was "markedly longer" than the four and a half year period of absence in *Kurt* (§ 85). In addition, in *Kurt*, it had never been established with certainty that the applicant's son had been taken to a place of detention by the authorities, whereas that fact was supported by witnesses in *Timurtas*. Finally, unlike in *Kurt*, it was actually established in *Timurtas* that the applicant's son was wanted by the authorities for his alleged PKK activities (§ 85). According to the Court, the detention of such a person could be life-threatening, given the state of security forces' activities in south-east Turkey. The inferences drawn from the facts of *Timurtas* were judged in a situation where the effectiveness of the criminal law was severely undermined by the lack of accountability of the security forces.

There has thus recently been something of a shift in the Court's attitude towards presuming death caused by the authorities in an enforced disappearance context. A dissenting opinion in *Timurtas* heavily criticized the reasoning for distinguishing *Kurt*, arguing particularly that the difference in significance between a four and half and six and

---

[151] *Timurtas v. Turkey*, E.C.H.R. 13 June 2000, at <http://hudoc.echr.coe.int/hudoc/ViewRoot.asp?Item=1&Action=Html&X=518132821&Notice=0&Noticemode=&RelatedMode=0>.

a half year detention period was meaningless.[152] Given the detailed knowledge the Court now has about the particular situation in southeastern Turkey, it seems to be moving towards the shifting of the burden of proof to the Government, as long as the evidence of the detention by the authorities of the person in question can be corroborated.

If an applicant wishes to bring a case of a forced disappearance before the Court, where the original apprehension into custody is uncorroborated, an allegation must be made either that the state failed to enforce its criminal law effectively in that it failed to protect the victim, failed to carry out an adequate investigation into the disappearance or death of the person in question or planned its operations in a grossly negligent way, which led to the death of the victim.[153] All of these allegations trigger positive duties of the state to protect the right to life, and if substantiated amount to a violation of Article 2.

3.1.2 Positive Obligations Under Article 2—Failure to Enforce the Criminal Law

In accordance with the findings of the Commission in past cases, notably cases involving allegations that the United Kingdom failed adequately to protect residents in Northern Ireland against IRA terrorist attacks,[154] the Court has held that:

> the first sentence of Article 2 § 1 enjoins the State not only to refrain from the intentional and unlawful taking of life, but also to take appropriate steps to safeguard the lives of those within its jurisdiction.[155] It is common ground that the State's obligation in this respect extends beyond its primary duty to secure the right to life by putting in place effective criminal-law provisions to deter the commission of offences against the person backed up by law-enforcement machinery for the prevention, suppression and sanctioning of breaches of such provisions.

Indeed, Article 2 § 1 requires in certain circumstances a positive obligation on the authorities to take measures to protect an individual whose life is at risk from the criminal acts of another individual, whether

---

[152] Judge Gölkücklu, dissenting in *Timurtas v. Turkey, supra* note 151.
[153] *McCann and Others v. United Kingdom, supra* note 46, and *Ergi v. Turkey, supra* note 80.
[154] App. No. 9348/81, 32 Eur. Comm'n H.R. Dec. & Rep. 162 (1983).
[155] See *L.C.B. v. the United Kingdom*, 1998-III Eur. Ct. H.R. 1403 § 36.

those individuals are agents of the state or not.[156] This obligation attaches only where the authorities knew or ought to have known of the existence of a real and immediate risk to the life of an identified individual or individuals from the criminal acts of a third party and where there were measure within the scope of the authorities' powers that might reasonably have avoided the risk.

The applicant must show that the authorities *did not do all that could reasonably be expected of them to avoid a real and immediate risk of life of which they had or ought to have had knowledge.* Their failure to avoid the risk does not have to amount to gross negligence. The Court has held that such a rigid standard would violate Article 1 of the ECHR, which requires that all High Contracting Parties secure to all those within their jurisdiction the "practical and effective protection of the rights and freedoms laid down in the ECHR."[157]

Osman[158] indicates that the Court will have regard to the difficulties involved in policing, the unpredictability of human conduct, operational choices, as well as priorities and resources. The Court will not interpret the obligation either so as to place a disproportionate burden on the authorities,[159] or so as to require that a police crime-prevention exercise violate other ECHR rights, such as the right to due process (Articles 5 and 6) and the right to a private life (Article 8). The measures taken by the police will always be judged against a standard of reasonableness.

In *Osman*, the family of a murder victim alleged that the police could have prevented the crime if they had been more diligent in tracking the suspect, who was continually harassing and behaving in an extremely alarming manner towards the Osman family. The state does not have a general obligation to deploy its security forces so as to negate the possibility of violence altogether, and the Court found that the applicant failed to identify a specific point during the course of police operations when the police could reasonably be expected to know or did know that a member of the Osman family was in real and immediate risk of his life. Other actions the police could have taken to detain the murderer earlier could not, judged reasonably, have produced "concrete results" (§ 121) and thus prevented the killing of Mr. Osman. Indeed, the Court found that to have taken such actions risked revers-

---

[156] *Osman v. United Kingdom, supra* note 129.
[157] *Id.* at § 116.
[158] *Osman v. United Kingdom*, 1998 VIII Eur. Ct. H.R, *supra* note 129.
[159] In "bodyguard" cases, where someone had been the victim of a terrorist attack and been given police protection, there was no obligation for that protection to be indefinite. HARRIS, *supra* note 62, at 95.

ing the presumption of innocence (Article 6 § 2) or overreaching the police's search and seizure powers.[160]

When this test is applied to a state or region where the criminal law is not enforced effectively, it is applied rather less strictly. The findings of the Court with regard to the situation in south-eastern Turkey clearly indicate a breakdown in the effective enforcement of the law. Where this general situation is severe, and is known to the authorities, the Court has held that the authorities cannot reasonably claim to be unaware of the heightened risk to targeted individuals.

In the case of *Mahmut Kaya v. Turkey*,[161] the Court found that the authorities had failed to protect the applicant's husband from a risk to his life under Article 2 § 1. The applicant's husband was a doctor who was under suspicion, according to a witness, of treating wounded PKK members. The doctor had complained on several occasions that he was under surveillance, had been questioned and threatened by police, and believed that his life was at risk. The Court did not accept the argument that Dr. Kaya was under the same degree of risk as any other person in that conflict-ridden region. It was satisfied that, as a doctor suspected of aiding and abetting the PKK, he was at a particular, immediate and real risk of an unlawful attack, of which the authorities should reasonably have been aware. Biased and dilatory investigations, inability to bring these cases before a judicial body, and the failure to investigate and prosecute these complaints were evidence of a collapse of the rule of law.[162]

3.1.3 Failure to Investigate or Prosecute

A member state can also be held liable for breach of its Article 2 obligations where it fails to carry out an adequate investigation into the disappearance or death of an individual within its jurisdiction. The rationale for this duty was explained by the Court in *McCann and Others v. the United Kingdom:*

> a general legal prohibition of arbitrary killing by the agents of the State would be ineffective, in practice, if there existed no procedure for reviewing the lawfulness of the use of lethal force by State authorities.[163]

---

[160] Art. 5.
[161] *Mahmut Kaya v. Turkey*, 28 March 2000, at <http://hudoc.echr.coe.int/hudoc/ViewRoot.asp?Item=1&Action=Html&X=518133503&Notice=0&Noticemode=&RelatedMode=0>.
[162] *Id.* at §§ 98–101.
[163] *McCann, supra* note 46, at § 161.

The duty to secure to everyone within its jurisdiction the rights and freedoms protected by the ECHR obliges signatories to provide some form of effective official investigation when individuals have been killed as a result of the use of force by agents of the State.

As to the elements of an effective and adequate investigation, the following needs must be met:

- The significant elements of the incident must be established with impartiality, thoroughness, and care.[164]
- The investigation must be conducted in a diligent, systematic, and expeditious way,[165] such that the Court is satisfied that there is some "realistic prospect of the identification and apprehension of the perpetrators."[166]

The Court is not willing to excuse rushed reports and slapdash forensic examinations due the terrorist context of the alleged deaths.[167]

The obligation to investigate adequately is *not confined to cases were it has been established that a government agent was involved, nor is it triggered only by a formal complaint lodged by the family of the disappeared person.* The duty to investigate adequately begins from the moment when the authorities are appraised of the death[168] of the victim, and probably also from the report of his disappearance, though that has yet to be established specifically.

It should be noted here that allegations of the failure to carry out an effective and adequate investigation are most often made not only under Article 2 of the ECHR, but in conjunction with Article 13, concerning effective remedies. Article 13 has been described as "of autonomous but subsidiary character."[169] Although it is central to the application of Article 13 that the member states have a degree of discretion as to how to remedy a violation of the ECHR, the requirements of article 13 in case of a violation of Article 2 are strict. A violation of Article 13 taken together with Article 2 "entails in addition to the payment of compensation where appropriate, a thorough and effective investigation capable of leading to the identification and punishment of those responsible and including the effective access for the relatives

---

[164] From *Velikova, supra* note 145, at § 80.
[165] The Court has held that 5 years is too long between initiation and end of investigation, *Yasa v. Turkey, supra* note 149, at § 115.
[166] *Mahmut Kaya, supra* note 161, at § 108.
[167] *Id.* at § 91.
[168] *Yasa v. Turkey, supra* note 149, at § 100.
[169] HARRIS, *supra* note 62, at 461.

to the investigatory procedure."[170] The use of both articles together thus serves to strengthen a claim of failure to carry out a truly effective investigation, both in practice and law.[171]

The failure to prosecute also constitutes a violation of Article 2, as it is an integral part of the effective implementation of the criminal law. Prosecutorial discretion may be exercised, but a determination whether or not to prosecute must be made fairly and promptly.[172]

3.1.4 Extradition, Expulsion, and Article 2

Extradition orders have not been successfully challenged on Article 2 grounds. Successful challenges to extradition or expulsion orders have been made under Article 3, the prohibition on torture and inhuman and degrading treatment.

3.2 Torture and Inhuman and Degrading Treatment

> **Chen**—in Scenario 1 has a claim under Article 3 for the torture she suffered in prison in her state of origin. She may also have a claim of inhuman or degrading treatment regarding the violent attacks she suffered in the asylum state at the hands of the police.
> **Ibrahim**—in Scenario 2 has a claim under Article 3 against his own government for torture while in detention, and, like Chen, he may have another claim against his asylum state for the beatings inflicted upon him by the police and members of the local community, if the police failed to enforce domestic criminal law effectively.
> **Maria**—in Scenario 3, depending on the circumstances of the death of her oldest son, may have an Article 3 claim for the "inhuman punishment" she endured watching him being killed by security forces.

The Court has reiterated that Article 3:

> enshrines one of the most fundamental values of democratic societies. Even in the most difficult circumstances, such as the fight against terrorism and organized crime, the ECHR prohibits in absolute terms torture or inhuman or degrading treatment or punishment. Unlike most of the substan-

---

[170] *Kaya, supra* note 161, at § 107.
[171] *Velikova, supra* note 145, at § 89.
[172] HARRIS, *supra* note 62, at 39.

tive clauses of the ECHR and of Protocols No.1 and 4, Article 3 makes no provision for exceptions and no derogation from it is permissible under Article 15 § 2 even in the event of a public emergency threatening the life of the nation.[173]

3.2.1 Standard of Proof

The standard of proof for an alleged violation of Article 3 is the same as that employed in the enforced disappearance context. The standard is *"beyond a reasonable doubt,"* though "such proof may follow from the coexistence of sufficiently strong, clear and concordant inferences or of similar unrebutted presumptions of fact."[174] The Court has held that where a person in good health is taken into police custody and emerges with injuries, it will look to the state to furnish a plausible explanation of how the injuries were caused.[175]

Ordinarily, the Court makes the distinction between degrading treatment, inhuman treatment and torture based on degree. Cases where it has found torture have been comparatively rare.

3.2.2 Torture

Torture is defined as inhuman treatment that causes "very serious and cruel suffering,"[176] and thus has attached to it a special stigma. Most often, torture will be found in cases where the treatment suffered " could only be described as torture."[177] Where a state practices a policy of torture, a successful complaint can be brought against it for breach of Article 3 provided that there is evidence that the practice is sufficiently widespread and officially tolerated.[178] The same logic applies to policies of inhuman treatment.

3.2.3 Inhuman Treatment

Inhuman treatment is defined as the infliction of intense physical and mental suffering without justification. The question of what is the requisite intent for a holding of inhuman and/or degrading treatment has not been answered clearly, though mention of "deliberate

---

[173] *Ireland v. the United Kingdom supra* note 142, at §163.
[174] *Id.* at § 161.
[175] *Selmouni v. France*, supra note 144, citing *Tomasi v. France*, 214-A Eur. Ct. H.R. (ser. A) 40–41, §§ 108–111 (1992).
[176] *Ireland v. United Kingdom, supra* note 142, at § 167.
[177] *Selmouni v. France, supra* note 144, at § 101.
[178] *The Greek Case, supra* note 119, at § 28–29.

conduct" has been made by the Court and Commission.[179]

Inhuman treatment has been held to include physical assault, force disproportionate to the amount needed to effect an arrest; the use of the psychological interrogation techniques;[180] dangerous, unsanitary, and unhealthy conditions of detention imposed by the state, where inmates are deprived of food, water, adequate personal space, and recreation; and failure to provide adequate medical treatment to persons in detention. A margin of appreciation is given to states when controlling detention conditions in the context of terrorist activities, thought the basic standards must be met.[181]

3.2.4 Degrading Treatment

To classify as degrading treatment, the acts complained must "arouse in the applicant feelings of fear, anguish and inferiority capable of humiliating and debasing him and possibly breaking his physical and moral resistance."[182] When someone is deprived of his liberty, the Court has held that recourse to any physical conduct, not made strictly necessary by the victim's own conduct, diminishes human dignity and is in principle an infringement of the right set forth in Article 3.[183]

It can be very difficult to reach the threshold of "degrading" treatment to the Court's satisfaction. This is particularly the case where the treatment is a series of events and cumulative in its impact. Over the last ten years, however, the Court has extended the notion to cover a series of cumulative factors working together to render the treatment of the applicant degrading. The main case is *Herczegfalvy v. Austria*,[184] which concerned the treatment of a Hungarian patient in detention in an Austrian psychiatric hospital. The Commission held that the compulsory medical treatment of the applicant, administered forcibly and involving him being tethered to his bed, combined with the artificial feeding and isolation he had to endure, even though as a result of a

---

[179] *Id.* at 186.

[180] In *Ireland v. the United Kingdom*, *supra* note 142, the Court regarded interrogation techniques which deprived the applicants of sleep, food, and drink, forced them to stand for hours against a wall in an extremely uncomfortable way, wear a dark hood during interrogations and endure a great deal of noise, as amounting to inhuman and degrading treatment rather than torture.

[181] *See Ensslin, Baader and Raspe v. the Federal Republic of Germany*, App. No. 7572/76, 14 DR 64 at 109, and HARRIS, *supra* note 62, at 69.

[182] *Ireland v. the United Kingdom*, *supra* note 142 at § 167 and *Tomasi v. France*, *supra* note 175, at § 115.

[183] *Ribitsch v. Austria*, 336 Eur. Ct. H.R. (ser. A) § 38 (1995).

[184] *Herczegfalvy v. Austria*, App. No. 10533/83(1991).

hunger strike, had a cumulative effect constituting inhuman and degrading treatment.

In finding a breach of Article 3, the Court will judge each case with reference to the prevalent views of the time.[185] Treatment once regarded as inhuman or degrading may in certain circumstances rise to the level of torture. This happened in the case of *Selmouni v. France*, which distinguished an earlier case involving ill-treatment in custody, *Tomasi v. France*.[186]

3.2.5 Article 3 and Extradition, Expulsion, and Deportation—Non-Refoulement

> A claim under Article 3 of the ECHR is especially important to **Ibrahim** in Scenario 2. If he can meet the requisite burden of proof he could use this article to stop his asylum state from sending him back home, as long as persecutory situation persists. As is clear below, Ibrahim's advocate would have to produce fairly compelling evidence that Ibrahim would not be safe in another province at home and in some way belong to an identified and persecuted group of people. In this connection, his advocate is advised to go to human rights resources on the web, such as Amnesty International's country reports, to obtain the sort of evidence required by the Court. In Scenario 5, where Ibrahim is part of a mass influx, his advocate has a much better chance of staying his deportation through recourse to the Court by applying to the Court for emergency interim measures before he is repatriated.

There is no right in the ECHR either to political asylum or lawful entry into another country. The Court, however, has enshrined a principle of non-refoulement where return would result in an indirect breach of Article 3. In this way, Article 3 has become a powerful shield against certain expulsion, extradition, or deportation orders. This protection is especially important for asylum-seekers whose claims have been rejected.

The Court must strike a balance between state and community interests on the one hand and the rights of the individual on the other. The fact that "Contracting States have the right . . . to control the entry, residence and expulsion of aliens" on their territory is apparent to the Court.[187] Cases where a breach of Article 3 will occur on return impose

---

[185] GOMIEN, *supra* note 18, at 105–106.
[186] *Tomasi v. France, supra* note 175.
[187] *Vilvarajah v. the United Kingdom, supra* note 83, at § 102.

an absolute duty on states not to expel or extradite, regardless of national interest. However, the diplomatic complexity and sensitivity of cases involving an evaluation of the criminal justice system of the receiving state places the Court in a difficult situation. The Court, under rule 62, will do its utmost to secure a friendly settlement or encourage an accommodation whereby the extraditing state grants some form of residence to the applicant, or diplomatically secures entry for the applicant into a third country.[188]

The test is whether it has been shown that there are *substantial* grounds for believing that the person concerned, if extradited, would face a *real* risk of being subjected to torture or to inhuman or degrading treatment or punishment in the requesting country. The Court does not focus on whether the risk is one of torture or cruel treatment.

The risked breach can occur either at the hands of public or private individuals. It is the foreseeability of harm that triggers states' duties not to extradite. In *Vilvarajah and Others v. the United Kingdom*, the Court stated:[189]

> It is not normally for the ECHR institutions to pronounce on the existence or otherwise of potential violations of the ECHR. However, where an applicant claims that a decision to extradite him would, if implemented, be contrary to Article 3 by reason of its *foreseeable consequences* in the requesting country, a departure from this principle is necessary, in view of the serious and irreparable nature of the alleged suffering risked. . . .

A "real" risk is not a certainty, but a fact very likely to occur, judged from an objective standpoint. It is generally easier to establish a real risk in an expulsion case when the receiving state is not a member of the ECHR.

The existence of a risk of suffering torture, inhuman and/or degrading treatment falls to be determined, if the applicant has not yet been deported, not at the time when the deportation or extradition order was issued, but when the case comes before the Court. This allows the Court to take into account information that may have come to light in the interim, or to adjust to a changed situation in the receiving state. The Court has observed that "although the historical position is of

---

[188] As in the case of *Giama v. Belgium*, Comm. Report 17.7.80, §§ 43–55, D.R. 21, at 71.

[189] *Vilvarajah v. the United Kingdom*, supra note 83, at §§ 90–91 (emphasis added).

interest in so far as it may shed light on the current situation and its likely evolution, it is the present conditions which are decisive."[190]

Where an applicant has been expelled, as occurred in the case of *Cruz Varas and Others v. Sweden*,[191] the Court will primarily analyze the facts known to the state *at the time of extradition* to see if they indicated a real risk. In that case, a Chilean national who had been refused refugee status in Sweden argued that he would be subjected to torture, inhuman and/or degrading treatment on return. He claimed to have been tortured previously in Chile, due to membership of a militantly anti-Pinochet organization. Medical evidence indicated that he had been subject to such treatment in the past, but the Court found that there had been no substantial grounds evident to the state that his expulsion would breach Article 3. The applicant had said nothing of his political clandestine activities for eighteen months after his first interrogation in Sweden. Moreover, his story continually changed in the course of questioning. There are obviously problems with rejecting the risk of inhuman treatment based purely on a lack of credibility of the applicant's testimony, when the applicant is of foreign origin, may be intimidated by the interrogation setting and have language difficulties. Reassuringly, in *Cruz Varas*, the Court weighed heavily the fact that the political situation in Chile was improving, that some refugees had voluntarily returned, and that it considered the National Immigration Board to have made a sufficiently thorough examination of the case.[192] Nevertheless, the applicant's family did go into hiding in Sweden to avoid expulsion, and there was evidence that the applicant suffered a deterioration in mental health on his return.

Even where returned asylum applicants suffer inhuman treatment, the legitimacy of the decision to expel them will not be impugned with hindsight, unless it is established that it was taken in disregard of the existence of "substantial grounds" established at the time. This point is illustrated by the case of *Vilvarajah v. the United Kingdom*, where several Tamil applicants from Sri Lanka were denied political asylum and returned to Sri Lanka although they argued that they would be subjected to persecution and excessive violence if returned. Several of the applicants were ill-treated on return. Nevertheless, the Court determined that the decision to expel made by the United Kingdom authorities did not fall foul of the "substantial grounds" standard, however real the risk might have proven to be. There was once again evidence

---

[190] *Ahmed v. Austria*, 1996, §43, citing *Chahal v. the United Kingdom*, supra note 84, at § 86.
[191] *Cruz Varas and Others v. Sweden*, supra note 17.
[192] *Id.* at §§ 68–86.

that the situation in Sri Lanka was improving markedly, and voluntary repatriation was underway under UN auspices. The Court deferred to the experience of the Home Secretary in choosing to grant or refuse asylum, on the grounds that he had carefully considered the case, and had granted leave to stay in the case of many asylum-seekers.[193] The important feature appears to be that there was "no special distinguishing feature" in the circumstances of the particular applicants to suggest that they would be exposed to a greater risk of inhuman treatment than any Tamil resident in Sri Lanka.

The "special distinguishing feature" element defers to state discretion in granting asylum. Particular danger was found in the case of *Chahal v. the United Kingdom*.[194] The applicant was a prominent member of the British Sikh Community whose indefinite leave to remain was revoked on national security grounds, after he was arrested for involvement in terrorist activities. The charges had not been substantiated. The Court noted that "the applicant's high profile would be more likely to increase the risk to him of harm than otherwise" (§ 106). This, taken together with a rigorous examination of persons in a similar position led the Court to find that the British Government had violated its Article 3 duty towards Mr. Chahal. That examination involved consideration of reports submitted by non-governmental organizations, such as Amnesty International. Those reports established that although the situation in India was improving, and although criminal justice provisions were adequate, there were still too many incidences of inhuman treatment, including disappearances and extrajudicial killing of Sikhs by the Punjabi police and security forces, to render Mr. Chahal safe from serious risk of inhuman treatment anywhere in India. "[No] concrete evidence" was produced of "any fundamental reform or reorganization of the Punjab police in recent years" (§ 103), and the Punjab security forces remained "a recalcitrant and enduring problem" (§ 105). This was so despite the good faith efforts of the United Kingdom government to secure Mr. Chahal's return to a region far from the Punjab.

3.2.6 Non-Derogability of Article 3

Article 3 ... enshrines one of the most fundamental values of democratic society.... The Court is well aware of the immense difficulties faced by States in modern times in protecting their communities from terrorist violence. However,

---

[193] *Vilvarajah v. The United Kingdom, supra* note 83, at § 114.
[194] *Chahal v. the United Kingdom, supra* note 84.

even in these circumstances, the Convention prohibits in absolute terms torture or inhuman or degrading treatment or punishment, irrespective of the victim's conduct . . .

The prohibition provided by Article 3 . . . against ill-treatment is equally absolute in expulsion cases.[195]

Thus, it did not matter that Mr. Chahal was considered to pose a threat to national security. There is no balancing of competing interests involved when a breach of Article 3 is made out.

3.2.7 Capital Punishment and Article 3

An argument might be made that the death penalty is inhuman and degrading treatment and contrary to Article 3, when applied by a member state or a state to which a member state is extraditing a fugitive criminal. In *Soering*, this argument was raised, but dropped in favor of a line of reasoning which classified the "death row phenomenon" associated with the imposition of the death penalty as inhuman and degrading treatment

The Court's decision on Article 3 and the death penalty in *Jabari v. Turkey*[196] muddies the distinction between the inhuman and degrading character of the circumstances surrounding the death penalty and capital punishment itself. In *Jabari*, an Iranian national challenged her extradition to Iran from Turkey on the grounds that there was a real risk that she would be convicted of adultery under local law and be flogged, whipped or stoned to death on return. The Court, giving due weight to the findings of UNHCR, found that Turkey would be in violation of Article 3 of the ECHR if she were returned.[197] It is unclear how far an advocate could push the Court's reasoning in *Jabari*. The Court has certainly extended the ambit of Article 3 in an extradition and expulsion context to include types of capital punishment it regards as a form of torture, inhuman and degrading treatment or punishment.

Furthermore, the Court in *Jabari* proved itself willing to reevaluate Turkey's decision not to grant asylum, where that decision was tantamount to a violation of Article 3. It found that the Ankara Administrative Court had failed to conduct adequate judicial review of the asylum application in that it:

---

[195] *Id.* at §§ 78–79.
[196] E.C.H.R. July 11, 2000, at <http://hudoc.echr.coe.int/hudoc/ViewRoot.asp?Item=0&Action=Html&X=511053402&Notice=0&Noticemode=&RelatedMode=0>.
[197] *Id.* at § 41.

limited itself to the issue of the formal legality of the applicant's deportation rather than the more compelling question of the substance of her fears, even though by that stage the applicant must be considered to have had more than an arguable claim that she would be at risk if removed from her country of origin.[198]

This is the closest the Court has come to an evaluation of a member state's review of an asylum application. The language of *Jabari* opens a door for advocates in the future.

3.2.8 Health Care and Article 3

In *D. v. the United Kingdom*,[199] an expulsion order was issued for a man in the late stages of AIDS. He was due to expelled to St. Kitts, where the shelter, sanitation, and medication, and counseling were unlikely to be available to him. The Court found that "[a]lthough it cannot be said that the conditions which would confront [the applicant] in the receiving country are themselves a breach of the standards of Article 3 . . . , his removal would expose him to dying under most distressing circumstances and would thus amount to inhuman treatment" (§ 53).

The Court noted that the duty not to cause a real risk of a breach of Article 3 had normally been applied to a risk of "intentionally inflicted acts of the public authorities in the receiving country or from those of non-State bodies in that country when the authorities there are unable to afford [the applicant] appropriate protection."[200] Further, the Court stated:

> Aside from these situations and given the fundamental importance of Article 3 in the ECHR system, the Court must reserve to itself sufficient flexibility to address the application of that Article in other contexts which might arise. It is not therefore prevented from scrutinizing an applicant's claim under Article 3 where the source of the risk of proscribed treatment in the receiving country stems from factors which cannot engage either directly or indirectly the responsibility of the public authorities of that country, or which, taken alone, do not in themselves infringe the standards of that article.

---

[198] *Id.* at § 40.
[199] *D. v. the United Kingdom*, 1997-III Eur. Ct. H.R. 777.
[200] *Id.* at § 49.

To limit the application of Article 3 in this manner would be to undermine the absolute character of its protection. In any such contexts, however, the Court must subject all the circumstances surrounding the case to a rigorous scrutiny, especially the applicant's personal situation in the expelling State.[201]

3.3 Article 8—The Right to Private Life

One of the few other articles of the ECHR of direct applicability to extradition, expulsion, and deportation cases is Article 8. Claims under Article 8 may be brought when the impugned treatment does not rise to the level of torture, inhuman or degrading treatment or punishment, but still constitutes an interference with an individual's right to personal and physical integrity. In the case of *X and Y v. the Netherlands*, it was held that any forced physical treatment of an individual amounts to an interference with private life.[202] The interference must affect the well-being of the applicant.[203] Actions that were expected or impliedly consensual[204] do not implicate Article 8. "Consent" is not used here as a legal term of art, but rather to connote an action that is either truly voluntary or an accepted risk involved in a particular activity.

The state is under a positive duty to create conditions that protect the private life of the individual or compensate the individual for the damage caused.[205] The ECHR does not ensure, however, that the applicant has a home, food, or a private life to enjoy in the first place. There is some truth in the assertion that in the area of family life, the ECHR protects vested rights (i.e. pre-existing families) much more efficiently than newly-asserted asserted rights (the right to found a family, for example, under Article 12).

3.4 Equality and Non-Discrimination

> Claims under Article 14 against her state of origin are of prime importance to Chen in Scenario 1, for her imprisonment, the torture she suffered, her involuntary expatriation, and the seizure of her home and personal property. She may have further claims under Article 14 against her asylum state for discrimination in education.

---

[201] *Id.*
[202] 91 Eur. Ct. H. R. (ser. A) (1985).
[203] *López Ostra v. Spain, supra* note 34.
[204] *Costello-Roberts v. United Kingdom*, 247-C Eur. Ct. H.R. (ser. A) (1993).
[205] The injury in *López Ostra, supra* note 34, did involve actual physical harm.

> **Note:** At least until Protocol 12 comes into force and depending on the remedy sought, the advocate is advised to pursue cases involving discrimination in access to social support and any case of discriminatory treatment involving a right not protected by the ECHR under the ICCPR, or, depending on the state, through European Union machinery (see Section 5). Article 26 ICCPR is wider in scope than Article 14 of the ECHR as it is a free-standing provision on equality, not limited to any category of rights.

Often, the mistreatment that causes flight or is found on arrival in a host country has at its core an element of discrimination. This was amply illustrated by the *East Africa Cases*[206] in which the United Kingdom refused entry to holders of its passport based purely on their country of origin. Article 14 does not oblige states to prohibit all discrimination, but only to protect against discrimination in securing the rights and freedoms guaranteed by the ECHR. Its has been described by commentators as having an "accessory nature and autonomous status."[207] Even where no violation of the right in issue can be established, if the measures being examined are discriminatory, a violation of Article 14 may be found.

The Court's analytical approach to Article 14 was set out in the *Belgian Linguistics Case*:[208]

- Do the facts disclose a differential treatment?
- Did the distinction have a reasonable justification, having regard to the aims and effects of the measure under consideration?
- Is there reasonable proportionality between the means employed and the aim sought to be realized?[209]

A law barring all children of one religion from school in a Contracting Party to the ECHR would be prohibited under article 14. When the United Kingdom refused to allow holders of its own passport into its territory after they had been expelled from a number of countries in East Africa, the Commission found that the exclusion was racially motivated.[210] There was even a suggestion in that case that the discrimination

---

The symptoms of her daughter were confirmed by a pediatrician—nausea, vomiting, allergic reactions, anorexia, and acute bronchopulmonary infections.

[206] Nos. 4715/70, 4783/71, 4827/71, Dec. 6.3.78, DR 13 at 17.
[207] GOMIEN, *supra* note 18, at 346.
[208] *Belgian Linguistics Case, supra* note 121.
[209] GOMIEN, *supra* note 18, at 350.
[210] Nos. 4715/70, 4783/71, 4827/71, Dec. 6.3.78, D.R. 13 p.17.

might itself have amounted to a breach of Article 3, though the case ended in friendly settlement and the question has gone unanswered.

Thus, the finer intricacies of the operation of Article 14 often need not be addressed in situations at issue for refugees, asylum-seekers, and internally displaced persons, given that exclusions are likely to be transparently based on some identity-based classification. The legitimate aims and proportionality concerns will accord states a wide margin of appreciation where such apparent prejudice is not at issue, due to the immigration context.

In November 2000, Protocol 12 to the ECHR opened for signature. The new wording covering cases of discrimination provides:

Article 1—General Prohibition of Discrimination

1. The enjoyment of any right set forth by law shall be secured without discrimination on any ground such as sex, race, color, language, religion, political or other opinion, national minority, property, birth or other status.
2. No one shall be discriminated against by any public authority on any ground such as those mentioned in paragraph 1.

The addition of § 2 is intended to bring the following situations, where there is evidence of discrimination, within the purview of the ECHR:

- the enjoyment of a right, which may be inferred from a clear obligation of a public authority under national law, to behave in a particular manner
- the exercise of discretionary power by a public authority
- by any other act or omission by a public authority (for example, the behavior of law enforcement officers when controlling a riot)[211]

The scrutiny of discretionary acts of public authorities arguably could extend to decisions in certain countries to grant asylum. Protocol 12 may entail a duty to take positive anti-discrimination measures in certain instances. States may also be under an obligation to protect, in limited instances, certain individuals from the discriminatory acts of other private citizens.

---

[211] § 22 to Explanatory Report on Protocol 12, at <http://www.humanrights.coe.int/Prot12/Protocol%2012%20and%20Exp%20Rep.htm>.

3.5 Personal Liberty

The process of seeking asylum, and of being deported or extradited, often involves periods of detention. Lawfulness of detention and procedural safeguards relating to detention are laid down in Article 5 of the ECHR. Provisions covering conditions while in detention are not covered by Article 5, but by Article 3. The right to humane treatment has been described, with obvious reason, as a "cornerstone of the protection of the individual."[212]

3.5.1 Article 5 and Internally Displaced Persons

Article 5 addresses physical detention, and its purpose is to protect against *arbitrary* deprivations of liberty.[213] Detention must be *lawful* (Article 5 § 1). The requirement of lawfulness not only demands that detention be carried out in accordance with the domestic law of the detaining state, but also that the laws governing detention themselves conform to "recognized European" standards[214] which militate against arbitrariness.

The arbitrary, often unacknowledged, detention suffered by internally displaced persons at the hands of the authorities has been outlawed by the Court, provided a relatively low standard of proof of detention can be met. In the case of *Kurt v. Turkey*,[215] even though the applicant was the only witness to her son's detention by security forces, the Court found a violation of article 5, given that the Government denied that he had ever been detained in the first place. Article 5 § 4 guarantees the right to seek habeas corpus for every detainee.

3.5.2 Article 5 and Asylum-Seekers and Refugees

In contrast to a situation involving an internally displaced person, Article 5 § 1 § f excepts detention to stop illegal immigration and during extradition or deportation proceedings from most of the safeguards of Article 5. The issues it raises were examined by the Court in the case of *Amuur v. France*,[216] which concerned four Somali nationals, who fled their country via Syria to France in 1992. They believed that their lives were in danger if they stayed, and several members of their family had been murdered in Somalia. Upon arrival, the four applicants were found

---

[212] GOMIEN, *supra* note 18, at 127.
[213] HARRIS, *supra* note 62, at 97.
[214] *Id.*
[215] *Kurt v. Turkey*, *supra* note 150.
[216] 22 E.H.R.R. 533, 1996-III, Vol. 10, June 25, 1996.

to have forged passports and were denied entry into France. They spent the next 20 days in the International Section of Orly Airport, under surveillance and spent their nights at a hotel, a floor of which had been set up as an extension of the international zone of the airport. They were not allowed access to any social, legal, or humanitarian assistance, did not have their cases examined by the Refugee Appeals Board and were deported to Syria after the 20 days had passed.

The applicants had to establish first that the circumstances under which they were held constituted a *deprivation of liberty* according to the meaning of Article 5 § 1. They then had to satisfy the Court that their detention was not, even though with a view towards deportation, *"lawful."* The Court held that the detention of the applicants constituted a deprivation of liberty. While the Contracting Parties had the "undeniable sovereign right to control aliens' entry and residence in their territory, . . . [that] right must be exercised in accordance with the provisions of the ECHR, including Article 5."[217] The Court held that:

> In order to determine whether someone has been "deprived of his liberty" within the meaning of Article 5, the starting-point must be his concrete situation, and account must be taken of a whole range of criteria, such as the type, duration, effects and manner of implementation of the measure in question. The difference between deprivation of and restriction upon liberty is merely one of degree or intensity, and not one of nature or substance.[218]

The holding of aliens in the international zone of the airport was ruled acceptable only in order to enable States to prevent unlawful immigration, and had to be accompanied by suitable safeguards. These safeguards included a length of detention corresponding only to the legitimate time needed to process an asylum claim. The Court emphasized the need to respect the 1951 Convention relating to the Status of Refugees and access to refugee status determination for those who have been forced to flee for their lives. The Court distinguished the case of persons who have committed criminal offenses. The fact that the applicants had no access to a lawyer or any other assistance, nor any chance to have their claim to asylum application brought before a court, rendered their confinement a deprivation of liberty. The Court noted that freedom of movement was a fairly hollow concept, when one could leave one's own country, but find no safe haven elsewhere. Even where

---

[217] *Id.* at § 41.
[218] *Id.* at § 44.

such a safe country could be found, the Court was not prepared to legitimize detention conditions on the strength of an outcome dependent upon "the vagaries of diplomatic relations."[219]

The Court then turned to the lawfulness of the deprivation of liberty. When examining the application of a national law, the Court defers in large measure to the judgments and interpretations of the domestic courts. However, there are certain base requirements that national laws must meet. These include: compatibility with the doctrine of the rule of law, which requires open, clear, and prospective legislation, as well as compatibility with the provisions of the ECHR. The Court considered that particularly with respect to asylum-seekers detained at airports, there was a need to reconcile fundamental rights with the requirements of immigration regulation. This is evocative of the practical proportionality requirements that have been generally imputed to "lawfulness" in Article 5 by the Court.[220]

From *Amuur*, it is clear that, in cases of airport detention of asylum-seekers:

- there must be a clear law in force at the time of detention, not a circular nor regulation;
- the asylum-seekers have access to that law;
- the law must pertain to the particular circumstances of their detention;
- the asylum-seeker must be given access within a reasonable time to procedures for review of the asylum application; and
- the asylum-seeker must be given access within a specific time-limit to legal, humanitarian, and social assistance during detention.

Even in cases where detention pending extradition or deportation is found lawful, that detention is still subject to the requirements of Article 5 § 4, which demand that the detainee be given a chance to challenge that lawfulness and have it decided upon speedily before a court. The scope of review under Article 5 § 4 is not as wide as that of the actual decision-making authority in the matter for which the person is detained. Moreover, it is adjusted in scope depending on the level of judicial review ultimately undertaken by the decision-making authority.[221] In all cases, however, Article 5 § 4 review must be wide enough to satisfy the essential conditions of "lawfulness" under Article 5.

---

[219] *Id.* at § 49.
[220] HARRIS, *supra* note 62, at 105.
[221] *Bouamar v. Belgium*, February 29, 1988, § 60.

In addition, detention cannot last for a "length of time bound to give rise to serious concern."[222] Precisely the length of time involved is unclear. By way of comparison, in a suspected terrorism context, where the applicants had been detained but not yet charged, the Court held that 4 days and six hours was too long a period to wait before bringing the applicants before a competent judge.[223] Thus, the discretion involved in detention pending extradition or deportation is markedly wider than in case which does not fall under the article 5 § 1 §§ a-f exceptions.

The logic of *Amuur* equally applies to detention camps, although "reasonable" time limits may be interpreted differently in a mass influx situation. Although the Court noted that the situation of airport detention "was not in every respect comparable to that which obtains in centers for the detention of aliens pending deportation" (§ 43), the general guarantees against arbitrariness which go to the core of Article 5 must apply in that situation also.

With regard to extradition, the Court is not prepared to find lawful a case of prolonged detention pending deportation to a country that has requested extradition and been refused by national courts in the host state. This is regarded as disguised extradition and therefore in violation of the ECHR.[224]

3.6 Right to a Fair Trial and Due Process of Law

3.6.1 Article 6—The Right to a Fair Trial and Asylum Applications

Article 6 enshrines the right to a fair trial, in public, within a reasonable time by an independent and impartial tribunal, established by law. Fairness itself is held to extend to ensuring that both parties to a dispute are given the same opportunities to make their case and defend themselves. This principle is known as "the equality of arms."[225] The two areas to which the right applies, criminal charges and the determination of civil rights and obligations, do not encompass extradition or asylum petitions. Extradition obviously involves criminal charges, but the Commission has held that extradition is not actually a criminal process, in that the proceedings do not themselves determine the guilt or innocence of the accused.[226] In *Soering*, however, the Court did leave

---

[222] *Chahal*, supra note 84, at § 123.
[223] *Brogan and Others v. the United Kingdom* 145-B Eur. Ct. H.R. (ser. A) 11 (1988).
[224] *Bozano v. Italy*, December 18, 1956, §§ 59–60.
[225] *Dombo Beheer v. the Netherlands*, 27 October, 1993, § 35.
[226] *Farmakopoulos v. Belgium*, No. 11683/85, 1986.

open the question of whether Article 6 could apply to render extradition a violation of the ECHR, where the applicant would face a trial deficient as to the guarantees of Article 6 on return.

The word "civil" in "civil rights and obligations" is analyzed by the Court as connoting private law rights and obligations, as opposed to public law rights. This distinction is taken, in general terms, from a civil law distinction, but also reflects concepts in United Kingdom administrative law. Unless another right could be attached to a case involving a hearing for asylum application, immigration lies in the sphere of public law and outside the purview of Article 6. However, a dispute concerning the right to family life has been recognized as within the ambit of "civil rights and obligations," but not yet in the context of extradition or family reunification.

Furthermore, in many European countries, the decision on whether or not to grant asylum is taken by an administrative, not judicial body. Article 6 does apply to administrative decisions, but at most demands judicial review by a competent tribunal offering the guarantees of Article 6.[227]

3.6.2 Procedural Protections for Aliens Facing Expulsion, Article 1 Protocol 7

As a reaction against the exclusion of fair hearing rights in cases of expulsion and extradition, Article 1 of Protocol 7 to the ECHR was adopted "in order to afford minimum guarantees."[228] Since its entry into force, there has been virtually no consideration of Article 1 of Protocol 7 by the Court. It provides fairly weak protection for asylum-seekers. First, it demands that the alien be lawfully resident to invoke the procedural safeguards it offers. Thus, an asylum seeker in detention might not qualify, as the lawfulness of his stay is as yet undetermined. Second, it does not apply to aliens whose leave to remain was on terms which were subsequently broken.

There is no guarantee under Article 1 of Protocol 7 that the resident can stay on the territory of the respondent state while his appeal is pending, and the form of representation and of the authority which will review his case is also left to the discretion of the state. Review does not have to assume a judicial guise. Lastly, there is no indication that the two exceptions in subsection 2, public order and national security,

---

[227] *Zumtobel v. Austria*, 1993, § 32.
[228] Explanatory Report on Protocol No.7 to the ECHR for the Protection of Human Rights and Fundamental Freedoms, p.7, §7, from GOMIEN, *supra* note 18, at 364.

are subject to any proportionality-based balancing test. It has, however, been asserted that exempting subsection 2 from such limitations would fly against the spirit of the ECHR itself.[229]

3.6.3 The Right to a Fair Trial

As stated above, the guarantees of Article 6 of the ECHR apply to two types of dispute:

- criminal matters
- the determination of one's civil rights and obligations

Civil rights and obligations included rights acquired in relation to one's private dealings and business, such as the right to a good reputation,[230] to practice a profession[231] (as long as not a administrative post[232]) and decisions concerning children, such as custody and paternity.[233] The following protections are provided in the context of criminal matters:

- access to the courts[234]
- a fair and public hearing at all stages of proceedings[235]
- public pronouncement of judgments[236]
- the length of proceedings must be reasonable in the circumstances[237]
- trial by an independent[238] and impartial[239] tribunal
- right to a hearing in the presence of the accused[240]
- freedom from self-incrimination[241]
- right to adversarial proceedings
- right to a reasoned judgment[242]

---

[229] GOMIEN, *supra* note 18, at 366.
[230] *Golder v. the United Kingdom*, Eur. Ct. H.R. (ser. A) 18 (1975).
[231] *H. v. Belgium*, Eur. Ct. H.R., (ser. A) 127 (1987).
[232] *Neigel v. France*, 10 E.H.R.R. 1997-II No. 32.
[233] *Olsson v. Sweden*, Eur. Ct. H.R. (ser. A) 130 (1988).
[234] *Golder v. the United Kingdom*, *supra* note 230.
[235] *Hornsby v. Greece* Eur. Ct. H.R. (ser. A) 1997.
[236] *Sutter v. Switzerland*, Eur.Ct. H.R. (ser. A) 74 (1984).
[237] *Buchholz v. Germany*, Eur. Ct. H.R. (ser. A.)42 (1981).
[238] *Campbell and Fell v. the United Kingdom*, Eur. Ct. H.R. (ser. A) 80 (1984).
[239] *Piersack v. Belgium*, Eur. Ct. H.R. (ser. A) 53 (1982).
[240] *Ekbatani v. Sweden*, Eur. Ct. H.R. (ser. A) 134 (1988).
[241] *Saunders v. the United Kingdom*, Eur. Ct. H.R. (ser. A) (1996).
[242] *Helle v. Finland* 26 E.H.R.R. 159 (1997).

The ECHR specifically protects an individual's rights to be presumed innocent under Article 6 § 2.[243] Under Article 6 § 3, charges must be communicated promptly and intelligibly. An adequate time for defense is guaranteed (subsection b), as is the right to representation and legal aid, the right to examine witnesses and to an interpreter (subsection c).

3.7 The Right to Vote and to Participate in the Political Process

Internally displaced persons may face obstacles in voting as result of their dislocation. Refugees and asylum-seekers generally do not qualify for voting rights or to run for political office.

3.7.1 The Right to Vote and Citizens

Article 3 of Protocol 1 guarantees that its parties will hold "free and fair elections at reasonable intervals by secret ballot." The principle at the core of Article 3 Protocol 1 is an extension of freedom of expression and requires states to put in place "conditions which ensure the free expression of the people in the choice of legislature." That right inheres in *citizens*, not temporary residents, whether asylum-seekers or refugees.

The article has been interpreted to cover two rights:

- the right to vote and
- the right to stand for election to the legislature[244]

Whiles states enjoy a margin of appreciation, citizens may not be disqualified from standing for elected office based on discriminatory grounds, such as their religious affiliation.[245]

---

[243] *Barbara, Messegue and Jabardo v. Spain*, Eur. Ct. H.R. (ser. A) 146 (1989).

[244] CLEMENTS, *supra* note 20, at 233, citing *Mathieu-Mohin and Clerfayt v. Belgium*, Eur. Ct. H.R. (ser. A) 113 (1987).

[245] Contrast the situation in *Gitonas v. Greece*, Eur. Ct. H..R. (ser. A) 42 (1997), where the Court upheld the disqualification of the applicants from running for election because they already held public office. The Court regarded the Government's rationale that holding public office within 3 years of running for election as a member of parliament accorded the candidates unfair influence over the outcome of the election.

3.7.2 The Right to Vote and Non-Citizens (Refugees and Asylum-Seekers)

Beyond the rights to freedom of expression and association enshrined in Articles 10 and 11 respectively, the ECHR does not speak to the right of aliens to participate directly in the political process. In fact, Article 16 of the ECHR specifically states that "nothing in Articles 10, 11 and 14 shall be regarded as preventing the High Contracting Parties from imposing restrictions on the political activities of aliens." Where it can, the Court has shown willingness to interpret "aliens" as narrowly as possible, so as to limit the ambit of Article 16. Thus far, however, that interpretation has done little to aid refugees or asylum-seekers. While Article 16 has been held not to apply to citizens of the European Union, few refugees or asylum-seekers benefit from this clarification.[246]

3.8 Freedom of Religion, Thought, and Conscience

> A claim against her state of origin under Article 9 of the ECHR is relevant to Chen in Scenario 1, who is tortured, imprisoned, and involuntarily expatriated specifically in order to silence her religious beliefs and stop her religious activities (see also under freedom of expression and association below, Sections 3.9 and 3.10)
>
> She may also have an Article 9 claim against her asylum state, if the reason for her suffering discrimination in employment and housing is not her status as a refugee, but the actual substance of her beliefs. This latter claim may considerably harder to make out.

3.8.1 Article 9 and Proof of a Subjective Belief

Most often, breaches of Article 9 are asserted in concert with alleged breaches of the rights to freedom of expression and association under Article 10, as there is often a degree of substantive overlap. It is difficult to meet the high burden of proof required by Article 9 § 1. The holding of beliefs is a personal, subjective matter, almost impossible to prove objectively without recourse to the "manifestation of religion" wing of Article 9 § 1. Indeed, it can be inferred from the Court's approach to census-taking that the compulsory divulgence of those beliefs is itself a violation of Article 9.[247]

---

[246] *Piermont v. France*, Eur. Ct. H.R. (ser.A) 314 (1995).
[247] HARRIS, *supra* note 62, at 361.

It is, however, useful to be able to make the distinction between a case where the applicant's very right to hold a belief and his ability to manifest that belief are at issue. The latter is subject to the usual proportionality test of Articles 8–11, with the exception of measures taken for national security reasons, which are not permissible limitations under Article 9 § 2. The freedom to *hold* a belief in Article 9 § 1 is absolute.

3.8.2 Limitations on the Ability to Manifest a Religious Belief

The Court has never addressed a widespread mass persecution of a religious minority group that has been forcibly displaced. It has never defined religion for the purposes of Article 9. It has, however, been established that any indoctrination of religion by the state,[248] or compulsion to accept a state religion[249] violates Article 9 § 1. Any violent oppression of religion probably will amount to indoctrination for the purposes of Article 9, if it reaches the requisite level of severity.

The balancing test of Article 9 § 2 is thus more likely to be applied to a case in which the applicants have been prevented from engaging in particular religious practices by the state, rather than stopped, wholesale, from expressing their beliefs at all. In the seminal case of *Kokkinakis v. Greece*,[250] the Court found that conviction for proselytism and subsequent imprisonment of a couple, who as Jehovah's Witnesses entered an Orthodox Christian's home in order to speak to her about their beliefs and attempt to convert her, was neither supported by a pressing social need, nor proportionate to the legitimate aim pursued. It is significant that in *Kokkinakis*, the Court identified the legitimate aim of Article 9 as the provision of protection against religious indoctrination and brainwashing. On the other hand, the Commission has held that members of the Sikh religion were not subject to a violation of Article 9, when forced by British motorcycle helmet laws to wear a helmet, even though it interfered with their ritual wearing of a turban.[251]

3.8.3 Article 9 and Non-State Actors

In order to be a true shield for displaced persons, Article 9 must also entail a positive duty for the state to protect groups against private acts that violate religious freedoms, and ideally also impose upon states

---

[248] *Id.* at 360.
[249] *Darby v. Sweden*, 187 Eur. Ct. H.R. (ser. A) (1991).
[250] *Kokkinakis v. Greece*, 260-A Eur. Ct. H.R. (ser. A) (1993).
[251] No. 7992/77, Dec. 12.7.78, GOMIEN, *supra* note 18 at 266.

a duty to create conditions whereby groups of refugees, asylum-seekers, or displaced persons are able to manifest their religion, even while in temporary accommodation or camps. The former duty was established to some extent in the case of *Otto-Preminger-Institut v. Austria*,[252] which involved the screening by a private institute of a film deeply offensive to the Catholics, in a region where Catholicism was the majority religion. The Court found the state could lawfully prohibit conduct that was gratuitously offensive to religious beliefs. Although a majority religion was protected in that case, the principle could be seen as a broader one of tolerance. The Court has not yet gone so far, however, as to impose upon the state the duty to create conditions in which groups can manifest their religion.

3.9 Freedom of Expression

> A claim under Article 10 is especially relevant to **Ibrahim** in Scenario 2, who has been forced to flee his state of origin because he cannot express his political beliefs there.

The right to freedom of expression is central to the scheme of rights guaranteed by the ECHR.[253] The persecution suffered by refugees, asylum-seekers, and internally displaced persons frequently includes being prevented from expressing their political, religious, or cultural views or beliefs. Freedom of expression in Article 10 overlaps significantly with the right to freedom of thought, conscience, and religion in Article 9. Both guarantees cover cases where the victim is being prevented from holding an opinion. There is also significant overlap with Article 11, the right to freedom of association. Any public demonstration is both a form of "peaceful assembly" under Article 11 and an exercise of freedom of expression under Article 10.[254]

> **Tip:** In a case involving the disruption of a public demonstration, the advocate is advised to look to Article 11 before Article 10.

"Expression" in Article 10 extends to all information or ideas, regardless of how favorably they are received.[255] Specifically, Article 10 has applied to:

---

[252] *Otto-Preminger-Institut v. Austria*, 295 Eur. Ct. H.R. (ser. A) § 47.
[253] *Handyside v. U.K.*, 24 Eur. Ct,.H.R. (ser. A.) (1976).
[254] CLEMENTS, *supra* note 18, at 192.
[255] *Handyside v. U.K.*, *supra* note 253.

- freedom of the press
- broadcasting, television, and cinema
- the right to receive information (freedom of information)
- advertising and commercial activities
- political speech

For a state's interference to be justified every condition, restriction, or penalty must be:

- prescribed by law
- necessary in a democratic society
- imposed in the interests of national security, territorial integrity, or public safety, for the prevention of disorder or crime, for the protection of health or morals, for the protection of the reputation or rights of others, for preventing the, disclosure of information received in confidence or for maintaining the authority and impartiality of the judiciary

3.9.1 Establishing the Existence of an Interference with Article 10

Imprisonment, a financial penalty imposed upon an individual, confiscation of a newspaper or literary work, or other effort to prevent an individual from expressing his views will constitute an "interference" for the purposes of Article 10 of the ECHR.[256]

3.9.2 Justification for the Interference

The requirement that the interference with the right of freedom of expression be prescribed by law is not a difficult one for the state to meet. It must merely show that the consequences suffered by the victim were legally mandated, and that the law in question met several fundamental tests. The law in question must:

- be adequately accessible
- be formulated with sufficient precision to enable the person to regulate his conduct. It must be possible to foresee, to a degree that is reasonable in the circumstances, the consequences that a given action may entail. Absolute certainty, however, is not required. In practice, the Court is relatively flexible

---

[256] *Engels and Others v. the Netherlands*, Eur. Ct. H.R. (ser. A) 22 (1976), and *Müller and Others v. Switzerland*, Eur. Ct. H.R. (ser A.) 133 (1988).

on this issue, and has found an interference to be "prescribed by law" even where the law in question had been criticized for vagueness by the Commission.[257]
- be limited in effect where the application of the law is left to executive discretion

The Court will turn next to the motivation behind state interference with an individual's right to freedom of expression. A list of permissible grounds for interference is contained within Article 10 § 2. Once again, this threshold is not difficult for states to meet.

Mass internal displacement and refugee flows often occur in countries experiencing a degree of internal civil strife. The most relevant cases from a member state in this situation concern efforts by the Turkish government in the southeastern region of Turkey to control pro-Kurdish expression in the context of Kurdish assertions of independence and ongoing violent confrontations between the government and the PKK.[258] The Turkish government has continually justified its actions under Article 10 § 2 of the ECHR as intended to protect national security, preserve territorial integrity, and prevent crime. In those cases, the Court has found that the government's aim in imposing restrictions on freedom of expression is legitimate.

As will be discussed below, an interference that is in violation of Article 10 usually fails on the grounds that it is not regarded by the Court as "necessary in a democratic society," rather than illegitimate as to its aim. It is under the "necessary in a democratic society" prong of Article 10 § 2 that the Court subjects the interference to the most rigorous balancing test, judging the proportionality of the restrictive measures taken against the nature and effect of the form of expression. The Court will, nevertheless, undertake a cursory examination of the general nature of the interference when evaluating the legitimacy of the aim it was intended to serve. For example, in *Zana v. Turkey*,[259] the Court commented on the fact that the victim was the former mayor of

---

[257] *Polat v. Turkey*, Application no. 23500/94, at <http://hudoc.echr.coe.int/hudoc/ViewRoot.asp?Item=0&Action=Html&X=518135558&Notice=0&Noticemode=&RelatedMode=0>.

[258] The Court has continually reiterated that "since approximately 1985, serious disturbances have raged in the south-east of Turkey between the security forces and the members of the PKK (Worker's Party of Kurdistan). This confrontation has so far, according to the Government, claimed the lives of 4,036 civilians and 3,884 members of the security forces." *Zana v. Turkey*, 1997-VII Eur. Ct. H.R. 2553 § 10.

[259] *Id.*

Diyarbakir and long-time political activist for Kurdish independence. It stated when evaluating the legitimacy of the government's aim in suppressing the speech that his words "coming from a political figure well known in the region—could have an impact such as to justify the national authorities' taking a measure designed to maintain national security and public safety."[260]

In assessing whether a measure is "necessary in a democratic society" under Article 10 § 2, the Court undertakes a sophisticated balancing exercise. Under this head, two questions must be answered:

- Was there a "pressing social need" for the interference and
- Were the measures taken "proportionate to the legitimate aim pursued and did the authorities give "relevant and sufficient" reasons to justify it?

Although states have a certain margin of appreciation when assessing the existence of a pressing social need, the final determination of whether or not a restriction can be reconciled with that need lies with the Court. The Court's approach to this inquiry is best addressed in the context of the different forms of expression protected by Article 10.

Freedom of the Press

The Court has time and again made clear the essential position of the press to the proper functioning of a political democracy:[261]

> While the press must not overstep the bounds set, *inter alia*, for the protection of the vital interests of the State such as national security or territorial integrity against the threat of violence or the prevention of disorder or crime, it is nevertheless incumbent on the press to impart information and ideas on political issues, including divisive ones. Not only has the press the task of imparting such information and ideas; the public has a right to receive them. Freedom of the press affords the public one of the best means of discovering and forming an opinion of the ideas and attitudes of political leaders.[262]

---

[260] *Id.* at § 50.
[261] *Lingens v. Austria*, Eur. Ct. H.R. (ser.A.) 103 (1986).
[262] *Id.* at §§ 41–42.

When balancing this pressing social need served by the press against those of the state, the Court will look to the subject matter, context, and language of the articles in question.

In the landmark case *Sunday Times v. United Kingdom*,[263] the Government argued that it was justified in preventing the Sunday Times newspaper from publishing a report emphasizing the difficulties faced by families whose children had suffered from severe birth defects after their mothers had taken the drug Thalidomide during pregnancy. The article in question was published while a case concerning the quantum of damages to be awarded to the parents was pending in U.K. courts and the government considered that the publication of the piece would lead to trial by media and constitute a threat to the authority and impartiality of the judiciary. The Court held that the interference with the Times' freedom to publish the article and the public's freedom to receive the information it contained was not "necessary in a democratic society" within the meaning of the ECHR. The defects caused by Thalidomide were a matter of public concern and raised issues of greater importance concerning damage caused by pharmaceutical drugs and the compensation available.

In the context of ongoing and violent civil strife, the Court has undertaken very careful analyses of the language used and purpose behind impugned press articles. The Court has considered the following factors to be relevant when distinguishing between an article that amounts to "hate speech and the glorification of violence" and is therefore not protected by Article 10, and an article the state cannot suppress for a legitimate aim:

- the purpose of the report, whether informative[264] (protected) or inflammatory (restricted);
- identification and incrimination of individuals by name in a context which is either accusatory and uncorroborated or endangers the individuals in question;[265]

---

[263] 30 Eur. Ct. H.R. (ser. A.) (1979).

[264] *Jersild and Others v. Denmark*, Eur. Ct. H.R. (ser A.) 298 (1994); *Gerger v. Turkey*, Eur. Ct. H.R. (1999), at <http://hudoc.echr.coe.int/hudoc/ ViewRoot. asp?Item=0&Action=Html&X=518135734&Notice=0&Noticemode=&RelatedMo de=0>, where the journalist did not publish the material in question in the newspaper, but read it aloud to a select group of people at a commemorative celebration.

[265] *Sürek v. Turkey No. 1*, Eur. Ct. H.R. (1999), at <http://hudoc. echr.coe.int/ hudoc/ViewRoot.asp?Item=1&Action=Html&X=518135848&Notice=0&Noticemo de=&RelatedMode=0>.

- use of violent language or language intended to incite others to violence (such as "massacres," "brutalities," "slaughter," "the hired killers of imperialism")[266] as opposed to merely "colorful and pejorative" language;[267]
- the fact that the information is already out in the public domain, such that it cannot cause any additional significant harm.[268]

Equally important to a determination of the justifiability of state interference with the freedom of the press under Article 10 is the question of proportionality. The Court must balance the measures taken to protect any of the interests enumerated in Article 10 § 2 against the extent of the danger posed to that interest by the report in question.

The Court demands a reasonably high degree of proportionality in these circumstances. In the Turkish context, it has repeatedly held that incarceration of the writer, editor, or publisher of the material in question or the imposition personal fine considered more than "moderate" in the circumstances will render the measures taken disproportionate and thus in violation of the ECHR.

The Court, while recognizing that it lies within the discretion of states to impose criminal penalties for activities endangering legitimate social interests, requires the state not only to exercise tolerance in accepting criticism, but also to give adequate reasons for all criminal sanctions taken against individual citizens in the name of protecting those interests.[269]

Political Figures

The Court has stated on numerous occasions that "there is little scope under article 10 § 2 . . . for restrictions on political speech or on debate on questions of public interest."[270] Where, however, a public figure uses his or her role to incite a group to violence, even if the precise wording of the incitement is ambiguous, the Court will evaluate the words in the context of the person's position and sphere of influence.

---

[266] *Id.*
[267] *Özgür Gündem v. Turkey*, Eur. Ct. H.R. (2000), at <http://hudoc.echr.coe.int/hudoc/ViewRoot.asp?Item=0&Action=Html&X=518135939&Notice=0&Noticemode=&RelatedMode=0>.
[268] *Sürek v, Turkey No. 2*, Eur. Ct. H.R. (1999), at <http://hudoc.echr.coe.int/hudoc/ViewRoot.asp?Item=2&Action=Html&X=518140015&Notice=0&Noticemode=&RelatedMode=0>.
[269] *Özgür Gündem v. Turkey*, *supra* note 267.
[270] *Sürek v, Turkey No. 1*, *supra* note 265.

Thus, in *Zana v. Turkey*,[271] when a long-time activist and former mayor of Diyarbakir made "ambiguous" and even contradictory statements about the PKK and resort to violence to achieve independence, the Court considered that Mr. Zana was rightfully prevented from publishing his views in an interview, given the explosive situation in the region. The Court is strongly influenced by the precise position held by the person making the statements in question and the nature of the language used. In *Ceylan v. Turkey*,[272] the head of a trade union in the same area published an article adjudged political speech by the Court. It used a Marxist tone and virulent language to criticize the state's actions in southeastern Turkey. The Court observed "that the applicant was writing in his capacity as a trade-union leader, a player on the Turkish political scene, and the article in question, despite its virulence, does not encourage the use of violence or armed resistance or insurrection."[273]

Literary Works

Similar language, however, written in the context of a literary memoir or work of non-fiction by a private individual, is not evaluated as posing such a danger to the interests protected by Article 10 § 2, even if it does not qualify as a "neutral description of historical facts."[274]

Broadcasting

Article 10 § 1 specifically preserves the right of states to regulate television and cinematic broadcasting by requiring a license. For the purposes of a group being discriminated against on the grounds of their beliefs, it is important that Article 10 prevent the state from using this discretion in order to stop that group's views being broadcast. Article 10 has been interpreted by the Court as preventing a broadcast from being stopped or jammed by the state.[275] It has also been held under Article 10 that a licensing scheme must be sufficiently narrowly tailored

---

[271] *Supra* note 258.
[272] *Ceylan v. Turkey*, Eur. Ct. H.R. (1999), at <http://hudoc.echr.coe.int/hudoc/ViewRoot.asp?Item=0&Action=Html&X=518140200&Notice=0&Noticemode=&RelatedMode=0>.
[273] *Id.*
[274] *Arslan v. Turkey*, Eur. Ct. H.R. (1999), at <http://hudoc.echr.coe.int/hudoc/ViewRoot.asp?Item=0&Action=Html&X=518140240&Notice=0&Noticemode=&RelatedMode=0>.
[275] *Autotronic AG v. Switzerland*, Eur. Ct. H.R. (ser. A) 178 (1990).

so as to allow legal and natural persons the opportunity to set up cable and radio stations separate from those run by the state.[276]

Advertising

States enjoy a wider margin of appreciation over the regulation of commercial speech than political speech. However, measures taken to curb commercial speech must still be strictly proportionate to the aim they seek to achieve.[277]

3.9.3 Positive Duties Under Article 10

In the case of *Özgür Gündem v. Turkey*,[278] a pro-Kurdish Turkish-language newspaper with a circulation of up to 45,000 copies and some international circulation was the target of serious attacks and harassment over the course of two years. The attacks resulted in several killings of staff and persons present in the newspaper offices. The newspaper was never able to identify the perpetrators. Repeated petitions to local police and authorities resulted only in an independent prosecutor taking unilateral investigative action into the incidents. The police did nothing to protect the newspaper, but instead eventually searched its premises and made arrests there in a forceful manner. The paper eventually closed down. The Court found a positive duty for the state to protect the newspaper's freedom of expression under Article 10. The Court was not persuaded that the government had provided adequate or effective responses to the applicant's allegations that the attacks were part of a campaign either supported or tolerated by the government. To that extent, therefore, a positive duty to protect the right to freedom of expression exists under Article 10.

3.10 Freedom of Assembly and Association

Article 11 enshrines the right to assemble as well as to associate. The Court has interpreted the right to include some positive duties on states, which may have implications for asylum states. Article 11 also applies to the freedom to choose to belong, or not to belong, to a particular political party. Interference with this choice is often central to the abuse suffered by political refugees and internally displaced persons because of their political affiliations.

---

[276] *Informationsverien Lentia v. Austria*, Eur. Ct. H.R. (ser. A) 276 (1993).
[277] *Dublin Well Woman and Others v. Ireland*, supra note 28.
[278] *Supra* note 267.

3.10.1 Freedom to Assemble Peacefully

The freedom to assemble under the ECHR is not unlimited. Quite apart from the restrictions that can be placed on its exercise by the state under Article 11 § 2 of the ECHR, the freedom is only limited to *peaceful* assembly. It is this aspect of the freedom, which imposes a positive duty on states under Article 11. In *Platform "Ärtzte für das Leben" v. Austria*,[279] the Court held that states have an obligation to take "reasonable and appropriate" measures to ensure that lawful demonstrations can proceed peacefully.[280] Article 11 does not require states to guarantee absolutely that demonstrations will occur without disruption. In that case, although counter-demonstrators interrupted the march in question, no demonstrators suffered any violence to their person. The Court held that the state had taken appropriate protective measures within the ambit of its discretion to protect the marchers. This positive duty not only has implications for internally displaced persons, but also for asylum-seekers and refugees in their asylum state.

3.10.2 Restrictions on the Right to Assemble Peacefully

Article 11 prevents states from imposing unreasonable and arbitrary restrictions on the right to assemble.[281] The Court approaches its analysis of Article 11 in a very similar way to its analysis of Article 10. When evaluating a state restriction on the right to assemble or to associate freely, the Court considers whether the state interfered with those rights, whether the interference was prescribed by law and pursued a legitimate aim, as enumerated in Article 11 § 2. The legitimate state aims set out in Article 10 § 2 are almost identical. Additionally, Article 11 § 2 allows the state further discretion to restrict the rights of members of the armed forces, police and administration of the state to assemble peacefully and associate freely.[282] However, there is some indication that the Court will construe administration of the state as narrowly as

---

[279] Eur. Ct. H.R. (ser. A) 139 (1988).
[280] CLEMENTS, *supra* note 20, at 203.
[281] *Ezelin v. France*, Eur. Ct. H.R. (ser. A) 202 (1991). The Bar Association reprimanded a lawyer for protesting judicial decisions in public. The Court found a violation of Article 11. CLEMENTS, *supra* note 20, at 204.
[282] The Commission has made this distinction in discretion by applying a slightly different test. Instead of requiring that the measures taken be strictly proportional to the pressing social need in question, the Court asks only if the interference was prescribed by law and in pursuit of a legitimate aim: *Council of Civil Service Unions v U.K.* 50 DR 228; CLEMENTS, *supra* note 20, at 207.

possible.[283] Finally, as under Article 10, the Court will balance the "pressing social need" justifying the aims in question against the severity of the measures taken to restrict Article 11 rights.

3.10.3 Freedom of Association

Freedom of association includes freedom to associate and choose not to associate.[284] The only bodies exempted from this choice are professional bodies and associations that guarantee the qualifications of their members, such as bar and medical associations.[285]

Of particular significance for groups frequently subject to persecutory harm is the Court's approach under Article 11 applied to minority groups. For example, the Court held in the case of *Sidoropoulos and Others v. Greece*[286] that the Greek authorities could not justifiably shut down an association of ethnic Macedonians calling themselves "Home of Macedonian Civilization" on the grounds that they threatened the territorial integrity of the state. The Court stated that "the inhabitants of a region in a country are entitled to form associations in order to promote the region's special characteristics, for historical as well as economic reasons."[287]

3.10.4 The Freedom to Form and Join Political Parties

The example of *Ibrahim* above illustrates the importance of Article 11 to political asylum-seekers and refugees. The Court has on a number of occasions addressed this issue. The Court has repeatedly held that political parties that do not advocate violence as a means for achieving their ends cannot be suppressed on the grounds that they endanger national security or the territorial integrity of the state. In *Özdep v. Turkey*, the Court stated that:

> the fact that such a political project is considered incompatible with the current principles and structures of the Turkish State does not mean that it infringes democratic rules. It is of the essence of democracy to allow diverse political

---

[283] *Vogt v. Germany*, Eur. Ct. H.R. (ser. A) 323 (1995).
[284] CLEMENTS, *supra* note 20 at 204.
[285] *Le Compte v. Belgium*, Eur. Ct. H.R. (ser. A) 44 (1981).
[286] E.C.H.R. July 10, 1998, at <http://hudoc.echr.coe.int/hudoc/ViewRoot.asp?Item=0&Action=Html&X=518140521&Notice=0&Noticemode=&RelatedMode=0>.
[287] *Id.* at § 44.

projects to be proposed and debated, even those that call into question the way a State is currently organised, provided that they do not harm democracy itself.[288]

3.11 Freedom of Movement

There is no right more central in theory to refugees, asylum-seekers, and internally displaced persons than freedom of movement, namely the right to move freely within their own country, to leave where necessary and to enter another. The provisions of Protocol 4 can only be invoked against states that have ratified it. Article 2 of Protocol 4 protects only applicants lawfully on the territory of the respondent state, as determined by local law. In *Piermont v. France*,[289] the applicant, a Member of the European Parliament, was served with an expulsion order as she was seated in the plane to leave French Polynesia. The service of the order was valid in local law, and therefore, absent arbitrariness was valid.

3.11.1 Expulsion of Nationals

An interesting issue raised under Article 3 of Protocol 4 is the situation where a state deprives one of its nationals of their nationality for the purposes of expulsion. To allow such behavior "would make the protection of Article 3 illusory."[290]

3.11.2 Collective Expulsion of Aliens

Article 4 of Protocol 4 prohibits the collective expulsion of aliens. The article does not protect individuals from expulsion, unless they form part of an expelled group, but it does apply to those illegally present. The only indication in the case law of the Court as to what might constitute a group expulsion comes from a case before the Commission in 1975, which was brought on behalf of a group of repatriated Vietnamese children. The Commission held that they had not been expelled as a group, because although the expulsion orders were iden-

---

[288] E.C.H.R. December 8, 1999, at <http://hudoc.echr.coe.int/hudoc/ViewRoot.asp?Item=0&Action=Html&X=518140624&Notice=0&Noticemode=&RelatedMode=0>, *citing Socialist Party and Others v. Turkey*, 25 May 1998 at <http://hudoc.echr.coe.int/hudoc/ViewRoot.asp?Item=0&Action=Html&X=518140729&Notice=0&Noticemode=&RelatedMode=0>.
[289] *Piermont v. France, supra* note 246.
[290] GOMIEN, *supra* note 18, at 362.

tical in format, each application was reviewed, as far as practicable, separately, and on its merits.[291]

3.11.3 The Right to Asylum

As has been stated above, there is no right to asylum specifically enshrined in the ECHR.

3.12 The Right to Family and Private Life

Not allowing a family member into a member state or extraditing one family member so as to separate is the family may, under certain circumstances, violate the right to family and private life. Article 8, which guarantees the right to family life and private life, is also of great potential significance for internally displaced persons, as the destruction of family life and private life is at the core of being forced to flee from one's home.

Like Articles 2, 3, 10, and 11, Article 8 has positive and negative aspects.[292] In *Kroon v. the Netherlands*,[293] the Court defined the "essential object" of Article 8 as:

> to protect the individual against arbitrary action by the public authorities. There may in addition be positive obligations inherent in "effective" respect for family life [and other Article 8(1) values].

3.12.1 Limitations on Article 8

Article 8 is subject to limitation. An interference will be legitimate if it occurs "in accordance with the law" and has a "legitimate aim" and is "necessary in a democratic society." The limitations in Article 8 § 2 apply also to Articles 9, 10, and 11. They are interpreted with reference to and evoke the doctrines of the margin of appreciation and proportionality. The Court engages in a balancing test between the interests of the community as a whole and the rights of the individual.

---

[291] No. 77014/76, Dec. 11.3.77, unpublished.
[292] *Johnston and Others v. the United Kingdom*, 112 Eur. Ct. H.R. (ser. A) 25, § 55 (1986).
[293] *Kroon v. the Netherlands*, 297-C Eur. Ct. H.R. (ser. A) § 31 (1994).

3.12.2 The Home

> **Maria** in Scenario 3 has been evicted from her home by security forces and has a claim under Article 8.

The ECHR does not guarantee the right to a home per se. Article 8 deals with situations where home life is forcibly interrupted by the state, either by interference with physical enjoyment of one's home and ownership rights, or with lifestyle. For a particular property to be regarded as a home, either the building or the land must be legally owned by the applicant, the applicant must have resided there for a period, with a view towards living there permanently, and must evince an intention not to establish a primary residence elsewhere.[294]

A place where the applicant has lived for a prolonged period of time will generally be regarded as his "home."[295] In contrast, a plot of land bought by an applicant for the purpose of setting up home, but upon which he never resided and where the home in question is not yet built, will not be so regarded, even if it is situated in the applicant's family's "home town."[296]

There is, above and beyond the definitional issues, one complaint wherein the Commission spoke directly to a situation of forcible evictions en masse. In the interstate complaint of *Cyprus v. Turkey*, the Commission declared that:

---

[294] These elements are drawn from two very different cases. The first is *Gillow v. the United Kingdom*, Eur. Ct. H.R. (ser. A) 109 (1986), where the applicants challenged the revocation of their license to live on Guernsey, where they had resided in a house they still owned, before moving constantly for work for a period of eighteen years. The important issue in the case was the establishment of their intent to set up home there. In that case, the applicants argued that the Guernsey house was always intended to be the center of their home life.

The second case is that of *Buckley v. the United Kingdom*, 23 E.H.R.R. 101 (1996), where the applicant unsuccessfully challenged planning laws, which prohibited her from carrying on her "traditional Gypsy lifestyle." The applicant did not intend to be peripatetic, but live, in her caravan, on a plot of land she owned, and where she had resided for eight years. Application No. 46346/99, E.C.H.R. May 25, 2000.

[295] *Larkos v. Cyprus*, E.C.H.R. 18 February 1999, at <http://hudoc.echr.coe.int/hudoc/ViewRoot.asp?Item=0&Action=Html&X=518141226&Notice=0&Noticemode=&RelatedMode=0>.

[296] *Loizidou v. Turkey, supra* note 88, at § 65.

[T]he prevention of the physical possibility of the return of Greek Cypriot refugees to their homes in the north of Cyprus amounts to an infringement, imputable to Turkey, of their right to respect of their homes as guaranteed in Article 8 § 1 of the ECHR.[297]

As regards the specific rights appertaining to respect of the home, these appear to be: the right to occupy in peace, and the rights not to be subjected to an unjustified arrest, search, seizure, or inspection of one's home by the authorities.

It has not actually been firmly established that the right to occupy involves a choice of lifestyle. However, the fact that the definitions of "home" both in *Loizidou* and *Buckley* include an inference with "home life" if not "lifestyle," does suggest that the protection of a lifestyle is within the ambit of Article 8. This also serves to distinguish Article 8 from Article 1 of Protocol 1, which protects property rights generally in movable and immovable property. Thus, where internal displacement results from a state policy of eviction in the course of widespread persecution aimed to destroy a particular group's lifestyle, Article 8 would be triggered.

As far as Article 8 § 2 is concerned in an eviction context, a relatively wide margin of appreciation will usually be accorded to the states, unless the state is clearly acting in a disproportionate or persecutory manner or if, in a situation of armed conflict, the state is the aggressor. In *Loizidou*,[298] the Court held that eviction of Greek Cypriots by invading Turkish soldiers could not be justified by an interest in providing shelter for Turkish citizens. Where destruction of property occurs in the course of an anti-terrorist campaign, however, the situation is less clear-cut. Article 8 is not absolute.

3.12.3 The Right to a Personal Identity

> **Maria** in Scenario 3 is being deprived of the identity documents she needs to leave her country, and will therefore look to Article 8 for redress.

Internally displaced persons may be denied the right to an identity, through the refusal or removal of identity documents, which in turn makes it very difficult to seek refuge outside their country of residence.

---

[297] Comm. Report, 10.7.76, § 208, unpublished, cited from GOMIEN, *supra* note 18, at 247.

[298] *Loizidou v. Turkey*, *supra* note 88.

The right to an identity is not specifically enshrined in the ECHR. A positive general duty to provide to everyone the requisite information to establish a personal identity is not protected by the ECHR, but a permutation of it is. In the case of *Gaskin v. the United Kingdom*,[299] the applicant challenged a British law, which prevented him from having access to files, which documented his childhood experiences in public care, on confidentiality grounds. The Court recognized that a balance had to be struck, in the interests of protecting third persons, between Gaskin's rights and the confidentiality rights of the contributors to the files. It found, however, that "persons in the situation of the applicant have a vital interest, protected by the ECHR, in receiving the information necessary to know and understand their childhood and early development" (§ 49). Having weighed up the competing interests, the Court came to the conclusion that, where confidentiality had not been requested or had been erroneously requested, the applicant was entitled to access to the documents.

Applying this to the right to identification papers in a displacement situation, it appears that, the state has no duty to provide the papers in the first place. However, it may have a duty to give the applicants access to such a papers as exist and presumably a duty not to destroy existing papers. In order to argue for a greater positive duty, an claim made under Article 8 on these grounds would have to be bolstered by other provisions, such as Protocol 4, Article 2, which enshrines the right to leave one's country of residence, and Article 13, the right to an effective remedy under national law.

3.12.4 Article 8, Deportation, and Expulsion

Very few cases have come before the Court concerning refugees making claims under Article 8. The jurisprudential trends are gleaned from cases concerning immigrants.[300] The interests to be balanced in immigration situations, versus refugee or displacement situations, may create confusion.

Two paradigms for immigrants who are not forced migrants have emerged:

(1) An immigrant or refugee challenging an expulsion or extradition order on the grounds that it would violate his family life by separating him from his family (*expulsion scenario*) or

---

[299] *Gaskin v. the United Kingdom*, Eur. Ct. H.R. (ser. A) 160 (1989).

[300] Hélène Lambert, *The European Court of Human Rights and the Right of Refugees and Other Persons in Need of Protection to Family Reunion*, 11 INT'L J. REFUGEE L. 427, 433 (1999).

(2) An immigrant or refugee requesting that a family member be allowed into the territory in question, so as to respect the right to family life and not keep a family apart (*family reunion scenario*).

The general approach of the Court to these cases was laid down in the case of *Gül v. Switzerland*.[301] Article 8 protects the individual against arbitrary interference by the public authorities. Article 8 has negative and positive aspects requiring the Court to balance the interests of the individual against those of the community.

Every nation has the right to control the entry of non-nationals onto its territory and no nation is obliged to let whole families enter its territory purely because they choose to move there, particularly if normal family life can realistically be established somewhere else.[302]

When non-citizens challenge expulsion orders on grounds of interference with family life, the Court tends to be more liberal than when entry of family members is sought. The expulsion cases trigger the negative obligation not to interfere with family life, rather than the positive duty to protect it, and in the expulsion cases by and large the applicant has lived with his family, in a settled situation, on the territory of the state for some time. In family reunion cases, only where the respondent state is the last and only resort for family life, is the Court inclined to grant relief.

In expulsion cases, the Court routinely finds that, where family and private life exist, expulsion constitutes an interference under Article 8.[303] The legitimacy of that interference is assessed with reference to Article 8 § 2, as justified only when "in accordance with the law," pursuant to a legitimate aim and "necessary in a democratic society." The Court has acknowledged, particularly in cases involving revocation of residency after repeated criminal convictions, that Article 8 § 2 considerations of public safety and prevention of disorder and crime are relevant in evaluating pressing social need and the state's legitimate aim.[304]

---

[301] *Gül v. Switzerland*, 22 E.H.R.R. 228 (1996).
[302] Lambert, *supra* note 300, at 433–434.
[303] *Id.* at 441.
[304] *See Beldjoudi v. France* Eur. Ct. H.R. (ser. A) 234-A (1992), *Broughanemi v. France*, 22 E.H.R.R. 93 (1996) *Moustaquim v. Belgium*, 191-B Eur. Ct. H.R. (ser. A) § 11–12 (1991).

The Court is influenced by the following considerations:

- the personal circumstances of the applicant, including his age, health, and the existence or non-existence of any family in the receiving country;
- the fact that the applicant is a settled, integrated non-citizen. Length of time of residence, birth in that country, establishment of the intention to acquire nationality, immigration status, and nationality of the applicant's spouse, may all be relevant;
- the strength of the ties to the country of origin may be important, including language and the retention of that country's nationality;
- whether minor children whose relationship with the parent would be disrupted by the expulsion;
- where expulsion occurs due to criminal conviction(s), the nature and gravity of the crimes committed.

In *Moustaquim v. Belgium*,[305] a minor of Moroccan descent with a severe history of criminality and posing a real danger to society and public order who had lived in Belgium since the age of two, spoke little Arabic and with few family ties in Morocco was given relief under Article 8. In *Nasri v. France*,[306] the applicant was severely disabled (deaf and mute) and had lived in France since the age of four. Despite the severity of his crime, he was also given relief under Article 8.

Ties with the state of residence may also influence the Court, as indicated in *Beldjoudi v. France*.[307] Beldjoudi was born in France, had lost his French nationality after conviction for serious crimes, but had also taken steps to recover it, thus evincing a clear intention to identify with France. He had been married to French woman for many years, who knew no Arabic and could not be expected to cope in Algeria. In these circumstances the deportation order was ordered cancelled by the Court.

Where the applicant is an integrated member of society and has a child whose other parent is not subject to expulsion, the maintenance of the parent-child relationship may render expulsion a violation of Article 8. In *Berrehab v. the Netherlands*,[308] the Dutch Government refused to grant a residence permit to a foreign man who had married a Dutch woman and had a child with her. They had subsequently divorced, but

---

[305] *Moustaquim v. Belgium, supra* note 304.
[306] *Nasri v. France*, Eur. Ct. H.R. (ser. A) 320-B (1995).
[307] *Beldjoudi v. France, supra* note 304.
[308] *Berrehab v. the Netherlands*, Eur.Ct. H.R. (ser.A) 138 (1998).

he continued to see the child a number of times a week, and his connection to the child remained very close. The Court held that his expulsion would disrupt that tie so much as to violate Article 8.

There have been cases, however, where the Court had found that the pressing social need for the expulsion is not outweighed by family considerations. In *Boughanemi v. France*,[309] despite applicant's ties to his girlfriend and her child, his parents and ten sisters and brothers, the Article 8 claim was denied. The applicant had legally resided in France for twenty years and then resided there as an illegal immigrant for another six years. The Court noted, however, that:

> ... he kept his Tunisian nationality and, so it would seem, never manifested a wish to become French. ... It is probable, as the Government pointed out, that he retained links with Tunisia that went beyond the mere fact of his nationality. Before the Commission he did not claim that he could not speak Arabic, or that he had cut all his ties with his country of birth, or that he had not returned there after his deportation.(§ 44)

These cases may be of little value to displaced applicants in danger of expulsion who have not resided in the expelling country for a prolonged period of time.

3.12.5 The Right to Reunification

> A claim under this head is relevant to **Chen**, a refugee seeking to be reunited with her children, and **Ibrahim**, whose asylum state has refused permission for his children to join him there.

Article 8 protects vested rights better than prospective ones. The first case on family reunification, *Abdulaziz, Cabales and Balkandali v. the United Kingdom*[310] presented a question of prospective family unity. Three long-term residents of the United Kingdom applied for permission from the Home Office for their husbands to join them, and were refused. That refusal was upheld by the Court, although the law violated the prohibition on gender discrimination contained in Article 14. The Court held that "by guaranteeing the right to respect for family life,

---

[309] *Broughanemi v. France, supra* note 304.
[310] *Abdulaziz, Cabales and Balkandali v. the United Kingdom*, Eur. Ct. H.R. (ser. A) 94 (1983).

article 8 'presupposes the existence of a family.'"[311] The Court further held that:

> the duty imposed by Article 8 . . . cannot be considered as extending to a general obligation on the part of a Contracting State to respect the choice by married couples of the country of the matrimonial residence and to accept their non-national spouses for settlement in that country.
>
> In the present case, the applicants have not shown that there were obstacles to establishing family life in their own or their husbands' home countries or that there were special reasons why that could not be expected of them.[312]

Family life may exist between a parent and child, whether the child was born inside or outside of marriage,[313] whether or not the biological parents of the child cohabit and whether or not they live in the same jurisdiction.[314] In the case of *Nsona v. the Netherlands*,[315] the Court left open the issue with regard to the relationship between a child and her aunt, or close relative outside of the Western concept of a nuclear family.

The "home of last resort" rule has been applied fairly strictly. Three requirements must be met before a family member will be allowed entry on reunification grounds:

- "family life" must exist;
- obstacles must exist against the establishment of a normal family life elsewhere, particularly in the home state of the applicant;
- the interference with family life must have been committed by the respondent state and no other party.[316]

States are given substantial discretion in family unity admission cases. In *Gül v. Switzerland*, the Court held that even though family ties existed between the applicant and his eight-year old son, the applicant

---

[311] *Id.*
[312] *Id.* at § 68.
[313] *Broughanemi v. France supra* note 304.
[314] *Gül v. Switzerland, supra* note 304; and *Ahmut v. the Netherlands* E.C.H.R. 28 November 1996, at <http://hudoc.echr.coe.int/hudoc/View Root.asp?Item=0&Action=Html&X=518141226&Notice=0&Noticemode=&RelatedMode=0>.
[315] *Nsona v. the Netherlands*, E.C.H.R. 28 November, 1996, at <http://hudoc.echr.coe.int/hudoc/ViewRoot.asp?Item=0&Action=Html&X=518142054&Notice=0&Noticemode=&RelatedMode=0>.
[316] Lambert, *supra* note 300, at 438.

had been granted a temporary residence permit in Switzerland on humanitarian grounds, and his wife had come to join him to obtain medical treatment otherwise unavailable in Turkey, family life could be re-established in Turkey. The Court stated that "it would admittedly not be easy for the applicants to return to Turkey," but there were "strictly speaking no obstacles preventing them from developing family life in Turkey" (§ 42).

A positive duty to respect family life by allowing family reunification, may also be discerned from the case of *Nsona v. the Netherlands*. Miss Nsona, the applicant, received a temporary residence permit from the Netherlands to come from Zaïre on humanitarian grounds. She brought with her son and her niece, whom she claimed, by forgery, was her daughter. Having discovered the forgery, the authorities in the Netherlands refused admission to the child and sent her back. Although there appears little evidence that the authorities actually considered whether or not the child would be subjected to inhuman or degrading treatment if returned, the Court did consider the evidence post-return and come to the conclusion that the child was being cared for and thus no violation of Article 8 had occurred. The applicant's deceit was regarded as relevant in justifying the state's action. The margin of appreciation in family reunion cases may make it very difficult, though not impossible, to establish a claim of violation of the right to family life where the entry of family members is refused.

3.13 The Right to Marry

In a recent colloquy on the asylum-related jurisprudence of the Court,[317] Article 12 was identified as being of special significance. There is at present, however, no detailed case law on Article 12 and refugees, asylum-seekers, or displaced persons. Article 12 refers to marriages contracted according to "national laws." The state thus has no positive duty to allow marriage in any particular form, nor to promote it in any way. Article 12 does not require the state to allow marriages according to a particular religious ceremony.[318]

For internally displaced persons suffering under an arbitrary law which makes it impossible to marry, merely because of the social, religious, ethnic, or other group to which they belong, the ECHR does

---

[317] 19–20 May 2000, held at the Human Rights Building, Council of Europe, Strasbourg, "Second Colloquy on the European Convention on Human Rights and the Protection of Refugees, Asylum-seekers and Displaced Persons."

[318] Harris, *supra* note 62, at 436.

subject national laws on marriage to scrutiny. Such laws flagrantly violate the ECHR if they are arbitrary or rob the right itself of its content.[319]

Where no violation of Article 8 is found, the Court is reluctant to find a violation of Article 12. One Commission decision in 1975[320] stated that the right to found a family is absolute, in the sense that, unlike Article 8, Article 12 states no grounds for lawful interference.

3.14 The Prohibition Against Slavery, Servitude, and Forced or Compulsory Labor

A recent report published by the Office of Democratic Institutions and Human Rights of the OSCE, entitled "Trafficking in Human Begins: Implications for the OSCE," details the surprising extent to which residents of member states, particularly in Central and Eastern Europe, are being displaced from their homes and sold, either for labor or into the sex industry. This is not a problem with which the Court has yet been confronted, but may be an issue for the future.

"Slavery" under Article 4 has never been defined for the purposes of the Convention. It is most likely that the Court would adopt the definition of the 1926 Slavery Convention, which defines slavery as " the status or condition of a person over whom any or all of the powers attaching to the right of ownership are exercised."[321] With respect to forced or compulsory labor, the Court adopted, as a starting point, the definition of forced labor found in the I.L.O. Forced Labor Convention, No. 29: "all work or service, which is exacted from any person under the menace of any penalty and for which the said person has not offered himself voluntarily."[322] Most human trafficking scenarios easily fit within this definition. A proportionality test for the legitimacy of consent allegedly given by the victim may be applied.

The biggest hurdle in bringing a case under Article 4 is establishing that the state had a positive duty to protect those under its jurisdiction from trafficking, as the perpetrators are usually private citizens or organized crime cartels. In the case of *Van der Mussele v. Belgium*,[323] the Court found the state in breach of its Article 6 obligation to provide legal aid by delegating that responsibility to the Bar Association, and found the state was obliged to protect private citizens (in that case, pupil advocates) against the imposition of rules by other private citi-

---

[319] *Van Oosterwijk v. Belgium, Commission*, Eur. Ct. H.R. (ser. A) 40 (1980).
[320] HARRIS, *supra* note 62, at 440.
[321] *Id.* at 91–92.
[322] *Id.* at 92.
[323] (Ser. A) 70 (1983).

zens that required them to do forced labor (providing free legal aid services).[324] This is the closest the Court has come to inferring a positive duty under Article 4.

Article 4 is not subject to derogation under Article 15. Under nonderogable Articles 2 and 3, the Court has found that the state has positive duties. It could be argued, therefore, that Article 4 obliges states to enact and enforce laws against human trafficking and to take all reasonable and proportionate measures to protect vulnerable, identifiable groups from trafficking.

3.15 Access to Food, Clothing, Social Support, and Shelter

As stated above in connection with Article 3, the ECHR does not include positive rights to food, clothing, social support, or shelter, except in the case of a specific undertaking or particularly severe injury, such as degrading treatment. Deliberately starving a family or depriving its members of necessary medical attention, however, as may be the case with *Maria's* family, could amount to a violation of Article 3.

3.16 Access to Education

Of inestimable importance to all displaced and refugee children is the continuance of as stable an education as possible in the environment of insecurity surrounding their flight. Article 2 of Protocol 1 imposes an obligation to ensure access to such educational institutions as exist, an effective education and recognition of completed studies.[325] This is of direct relevance to internally displaced persons, whose children are unable to attend school safely. Moreover, if those children are being deprived of an education in their language, provided it is an official language of the country in question, a claim under Article 14 may be made, provided that children of other official languages in other areas are being allowed to be educated primarily in those languages.

Article 2 of Protocol 1 refers to the religious and philosophical convictions of parents, in order to guard against indoctrination by the state and teachers.[326] Where schools are teaching intolerance of a particular group, Article 2 of Protocol 1 is implicated.

In relation to refugee children, the article is disappointing. Originally, it was framed in the positive terms of a right to education, but during the drafting process, became the right "not to be denied

---

[324] HARRIS, *supra* note 62, at 93.
[325] *Id.* at 542.
[326] HARRIS, *supra* note 62, at 544.

the right to an education." Thus a positive right to education was not intended. A refugee child could not be denied access to a local school under the ECHR, but where the family is seeking asylum and is in detention, or cannot speak the national language or does not have the means to get the child to the relevant establishment, they are unprotected.

3.17 Protection of Property: The Right to the Enjoyment of One's Possessions

Displacement often involves leaving behind much of one's property, including the family home. Refugees, asylum-seekers, and internally displaced persons therefore need protection, not just for the property they leave behind, but also for everything they acquire during displacement or flight. Often, on return, they will find their property occupied by another person or seized by the state, and thus need a right to compensation.

The ECHR in its original form did not protect property rights at all. However, this omission was hastily remedied in Protocol 1, which came into force in 1952. Article 1 of Protocol 1 reflects a compromise achieved after much negotiation. The article neither guarantees the right to own property, nor prohibits dispossession of one's property in absolute terms. It also contains no express right to compensation.

3.17.1 Meaning of "Possessions"

Although the Court will be guided by the interpretation of a right made by national law, "possessions" have an autonomous ECHR meaning.[327] The Court has interpreted the word "possessions" broadly, so as to cover private movable and immovable property, and incorporeal as well as corporeal interests, including contractual rights, leases, and company shares. Accordingly, this is the only ECHR right where legal persons (companies) as well as natural persons can apply to the Court as victims. The individual interest must have an "acquired economic value."[328] Future rights and expectations are not protected by the article.

3.17.2 A "Deprivation" of Property

The Court very seldom finds that there has been a deprivation of property within the meaning of Article 1, Protocol 1. It held in the case of the *Holy Monasteries v. Greece*, that proof of title on the part of the

---
[327] *Id.* at 518.
[328] *Id.* at 517.

applicant is required for such a finding. Given that most displaced persons flee without identification documents, such a threshold is not easily met. That case also illustrated that a formal, legal extinction of the rights of the applicant is the clearest indication that a deprivation has occurred. The Court will evaluate expropriation laws according to safeguards against arbitrariness, and will apply a "fair balance" test. *De facto* deprivation, in the absence of expropriation provided for by law has also been found by the Court.[329]

The second sentence of the first paragraph of Article 1, Protocol 1, allows for state deprivation of property only when the deprivation is in the public interest, subject to conditions provided for law and in accordance with the general principles of international law.

3.17.3 Limitations on the Enjoyment of One's Property

Interferences with the right to the enjoyment of one's possessions are not restricted to deprivations by the state. Any state restriction on the use, ownership, possession, or the ability to divest oneself on of one's property will be evaluated using a "fair balance" test, involving the general interest of the community and the individual's interests.

The limitations on the right protected by Article 1, Protocol 1 are not laid out specifically. In *Sporrong and Lönnroth v. Sweden*,[330] the Court established that:

- there is a general right to the peaceful enjoyment of one's possessions;
- when a state deprives someone of those possessions, the Protocol has been violated, unless that deprivation can be justified by the conditions laid out in the second sentence of the first paragraph of Article 1, Protocol 1 (public interest, conditions provided for by law, general principles of international law);
- states are allowed to control the use of property, but only in the general interest (paragraph 2 of Article 1, Protocol 1).

The width of the margin of appreciation will depend on the context of the case. In *Sporrong*, the Court acknowledged that states enjoyed a high degree of discretion in the area of town planning, but also evaluated the way in which the planning scheme had been implemented. In *Sporrong*, one of the properties had been subject to an expropriation for twenty-five years, without means of review. The Court found that

---

[329] *Papamichalopolous v. Greece*, Eur. Ct. H.R. (ser. A) 260-B (1993).
[330] *Sporrong and Lönnroth v. Sweden*, Eur. Ct. H.R.(ser. A) 52 (1961).

the inflexibility of the Swedish system for the issuance of expropriation permits failed to strike a sufficiently fair balance between the interests of the community and the rights of the individual.

In a case more analogous to the situation in which the displaced would find themselves, the Court also found an interference with the right to enjoyment of one's possessions. In *Loizidou v. Turkey*, the Turkish occupation of Northern Cyprus resulted in the applicant, a Greek Cypriot, being deprived of access to her property in the northern part of Cyprus for over twenty years. The Turkish Government argued that deprivation of access to her property was a freedom of movement issue Protocol 4) and not a question of the right to property. The Court was not persuaded by the contention, and found that the applicant had "effectively lost all control over, as well as all possibilities to use and enjoy, her property" (§ 63). Applying the fair balance test, the Court considered that no explanation had been given as "to how the need to re-house displaced Turkish Cypriot refugees . . . could justify the complete negation of the applicant's property rights in continuous denial of access and a purported expropriation without compensation" (§ 64).

The public interest involved in each deprivation falls to be delineated by the state, not the Court,[331] although the Court will evaluate whether or not a "fair balance" has been achieved. In a displacement context, that balancing will be undertaken as in *Loizidou*.

3.17.4 State Control of Property

The language of the second paragraph of Article 1, Protocol 1 is less restrictive than that covering deprivation of property by the state. It allows the state to control the use of private property "as it deems necessary" in the general interest. However, the Court has not left the state unlimited discretion in this area. It has repeatedly applied the fair balance test. Therefore, although in theory it is often difficult to distinguish between a deprivation of property and the control of its use, the distinction is not of great practical significance. Though in matters such as rent control[332] and town planning[333] the margin of appreciation is very wide, the Court has ruled that no laws that control the use of private property can violate the anti-discrimination clause of the ECHR, Article 14.[334] Since displacement is usually classification-based,

---

[331] *James v. the United Kingdom*, Eur. Ct. H.R. (ser. A) 98 (1986).
[332] *Mellacher v. Austria*, Eur. Ct. H.R. (ser. A) 169 (1989).
[333] *Allan Jacobsson v. Sweden*, Eur. Ct. H.R. (ser. A) 163 (1989).
[334] *Pine Valley Developments v. Ireland*, Eur. Ct. H.R. (ser. A) 222 (1991).

it is this holding that is of prime importance for refugees, asylum-seekers, and internally displaced persons.

3.17.5 International Law and Expropriation of the Property of an Alien

The general principles of international law could in theory be extremely useful to refugees, asylum-seekers, and internally displaced persons in a deprivation of property context. International law protects the property of *aliens* against expropriation or nationalization by the state without compensation. In *James v. the United Kingdom*,[335] it was established that the ECHR was not intended to apply general international legal principles to nationals as to non-nationals, but the Court did infer a right to compensation in Article 1, Protocol 1. To date, the rules of international law have not been applied to cases of the deprivation of property of non-nationals. The only case concerning expropriation of non-nationals' property came before the Commission in 1995.[336] The Commission analyzed the case according to the usual test, balancing fairly the public interest against individual rights. It regarded the case as incomparable to the class of cases of "confiscation, nationalization or expropriation in regard to which international law provides special protection to foreign citizens and companies" (§ 63). Therefore, rather than introduce a different standard in this area for non-nationals, the reference to general principles of international law in the ECHR serves the dual purpose of ensuring access to the ECHR organs of non-nationals who have been deprived of their property by one of the Contracting Parties, and guarantees them the same degree of protection accorded to nationals of state parties. This was confirmed by the Court in *James* (§ 39).

3.17.6 Compensation

The Court has found that where there is a disproportionate interference with private property by the state, some compensation should be awarded.[337] The provision of compensation is included as a significant factor in the assessment of whether or not an interference strikes a fair balance between the public interest and individual's rights. In

---

[335] *Supra* note 331.
[336] *Gasus Dosier-und Fördertechnik v. the Netherlands*, Eur. Ct. H.R. (ser. A) 306-B (1995).
[337] *James v. the United Kingdom*, *supra* note 331, *Lithgow and Others v. the United Kingdom*, Eur. Ct. H.R. (ser. A) 102 (1986).

James, the Court described a sufficient level of compensation as one reasonably related to the value of the property, as affected by the state's actions (§ 36). However, there is no uniform amount or standard. Full compensation is not required for all deprivations. The Court has left open the possibility that in exceptional circumstances a fair balance between community and individual interests may be struck without the provision of any compensation, though the content of those circumstances has not yet been worked out.

4. Other European Human Rights Mechanisms

4.1 The 1961 European Social Charter

Whereas the 1950 European Convention on Human Rights protects against violations of civil and political rights, its companion instrument, the 1961 European Social Charter, protects economic, social, and cultural rights. The Charter entered into force in February 1965 and currently has 25 states parties. It is therefore applies to just over half the High Contracting Parties to the ECHR.

The Charter has never been regarded as a binding legal instrument in the same way as the ECHR. Historically, political will and agreement on the enforcement of economic, social, and cultural rights is much harder to achieve. Civil and political rights are regarded as the cornerstone of democratic society, which the Council of Europe was set up to promote. The Charter was more of a common European agenda for development. This is particularly evident in the scheme set up for accession to the Charter.

Part I of the Charter is essentially a declaration of its aims, as follows:

(1) Everyone shall have the opportunity to earn his living in an occupation freely entered upon.
(2) All workers have the right to just conditions of work.
(3) All workers have the right to safe and healthy working conditions.
(4) All workers have the right to a fair remuneration sufficient for a decent standard of living for themselves and their families.
(5) All workers and employers have the right to freedom of association in national or international organizations for the protection of their economic and social interests.
(6) All workers and employers have the right to bargain collectively.
(7) Children and young persons have the right to a special protection against the physical and moral hazards to which they are exposed.

(8) Employed women, in case of maternity, and other employed women, as appropriate, have the right to a special protection in their work.
(9) Everyone has the right to appropriate facilities for vocational guidance with a view to helping him choose an occupation suited to his personal aptitude and interests.
(10) Everyone has the right to appropriate facilities for vocational training.
(11) Everyone has the right to benefit from any measures enabling him to enjoy the highest possible standard of health attainable.
(12) All workers and their dependents have the right to social security.
(13) Anyone without adequate resources has the right to social and medical assistance.
(14) Everyone has the right to benefit from social welfare services.
(15) Disabled persons have the right to vocational training, rehabilitation and resettlement, whatever the origin and nature of their disability,
(16) The family as a fundamental unit of society has the right to appropriate social, legal and economic protection to ensure its full development.
(17) Mothers and children, irrespective of marital status and family relations, have the right to appropriate social and economic protection.
(18) The nationals of any one of the Contracting Parties have the right to engage in any gainful occupation in the territory of any one of the others on a footing of equality with the nationals of the latter, subject to restrictions based on cogent economic or other social reasons.
(19) Migrant workers who are also nationals of a Contracting Party and their families have the right to protection and assistance in the territory of any other Contracting Party.

Under Article 20 of the Charter, a party undertakes not only to consider pursuit of these aims by all appropriate means, but also to "consider itself bound" by at least ten of the nineteen aims, which are stated and elaborated upon as rights in part II of the Charter. This opt-in mechanism makes the Charter's operation very different from the Court's, but is in line with the "agenda towards development" theme.

On first glance, it seems evident that a number of the rights enshrined in the Charter could be of great use to refugees, asylum-seekers, and internally displaced persons. Their wording obviously did not foresee that application, but rights such as access to health care, work, and social security can be of vital importance, particularly as the Charter does not apply to lawful residents, but to everyone within the jurisdiction of the state party.

From the beginning, the Social Charter required its members to submit reports on the application of the provisions accepted. The reporting mechanism was modified by a 1991 protocol, to make it less labored. Comments on country reports are submitted by trade unions as part of the reporting process and then examined by a series of oversight bodies, including a Committee of Experts and Governmental Committee.

In 1996, the Social Charter was revised so as to make it more comprehensive. The list of aims was expanded to 31, including the right to housing and protection against poverty and social exclusion. As of July 2001, the revised Charter had received 11 ratifications.

4.1.1 Collective Complaints Mechanism

Perhaps the most important Charter development of recent years is the establishment of a collective complaints mechanism, which entered into force in January 1998. The mechanism is modeled somewhat on ILO procedures, and although it does not allow for individual complaints, it does permit certain categories of organization to bring complaints against parties to the Protocol. There are at present eight such parties and eight complaints lodged with the Committee of Independent Experts, submitted by NGOs and labor organizations on issues ranging from collective bargaining to child labor. There is, in principle, no reason why an NGO could not bring such a complaint by way of clarification of the Charter's application to, for instance, refugees' rights to health care, although the Committee of Expert's findings are not enforceable.

4.2 The 1987 European Convention for the Prevention of Torture and Inhuman or Degrading Treatment or Punishment

In order to target instances of torture and inhuman or degrading treatment, as defined in Article 3 of the ECHR, a further Convention for the Prevention of Torture and Inhuman or Degrading Treatment or Punishment was drafted by the Council of Europe in 1987. Today, all 41 member states have ratified the Convention for the Prevention of Torture. The First Protocol to that Convention, which has not yet entered into force, allows non-member states invited by the Committee of Ministers to accede to the Convention for the Prevention of Torture.

There is no individual complaints mechanism provided in the Convention for the Prevention of Torture. Instead, protection for detainees is based on a system of on-site visits by members of the European Committee for the Prevention of Torture and Inhuman or Degrading Treatment or Punishment (CPT). The CPT is made up of independent experts, with a variety of expertise from medicine to prison affairs. CPT members are elected by the Committee of Ministers for four-year terms.[338]

The CPT visits places of detention in member states, including prisons, army barracks and psychiatric hospitals. Delegations are comprised of at least two CPT members, members of the CPT's Secretariat, and interpreters. The member elected from the country being visited is never permitted to join that delegation. Visits may be either periodic or in the form of spot checks. Advance notice must be given to the state being visited, but there is no time limit as to exactly when this must be done. The Convention for the Prevention of Torture provides that Governments can legitimately object to the time of the visit, but only on the grounds of national defense, public safety, serious disorder, the medical condition of a person, or on the grounds that an urgent interrogation relating to a serious crime is in progress. Even when such an objection is legitimately made, the state must take steps to facilitate the visit as soon as possible. By the time of writing, 72 periodic visits and 31 ad hoc visits have been made. During an on-site visit, the CPT interviews detainees and any other person whom it considers to have relevant information.

Given that the CPT relies heavily on state co-operation for its monitoring work, it is logical that its post-visit reports should be issued confidentially. This is the official practice, although the CPT retains the ability to publish a public statement concerning any state that fails to implement its recommendations. An informal practice has also developed whereby the CPT publishes reports and Government responses to their findings, with the consent of the state in question.

As mentioned above, the CPT has no individual complaints mechanism. However, it is an extremely useful evidentiary source for advocates bringing cases before the European Court of Human Rights and activists lobbying the Parliament of the European Union or the OSCE.[339]

---

[338] A second Protocol to the Convention for the Prevention of Torture is currently open for signature, which allows for membership of the CPT to be renewed every two years, rather than four, and for members to be re-elected for a second term, rather than just one, as is now the case. The Protocol has not yet entered into force.

[339] Boyle, *supra* note 14, at 154.

Information about the CPT's activities and copies of its published reports are available on-line through the Council of Europe web-site,[340] or by contacting the Secretariat at:
Secretariat of the CPT
Human Rights Building
Council of Europe
F 67075 Strasbourg CEDEX
France
Tel: +33 3 88 41 23 88
Fax: +33 3 88 41 27 72
E-mail: *cptdoc@coe.int*

4.3 The 1995 Framework Convention for the Protection of National Minorities

Often, displaced groups are discrete minorities. The Council of Europe has recognized the need for the protection of these groups by drafting the Framework Convention for the Protection of National Minorities (hereinafter "Framework Convention"), which entered into force on February 1, 1998. The Framework Convention has been ratified by 34 countries, 2 of which are non-members of the Council of Europe.[341]

The Framework Convention protects a wide variety of rights specific to minority groups, such as choice of personal identity and the exercise thereof (Article 3), equality before the law (Article 4), the right to cultural preservation (Article 5), the right to freedom of expression (Article 9) and religion (Article 8), the right to use a minority language (Article 10) and the duty of states to provide for the effective participation of persons belonging to minority groups in cultural, economic, and social life, as well as in public affairs (Article 15).

Like the Convention for the Prevention of Torture, the Framework Convention has no individual complaints mechanism. States submit reports to an Advisory Committee, detailing the measures they have taken to comply with the Framework Convention. Exactly how this mechanism will function is as yet unclear, though there is provision for NGOs and minority groups to inject their comments of the governments' reports into the process.[342]

---

[340] *See* <http://www.coe.int>.

[341] The three non-member state parties are Armenia, Azerbaijan, and Bosnia Herzegovina.

[342] Boyle, *supra* note 14, at 155.

4.4 Commissioner for Human Rights

On May 7, 1999, the Council of Europe established the institution of the Commissioner for Human Rights. The purpose of the office is to promote the concept of human rights and to ensure effective respect and full enjoyment of those rights in the Council of Europe.

The Commissioner is charged with promoting human rights education, identifying possible shortcomings in the law and practice of member states with regard to compliance with human rights standards, and helping promote the effective observance of the Council of Europe human rights instruments.

To this end, the Commissioner makes on-site visits and issues reports on compliance in member states, provides information on the protection of human rights and prevention of abuses, co-operates with national ombudsmen, and works directly with governments of member states. The office does not have an individual complaints mechanism, and is non-judicial in character. Details of the reports (of great evidentiary use for advocates) of the Commissioner can be found at <www.commissioner.coe.int>.

4.5 Organization for Security and Cooperation in Europe (OSCE)

The OSCE began as the Conference on Security and Co-operation in Europe, a pan-European security conference whose 35 original members from Europe and North America met for the first time in Finland in 1972. Its meetings led to the adoption of the Helsinki Final Act in 1975, which encompasses three main sets of recommendations or "baskets." The third "basket" of the Act deals with "co-operation in humanitarian and other fields," human rights (referred to as "human contact") and fundamental freedoms, including freedom of thought, conscience, religion and belief,[343] self-determination, and freedom of movement. Prior to the collapse of Communism, the CSCE remained a diplomatic process,[344] dealing in a unitary fashion with bipolarized politics and bloc-to-bloc security threats. The collapse of Communism transformed European security, and the CSCE with it. In 1994, the CSCE became, through a series of diplomatic conferences, the OSCE, the Organization for Security and Co-operation in Europe.

The OSCE now comprises all European States, all the States of the former USSR, as well as the United States and Canada (55 members

---

[343] No. 7 of the "Helsinki Decalogue," which is actually included in the first basket of the Act.

[344] Boyle, *supra* note 14, at 157.

in all). The Secretary General of the OSCE and Permanent Council of participating states are based in Vienna. Its documentation and information center is in Prague.

The OSCE holds summits once every two years. Its Permanent Council meets every week in Vienna to supervise daily operations. This process is in turn overseen by a Chairman-in-Office, who is chosen from among the participating States, and serves for a period of a year before the next state's Foreign Minister takes over.

The basic priorities of the OSCE are as follows:

- to consolidate the participating states' common values and help in building fully democratic civil societies based on the rule of law;
- to prevent local conflicts, restore stability and bring peace to war-torn areas;
- to overcome real and perceived security deficits and to avoid the creation of new political, economic or social divisions by promoting a co-operative system of security.[345]

First and foremost a conflict resolution body, the OSCE has established a substantial field presence in areas experiencing migration crises such as in Kosovo. The OSCE has a number of features and institutions specific to human rights protection and monitoring. Principal among these is the Office for Democratic Institutions and Human Rights (ODIHR), which is situated in Warsaw. This office is divided into two sections, the Election Section and Democratization Section. The office as a whole, in addition to election monitoring, works to "provide practical support in consolidating democratic institutions and human rights and strengthening civil society and the rule of law" and to "contribute to early warning and conflict prevention, in particular by monitoring the implementation of human dimension commitments."[346]

Of most relevance to the plight of refugees, asylum-seekers, and internally displaced persons is the monitoring work of the ODIHR. This is carried out by a subsection of the Democratization Group. The reports compiled are used to advise the Chairman-in-Office and to plan OSCE policies. Reports are issue- and region-specific and are invaluable as an evidentiary source for advocates and activists alike.[347] There is in addi-

---

[345] OSCE Handbook, p. 8 of " History," Section 2, at <www.osce. org/publications/handbook>.

[346] *Id.* at 4.

[347] A good example of such a report is the paper on human trafficking in Europe, referred to in connection with Article 4 of the ECHR, above.

tion a specific sub-group on Freedom of Movement, which publishes useful and informative reports.

The Democratization group is also responsible for strengthening regional NGO networks for the purpose of information gathering. The ODHIR has a web-site, and is otherwise contactable at:

OSCE Office for Democratic Institutions and Human Rights,
Aleje Ujazdowskie 19,
00-557 Warsaw, Poland
Tel: +48-22 520 06 00
Fax: +48-22 520 06 05
E-mail: *office@odihr.osce.waw.pl*

In 1992, the OSCE created the post of High Commissioner on National Minorities. The position was designed mainly for conflict prevention. In order to identify and deal with burgeoning minority rights problems in Europe, the office is empowered to collect data from any source. Reports on these situations, such as those of the Roma or Sinti, are prepared. In theory the work of the High Commissioner is confidential, but the practice has been to publish the majority of his recommendations.[348]

In terms of the relations between states in the OSCE, the Vienna Mechanism, adopted in 1989, provides for the exchange of information between participating states, the holding of bilateral meetings and the ability for one participating state to request a response from another on an issue of non-compliance by the latter with an OSCE norm. Under the mechanism, responding states have ten days to reply to such a request. If they fail to do so, they must invite a fact-finding mission on to their territory. If that does not occur, then a quorum of six OSCE members may demand the admission of OSCE fact-finders. Recommendations are then made on the basis of the fact-finders' report. The mechanism is less useful now that most European states have ratified the European Convention on Human Rights, but is still an effective diplomatic tool.[349]

4.6 The European Union

The predecessor to the European Union, the European Economic Community, was established by the Treaty of Rome in 1957. It began as an attempt to open to other European countries participation in the

---

[348] Boyle, *supra* note 14, at 158.

[349] *See* <www.osce.org>; Boyle, *supra* note 14, at 158–159; and *Methodology for implementing mechanisms for monitoring commitments by member states of the Council of Europe and the OSCE*, Council of Europe Publications, 1997.

French and German coal and steel industry.[350] What started as a form of industrial partnership has become over the last 15 years an ever-closer political union. This was accomplished by a series of amendments found in the Single European Act of 1986, the Maastricht Treaty or Treaty of the European Union (TEU) of 1992 and the Treaty of Amsterdam of 1997. The European Union is now best described as a supranational legal and political institution. It has its own Court, the European Court of Justice (ECJ), charged with interpreting the EU treaties, and EU law prevails over the domestic law of the 15 member states.

4.6.1 The European Union and Human Rights

Before the TEU, the treaties establishing the EU made little express reference to human rights. The European Union created by the TEU pursued co-operation in the fields of justice and home affairs and a common foreign and security policy.[351] The TEU also established that the Union "shall respect fundamental rights, as guaranteed by the European Convention on Human Rights . . . and as they result from the constitutional traditions common to the Member States, as general principles of Community Law."[352]

The accession of the European Union as an entity to the ECHR has been discussed and debated on many occasions and suggested a number of times by the Commission of the EU since 1978. Although ECJ jurisprudence makes many references to ECHR principles,[353] in its *Opinion 2/94*,[354] the ECJ held that the EU's accession to the ECHR would not be possible without a treaty amendment. Such an amendment was not accomplished in the Treaty of Amsterdam.

In Nice in December 2000, the Council of the EU adopted as a solemn declaration of principles the Charter of Fundamental Rights of the European Union. How the Charter will be used and interpreted is as yet unclear. In so far as the ECJ had applied ECHR principles in its jurisprudence, and to the extent that the principles embodied in the Charter overlap with those in the ECHR, it seems clear that the ECJ will still interpret those rights in conformity with ECHR jurisprudence.

---

[350] THE COURT OF JUSTICE OF THE EUROPEAN COMMUNITIES 1 (NEVILLE BROWN AND TOM KENNEDY, EDS. 2000).
[351] Title V TEU.
[352] Article 6 TEU.
[353] CLEMENTS, *supra* note 20, at 109.
[354] *Opinion 2/94* of the Court of March 28, 1996 on Accession by the Community to the European Convention for the Protection of Human Rights and Fundamental Freedoms [1996] ECR I-1195.

However, in certain ways, the Charter is much wider than the ECHR. It is a precondition to accession to the EU that domestic respect for fundamental human rights be demonstrated to the existing members' satisfaction. The Charter includes an expanded list of rights, such as:

- the right to asylum (Article 18);
- positive protection in the event of removal, expulsion, or extradition (Article 19);
- the freedoms of expression, information, assembly, and association are enshrined in Articles 11 and 12 respectively without qualifications aimed at giving discretion to member states;
- the right to education is not phrased negatively. Everyone is accorded the right to receive free compulsory education (Article 14);
- the right to engage in work (Article 15);
- a strong free-standing provision against discrimination (Article 21);
- protection of cultural, religious, and linguistic diversity (Article 22);
- the right to fair and just working conditions (Article 31);
- the right of legal, economic, and social protection for the family (Article 33);
- the right to preventive health care (Article 35);
- the right for anyone registered in the EU to have access to their documentation (Article 42);
- freedom of movement and of residence Article 46).

4.6.2 Individuals and the ECJ

Unlike the European Court of Human Rights, individuals have only limited rights of petition to the courts of the EU (in addition to the ECJ, there is also a Court of First Instance).[355] Disputes between individuals or between individuals and national authorities can only be referred to the ECJ by member states. Ordinarily, they fall to national courts to be decided in accordance with EU law. "Thus a person claming the right to enter a Member State, under the Treaty provisions on the free movement of workers and the implementing Community legislation, must seek his remedy before the courts of that State against the immigration authorities who have refused the right he claims."[356]

---

[355] BROWN, *supra* note 350, at 10.
[356] *Id.*, citing Case 41/74 *Van Duyn v. Secretary of State for Home Affairs* (1974) ECR 1337; (1975) 1 C.M.L.R. 1.

The body of cases and Community legislation on migrant workers is of some relevance to refugees and asylum-seekers, in that it relates to the right of family reunification in EU countries.[357]

4.6.3 EU Policies on Refugees and Asylum-Seekers

The EU member states are currently in the process of harmonizing their immigration and asylum policies, as required under Title IV of the Amsterdam Treaty. The resulting Commission-proposed Migration Convention[358] is the subject of debate and lobbying on the part of NGOs representing asylum-seekers and refugees. It has been criticized, *inter alia*, on the grounds that:

- it will further the gulf between EU nationals and non-nationals by concentrating all its efforts on the protections accorded to EU nationals and citizenship;
- it conflates the considerations behind immigration policy on the one hand and asylum policy on the other;
- it will promote practices of "passing off" of asylum-seekers to safe third countries in such a way as to further weaken the right to family reunification and increase instances of failure to uphold the obligation of non-refoulement contained in Article 33 of the 1951 UN Refugee Convention;
- while the Convention may be progressive in including 1951 Convention refugees within its scope, it still fails to address those granted temporary leave to stay on humanitarian grounds;
- it fails to address all aspects of voluntary repatriation and detention pending the outcome of the asylum application.[359]

Although these developments are not directly relevant to the legal claims of asylum-seekers and refugees at present, they will certainly be of central importance to their future interests in EU countries. There

---

[357] That body of jurisprudence is beyond the scope of a Guide on international human rights mechanisms, but see 5th Recital of the Preamble to the Council regulation 1612/68 on freedom of movement for workers within the Community, in Nicholas Blake, *Family Life in Community Law: The Limits of Freedom and Dignity*, in THE LEGAL FRAMEWORK AND SOCIAL CONSEQUENCES OF FREE MOVEMENT OF PERSONS IN THE EUROPEAN UNION (ELSPETH GUILD ED. 1999). Blake provides an interesting and useful examination of the development of ECJ jurisprudence on the rights of migrant workers with non-EU national families.

[358] Steven Peers, *Raising Minimum Standards, or Racing for the Bottom? The Commission's Proposed Migraton Convention*, in GUILD, *supra* note 357, at 149.

[359] *Id.*

is work here to be done now by activists, to ensure that the proposed Convention does not enshrine any regressive measures in the development of legal protections for these vulnerable groups.

5. Conclusion

Comparatively speaking, the human rights mechanisms available in Europe are well-established, developed, and, in the case of the European Court of Human Rights, provide a forum for advocates where individual complaints can be heard and the execution of judgments supervised. It is only in recent years, however, that recognition of the particular needs of asylum-seekers is beginning to pervade the Council of Europe system. There are indications that both the European Union and European Court of Human Rights are beginning to see, through individual cases and the need to set broader policies alike, that the traditional conflation of domestic concerns about immigration and asylum is inaccurate and misleading. It is for advocates and activists to ensure that this realization is reflected in the developing jurisprudence of the Court in areas such as family reunification and anti-discrimination, and in the future EU Common Asylum Policy mandated by the Amsterdam Treaty.

Regional mechanisms inform the jurisprudence of other regional and UN bodies. In areas such as the right to family life in expulsion cases or forced disappearance, the case law of one human rights tribunal can be cited to influence the interpretation of similarly phrased rights. Therefore, when considering bringing a case before a European mechanism, look beyond the confines of its law. Likewise, advocates outside Europe may draw upon the rich case law the European Court has developed over five decades.

Bibliography

Books

BROWN, L. NEVILLE AND TOM KENNEDY, EDS., THE COURT OF JUSTICE OF THE EUROPEAN COMMUNITIES (5th ed. 2000).

CLEMENTS, LUKE, ET AL., EUROPEAN HUMAN RIGHTS: TAKING A CASE UNDER THE CONVENTION (2d ed. 1999).

GOMIEN, DONNA, DAVID HARRIS AND LEO ZWAAK, LAW AND PRACTICE OF THE EUROPEAN CONVENTION ON HUMAN RIGHTS AND THE EUROPEAN SOCIAL CHARTER (1996).

HARRIS, DAVID J., MICHAEL O'BOYLE AND COLIN WARBRICK, LAW OF THE EUROPEAN COURT OF HUMAN RIGHTS (1995).

METHODOLOGY FOR IMPLEMENTING MECHANISMS FOR MONITORING COMMITMENTS BY MEMBER STATES OF THE COUNCIL OF EUROPE AND THE OSCE (Council of Europe Publications 1997).

Chapters

Blake, Nicholas, *Family Life in Community Law: The Limits of Freedom and Dignity*, in THE LEGAL FRAMEWORK AND SOCIAL CONSEQUENCES OF FREE MOVEMENT OF PERSONS IN THE EUROPEAN UNION, (ELSPETH GUILD ED., 1999).

Boyle, Kevin, *Europe: The Council of Europe, the OSCE, and the European Union*, in GUIDE TO INTERNATIONAL HUMAN RIGHTS PRACTICE 135 (HURST HANNUM ED., 3d ed. 1999).

Peers, Steven, *Minimum Standards, or Racing for the Bottom? The Commission's Proposed Migration Convention*, in THE LEGAL FRAMEWORK AND SOCIAL CONSEQUENCES OF FREE MOVEMENT OF PERSONS IN THE EUROPEAN UNION (ELSPETH GUILD ED., 1999).

Journal Articles

Lambert, Hélène, *The European Court of Human Rights and the Right of Refugees and Other Persons in Need of Protection to Family Reunion*, 11 INT'L J. REFUGEE L. 427 (1999).

IGO Documents

Explanatory Report on Protocol No. 7 to the ECHR for the Protection of Human Rights and Fundamental Freedoms.

Explanatory Report of the Council of Europe to Protocol No. 11 (Council of Europe Publishing, May 1994).

Explanatory Report on Protocol 12, available at <http://www.human-rights.coe.int/Prot12/Protocol%2012%20and%20Exp%20Rep.htm>.

OSCE Handbook, "History", Sec. 2, available on-line at <www.osce.org/publications/handbook>.

Cases

Abdulaziz, Cabales and Balkandali v. the United Kingdom, Eur. Ct. H.R. (ser. A) 94 (1983).

Ahmed v. the United Kingdom, 1996-III Eur. Ct. H.R. 846.

Ahmut v. the Netherlands E.C.H.R. 28 November 1996, at <http://hudoc.echr.coe.int/hudoc/ViewRoot.asp?Item=0&Action=Html&X=518141226&Notice=0&Noticemode=&RelatedMode=0>.

Akdivar v. Turkey, 1996-IV, No. 15, 23 E.H.R.R. 150.
Altun v. Federal Republic of Germany, No. 10308/83, 36 DR 236 (1983).
Amuur v. France, 22 E.H.R.R. 491 (1996).
Angelini v. Sweden, No. 10491/83.
Arslan v. Turkey, Eur. Ct. H.R. (1999), at <http://hudoc. echr.coe.int/ hudoc/ViewRoot.asp?Item=0&Action=Html&X=518140240&Notice =0&Noticemode=&RelatedMode=0>.
Autotronic AG v. Switzerland, Eur. Ct. H.R. (ser. A) 178 (1990).
Aydin v. Turkey, 1997-VI 25 E.H.R.R. 251.
Barbara, Messegue and Jabardo v. Spain, Eur. Ct. H.R. (ser. A) 146 (1989).
Dombo Beheer v. the Netherlands, (27 October, 1993).
Beis v. Greece, 25 E.H.R.R. 335 (1997).
Beldjoudi v. France Eur. Ct. H.R. (ser. A) 234-A (1992).
Belgian Lingusitics (No.1), Eur. Ct. H.R. (ser. A) 5 (1967).
Berrehab v. the Netherlands, Eur.Ct. H.R. (ser.A) 138 (1998).
Bouamar v. Belgium, (29 February, 1988).
Bozano v. Italy, (18 December 1956).
Brogan and Others v. the United Kingdom, 145-B Eur. Ct. H.R. (ser. A) 11 (1988).
Broughanemi v. France, 22 E.H.R.R. 93 (1996).
Buchholz v. Germany, Eur. Ct. H.R. (ser. A.) 42 (1981).
Buckley v. the United Kingdom, 23 E.H.R.R. 101 (1996).
Cakici v. Turkey, Eur. Ct. H.R. (July 1999), at <http://hudoc.echr. coe.int/hudoc/ViewRoot.asp?Item=0&Action=Html&X=518122224 &Notice=0&Noticemode=&RelatedMode=0>.
Campbell and Fell v. the United Kingdom, Eur. Ct. H.R. (Ser. A) 80 (1984).
Castells v. Spain, 236 Eur. Ct. H.R. (ser. A) (1992).
Ceylan v. Turkey, Eur. Ct. H.R. (1999), at <http://hudoc.echr.coe.int/ hudoc/ViewRoot.asp?Item=0&Action=Html&X=518140200&Notice =0&Noticemode=&RelatcdMode-0>.
Chahal v. United Kingdom, 23 E.H.R.R. 413 (1996).
Chappell v. United Kingdom, 152 Eur. Ct. H.R. (ser. A) (1989).
Costello-Roberts v. United Kingdom, 247-C Eur. Ct. H.R. (ser. A) (1993).
Council of Civil Service Unions v U.K. 50 DR 228.
Cunningham v. U.K., DR 43/171.
Cyprus v. Turkey, 4 E.H.R.R. 282.
Dalban v. Romania, Eur. Ct. H.R. (September 1999), at <http://hudoc. echr.coe.int/hudoc/ViewRoot.asp?Item=0&Action=Html&X=51812 3315&Notice=0&Noticemode=&RelatedMode=0>.
Darby v. Sweden, 187 Eur. Ct. H.R. (ser. A) (1991).
Deweer v. Belgium, 35 Eur. Ct. H.R. (ser. A) 19 (1980).
De Wilde, Oomas and Versyp ("Vagrancy" Cases), 12 Eur. Ct. H.R. (ser. A) 36 (1971).

Donnelly v. the United Kingdom, DR 4/4.
Gasus Dosier-und Fördertechnik v. the Netherlands, Eur. Ct. H.R. (ser. A) 306-B (1995).
Dudgeon v. the United Kingdom, 45 Eur. Ct. H.R. (ser. A) (1981).
Ekbatani v. Sweden, Eur. Ct. H.R. (ser. A) 134 (1988).
Engels and Others v. the Netherlands, 22 Eur. Ct. H.R. (ser. A) 22 (1976).
Ensslin, Baader, and Raspe v. the Federal Republic of Germany, App. No. 7572/76, 14 DR 64.
Ergi v. Turkey, Eur. Ct. H.R. (July 1998), at <http://hudoc.echr.coe.int/hudoc/ViewRoot.asp?Item=0&Action=Html&X=518123525&Notice=0&Noticemode=&RelatedMode=0>.
Ezelin v. France, Eur. Ct. H.R. (ser. A) 202 (1991).
Handyside v. U.K., 24 Eur. Ct. H.R. (ser. A.) (1976).
Helle v. Finlan, 26 E.H.R.R. 159 (1997).
Ismail Ertak v. Turkey, (9 May 2000).
Farmakopoulos v. Belgium, No. 11683/85 (1986).
Gaskin v. the United Kingdom, Eur. Ct. H.R. (ser. A) 160 (1989).
Gerger v. Turkey, Eur. Ct. H.R. (1999), at <http://hudoc.echr.coe.int/hudoc/ViewRoot.asp?Item=0&Action=Html&X=518135734&Notice=0&Noticemode=&RelatedMode=0>.
Giama v. Belgium, Comm. Report 17.7.80, D.R. 21.
Gillow v. the United Kingdom, Eur. Ct. H.R. (ser. A) 109 (1986).
Gitonas v. Greece, Eur. Ct. H.R. (ser. A) 42 (1997).
Golder v. the United Kingdom, 18 Eur. Ct. H.R. (ser. A) (1975).
Granger v. U.K., 174 Eur. Ct. H.R. (ser. A) (1990).
Greece v. the United Kingdom, no. 176/56, Dec. 2.6.56, YEARBOOK 2 (176).
Greek Case, 12 YEARBOOK 1 (1969).
Gül v. Switzerland, 22 E.H.R.R. 228 (1996).
Özgür Gündem v. Turkey, Eur. Ct. H.R. (2000), at <http://hudoc.echr.coe.int/hudoc/ViewRoot.asp?Item=0&Action=Html&X=518135939&Notice=0&Noticemode=&RelatedMode=0>.
H. v. Belgium, Eur. Ct. H.R., (ser. A) 127 (1987).
Handyside v, the United Kingdom, Eur. Ct. H.R. (ser. A) 24 (1976).
Hatami v. Sweden, (9 October 1998).
Hauschildt v. Switzerland, 154 Eur. Ct. H.R. (ser. A) (1989).
Herczegfalvy v. Austria, App. No. 10533/83 (1991).
The Holy Monasteries v. Greece, Eur. Ct. H.R. (ser. A) 310-A (1994).
Hornsby v. Greece, Eur. Ct. H.R. (ser. A) (1997).
Hurtado v. Switzerland, (ser. A 280-A).
Informationsverien Lentia v. Austria, Eur. Ct. H.R. (ser. A) 276 (1993).
Ireland v. United Kingdom, 25 Eur. Ct. H.R. (ser. A) (1978).
Allan Jacobsson v. Sweden, Eur. Ct. H.R. (ser. A) 163 (1989).
James v. the United Kingdom, Eur. Ct. H.R. (ser. A) 98 (1986).
Jersild and Others v. Denmark, Eur. Ct. H.R. (ser A.) 298 (1994).

Johnston v. Ireland, 112 Eur. Ct. H.R. (ser. A) (1986).
Johnston and Others v. the United Kingdom, 112 Eur. Ct. H.R. (ser. A) 25 (1986).
Kaya v. Turkey, Reports I Eur. Ct. H.R. (1998), at <http://hudoc.echr.coe.int/hudoc/ViewRoot.asp?Item=0&Action=Html&X=518133632&Notice=0&Noticemode=&RelatedMode=0>.
Mahmut Kaya v. Turkey, (28 March 2000), at <http://hudoc.echr.coe.int/hudoc/ViewRoot.asp?Item=1&Action=Html&X=518133503&Notice=0&Noticemode=&RelatedMode=0>.
Kilic v. Turkey, Eur. Ct. H.R. (28 March 2000), at <http://hudoc.echr.coe.int/hudoc/ViewRoot.asp?Item=0&Action=Html&X=518133949&Notice=0&Noticemode=&RelatedMode=0>.
Kjeldsen, Busk, Madsen and Pedersen v. Denmark, (1976).
Kofler v. Italy, Comm. Report, D.R. 30 (9 October 1982).
Kokkinakis v. Greece, 260-A Eur. Ct. H.R. (ser. A) (1993).
Kroon v. the Netherlands, 297-C Eur. Ct. H.R. (ser. A) (1994).
Kurt v. Turkey, Eur. Ct. H.R. (1998), at <http://hudoc.echr.coe.int/hudoc/ViewRoot.asp?Item=0&Action=Html&X=518132821&Notice=0&Noticemode=&RelatedMode=0>.
L.C.B. v. the United Kingdom, III Eur. Ct. H.R. 1403 (1998).
Le Compte v. Belgium, Eur. Ct. H.R. (ser.A) 44 (1981).
Larkos v. Cyprus, Eur. Ct. H.R. (18 February 1999), at <http://hudoc.echr.coe.int/hudoc/ViewRoot.asp?Item=0&Action=Html&X=518141226&Notice=0&Noticemode=&RelatedMode=0>.
Lawless v. the United Kingdom, Eur. Ct. H.R. (ser. A) 3 (1961).
Leander v. Sweden, Commission phase, No. 92148/81 (1983).
Lingens v. Austria, Eur. Ct. H.R. (ser. A.) 103 (1986).
Lithgow and Others v. the United Kingdom Eur. Ct. H.R. (ser. A) 102 (1986).
Loizidou v. Turkey, 310 Eur. Ct. H.R. (ser. A) (1995).
López-Ostra v. Spain, 303-C Eur. Ct. H.R. (ser A) (1994).
Lüdi v. Switzerland, 238 Eur. Ct. H.R. (ser. A) (1992).
M v. UK, DR 57/136 (1986).
Mahmut v. Turkey, (28 March 2000).
Marckx v. Belgium, 31 Eur. Ct. H.R. (ser. A) (1979).
Mathieu-Mohin and Clerfayt v. Belgium, Eur. Ct. H.R. (ser. A) 113 (1987).
McCann and Others v. the United Kingdom, 324 Eur. Ct. H.R. (ser. A) (1995).
Mellacher v. Austria, Eur. Ct. H.R. (ser. A) 169 (1989).
Moustaquim v. Belgium, 191-B Eur. Ct. H.R. (ser. A) § 11–12 (1991).
Moustaquim v. Belgium, 193 Eur. Ct. H.R. (ser. A) (1991).
Müller and Others v. Switzerland, Eur. Ct. H.R. (ser A.) 133 (1988).
Nasri v. France, 320-B Eur. Ct. H.R. (ser. A) (1995).
Neigel v. France, 10 E.H.R.R. 1997-II No. 32 (1997).
Norris v. Ireland, 142 Eur. Ct. H.R. (ser. A) 34 (1988).

Nsona v. the Netherlands, Eur. Ct. H.R. (28 November 1996), at <http://hudoc.echr.coe.int/hudoc/ViewRoot.asp?Item=0&Action=Html&X=518142054&Notice=0&Noticemode=&RelatedMode=0>.
Olsson v. Sweden, Eur. Ct. H.R. (ser. A) 130 (1988).
Open Door and Dublin Well Woman v. Ireland, 246-A Eur. Ct. H.R. (ser. A) (1992).
Opinion 2/94 of the Court of an Accession by the Community to the European Convention for the Protection of Human Rights and Fundamental Freedoms [1996] ECR I-1195 (28 March 1996).
Osman v. United Kingdom, VIII Eur. Ct. H.R. (1998).
Otto-Preminger-Institut v. Austria, 295 Eur. Ct. H.R. (ser. A).
López Ostra v. Spain, 303-C Eur. Ct. H.R. (ser. A) (1994).
Pakelli v. Germany, 64 Eur. Ct. H.R. (ser. A) (1983).
Papamichalopolous v. Greece, Eur. Ct. H.R. (ser. A) 260-B (1993).
Paton v. United Kingdom, No. 8416/78, 19 DR 211 (1980).
Philis v. Greece, 209 Eur. Ct. H.R. (ser. A) (1991).
Piermont v. France, Eur. Ct. H.R. (ser.A) 314 (1995).
Piersack v. Belgium, Eur. Ct. H.R. (Ser. A) 53 (1982).
Pine Valley Developments v. Ireland, Eur. Ct. H.R. (ser. A) 222 (1991).
Polat v. Turkey, Application no. 23500/94, at <http://hudoc.echr.coe.int/hudoc/ViewRoot.asp?Item=0&Action=Html&X=518135558&Notice=0&Noticemode=&RelatedMode=0>.
Rekvényi v. Hungary, (20 May 1999), at <http://hudoc.echr.coe.int/hudoc/ViewRoot.asp?Item=0&Action=Html&X=518135647&Notice=0&Noticemode=&RelatedMode=0>.
Ribitsch v. Austria, 336 Eur. Ct. H.R. (ser. A) (1995).
Ringeisen (no 3) v. Austria, 16 Eur. Ct. H.R. (ser. A) (1973).
Saunders v. the United Kingdom, Eur. Ct. H.R. (Ser. A) (1996).
Selmouni v. France, Eur. Ct. H.R. (28 July 1999), at <http://www.dhcour.coe.fr/hudoc/ViewRoot.asp?Item=0&Action=Html&X=1025023138&Notice=0&Noticemode=&RelatedMode=0>.
Socialist Party and Others v. Turkey, (25 May), at <http://hudoc.echr.coe.int/hudoc/ViewRoot.asp?Item=0&Action=Html&X=518140729&Notice=0&Noticemode=&RelatedMode=0>.
The Society for the Protection of Unborn Children Ireland Ltd. v. Grogan and Others, C-159/90, E.CR. I-4685 (1991).
Soering v. the United Kingdom, 161 Eur. Ct. H.R. (ser. A) (1989).
Sporrong and Lönnroth v. Sweden, Eur. Ct. H.R. (ser. A) 52 (1961).
Stewart v. UK, No.20044/82, 39 DR 162 (1984).
Stran Greek Refinieries & Straits Andreadis v. Greece, Eur. Ct. H.R. (ser. A) (1994).
Sunday Times v. the United Kingdom (No.2), 217 Eur. Ct. H.R. (ser. A) (1991).

Sürek v, Turkey No. 1, Eur. Ct. H.R. (1999), at <http://hudoc.echr.coe. int/hudoc/ViewRoot.asp?Item=1&Action=Html&X=518135848&N otice=0&Noticemode=&RelatedMode=0>.
Sürek v, Turkey No. 2, Eur. Ct. H.R. (1999), at <http://hudoc.echr.coe.int/ hudoc/ViewRoot.asp?Item=2&Action=Html&X=518140015&Notice =0&Noticemode=&RelatedMode=0>.
Sutter v. Switzerland, Eur.Ct. H.R. (ser. A) 74 (1984).
Swedish Engine Drivers Union v. Sweden, Eur. Ct. H.R. (ser. A) 20 (1976).
Tanrikulu v. Turkey, Eur. Ct. H.R. (17 June 1999), at <http://hudoc.echr. coe.int/hudoc/ViewRoot.asp?Item=3&Action=Html&X=518133949 &Notice=0&Noticemode=&RelatedMode=0>.
Tomasi v. France, 214-A Eur. Ct. H.R. (ser. A) (1992).
Timurtas v. Turkey, Eur. Ct. H.R. (13 June 2000), at <http://hudoc. echr.coe.int/hudoc/ViewRoot.asp?Item=1&Action=Html&X=51813 2821&Notice=0&Noticemode=&RelatedMode=0>.
Tomasi v. France, 214-A Eur. Ct. H.R. (ser. A) 40–41 (1992).
Tryer v. United Kingdom, 26 Eur. Ct. H.R. (ser. A) (1978).
Van der Mussele v. Belgium, 70 Eur. Ct. H.R. (ser. A) (1983).
Van Duyn v. Secretary of State for Home Affairs, Case 41/74, ECR 1337 (1974); 1 C.M.L.R. 1 (1975).
Van Oosterwijk v. Belgium, Commission, Eur. Ct. H.R. (ser. A) 40 (1980).
Van Vlimmeren and Van Ilneerenbeck v. the Netherlands, Eur. Ct. H.R. (29 Sept. 2000), at <http://www.dhcour.coe.fr/hudoc/ViewRoot.asp? Item=0&Action=Html&X=1108041737&Notice=0&Noticemode=&R elatedMode=0>.
Cruz Varas and Others v. Sweden, 201 Eur. Ct. H.R. (ser. A) (1991).
Velikova v. Bulgaria, Eur. Ct. H.R. (18 May 2000), at <http://www. dhcour.coe.fr/hudoc/ViewRoot.asp?Item=0&Action=Html&X=102 5023358&Notice=0&Noticemode=&RelatedMode=0>.
Vermelen v. Belgium, Eur. Ct. II.R. (1996).
Vijayanathan and Puspurajah v. France, 241-B Eur. Ct. H.R. (ser. A) (1992).
Vilvarajah v. United Kingdom, Eur. Ct. H.R. (ser. A) 215 (1991).
Vogt v. Germany, Eur. Ct. H.R. (ser. A) 323 (1995).
Mrs. W. v. United Kingdom, 9348/81, 32 DR 211 (1983).
X and Church of Scientology v. Sweden, No. 7805/77, Dec. 5.5.79, D.R. 16.
X v. FRG, 6167/73, 1 DR (1974).
X v. France, Eur. Ct.H.R. (ser.A) 234-C (1992).
X and Y v. Netherlands, 91 Eur. Ct. H. R. (ser. A) 33 (1985).
Yasa v. Turkey, VI Eur. Ct. H.R. (1998), at <http://hudoc.echr.coe.int/ hudoc/ViewRoot.asp?Item=0&Action=Html&X=518132714&Notice =0&Noticemode=&RelatedMode=0>.
Young, James and Webster v. the United Kingdom, 44 Eur. Ct. H.R. (ser. A) (1981).
Zana v. Turkey, Eur. Ct. H.R. (25 November 1997).

Chapter 6
The Inter-American Mechanisms

Beth Lyon
Soren Rottman

1. The Major Bodies

In the Americas, the protection of refugees, asylum-seekers, and internally displaced persons may be promoted through the mechanisms of the Organization of American States (OAS) and its organs, in particular the Inter-American Commission on Human Rights ("the Commission") and the Inter-American Court of Human Rights ("the Court").[1] However, the OAS has not traditionally dealt with massive displacements and other humanitarian emergencies, and thus its initiatives in this area are still in the early stages of development. In fact, while various extradition and asylum conventions have been adopted in the Americas, there is to date no comprehensive regional agreement specifically relating to the status of refugees or internally displaced people. Nevertheless, this chapter will provide a description of the available human rights complaint mechanisms, procedures, and jurisprudence, with a view to exploring both existing and emerging avenues for the protection and relief of refugees, asylum-seekers, and the internally displaced in the hemisphere.

1.1 The Organization of American States (OAS)

The OAS, the world's oldest regional organization, traces its origin back to the First International Conference of American States that established the International Union of American Republics in 1890. Headquartered in Washington, D.C., the OAS has among its purposes

---

[1] The authors thank Christina Cerna, Juan Méndez, Robert K. Goldman, Elizabeth Abi-Mershed, Verónica Gómez, Stella Villagrán, Hiram Ruiz, Robin Kirk, Lorraine Eide, Volker Türk, Richard Wilson, Claudia Martin, Diego Rodriguez, Bernadette Passade Cissé, Alejandro Cedeño, Alison Posner, Lynda Cevallos, Quoc Vuong, and Sherilyn Holcombe.

the strengthening of peace and security in the hemisphere, the promotion of representative democracy, the peaceful settlement of disputes between its members, and providing for common action on behalf of those states in the event of aggression. In addition, the OAS seeks economic, social, and cultural development through cooperative action, and the achievement of an effective limitation of the use of conventional weapons. The OAS has 35 member states, and 45 states as well as the European Union have been granted permanent observer status.[2]

The majority of OAS member states are parties to the American Convention on Human Rights, which was adopted in 1969. States that have not ratified the 1969 American Convention remain bound by the 1948 OAS Charter and the 1948 American Declaration on the Rights and Duties of Man. The Declaration recognizes a broad range of fundamental human rights, including less detailed versions of many of the rights embodied in the American Convention.

1.2 The Inter-American Commission on Human Rights

The Inter-American Commission on Human Rights, a charter organ of the OAS and a treaty body of the 1969 American Convention on Human Rights, was formally established in 1960. The principal function of the Commission is to promote the observance and protection of human rights and to serve as consultative organ of the OAS in these matters. The Commission represents all the member states of the OAS and is composed of seven members elected by the General Assembly of the OAS in their personal capacity.[3] The Commission is a part-time body that meets in session for eight weeks in a year. Its offices are at OAS headquarters in Washington, D.C.

Historically, the Commission has carried out its mission primarily through the preparation of country reports on the human rights conditions within a country, usually published following on-site visits and hearings in the country in question. Through both visits and reports, an improvement in the human rights conditions is frequently achieved. Though not binding as a matter of international law, the recommendations issued by the Commission at the conclusion of a visit or a report

---

[2] *See* Appendix 6C for a list of OAS Member States. *See* Bibliography of Cited International Instruments for full citations to the international instruments mentioned in this chapter.

[3] The current officers of the Commission are: Dr. Hélio Bicudo, Chairman; Dean Claudio Grossman, First Vice Chairman; Dr. Juan E. Méndez, Second Vice Chairman, Dra. Marta Altolaguirre, Prof. Robert K. Goldman, Dr. Peter Laurie, and Dr. Julio Prado Vallejo.

are highly persuasive and taken very seriously by member states. More recently, the examination of individual petitions has come to play a more important role, particularly since the American Convention made possible the referral of cases to the Inter-American Court for final, legally binding decisions.[4] For further discussion of country reports and on-site visits, see section 5 of this chapter.

1.3 The Inter-American Court of Human Rights

The Inter-American Court of Human Rights is an autonomous judicial institution of the OAS with both contentious and advisory jurisdiction whose purpose is to interpret and apply the 1969 American Convention on Human Rights. The Court is composed of seven jurists elected in a personal capacity by states parties to the American Convention.[5] From its seat in San José, Costa Rica, the Court heard its first case in 1981. While the contentious jurisdiction of the Court depends on the acceptance of its jurisdiction by the member states, its advisory jurisdiction is broad and may be invoked by a member of the OAS or any of its organs. As part of its advisory jurisdiction, the Court is competent to rule on the compatibility of human rights treaties with domestic laws of the member states, much like the European Court of Justice.[6]

It is only through reference to the Court by the Commission or by a state party that a complaint may be heard by the Court. In other words, the petitioner cannot take an appeal directly to the Court. After being notified of the decision to refer the case to the Court, the petitioner will have the opportunity to submit observations and to request any measures that may be needed to avoid irreparable harm, recommend particular witnesses, or authorize an attorney to assist the delegates of the Commission in presenting the case. The Commission generally will send a delegate to argue the case on the petitioner's behalf. However, the Court will also permit an advisor to represent the

---

[4] David Harris, *Regional Protection of Human Rights: The Inter-American Achievement, in* THE INTER-AMERICAN SYSTEM OF HUMAN RIGHTS 1, 21 (DAVID J. HARRIS AND STEPHEN LIVINGSTON EDS., 1998).

[5] The Court is currently composed by: Antônio A. Cançado Trindade (Brazil), President; Máximo Pacheco Gómez (Chile), Vice-president; Hernán Salgado Pesantes (Ecuador); Oliver Jackman (Barbados); Alirio Abreu Burelli (Venezuela); Sergio García Ramírez (México) and Carlos Vicente de Roux Rengifo (Colombia). The Court's Secretary is Manuel E. Ventura Robles (Costa Rica) and its Deputy Secretary is Mr. Renzo Pomi (Uruguay).

[6] SCOTT DAVIDSON, THE INTER-AMERICAN COURT OF HUMAN RIGHTS 2 (1992).

petitioners at hearings, which can be especially valuable if the advisor is an expert in the law of the state concerned or international human rights law. The proceedings before the Court involve presentation of a memorial and counter-memorial. The Court is not bound by the findings made earlier by the Commission and is free to make its own findings of fact. Its hearings are usually public, but its deliberations are secret. The judgment of the Court is public and copies of the decision are sent to the parties, the Commission, the Secretary General of the OAS, and any other concerned parties.

If the Court finds a violation of a right protected by the American Convention, it may rule that the situation be remedied and the compensation be paid to the victim. The decisions by the Court are final and binding on the states, and the OAS General Assembly is responsible for enforcement of the Court's orders. The Court has the power to order compensation and can also impose specific injunctive relief. In fact, it has ordered a variety of injunctive measures, including the establishment of trust funds and schools. Under Article 63(1) of the American Convention, the Court has the power to award legal fees and costs.

1.4 Inter-Institutional Coordination

The Inter-American Commission on Human Rights has occasionally treated the issue of refugees and internally displaced persons in its reports to the General Assembly, which in turn has regularly issued resolutions stressing its concern for the plight of forced migrants in the region.[7] However, UNHCR is the international body that has played the largest role in giving assistance and emergency relief, as well as in developing projects for refugees in the region, especially in Central America. Inter-institutional coordination between UNHCR and the OAS and agencies such as the International Labor Organization (ILO) and the International Organization for Migration (IOM) has attempted to provide durable solutions for refugees, focusing in particular on their social and economic integration and on resettlement both inside and outside the region.[8] Such coordination has yielded the fruits of

---

[7] *See, e.g.*, The Situation of Refugees, Returnees, and Internally Displaced Persons in the Americas, AG/RES. 1602 XXVIII-0/98 (June 3, 1998) (mentioning the role of the OAS in cooperation with UNHCR in working to strengthen regional and national protection systems, but emphasizing its role of providing "advisory support" to states, which are "the entities primarily responsible for the effective application of humanitarian principles and rules of refugee law").

[8] Lelio Mármora, *Social Integration and Employment of Central American Refugees, in* WHEN BORDERS DON'T DIVIDE: LABOR MIGRATION AND REFUGEE MOVEMENTS IN THE AMERICAS 149 (PATRICIA R. PESSAR ED., 1988).

greater protection for refugees and rational planning for social integration and employment of refugees. At the same time, excessive bureaucratization and duplication of efforts among agencies has tended to pull vital resources away from the principal objective of assisting refugees.[9]

2. Admissibility Criteria for Individual Complaints

"Admissibility" applies to the individual petition system[10] in the Commission and Court, and refers to the formal procedural requirements that an individual petitioner must meet before the Commission and Court will agree to examine the strength of the underlying human rights claim.

The rules about admissibility are contained in the 1969 American Convention, the Statute and the Rules of Procedure of the Commission, and the Statute and Rules of the Court.[11] Admissibility requirements include the limitations on who can file a petition, against what government they can complain, when they can file, what kind of violation they must allege, and what other entity has or must examine the claim before it was filed with the Commission. The procedural requirements for filing individual petitions in the Inter-American mechanisms are quite flexible, among other things allowing for non-victim petitioners, presumptions of fact against non-responsive governments, and flexible exhaustion rules, all of which are particularly important to forcibly displaced petitioners.

When the Commission receives a petition, it conducts an initial admissibility review, and, if it meets the requirements of admissibility under article 28 of the Rules of Procedure, forwards it to the government against which the petition was lodged and requests that the government provide information on the case.[12] After a round of replies ending with the opportunity for final written observations by both parties,[13]

---

[9] *Id.*

[10] The Court refers to the individual petition function as its "adjudicatory jurisdiction" as opposed to its "advisory jurisdiction." *See* Statute of the Inter-American Court of Human Rights, 1979, art. 2, *reprinted in Basic Documents Pertaining to Human Rights in the Inter-American System*, OAS/Ser.L/V/I.4 Rev.7 (February 2, 2000) [hereinafter Court Statute].

[11] *See* Rules of Procedure of the Inter-American Commission on Human Rights, art. 27, (entered into force on May 1, 2001) at <http://www.cidh.org/Básicos/newregulations.htm> [hereinafter Commission Rules].

[12] *Id.*, art. 30.

[13] *Id.* If the government entirely fails to respond and no other conflicting information comes to light, the Commission presumes that the allegations contained in the petition are true. *Id.* art. 39.

the Commission then examines the case and makes its formal admissibility determination.[14] If the case is admissible, the Commission "opens" it.

Because the Court has jurisdiction only over contentious cases referred by the Commission and states parties to the Convention, admissibility requirements are most likely to be given final adjudication at the Commission stage. The Court is not required to make a formal inquiry as to admissibility, but the Convention specifically states that the Court cannot hear a case that has not gone through the full pre-hearing procedures at the Commission, including an admissibility finding.[15]

Due to the incomplete state of Convention ratifications, the admissibility requirements vary slightly depending on whether a petition was filed against governments that have ratified the Convention ("Convention States") or against governments who have not ratified the Convention ("Declaration States").[16] Except where otherwise noted, the following admissibility rules apply to both Convention and Declaration States.

2.1 Jurisdiction Ratione Personae—The Parties to an Individual Complaint

In the individual petition system at the Commission, *petitioners* file complaints against a *state party* about human rights violations suffered by *victims*. One of the admissibility requirements is that the Commission must have both active and passive jurisdiction. Active jurisdiction refers to the identity of the petitioner and the victim.[17] Passive jurisdiction refers to the Commission's authority to decide complaints against a particular state party.

2.1.1 Who Can Bring a Complaint?

In the Inter-American human rights system, it does not have to be the victim who files a petition regarding her situation. The Convention establishes that "[a]ny person or group of persons, or any nongovernmental entity legally recognized in one or more member states

---

[14] *Id.*, art. 37.
[15] *See* American Convention on Human Rights art. 61(1).
[16] *See* Commission Rules, *supra* note 11, at art. 52. Supplementary procedures for Declaration States are laid out in Chapter III of the Commission Rules. *Id.*, arts. 49–50.
[17] *See, e.g., Bendeck-Cohdinsa*, Petition, Report No. 106/99 [Honduras], IACHR 1999 Annual Report 311, 313 ¶ 15 (September 27, 1999).

of the Organization" can lodge an individual petition with the Commission.[18] The Commission interprets this phrase to mean "natural persons and NGOs."[19] The definition does not, however, include business entities.[20] Even when an individual petitioner appears to meet the criteria, the Commission actively examines the petitioner's exhaustion record to learn whether he appears to be filing on behalf of a private company. If a business entity rather than the individual petitioner exhausted the domestic remedies, then the Commission will dismiss the case on the grounds that it does not have active jurisdiction *ratione personae*.[21]

> **Focus on: Maria**
> As described in Chapter 1, Maria has been forcibly evicted from her farmland and is living in an abandoned warehouse. The petitioner-victim distinction means that someone, for example a non-governmental organization in her hometown, could file a petition on Maria's behalf, even if she is not available to give her consent.

Only states parties to the Convention, and the Commission, have the right to submit a case to the Court.[22] Therefore, when pursuing an individual petition at the Commission, one important advocacy goal is

---

[18] American Convention, art. 44. Indeed, the Commission has held that the petitioner does not need the victim's permission to initiate an action with the Commission. *See* Case 1954, Resolution No. 59/81 [Uruguay], IACHR 1981–1982 Annual Report 96, 96 (October 16, 1981); *Raquel Martín de Mejía*, Case 10.970, Report No. 5/96 [Peru], IACHR 1995 Annual Report 157, 193 (March 1, 1996).

[19] *See Monsignor Oscar Arnulfo Romero y Galdámez*, Case 11.481, Report No. 37/00 [El Salvador], IACHR 1999 Annual Report 671, 676 ¶ 21 (April 13, 2000).

[20] *See, e.g., Banco de Lima*, Case 10.169, Report No. 10/91 [Peru], IACHR 1990–1991 Annual Report 423, 425 ¶¶ 1–3 (February 22, 1991); *Tabacalera Boquerón*, Report No. 47/97 [Paraguay], IACHR 1997 Annual Report 225, 229 ¶¶ 24–25 (October 16, 1997); *Mevopal, S.A.*, Petition, Report No. 39/99 [Argentina], 1998 Annual Report 297, 299 ¶ 16 (March 11, 1999); *Bernard Merens and Family*, Petition, Report No. 103/99 [Argentina], IACHR 1999 Annual Report 307, 309 ¶ 15 (September 27, 1999); *Bendeck-Cohdinsa*, Petition, Report No. 106/99 [Honduras], IACHR 1999 Annual Report 311, 314 ¶ 17 (September 27, 1999).

[21] *Id.* This doctrine is known as the "human personality restriction." *Bernard Merens and Family*, Petition, Report No. 103/99 [Argentina], IACHR 1999 Annual Report 307, 309 n.2 (September 27, 1999).

[22] American Convention, art. 61(1); *see also* Court Statute, *supra* note 10, at art. 28.

to convince the Commission to proceed further with its own ruling on your case by lodging the case at the Court.

Individual Victims

The Declaration and the Convention refer repeatedly to the rights of "every person," defined in Convention Article 1(2) as "every human being."[23] Accordingly, a victim does not have to possess a particular nationality to invoke the Convention.[24]

> **Focus on: Ibrahim**
> Ibrahim has crossed an international border and suffered various human rights violations in the new country where he is residing . He can file a petition against the government of the new country even though he is not a citizen of that country.

As stated above, only states parties to the Convention, and the Commission, have the right to submit a case to the Court.[25] However, when appearing before the Court, the Commission may designate a "Delegate" to represent the Commission at the Court, and the Delegate may be "assisted by the persons of [the Commissioners'] choice."[26] With the Court's approval, the Commission may appoint the victim or the victim's next of kin as Delegates.[27] Victims and next of kin, or their chosen representatives, are also permitted to submit evidence and arguments independent of the Commission at the reparations stage,[28] and the Court notifies the victim or victim's next of kin of the existence of an application regarding her situation.[29]

---

[23] American Convention, art. 1(2).

[24] *See id.*, preamble ("*Recognizing* that the essential rights of man are not derived from one's being a national of a certain state, but are based upon attributes of a human personality . . ."); Harris, *supra* note 4, at 16. Although the word "man" is used in various points in the early documents, including most notably in the title of the Declaration, women and children are included under the Declaration's protection.

[25] American Convention, art. 61(1); *see also* Court Statute, *supra* note 10, at art. 28.

[26] American Convention, art. 22(1).

[27] *Id.*, art. 22(2).

[28] *Id.*, art. 23.

[29] Rules of Procedure of the Inter-American Court of Human Rights, art. 35(e), *reprinted in Basic Documents Pertaining to Human Rights in the Inter-American System*, OAS/Ser.L/V/I.4 Rev.7 (January 2000), at <http://www.cidh.oas.org/

The Court has stated that governments are responsible only for the immediate effects of their unlawful acts.[30] Generally the victim's larger community will not qualify for reparations unless the community has suffered a proven, direct damage.[31] However, "society" has the right to know the truth about what happened to a particular victim.[32]

Indirect Victims

The Court has established that a deceased victim's right to compensation passes to her successors.[33] The term successors is construed broadly to include family members generally, not just those who qualify under national laws of succession.[34]

The family members of a victim have distinct rights in addition to their rights as the successors of a deceased victim. They have the right to know the truth about what happened to the victim.[35] Family members also have the right to compensation for the actual and moral damages they themselves suffered.[36] The Court has awarded non-

---

Básicos/Basic%20Documents/enbas10.htm> [hereinafter Court Rules].

[30] *Aloeboetoe Case*, Judgment on Reparations [Suriname], Inter-Am Ct. H.R. (ser. C) No. 15, 57, 68–69 ¶ 49 (September 10, 1993).

[31] *See, e.g., id.* at 82 ¶ 83.

[32] *See* IACHR 1985–86 Annual Report 205 (relying on *Castillo Páez Case* [Peru], Inter-Am. Ct. H.R. (ser. C) No. 34, 39, 69 ¶ 86 (November 3, 1997); *see also Lucio Parada Cea*, Case 10.480, Report No. 1/99 [El Salvador], IACHR 1998 Annual Report 531, 568–70 ¶¶ 148–58 (January 27, 1999); *Monsignor Oscar Arnulfo Romero y Galdámez*, Case 11.4811, Report No. 37/00 [El Salvador], IACHR 1999 Annual Report 671, 711 ¶ 142 (April 13, 2000).

[33] *See, e.g., Aloeboetoe Case*, Judgment on Reparations [Suriname], Inter-Am. Ct. H.R. (ser. C) No. 15, 51, 70 ¶ 54 (September 10, 1993).

[34] *Velásquez Rodríguez Case*, Interpretation of the Compensatory Damages Judgment [Honduras], Inter-Am. Ct. H.R. (ser. C) No. 9, 25, 37 ¶ 27 (August 17, 1990).

[35] *See* IACHR 1985–86 Annual Report 205 (relying on *Castillo Páez Case* [Peru], Inter-Am. Ct. H.R. (ser. C) No. 34, 39, 69 ¶ 86 (November 3, 1997); *see also Lucio Parada Cea*, Case 10.480, Report No. 1/99 [El Salvador], IACHR 1998 Annual Report 531, 568–70 ¶¶ 148–58 (January 27, 1999); *Monsignor Oscar Arnulfo Romero y Galdámez*, Case 11.4811, Report No. 37/00 [El Salvador], IACHR 1999 Annual Report 671, 711, ¶ 142 (April 13, 2000).

[36] *See* American Convention, art. 63(1); *Velásquez Rodríguez Case*, Interpretation of the Compensatory Damages Judgment [Honduras], Inter-Am. Ct. H.R. (ser. C) No. 9, 25, 37 ¶ 27 (August, 17, 1990); *Godínez Cruz Case*, Interpretation of the Compensation Damages Judgment [Honduras], Inter-Am. Ct. H.R. (ser. C) No. 10, 25, 37 ¶ 27 (August 17, 1990); *see also Aloeboetoe Case*, Judgment on Reparations [Suriname], Inter-Am. Ct. H.R. (ser. C) No. 15, 51, 83

monetary reparations to family members, in one case ordering the government of Suriname to start a foundation and re-open a school for the benefit of the victims' children and tribe.[37]

> **Focus on: Chen**
> Chen was involuntarily expatriated from her home country, and her children remain there. The new country where she is living will not let her bring her children to live with her. As dependents of Chen, her children may have the right to compensation from both governments.

The authors are not aware of contentious case law addressing potential violations of an Inter-American treaty provision. However, the advisory jurisdiction of the Court can serve this function, as shown in its opinion on the "Compatibility of Draft Legislation with Article 8(2)(h) of the American Convention on Human Rights."[38]

Groups and NGOs

The American Convention establishes that "[a]ny person or group of persons, or any nongovernmental entity legally recognized in one or more member states of the Organization" can lodge an individual petition with the Commission.[39] The Commission interprets this phrase to mean "natural persons and NGOs," but not business entities. Court participation is very greatly limited, and the right of petition at the Court is limited to the Commission and states parties.[40]

2.1.2 Against Whom Can a Claim Be Brought?

Petitions may be filed with the Commission against any member state of the Organization of American States. The Commission is competent to decide petitions against *Declaration States* by virtue of their

---

¶ 85 (September 10, 1993). For a helpful summary of the types of possible compensation, *see* Dinah Shelton, *Reparations in the Inter-American System, in* THE INTER-AMERICAN SYSTEM OF HUMAN RIGHTS, *supra* note 4 at 151, 161–63.

[37] *Aloeboetoe Case,* Judgment on Reparations [Suriname], Inter-Am. Ct. H.R. (ser. C) No. 15, 51, 94 ¶ 116 (September 10, 1993).

[38] Advisory Opinion OC-12/91, *Compatibility of Draft Legislation with Article 8(2)(h) of the American Convention on Human Rights,* Inter-Am. Ct. H.R. (ser. A) No.12, 18 (December 6, 1991).

[39] American Convention, art. 44.

[40] *See supra* Section 1.1.2.

being states parties to the Organization of American States Charter.[41] *Convention States* additionally subject themselves to the Commission's jurisdiction by ratifying the American Convention.[42]

The Commission is limited to hearing state-to-state complaints initiated by, and lodged against, governments that have deposited a "declaration concerning recognition of competence" affirmatively accepting the Commission's jurisdiction over state-initiated cases alleging violations of the Convention.[43]

Declaration States are not subject to the jurisdiction of the Court. States parties to the American Convention that have made a declaration under Article 62 recognizing the jurisdiction of the Court can be the subject of a petition.[44] A state party can accept jurisdiction for limited purposes, such as one case, and by special agreement.[45]

Federal governments, such as Brazil and the United States, are responsible for the actions of constituent entities.[46] This rule fits into a more general doctrine that the "action or omission of any public authority constitutes an act imputable to the State."[47]

---

[41] *See Roach and Pinkerton Cases*, Case 9647, Resolution No. 3/87 [United States], IACHR 1986–1987 Annual Report 147, 165 ¶¶ 46–47 (March 27, 1987); *Armando Alejandre Jr., et al.*, Case 11.589, Report No. 86/99 [Cuba], IACHR 1999 Annual Report 586, 593 ¶ 18 (September 29, 1999); Case 2141, Resolution No. 23/81 [United States], IACHR 1980–1981 Annual Report 25 (March 6, 1981); Advisory Opinion OC-13/93, *Certain Attributes of the Inter-American Commission on Human Rights (Arts. 41, 42, 44, 46, 47, 50 and 51 of the American Convention on Human Rights)*, Inter-Am. Ct. H.R. (ser. A) No.13, 25, 39–40 ¶¶ 42, 45 (July 16, 1993); Harris, *supra* note 4, at 6.

[42] American Convention, art. 44.

[43] *Id.*, art. 45.

[44] *Id.*, art. 62(1).

[45] *Id.*, arts. 62(2)–(3).

[46] *Id.*, art. 28; *see also Alonso Eugénio da Silva*, Case No. 11.598, Report No. 9/00 [Brazil], IACHR 1999 Annual Report 399, 403 ¶¶ 20–21 (February 24, 2000); *Marcos Aurelio de Oliveira*, Case 11.599, Report No. 10/00 [Brazil], IACHR 1999 Annual Report 413, 417 ¶ 21 (February 24, 2000).

[47] *Marcos Aurelio de Oliveira*, Case 11.599, Report No. 10/00 [Brazil], IACHR 1999 Annual Report 413, 416–17 ¶ 20 (February 24, 2000) (citing *Velásquez Rodríguez Case*, Inter-Am. Ct. H.R. (ser. C) No. 4, 91, 151 ¶ 164 (July 29, 1988)).

2.2 Jurisdiction Ratione Materiae—What Must the Complaint Concern?

2.2.1 Rights Protected by Regional Instruments

The Declaration or the Convention?

The Court and Commission have jurisdiction to enforce several regional human rights treaties. Where the respondent state has not ratified any relevant treaties other than the OAS Charter, petitions filed with the Commission must allege a violation of the Declaration.[48] Petitions filed with the Commission alleging violations of the American Convention must set forth the relevant provisions.[49] Against Convention States, if the relevant right in the Convention is "substantially identical" to a right in the Declaration, the Commission and Court will only consider violations of that right under the Convention.[50] The Inter-American Court and Commission have established that the American Declaration is a source of international obligations for OAS member states[51] and that American Convention norms will be relied on "insofar as [petitioners allege] violations of *substantially identical rights* set forth in both instruments."[52] These decisions establish a complementary principle by which individual petitioners should fill substantive gaps in the American Convention with arguments under the American Declaration.

---

[48] *See* Commission Rules, *supra* note 11 at art. 49; *see also id.* art. 23. Interestingly, the Statute of the Commission in art. 20 (b) instruct the Commission to "pay particular attention" to specific provisions of the Declaration when dealing with Declaration States, namely Articles I (life, liberty, and personal security); II (equality before the law); III (religious freedom and worship); IV (freedom of investigation, opinion, expression, and dissemination); XVIII (fair trial); XXV (protection from arbitrary arrest); and XXVI (due process of law).

[49] American Convention, art. 44; *see also id.*, art. 47(b); *see also* Commission Rules, *supra* note 11, at art. 28(f).

[50] *Paul Lallion*, Case 11.765, Report No. 124/99 [Granada], IACHR 1999 Annual Report 225, 230 ¶ 26 (September 27, 1999).

[51] *See* Advisory Opinion OC-10/89, *Interpretation of the American Declaration on the Rights and Duties of Man within the framework of Article 64 of the American Convention on Human Rights* 109, 121 ¶¶ 44–47, Inter-Am. Ct. H.R.(ser. A) No. 10 (July 14, 1989).

[52] *Paul Lallion*, Case No. 11.765, Report No. 124/99 [Granada], IACHR 1999 Annual Report 225, 230 ¶ 26 (September 27, 1999).

Other Regional Treaties

The Commission and Court have jurisdiction over alleged violations of two provisions of the 1988 Additional Protocol to the American Convention on Human Rights in the Area of Economic, Social and Cultural Rights (involving protection of trade unions and the right to education).[53] Three other regional treaties are in force and can be used in petitions against their signatories: the 1994 Inter-American Convention on the Prevention, Punishment and Eradication of Violence Against Women;[54] the 1985 Inter-American Convention to Prevent and Punish Torture;[55] and the 1994 Inter-American Convention on Forced Disappearance of Persons.[56]

International and Non-OAS Regional Precedent

Although Declaration States cannot be held to the American Convention or to the jurisprudence of the Court, it is important to note that the Commission typically looks to other international and regional human rights authority it finds to be "relevant in informing an interpretation of the principles of the Declaration."[57] The Court endorsed this practice in a 1982 advisory opinion,[58] and itself uses the same approach.[59]

---

[53] Also known as the "Protocol of San Salvador" [hereinafter ESCR Protocol]. *See* Bibliography of Cited International Instruments.

[54] Also known as the "Convention of Belem Do Para" [hereinafter Convention on Violence Against Women]. *See* Bibliography of Cited International Instruments.

[55] Hereinafter "Convention Against Torture." *See* Bibliography of Cited International Instruments.

[56] Hereinafter "Convention on Forced Disappearances." *See* Bibliography of Cited International Instruments.

[57] IACHR, REPORT ON THE SITUATION OF HUMAN RIGHTS OF ASYLUM SEEKERS WITHIN THE CANADIAN REFUGEE DETERMINATION SYSTEM, OEA/Ser.L/V/II.106 Doc. 40 rev. ¶ 38 (2000).

[58] Advisory Opinion OC-1/82, *Other Treaties" Subject To The Advisory Jurisdiction Of The Court (Art. 64 American Convention On Human Rights)*, Inter-Am. Ct. H.R. (ser. A) No. 1 (September 24, 1982).

[59] *See Velásquez-Rodríguez Case*, [Honduras], Inter-Am. Ct. H.R. (ser. C) No. 4, 91, 134, 135 ¶ 127 (July 29, 1988).

2.2.2 Acts or Omissions Committed by a State, Its Agents, Officials, Etc.

In its landmark case *Velásquez Rodríguez*,[60] the Court held that a state party is responsible not only for human rights violations committed by public officials, but also by people acting under color of law.[61] States parties are also held accountable for acts involving their failure to exercise due diligence to prevent, investigate, or punish violations.[62]

> **Focus on: Chen**
> Chen has suffered discrimination in employment, housing and education in the new country where she is has asylum. Although the people discriminating against her may not be government officials, the government has a responsibility to prevent, investigate, and punish discrimination.

2.2.3 Court of Fourth Instance Rule

The Inter-American human rights bodies are not permitted to act as a supra-national "appeals" court. This means that the Commission cannot pass judgment on a decision by a domestic court "acting within [its] competence and with due judicial guarantees," unless the decision itself constitutes a violation of a right protected by an applicable Inter-American human rights instrument.[63]

2.3 Jurisdiction Ratione Temporis

The facts alleged in the petition must have taken place at a time when the state party's obligation to respect and ensure the rights in the relevant treaty was already in force.[64] For violations of the American Convention, for example, the relevant date would be the date the country deposited its instrument of ratification.[65] Under the doctrine of *con-*

---

[60] *Id.* at 158, ¶ 182.
[61] *Id.*, ¶ 172.
[62] *Id.*, ¶¶ 172–173.
[63] *Santiago Marzioni*, Case 11.673, Report No. 39/96 [Argentina], IACHR 1996 Annual Report 76, 85–91 ¶¶ 48–71 (October 15, 1996); *see also Narciso Palacios*, Case 10.194, Report No. 105/99 [Argentina], IACHR 1999 Annual Report, 355, 363 ¶ 45 (September 29, 1999); *Rudolph Baptiste*, Case 11.743, Report No. 38/00 [Grenada], IACHR 1999 Annual Report 721, 739 ¶ 65 (April 13, 2000).
[64] *See "Ojo de Agua" Cooperative*, Case 11.701, Report No. 73/99 [Mexico], IACHR 1999 Annual Report 316, 318 ¶ 10 (May 4, 1999).
[65] *See id.*, n.4.

tinuing violation, it may be possible to argue that the violation of the right extended past the relevant ratification date. Violations of the judicial guarantees and due process protections in Articles 8 and 25 of the American Convention may be especially suitable for a continuing violation argument.[66]

2.4 Jurisdiction Ratione Loci

The American Convention protects people who are "subject to [the] jurisdiction" of the states parties,[67] whether or not they are within the geographic boundaries of that state.[68] This phrase has been interpreted to include individuals interdicted on the high seas,[69] shot down in international airspace,[70] injured in invasions by the respondent state,[71] or attacked by agents of the respondent state in another country.[72]

2.5 Must Domestic Remedies Have Been Exhausted?

Before the Commission and the Court will consider a case, the petitioner must prove that the accused state had an opportunity to remedy the problem at the domestic level.[73] This is a common defense raised by respondent states against petitions filed with the Commission.[74]

---

[66] *See Alonso Eugénio da Silva*, Case 11.598, Report No. 9/00 [Brazil], IACHR 1999 Annual Report 399, 402, n.2 (February 24, 2000); *Andres Aylwin Azocar et al.*, Case 11.863, Report No. 137/99 [Chile], IACHR 1999 Annual Report 536, 542 (December 27, 1999).

[67] American Convention, art. 1(2).

[68] Harris, *supra* note 4, at 16.

[69] *Haitian Interdiction*, Case 10.675, Report No. 51/96 [United States], IACHR 1996 Annual Report 550, 605 ¶ 171 (March 13, 1997).

[70] *Armando Alejandre Jr., et al.*, Case 11.589, Report No. 86/99 [Cuba], IACHR 1999 Annual Report 586, 594, 595 ¶ 23 (September 29, 1999).

[71] Application No. 9213 [United States], IACHR 1986–1987 Annual Report 184 (April 17, 1986) (U.S. forces in Granada, case admissible); *Richmond Hill*, Case 9213, Report No. 3/96 [United States], IACHR 1995 Annual Report 201 (March 1, 1996) (U.S. forces in Granada, case settled); *Salas and Others*, Case 10.573, Report No. 31/93 [United States], IACHR 1993 Annual Report 312 (February 11, 1994) (U.S. forces in Panama).

[72] IACHR, REPORT ON THE SITUATION OF HUMAN RIGHTS IN CHILE, OEA Ser.L/V/II.66, Doc. 17 (1985) (Letelier murder in Washington, D.C.); IACHR, SECOND REPORT ON THE SITUATION OF HUMAN RIGHTS IN SURINAME, OEA Ser.L/V/II.66, Doc. 21, rev. 1 (1985) (harassment of Surinamese residents of Holland by agents of the government of Suriname).

[73] *See* American Convention, arts. 46(1)(a), 61(2); Court Statute, *supra* note 10, at arts. 19(a), 20(c); Commission Rules, *supra* note 11, at arts. 28(h), 31, 50.

[74] Christina Cerna, *The Inter-American Commission on Human Rights: Its*

Which remedies is a petitioner expected to exhaust? This is a question with which nearly all potential petitioners struggle. When preparing a case that might involve exhaustion or timeliness of the petition, it is particularly important to investigate the latest case law and talk over the case with mentors who regularly interact with the Commission and Court. There are several general exceptions to exhaustion in the American Convention and the Commission Rules,[75] and advocates should be prepared to develop creative arguments to use these exceptions to get their cases examined by the Commission. A petitioner does not have to prove exhaustion if the available remedies are not *"adequate and effective."*[76] The Commission conducts a case-by-case analysis of exhaustion to determine whether the petitioner enjoys a "reasonable possibility of obtaining a remedy."[77]

As described in greater detail below, the Convention lays out three broad *"denial of justice"*[78] exceptions to exhaustion:

(1) domestic legislation does not "afford due process of law for protection of the [rights] . . . allegedly violated;"
(2) the petitioner was denied access to domestic remedies or otherwise "prevented" from exhausting them; or
(3) there was an "unwarranted delay" in getting a decision from the domestic authorities.[79]

The initial burden of proof regarding exhaustion lies with the respondent state.[80] In other words, a petitioner does not have to provide affirmative proof that domestic remedies have been exhausted. If the petitioner alleges that domestic remedies have been exhausted, "it shall be up to the State concerned to demonstrate to the Commission that the remedies under domestic law have not been previously exhausted, unless it is clearly evident from the record."[81] The Court

---

Organization and Examination of Petitions and Communications, in THE INTER-AMERICAN SYSTEM OF HUMAN RIGHTS, *supra* note 4, at 85.

[75] Commission Rules, *supra* note 11, at art. 31(2).

[76] *Velásquez Rodríguez Case*, [Honduras], Inter-Am. Ct. H.R. (ser. C) No. 4, 91, 113 ¶ 60 (July 29, 1988).

[77] *Godínez Cruz Case*, Preliminary Objections [Honduras], Inter-Am. Ct. H.R. (ser. C) No. 3, 45, 70 ¶ 95 (June 26, 1987).

[78] Cerna, *supra* note 74, at 85.

[79] American Convention, art. 46(2); *see also* Commission Rules, *supra* note 11, at art. 31(2).

[80] Commission Rules, *supra* note 11, at art. 31(3).

[81] *Id.*

has endorsed this burden of proof formula.[82] If the respondent state does not raise the exhaustion issue in the "initial stages of procedure,"[83] before the Commission, the objection is presumed *tacitly waived*.[84] The Commission or Court will also consider the exhaustion objection to be waived if the respondent state acknowledges responsibility for the actions alleged in the petition.[85]

Even if the Commission decides that a petitioner has not taken sufficient steps at the local level, the petition may be renewed later after further attempts to exhaust domestic remedies.[86] After one petition

---

[82] *Velásquez Rodríguez Case*, Preliminary Objections [Honduras], Inter-Am. Ct. H.R. (ser. C) No. 1 ¶ 88 (June 26, 1987); *Fairén Garbi y Solis Corrales Case*, Preliminary Objections [Honduras], Inter-Am. Ct. H.R. (ser. C) No. 2, 47, 81, ¶ 87 (June 26, 1987); *Godínez Cruz Case*, Preliminary Objections [Honduras], Inter-Am. Ct. H.R. (ser. C) No. 3, 45, 70 ¶ 95 (June 26, 1987).

[83] *Monsignor Oscar Arnulfo Romero y Galdámez*, Case 11.481, Report No. 37/00 [El Salvador], IACHR 1999 Annual Report 671, 677 ¶ 26 (April 13, 2000).

[84] *Velásquez Rodríguez Case*, [Honduras], Inter-Am. Ct. H.R. (ser. C) No. 4, 91, 123 ¶ 88 (July 29, 1988); *Fairén Garbi y Solis Corrales Case*, Preliminary Objections [Honduras], Inter-Am. Ct. H.R. (ser. C) No. 2, 47, 81 ¶ 87 (June 26, 1987); *Caballero Delgado y Santana Case*, Preliminary Objections [Colombia], Inter-Am. Ct. H.R. (ser. C) No. 17, 33, 159 ¶ 66 (January 21, 1994); *Godínez Cruz Case*, Preliminary Objections, [Honduras], Inter-Am. Ct. H.R. (ser. C) No. 3, 45, 77 ¶ 90 (June 26, 1987); *Viviana Gallardo Case*, [Costa Rica], Inter-Am. Ct. H.R. (ser. A) No. G 101/81, 77, 87, 88 ¶ 26 (November 13, 1981); *Castillo Páez Case*, Preliminary Objections [Peru], Inter-Am. Ct. H.R. (ser. C) No. 24, 29, 44, ¶ 41 (January 30, 1996); *Alonso Eugénio da Silva*, Case 11.598, Report No. 9/00 [Brazil], IACHR 1999 Annual Report 399, 404 ¶ 26 (February 24, 2000); *Marcos Aurelio de Oliveira*, Case 11.599, Report No. 10/00 [Brazil], IACHR 1999 Annual Report 413, 417–18 ¶ 25 (February 24, 2000); *"Los Uvos" Massacre*, Case 11.020, Report No. 35/00 [Colombia], IACHR 1999 Annual Report 446, 454 ¶ 29 (April 13, 2000); *"Caloto" Massacre*, Case 11.101, Report No. 36/00 [Colombia], IACHR 1999 Annual Report 468, 478 ¶ 32 (April 13, 2000); *Armando Alejandre Jr., et al.*, Case 11.589, Report No. 86/99 [Cuba], IACHR 1999 Annual Report 586, 596 ¶ 27 (September 29, 1999); *Ignacio Ellacuría, et al.*, Case 10.488, Report No. 136/99 [El Salvador], IACHR 1999 Annual Report 608, 618 ¶ 44 (December 22, 1999); *Monsignor Oscar Arnulfo Romero y Galdámez*, Case 11.481, Report No. 37/00 [El Salvador], IACHR 1999 Annual Report 671, 677 ¶ 26 (April 13, 2000); *Rudolph Baptiste*, Case 11.743, Report No. 38/00 [Grenada], IACHR 1999 Annual Report 721, 737 ¶ 58 (April 13, 2000); *Joaquín Ortega et al. ("Extrajudicial Executions")*, Case 10.586 et al., Report No. 39/00 [Guatemala], IACHR 1999 Annual Report 772, 820 ¶ 197 (April 13, 2000).

[85] See *"Caloto" Massacre*, Case 11.101, Report No. 36/00 [Colombia], IACHR 1999 Annual Report 468, 478 ¶ 32 (April 13, 2000).

[86] *Salvador Jorge Blanco*, Case 10.208, Resolution No. 15/89 [Dominican Republic], IACHR 1988–1989 Annual Report 67, 103 ¶ 21 (April 14, 1989).

was filed, alleging that the United States had refused to grant citizenship to the biological son of a U.S. citizen, the Commission helped the petitioner find a volunteer lawyer and suspended the case while the petitioner sought judicial remedies.[87] In keeping with this procedure, if it appears that a petition was filed before exhaustion occurred, the Commission will not penalize the petitioner but will simply examine exhaustion as of the date the Commission "pronounces" on admissibility.[88]

A decision about what constitutes exhaustion may also be affected by the seriousness of the alleged violation and the risk associated with delaying the case for further domestic efforts to remedy the situation.[89] Generally, in cases regarding disappearance or extrajudicial execution, the appropriate remedy is a criminal investigation and judicial process *by the government* unless that government can prove that some other remedy should be invoked.[90] A petitioner is not required to seek out every public forum to air her grievance.[91] Moreover, available domestic remedies may not address every issue raised in a petition, rendering them ineffective as regards those issues.[92] A petitioner can satisfy the exhaustion requirement if she shows an amnesty has been declared that "has the effect of deciding the . . . case."[93]

A business entity cannot exhaust domestic remedies on behalf of the petitioner or victim.[94]

---

[87] Cerna, *supra* note 74, at 88–89 (ultimately the U.S. government agreed to issue a passport and the case was closed. *Id.* at 89).

[88] *Dismissed Congressional Employees*, Cases 11.830 & 12.038, Report No. 52/00 [Peru], *to be published in* IACHR 2000 Annual Report ¶ 19 (June 15, 2000).

[89] Cerna, *supra* note 74, at 89 (describing the Commission's decision not to apply an exception to a petitioner both because it was able to assist the petitioner in finding a volunteer lawyer and because "his life and liberty were not at risk.").

[90] *See, e.g., Joaquín Ortega et al. ("Extrajudicial Executions")*, Case 10.586 et al., Report No. 39/00 [Guatemala], IACHR 1999 Annual Report 772, 820 ¶ 200 (April 13, 2000).

[91] *See, e.g., "Ojo de Agua" Cooperative*, Case 11.701, Report No. 73/99, IACHR 1999 Annual Report 316, 319–20, ¶ 15–16 (May 4, 1999) (domestic body that makes only non-binding recommendations and petitions to other authorities not a "suitable remedy" for violations alleged by the petitioner, including right to humane treatment, fair trial, property, and judicial protection).

[92] *See* Cerna, *supra* note 74, at 87–88 (describing Case 3228 [United States], a petition concerning U.S. detention and deportation of Haitian asylum-seekers. The case was closed without a decision because the Commission could not reach a consensus on the merits of the case.).

[93] *See, e.g., Monsignor Oscar Arnulfo Romero y Galdámez*, Case 11.481, Report No. 37/00 [El Salvador], IACHR 1999 Annual Report 671, 677 ¶ 25 (April 13, 2000).

[94] *See, e.g., Banco de Lima*, Case 10.169, Report No. 10/91 [Peru], IACHR

2.5.1 Due Process of Law

A petitioner does not have to prove exhaustion if domestic legislation does not "afford due process of law for protection of the right or rights that have allegedly been violated."[95] The Commission has utilized this provision in many cases in which "there is good evidence that there is no independent judiciary that is competent to provide an effective remedy. . . ."[96] Citing "the total ineffectiveness of the [Honduran] judiciary," the Court applied the due process of law and denial of access/prevention exceptions against Honduras in the landmark cases *Velásquez Rodríguez*,[97] *Fairén Garbi and Solís Corrales*.[98] and *Godínez Cruz*.[99]

2.5.2 Denial of Access to Domestic Remedies or Prevention

If the petition argues denial of access to domestic remedies, the burden shifts to the respondent state to "[show] what domestic remedies remain to be exhausted, and [to offer] an effective remedy to make reparations for the alleged damage. . . ."[100] Many cases to which the "due process of law" exception applies will also involve this exception. The denial of access/prevention exception includes an important circumstance: petitioners who cannot find a lawyer. A petitioner

---

1990–1991 Annual Report 423, 425, ¶ 3 (February 22, 1991); *Tabacalera Boquerón, S.A.*, Report No. 47/97 [Paraguay], IACHR 1997 Annual Report 225, 231, ¶¶ 35, 36 (October 16, 1997); *Mevopal, S.A.*, Report No. 39/99 [Argentina], IACHR 1998 Annual Report 297, 300 ¶¶ 18, 19 (March 11, 1999); *Bernard Merens and Family*, Petition, Report No. 103/99 [Argentina], IACHR 1999 Annual Report 307, 309 ¶ 15 (September 27, 1999); *Bendeck-Cohdinsa*, Petition, Report No. 106/99 [Honduras], IACHR 1999 Annual Report 311, 314, ¶ 18 (September 27, 1999).

[95] American Convention, art. 46(2); Commission Rules, *supra* note 11, at art. 31(2)(a).

[96] Cerna, *supra* note 74, at 87.

[97] *Velásquez Rodríguez Case*, Preliminary Objections [Honduras], Inter-Am. Ct. H.R. (ser. C) No. 1, ¶ 88 (June 26, 1987).

[98] *Fairen Garbi y Solis Corrales Case*, Preliminary Objections [Honduras], Inter-Am. Ct. H.R. (ser. C) No. 2, 47, 78 ¶ 81 (June 26, 1987).

[99] *Godinez Cruz Case*, Preliminary Objections [Honduras], Inter-Am. Ct. H.R. (ser. C) No. 3, 45, 79, 80 ¶ 95 (June 26, 1987). For a recent case finding a "due process of law" exception, see *Damion Thomas*, Case 12.069, Report No. 54/00 [Jamaica], *to be published in* IACHR 2000 Annual Report ¶¶ 28–33 (June 15, 2000).

[100] *Joaquín Ortega et al. ("Extrajudicial Executions")*, Case 10.586 et al., Report No. 39/00 [Guatemala], IACHR 1999 Annual Report 772, 820 ¶ 199 (April 13, 2000) (citing *Velásquez Rodríguez Case*, [Honduras], Inter-Am. Ct. H.R. (ser. C) No. 4, 91, 113, 123 ¶¶ 59, 88 (July 29, 1988)).

is exempted from the exhaustion requirement if indigency or a "generalised fear in the legal community" prevents her from getting the legal assistance she needs to exhaust domestic remedies.[101] If prevailing case law indicates that a particular domestic remedy provides "no reasonable prospect of success," it can be argued that the remedy is not effective.[102]

2.5.3 Unwarranted Delay of Domestic Remedies

The Convention also excuses petitioners from proving exhaustion if their government subjects their domestic claims to "unwarranted delay."[103] Unwarranted delay has no set definition, but in cases of alleged torture and extrajudicial executions, as few as two years for investigation has been deemed to constitute unwarranted delay.[104]

The Commission ties the rule of unwarranted delay to the concept of effectiveness, pointing out that delay causes evidence to dete-

---

[101] Advisory Opinion OC-11/90, *Exceptions to the Exhaustion of Domestic Remedies (Art. 46(1), 46(2)(a), 46(2)(b) American Convention on Human Rights*, Inter Am Ct. H.R. (ser. A) No. 11, 37, 42 ¶ 18 (August 10, 1990).

[102] *See Gary T. Graham, now known as Shaka Sankofa*, Case 11.193, Report No. 51/00 [United States], *to be published in* IACHR 2000 Annual Report ¶ 60 (June 15, 2000) (citing *De Wilde, Oomas and Versyp ("Vagrancy Cases")*, 12 Eur. Ct. H.R. (ser. A) at 34 ¶¶ 37, 62 (1971).

[103] American Convention, art. 46(2); *see also* Commission Rules, *supra* note 11, at art. 31(2)(c).

[104] *See, e.g.*, Case 9755, Resolution No. 01a/88 [Chile], IACHR 1987–1988 Annual Report 132, 137 ¶ 7(a) (September 12, 1988); *see also Carandiru*, Case 11.291, Report No. 34/00 [Brazil], IACHR 1999 Annual Report 370, 380–81 ¶¶ 49–51 (April 13, 2000) (seven years without punishment for one perpetrator or compensation to any of the more than 111 prisoners killed or injured by military police was unwarranted delay); *Alonso Eugénio da Silva*, Case 11.598, Report No. 9/00 [Brazil], IACHR 1999 Annual Report 399, 404 ¶ 26 (February 24, 2000) (three-and-a-half year long investigation of fatal police shooting of a suspect, without required motion to judge to extend the investigation beyond thirty days, constituted unwarranted delay); *Marcos Aurelio de Oliveira*, Case 11.599, Report No. 10/00 [Brazil], IACHR 1999 Annual Report 413, 417 ¶ 24 (February 24, 2000) (two years between fatal police shooting of a minor and filing of IACHR petition, without completion of a police investigation, request to court for extension, or intervention by Office of the Attorney General, constituted unwarranted delay); *Joaquín Ortega et al. ("Extrajudicial Executions")*, Case 10.586 et al., Report No. 39/00 [Guatemala], IACHR 1999 Annual Report 772, 820–21 ¶ 201 (April 13, 2000) (7–8 years after 29 extrajudicial executions without any final decisions "clarifying the alleged facts and corresponding responsibility," and no explanation or justification from the government, constituted unwarranted delay).

riorate,[105] so it may be persuasive to make a record on loss of evidence when arguing for this exception.

2.6 Once Domestic Remedies Have Been Exhausted, Is There a Time Limit Within Which a Complaint Must Be Brought in Order to be Admissible?

Petitions should be filed with the Commission within six months of notification of a "final ruling" from the domestic system,[106] or within a "reasonable period of time" after the alleged violation if the petitioner was prevented from using domestic remedies.[107] One potential argument against the *timeliness of petition* defense is that even though domestic remedies were exhausted more than six months before the filing of the petition, the situation complained of in the petition is "continuing and ongoing."[108]

As with exhaustion of domestic remedies, the timeliness requirement is considered to exist for the benefit of the respondent state. If the state does not explicitly raise its objection to the timeliness of the petition within the ordinary briefing schedule, the Commission will rule that the government *tacitly waived* the argument.[109]

---

[105] See *Carandiru*, Case 11.291, Report No. 34/00 [Brazil], IACHR 1999 Annual Report 370, 380 ¶ 49 n.19 (April 13, 2000).

[106] American Convention, art. 46(b); Commission Rules, *supra* note 11, at art. 32(1). For recent cases analyzing the timeliness requirement, *see Joaquín Ortega et al. ("Extrajudicial Executions")*, Case 10.586 et al., Report No. 39/00 [Guatemala], IACHR 1999 Annual Report 772, 820 ¶ 199 (April 13, 2000) and *Mary and Carrie Dann*, Case 11.140, Report No. 99/99 [United States], IACHR 1999 Annual Report 286, 305 ¶ 87 (September 27, 1999).

[107] Commission Rules, *supra* note 11, at art. 32(2). For recent cases analyzing the reasonable period requirement, *see Carandiru*, Case 11.291, Report No. 34/00 [Brazil], IACHR 1999 Annual Report 370, 381 ¶¶ 51–53 (April 13, 2000), *Marcos Aurelio de Oliveira*, Case 11.599, Report No. 10/00 [Brazil], IACHR 1999 Annual Report, 413, 418 ¶ 26 (February 24, 2000) and *Andres Aylwin Azocar et al.*, Case 11.863, Report No. 137/99 [Chile], IACHR 1999 Annual Report 536, 542 ¶ 27 (December 27, 1999).

[108] *See, e.g., Mary and Carrie Dann*, Case 11.140, Report No. 99/99 [United States], IACHR 1999 Annual Report 286, 305 ¶ 87 (September 27, 1999).

[109] *Velásquez Rodriguez Case*, Preliminary Objections [Honduras], (ser. C) No 1 ¶ 88 (June 26, 1987); *Ramón Mauricio García-Prieto Giralt*, Case 11.697, Report No. 27/99 [El Salvador], IACHR 1998 Annual Report 111, 116–17 ¶ 35 (March 9, 1999). For recent Commission cases applying the tacit waiver of timeliness doctrine, *see Monsignor Oscar Arnulfo Romero y Galdámez*, Case 11.481, Report No. 37/00 [El Salvador], IACHR 1999 Annual Report 671, 677 ¶ 26 (April 13, 2000); *Rudolph Baptiste*, Case 11.743, Report No. 38/00 [Grenada], IACHR 1999 Annual

2.7 Concurrent Jurisdiction—If Another International Body Is Examining the Matter, Can the Mechanism in Question Still Admit It?

The Commission and the Court will not consider a petition if it is "pending in another international proceeding for settlement."[110] This doctrine is generally known as *duplication of procedures*.[111] Extraconventional procedures and mechanisms, such as Working Groups and Special Rapporteurs of the UN Commission on Human Rights (see Chapter 3), are not considered to constitute "international proceedings," because they do not provide "a mechanism whereby the violation denounced can be effectively resolved between the petitioner and the authorities of the State or . . . lead to a decision that ends the litigation and/or gives other bodies jurisdiction."[112] If a case is before a body that is considered to conduct "international proceedings," for example the Human Rights Committee or the Committee Against Torture (see Chapter 2), the key issue is whether the body examined the same violation as the one alleged at the Commission. The fact that a different petitioner filed the complaint in the Inter-American system does not eliminate the duplication, if the underlying victim and violation are the same.[113] The Commission and the Court will not consider

---

Report 721, 737 ¶ 59 (April 13, 2000); *Joaquín Ortega et al. ("Extrajudicial Executions")*, Case 10.586 et al., Report No. 39/00 [Guatemala], IACHR 1999 Annual Report 772, 822 ¶ 205 (April 13, 2000).

[110] American Convention, art. 46(1)(c); Commission Rules, *supra* note 11, at art. 33(1)(a); *see, e.g., Peter Blaine*, Case 11.827, Report No. 96/98 [Jamaica], IACHR 1998 Annual Report 312, 319 ¶ 40 (December 17, 1998).

[111] *See, e.g., Mariela Barreto Riofano*, Case 12.095, Report No. 30/00 [Peru], IACHR 1999 Annual Report 270, 275 ¶ 24 (February 23, 2000). The Commission has also referred to this concept as *internationalitis litispendeus* and *res judicata*. *Marcos Aurelio de Oliveira*, Case 11.599, Report No. 10/00 [Brazil], IACHR 1999 Annual Report 413, 418 ¶ 27 (February 24, 2000).

[112] *Clemente Ayala Torres et al*, Case 10.545, Report No. 33/98 [Mexico], IACHR 1998 Annual Report 172, 180 ¶ 43 (finding that consideration of the same matter by the United Nations Working Group on Enforced or Involuntary Disappearances did not trigger Convention Article 46(1)(c)); *Mariela Barreto Riofano*, Case 12.095, Report No. 30/00 [Peru], IACHR 1999 Annual Report 270, 275, 276 ¶¶ 25–27 (February 23, 2000) (finding that consideration of the same matter by the Special Rapporteur for Extrajudicial, Summary or Arbitrary Executions of the UN Commission on Human Rights did not trigger American Convention Article 46(1)(c)).

[113] *Victor Alfredo Polay Campos*, Case 11.048, Report No. 32/00 [Peru], IACHR 1999 Annual Report 330, 333–335 ¶¶ 16–23 (March 10, 2000) (dismissing a case owing to a Human Rights Committee decision concerning the same petitioner).

a case if the petition is "substantially the same" as a petition that has already been studied by the Commission or another international organization.[114] The duplication of procedures restriction is tacitly waived if the respondent state does not raise it affirmatively.[115]

2.8 Other Admissibility Criteria

The Convention sets forth three related grounds for dismissing a non-meritorious petition. Petitions to the Commission that are *"manifestly groundless"* or *"out of order"* will be considered inadmissible and closed.[116] Petitioners must also "provide factual allegations that tend to establish that the alleged violations may be *well-founded.*"[117] The Complaint Form provided by the Commission also requests that petitions be "free of political rhetoric."[118] The Commission does not accept "conclusory arguments" by the respondent state that call for an adjudication of the underlying violations to defeat admissibility.[119]

---

[114] American Convention, art. 47(d); Commission Rules, *supra* note 11, at art. 33(1)(b).

[115] *See Rudolph Baptiste*, Case 11.743, Report No. 38/00 [Grenada], IACHR 1999 Annual Report 721, 738 ¶ 60 (April 13, 2000).

[116] American Convention, art. 47(c); Commission Rules, *supra* note 11, at art. 34(b).

[117] American Convention, art. 47(b). For a recent decision applying these provisions, *see Lino César Oviedo*, Case 12.013, Report No. 88/99 [Paraguay], IACHR 1999 Annual Report 322, 326–29 ¶¶ 24–36 (September 27, 1999) (finding the petition inadmissible, in part because the allegation of a violation of the right to be tried by a tribunal previously established by law was undermined by facts alleged by the petitioner demonstrating that the tribunal in question had been legislated before the petitioner's trial).

[118] *Complaint Form, in* Basic Documents Pertaining to Human Rights in the Inter-American System OAS/Ser.L/V/I.4 Rev.7 at 197 (January 2000), *available at* <http://www.cidh.oas.org/email.htm>. The complaint form is reproduced in Appendix 6–A.

[119] *Joaquín Ortega et al. ("Extrajudicial Executions")*, Case 10.586 et al., Report No. 39/00 [Guatemala], IACHR 1999 Annual Report 772, 824 ¶ 210 (April 13, 2000) (Guatemalan government's allegation that the cases were inadmissible for "failing to state a cognizable claim," based "exclusively" on the argument that the killings in question were not committed by state agents, called for an analysis that should be made at the merits stage, not the admissibility stage).

3. Substantive Rights and Important Jurisprudence

3.1 Civil and Political Rights

3.1.1 Right to Seek and Receive Asylum

In 1948, Article XXVII of the American Declaration established the right to seek asylum in the Americas, stating that: "Every person has the right, in case of pursuit not resulting from ordinary crimes, to seek and receive asylum in foreign territory, in accordance with the laws of each country and with international agreements."[120] The 1969 American Convention reiterated the right to seek asylum in Article 22(7): "Every person has the right to seek and be granted asylum in a foreign territory, in accordance with the legislation of the state and international conventions, in the event he is being pursued for political offenses or related common crimes."[121]

Despite this early establishment of refugee rights, the OAS has never conceived of refugee protection as one of its key missions or goals. OAS organs have become involved with various refugee situations, but the OAS has had no uniform or consistent approach to the question of refugees in the Americas. Instead, the regional body has repeatedly ceded responsibility and authority over refugee situations to the United Nations, or, in one important migration emergency, a sub-regional arrangement. These statements apply as well to the Commission's approach. The Commission's refugee protection activities have taken place almost exclusively through its report writing functions, and reflect the decision of the refugee rights advocacy community not to utilize the mechanisms extensively. Following is a description of the Inter-American human rights system's major contributions categorized into contentious cases, country reports, and annual reports.

Contentious Cases

The right to asylum is protected in American Declaration Article XXVII. The Commission's first published deportation case involved a Costa Rican citizen of Polish origin being removed from the United States. The case was declared inadmissible "inasmuch as the events denounced bore no relation to a disregard of human rights by the government against which it was directed."[122]

---

[120] American Declaration on the Rights and Duties of Man, art. XXVII, *in* Bibliography of Cited International Instruments.
[121] American Convention, art. 22(7).
[122] Communication No. 1593 [United States], IACHR Report on the Work

In 1970, two Cuban nationals detained in Nicaragua for lack of travel documents petitioned the Commission.[123] The Nicaraguan government had ordered both men deported but, unable to send them to Cuba, held them in indefinite detention.[124] The Commission referred the cases to the Regional Office of the UNHCR in Latin America.[125] Case 1687 was referred to UNHCR "so that a solution favorable to the interested party might be sought, inasmuch as there had been no violation of a human right by the Government of Nicaragua." In case 1699, the Regional Representative of UNHCR stated that "he hoped to ascertain from the Nicaraguan authorities whether the interested party was a 'refugee' within the mandate of the High Commissioner; and that if this were the case, he would try to facilitate his repatriation provided there were assurances 'that such repatriation is completely voluntary on the part of the interested party.'"[126] The case report ended with the Commission's decision to maintain contact with UNHCR, but the case does not reappear in subsequent annual reports, and there is no clarification about why UNHCR would seek to repatriate someone who had been determined to be a refugee. In neither case did the Commission invoke or analyze the implications for the case of Declaration Article XXVII.

In 1972, the Commission reported that "several Haitian political refugees" had complained of arbitrary arrest by the authorities in the Dominican Republic.[127] The government failed to respond to the

---

Accomplished by the Inter-American Commission on Human Rights During Its Twenty-First Session, OEA/Ser.L/V/II.21, Doc. 27, 21–22 (April 7 through 17, 1969).

[123] Communication No. 1687 [Nicaragua], IACHR Report on the Work Accomplished by the Inter-American Commission on Human Rights During Its Twenty-Fifth Session 34–35 (March 1 through 12, 1971), *available at* <http://www.wcl.american.edu/pub/humright/digest/inter-american/english/annual/71part3/comm1687.html>; Communication No. 1699 [Nicaragua], IACHR Report on the Work Accomplished by the Inter-American Commission on Human Rights During Its Twenty-Sixth Session 38–39 (October 27 through November 4, 1971) *available at* <http://www.wcl.american.edu/pub/humright/digest/inter-american/english/annual/71part3/comm1699.html>.

[124] *Id.*
[125] *Id.*
[126] Communication No. 1699, *supra* note 123.
[127] Communications Nos. 1526 and 1545 [Dominican Republic], IACHR Report on the Work Accomplished by the Inter-American Commission on Human Rights During Its Twenty-Sixth Session 39–40 (October 27 through November 4, 1971) *available at* <http://www.wcl.american.edu/pub/humright/digest/interamerican/english/annual/71part3/comm1526,1545.html>.

Commission's requests for information, but after the Commission announced it was presuming the accuracy of the facts contained in the petition, UNHCR informed the Commission that "according to information in that office," the refugees had been released by the Dominican authorities "without requiring that they leave the country."[128] UNHCR provided other general assurances about treatment of Haitian refugees in the Dominican Republic, and the Commission closed the file.[129]

In 1974, the Commission released a set of decisions on individual petitions against Chile.[130] The petitions described groups of petitioners who had been arrested and tortured.[131] Many of them were missing and some had already been found dead.[132] The Chilean authorities participated in the Commission process, denying responsibility for violations.[133] Refugee issues arose tangentially in some of these cases. Case 1774 involved a petition filed by Amnesty International and the International Commission of Jurists on behalf of political opponents and "political refugees from other countries" subjected to mass arrests and summary executions.[134] The Chilean government asserted as to one Uruguayan national believed by the petitioners to have been disappeared, "the whereabouts [are] not known."[135] The Chilean government also stated that two women who had been arrested without being informed for the reasons of their arrest, "had sought asylum."[136] There is no further information given to explain this statement; for example, whether the women were arrested because they were seeking

---

[128] Id.
[129] Id.
[130] Case 1774 [Chile], IACHR 1974 Annual Report 35; Case 1786 [Chile], IACHR 1974 Annual Report 7 (Oct. 25, 1973); Case 1790 [Chile], IACHR 1974 Annual Report 8 (Nov. 9, 1973); Case 1803 [Chile], IACHR 1974 Annual Report 10 (March 2 1974); Case 1809 [Chile], IACHR 1974 Annual Report 11 (March 18, 1974); Case 1810 [Chile], IACHR 1974 Annual Report 12 (March 26, 1974).
[131] Id.
[132] Id.
[133] See Case 1799 [Chile], IACHR 1974 Annual Report 9 (Feb. 21, 1974). (quoting the Chilean government note of March 14, 1974 ("That the Government of Chile is not violating nor will it ever violate human rights and will remain faithful to the principles of justice and equity that make it possible and compulsory to investigate and prosecute the criminal activities of anti-social elements.... That the terms of the [Commission] report were unacceptable and the Government of Chile rejected them categorically ... supported by the traditional Chilean policy of respect for human rights.").
[134] Case 1774, *supra* note 130.
[135] Id.
[136] Id.

asylum or whether the government wanted to show that the women must be in good condition if they were asking to remain in Chile. Nor did the Commission make a factual finding that the women actually had asked for asylum.

Another case of mistreatment of a political refugee by the country of asylum was reported in 1980. A Cuban national granted asylum in the United States accused the United States of kidnapping him in the Dominican Republic for prosecution.[137] The case was closed because the petitioner failed to respond to requests for additional information.[138] The Commission found that Cuba violated the right to asylum of one of its own nationals in 1982 by refusing to allow her to travel abroad for the purposes of seeking asylum.[139]

In 1988, the Commission launched an emergency effort on behalf of a group of Salvadoran refugees in Colomoncagua, Honduras, a number of whom were reported to have been killed, wounded, arrested, raped, and tortured by members of the Honduran army. The petitioners requested that the Commission act to secure the safety of the refugees, including those detained. The Commission requested Honduras to adopt precautionary measures to ensure that the acts covered by the denunciation would be actively and rapidly investigated, as well as to safeguard the victims and to preserve evidence for investigation. It further requested that the government adopt timely measures to prevent a repetition of the occurrences and ensure respect for the principle of "no return" (non-refoulement) stipulated in Article 22(8) of the American Convention. The government provided certain information, which was considered unsatisfactory by the petitioners. The Commission, employing the "presumption of truth rule" of Article 39 of its Rules of Procedure, requested that the government of Honduras conduct an investigation and to indicate the measures it proposed to indemnify the victims or their heirs.[140] When the Commission's request was ignored, the Commission requested that the Court take provisional measures, which it did. However, while the case was still pending, the Court was informed of the assassination of two witnesses in the proceedings. Additional measures were ordered, and Honduras submitted proof to the Court that it was conducting investigations into the killings of these individuals.[141]

---

[137] Case 1983 [United States] adopted by the IACHR at its 656th meeting, April 8, 1980. OEA/Ser.L/V/II.49, Doc. 39, (14 April 1980).

[138] *Id.*

[139] Case 7602 [Cuba] IACHR 1982 Annual Report 79 (March 8, 1982).

[140] Case 9619 [Honduras] IACHR 1986–1987Annual Report 75; *see also* Cerna, *supra* note 74, at 108–109.

[141] Case 9619, *supra* note 140.

In 1993, a petition protesting a pending deportation from Canada ended in an inadmissibility finding, but the Commission made some indicative statements regarding the application of Declaration Article XXVII. In that case, a citizen of Trinidad whose Canadian husband died and left her without status, faced deportation with her five children.[142] She sought asylum, in addition to other immigration remedies, but was found by an administrative body not to have a credible basis for the claim. The Commission found the petition inadmissible for failure to exhaust domestic remedies,[143] but not without stating that the petitioner "did not receive asylum because an independent, and impartial panel determined that she had not demonstrated a credible basis on which she might be found to be a Convention refugee."[144] The Commission cited *Maroufidou v. Sweden*[145] for the proposition that a deportation is acceptable if arrived at in accordance with a domestic legal procedure with "no evidence of bad faith or abuse of power."[146] The Commission also noted that the petitioner had received "several humanitarian and compassionate reviews" to determine whether extraordinary circumstances justified her continued stay in Canada.[147] The Commission did not make clear whether this additional process would be a necessary factor in satisfying a *Maroufidou*-based analysis.

In 1997, the Commission published its most important contentious refugee decision, the Haitian Interdiction Case. This case concerned the United States' practice of interdicting and repatriating Haitian boat people.[148] By the time of the decision, U.S. policy toward Haitian boat people had evolved through several stages, and the Commission examined essentially four practices: interdiction of boats and refugee processing on board boats or at Guantanamo Bay, in place from 1981 through May 1992; interdiction and direct repatriation coupled with in-country processing of refugee claims, in place from May 1992 through May 1994; interdiction and processing aboard the U.S. naval ship Comfort, which operated from May 1994 through July 1994, and interdiction and removal for processing to "safe haven" camps in various

---

[142] Case 11.092 Decision of the Commission as to the Admissibility, [Canada], IACHR 1994 Annual Report 32 (October 6, 1993).
[143] *See id.*, ¶ 29 and final Conclusion.
[144] *Id.*, ¶ 31.
[145] Anna Maroufidou v. Sweden, United Nations Human Rights Committee Communication No. R.13/58 (5 September 1979), U.N. Doc. Supp. No. 40 (A/36/40) at 160 (1981), *cited in* Case No. 11.092, *supra* note 142, ¶¶ 32–34.
[146] *Id., cited in* ¶ 33.
[147] Case No. 11.092, *supra* note 142, ¶ 31.
[148] *Haitian Interdiction*, Case 10.675, Report No. 51/96 [United States], IACHR 1996 Annual Report 550 (March 13, 1997).

third countries, which began in July 1994.[149] The petitioners provided extensive documentation and witness testimony demonstrating that people returned to Haiti as a result of these programs had been arrested, tortured, and killed. The petitioners supplied statistics showing that a Haitian asylum applicant enjoyed a drastically lower likelihood of prevailing if the claim was processed through the interdiction program rather than in the U.S. domestic asylum adjudication system.[150] Statements by U.S. government officials were also introduced to the effect that an estimated one third of the people fleeing Haiti in boats were not bound for the United States but were planning to seek asylum in other countries.[151]

The Commission held that the United States violated the rights of both named petitioners and unknown refugees who had been subjected to the interdiction policy. The Commission found a violation of Declaration Article XXVII, using a "dual cumulative criteria" test patterned on the "in accordance with the laws of each country and with international agreements" phrase in the Declaration.[152] The decision conceded that this language, which did not appear in an initial draft of the Declaration, was inserted to protect OAS member states' sovereignty over the asylum process.[153] The Commission stated that the effect of this language is to condition Article XXVII protection on a finding of both international and domestic law obligations operating on the country in question.[154]

First, the Commission found that the interdiction policy violated international law, accepting UNHCR's position that Article 33 of the Refugee Convention extends to the high seas.[155] The Commission also found that the interdiction policy violated customary law of *nonrefoulement*.[156] Second step, the Commission found that the United States was responsible under Declaration Article XXVII,[157] because throughout the policy changes and domestic litigation the United States "recognized and acknowledged the right of Haitian refugees to seek and receive asylum in the United States."[158] The Commission also noted

---

[149] *See id.*, ¶¶ 57, 160.
[150] *Id.*, ¶ 6.
[151] *Id.*, ¶ 161.
[152] *Id.*, ¶ 153.
[153] *Id.*, ¶ 152.
[154] *Id.*, ¶ 158.
[155] *Id.*, ¶¶ 156–157.
[156] *Id.*, ¶ 88.
[157] *Id.*, ¶¶ 159–163.
[158] *Id.*, ¶ 160.

that Article XXVII establishes the right "to seek and receive asylum in *foreign territory*,"[159] and the potential illegality of preventing Haitian boat people from traveling to countries other than the United States.[160]

Apart from Declaration Article XXVII, the Commission also found that the United States had breached the Article I rights to life, liberty, and security, Article II right to equality before the law, and the Article XVIII right to resort to the courts,[161] and recommended that the United States pay compensation to the victims.[162]

In 1998, the Center for Justice and International Law (CEJIL) and the Open Society Institute's Forced Migration Projects filed a petition on behalf of 120 Cuban nationals detained in the Bahamas, a Declaration State.[163] The petition argued that the Bahamian authorities' refusal to consider the Cubans' refugee claims violated the same provisions addressed in the Haitian interdiction case: Article I, Article II, Article XVIII, and Article XXVII.[164] The petition also raised the Article XXV prohibition on arbitrary detention, citing the Bahamas' failure to establish a "mechanism for determining the reasonableness and necessity of detaining asylum seekers."[165] At the time of writing, this petition had not been decided.

CEJIL, Human Rights Watch/Americas, the Iniciativa de Solidaridad con Colombia, and the U.S. Committee for Refugees filed a petition in July 1999 against the Venezuelan government on behalf of 1000 displaced Colombian villagers who had crossed into Venezuelan territory four days earlier.[166] The international community was not given access to the group, which included children and elderly people, and the petition expressed concern about their living conditions.[167] The petition also warned of the possibility of the group's imminent deportation to Colombian territory, where dozens of villagers had been killed in violent attacks by paramilitary troops.[168] This petition also remained pending at the time of writing.

---

[159] *Id.*, ¶¶ 161–162.
[160] *Id.*
[161] *Id.*, ¶¶ 183–188.
[162] *Id.*, ¶ 189.
[163] Arthur C. Helton, *Securing Refugee Protection in the Americas: The Inter-American System on Human Rights and the Rights of Asylum seekers*, 6 SW J.L. TRADE AM. 129, 134–135 (1999).
[164] *Id.* at 136–38.
[165] *Id.* at 138.
[166] Letter of CEJIL, Human Rights Watch/Americas, Iniciativa de Solidaridad con Colombia, and U.S. Committee for Refugees, to the Inter-American Commission on Human Rights (July 1, 1999), at 1 (on file with authors).
[167] *Id.* at 2.
[168] *Id.*

Country Reports

The Inter-American human rights system's primary response to refugee crises has been through the reporting activities of the Commission. Since the Commission published its first country report in 1962,[169] it has developed country visits and reporting into a powerful tool for protection. The Commission has published roughly 53 country reports.[170] A description of the most recent and significant refugee reporting by the Commission follows.

In 1983, the Commission settled a contentious case by publishing a report on "the Situation of Human Rights of a Segment of the Nicaraguan Population of Miskito Origin."[171] This report was organized with reference to particular rights.[172] Under a discussion of the right to residence and movement, the Commission found that the forced relocation of nearly 8,500 Miskito people was not carried out in a discriminatory fashion but that they should be helped to return to their ancestral region.[173]

In 1993, the Commission devoted a chapter of its country report on Guatemala to the situation of refugees and displaced persons in Guatemala.[174] The report noted "numerous allegations . . . that it is difficult for these people to exercise the human rights recognized in the American Convention, particularly the right to humane treatment (Article 5), the right to personal liberty (Article 7), the right to a fair trial (Article 8), freedom of movement and residence (Article 22), the right to property (Article 21), their right to participate in government, the right of assembly and of association (Articles 15, 16, and 23)."[175] The report listed six conditions for a safe and dignified return:[176]

---

[169] *See* IACHR, REPORT ON THE SITUATION REGARDING HUMAN RIGHTS IN CUBA, OEA/Ser.L/V/II.4 Doc. 2 (1962); *see also* Cecilia Medina, *The Role of Country Reports in the Inter-American System of Human Rights, in* THE INTER-AMERICAN SYSTEM OF HUMAN RIGHTS, *supra* note 4, at 115, 118.

[170] *See Publications of the Inter-American Commission on Human Rights, in* Basic Documents Pertaining to Human Rights in the Inter-American System 185 (January 2000).

[171] IACHR, *Right to Residence and Movement*, in REPORT ON THE SITUATION OF HUMAN RIGHTS OF A SEGMENT OF THE NICARAGUAN POPULATION OF MISKITO ORIGIN, OEA/Ser.L/V/11.62 (1983).

[172] *Id.* at 112.

[173] *Id.*, ¶ 31.

[174] IACHR, *The Situation of Refugees and Displaced Persons in Guatemala, in* REPORT ON THE SITUATION OF HUMAN RIGHTS IN GUATEMALA, OEA/Ser.L/V/11.83 (1993); *see also* IACHR, *Freedom of Movement and Residence, in* REPORT ON THE SITUATION OF HUMAN RIGHTS IN GUATEMALA, OEA/Ser.L/V/11.61 (1983).

[175] *Id.*

[176] *Id.* at 63–64.

- Be a voluntary, individual decision
- Guarantee that refugees will be allowed to return to their lands "to take possession of them"
- Recognition of the refugees' rights to organize and associate freely
- Right to life, to humane treatment, and community
- Accompaniment and ongoing access by UNHCR
- Freedom of movement, both national and international

> **Focus on: Maria**
> Maria has been forced from her home by security forces. She and her younger children are living in an abandoned warehouse. The Commission has referred to standards of return that should allow her to go back only when she is willing to do so and when it is safe for her to do so.

Actions by paramilitary groups, along with those of guerrillas and the armed forces, have been primary causes of internal displacement during the last decade in Colombia. Many families flee from their homes in order to avoid the forced recruitment of their children into any of these three armed groups. In 1998, approximately 1.4 million Colombians were internally displaced. Though few sought recognition as refugees in neighboring countries, more than 180,000 who did seek refuge were living in Venezuela, Ecuador and Panama.[177]

In 1999, the IACHR published its "Third Report on the Human Rights Situation in Colombia" following an on-site visit to the country in 1997.[178] The Report devoted a chapter to the situation of the internally displaced in Colombia in which the Commission recognized the seriousness of the situation of the displaced in Colombia and usefulness of designating a special rapporteur to strengthen relations between the IACHR and the UN Representative to the Secretary General on Displaced Persons. Most importantly, the report admits that, while IDPs are entitled to enjoy the fundamental guarantees provided for in the American Convention, certain shortcomings exist in the application of human rights and humanitarian law to IDPs.[179] These "gray areas" of the law are addressed by the Guiding Principles on Internal Displacement (see Appendix 3-C), which the Commission supports as

---

[177] U.S. COMMITTEE FOR REFUGEES, WORLD REFUGEE SURVEY 1999 258 (1999).
[178] IACHR, *Chapter VI-Internal Displacement*, in THIRD REPORT ON THE SITUATION OF HUMAN RIGHTS IN COLOMBIA, OEA/Ser. L/V/II.102 Doc. 9 rev. 1 (1999).
[179] *Id.*, ¶¶ 6–8.

the "most comprehensive restatement of norms applicable to the internally displaced."[180]

The report emphasized the importance of preventing "the conditions that lead to forced internal displacement"[181] and the obligation to respect IDPs' "rights to life, physical integrity and personal security."[182] The report concluded with a number of specific recommendations to Colombia, including observation of the Guiding Principles and steps to ensure resettlement or return to habitual places of residence.[183]

> **Focus on: Maria**
> Maria is part of a mass internal displacement. She was forced from her home by security forces who suspect her of aiding an insurgent group. She can ask the Commission for protection of her rights as protected by the regional treaties and as described in the Guiding Principles on Internal Displacement. This means the government should help her go back to her home in safety and the government should respect her rights to life, physical integrity, and personal security.

In February 2000, the Commission published a *Report on the Situation of Human Rights of Asylum Seekers Within the Canadian Refugee Determination System* following an on-site visit carried out in October of 1997.[184] Written at the request of the Canadian government, the report recommended four improvements in the Canadian asylum system "to further enhance its compliance with the standards of the American Declaration . . . and the international instruments which assist in its interpretation."[185] The recommendations include first moving the initial determination on eligibility to enter the asylum screening process from the purview of border personnel to the jurisdiction of the refugee adjudication specialists.[186] The second recommendation is for expanded administrative and judicial review of negative asylum determinations, including legal aid.[187] The third recommendation urges various improve-

---

[180] *Id.*, ¶ 8.
[181] *Id.* at Recommendation 1.
[182] *Id.* at Recommendation 2.
[183] *Id.*, ¶ 8.
[184] IACHR, REPORT ON THE SITUATION OF HUMAN RIGHTS OF ASYLUM SEEKERS WITHIN THE CANADIAN REFUGEE DETERMINATION SYSTEM, OEA/Ser.L/V/II.106 Doc. 40 rev. (2000).
[185] *Id.*, ¶ 172.
[186] *Id.*, ¶ 173.
[187] *Id.*, ¶ 174.

ments in the adjudication and review procedures available to asylum-seekers being detained on public security grounds.[188] The Commission also made a fourth recommendation to the effect that recent improvements in the handling of family reunification issues be implemented at all levels of Canadian immigration adjudication.[189]

The Canadian asylum report reflects a significant evolution in the role of the Commission. Formerly focused on fact-finding concerning massive violations by repressive regimes, the Commission now may serve as a consultant on technical protection matters. The Canadian report offers some insight into the Commission's analysis of asylum-related norms. In its introduction, the Commission acknowledged the factors governments must weigh in identifying and protecting refugees within their borders. The Commission notes that its analysis of the situation of refugees is "necessarily grounded in the need to ensure that the fundamental human rights of refugees and asylum seekers are rigorously respected, in particular the right to seek asylum . . . and to respect for the full range of their protected civil and political, and economic, social and cultural rights."[190] The Commission "has taken into full account" the "right and . . . duty of the State . . . to manage the refugee system so as to deter abuse and safeguard the rights of persons genuinely at risk, as well as to control the ingress and egress of persons across its borders, and to protect related interests such as citizen and national security."[191]

In the Canada report, the Commission recognizes the UN Refugee Convention and Protocol as "the primary instruments governing the status and protection of asylum seekers . . . ,"[192] and relies on UNHCR's evaluation of Canadian border processing procedures.[193] Also as part of its discussion about the adjudication at the border, the Commission addresses underlying fairness issues. In the context of Canada's use of border personnel to determine initial entry into the asylum processing procedures, the Commission states that "the basic principles of equal protection and due process reflected in the American Declaration require predictable procedures and consistency in decision-making at each stage of the process."[194] The Commission notes that this initial determination at the border "potentially involves questions of life and

---

[188] *Id.*, ¶ 179.
[189] *Id.*, ¶ 180.
[190] *Id.*, ¶ 20.
[191] *Id.*
[192] *Id.*, ¶ 21.
[193] *Id.*, ¶ 55.
[194] *Id.*, ¶ 52.

death"[195] and "may involve sophisticated interpretations of fact and law,"[196] and that "it must necessarily be made pursuant to certain minimum guarantees."[197]

In making its recommendations to the Canadian government, the Commission invokes Declaration Articles II on equal protection,[198] V on protection of the family,[199] VI on the right to establish a family,[200] VII on special protection for minor children,[201] XVII on recognition of juridical personality and civil rights,[202] XVIII on fair trial,[203] XXVI on due process,[204] XXV on liberty,[205] and XXVII on asylum.[206] As in the Haitian Interdiction Case, the Commission derives the "right to be heard" from due process protections contained in the Declaration.[207] The Commission also relies on the "right of access" long recognized as "a necessary aspect" of the Article XVIII right to resort to the courts.[208]

3.1.2 The Right to Family and Private Life

Duty Not to Interfere with Family Life or Private Life

In two claims decided in the 1970s, the Commission found that the Cuban government violated the right to formation and protection of families by preventing the petitioners from leaving the country to join their spouses.[209] Recently, the Commission admitted a case arguing that the disappearance and subsequent adoption of a child constitutes a violation of the right to formation and protection of families.[210]

---

[195] *Id.*, ¶ 59.
[196] *Id.*, ¶ 60.
[197] *Id.*, ¶ 59.
[198] *See, e.g., id.*, ¶ 60.
[199] *See, e.g., id.*, ¶ 162.
[200] *See, e.g., id.*, ¶ 162.
[201] *See, e.g., id.*, ¶ 163.
[202] *See, e.g., id.*, ¶ 60.
[203] *See, e.g., id.*
[204] *See, e.g., id.*
[205] *See, e.g., id.*, ¶ 137.
[206] *See, e.g., id.*
[207] *See id.*, ¶ 60.
[208] *See id.*, ¶ 125 & n.64.
[209] *Calvar Rivero Family*, Case 7602, Resolution. No. 6/82 [Cuba], IACHR 1981–1982 Annual Report 79 (March 8, 1982); *Álvarez Hernández*, Case 7898, Resolution. No. 11/82 [Cuba], IACHR 1981–1982 Annual Report 68 (March 8, 1982).
[210] *Emiliano Castro Tortrino*, Case 11.597, Report No. 7/98 [Argentina], IACHR 1997 Annual Report 51(March 2, 1998).

The Commission is also considering a case alleging a violation of the right to protection of mothers in children in the context of an extra-judicial execution.[211]

> **Focus on: Chen**
> Chen has been involuntarily expatriated from her country. If her country refuses to let her children leave to join her, she can ask the Commission to rule that it has violated her right to the formation and protection of families.

3.2 Social and Economic Rights

3.2.1 Access to Food, Clothing, and Shelter

To the best of the authors' knowledge, there are no contentious cases about these rights in the Inter-American system. The Commission has addressed these rights in the context of country reports.[212]

> **Focus on: Maria**
> Maria is part of a mass internal displacement. She and her younger children are living in an abandoned warehouse, where they lack adequate food, shelter, medical care, and education. Under the American Declaration, Maria has a right to all these things. She can file an individual petition asking the Commission for immediate assistance, but the Commission is most likely to help her by examining the plight of everyone in her situation. The Commission could carry out a mission to examine the living conditions of Maria and the other displaced persons, holding a hearing asking the government to explain why the situation exists, and writing a report about that will be adopted by the OAS General Assembly. The Commission can also write follow-up reports tracking whether the government is implementing its recommendations.

---

[211] *Village of Moiwana*, Case 11.821, Report No. 26/00 [Suriname], IACHR 1999 Annual Report 278 (March 7, 2000).

[212] See IACHR, REPORT ON THE SITUATION OF HUMAN RIGHTS IN CUBA, OEA/Ser.L/V/II.61 Doc.29 rev. 1, Conclusions ¶¶ 19–21 (1983); IACHR, SPECIAL REPORT ON HUMAN RIGHTS IN THE SO-CALLED "COMMUNITIES OF PEOPLES IN RESISTANCE" IN GUATEMALA, OEA/Ser/L/V/II.86 Doc.5 Rev. 1, Measures Recommended ¶¶ e, m, ñ, o, p, q (1994); IACHR, REPORT ON THE SITUATION OF HUMAN RIGHTS IN MEXICO, OEA/Ser. L/V/II.100 Doc. 7 rev. 1 ¶¶ 605–608, 639, 644 (1998); IACHR, THIRD REPORT ON THE SITUATION OF HUMAN RIGHTS IN COLOMBIA, OEA/Ser. L/V/II.102 Doc. 9 rev., Chapter on Economic, Social and Cultural Rights, Recommendations on the Rights of Women ¶¶ 6, 8, 13, Recom-

3.2.2 Access to Health Care

The Commission has found violations of the right to the preservation of health in the context of unhygienic prison conditions.[213] In 1977, the Commission ruled that assimilationist and child labor policies violated the health rights of the Aché indigenous people in Paraguay.[214]

3.2.3 Access to Education

The right to education has arisen in a few decided petitions; the most detailed of these involved the expulsion of Jehovah's Witness children from Argentine schools.[215] The Commission recently granted precautionary measures to prevent an immigrant child living in the Dominican Republic "from being deprived of her right to attend school and to receive the education provided to other children of Dominican nationality."[216]

> **Focus on: Maria**
> Maria is an internally displaced person. Her identity documents were seized. Even though Maria is not an immigrant in her country, her children lack documentation. She can ask the Commission for emergency measures requiring the government to permit her children to go to school.

3.2.4 Property Rights

The law on the right to property is mixed and a number of cases are pending that will help shape the law. Most of the published cases were declared inadmissible. Admissibility requirements that have proven

---

mendations on The Rights of Persons Deprived of Their Liberty, ¶¶ 6, 9 (1999); IACHR, REPORT ON THE SITUATION OF HUMAN RIGHTS IN PERU, OEA/Ser. L/V/II.106 Doc. 59, Chapter on Economic, Social and Cultural Rights, and Prison Situation, Chapter on Women's Rights ¶¶ 27(6), 27(19), Chapter on the Rights of Indigenous Communities ¶¶ 39(2)–39(7) (2000).

[213] For example, *see* Case 6091, Resolution No. 3/82 [Cuba], IACHR 1981–1982 Annual Report 71, 76 (March 8, 1982).

[214] Case 1802 [Paraguay], IACHR 1977 Annual Report, 36, 37 (May 27, 1977).

[215] Case 2137 [Argentina], IACHR 1978 Annual Report, 43 (November 18, 1978).

[216] *Petitions and cases before the Inter-American Commission on Human Rights, Precautionary measures granted or extended by the Commission,* IACHR 1999 Annual Report 57 ¶ 27.

to be particular challenges in right to property cases include, first, the "natural person" rule, meaning that petitioners and victims must be natural persons, not business entities.[217] The second common admissibility problem for property claims is timeliness of the petition. For example, in a 1998 decision, the loss of a Supreme Court appeal marked the point of exhaustion for the purposes of the six month deadline. However, the petitioners went on to request an internal investigation, which the Commission decided was not a "jurisdictional recourse," and the six months time ran while the petitioners pursued the investigation.[218]

Another issue that arises in the admissibility context is the definition of property. The petitioner's underlying right to the property in question must be an absolute, acquired right.[219] The Commission has held that in order for an alleged taking to constitute a "potential direct violation" of the right to property under the Convention, it must have been the result of a state action constituting "clear arbitrariness."[220] If the petitioner/victim recovers her property to her satisfaction, the claim will be ruled inadmissible.[221]

In its report on the displaced Miskito Indians, the Commission invoked the right to property with regard to both the right of indigenous people to ancestral land and possible violations arising from the destruction of the Miskitos' homes, crops, livestock, and other belongings in the course of the forced relocation.[222]

Petitioners used artful arguments in a recent positive admissibility decision. In *Eolo Margaroli and Josefina Ghiringhelli de Margaroli*, the Commission admitted a right to property claim when the petitioners laid out and rebutted possible justifications for the government taking at issue, including "social interest" and "eminent domain."[223] The peti-

---

[217] For a recent example, *see Bendeck-Cohdinsa*, Petition, Report No. 106/99 [Honduras], IACHR 1999 Annual Report 311 ¶ 30 (September 27, 1999).

[218] *See Anselmo Rios Aquilar*, Case 11.507, Report No. 32/98 [Mexico], IACHR 1998 Annual Report 362 ¶ 3 (May 5, 1998).

[219] *See Carlos García Saccone*, Case 11.671, Report No. 8/98 [Argentina], IACHR 1997 Annual Report 193, 199 (March 2, 1998). For example, the mere possibility of a money award does not by itself constitute property. *Id.*, ¶ 32.

[220] *Id.*, ¶ 37.

[221] *Norma Dominga Carpi de Szukalo (Widowed)*, Case 11.707, Report No. 69/99 [Argentina] IACHR 1999 Annual Report 99, 108 ¶¶ 48–49 (May 4, 1999).

[222] IACHR, REPORT ON THE SITUATION OF HUMAN RIGHTS OF A SEGMENT OF THE NICARAGUAN POPULATION OF MISKITO ORIGIN, OEA/Ser.L/V/11.62, 125, Right to Property (1983).

[223] *Eolo Margaroli and Josefina Ghiringhelli de Margaroli*, Case 11.400, Report No. 104/99 [Argentina], IACHR 1999 Annual Report 76, 81 ¶ 27 (September 27, 1999).

tioners further argued that "they do not want to undermine the State's discretionary right to conduct economic, social, and cultural policies, but rather to show that the principles followed in the case are unreasonable. A fair balance between the general interest and basic rights is missing."[224] Arguments such as these are critical to guide adjudicators and situate them in their appropriate role of balancing interests as they establish the substantive criteria of previously unexplored rights.

> **Focus on: Maria**
> Maria was forced from her home by security forces who suspect her of aiding an insurgent group. Maria can argue that the government violated her rights under American Declaration Article XXIII and American Convention Article 21. Maria should be careful to explain that the government has the right to take property in the public interest but that in her case the government's needs were not as important as Maria's basic rights. She should also point out that the violent way the government took her property shows it was not a lawful taking.

4. Effectiveness of Inter-American Mechanisms

The Inter-American human rights mechanisms' potential usefulness for refugees, asylum-seekers, and internally displaced persons lies in the Commission's agility and the Court's proven effectiveness in gaining compliance with its orders. Once described as the "Hemispheric Grand Jury,"[225] the Commission's missions and reporting powers, combined with its ability to take precautionary measures, render it uniquely able to gather information on emerging mass migration situations and apply pressure in individual cases.

At the same time, the case-decision function is relatively slow, often several years from filing to resolution, and the Commission's and Court's record in preventing deportations is not very encouraging. As one commentator observed of the Haitian refugee crisis, "IACHR consideration of the US policy of interdiction and forced repatriation of Haitian asylum-seekers seemed little more than a side-show, even though the refugee situation influenced the United States' eventual decision to intervene forcefully. However, the IACHR reports remained an integral aspect of the OAS response to the Haitian crisis."[226]

---

[224] *Id.*
[225] Tom Farer, *The Rise of the Inter-American Human Rights Regime: No Longer a Unicorn, Not Yet an Ox*, in THE INTER-AMERICAN SYSTEM OF HUMAN RIGHTS, *supra* note 4 at 31, 32.
[226] Joan Fitzpatrick, *States of Emergency in the Inter-American Human Rights*

Compliance with Commission precautionary measures and recommendations is also a problem. One advocate who joined in the petition on behalf of the Colombian refugees in Venezuela stated that they had finally given up on the case because they felt that the time spent did not translate into any improvements on the ground.[227] She stated that the Commission's missions and reports were the most helpful product of the system in terms of augmenting pressure on governments to respect the rights of refugees.[228]

The overloaded Commission, comprised of seven part-time Commissioners and fifteen staff attorneys, is wary of adding new missions to its plate, and in that regard the appointment of a rapporteur for refugee issues to complement the IDP rapporteurship is unlikely, as are the other indicia of high-profile issues, such as a thematic report or spontaneous missions. However, the joining of CEJIL on two major recent refugee protection individual petitions is a promising sign that the most influential NGO in the Inter-American human rights system is concerned with refugee issues. The Canadian report also demonstrates that the Commission is increasingly literate in refugee law and concepts.

UN human rights protection mechanisms, though worth strengthening, still "leave much to be desired."[229] One often suggested alternative is the building and strengthening of regional complaint mechanisms, which could offer the advantages of flexible logistics, familiarity, and local confidence. The need for a more systematic regional arrangement for refugees, asylum-seekers, and IDPs in the Americas is apparent. The absence of an inter-American convention regulating the status of refugees, and of an agency with authority suitable to carry out international protection of refugees, has resulted in sometimes inadequate responses to past refugee and migration emergencies. This absence has not gone unnoticed or unmentioned both within and without the structures of the OAS. In 1965, for example, the Commission conducted a full report on the situation of political refugees in the hemisphere and charged the Juridical Committee with the preparation of a draft convention on refugees.[230] Such a convention was never concluded.

System, in THE INTER-AMERICAN SYSTEM OF HUMAN RIGHTS, *supra* note 4, at 371, 389.

[227] Telephone Interview with Robin Kirk, Human Rights Watch (November 1, 2000).

[228] *Id.*

[229] *See, e.g,* FRANCISCO FORREST MARTIN ET AL., INTERNATIONAL HUMAN RIGHTS LAW AND PRACTICE 13 (1997).

[230] OAS, THE ORGANIZATION OF AMERICAN STATES AND HUMAN RIGHTS 59 (1972).

Another call for an hemispheric arrangement occurred in the early 1980s, when the U.S. government turned to the OAS in an effort to obtain assistance in resettling the thousands of displaced Cubans and Haitians arriving at its shores. Hinting at the government's desire to arrive at an inter-American convention on refugees, Secretary of State Warren Christopher addressed the OAS Permanent Council and outlined a number of challenges which, in his view, required "a concerted response in this hemisphere and in the world community."[231] Pointing to the lack of a mechanism for coping with the displaced or with countries that induce such displacement, Christopher suggested that the OAS was well-situated to provide an "institutional framework for insuring that appropriate legal obligations are carried out and that member nations get the help they need to meet their responsibilities to displaced people."[232]

The United States Committee for Refugees (USCR) has also noted how the OAS remained on the sidelines of conflicts in Central America, which produced large numbers of refugees and internally displaced persons. USCR called for the OAS to accompany the return of refugees and verify the Guatemalan government's adherence to the terms of its agreements and to take on a vital, positive role.[233] More recently, other authorities have pointed to the feasibility of a regional solution, particularly given the success of prior cooperative efforts such as 1989–1994 International Conference on Central American Refugees (CIREFCA) and the 1984 Declaration of Cartagena on Refugees. As one analyst suggests, "the nations of the Americas should expand upon earlier regional efforts and conclude a temporary refuge agreement. This would provide a rapid, efficient, and humane response to refugee and migration emergencies, while ensuring that no one nation would be left to deal with a crisis alone. Such an agreement would provide a genuine measure of security both for individuals and for states."[234] Both the OAS and the Caribbean Community and Common Market (CARICOM) have been suggested as appropriate institutions to deal with refugee and

---

[231] Bureau of Public Affairs, U.S. Department of State, Current Policy No. 201, *Refugees: A Global Issue,* July 23, 1980.

[232] *Id.*

[233] United States Committee on Refugees, Issue Paper, *El Retorno: Guatemala's Risky Repatriation Begins,* February 1993 (on file with authors).

[234] Arthur C. Helton, *Establishing a Comprehensive Scheme for Refugee and Migration Emergencies in the Caribbean Region: Lessons from Recent Haitian and Cuban Emergencies, in* FREE MARKETS, OPEN SOCIETIES, CLOSED BORDERS? TRENDS IN INTERNATIONAL MIGRATION AND IMMIGRATION POLICY IN THE AMERICAS 256 (MAX J. CASTSTRO ED., 1999).

migration emergencies through a treaty scheme that includes reception, ceilings, conditions of stay, duration of stay, and solutions for those in need of permanent homes.[235]

Regional bodies such as the OAS are expected to cooperate with international organizations in addressing situations of refugees, asylum-seekers, and the internally displaced to ensure protection, assistance, and reintegration. Yet regional political bodies body are constrained by a lack of resources and political will, as well as a reluctance to interfere with the domestic affairs of member states. Political rivalries within regional organizations can also limit their effectiveness. There may also be a significant lack of experience and expertise within the organizations in dealing with refugee and displacement issues.[236] In the case of the IACHR, a significant constraint is the existing backlog of cases. Presently, the amount of time elapsing from filing of a petition to final decision ranges from three to five years. Capacity to deal with emergency situations is thus problematic.

The Inter-American system has been widely praised for its contributions to the promotion of human rights. It has been deemed "surprisingly effective" for its ability to conduct work among 35 members states of varying size and interests, to deal with undemocratic governments, and to operate despite serious financial and staff restraints.[237] With regards to IDPs, as one analyst commented that "greater progress has been made in the Americas than perhaps any other continent."[238] But the pace of the progress may require acceleration, since it is expected that new waves of sudden forced migration will continue to occur in the Americas. Governments, non-governmental organizations, and academics must engage in a "systematic analysis of past experiences" and in a "learning process that can prepare all of us better for the next contingency."[239]

---

[235] *Id.*

[236] Roberta Cohen, *The Response of Regional Organizations to Internal Displacement in the Americas*, Conference on Sudden Forced Migration Emergencies in the Americas, Washington, D.C., September 30–October 1, 1997 (on file with authors).

[237] *See* Martin, *supra* note 229, at 17.

[238] *See* Cohen, *supra* note 236, at 2.

[239] Juan E. Méndez, *A Proposal for Action on Sudden Forced Migrations*, Conference on Sudden Forced Migration Emergencies in the Americas, Washington, D.C., September 30–October 1, 1997, at 4 (on file with authors).

5. Other Avenues for Advocacy

Unlike most other regional mechanisms, the Inter-American Commission on Human Rights has the ability *sua sponte* to prepare special reports on the human rights situation in a particular country and/or conduct on-site fact-finding visits. This may occur especially in cases where the seriousness or scale of the human rights violations at issue leads the Commission to believe that the individual complaint mechanism may not produce satisfactory results. Thus, these two features can be considered useful tools as well as viable alternatives to the individual complaint for refugee, asylum-seeker, and IDP advocates alike. Another positive feature of the Inter-American system is the ability of the Court to issue advisory opinions, though these must come at the request of an OAS member state or competent organ.

5.1 On-Site Visits and Country Reports

The Commission has conducted more *in loco* visits than any similar body in the world. On-site visits are conducted to investigate an individual case or to study the general human rights situation in a particular country. Delegations have been sent with this purpose to both OAS member states and to non-member states. The Commission has also in the past sent delegations to third countries to interview refugees who fled repression in their home state. On-site visits and country reports are initiated usually after a large number of complaints against a particular government are received by the Commission. These complaints may come from individuals, NGOs, churches, or other credible sources. A country study may also come at the request of the General Assembly or another political organ of the OAS, or at the invitation of a government to visit its own territory.

During an on-site visit, the delegation generally relies on the government to arrange meetings with important officials, including the president, ministers, and chief of police, and on local NGOs to suggest persons and groups whose testimony they believe the Commission should hear. In addition, the Commission always seeks assurances from the host government that the delegation will have freedom of mobility, access to prisons, and privacy to meet with both individuals and organization leaders. The Commission also expects the government to issue a public expression that persons cooperating with the Commission will not be subject to reprisals for coming forward. However, despite these measures, there have been instances where human rights monitors or witnesses have been killed, disappeared, or exiled for providing testimony to the Commission.

Before traveling to a country for an on-site visit, the Commission must first request the government's permission to visit the country. Following its admission, the Commission will normally travel extensively within the country, holding hearings, calling for meetings, and setting up temporary offices where it can accept further complaints related to its visit. Hearings may be called at any point during an investigation, and are normally adversarial in nature, and in exceptional instances ex-parte. There are no formal requirements; the Commission may request that the state involved supply any necessary information and the parties may be requested to present written or oral statements.

The contents of a country report will generally include a chapter on background information, followed by a description of the current legal and political regime currently in place in that country. Then, specific rights about which the Commission has received petitions are addressed. The results of the Commission's examination of the actual situation are then presented, including all evidence. Finally, the report ends with a series of conclusions and recommendations, which may request that a state take certain preventative measures, conduct investigations into past violations, punish those responsible and grant reparations to the victims and their families.

Once a report is concluded it is published and may be transmitted to the OAS General Assembly for its consideration. Reference to and discussion of a country report at the General Assembly level, sometimes followed by a related resolution, can have a strong impact on a government's behavior. In fact, the very presence of the Commission within a country can have a positive effect on human rights conditions. Should conditions not improve, however, the Commission can later undertake a country study to follow-up on an earlier recommendation to a subject state. This procedure has come to be accepted by the OAS member states.

5.2 The Inter-American Court Advisory Opinion

The Court is empowered to grant advisory opinions in three categories of the American Convention: it may be requested to interpret the Convention by any OAS member state or OAS organ; the Court may also be asked by an OAS member or organ to interpret any other human rights treaty in the hemisphere; finally, the Court may accept a request by a member state to give an opinion regarding the compatibility of that state's domestic laws with the Convention or another human rights treaty. The Court also has wide discretion to refuse a request for advisory opinion if it appears to be a contentious case in disguise or is designed to circumvent the Convention system.

6. Specific Guidance for Advocates

6.1 Framing the Complaint

Familiarity with the format and methods of analysis of the Commission can be of benefit when framing individual denunciations. Relevant portions of an existing report, such as the chapter on IDPs in the 1998 Report on the Situation of Human Rights in Colombia, can be both useful as a model to the advocate and of service to the Commission.

6.2 Supportive Documentation

When filing complaints with the Inter-American Commission on Human Rights, it is important to attach any and all documentation available to support the facts alleged, including newspaper stories, legislation, decisions, and official statements. The petitioner should also include statements by witnesses to the act in question, if possible signed and notarized. Additional information can be sent to the Commission as it becomes available.[240]

6.3 Confidentiality

Traditionally, the Inter-American system operated with a high degree of transparency, with the Commission automatically forwarding all government briefs and Commission decisions to the petitioner, with no restrictions on publicity. In a clearly disadvantageous decision for petitioners, the Court ruled that an Article 50 report, which contains the Commission's preliminary findings, should be sent only to the government involved, handicapping the petitioner at a crucial moment.[241] The motivation for this decision arose from government complaints of petitioners leaking Article 50 reports to the press, though no evidence of such leaks due to petitioners violating the confidentiality requirements of the Convention has been found.[242] In October 1996, the

---

[240] Robert E. Norris, *The Individual Petition Procedure of the Inter-American System for the Protection of Human Rights, in* GUIDE TO INTERNATIONAL HUMAN RIGHTS PRACTICE 123 (HURST HANNUM ED., 1984).

[241] Advisory Opinion OC-13/93 of, *Certain Attributes of the Inter-American Commission on Human Rights (Arts. 41, 42, 44, 46, 47, 50 and 51 of the American Convention on Human Rights)*, Inter-Am. Ct. H.R. (ser. A) No.13 47, 56 ¶¶ 48–49 (July 16, 1993).

[242] Article 50 of the Convention states: "The report shall be transmitted to the states concerned, which shall not be at liberty to publish it." The petitioner is not mentioned.

Commission narrowed its confidentiality requirement by sending preliminary reports to the state in question for a determined period of time (60 days) while also addressing a note, without a full report, to the petitioner informing of the decision in the case.[243] The confidentiality practice of the Commission has received its share of criticism, and is under review to insure that the process is fair.

6.4 Settlements

Throughout the process, the Commission will attempt to seek a friendly settlement between the parties. If such a settlement is reached, a brief report is sent to the Secretary General of the OAS. If no settlement can be achieved, the Commission will normally draft a report of its findings and recommendations, and submit it to the state party only. If, after a three month time period, the matter still has not yet been settled, the Commission will either publish the report in its Annual Report or, if the state party is subject to the jurisdiction of the Inter-American Court, will refer the case to the Court for adjudication.

6.5 Temporary Protective Orders

Perhaps one of the most significant actions that can be taken by the Commission once a case has been admitted is to request that the Inter-American Court issue a temporary or interim protective order against the state in question, to ensure the physical and mental safety of the petitioner(s) or witnesses. The relevant provision lies in Article 63(2) of the American Convention:

> In cases of extreme gravity and urgency, and where necessary to avoid irreparable damage to persons, the Court shall adopt such provisional measures as it deems pertinent in matters it has under consideration. With respect to a case not yet submitted to the Court, it may act at the request of the Commission.

Such temporary protective orders have been frequently requested by the Commission and granted by the Court. While the Commission itself can only *request* that a state adopt certain measures, Article 63(2) of the American Convention and Article 23(4) of the Rules of Procedure of the Inter-American Court give the president of the Court the power

---

[243] Jose Miguel Vivanco & Lisa Bhansali, *Procedural Shortcomings in the Defense of Human Rights: An Inequality of Arms, in* THE INTER-AMERICAN SYSTEM OF HUMAN RIGHTS, *supra* note 4, at 437.

to issue temporary and protective orders.[244] This holds true not only for cases before the Court but also for cases that have not yet been submitted to the Court but are nevertheless referred by the Commission. It has also been suggested that the use of the word "matters" in Article 63(2) also enables the Court to issue provisional measures when an advisory opinion is requested.[245]

Prior to ordering provisional measures for protection, the Court will verify that the State involved recognizes the contentious jurisdiction of the Court under Article 62(2) of the Convention. The granting of provisional measures is a feature that is unique to the Inter-American system and one that is considered an "increasingly important aspect of the contemporary case-law of the Court," particularly given the emergency relief it has secured and the lives it has saved.[246]

6.6 Amicus Curiae ("Friend of the Court") Briefs

While there is no explicit provision for the Court's taking notice of amicus curiae briefs, Article 34(2) of the Court Rules states that the Court "may, in consultation with the parties, entrust any body, office, commission or authority of its choice with the task of obtaining information expressing an opinion, or making a report upon any specific point." In the past, NGOs have provided the Court with such briefs and, on one occasion, the Court made a direct reference to an amicus brief in its decision. The Court has appeared not to have ever rejected an amicus filing. Thus, it may be very helpful to bolster your arguments with submissions from UNHCR or from NGOs concerned with human rights protection for the forcibly displaced.

Bibliography

Books

DAVIDSON, SCOTT, THE INTER-AMERICAN COURT OF HUMAN RIGHTS (1992).
DAVIDSON, SCOTT, THE INTER-AMERICAN HUMAN RIGHTS SYSTEM (1997).
MARTIN, FRANCISCO FORREST ET AL., INTERNATIONAL HUMAN RIGHTS LAW AND PRACTICE (1997).
OAS, THE ORGANIZATION OF AMERICAN STATES AND HUMAN RIGHTS (1972).

---

[244] *See Bustios-Rojas Case*, Provisional Order [Peru], Inter-Amer. Ct. H.R. (ser. E) No.1 (August 8, 1990).
[245] SCOTT DAVIDSON, THE INTER-AMERICAN HUMAN RIGHTS SYSTEM 139 (1997) (referring to the observations of Dunshee de Abranches).
[246] Antônio A. Cançado Trindade, *The Operation of the Inter-American Court of Human Rights, in* THE INTER-AMERICAN SYSTEM OF HUMAN RIGHTS, *supra* note 4, at 146.

Chapters

Cerna, Christina, *The Inter-American Commission on Human Rights: Its Organization and Examination of Petitions and Communications, in* THE INTER-AMERICAN SYSTEM OF HUMAN RIGHTS 85 (DAVID J. HARRIS AND STEPHEN LIVINGSTONE EDS., 1998).

Farer, Tom, *The Rise of the Inter-American Human Rights Regime: No Longer a Unicorn, Not Yet an Ox, in* THE INTER-AMERICAN SYSTEM OF HUMAN RIGHTS 31 (DAVID J. HARRIS AND STEPHEN LIVINGSTONE EDS., 1998).

Fitzpatrick, Joan, *States of Emergency in the Inter-American Human Rights System, in* THE INTER-AMERICAN SYSTEM OF HUMAN RIGHTS 371 (DAVID J. HARRIS AND STEPHEN LIVINGSTONE EDS., 1998).

Harris, David, *Regional Protection of Human Rights: The Inter-American Achievement, in* THE INTER-AMERICAN SYSTEM OF HUMAN RIGHTS 16 (DAVID J. HARRIS AND STEPHEN LIVINGSTONE EDS., 1998).

Helton, Arthur C., *Establishing a Comprehensive Scheme for Refugee and Migration Emergencies in the Caribbean Region: Lessons from Recent Haitian and Cuban Emergencies, in* FREE MARKETS, OPEN SOCIETIES, CLOSED BORDERS? TRENDS IN INTERNATIONAL MIGRATION AND IMMIGRATION POLICY IN THE AMERICAS 256 (MAX J. CASTRO ED., 1999).

Mármora, Lelio, *Social Integration and Employment of Central American Refugees, in* WHEN BORDERS DON'T DIVIDE: LABOR MIGRATION AND REFUGEE MOVEMENTS IN THE AMERICAS 149 (PATRICIA R. PESSAR ED., 1988).

Medina, Cecilia, *The Role of Country Reports in the Inter-American System of Human Rights, in* THE INTER-AMERICAN SYSTEM OF HUMAN RIGHTS 115 (DAVID J. HARRIS AND STEPHEN LIVINGSTONE EDS., 1998).

Norris, Robert E., *The Individual Petition Procedure of the Inter-American System for the Protection of Human Rights, in* GUIDE TO INTERNATIONAL HUMAN RIGHTS PRACTICE 123, (Hurst Hannum ed., 1984).

Shelton, Dinah, *Reparations in the Inter-American System, in* THE INTER-AMERICAN SYSTEM OF HUMAN RIGHTS 151 (DAVID J. HARRIS AND STEPHEN LIVINGSTONE EDS., 1998).

Trinidade, Antonio Augusto Cancado, *The Operation of the Inter-American Court of Human Rights, in* THE INTER-AMERICAN SYSTEM OF HUMAN RIGHTS 146 (DAVID J. HARRIS AND STEPHEN LIVINGSTONE EDS., 1998).

Vivanco, Jose Miguel & Lisa Bhansali, *Procedural Shortcomings in the Defense of Human Rights: An Inequality of Arms, in* THE INTER-AMERICAN SYSTEM OF HUMAN RIGHTS 437 (DAVID J. HARRIS AND STEPHEN LIVINGSTONE EDS., 1998).

Articles

Helton, Arthur C., *Securing Refugee Protection in the Americas: The Inter-American System on Human Rights and the Rights of Asylum Seekers*, 6 Sw. J. L. Trade Am. 129 (1999).

Organization of American States Documents

Complaint Form, in Basic Documents Pertaining to Human Rights in the Inter-American System OAS/Ser.L/V/I.4 Rev.7 (January 2000).

Publications of the Inter-American Commission on Human Rights, in Basic Documents Pertaining to Human Rights in the Inter-American System OAS/Ser.L/V/I.4 Rev.7, 185 (January 2000).

Regulations of the Inter-American Commission on Human Rights, *reprinted in Basic Documents Pertaining to Human Rights in the Inter-American System*, OAS/Ser.L/V/I.4 Rev.7 (January 2000).

Rules of Procedure of the Inter-American Court of Human Rights, *reprinted in Basic Documents Pertaining to Human Rights in the Inter-American System*, OAS/Ser.L/V/I.4 Rev.7 (January 2000).

Situation of Refugees, Returnees, and Internally Displaced Persons in the Americas, AG/RES. 1602 XXVIII-0/98 (June 3, 1998).

Statute of the Inter-American Commission of Human Rights, *reprinted in Basic Documents Pertaining to Human Rights in the Inter-American System*, OAS/Ser.L/V/I.4 Rev.7 (February 2, 2000).

Statute of the Inter-American Court of Human Rights, *reprinted in Basic Documents Pertaining to Human Rights in the Inter-American System*, OAS/Ser.L/V/I.4 Rev.7 (February 2, 2000)

IACHR:

Annual Report of the IACHR 1999, OEA/Ser.L/V/II.106 Doc. 6 rev. (1999).

Report on the Situation of Human Rights in Chile, OEA Ser.L/V/II.66, Doc. 17 (1985).

Report on the Situation Regarding Human Rights in Cuba, OEA/Ser.L/V/II.4 Doc. 2 (1962).

Report on the Situation of Human Rights in Guatemala, OEA/Ser.L/V/11.61 (1983).

Report on the Situation of Human Rights in Guatemala, OEA/Ser.L/V/11.83 (1993).

Report on the Situation of Human Rights in Mexico, OEA/Ser.L/V/II.100 Doc. 7 rev. 1 (1998).

Report on the Situation of Human Rights in Perú, OEA/Ser. L/V/II.106 Doc. 59 (2000).

Report on the Situation of Human Rights of a Segment of the Nicaraguan Population of Miskito Origin, OEA/Ser.L/V/11.62 (1983).
Report on the Situation of Human Rights of Asylum Seekers within the Canadian Refugee Determination System OEA/Ser.L/V/II.106 Doc. 40 rev. (2000).
Second Report on The Situation of Human Rights in Suriname, OEA Ser.L/V/II.66, Doc. 21, rev. 1 (1985).
Special Report on the Human Rights in the So-Called "Communities of Peoples in Resistance" in Guatemala, OEA/Ser/L/V/II.86 Doc.5 Rev. 1 (1994).
Third Report on the Situation of Human Rights in Colombia, OEA/Ser. L/V/II.102 Doc. 9 rev. 1 (1999).

Cases

European Court of Human Rights:

De Wilde, Oomas and Versyp ("Vagrancy Cases"), 12 Eur. Ct. H.R. (ser. A) (1971).

Inter-American Court of Human Rights:

Advisory Opinions

Advisory Opinion OC-12/91, *Compatibility of Draft Legislation with Article 8(2)(h) of the American Convention on Human Rights*, Inter-Am. Ct. H.R. (ser. A) No.12 (December 6, 1991).
Advisory Opinion OC-13/93, *Certain Attributes of the Inter-American Commission on Human Rights (Arts. 41, 42, 44, 46, 47, 50 and 51 of the American Convention on Human Rights)*, Inter-Am. Ct. H.R. (ser. A) No.13 (July 16, 1993)
Advisory Opinion OC-10/89, *Interpretation of the American Declaration on the Rights and Duties of Man within the framework of Article 64 of the American Convention on Human Rights*, Inter-Am. Ct. H.R.(ser. A) No. 10 (July 14, 1989).
Advisory Opinion OC-1/82, *Other Treaties" Subject To The Advisory Jurisdiction Of The Court (Art. 64 American Convention On Human Rights)*, Inter-Am. Ct. H.R. (ser. A) No.1 (September 24, 1982).
Advisory Opinion OC-11/90, *Exceptions to the Exhaustion of Domestic Remedies (Art. 46(1), 46(2)(a), 46(2)(b) American Convention on Human Rights)*, Inter Am Ct. H.R. (ser. A) No. 11 (August 10, 1990).

Contentious Cases:

Aloeboetoe Case, Judgment on Reparations [Suriname], Inter-Am. Ct. H.R. (ser. C) No. 15 (September 10, 1993).
Bustios-Rojas Case, Provisional Order [Peru], Inter-Amer. Ct. H.R. (ser. E) No.1 (August 8, 1990).
Caballero Delgado y Santana Case, Preliminary Objections [Colombia], Inter-Am. Ct. H.R. (ser. C) No. 17 (January 21, 1994).
Castillo Páez Case, Preliminary Objections [Peru], Inter-Am. Ct. HR (ser. C) No. 24 (January 30, 1996).
Castillo Páez Case [Peru], Inter-Am. Ct. H.R. (ser. C) No. 34 (November 3, 1997).
Fairén Garbi y Solis Corrales Case, Preliminary Objections [Honduras], Inter-Am. Ct. H.R. (ser. C) No. 2 (June 26, 1987).
Godínez Cruz Case, Preliminary Objections [Honduras], Inter-Am. Ct. H.R. (ser. C) No. 3 (June 26, 1987).
Godínez Cruz Case, Interpretation of the Compensation Damages Judgment [Honduras], Inter-Am Ct. H.R. (ser. C) No. 10 (August 17, 1990).
Velásquez Rodríguez Case, Preliminary Objections [Honduras], Inter-Am Ct. H.R. (ser. C) No. 1, Doc. VI (June 26, 1987).
Velásquez-Rodríguez, [Honduras], Inter-Am. Ct. H.R. (ser. C) No. 4 (July 29, 1988).
Velásquez Rodríguez Case, Interpretation of the Compensatory Damages Judgment [Honduras], Inter-Am. Ct. H.R. (ser. C) No. 9 (August 17, 1990).
Viviana Gallardo Case [Costa Rica], Inter-Am. Ct. H.R. (ser. A) No. G 101/81 (November 13, 1981).

Inter-American Commission on Human Rights:

Alonso Eugénio da Silva, Case No. 11.598, Report No. 9/00 [Brazil], IACHR 1999 Annual Report 399 (February 24, 2000).
Álvarez Hernández, Case 7898, Resolution. No. 11/82 [Cuba], IACHR 1981–1982 Annual Report 68 (March 8, 1982).
Andres Aylwin Azocar et al., Case 11.863, Report No. 137/99 [Chile], IACHR 1999 Annual Report 536 (December 27, 1999).
Anselmo Rios Aquilar, Case 11.507, Report No. 32/98 [Mexico], IACHR 1998 Annual Report (May 5, 1998).
Armando Alejandre Jr. et al., Case 11.589, Report No. 86/99 [Cuba], IACHR 1999 Annual Report 586 (September 29, 1999).
Banco de Lima, Case 10.169, Report No. 10/91 [Peru], IACHR 1990–1991 Annual Report 423 (February 22, 1991).

Bendeck-Cohdinsa, Petition, Report No. 106/99 [Honduras], IACHR 1999 Annual Report 311 (September 27, 1999).
Bernard Merens and Family, Petition, Report No. 103/99 [Argentina], IACHR 1999 Annual Report 307 (September 27, 1999).
"Caloto" Massacre, Case 11.101, Report No. 36/00 [Colombia], IACHR 1999 Annual Report 468 (April 13, 2000).
Calvar Rivero Family, Case 7602, Resolution. No. 6/82 [Cuba], IACHR 1981–1982 Annual Report 79 (March 8, 1982).
Carandiru, Case 11.291, Report No. 34/00 [Brazil], IACHR 1999 Annual Report 370 (April 13, 2000).
Carlos García Saccone, Case 11.671, Report No. 8/98 [Argentina], IACHR 1997 Annual Report (March 2, 1998).
Clemente Ayala Torres et al., Case 10.545, Report No. 33/98 [Mexico], IACHR 1998 Annual Report 172 (May 5, 1998).
Damion Thomas, Case 12.069, Report No. 54/00 [Jamaica], *to be published in* IACHR 2000 Annual Report (June 15, 2000).
Dismissed Congressional Employees, Cases 11.830 & 12.038, Report No. 52/00 [Peru], *to be published in* IACHR 2000 Annual Report (June 15, 2000).
Emiliano Castro Tortrino, Case 11.597, Report No. 7/98 [Argentina], IACHR 1997 Annual Report (March 2, 1998).
Eolo Margaroli and Josefina Ghiringhelli de Margaroli, Case 11.400, Report No. 104/99 [Argentina], IACHR 1999 Annual Report (September 27, 1999).
Gary T. Graham, now known as Shaka Sankofa, Case 11.193, Report No. 51/00 [United States], *to be published in* IACHR 2000 Annual Report (June 15, 2000).
Haitian Interdiction, Case 10.675, Report No. 51/96 [United States], IACHR 1996 Annual Report 550 (March 13, 1997).
Ignacio Ellacuría, et al., Case 10.488, Report No. 136/99 [El Salvador], IACHR 1999 Annual Report 608 (December 22, 1999).
Joaquín Ortega et al. ("Extrajudicial Executions"), Case 10.586 et al., Report No. 39/00 [Guatemala], IACHR 1999 Annual Report 772 (April 13, 2000).
Lino César Oviedo, Case 12.013, Report No. 88/99 [Paraguay], IACHR 1999 Annual Report 322 (September 27, 1999).
"Los Uvos" Massacre, Case 11.020, Report No. 35/00 [Colombia], IACHR 1999 Annual Report 446 (April 13, 2000).
Lucio Parada Cea, Case 10.480, Report No. 1/99 [El Salvador], IACHR 1998 Annual Report 531 (January 27, 1999).
Marcos Aurelio de Oliveira, Case 11.599, Report No. 10/00 [Brazil], IACHR 1999 Annual Report 413 (February 24, 2000).
Mariela Barreto Riofano, Case 12.095, Report No. 30/00 [Peru], IACHR 1999 Annual Report 270 (February 23, 2000).

Mary and Carrie Dann, Case 11.140, Report No. 99/99 [United States], IACHR 1999 Annual Report 286 (September 27, 1999).
Mevopal, S.A., Petition, Report No. 39/99 [Argentina], 1998 Annual Report 297 (March 11, 1999).
Monsignor Oscar Arnulfo Romero y Galdámez, Case 11.481, Report No. 37/00 [El Salvador], IACHR 1999 Annual Report 671 (April 13, 2000).
Narciso Palacios, Case 10.194, Report No. 105/99 [Argentina], IACHR 1999 Annual Report 355 (September 29, 1999).
Norma Dominga Carpi de Szukalo (Widowed), Case 11.707, Report No. 69/99 [Argentina] IACHR Annual Report (May 4, 1999).
"Ojo de Agua" Cooperative, Case 11.701, Report No. 73/99 [Mexico], IACHR 1999 Annual Report 316 (May 4, 1999).
Paul Lallion, Case 11.765, Report No. 124/99 [Granada], IACHR 1999 Annual Report 225 (September 27, 1999).
Peter Blaine, Case 11.827, Report No. 96/98 [Jamaica], IACHR 1998 Annual Report 312 (December 17, 1998).
Ramón Mauricio García-Prieto Giralt, Case 11.697, Report No. 27/99 [El Salvador], IACHR 1998 Annual Report 111 (March 9, 1999).
Raquel Martín de Mejía, Case 10.970, Report No. 5/96 [Peru], IACHR 1995 Annual Report 157 (March 1, 1996).
Richmond Hill, Case 9213, Report No. 3/96 [United States], IACHR 1995 Annual Report 201 (March 1, 1996).
Roach and Pinkerton Cases, Case 9647, Resolution No. 3/87 [United States], IACHR 1986–1987 Annual Report 147 (March 27, 1987).
Rudolph Baptiste, Case 11.743, Report No. 38/00 [Grenada], IACHR 1999 Annual Report 721 (April 13, 2000).
Salas and Others, Case 10.573, Report No. 31/93 [United States], IACHR 1993 Annual Report 312 (February 11, 1994).
Salvador Jorge Blanco, Case 10.208, Resolution No. 15/89 [Dominican Republic], IACHR 1988–1989 Annual Report 67 (April 14, 1989).
Santiago Marzioni, Case 11.673, Report No. 39/96 [Argentina], IACHR 1996 Annual Report 76 (October 15, 1996).
Tabacalera Boquerón S.A., Petition, Report No. 47/97 [Paraguay], IACHR 1997 Annual Report 225 (October 16, 1997).
Victor Alfredo Polay Campos, Case 11.048, Report No. 32/00 [Peru], IACHR 1999 Annual Report 330 (March 10, 2000).
Village of Moiwana, Case 11.821, Report No. 26/00 [Suriname], IACHR 1999 Annual Report 278 (March 7, 2000).

Commission Cases (parties unnamed):

Application No. 9213 [United States], IACHR 1986–1987 Annual Report 184 (April 17, 1986).

Case 1774 [Chile], IACHR 1974 Annual Report 35.
Case 1786 [Chile], IACHR 1974 Annual Report 7 (Oct. 25, 1973).
Case 1790 [Chile], IACHR 1974 Annual Report 8 (Nov. 9, 1973).
Case 1799 [Chile], IACHR 1974 Annual Report 9 (Feb. 21, 1974).
Case 1802 [Paraguay], IACHR 1977 Annual Report, 36, 37 (May 27, 1977).
Case 1803 [Chile], IACHR 1974 Annual Report 10 (March 2 1974).
Case 1809 [Chile], IACHR 1974 Annual Report 11 (March 18, 1974).
Case 1810 [Chile], IACHR 1974 Annual Report 12 (March 26, 1974).
Case 1954, Resolution No. 59/81 [Uruguay], IACHR 1981–1982 Annual Report 96 (October 16, 1981).
Case 1983 [United States] adopted by the IACHR at its 656th meeting, April 8, 1980. OEA/Ser.L/V/II.49, doc. 39, (14 April 1980).
Case 2137 [Argentina], IACHR 1978 Annual Report, 43 (November 18, 1978).
Case 2141, Resolution No. 23/81 [United States], IACHR 1980–1981 Annual Report 25 (March 6, 1981).
Case 6091, Resolution No. 3/82 [Cuba], IACHR 1981–1982 Annual Report 71, 76 (March 8, 1982).
Case 7602 [Cuba] IACHR 1982 Annual Report 79 (March 8, 1982).
Case 9755, Resolution No. 01a/88 [Chile], IACHR 1987–1988 Annual Report 132 (September 12, 1988).
Case 9619 [Honduras] IACHR 1986–1987 Annual Report 75.
Case 10109, Resolution No. 26/88 [Argentina], IACHR 1987–1988 Annual Report 102 (September 13, 1988)
Case 11.092 Decision of the Commission as to the Admissibility, [Canada], IACHR 1994 Annual Report 32 (October 6, 1993).

United Nations Human Rights Committee:

Anna Maroufidou v. Sweden, Communication No. R.13/58, U.N. Doc. A/36/40 (1981).

Miscellaneous

Bureau of Public Affairs, U.S. Department of State, *Current Policy No. 201*, REFUGEES: A GLOBAL ISSUE (July 23, 1980).
Letter of CEJIL, Human Rights Watch/Americas, Iniciativa de Solidaridad con Colombia, and U.S. Committee for Refugees, to the Inter-American Commission on Human Rights (July 1, 1999) (on file with authors).
Cohen, Roberta, *The Response of Regional Organizations to Internal Displacement in the Americas, Forced Migrations*, Conference on

Sudden Forced Migration Emergencies in the Americas, Washington, D.C., Sept.30–Oct.1, 1997 (on file with authors).

Méndez, Juan E., *A Proposal for Action on Sudden Forced Migrations*, Conference on Sudden Forced Migration Emergencies in the Americas, Washington, D.C., Sept.30–Oct.1, 1997 4 (on file with the authors).

United States Committee on Refugees, Issue Paper, El Retorno: Guatemala's Risky Repatriation Begins, February 1993 (on file with authors).

U.S. Committee for Refugees, World Refugee Survey (1999).

Chapter 7
International Criminal Tribunals: Refugees and Internally Displaced Persons Who May Be Witnesses Before The Tribunals

Åsa Rydberg
Kelly D. Askin

1. Introduction

The 20th century was marked by scores of conflicts that raged in all corners of the world.[1] As a result of these conflicts, millions of refugees and displaced persons fled into neighboring regions and beyond, a host of persons seeking safe haven from the conflicts. Many persons who have fled or been expelled from conflict regions have been victims of or witnesses to serious violations of international humanitarian law. While all such persons may have certain expectations with regard to international criminal justice, refugees, asylum-seekers, and internally displaced persons in particular may want to participate in bringing the perpetrators of the crimes to justice or to seek compensation for their losses. This chapter focuses on the work of the existing *ad hoc* international criminal tribunals and on the anticipated International Criminal Court (ICC). More specifically, it will try to explain what a victim should expect from the *ad hoc* tribunals and the ICC in terms of prosecution of alleged perpetrators, witness testimony, and victim compensation.

As of October 2000, there are two *ad hoc* tribunals, the International Criminal Tribunal for the former Yugoslavia (ICTY)[2] and the

---

[1] The views in this article are those of the authors and do not necessarily represent those of the International Criminal Tribunal for the former Yugoslavia or the United Nations.

[2] *International Tribunal for the Prosecution of Persons Responsible for Serious Violations of International Humanitarian Law Committed in the Territory of the Former*

International Criminal Tribunal for Rwanda (ICTR).[3] The Security Council is currently in the process of establishing a similar Special Court for Sierra Leone[4] and there are ongoing discussions for the establishment of a tribunal for Cambodia.[5] While differences certainly exist, the ICTY and ICTR nonetheless have similar, sometimes identical, provisions in their Statutes and Rules of Procedure and Evidence. With regard to the *ad hoc* tribunals, this article will focus primarily on the relevant provisions and practices of the ICTY and highlight any significant differences with the ICTR, as appropriate. The ICC has not yet entered into force. However, the ICC Statute has been finalized and the Rules of Procedure and Evidence have been adopted by the Preparatory Commission, so the most relevant provisions will be examined here.

This chapter will begin with an examination of the functioning of the tribunals. After a brief background on the establishment of the tribunals, the pre-trial phase, including the powers of the prosecutor, will be explained. The work of the Victims and Witnesses Section (VWS) will then be described and the trial and the post-trial phase will be examined. The possibilities of requesting restitution of stolen property and victim compensation will be briefly discussed. Because a refugee or an internally displaced person is most likely to come into contact with the ICTY as a witness before the court, the examination of the work of this institution will be done mainly from the point of view of a witness. Special focus will be placed on the practices developing in the ICTY related to practical, logistical, and protective arrangements that may be particularly relevant to victims or witnesses who are permanently or temporarily displaced. Explanations will also be given as to how the practices are implemented in the context of prosecutions in international criminal tribunals situated far from the conflict region. It should be noted that much of the material discussed in this chapter concerns

---

Yugoslavia since 1991, U.N. Doc. S/25704, annex (1993), *reprinted in* 32 I.L.M. 1192 (1993).

[3] *International Criminal Tribunal for the Prosecution of Persons Responsible for Genocide and Other Serious Violations of International Humanitarian Law Committed in the Territory of Rwanda and Rwandan Citizens responsible for genocide and other such violations committed in the territory of neighboring States, between 1 January 1994 and 31 December 1994*, SC Res. 955, annex, UN SCOR, 49th Sess., Res. & Dec., at 15, U.N. Doc. S/INF/50 (1994), *reprinted in* 33 I.L.M. 1602 (1994).

[4] Security Council resolution 1315, U.N. Doc. S/RES/1315 (2000) (14 August 2000), available at <http://www.un.org/Docs/scres/2000/res1315e.pdf>. *See further the Report of the Secretary-General on the establishment of a Special Court for Sierra Leone*, U.N. Doc. S/2000/915 (4 October 2000).

[5] *See especially Group of Experts Report, Cambodia*, U.N. Doc. A/53/850 (16 March 1999).

practices and not necessarily formal policies. Practices continue to change and evolve as circumstances dictate and needs require. They also tend to be flexible in order to meet the needs of each particular witness or situation. Finally, the most pertinent ICC Statute and Rules will be highlighted.

2. The Establishment of the Ad Hoc Tribunals

The ICTY and ICTR were established in 1993 and 1994, respectively, in response to serious violations of international humanitarian and criminal law committed during recent armed conflicts in the former Yugoslavia and in Rwanda. Acting under Chapter VII of the UN Charter, the United Nations Security Council established the tribunals to prosecute persons accused of genocide, crimes against humanity, or war crimes in these conflicts. These extraordinary measures were taken primarily in an attempt to contribute to peace and reconciliation, and to end the cycle of impunity that historically characterizes these crimes.

In resolutions 808 and 827 (1993), the Security Council expressed its grave alarm at continuing reports of widespread and flagrant violations of international humanitarian law occurring within the territory of the former Yugoslavia and especially in the Republic of Bosnia and Herzegovina. It determined that the situation continued to constitute a threat to international peace and security and undertook to institute effective measures to put an end to such crimes and bring to justice the persons who are responsible for them. The Security Council was "[c]onvinced that in the particular circumstances of the former Yugoslavia the establishment as an ad hoc measure by the Council of an international tribunal and the prosecution of persons responsible for serious violations of international humanitarian law would enable this aim to be achieved and would contribute to the restoration and maintenance of peace."[6]

Similarly, in Security Council resolution 955 (1994), the Council expressed its grave concern at reports of genocide and other serious crimes committed in Rwanda and determined to establish an *ad hoc* tribunal to prosecute the perpetrators. It was intended and expected that such a tribunal would facilitate a process of national reconciliation and contribute to the restoration of peace in the region.[7]

---

[6] *Security Council resolution 827*, U.N. Doc. S/RES/827 (1993) (25 May 1993), at <http://www.un.org/Docs/scres/1993/827e.pdf>.

[7] *Security Council resolution 955*, U.N. Doc. S/RES/955 (1994) (8 November 1994), at <http://www.un.org/Docs/scres/1994/9443748e.htm>.

The ICTY and ICTR do not have the capacity to prosecute all perpetrators of serious crimes, so their goal is generally broader: to bring those must culpable to justice and to heighten awareness of the crimes committed during the conflicts. A primary purpose in the establishment of the *ad hoc* tribunals was to facilitate peace and reconciliation by prosecuting those who were most responsible for violations of international humanitarian law, rather than to prosecute all alleged perpetrators or provide redress for individual victims of these violations.

The statutes of the tribunals establish the guidelines and scope of their mandates. The ICTY Statute provides that the ICTY has jurisdiction over the following crimes: grave breaches of the Geneva Conventions of 1949; violations of the laws or customs of war; genocide; and crimes against humanity.[8] The ICTR Statute provides that the ICTR has jurisdiction over genocide; crimes against humanity; and violations of Article 3 common to the Geneva Conventions and of Additional Protocol II.[9] The statutes further stipulate that the judges are responsible for devising the rules of procedure and evidence to be applied by the tribunals.[10] The rules have been amended several times to take into account evolving needs and unforeseen circumstances of pre-trial, trial, and post-trial proceedings.[11] The statutes explicitly require that the tribunals "shall provide in [their] rules of procedure and evidence for the protection of victims and witnesses. Such protection measures shall include, but shall not be limited to, the conduct of in camera proceedings and the protection of the victim's identity."[12]

Individual and joint trials continue to be held in both tribunals. Trials of persons accused of individual criminal responsibility, including superior responsibility, from the recent Balkan conflicts are held

---

[8] *Statute of the International Tribunal for Yugoslavia*, arts. 2–5, *adopted* May 25, 1993, at <http://www.un.org/icty/basic/statut/statute.htm>.

[9] *Statute of the International Criminal Tribunal for Rwanda*, arts. 2–4, 1994, at <http://www.ictr.org/>.

[10] ICTY Statute, *supra* note 8 ,at art. 15, which provides: "The judges of the International tribunal shall adopt rules of procedure and evidence for the conduct of the pre-trial phase of the proceedings, trials and appeals, the admission of evidence, the protection of victims and witnesses and other appropriate matters."

[11] *See further International Criminal Tribunal for Yugoslavia, Rules of Procedure and Evidence, adopted* February 11, 1994, IT/32/Rev.18, at <http://www.un.org/icty/basic/rpe/IT32_rev18con.htm>; and *International Criminal Tribunal for Rwanda, Rules of Procedure, adopted* July 5, 1995, last amended at the ICTR Eighth Plenary Session of 26 June 2000, at <http:// www.ictr.org/>.

[12] ICTY Statute, *supra* note 8, at art. 22; ICTR Statute, *supra* note 9, at art. 21.

in The Hague, The Netherlands, where the Office of the Prosecutor (OTP) is also based. Persons accused of the enumerated crimes during the Rwandan genocide are tried in Arusha, Tanzania, although the OTP is based in Kigali, Rwanda, for logistical reasons. The prosecutor is common to both tribunals, and each has three trial chambers and an appeals chamber.[13] Judgment is rendered by a panel of three judges at the trial level and a panel of five judges at the appeals level. There is no jury system at the tribunals.

As of October 2000, the ICTY had rendered judgments against 12 accused after trials on the merits, and made four appeal judgments.[14] Thus far, some 1,450 witnesses have been called before the ICTY.[15] While it is unknown precisely how many of these witnesses are refugees, asylum-seekers, or internally displaced persons, the Victims and Witnesses Section estimates that such persons constitute well above half of all the witnesses.[16] While most ICTY witnesses have come from Bosnia and Herzegovina, witnesses have also come from all other regions of the world, totaling thus far 24 states.[17] The ICTR has had some 200 witnesses from 12 African, European, and American countries.[18] At both tribunals, some witnesses may have served as UN peacekeepers or journalists during the conflicts. Others may be victim witnesses now living as refugees in a state far away from their country of origin.

3. Investigation and Pre-Trial Stages

The common prosecutor is tasked with investigating and prosecuting crimes within the jurisdictions of the tribunals.[19] Because the tribunals have limited mandates, scopes of jurisdiction, and resources,

---

[13] The Judges of the ICTY Appeals Chamber also serve on the ICTR Appeals Chamber.

[14] In addition, two accused have been sentenced on guilty pleas and there have been three contempt proceedings. *See further* the ICTY web-site, at <http://www.un.org/icty/glance/>.

[15] Information obtained from the Victims and Witnesses Section of the ICTY. *See further* <http://www.un.org/icty/glance/keyfig-e.htm>.

[16] Information obtained from the Victims and Witnesses Section of the ICTY.

[17] *Id.*

[18] *See further* the International Criminal Tribunal for Rwanda, Witnesses and Victims Support Section, Fact Sheet No. 9, (August 2000), at <http://www.ictr.org/ENGLISH/factsheets/9.htm>.

[19] ICTY Statute, *supra* note 8, at art. 16(1); and ICTR Statute, *supra* note 9 at art. 15(1). The current Prosecutor is Carla Del Ponte, former Attorney-General of the Confederation of Switzerland. *See* <http://www.un.org/icty/

as a general rule the tribunals attempt to prosecute primarily, but not exclusively, the leaders and most serious offenders. Indictments and trials may be based on discovery of evidence and gaining custody over an accused. For strategic, logistical, or resource-related reasons, many suspected perpetrators will not be prosecuted even when there is sufficient evidence against them to sustain a prosecution. In this connection it should be noted that the statutes of the tribunals provide for concurrent jurisdiction with national courts. Thus, while the respective statutes grant the tribunals primacy over national courts, allowing for the tribunals to formally request that national courts defer to their competence, cases that are not prosecuted by the tribunals can be prosecuted before national courts.[20]

Although the tribunals were not principally intended to prosecute lower-level actors in general, the precedent established in prosecuting perpetrators at all levels of the hierarchy of command or responsibility is important. It is often the lower-level actors who carry out the orders or policies of the leaders and physically commit the crimes. Indeed, it is usually those actors whom witnesses are most able to point to in court as the direct victimizers.

Indictments, which are not always available to the public,[21] are brought solely by the common prosecutor. Thus, individuals, states, or organizations cannot bring cases before the tribunal. They may, however, contact or provide information to the Office of the Prosecutor regarding any information about crimes that have been committed. According to the statutes of the tribunals, the "Prosecutor shall initiate investigations ex-officio or on the basis of information obtained from any source, particularly from Governments, United Nations organs, intergovernmental and non-governmental organizations."[22] The statutes stipulate that the prosecutor shall act independently as a separate organ of the tribunals and shall not seek or receive instructions from any gov-

---

glance/keyfig-e.htm>. The previous Prosecutors were Justice Louise Arbour, from Canada, and Justice Richard Goldstone, from South Africa.

[20] ICTY Statute, *supra* note 8, at art. 9; and ICTR Statute, *supra* note 9, at art. 8.

[21] ICTY Rules of Procedure and Evidence, *supra* note 11, at Rule 53; and ICTR Rules of Procedure, *supra* note 11, at Rule 53. Rule 53, Non-disclosure, allows a Judge or Trial Chamber in exceptional circumstances and in the interests of justice to order the non-disclosure of all or parts of an Indictment until it is served on the accused. So-called sealed indictments are kept confidential in order to increase the chances of arrest of the accused.

[22] ICTY Statute, *supra* note 8, at art. 18(1); and ICTR Statute, *supra* note 9, at art. 17(1).

International Criminal Tribunals   501

ernment or other source.[23] However, because the tribunals do not have their own police or enforcement units, they must often depend on states or other entities, such as NATO, for cooperation in general and with regard to arrests of the indicted people in particular. While most evidence is gained from the investigations by the OTP, it is also possible for a person having information about a crime to contact the OTP directly.[24] Although the prosecutor will make an assessment of received complaints and allegations of crimes falling within the jurisdiction of the respective tribunals,[25] it should be emphasized that in the end it is always the prosecutor who decides whether the information warrants further investigation or whether an indictment should be prepared.[26] Normally, the prosecutor will not make public the details about investigations or allegations received but not investigated, as the standard practice is to comment only on indictments that have been made public.[27]

There is not much documentary evidence on the crimes committed in the former Yugoslavia, so witnesses have played and will continue to play a crucial role in most proceedings before the ICTY. During the investigation of alleged crimes and the preparation for trial, the OTP is usually in contact with a large number of people who provide information or give statements relating to the alleged crimes. However, while most of the information given to the prosecutor is useful, only a

---

[23]   ICTY Statute, *supra* note 8, at art. 16(2); and ICTR Statute, *supra* note 9, at art. 15(2).

[24]   For the contact details of the ICTY and the ICTR, please refer to Appendix 7A.

[25]   *See, e.g.*, the ICTY press release, *Prosecutor's Report on the NATO bombing campaign*, Final Report to the Prosecutor by the Committee Established to Review the NATO Bombing Campaign Against the Federal Republic of Yugoslavia, U.N. Doc. PR/P.I.S./510-E (13 June 2000), at <http://www.un.org/icty/pressreal/p510-e.htm>.

[26]   ICTY Statute, *supra* note 8, at art. 18(4); and ICTR Statute, *supra* note 9, at art. 17(4). ICTY Statute, art. 18(4) and ICTR Statute, art. 17(4) provide that upon a determination that a *prima facie* case exists, the Prosecutor shall prepare an indictment.

[27]   However, on June 2, 2000, the Prosecutor made public that she had decided not to open criminal investigation into any aspect of NATO's 1999 air campaign against the Federal Republic of Yugoslavia. *See further the ICTY press release, Prosecutor's Report on the NATO bombing campaign*, Final Report to the Prosecutor by the Committee Established to Review the NATO Bombing Campaign Against the Federal Republic of Yugoslavia, U.N. Doc. PR/P.I.S./510-E (13 June 2000), at <http://www.un.org/icty/pressreal/p510-e.htm>.

few of the persons providing evidence will eventually appear as witnesses before the tribunals.[28]

For the persons who are called to testify, there is an interim period between the contact with the OTP, the giving of a statement, and the arrival at the tribunal to testify. This interim period may encompass a matter of weeks or several years, depending on the arrest and detention of indictees, prosecutorial strategy, courtroom availability, and other factors. Once a trial begins, it may still be some time before a person on the witness list is called to testify; the Blaskić trial at the ICTY, for example, lasted just over two years. Some indictments are against a single person, while others contain allegations against several accused in one joint indictment. In some circumstances, a witness may need to testify in more than one trial if there are more than one accused and they are not tried jointly.

During the interim period between the giving of a statement to the OTP and arriving at the tribunals, the potential witness will normally have very little contact with the OTP. Potential witnesses are unfortunately afforded little protection and may thus be more vulnerable, especially if they remain in the conflict territory, the indictee has not yet been arrested, and the case does not go to trial for some time. Normally, a witness is not truly at great risk, because it is not known whether that person will testify or give evidence about the alleged crime.[29] However, a public indictment may indicate to the accused perpetrator the crimes for which he is being charged, and he may conceivably make an attempt to threaten, discredit, bribe, or perhaps even eliminate potential witnesses. Generally, these issues are considered by the OTP before a public indictment is issued and, if a person is considered to be at substantial risk, protective measures are taken on his or her behalf, such as relocation, non-disclosure of the indictment, and so on. Realistically, however, as in domestic crimes, a victim or witness may always be vulnerable before the perpetrators are arrested and convicted, regardless of whether they choose to provide information to the OTP

When a potential witness is contacted by the OTP, an OTP investigator will first identify his or her security and confidentiality needs and then determine whether his or her testimony might be useful to cases coming before the tribunal. As explained above, there are many

---

[28] As in most criminal processes, it depends on prosecutorial strategy, testimony of previous witnesses, logistical arrangements, etc. as to who will ultimately be called to testify.

[29] Also, for logistical or practical reasons, a perpetrator may not know the identity or whereabouts of potential witnesses against him or her, or may realistically have too many victims to intimidate.

crimes that will not be pursued by the OTP because of their relative gravity or lack of resources. For example, a person may contact the OTP to tell that a person entered their home, shot and wounded family members, evicted them, and is now living in their home. Such a crime, however awful, will not automatically generate an investigation by the OTP. Thus, while statements from many victims and witnesses will be helpful to the OTP by providing background information or leading to other sources, they will not necessarily be called to testify or give direct evidence at trial.

4. The Victims and Witnesses Section

The Victims and Witnesses Section (VWS) of the ICTY was the first of its kind in any international context. At an early stage of its existence, the ICTY recognized that in giving testimony before it, witnesses will have to re-live their experiences in a country far away from their own and without the support of relatives and friends that they would normally receive if they were testifying in an ordinary court of law in their own country in time of peace. Moreover, it was also recognized that some witnesses may have legitimate concerns about reprisals.[30] The VWS was established to alleviate these anxieties as far as possible and to create an environment in which witnesses can testify with dignity and in safety.[31] Thus, the VWS is tasked with the support and protection of victims and witnesses, as provided in Rule 34 of the ICTY Rules, and is responsible for the administrative and logistical arrangements related to the witnesses' travel to The Hague. The Victims and Witnesses Section deals with any witness, whether for the defense or for the prosecution.[32] The VWS is placed within the Registry of the ICTY—a neutral place—which enables it to take into consideration the interests of the witness, rather than those of the accused or the prosecutor, regardless of the role the witness will play in the trial.[33] A chamber of the tribunal can consult with the Victims and Witnesses Section on what protective

---

[30] *Secretary-General's Second Annual Report*, ¶ 109, U.N. Doc. A/50/365 (1995).

[31] *Id.* para 110.

[32] A Chamber can also call witnesses on its own initiative; Rule 98 of the Rules provides that a Trial Chamber may *proprio motu* summon witnesses and order their attendance. ICTY Rules of Procedure and Evidence, *supra* note 11, at Rule 98. The Victims and Witnesses Section also deals with these so-called court witnesses. It should be noted that witnesses appearing for the Defense also may have legitimate security concerns.

[33] *See further* Åsa Rydberg., *The Protection of the Interests of Witnesses: The ICTY in Comparison to the Future ICC*, 12 LEIDEN J. INT'L L. 455, 459 (1999).

measures would be appropriate in a particular situation. It is noteworthy that Rule 75 allows for the VWS to independently request of the chamber the implementation of certain protective or privacy measures for victims and witnesses.[34] The ICTR has a similar section called the Witnesses and Victims Support Section.[35]

Once a determination is made by either the OTP or a defense counsel that the testimony of a witness may be useful to the trial, that person will be put on a potential witness list. Only after a witness is included on this list will he or she come within the mandate of the VWS, as it cannot offer services to people who have witnessed crimes that are not prosecuted before the ICTY. In this connection, it should be noted that it is not uncommon for the OTP or the defense, for strategic, logistical, or practical purposes, to put a person's name on the witness list—and even have the witness transferred to The Hague or Arusha for the trial—and then decide not to call the witness to give testimony at trial.

The tribunal attempts to protect the privacy and dignity of all persons called by the defense and prosecution, and enable them to testify in a safe environment conducive to relieving unnecessary stress. The VWS and the Registry of the ICTY are experienced in resolving legal and practical problems relating to visas or identification papers. While the tribunals strive to ensure that any assistance provided not appear as providing benefits to a witness in exchange for testimony, it also attempts to ensure, as much as possible, that witnesses are not made worse off because of their testimony.

5. Trial Phase

A person who is requested by the OTP or a defense counsel to travel to the tribunal to testify may have various concerns or questions in relation to testifying. Indeed, there may be compelling reasons why victims or witnesses would be reluctant to give testimony to an international tribunal: perhaps they have moved on with their lives and do not want to re-live their experiences by talking about them in a courtroom; they may have family problems associated with leaving their home

---

[34] The Victims and Witnesses Section's standing was made significantly stronger at the seventh plenary session of the ICTY when Rule 75 was amended to provide that in addition to a witness or the parties concerned, the Victims and Witnesses Section can request measures for privacy or protection of the witness. ICTY Rules of Procedure and Evidence, *supra* note 11, at Rule 75.

[35] On the work of the ICTR Witnesses and Victims Support Section, *see further* the International Criminal Tribunal for Rwanda web-site, at <http://www.ictr.org/ENGLISH/factsheets/9.htm>.

for a week or more, especially if they have small children; they might not be compensated adequately for work time lost or they may not have revealed their background to their employer or superiors and would prefer to keep it that way; they may be seeking refugee status in another country; etc. Before discussing practical solutions to the concerns a witness may have, the question whether a person has a legal obligation to testify will be examined.

In most domestic systems, a citizen has a civic duty to cooperate with legal authorities and may be compelled to testify, regardless of their wishes. In the context of the tribunal, a person is not under a legal obligation to testify simply because he or she has been requested to do so by the OTP or a defense counsel, although the OTP or the defense can request a judge or a trial chamber to issue a subpoena to compel him or her to testify.[36] If subpoenaed, the witness has a legal duty to attend before the tribunal. In the event that the witness fails to do so without just excuse, he or she may be found in contempt of the tribunal.[37] However, the ability of the tribunal to enforce orders and subpoenas generally depends on the implementing legislation of the state for providing assistance to the tribunal or on any cooperation agreements the tribunal may have with the state.[38]

The Victims and Witnesses Section endeavors to alleviate, as much as is practically possible, the anxieties and concerns of witnesses related to their testimony. The support officers of the VWS will try to solve any practical problems the witness may face in connection with having to be absent from his or her place of residence. For example, the support officers will try to arrange for someone to care for the witness's elderly father or for someone to feed the cattle while the witness is in The Hague. A number of policies have been developed in order to address the most common needs of witnesses. They establish, *inter alia*, under what circumstances a witness should be entitled to be accompanied by a support person when traveling to The Hague, child care, compensation

---

[36] ICTY Rules of Procedure and Evidence, *supra* note 11, at Rule 54. ICTY Rule 54 provides that at the request of either party or *proprio motu*, a Judge or a Trial Chamber may issue such orders, summonses, subpoenas, warrants, and transfer orders as may be necessary for the purposes of an investigation or for the preparation or conduct of the trial.

[37] *Id.* at Rule 77(A)(iii), which provides that any person who without just excuse fails to comply with an order to attend before or produce documents before a Chamber, commits a contempt of the tribunal. Thus far, no such contempt proceedings have been initiated against a witness at the ICTY.

[38] It should be noted that UN member States are under a legal obligation to co-operate with the tribunal. *See further* ICTY Statute, *supra* note 8, at art. 29; and ICTY Rules of Procedure and Evidence, *supra* note 11, at Rule 7.

for lost wages, and a daily allowance.[39] The VWS informs witnesses how to apply for such support or services so that appropriate arrangements can be made in accordance with these policies.[40] It will also make arrangements for the trip to The Hague, including providing a pre-paid ticket; it will even cover the cost of a passport photo, if one is needed. If necessary, a VWS field officer will escort the witness from his or her place of residence to The Hague. In other cases, the VWS staff will assist and meet the witness at the relevant airport or entry point.

In the event that there are safety concerns involved, the party calling the witness (normally the OTP) will meet with the protection officers of the Victims and Witnesses Section at an early stage in order to discuss and make appropriate arrangements. Rule 69(A) provides that the prosecutor may apply to the trial chamber to order non-disclosure of the identity of a victim or witness who may be in danger or at risk until such person is brought under the protection of the tribunal.

For the most vulnerable witnesses, the VWS provides 24-hour, live-in support at their place of accommodation during their stay in The Hague. The witness assistants who work in this support program all speak Serbo-Croatian, but are not themselves from the areas involved in the conflict of the former Yugoslavia.[41] These assistants will accompany witnesses outside the trial chamber; provide emotional support, if necessary; take care of all practical details to ensure that the witness shows up for the trial at the right time and place; or assist the witness in making international phone calls.

A witness normally receives some basic information about testifying from the party calling the witness. The ICTY has produced an informative video about testifying before the tribunal, which is shown to the witness before his or her trip to The Hague, if possible. Informational leaflets are also available. The video and the leaflets are produced in the relevant languages.[42]

Once the witness arrives at the tribunal, the party calling the witness will normally prepare—but should not "coach"—the witness, so that he or she understands the procedures and basics of testimony. If

---

[39] *See further* leaflets issued by the Victims and Witnesses Section: *Information on VWS; Child Care Provisions; Compensation for Lost Wages; Daily allowance Policy; Accompanying Support Person; and Provisions for Dependants.*

[40] In general, the VWS encourages the witness to make child care arrangements at the residence of the witness.

[41] *Secretary-General's Fourth Report,* ¶ 94, U.N. Doc. A/52/375 (1997). The Witness Assistants also speak English and Dutch.

[42] Currently, the leaflets are available in Albanian, Bosnian, Croatian, and Serbian. The video is available in English, B/C/S and French.

time allows, the witness will be given a tour of a courtroom and walked through the trial process. There are separate waiting rooms for defense and prosecution witnesses that contain coffee, tea, and light snacks, so that the wait before the testimony is as comfortable as possible under the circumstances.

Scheduling is not always predictable. Prolonged questioning, a change in strategy, or various other unforeseen events may delay, disrupt, or preclude the giving of evidence by the witness. In general, the witness tends to be in The Hague for an average of seven days, even though his or her testimony may take only a matter of minutes or hours.[43]

When it is time for the testimony, a court usher from the Registry of the tribunal will escort the witness into the courtroom. In court, the court usher will, among other things, assist the witness with any practical issues, such as how to put on the headphones, or ensure that the witness has the right document in front of him or her. The witness will normally testify in his or her native language. At the ICTY, the judges and the prosecution will speak either English or French, with simultaneous interpretation into Bosnian/Croatian/Serbian (B/C/S). Thus, simultaneous interpretation into English, French, and B/C/S is available at all times through the headphones, which are worn by everybody in the courtroom. Unlike most domestic courtrooms, the public gallery is separated from the courtroom by bulletproof glass and the trials are televised. The airing of the trials on the video monitors within the tribunal and the release of the broadcast to the outside world is delayed by 30 minutes, so that any accidental disclosure of confidential information can be redacted from the broadcast. The transcript of the court session will also be redacted accordingly.[44]

Before giving evidence, every witness must make a solemn declaration to speak the truth.[45] As a general rule, the hearings are held in

---

[43] Information obtained from the Victims and Witnesses Section of the ICTY.

[44] This precaution however, does not prevent anyone sitting in the public gallery of the Courtroom from hearing the testimony during open sessions.

[45] ICTY Rules of Procedure and Evidence, *supra* note 11, at Rules 90(B) and 90(C). Rule 90(B) of the Rules provides the following solemn declaration: "I solemnly declare that I will speak the truth, the whole truth and nothing but the truth." Rule 90(C) provides that a child who, in the opinion of the Chamber, does not understand the nature of a solemn declaration, may be permitted to testify without that formality, if the Chamber is of the opinion that the child is sufficiently mature to be able to report the facts of which the child had knowledge and understands the duty to tell the truth.

public with full disclosure of the identity and address of the witness.[46] A chamber may, in exceptional circumstances and in the interests of justice, authorize the receipt of testimony via live video-conference link.[47] In this way, the chamber can examine a witness who was unable or unwilling to travel to the tribunal to testify.[48]

As noted above, a chamber may grant protective measures in court. In accordance with Rule 75, a chamber may order various measures for the privacy or protection of the witness, provided that the measures are not inconsistent with the rights of the accused.[49] Some of the measures that are frequently applied in court have also been developed in practice.[50] A judge or chamber can order that the witness's name and identifying information be expunged from the chamber's records.[51] In such a case, the witness will be assigned a pseudonym, e.g., "Witness R," which will be used for all purposes at the tribunal.[52] Moreover, a judge or chamber can order non-disclosure to the public of any records identifying the victim.[53] The chamber can also order image-altering and/or voice-distortion measures so that the witness's appearance or voice is unrecognizable on the court television and in the public gallery of the tribunal. In an early decision by the trial chamber in the *Tadić* case, a witness was allowed

---

[46] ICTY Statute, *supra* note 8, at art. 20(4); *and* ICTY Rules of Procedure and Evidence, *supra* note 11, at Rule 78.

[47] ICTY Rules of Procedure and Evidence, *supra* note 11, at Rule 71.

[48] *See further Prosecutor v. Tadić, Decision on the Defense Motion to Summon and Protect Defense Witnesses, and on the Giving of Evidence by Video-Link*, Case No. IT-94-1-PT, Tr. Ch. II, para. 19 (June 25, 1996). However, it should be noted that Decision was made prior to (the existence of) Rule 71 *bis* of the Rules.

[49] On the rights of the accused, *see further* Article 21 of the ICTY Statute.

[50] *See further e.g. Prosecutor v. Tadić, Decision on the Prosecutor's Motion, Protective Measures for Victims and Witnesses*, Case No. IT-94-I-T, Tr. Ch. II (August 10, 1995).

[51] ICTY Rules of Procedure and Evidence, *supra* note 11 at Rule 75(B)(i)(a).

[52] For instance, in the *Foca* case, where the identities of many victims were not disclosed, a chart was given to each witness that identified the protected witnesses and their pseudonyms, so that Witness X is Jane Doe, Witness Y is Jill Smith, etc. In giving testimony at trial, the witness would refer to the chart when saying who was taken out of the room and raped or who was being raped in the same room at the same time as the testifier, thus avoiding naming the victim but satisfying issues of credibility and consistency. Ways and means are creatively devised in an attempt to protect the identity of a protected witness. *Foca*, IT-96-23/2 (2000), at <http://www.un.org/icty/ind-e.htm>.

[53] ICTY Rules of Procedure and Evidence, *supra* note 11, at Rule 75(B)(i)(b).

"confidentiality," which was basically a combination of the protective measures described above.[54] The trial chamber carefully considered the need to balance matters of witness protection and the procedural rights of the accused. In the case in question, the trial chamber held that the confidentiality of the witness was justified if there were special considerations, such as in cases involving sexual assault.[55] The same decision also allowed for witness anonymity, which, if granted, results in the withholding of a witness's name and identifying data not only from the public, but also even from the other party to the proceedings.[56] Pursuant to Rule 79(a)(ii), a trial chamber may also order that the press and the public be excluded from all or part of the proceedings so that a witness can testify in closed session because of, for example, safety and security concerns or to protect a victim's or witness's identity. While witness confidentiality is a relatively common protective measure, witness anonymity will only be granted in highly exceptional circumstances.[57] Thus far,

---

[54] A Chamber may allow for confidentiality by ordering that: a) the name, address, whereabouts and other information which may identify the witnesses be withheld from the public and the media; b) the identity of witnesses shall not be disclosed to the public and the media. In this case, the witnesses will be assigned a pseudonym by Chamber which shall be used in all trial proceedings and when all parties are discussing the trial; and, or c) the public and the media be ordered not to photograph, video record or sketch the witnesses while they are at the International tribunal.

[55] *Prosecutor v. Tadić, Decision on the Prosecutor's Motion, Protective measures for Victims and Witnesses*, Case No. IT-94-I-T, Tr. Ch. II (August 10, 1995). *See also* the Separate Opinion of Judge Stephen in the same case.

[56] The requirements that have to be met as stated in the *Tadić* decision were, in short, the following: there must be real fear for the safety of the witness and his or her family; the testimony must be important to the Prosecutor's case; the Trial Chamber must be satisfied that there is no *prima facie* evidence that the witness is untrustworthy; the availability of any witness protection program must be considered; and, any measures taken should be strictly necessary. *Prosecutor v. Tadić, Decision on the Prosecutor's Motion, Protective measures for Victims and Witnesses*, Case No. IT-94-I-T, Tr. Ch. II (August 10, 1995). The criteria for anonymity have subsequently been elaborated upon in a decision in the *Blaskić* case, where it was noted that the Trial Chamber would be willing to grant anonymity for certain witnesses according to the standards set out in the *Tadić* decision, provided that the Prosecution supported its assertions with relevant proof, especially with regard to the credibility of a witness. *Prosecutor v. Blaskić, Decision on the Application of the Prosecutor (dated 17 October 1996), Requesting Protective Measures for Victims and Witnesses*, Case No. IT-95-14-PT, Tr. Ch. I, para. 42 (November 5, 1996).

[57] For detailed commentaries on this Decision, *see e.g.* Monroe Leigh, *The Yugoslav tribunal: Use of Unnamed Witnesses Against Accused*, 90 AM J. INTL L. 235 (1996); Christine M. Chinkin, *Due Process and Witness Anonymity*, 91 AM. J. INT'L L.

anonymity has been granted only once in the ICTY.[58]

Which, if any, protective measures are granted will depend on a variety of factors, including the preference of the witness and the assessment of the physical or mental danger or threat of harm. Ultimately, however, the chamber has the final responsibility for determining which protective measures are most appropriate. It should be emphasized however, that pursuant to Article 21(2) of the ICTY Statute,[59] the preference is to keep trials open as much as possible. Given the availability of measures that can be used in open session, such as image and voice distortion, the need to go into closed session in order to protect a witness is minimized.

As explained above, a witness has a duty to comply with an order of attendance before a chamber; if the witness fails to do so, he or she can be found in contempt of the tribunal. A witness can also be found in contempt if he or she contumaciously refuses or fails to answer a question before the tribunal,[60] although a witness may legitimately object to making any statement that might tend to incriminate him- or herself.[61] The rule on contempt also protects witnesses: it provides for holding in contempt of the tribunal any person who threatens, intimidates, causes injury to, offers a bribe to, or otherwise interferes with a witness who is giving, has given, or may potentially give testimony.[62]

A witness who has not yet testified may not be present when the testimony of another witness is given.[63] As previously noted, a witness

---

75 (1997); Monroe Leigh, *Witness Anonymity is Inconsistent with Due Process*, 91 Am. J. Int'l L. 80 (1997); and Natasha A. Affolder, *Tadić, the Anonymous Witness and the Sources of International Procedural Law*, 19 MICH. J. INT'L L. 445 (1998).

[58] See Prosecutor v. *Tadić*, Decision on the Prosecutor's Motion, Protective Measures for Victims and Witnesses, Case No. IT-94-I-T, Tr. Ch. II (August 10, 1995).

[59] ICTY Statute, *supra* note 8, at art. 21(2), which provides: "[T]he accused shall be entitled to a fail and public hearing, subject to article 22 [Protection of Victims and Witnesses] of the Statute."

[60] ICTY Rules of Procedure and Evidence, *supra* note 11, at Rule 77(a)(i). The maximum penalty that may be imposed on a person who is found guilty of such contempt is a term of imprisonment not exceeding twelve months, a fine not exceeding Dfl. 40.000, or both.

[61] *Id.* at Rule 90(F). This Rule also provides: "The Chamber may, however, compel the witness to answer the question. Testimony compelled in this way shall not be used as evidence in a subsequent prosecution against the witness for any offence than perjury."

[62] *Id.* at Rule 77(B) and (H). These rules provide that the tribunal may impose on a person found guilty of such contempt a maximum term of imprisonment not exceeding seven years, or a fine not exceeding Dfl. 200.000, or both.

[63] *Id.* at Rule 90(D).

will be asked to pledge to tell the truth and must speak the truth to the best of his or her knowledge or recollection. In the event that a chamber has strong grounds for believing that a witness has knowingly and willfully given false testimony, it may conduct a trial of the witness.[64]

Memories and attention to detail vary, particularly regarding experiencing or witnessing traumatic events. Recollections of events will likely be less vivid and less accurate if an extensive period of time elapses between the commission of the crimes, the giving of a statement to an investigator, and testimony in court. Factual inaccuracies, an inability to recall details, or contradictions of previous testimony will often result and may affect the credibility of the witness or the reliability of his or her testimony. Sometimes, many years will have elapsed between the time statements are given to the OTP or a defense counsel and the time the witness is actually called to appear before the tribunal to give testimony. Perpetrators may look quite different because of hair style, facial hair, weight loss or gain, different clothing, aging, stress, illness—a large number of factors can make in-court identification difficult. A witness should never guess or try to fill in details, however. It is up to the chamber to assess the credibility of the witness's testimony, taking into account all surrounding circumstances. During cross-examination, the party not calling the witness is allowed to question the witness as to statements made and may attempt to undermine his or her credibility. Although witnesses are informed about the reasons for cross-examination prior to their testimony, some witnesses find this part of the testimony very demanding. Whenever necessary, the chamber will control the manner of questioning in order to avoid any harassment or intimidation.[65] In addition, the presence of security officers (at least one for each defendant) and cameras inside the courtroom serves to dissuade a defendant from attempting to intimidate a witness on the stand.

Sexual violence was widespread in the Yugoslavia and Rwanda conflicts. This was widely reported and documented and many witnesses before the tribunals are victims of or witnesses to various forms of sexual violence, particularly rape, sexual slavery, and sexual humiliation. Rule 96 endeavors to take into account the nature of these crimes and provide additional protection and privacy by disallowing attempts to needlessly undermine the credibility of victims of sexual violence. More precisely, Rule 96 provides, *inter alia*, that in cases of sexual assault, no corroboration of the victim's testimony shall be required, and that the prior sexual conduct of the victim shall not be admitted into evidence.

---

[64] The maximum penalty for false testimony is a fine of Dfl. 200.000 or a term of imprisonment of seven years, or both. *See further id.* at Rule 91.

[65] *Id.* at Rule 75(C).

The protective mechanisms that are available to other witnesses (discussed above) are also available to witnesses testifying about various forms of sexual violence.[66]

While security and confidentiality are taken extremely seriously by the tribunal, mistakes may be made in accurately assessing threats or in the performance of one's duties. Although every effort is made, confidentiality and safety cannot be guaranteed with absolute certainty.

6. Post-Trial Phase

As we have seen, measures for the protection of witnesses are mainly limited to the time during the testimony. The ICTY cannot guarantee the safety of a witness or his or her family after the testimony. However, it should be borne in mind that most of the protective measures have been designed to minimize the witness's need for protection in his or her country of residence after the testimony.[67]

In cases where a witness is in need of post-trial support, arrangements can be made with the local social services providers or with international or local NGOs for follow-up support. Similarly, arrangements can be made with local police authorities in the event that a witness needs post-trial protection. Furthermore, the VWS has a relocation program designed for witnesses who cannot return to their homes because of serious concerns for their safety as a result of their appearance before the tribunal.[68] For these rare cases, the ICTY has concluded a number of agreements with states that are willing to accept such witnesses and their close family members.[69] In some cases, witnesses can have their

---

[66] *Id.* at Rule 34(A)(ii). This rule provides that the Victims and Witnesses Section should have qualified staff to provide counseling and support for victims and witnesses, in particular in cases of rape and sexual assault.

[67] Rydberg, *supra* note 33, at 465.

[68] The Victims and Witnesses Section's leaflet "Information on VWS" at 3. It should be noted that this is a security measure under the authority of the Registrar, as the decision to relocate a witness is taken by the Registrar upon the recommendation of the Victims and Witnesses Section.

[69] *Cf. Secretary-General's Third Annual Report, Report of the International tribunal for the Prosecution of Persons Responsible for Serious Violations of International Humanitarian Law Committed in the Territory of the Former Yugoslavia since 1991*, para 124, U.N. Doc. A/51/292 (August 16, 1996). As the agreements concern the safety and security of witnesses, the terms and details of these agreements are confidential. *See further* the Press Release of the ICTY, *United Kingdom becomes first state to agree to provide enhanced assistance to witness protection efforts of International tribunal*, U.N. Doc. CC/PIO/258-E (November 7, 1997), *available at* <http://www.un.org/icty/pressreal/p258-e.htm>.

identities changed or be entered into a domestic witness-protection program, although relocation to another country normally provides the witness with sufficient protection.[70] At the ICTR, a similar post-trial witness program has already assured the relocation of those witnesses thought to be particularly at risk. Some have been relocated in countries outside Rwanda, while others have been relocated within Rwanda.[71]

7. Restitution of Property and Victim Compensation

The tribunals' statutes provide for recovery of property. In particular, Article 24, Penalties, stipulates that "[i]n addition to imprisonment, the Trial Chambers may order the return of any property and proceeds acquired by criminal conduct, including by means of duress, to their rightful owners." Rule 105 of the ICTY Rules provides that after a judgment of conviction containing a finding that unlawful taking of property was associated with the crime, the trial chamber shall, at the request of the prosecutor, or *proprio motu*, may after a special hearing, order the restitution of the property or the proceeds thereof.[72] In other words, under the current rules, the victim him- or herself does not have standing to request that the chamber order restitution of his or her property. Thus far, no orders for restitution have been made. However, the matter has been raised before the ICTR, where a request for restitution has been made in the *Bagosora* case.[73]

Victims cannot apply for compensation directly at the tribunals. However, Rule 106 provides that in the event that a victim or persons claiming through the victim bring an action in a national court or other competent body to obtain compensation, the judgment of the tribunal shall be final and binding as to the criminal responsibility of the convicted person for such injury.[74]

In this connection, it must be noted that the judges of the ICTY recently stated that they have recommended to the Security Council

---

[70] Rydberg, *supra* note 33, at 465.

[71] *See further* ICTR web-site, at <http://www.ictr.org/ENGLISH/factsheets/9.htm>.

[72] ICTY Rules of Procedure and Evidence, *supra* note 11, at Rules 106 and Sub-rule 98 ter (B).

[73] *Prosecutor v. Bagosora,* "*Request to appear before the tribunal and to testify as Amicus Curiae in the case of Théoneste Bagosora and others,*" *(by the Minister of Justice of the Republic of Rwanda, dated 20 April 1998),* Case No. ICTR-98-37 (1998).

[74] ICTY Rules of Procedure and Evidence, *supra* note 11 at Rules 106(B)–(C). *Id.* at Rule 106(A) provides that the Registrar shall transmit to the competent authorities of the States concerned the judgment finding the accused guilty of a crime which has caused injury to the victim.

and the Secretary-General that methods of compensating victims of crimes in the former Yugoslavia be seriously considered by the appropriate organs of the United Nations.[75]

8. The International Criminal Court

In July 1998, delegates of 120 countries signed the Rome Statute of the International Criminal Court (ICC), a permanent court that will have jurisdiction over a wide range of crimes in the territories of the state parties, including war crimes (whether committed in internal or international armed conflicts), crimes against humanity, genocide, and eventually aggression.[76] The ICC will enter into force following the deposit of the 60th instrument of ratification.[77]

The Rome Statute and the ICC Rules of Procedure and Evidence, which were subsequently adopted by the Preparatory Commission,[78] contain numerous provisions regarding victims and witnesses, which are far more extensive than those developed by the tribunals. Below is a summary of the most pertinent provisions regarding victims or witnesses who may be refugees or internally displaced.

Article 15 of the Rome Statute, concerning the investigations of the prosecutor, states that "[v]ictims may make representations to the Pre-Trial Chamber, in accordance with the Rules of Procedure and Evidence." Like the ICTY and ICTR, the Victim and Witnesses Unit is located in the Registry.[79] This unit, in consultation with the prosecutor, is required to provide:

---

[75] ICTY Press release, *The judges of the ICTY Acknowledge the Right of Victims of Crimes Committed in the Former Yugoslavia to Seek Compensation*, U.N. Doc. CC/P.I.S./528-E, (14 September 2000).

[76] *Rome Statute of the International Criminal Court*, Bibliography of Cited International Instruments.

[77] *Id.* at art. 126 (1), which provides: "This Statute shall enter into force on the first day of the month after the 60th day following the date of the deposit of the 60th instrument of ratification, acceptance, approval or accession with the Secretary-General of the United Nations."

[78] *See Report of the Preparatory Commission for the International Criminal Court, Addendum, Finalized draft text of the Rules of Procedure and Evidence*, UN Doc. PCNICC/2000/INF/3/Add.1, (12 July 2000). The final Rules must be adopted by the Assemblies of States Parties, once seventy nations have ratified the ICC Statute. For a general comparison of victim-related issues in the ICTY and ICC Statute, *see* Rydberg, *supra* note 33.

[79] ICC Statute, *supra* note 76, at art. 43.

protective measures and security arrangements, counselling and other appropriate assistance for witnesses, victims who appears before the Court, and others who are at risk on account of testimony given by such witnesses. The Unit shall include staff with expertise in trauma, including trauma related to crimes of sexual violence.[80]

Thus, the unit's mandate extends beyond protecting only persons testifying before the court. The unit is also required to take measures to protect others who are at risk because of witness testimony.

Article 68 of the Rome Statute, entitled "Protection of the victims and witnesses and their participation in the proceedings," is one of the statute's most important provisions and serves as the basis for the development of extensive rules for implementing its requirements. It is reproduced in its entirety below:

> 1. The Court shall take appropriate measures to protect the safety, physical and psychological well-being, dignity and privacy of victims and witnesses. In so doing, the Court shall have regard to all relevant factors, including age, gender . . . and health, and the nature of the crime, in particular, but not limited to, where the crime involves sexual or gender violence or violence against children. The Prosecutor shall take such measures particularly during the investigation and prosecution of such crimes. These measures shall not be prejudicial to or inconsistent with the rights of the accused and a fair and impartial trial.
>
> 2. As an exception to the principle of public hearings provided for in article 67, the Chambers of the Court may, to protect victims and witnesses or an accused, conduct any part of the proceedings *in camera* or allow the presentation of evidence by electronic or other special means. In particular, such measures shall be implemented in the case of a victim of sexual violence or a child who is a victim or a witness, unless otherwise ordered by the Court, having regard to all the circumstances, particularly the views of the victim or witness.
>
> 3. Where the personal interests of the victims are affected, the Court shall permit their views and concerns to be presented and considered at stages of the proceedings determined

---

[80] *Id.*

to be appropriate by the Court and in a manner which is not prejudicial to or inconsistent with the rights of the accused and a fair and impartial trial. Such views and concerns may be presented by the legal representatives of the victims where the Court considers it appropriate, in accordance with the Rules of Procedure and Evidence.

4. The Victims and Witnesses Unit may advise the Prosecutor and the Court on appropriate protective measures, security arrangements, counselling and assistance as referred to in article 43, paragraph 6.

5. Where the disclosure of evidence or information pursuant to this Statute may lead to the grave endangerment of the security of a witness or his or her family, the Prosecutor may, for the purposes of any proceedings conducted prior to the commencement of the trial, withhold such evidence or information and instead submit a summary thereof. Such measures shall be exercised in a manner which is not prejudicial to or inconsistent with the rights of the accused and a fair and impartial trial.

6. A State may make an application for necessary measures to be taken in respect of the protection of its servants or agents and the protection of confidential or sensitive information.

The statute thus requires the court to make extensive provisions on behalf of victims and witnesses while also balancing the rights of the accused and ensuring the trials are fair and impartial. The rules supplement the above provisions, containing guidelines and procedures that are designed to effectuate the prescriptions mandated in the statute.

Article 68(3) of the statute provides that the court permit the views and concerns of victims to be presented and considered during the proceedings. In other words, there is a participatory role for victims other than as witnesses. As seen above, this is not the case before the ICTY and the ICTR.

In the ICC Rules, the Victims and Witnesses Unit is required, *inter alia*, to provide "witnesses, victims who appear before the Court, and others who are at risk on account of testimony given by such witnesses" with appropriate protective and security measures and, if necessary, to formulate long-term or short-term plans for their protection.[81] Such plans would almost certainly require the cooperation of states and could

---

[81] *Id.* at Rule 17(2)(a)(i).

be of enormous assistance to refugees or internally displaced persons. It is important to emphasize, however, that while the court does not want to leave a person in a worse position for testifying, it also cannot be seen to reward witnesses by giving them special treatment, as such actions might call the veracity of the testimony into question.

Article 87 of the statute governs general provisions relating to requests for state cooperation. In particular, it stipulates in sub-article 4 that if assistance is requested for cooperation, the court may take necessary measures to ensure the "safety or physical or psychological well-being of any victims, potential witnesses and their families." Conceivably, this article could be used to protect the mental well-being of potential witnesses in a state by ensuring that they or their situation will not be jeopardized or otherwise put in a worse position by going to the court to testify or by providing other assistance in the investigation and prosecution.

Other important provisions with regard to victims are contained in Article 75, which concerns reparations to victims. It mandates the court to establish principles concerning reparations, restitution, compensation, and rehabilitation. The ICC would thus provide much more in terms of victim compensation than do the tribunals. Regarding reparations, for example, Rule 94 provides:

1. A victim's request for reparations under article 75 shall be made in writing and filed with the Registrar. It shall contain the following particulars:
   (a) The identity and address of the claimant;
   (b) A description of the injury, loss or harm;
   (c) The location and date of the incident and, to the extent possible, the identity of the person or persons the victim believes to be responsible for the injury, loss or harm;
   (d) Where restitution of assets, property or other tangible items is sought, a description of them;
   (e) Claims for compensation;
   (f) Claims for rehabilitation and other forms of remedy;
   (g) To the extent possible, any relevant supporting documentation, including names and addresses of witnesses.
2. At commencement of the trial and subject to any protective measures, the Court shall ask the Registrar to provide notification of the request to the person or persons named in the request or identified in the charges and, to the extent possible, to any interested persons or any interested States. Those notified shall file with the Registry any representation made under article 75, paragraph 3.

The rules of the ICC contain abundant stipulations specifically pertaining to victims and witnesses, in addition to the numerous other provisions that affect such persons. For example, four rules are devoted solely to the functioning of the Victim and Witnesses Unit, including details governing the responsibility of the Registrar, the functions of the unit, the responsibilities of the unit, and the expertise of the staff of the unit.[82] Further, the rules require the prosecutor to take steps necessary for the protection of victims and witnesses. For example, Rule 50 requires the prosecutor to inform known victims that he or she intends to seek authorization from a pre-trial chamber to initiate a particular investigation, unless the prosecutor determines that informing known victims "would pose a danger to the integrity of the investigation or the life or well-being of victims and witnesses." These alternatives may conflict, so the prosecutor will need to take measures to ensure that the requirements imposed are fulfilled.

Section III of the rules is made up of 15 rules exclusively pertaining to victims and witnesses. These rules address definitions and general principles (Rules 85–86), protection (Rules 87–88), participation of victims in the proceedings (Rules 89–93), and reparations to victims (Rules 94–99). The guidelines are rather extensive and detailed, and many are of a mandatory nature, particularly when having their basis in the statute.

Bibliography

Articles

Affolder, Natasha A., *Tadić, the Anonymous Witness and the Sources of International Procedural Law*, 19 MICH. J. INT'L L. 445 (1998).

Chinkin, Christine M., *Due Process and Witness Anonymity*, 91 AM. J. INT'L. L. 75 (1997).

Leigh, Monroe, *Witness Anonymity is Inconsistent with Due Process*, 91 AM. J. INT'L. L. 80 (1997).

Leigh, Monroe, *The Yugoslav Tribunal: Use of Unnamed Witnesses Against Accused*, 90 AM. J. INT'L. L. 235 (1996).

Rydberg, Åsa, *The Protection of the Interests of Witnesses—The ICTY in Comparison to the Future ICC*, 12 LEIDEN J. INT'L L. 455 (1999).

---

[82] *Id.* at Rules 16–19.

U.N. Documents

Final Report to the Prosecutor by the Committee Established to Review the NATO Bombing Campaign Against the Federal Republic of Yugoslavia, U.N. Doc. PR/P.I.S./510-E (2000).

Group of Experts Report, Cambodia, U.N. Doc. A/53/850 (1999).

International Criminal Tribunal for the Prosecution of Persons Responsible for Genocide and Other Serious Violations of International Humanitarian Law Committed in the Territory of Rwanda and Rwandan Citizens responsible for genocide and other such violations committed in the territory of neighboring States, between 1 January 1994 and 31 December 1994, SC Res. 955, annex, U.N. SCOR, 49th Sess., Res. & Dec., at 15, U.N. Doc. S/INF/50 (1994), *reprinted in* 33 I.L.M 1602 (1994).

International Tribunal for the Prosecution of Persons Responsible for Serious Violations of International Humanitarian Law Committed in the Territory of the Former Yugoslavia since 1991, U.N. Doc. S/25704, Annex (1993), *reprinted in* 32 I.L.M. 1192 (1993).

Judges of the ICTY Acknowledge the Right of Victims of Crimes Committed in the Former Yugoslavia to Seek Compensation, U.N. Doc. CC/P.I.S./528-E (2000).

Report of the International Tribunal for the Prosecution of Persons Responsible for Serious Violations of International Humanitarian Law Committed in the Territory of the Former Yugoslavia since 1991, U.N. Doc. A/51/292 (1996).

Report of the Preparatory Commission for the International Criminal Court, Addendum, Finalized draft text of the Rules of Procedure and Evidence, U.N. Doc. PCNICC/2000/INF/3/Add.1 (2000).

Report of the Secretary-General on the establishment of a Special Court for Sierra Leone, U.N. Doc. S/2000/915 (2000).

Rome Statute of the International Criminal Court, adopted by the United Nations Diplomatic Conference of Plenipotentiaries on the Establishment of an International Criminal Court on 17 July 1998, U.N. Doc. A/CONF. 183/9 (1998).

Security Council Resolution 827, U.N. Doc. S/RES/827 (1993), *available at* <http://www.un.org/documents>.

Security Council Resolution 955, U.N. Doc. S/RES/955 (1994).

Security Council Resolution 1315, U.N. Doc. S/RES/1315 (2000).

Secretary-General's Fourth Report, U.N. Doc. A/52/375 (1997).

Secretary-General's Second Annual Report, U.N. Doc. A/50/365 (1995).

United Kingdom Becomes First State to Agree to Provide Enhanced Assistance to Witness Protection Efforts of International Tribunal, U.N. Doc. CC/PIO/258-E (1997).

ICTR:

International Criminal Tribunal for Rwanda, *Witnesses and Victims Support Section, Fact Sheet No. 9* (February, 2001), *at* <http://www.ictr.org/ENGLISH/factsheets/9.htm>.

International Criminal Tribunal for Rwanda, *Rules of Procedure, adopted* July 5, 1995, last amended November 3, 2000, *available at* <http://www.ictr.org/>.

International Criminal Tribunal for Rwanda, *Statute of the International Criminal Tribunal for Rwanda, available at* <http://www.ictr.org>.

ICTY:

International Criminal Tribunal for Yugoslavia, *Rules of Procedure and Evidence, adopted* February 11, 1994, IT/32/Rev.18, *available at* <http://www.un.org/icty>.

International Criminal Tribunal for Yugoslavia, *Statute of the International Tribunal for Yugoslavia, adopted* May 25, 1993, *available at* <http://www.un.org/icty>.

Cases

Foca, IT-96-23/2 (2000), *available at* <http://www.un.org/icty/ind-e.htm>.

Prosecutor v. Bagosora, "*Request to appear before the Tribunal and to testify as Amicus Curiae in the case of Théoneste Bagosora and others*" *(by the Minister of Justice of the Republic of Rwanda, dated 20 April 1998)*, Case No. ICTR-98-37 (1998).

Prosecutor v. Blaskić, Decision on the Application of the Prosecutor (dated 17 October 1996), Requesting Protective Measures for Victims and Witnesses, Case No. IT-95-14-PT, Tr. Ch. I (November 5, 1996).

Prosecutor v. Tadić, Decision on the Defense Motion to Summon and Protect Defense Witnesses, and on the Giving of Evidence by Video-Link, Case No. IT-94-1-PT, Tr. Ch. II (June 25, 1996).

Prosecutor v. Tadić, Decision on the Prosecutor's Motion, Protective Measures for Victims and Witnesses, Case No. IT-94-I-T, Tr. Ch. II (August 10, 1995).

Miscellaneous

Victims and Witnesses Section Leaflets

"Accompanying Support Person"
"Child Care Provisions"
"Compensation for Lost Wages"
"Daily Allowance Policy"
"Information on VWS"
"Provisions for Dependants"

Chapter 8
Internationalized Legal Structures and The Protection of Internationally Displaced Persons

Marcus Cox
Christopher Harland

1. Introduction

The protection of internally displaced persons (IDPs) inside their country of origin poses particular difficulties for the international legal system. Because they are within the jurisdiction of their own state, IDPs are dependent on national institutions to safeguard their rights, under the watchful eye of the international human rights regime. All too often, however, the conflict that caused their displacement has also weakened or compromised the domestic legal structures, leaving international observers able to do little more than point out the lack of effective remedies for widespread human rights violations. International human rights standards are of limited practical value without institutions to apply them.

In recent years, an important new approach to addressing this problem has emerged. As part of peace settlements in countries such as Bosnia and Herzegovina, Kosovo, East Timor, Georgia, and Israel/Palestine, the parties have agreed to the establishment of specialized institutions to deal with the human rights consequences of population displacement. In a number of cases, these are "internationalized" bodies—that is, tribunals with domestic mandates but with the supervision or participation of international actors. This mixture of domestic and international jurisdiction represents an interesting new dimension to the in-country protection of human rights.

Special legal institutions may be required in the aftermath of mass displacement for one or more of several purposes. First, there may be a need for special legal remedies for people wishing to *return to their homes* in the aftermath of a conflict. Large-scale or protracted conflict may lead to a situation where property abandoned by refugees and IDPs is occupied by other persons. Often, the secondary occupants are other IDPs with genuine humanitarian needs. Where the destruction of housing has resulted in a shortage of housing space, the return of IDPs inevitably gives rise to property disputes that must be mediated by institutions that are able to resolve questions of property title, issue eviction orders, and identify emergency housing for vulnerable individuals. The Dayton Peace Agreement in Bosnia contains the most elaborate institutional structures for the return of refugees and IDPs to their homes. Second, there may be need for institutions to deal with the *human rights consequences* of displacement. IDPs are particularly vulnerable to a range of human rights abuses, from persecution by hostile authorities to discrimination and exclusion from public services and denial of social and economic rights. Third, peace agreements may incorporate mechanisms to address *historical injustices* that date back before the displacement. In South Africa and Kosovo, for example, special institutions have been created to remedy the discriminatory expropriation of property over a period of many years. Remedying historical injustices is often a necessary part of a comprehensive peace settlement and it requires legal institutions, often with external involvement, to act as impartial arbiters of complex factual and legal disputes.

The inclusion of international elements in these institutions may be of assistance, if it meets with the agreement of the parties. First, it may be necessary for reasons of *capacity*. Mass displacement can give rise to human rights violations on an enormous scale. Human rights claims, and particularly those involving questions of property title, are not easily resolved on a mass basis. In a post-conflict situation, the regular domestic court system may have limited capacity as a result of loss of personnel, destruction of infrastructure, and the collapse of public funding. Special bodies outside of the permanent judicial system, utilizing international management, personnel, and resources, may be created on a temporary basis to meet the exceptional needs of the displacement situation. Second, international involvement may be needed as a *neutral arbiter*, to overcome bias in domestic institutions. During protracted civil conflict, local courts and administrative bodies may become implicated in discrimination against minorities. Incorporating international supervision or control may be the only means of providing a legal framework acceptable to all sides.

Each mass displacement situation gives rise to a unique set of legal and institutional problems, and practitioners should be wary of standardized solutions. Selection of the appropriate institutional tools requires close knowledge of local conditions, including the legal culture, the institutional environment, and the particular legal problems caused by the displacement. Drawing mainly on the Bosnian experience, where there has been extensive experimentation with different institutional models, this chapter discusses the institutional choices available. The first part considers the legal problems raised by population displacement that such institutions are likely to encounter. The second part examines a number of existing institutional models. The third part draws some conclusions on the utility of internationalized institutions to address the human rights consequences of mass displacement.

2. Human Rights Issues in Population Displacement

2.1 The Right to Return Home

The rights of refugees and IDPs in their country of origin raise a very different set of legal problems than the traditional concerns of the refugee lawyer. Whereas the rights of refugees outside their country of origin are well established (protection, asylum, and non-refoulement), the rights of IDPs must be assembled from general principles of human rights and humanitarian law. In particular, the right of refugees and IDPs to return to their home of origin (as distinct from the right to repatriate to state of origin) is only just beginning to be discussed in the international legal system. Of the main binding human rights instruments,[1] only the 1950 European Convention for the Protection of Human Rights and Fundamental Freedoms and the 1969 American Convention on Human Rights[2] protect property rights. The right to return home must therefore be approached via norms of general application, such as the prohibition on forced displacement of civilian populations under the 1949 Geneva Conventions,[3] the rights to freedom of movement and protection of home and family life under the 1966 International Covenant on Civil and Political Rights,[4] and the right to adequate housing under the 1966 International Covenant on Economic, Social and Cultural Rights.[5] The authors of the *Guiding Principles on Internal Displacement* felt able to propose only a tentative duty on the

---

[1] See Bibliography of Cited International Instruments for full citations to these and other international instruments mentioned in this chapter.

[2] *European Convention on Human Rights*, art. 1, prot. 1; *American Convention on Human Rights*, art. 21.

[3] *Convention (IV) relative to the Protection of Civilian Persons in Time of War.*

[4] *International Covenant on Civil and Political Rights*, art. 17.

[5] *International Covenant on Economic, Social and Cultural Rights.* See also *International Convention on the Elimination of All Forms of Racial Discrimination*, art. 5(e)(iii).

part of domestic authorities to "establish the conditions and provide the means to allow IDPs to return to their homes."[6]

However, the right of refugees and IDPs to return to their homes may be asserted in the context of particular displacement situations. The Security Council has recognized the right of refugees and IDPs to return home in safety following the Kosovo,[7] East Timor,[8] Abkhazia,[9] and other conflicts. The most extensive statement of the right to return and to recover property lost through displacement is contained in the 1995 Dayton Peace Agreement in Bosnia and Herzegovina,[10] where it is elevated to a constitutional principle.[11] The document guarantees Bosnian citizens "the highest level of internationally recognised human rights and fundamental freedoms."[12] The European Convention on Human Rights (ECHR)[13] is incorporated as the highest law of the land, and a series of novel institutional mechanisms were created to promote human rights and refugee return, some of which included international control or participation. The parties to the Dayton Agreement also consented to the indefinite presence of a strong international peace implementation mission, including a military force led by NATO (initially 60,000 troops, and five years later still in excess of 20,000), a High Representative responsible for civilian coordination and political oversight, UNHCR as lead agency on refugee and humanitarian matters, OSCE with a human rights monitoring mission, over 2,000 international police monitors under the authority of the UN, and a wide range of other international organizations and NGOs.

Despite the constitutional and international guarantees, IDPs have faced great difficulty in recovering their property. At the fifth anniversary of the Dayton Agreement, only 17 percent of the 231,000 properties claimed by refugees and IDPs had been repossessed. IDPs and refugees have been confronted with a whole array of legal and administrative obstacles, illustrating that the right to return is in fact a composite of many different, interlocking legal rights.

---

[6] *Guiding Principles on Internal Displacement, Principle 28*, U.N. Doc E/CN.4/1998/53/Add.2 (1998). *Internally Displaced Persons: Compilation and Analysis of Legal Norms*, U.N. Doc. E/CN.4/1998/53/Add.1 (1998).

[7] U.N. Doc. S/RES/1244/1999/ (10 June 1999).

[8] U.N. Doc. S/RES/1319/2000/ (8 September 2000).

[9] U.N. Doc. S/RES/876/1993 (19 October 1993).

[10] *General Framework Agreement for Peace in Bosnia and Herzegovina.*

[11] Constitution of Bosnia and Herzegovina, art. II, para.5., *adopted* Dec. 1, 1995, at <http://www.uni-wuerzburg.de/law/bk00000_.html>.

[12] *Id.*, art. II, para.1.

[13] *European Convention on Human* Rights, *in* Bibliography of Cited International Instruments. Bosnia is not yet a party to the Convention itself.

2.1.1 Property Rights

By far the most extensive obstacle to return is interference with rights to residential property. During and after the war, all three regimes adopted laws, decrees, and administrative practices that prevented refugees and displaced persons from repossessing their homes. Adopted initially for humanitarian purposes in order to allow local authorities to allocate abandoned property to incoming displaced persons, these systems came to be applied in a corrupt and discriminatory manner. In some cases, property rights were canceled altogether and reallocated permanently to members of the ethnic majority. In other cases, the property right remained intact but the property was temporarily reallocated by administrative decision or simply taken over illegally. Displaced persons who had occupied other people's housing out of humanitarian need became, paradoxically, a powerful political lobby against return.[14]

2.1.2 Personal Security

Refugees and displaced persons seeking to return into areas controlled by another ethnic group faced threats to their personal safety to varying degrees throughout the country. Freedom of movement was restricted by illegal checkpoints, harassment by police and security forces, and ethnically motivated violence. Ethnically differentiated vehicle license plates and travel and identification documents greatly increased the vulnerability of citizens outside their own community.[15] Illegal arrest and detention of minorities, often on the pretext of war-related crimes, was widespread. Some detainees were subject to ill-treatment or torture, and there were cases of disappearances. Destruction of minority housing occurred extensively in certain areas.

2.1.3 Discrimination

IDPs returning into ethnically divided communities faced widespread discrimination in access to employment and public services. Public enterprises were divided territorially among the ethnic groups,

---

[14] *See* Marcus Cox, *The Right to Return Home: International Intervention and Ethnic Cleansing in Bosnia and Herzegovina*, 47 INT'L & COMP. L.Q. 599 (1998).

[15] A common vehicle license plate system was adopted under enormous international pressure in 1998, leading to a dramatic improvement in freedom of movement. *See Common License Plate / Vehicle Registration Document*, Office of the High Representative, Sarajevo, 29 May 1998, at <http://www.ohr.int/ docu/dr-lic1.htm>.

and IDPs were dismissed from their jobs under pre-war legislation for failure to report to work. Unemployment rates, which remain in excess of 50 percent for the population as a whole, exceeded 90 percent for minority returnees.[16] Access to pension funds was a major problem for elderly people attempting to return to their homes.[17] Minorities faced discrimination in access to humanitarian assistance and social services, and some of those who reconstructed their own houses were not permitted to reconnect to electricity and telephone services. Minorities enjoyed little freedom of expression or political participation outside their own ethnic group. Restrictions on freedom of religion were common, with widespread destruction of religious property and denial of access to places of worship and to burial grounds.[18]

2.2 Restitution and Transitional Justice

A feature of many protracted civil conflicts is the expropriation of property from minority groups as part of a campaign of discrimination or repression. Expropriation of property over an extended period of time gives rise to legal and practical problems of enormous complexity, which can pose a major obstacle to peace settlements. A number of recent peace agreements have incorporated measures for restitution of property. This can best be understood in the category of *transitional justice*. Together with war crimes tribunals and commissions of enquiry, restitution mechanisms are designed to address legal problems with broad symbolic and political implications. By recreating a common legal baseline, they allow the peace process to proceed on a solid foundation.

In Kosovo, for example, in the ten years following the abolition of Kosovo's autonomy within the former Yugoslavia in 1990, upwards of 400,000 ethnic Albanians were purged from jobs in the administration and public economy. In many cases, these individuals also lost publicly owned apartments given in connection with their employment. These apartments were then reallocated by the Serb authorities, and in subsequent years were privatized and sold on the open market. This

---

[16] See Michelle Alfaro, *Returnee Monitoring Study: Minority Returnees to the Republika Srpska-Bosnia and Herzegovina*, UNHCR Sarajevo Protection Unit (June 2000), at <http://www.unhcr.ba/Protection/PTB/rsminor.pdf>.

[17] *Id.*

[18] See *Islamic Community v. RS*, Human Rights Chamber (CH/96/29) (June 11, 1999) (finding an ECHR violation in the failure of Serb authorities in Banja Luka to provide permission to reconstruct mosques destroyed by vandalism in 1993).

gives rise to complex legal disputes between those who were dispossessed under discriminatory laws and subsequent *bona fide* purchasers.[19] The UN administration in Kosovo (UNMIK) has undertaken to reverse the effects of discriminatory laws over the past ten years.[20] To that end, it is in the process of establishing a Housing and Property Directorate, a quasi-judicial tribunal with both local and international participants.[21]

In South Africa, forced removals from land took place on a systematic basis from 1913 onward under the apartheid regime. The removals were carried out in order to establish zones where non-white populations were forbidden to own land. Land title was redistributed through expropriations, forced transactions, and dispossession by military means.[22] The South African authorities estimate that at least 3.5 million people lost land rights as a result of forced removals. The Interim Constitution of 1993 provided for the restitution of property by the state "in respect of which persons or communities were dispossessed under or for the purpose of furthering the objects of any racially based discriminatory law." A Commission on the Restitution of Land Rights was established to administer and, wherever possible, mediate restitution claims, and a specialized Land Claims Court was created for formal adjudication. The court has broad discretion to determine an equitable solution and may award claimants restitution in kind, or just and equitable compensation, or priority access to government housing and land development schemes. As of June 2000, a total number of 67,531 claims had been registered and 6,520 claims had been settled.[23]

In UN-administered East Timor, resolving historical disputes over property rights is an essential part of establishing the rule of law. Over the course of successive occupations, the property system has become highly irregular. The Indonesian regime carried out confiscation and redistribution of land on a large scale, including the forced resettlement of entire villages. Going back further in time, the Portuguese colonial authorities attempted various inconclusive land reforms, introducing new forms of title and displacing traditional communities. Certain elements

---

19   Hans Das, *Regularising Housing and Property Rights in Kosovo: The Housing and Property Claims Directorate*, UNMIK (Pristina, February 2000).

20   U.N. Doc. UNMIK/REG/1999/23 (15 November 1999), at <http://www.un.org/peace/kosovo/pages/regulations/reg23.html>.

21   Marcus Cox, *Principles of Law, Evidence and Procedure: The Housing and Property Directorate and Claims Commission*, UNMIK (Pristina, March 2000).

22   For a detailed account, *see* K. Henrard, *The Internally Displaced in South Africa. The Strategy of Forced Removals and Apartheid*, at <http://www.law.kuleuven.ac.be/jura>.

23   For the text of the Constitution and the principal acts, and for statistics, *see Interim Constitution* (1993), at <http://www.land.pwv.gov.za/restitution>.

of traditional land title continue to exist, but with uncertain legal status. In addition, the recent conflict has brought about secondary occupation of abandoned housing, as well as extensive destruction of property.[24] The UN mission in East Timor (UNTAET) is reportedly establishing a specialized commission to resolve property disputes.

The restitution of property is also reported to be on the agenda of Middle East peace negotiations, concerning Palestinians displaced during and after the creation of the State of Israel, and in recent proximity talks aimed at ending the partition of Cyprus.

3. Institutional Models for the Protection of IDPs

The international mission in Bosnia has experimented with various legal strategies and institutional structures for promoting human rights and return among the IDP population. Some of these were established in the Dayton Agreement itself; others were developed along the way in response to problems encountered in the field, using the High Representative's authority to impose laws. For the purpose of comparison, it is useful to divide the institutions into four categories.

Mass title determination. To deal with the enormous scale of dispossession of residential property, the Dayton Agreement created a Commission for Real Property Claims of Displaced Persons and Refugees to make decisions, through a fast-track administrative process, on property title for hundreds of thousands of individuals.

Human rights standards setting. The Human Rights Chamber and the state-level Human Rights Ombudsman were created as analogues of the European Court and former Commission of Human Rights, respectively, to make formal determinations of human rights claims against the state and the two entities.

Human rights mediation. There is a fully local ombudsman institution that investigates human rights complaints in the Bosniak-Croat Federation. Although its findings are not binding, the executive authorities have an obligation to permit them to engage in advocacy and mediation activities.

Management of the return process. An administrative claims process for repossession of property has been created at the municipal level. The administrative authority both rules on property rights and seeks to resolve the housing needs of the current occupant of the claimed property. This model is also being developed in Kosovo.

---

[24] Jean du Plessis and Scott Leckie, *Housing, Property and Land Rights in East Timor*, UNCHS-HABITAT (May 31, 2000).

3.1 Mass Property Title Determination: The Property Commission

The Commission for Real Property Claims of Displaced Persons and Refugees (CRPC) was established under Chapter 2 of Annex 7 of the Dayton Agreement as the principal legal mechanism for implementing the right to return. Its mandate is to "receive and decide any claims for real property in BiH, where the property has not voluntarily been sold or otherwise transferred since April 1, 1992, and where the claimant does not now enjoy possession of that property. Claims may be for return of the property or for just compensation in lieu of return."[25] The CRPC is authorized to disregard, although not to strike down, domestic legislation that is contrary to the Dayton Agreement, and to set aside property transactions made under duress. It operates as a quasi-judicial tribunal, with systems designed to register and decide claims in large numbers.

The CRPC has nine members, three of whom are foreigners appointed by the President of the European Court of Human Rights. The CRPC is supported almost entirely through foreign funding, principally from the European Commission and the US Government. With a staff of approximately 400 under a small international management team, the CRPC receives claims through eight offices and mobile teams within Bosnia and eight centers in refugee host countries. Because many refugees and IDPs have lost their title documents, CRPC staff investigate each claim using their right of access to official property records. Decisions are rendered on a mass basis, and there is no provision for oral evidence or public hearings. CRPC decisions are final and binding and cannot be reviewed in any court. However, the CRPC has established its own fairly liberal provisions for internal review.

By using only a single party administrative procedure and confining itself to questions of title, the CRPC has been able to achieve a high rate of efficiency in processing claims. With an annual budget of US $6.2 million,[26] a large investment of time and money was required to make the institution fully operational, and decision-making did not take place in large numbers until its third year of operation. As of July 2000, more than 270,000 claims had been registered, suggesting that the institution has successfully reached a high proportion of displaced persons and refugees. The commission has rendered decisions on over 120,000 claims and, with a rate of work now approaching 10,000

---

[25] *General Framework Agreement for Peace in Bosnia and Herzegovina, supra* note 10, at annex 7, art. XI.

[26] *Commission for Real Property Claims of Displaced Persons and Refugees*, at <http://www.crpc.org.ba/english/java/information.htm>.

decisions per month, it may complete its work within six to seven years of commencing operations.

Implementation of decisions has been a weakness of the CRPC model. The Dayton Agreement merely provides that the parties have an obligation "to respect and implement its decisions expeditiously and in good faith."[27] With no particular implementing mechanism specified, CRPC decisions were almost entirely ignored for the first three years of its operation. In October 1999, the High Representative imposed laws that create a domestic enforcement procedure through local administrative bodies, which is beginning to meet with some success. However, because it depends on local institutions for enforcement, the CRPC is not a self-contained remedy, and it remains hostage to the ethnic bias and inefficiency of local institutions.

3.2 Human Rights Standards Setting: The Human Rights Chamber and Ombudsman

The Human Rights Chamber and the state-level Ombudsman were created as two parts of a "Human Rights Commission" under Annex 6 of the Dayton Agreement, designed to mirror the functions of the European Court of Human Rights and the former European Commission on Human Rights in Strasbourg. Their mandate is to consider violations of the European Convention on Human Rights (ECHR) or discrimination under any other international human rights instrument occurring since the peace agreement. While the Chamber and the Ombudsman work mainly with individual complainants, their primary role is to assess the compliance of domestic laws and judicial and administrative practices with the ECHR, not to process return claims in large numbers. They are vehicles for introducing European human rights standards into Bosnia and Herzegovina, and in so doing prepare Bosnia for membership in the Council of Europe.

The Chamber has 14 members, eight of whom are appointed by the President of the European Court of Human Rights. It has broad power to issue final and binding orders against the two entity governments and the state to remedy violations.[28] It issues formal judgments on admissibility, and novel or factually complex cases are heard in public. Its rules of procedure are modeled closely on those of the European Court and, as in Strasbourg, the governments are represented in the

---

[27] *General Framework Agreement for Peace in Bosnia and Herzegovina, supra* note 10, at art. VIII, annex 7.

[28] *General Framework Agreement for Peace in Bosnia and Herzegovina, supra* note 10, at annex 6, art. XI, para. 6.

proceedings by agents. The Chamber may issue provisional measures, or interim injunctions, wherever the applicant is able to show both a *prima facie* case on the merits and that irreparable harm would result from inaction prior to trial. These injunctions have usually been respected by the authorities. The Chamber also issues financial awards against the governments to compensate for damages, such as the costs of medical treatment after police violence or income lost during illegal detention.

With a staff of 39 and an annual budget of around US $1.5 million, the Chamber issued its first decision in August 1996, but did not become fully operational until mid-1998. As of July 2000, it had decided over 650 cases,[29] and because many cases relate to similar facts and the same underlying human rights violations, it has been able to issue as many as 60 decisions each month. However, the Chamber's capacity remains well below demand. It has a backlog of over 4,000 cases, which continue to arrive at a rate of up to 400 per month. In a problem that mirrors that of the Strasbourg Court as the Council of Europe expands eastward, applicants may face a delay of up to seven years before they receive a decision.

The Ombudsman is a foreign national appointed by the Chairman-in-Office of the OSCE. He has jurisdiction over the same subject matter as the Chamber, but his reports contain only recommendations to the governments, which have an obligation to respond. He may mediate between the parties, keeping findings confidential while trying to reach an amicable settlement,[30] or he may forward complaints to the Chamber for formal adjudication. He has broad powers to investigate government authorities and public companies,[31] and may take up matters *ex officio*, issuing reports on any subject matter of concern. The rules of procedure are rather formal compared to "traditional ombudsmen" and modeled closely on the former Strasbourg Commission,[32] including exhaustion of local remedies, *rationae temporis*,[33] and strict

---

[29] For further details, *see* <http://www.gwdg.de/~ujvr/hrch/hrch.htm>.

[30] *See Fourth Annual Report of the Ombudsman*, Office of the Human Rights Ombudsperson for Bosnia and Herzegovina, p. 5, (1999), at <www.ohro.ba/index.htm>.

[31] *General Framework Agreement for Peace in Bosnia and Herzegovina, supra* note 10, at annex 6, art. VI, para. 1.

[32] The former European Commission on Human Rights was replaced by the expanded Strasbourg Court, under Protocol 11 of November 1998.

[33] Although most of the population displacement in Bosnia took place before the date when the temporal jurisdiction of the two human rights institutions begins, they have both found that interference with property rights is a continuing violation which falls within their jurisdiction: *Onic v. Federation BiH*,

filing deadlines. The institution has been criticized by some commentators on the grounds that its inflexible rules of procedure limit its effectiveness in the Bosnian environment.[34] A recent appointment to the post has, however, indicated that the institution may move toward a more "traditional" ombudsman role, approaching a broader range of issues in a less formal manner. With a staff of 40 and an annual budget of US $1.2 million, the institution has proved better able to manage its caseload than the Chamber, due in large part to the speedier and more flexible decision-making process inherent in a non-judicial body. The institution became fully operational by mid-1997, and, although it has issued findings on only 45 percent of its 5,300 cases, it is now able to keep up with its 200 to 300 new claims each month.

Following a decision of the Chamber or a recommendation of the Ombudsman, the respondent governments are given deadlines, ranging from one week to six months, to remedy the human rights violation. The dialogue on implementation is carried out between the institution and the "agents," government lawyers responsible both for representing the respondent and arranging for implementation. The implementation of the Chamber's decisions has been made one of the conditions of Bosnia's accession to the Council of Europe,[35] giving additional leverage. At July 2000, 139 of 207 cases (67 percent) had been implemented.[36] The implementation of recommendations of the Ombudsman is at 36 percent (approximately 250 of 600 cases in which violations were found), excluding cases resolved through mediation before a report was issued. It is important to note, however, that these implementation figures refer only to the resolution of the individual

---

CH/97/58 (February 12, 1999); *Lj.P v. Federation BiH*, CH/98/651, (October 15, 1998).

[34] Jessica Simor, *Tackling Human Rights Abuses in Bosnia and Herzegovina: The Convention is Up to It; Are its Institutions?* 6 EUR. HUM. RTS. L. REV.1 (1997); International Human Rights Law Group, *Human Rights Protection Mechanisms in Bosnia and Herzegovina: Effectiveness of the Human Rights Commission* (Sarajevo, 19 October 1998).

[35] Council of Europe Political Affairs Committee, *Bosnia and Herzegovina's Application for Membership of the Council of Europe* (26 May 1999) (on file with the authors).

[36] Of the 139 cases resolved, 99 relate to a single issue—that of military apartments, which has been partially resolved through legislation imposed by the High Representative. *See* Human Rights Commission Center, *HRCC Human Rights Quarterly Report*, OFFICE OF THE HIGH REPRESENTATIVE: HUMAN RIGHTS UPDATE (Feb. 2000–May 15, 2000), *available at* <http://www.ohr.int/hr-report/hr00-02.html>; Manfred Nowak, *Is Bosnia and Herzegovina Ready for Membership in the Council of Europe?* 20 HUM. RTS. L. J. 285, 288 (2000).

violation in question, rather than the wider human rights issue raised by the decision. On displacement-related cases, international pressure may succeed in returning the small number of individuals who have received a Chamber decision, but tens of thousands of identical cases remain unresolved. In the Strasbourg system, a case is not considered finalized until the Council of Ministers has determined that the likelihood of a similar violation occurring is low. If this standard were applied to the two human rights institutions, the implementation rate would be much lower.

The success of the two institutions in introducing European human rights standards into the Bosnian legal system is more difficult to measure. Although the institutions have contributed some 200 individual points of case law, it does not appear that this has been taken up by the domestic courts to any significant degree. In the old Yugoslav legal system, ordinary courts did not review legislation or executive acts according to human rights principles, nor did they use judicial precedent as a method of developing the law. Formal human rights adjudication may therefore not be the most effective way of introducing cultural change into the legal system. At the governmental level, several changes to laws and administrative practices are attributable to intervention by the human rights institutions. However, as with all human rights complaints mechanisms, the Bosnian institutions only pronounce upon the particular points of law raised before them. Such a system is designed for achieving incremental changes to established legal systems, rather than for large-scale reform, which may be better advanced by other means.

3.3 Human Rights Advocacy: The Federation Ombudsmen

The Office of the Federation Ombudsmen is a constitutional organ of the Bosniak-Croat Federation. Although similar in form to the State Ombudsman, it has flexible procedures and applies much broader standards. More akin to a traditional ombudsman institution, its strengths are in mediation, advocacy, and lobbying. Its mandate is to protect human dignity, rights, and liberties, and in particular to act to reverse the consequences of ethnic cleansing,[37] which enables it to intervene in a much broader range of social issues. It has the authority to examine the activities of the federation at any level of government, to intervene in court proceedings, and to examine official documents. It

---

[37] *Bosnia and Herzegovina: Constitution of the Federation—Chapter II(b), II. Human Rights and Fundamental Freedoms. B. Initial Appointment and Functions of the Ombudsmen*, Section 2 (b), art. 2, para.2, (December 1, 1995), at <http://www.bihfedomb.org/eng-cons/const2b.htm>.

responds to individual and group complaints, investigates issues of public importance, and produces periodic reports on the state of human rights in the federation.[38] A similar institution is currently being established in Republika Srpska and should be operational in November 2000.[39]

The office of the Federation Ombudsmen was established in late 1994 and became operational in 1995, while the conflict was still ongoing. It is a fully local institution, staffed solely by Bosnian nationals in 11 field offices. Importantly, the three ombudsmen were chosen by the OSCE through a rigorous selection process. They are highly respected members of the local community who serve in their personal capacities, rather than as representatives of the regimes. The institution receives 90 percent of its approximately US $1.7 million annual budget from the OSCE, together with strong political support. Through their reports, the ombudsmen have covered issues such as the dismissal of minority workers, the economic vulnerability of particular groups of citizens, pension rights, housing issues, the rights of children, access to education, freedom of the press, and the adequacy of health care.

The Federation Ombudsmen received 9,500 individual complaints in 1999, for a total of 29,707 complaints over their five-year history. Since its inception, some 265,000 citizens have made contact with the institution. Although the Federation Ombudsmen intervene in individual cases where appropriate, their procedures allow them to combine claims and to lobby governments for more general solutions to widespread problems. In contrast to the Dayton institutions, the Ombudsmen rely less on formal legal procedures than on engaging the regimes vigorously in public fora. As a fully domestic institution, they are better placed to carry out mediation than their international counterparts, and they claim a success rate of 56 percent in resolving individual complaints.[40] Their use of local media has been very effective, providing a voice to citizen grievances. Probing abuses of power at the local level has at times brought them into situations of some personal risk, and whether they could carry out their role without strong international backing is an open question. Nonetheless, the creation of a voice within the constitutional structure to promote human rights is a key institution-building initiative.

---

[38] *Id.* at Chapter II, arts. 5, 6, 7, 8.

[39] Human Rights Commission Center, *supra* note 36.

[40] *See* Federation of Bosnia and Herzegovina Ombudsman of the Federation of Bosnia and Herzegovina Office in Sarajevo, *Report on the State of Human Rights in the Federation of Bosnia and Herzegovina in 1999,* p. 12 (Sarajevo, February 2000), at <http://www.bihfedomb.org/eng-repo/rep99.htm>.

3.4 Managing Housing Stocks: Municipal Housing Offices

Strikingly, in its objective of helping IDPs to return to their homes, international strategy has focused more on local government structures than the special Dayton institutions. It is the local housing authorities who have actual control over the housing stocks, access to property records, and working relationships with police and other executive bodies. Although they remain inefficient, ethnically biased, and subject to improper political influence, it has proved more productive to try to influence their behavior than to bypass them using *ad hoc* institutions.

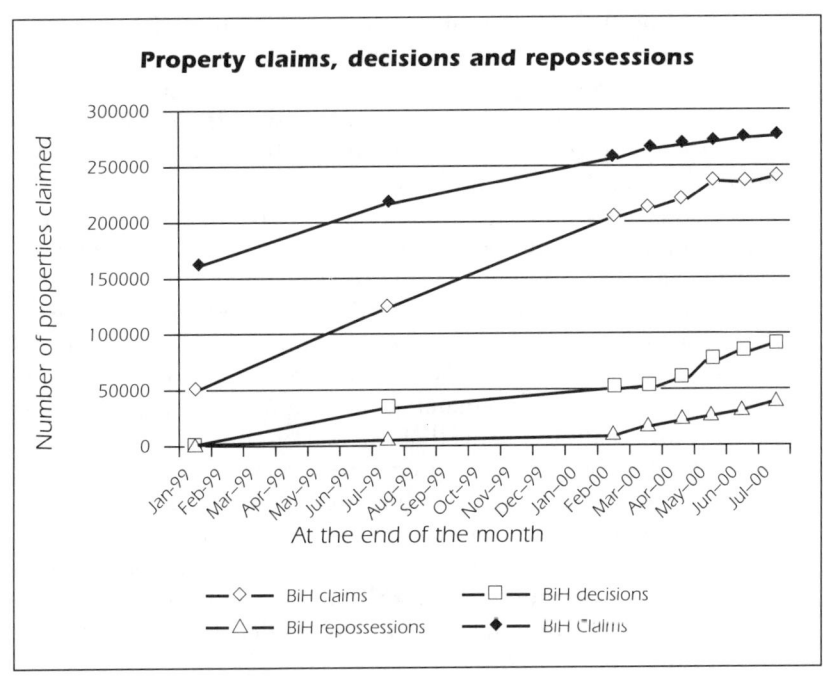

Property claims, decisions and repossessions

[Chart: Number of properties claimed (y-axis, 0 to 300000) vs. End of month from Jan-99 to Jul-00 (x-axis). Series: BiH claims, BiH decisions, BiH repossessions, BiH Claims.]

In 1998, legislation adopted in both entities under strong international pressure created a claims process at the municipal level for repossessing abandoned property, drawing on pre-war administrative procedure. Claims may be submitted in person, by proxy, or through the mail, using a simple claim form that was distributed widely throughout Bosnia and in refugee host countries. The local authorities have the dual function of ruling on the property rights of the claimants and of assessing and providing for the housing needs of the current occupants of the claimed property. By combining these two tasks, the authorities are able to manage the return process, balancing the humanitarian needs of both parties and trying to avoid the need to evict displaced families who have nowhere else to go.

Predictably, resistance to the new laws on the part of the administrative authorities themselves was widespread, and minority claimants met with a range of frustrations and bureaucratic inertia. After a slow start, the results have been gradually improving, although it is not yet possible to conclude that the process would continue to function without international supervision. As of the end of July 2000, some 83,000 positive decisions on the right to return have been issued on 231,000 claims, and 34,000 families have succeeded in repossessing their property.[41] Progress is uneven across the country, with Sarajevo well ahead of most parts of Republika Srpska, and Croat-controlled Herzegovina still maintaining staunch opposition to minority return.[42]

The benefit of working with local administrative bodies, as distinct from courts, is that they have the capacity to manage scarce housing stocks. The authorities should assess the housing needs of any person required to be evicted and try to identify alternative accommodation, although this should not delay repossession by the claimant. Where there is a shortage of housing, the international strategy has been to work on eliminating "multiple occupancy," where families have unlawfully acquired more housing space than they need. Another strategy has been to develop systems to detect when a property becomes available for return, either through reconstruction or by the departure of its current occupant, and to make sure that the owner vacates his temporary accommodation immediately. This then frees up space for a second return. By creating systems that can track and manage the return process effectively, it is possible to generate a cycle of returns, minimizing the need to evict genuine humanitarian cases.

Where administrative controls can be used to maximize the use of available housing space, there is less need for formal legal adjudication and forcible evictions, saving resources and diminishing conflict. For this reason, a similar institutional model is being developed for use in Kosovo.

4. Assessing the Institutional Choices

The international mission in Bosnia and Herzegovina has undertaken a series of remarkable experiments in "internationalizing" parts of the domestic legal system in order to provide direct assistance to

---

[41] Figures compiled by UNHCR and OHR, based upon official data from the municipalities and Entity governments.

[42] *See* European Stability Initiative, *Interim Evaluation of Reconstruction and Return Task Force (RRTF) Minority Return Programmes* (14 September 1999), at <www.esiweb.org>.

IDPs and the general population. The experience bears out the value of close international involvement in restoring a collapsed legal system. Without the strong and sometimes intrusive presence of the international community, the 2 million people displaced by the war would in all likelihood have been left permanently dispossessed. Bosnia could so easily have gone the way of other ethnically divided regions, from Cyprus to Kashmir to the Middle East, with the cease-fire lines between the ethnic groups hardening into permanent lines of partition, no freedom of movement, and arbitrary loss of property rights on a massive scale. Five years after the end of a bitter conflict, Bosnia now seems to be on the path to resolving these problems.

There is much to be learned about how to create institutions for the benefit of IDPs. In a situation of mass population displacement, where the domestic legal system itself has become a victim of the conflict, there may be a good case for establishing *ad hoc* bodies under international control and bypassing local institutions. Even a well-functioning judicial system is unlikely to cope with property-related claims in the tens or hundreds of thousands, and an institution under international control may be better placed to act as an impartial arbiter of disputes, acceptable to all sides of an ethnic conflict. Using international personnel working under mandates prepared by international lawyers, is a very direct way of ensuring that the highest international human rights standards are applied.

However, there are trade-offs involved in internationalizing legal institutions. What they gain in impartiality, they may lose in legitimacy among the local elites and administrative organs, whose support is necessary for them to function effectively. In the worst case, an internationalized body may produce legally correct decisions that have no impact on the ground—in effect, declaring legal rights but unable to provide legal remedies. To avoid this, care must be taken to ensure that the institution is integrated at a number of levels: with the bodies holding property and identity documents; with municipal authorities responsible for housing and humanitarian affairs; with courts of review; and with local police and enforcement bodies. An institution that is compatible with the rest of the legal system will be much more effective. The Bosnian experience also suggests that the efficiency gain of establishing an international body from scratch should not be over-estimated. Each of the Dayton institutions required a much greater investment of time and money to become operational than was originally anticipated.

Ad hoc institutions should aim to play a supporting or transitional role to the permanent legal structures, helping them to cope with the extraordinary circumstances of the conflict. The restoration of a self-sufficient legal system should always be the ultimate goal, and the process of transition should be built into the design of the institutions. At the outset, in the face of overt political resistance, strong international involvement may be necessary to make the legal system function. Over time, however, the international presence should take lighter forms while continuing to offer financial and political support.

In a post-conflict environment, creating institutions for formal human rights adjudication may not be the highest priority. If the legal system has substantially collapsed, institutions designed to pronounce upon the failure of legislative or executive bodies to comply with international standards may merely be stating the obvious. Bodies that hear individual human rights complaints can only adjudicate on the issues that come before them and are limited in the kind of reform proposals they can make. If there are no structures within the state to remedy violations at their source, the impact of judgments may be limited. Depending on the circumstances, it may be more appropriate to create institutions for human rights advocacy, which work in a more flexible fashion.

Where there are large numbers of IDPs seeking to return to their homes, there will be a need for administrative or quasi-judicial tribunals capable of processing claims in large numbers. It is vital to peace-building efforts to restore the rule of law in the housing field as soon as possible and to prevent the misappropriation of IDP property. There is a need for a process that results in an enforceable decision on property title. However, property rights are only one part of the equation. IDPs occupying claimed property may be unable to return to their own homes and may have a genuine humanitarian need. The institution must be able to balance the rights and housing needs of both parties, and should be linked with mechanisms for allocating humanitarian shelter. This is a wider set of tasks than a legal institution would usually undertake, and it requires a flexible mandate.

In sum, the legal and human rights problems raised by mass displacement are many and varied, and there is no such thing as a standard solution. Bosnia and a number of other current peace processes have resulted in a growing body of expertise among the international community for protecting IDPs. They reflect a growing awareness that effective human rights protection is not achieved solely by promulgating norms, but depends also on the promotion of effective institutions.

Bibliography

Journal Articles

Cox, Marcus, *The Right to Return Home: International Intervention and Ethnic Cleansing in Bosnia and Herzegovina*, 47 INT'L & COMP L. Q. 599 (1998).

Nowak, Manfred, *Is Bosnia and Herzegovina Ready for Membership in the Council of Europe?*, 20 HUM. RTS. L. J. 285 (2000).
Simor, Jessica, *Tackling Human Rights Abuses in Bosnia and Herzegovina: The Convention is Up to It; Are its Institutions?*, 6 EUR. HUM. RTS. L. REV. 1 (1997).

Documents

Alfaro, Michelle, UNHCR Sarajevo Protection Unit, *Returnee Monitoring Study: Minority Returnees to the Republika Srpska-Bosnia and Herzegovina* (June 2000), available at <http://www.unhcr.ba>.

Bosnia and Herzegovina: Constitution of the Federation, Dec. 14, 1995, 35 I.L.M. 75, available at <http://www.state.gov/www/regions/eur/bosnia/bosagree.html>.

Council of Europe Political Affairs Committee, *Bosnia and Herzegovina's Application for Membership of the Council of Europe* (May 26, 1999) (on file with the authors).

European Stability Initiative, *Interim Evaluation of Reconstruction and Return Task Force (RRTF) Minority Return Programmes* (1999).

Guiding Principles on Internal Displacement, Principle 28, U.N. Doc. E/CN.4/1998/53/Add.2 (1998).

Internally Displaced Persons: Compilation and Analysis of Legal Norms, U.N. Doc. E/CN.4/1998/53/Add.1 (1998).

Office of the High Representative in Bosnia and Herzegovinia, *Common License Plate / Vehicle Registration Document*, May 29, 1998, at <http://www.ohr.int/>.

Office of the High Representative, Human Rights Commission Center, *HRCC Human Rights Quarterly Report* (Feb. 2000–May 15, 2000), at <http://www.ohr.int/hr-report/hr00-02.html>.

Office of the Human Rights Ombudsperson for Bosnia and Herzegovina, *Fourth Annual Report of the Ombudsman* (1999), available at <www.ohro.ba/>.

Ombudsman of the Federation of Bosnia and Herzegovina Office in Sarajevo, *Annual Report on the State of Human Rights in the Federation of Bosnia and Herzegovina in 1999* (February 2000), available at <http://www.bihfedomb.org/>.

Regulation No. 1999/23 On the Establishment of the Housing and Property Directorate and the Housing and Property Claims Commission, U.N. Doc. UNMIK/REG/1999/23 (1999), available at <http://www.un.org/peace/kosovo/pages/regulations/reg23.html>.

Security Council Resolution 876, U.N. Doc. S/RES/876/1993 (1993).
Security Council Resolution 1319, U.N. Doc. S/RES/1319/2000 (2000).
Security Council Resolution 1244, U.N. Doc. S/RES/1244/1999/ (1999).

NGO Reports

Henrard, Kristin, *The Internally Displaced in South Africa. The Strategy of Forced Removals and Apartheid*, at <http://www.law.kuleuven.ac.be/jura>.

International Human Rights Law Group, *Human Rights Protection Mechanisms in Bosnia and Herzegovina: Effectiveness of the Human Rights Commission* (1998).

Cases

Islamic Community v. RS, Human Rights Chamber, CH/96/29 (June 11, 1999).
Lj.P v. Federation BiH, CH/98/651 (October 15, 1998).
Onic v. Federation BiH, CH/97/58 (February 12, 1999).

Internet Sources

Commission for Real Property Claims of Displaced Persons and Refugees, at <http://www.crpc.org.ba/>.
Human Rights Chamber, at <http://www.gwdg.de/~ujvr/hrch/hrch.html>.

Miscellaneous

Cox, Marcus, *Principles of Law, Evidence and Procedure: The Housing and Property Directorate and Claims Commission*, UNMIK (March 2000).
Das, Hans, *Regularising Housing and Property Rights in Kosovo: The Housing and Property Claims Directorate*, UNMIK (February 2000).
du Plessis, Jean, and Scott Leckie, *Housing, Property and Land Rights in East Timor*, UNCHS-HABITAT (May 31, 2000).

Appendix 1A
Relevant Human Rights Manuals/Resources

ASYLUM AND THE EUROPEAN CONVENTION ON HUMAN RIGHTS
By Nuala Mole, Human rights files No. 9 (revised), Council of Europe, 2000.

CIRCLE OF RIGHTS: ECONOMIC, SOCIAL AND CULTURAL ACTIVISM: A TRAINING RESOURCE
By International Human Rights Internship Program (IHRIP) and Asian Forum for Human Rights and Development. Available in English. Translations to follow in Arabic, French, Spanish. E-mail: *ihripescr@iie.org* or *forumasiabkk@mozart.inet.co.th* for notice of publication.

CLAIMING OUR PLACE (a training manual re: human rights for Muslim women)
By Women, Law & Development, 1993. Order from website at <www.wld.org>.

COMBATING RACISM TOGETHER: A GUIDE TO PARTICIPATING IN THE U.N. WORLD CONFERENCE AGAINST RACISM
By International Human Rights Law Group, May 2000. Available in French, Spanish, Portuguese, English.

HUMAN RIGHTS: A BASIC HANDBOOK FOR UN STAFF
By Office of the High Commissioner for Human Rights, United Nations Staff College Project.

HUMAN RIGHTS DEFENDER'S MANUAL
By John Scott-Murphy, Diplomacy Training Program, Ltd., 1994.

HUMAN RIGHTS MANUAL
By the University of New South Wales, Diplomacy Training Program, Ltd., January 2000.
Address: Faculty of Law, Sydney 2052 Australia. Tel: +61 (2) 313 6563. Fax: +61 (2) 385 1175. E-mail: *dtp@unsw.edu.au.*

HUMAN RIGHTS AND REFUGEE PROTECTION: PART I: GENERAL INTRODUCTION
By UNHCR. Training Module RLD 5, October 1995.

HUMAN RIGHTS AND REFUGEE PROTECTION: PART II: SPECIFIC ISSUES
By UNHCR. Training Module RLD 5, June 1996.

ORIENTATION MANUAL: THE U.N. COMMISSION ON HUMAN RIGHTS, ITS SUB-COMMISSION, AND RELATED PROCEDURES
By David Weissbrodt and Penny Parker, Minnesota Advocates for Human Rights and the International Service for Human Rights,

1993. Available in English and French. Minn. Advoc. Telephone: 612/341-3302. Send e-mail requesting infor. 7/22 to *hrights@mnadvocates.org*. (Also have a handbook on human rights in conflict situations).

PRACTICAL STRATEGIES FOR LOCAL HUMAN RIGHTS GROUPS
By the Center for Sustainable Human Rights Action (CeSHRA). Available in Spanish and English. Translations in French and Arabic to follow.

PUTTING GENDER ON THE AGENDA: A GUIDE TO PARTICIPATING IN U.N. WORLD CONFERENCES
By United Nations Non-Governmental Liaison Service. Telephone: 212/963-3125. See URL: *gopher://gopher.undp.org:70/11/unifem/public/gender*.

THE TORTURE REPORTING HANDBOOK: HOW TO DOCUMENT AND RESPOND TO ALLEGATIONS OF TORTURE WITHIN THE INTERNATIONAL SYSTEM FOR PROTECTION OF HUMAN RIGHTS
By Camille Giffard, Human Rights Centre, University of Essex, 2000.

THE UN AND REFUGEES' HUMAN RIGHTS: A MANUAL ON HOW UN HUMAN RIGHTS MECHANISMS CAN PROTECT THE RIGHTS OF REFUGEES
By Amnesty International and International Service for Human Rights, August 1997 (no publisher stated). Available in French and English. Tel: 022-733-5123 Inter. Serv. In Geneva. To dial Geneva, 011-41-22-733-5123.

THE UNITED NATIONS THEMATIC MECHANISMS-UPDATE 2000: AN OVERVIEW OF THEIR WORK AND MANDATES
By the Law Society, 113 Chancery Lane, London, WC2A 1PL, United Kingdom; and Amnesty International, International Secretariat, 1 Easton Street, London WC1X 0DW, United Kingdom, (1999).

WOMEN'S HUMAN RIGHTS STEP BY STEP: A PRACTICAL GUIDE TO USING INTERNATIONAL HUMAN RIGHTS LAW AND MECHANISMS TO DEFEND WOMEN'S HUMAN RIGHTS
By Women, Law & Development and Human Rights Watch Women's Rights Project, eds: Margaret A. Schuler and Dorothy Q. Thomas, 1997 (no publisher stated). Available in Spanish, English, Portuguese, Ukranian. Publication of the Albanian, Azeri, French, Indonesian, Macedonian, Mongolian, Polish, Russian, and Swahili versions are being finalized. Additional translations are currently underway in Arabic, Armenian, Bulgarian, Czech, Georgian, Kyrgyz, and Uzbek. Cost is 27.50+S/H; can order from website at <www.wld.org> or call 202/463-7477.

Appendix 1B
Participants at the Consultation on the International Human Rights Complaints Mechanisms Available to Refugees and Internally Displaced Persons

Queen Elizabeth House, Oxford
July 22, 2000
Sponsored by the Mellon Foundation

Participating Contributors:

Kelly Askin, International Criminal Tribunal for the Former Yugoslavia
Diane Atkinson-Sanford, University of Washington
Anne Bayefsky, York University
Marcus Cox, European Stability Initiative, University of Cambridge
Stephanie Farrior, Pennsylvania State University
Joan Fitzpatrick, University of Washington
Camille Giffard, University of Essex
Christopher Harland, Office of the High Representative to Bosnia and Herzegovina
Beth Lyon, American University
Chidi Anselm Odinkalu, Interights
Åsa Rydberg, International Criminal Tribunal for the Former Yugoslavia
Monette Zard, Refugee Studies Centre

Participating Experts:

Chaloka Beyani, London School of Economics
Nicholas Blake, Matrix Chambers, Gray's Inn, London
Carolyn Patty Blum, University of California, Berkeley
Peter Burns, Committee Against Torture
Christina Cerna, Organization of American States
Elizabeth Evatt, Human Rights Committee
Geoff Gilbert, University of Essex
Hurst Hannum, Fletcher School of Law and Diplomacy
Margaret Hauser, Refugee Studies Centre
Eckart Klein, Human Rights Committee
Andy McEntee, Amnesty International Lawyers Network

Kirsty Magarey, Human Rights Branch, Department of the Attorney General, Australia
Ada Maduakoh, United Nations High Commissioner for Refugees
Juan Méndez, University of Notre Dame
James Sloan, University of Glasgow
David Turton, Refugee Studies Centre, Oxford University

Appendix 1C
The Relevance of the Guiding Principles on Internal Displacement to the Individual Complaints Mechanisms of Human Rights Treaties in the United Nations System

Joan Fitzpatrick, Jeffrey & Susan Brotman Professor of Law, University of Washington, Seattle

Paper presented at the International Colloquy on the Guiding Principles on Internal Displacement, Vienna, Austria, September 20–23, 2000

I. Introduction

Internally displaced persons, lacking a specialized legal regime similar to refugee law, must find international protection primarily within the realm of human rights law. Many states experiencing serious problems of internal displacement have ratified one or more of the six major United Nations human rights treaties. Under three—and soon to be four—of these treaties, victims of human rights violations may file an individual complaint with a treaty body and obtain an adjudication of their rights, if their state has accepted this optional implementation mechanism. Under two of the treaties, states may also consent to an investigation of systematic violations.

The issues of primary interest at this Colloquy are two: (1) how the Guiding Principles on Internal Displacement may inform the UN treaty bodies' interpretation and application of the human rights within their jurisdiction, in the context of deciding individual complaints; (2) how—and whether—internally displaced persons, or persons at risk of forced displacement, should be encouraged to utilize these individual complaint mechanisms in order to protect their fundamental rights before, during, and after displacement.

The annotations to the Guiding Principles prepared by Professor Kälin indicate that the UN human rights treaties, especially the International Covenant on Civil and Political Rights (ICCPR), served as a major source of their normative content. Yet the Guiding Principles also identity important areas of ambiguity and gaps in protection. Thus, some potential exists that the Guiding Principles could assist the treaty bodies in explicating the meaning of relevant articles, such as those concerning freedom of movement, the right to family life, non-discrimination, and the right to recognition as a person. The Guiding Principles could also contribute substantially to the proper understanding of the limitations clauses that are attached to some articles and to derogation provisions.

In deciding individual cases, the UN treaty bodies do not tend to engage in elaborate or detailed legal analysis. The influence of the Guiding Principles on UN treaty body decisions may thus be more modest or succinct than would be the case if they were offered as an interpretive model to the European or Inter-American human rights courts. The UN treaty bodies may be more inclined to incorporate references to or to draw inspiration from the Guiding Principles in the drafting of general comments or the review of state reports. However, advocates who do invoke individual complaint mechanisms before UN treaty bodies on behalf of IDPs should be encouraged to draw upon the Guiding Principles where they helpfully interpret a generally worded provision of the treaty.

Individual complaint mechanisms may appear remote or ineffectual to advocates for the rights of internally displaced persons. Access to these procedures requires the satisfaction of complex and multiple admissibility criteria. Significant delays may occur before complaints are decided, although in some circumstances provisional measures may be sought. The treaty bodies have not focused on situations of internal displacement in their reported decisions of individual complaints.

This state of affairs could change if advocates for IDPs bring cases before the UN human rights treaty bodies that concern rights progressively interpreted by the Guiding Principles. By this means, a reciprocal relationship could develop between the Special Representative and the treaty bodies, redounding to the benefit of the internally displaced.

II. The Availability of Individual Human Rights Complaints Mechanisms under UN Human Rights Treaties

Treaties are consent-based sources of law, and no more so than in relation to complaint mechanisms that permit individual victims to challenge the international legality of a state's conduct. While acceptance of this enforcement mechanism is now *de rigeur* under the European Convention for the Protection of Human Rights and Fundamental Freedoms, it remains optional for four UN treaties and under discussion with respect to one of the other two.

Nevertheless, a surprising number of states experiencing serious problems of internal displacement have ratified the First Optional

Protocol to the ICCPR. Ninety-four of 143 states parties to the Covenant are subject to the First Optional Protocol. Of the 14 countries initially profiled in the Global IDP Database in December 1999, nine have accepted the Human Rights Committee's jurisdiction to consider individual communications (Angola, Bosnia and Herzegovina, Colombia, the Democratic Republic of the Congo, Peru, Sierra Leone, Somalia, Sri Lanka, and Uganda). Of the other states specifically mentioned in the Special Representative's report to the Fifty-sixth Session of the UN Human Rights Commission in 2000, El Salvador, the Russian Federation, Tajikistan, and the Federal Republic of Yugoslavia are also parties to the First Optional Protocol. This paper will emphasize the potential role of the Human Rights Committee (HRC) in promoting adherence to the Guiding Principles. The HRC has the most active docket of individual communications. Moreover, the ICCPR contains general provisions that could most benefit from interpretive insight drawn from the Guiding Principles.

Acceptance of individual complaint mechanisms is less widespread among states parties to the Convention Against Torture and Other Cruel, Inhuman and Degrading Treatment or Punishment (14 of 119 states parties) and the International Convention on the Elimination of All Forms of Racial Discrimination (27 of 156 states parties). The Optional Protocol to the Convention on the Elimination of All Forms of Discrimination Against Women will not enter into force until ten states become parties (as of July 2000, 5 states had ratified).

III. Using the Guiding Principles to Interpret Key Provisions of the ICCPR

The International Covenant on Civil and Political Rights provides for the protection of a number of rights included in the Guiding Principles. In this section, I will describe how the Human Rights Committee could draw upon the Guiding Principles to particularize the application of these guarantees to internally displaced persons.

A. Non-Discrimination

Article 2(1) of the ICCPR requires states to respect and to ensure to all persons the rights protected by the Covenant, "without distinction of any kind, such as race, colour, sex, language, religion, political or other opinion, national or social origin, property, birth or other status." Principle 1(1) and Walter Kälin in his *Guiding Principles on Internal Displacement: Annotations* (p. 83) clarify that internal displacement should be regarded as an "other status" protected against discrimination. Paired with other rights in the ICCPR, such as the right to family life under

Article 17 or the right to recognition as a person before the law in Article 16, Article 2 thus becomes an important protection for IDPs whose displacement subjects them to unfavorable treatment.

The detailed provisions of the Guiding Principles concerning treatment of IDPs can also assist the Human Rights Committee in applying the principle of proportionality with respect to measures that adversely affect IDPs. For example, Principle 12(2) provides that IDPs should not be interned or confined to camps unless "exceptional circumstances" exist, confinement is "absolutely necessary," and the restriction lasts no longer than required. Thus, discriminatory confinement of IDPs (as compared to the general population or other groups in society) would violate Article 2(1) if these strict conditions of proportionality are not satisfied.

Article 26 contains a broader non-discrimination guarantee on the basis of "other status," in that it is not limited to the enjoyment of rights specifically included in the ICCPR. Principle 3 protects the right to request and receive humanitarian assistance from the national government. Thus, if such assistance were selectively denied to IDPs by a state party to the First Optional Protocol, a claim could be brought under Article 26 even though the Covenant does not guarantee humanitarian assistance directly. The same analysis could be used by the Human Rights Committee to consider discriminatory denial to IDPs of subsistence needs identified in Principle 18(2) or medical care defined in Principle 19, even though the ICCPR does not itself guarantee economic and social rights. Article 26 is violated when denial is linked to the status of being internally displaced, and the state can offer no adequate justification for this discrimination.

Article 3 guarantees that men and women should equally enjoy the rights protected by the Covenant. The Guiding Principles contain several provisions that could assist the Human Rights Committee in applying this article to internally displaced women. For example, Principle 18(3) provides that states must take efforts to ensure the full participation of women in the planning and distribution of basic supplies. The exclusion of displaced women from such activities often has an adverse effect upon their health and safety. Principle 19(2) provides that the special health needs of internally displaced women must be addressed. The Human Rights Committee in its General Comment No. 28 (U.N. Doc. CCPR/C/21/Rev.1/Add. 10, paras. 3, 15 (2000)) has acknowledged that such accommodation is permissible under Article 3, and the Guiding Principles could assist the Committee to apply this normative framework in a context of internal displacement.

B. Freedom of Movement

The Guiding Principles supply a wealth of clarifying insight into the content of the freedom of movement. In applying Article 12 to individual communications, the Human Rights Committee may draw upon a number of the Guiding Principles, especially to assess the legitimacy of restrictions upon movement and derogations from Article 12 during states of emergency.

Persons who have been forcibly displaced from their homes by their government have suffered a loss of the "freedom to choose [one's] residence," guaranteed by Article 12(1). Principle 6(1) makes explicit what was previously implicit in this provision—that human beings have the right to be protected against being arbitrarily displaced from their homes or places of habitual residence. This right not to be internally displaced was recognized by the Human Rights Committee in its General Comment No. 27(67) (U.N. Doc. CCPR/C/21/Rev. 1/Add.9, para. 7 (1999)).

Whether the government has breached the ICCPR depends upon whether forced displacement can be justified on one of the limitations grounds in Article 12(3). These grounds are quite general—"national security" and "public health," for example. General Comment No. 27(67) stresses the principles of legality, necessity and proportionality (at paras. 11, 13–15), but also in fairly general terms.

Should the Committee receive a complaint concerning internal displacement, it could draw upon several of the Guiding Principles that explicate the principles of legality, necessity, and proportionality as they relate to the right not to be displaced. Imagine a situation analogous to that which prevailed in Burundi—Hutu farming families forced off their lands, out of their houses, and into closed camps ringing the city. The government asserted security reasons for the displacement—to deprive insurgents of the supplies these families might otherwise provide, willingly or unwillingly. General Comment No. 27(67) provides that "restrictions on access to military zones" are permissible national security measures (at para. 16). How should the Committee resolve a claim that the displacement violated Article 12(1)?

Principle 6(2)(a) provides that displacement is arbitrary when it is based upon the ethnicity of the displaced. Principle 6(2)(b) limits displacement during armed conflict to situations involving "imperative military reasons" or the security of civilians. Principle 6(2)(e) forbids forced displacement as a collective punishment. Principle 12(2) forbids confinement of the displaced unless "absolutely necessary" in "exceptional circumstances" and only for the briefest possible duration. Principle 7 asserts the principle of legality and specifies a number of procedural steps that should be taken prior to and following any forced displacement supposedly justified as a protective measure, such as consultation with those affected and access to compensation. Authorities are required to provide proper accommodation to the displaced pursuant to Principle 7(2), and the failure to do so may cast negative light on the decision to order evacuation. Further, Principle 9 cautions against the displacement of pastoralists and others with a special dependency on their land. All of these provisions could assist the Human Rights Committee in assessing the legitimacy and proportionality of state action involving a *prima facie* violation of Article 12(1) during armed conflict. The government forces' behavior following displacement could also be assessed under Principle 10(2), concerning the treatment of IDPs affected by armed conflict. Thus, the bare terms of Article 12(1) and the limitations clause of Article 12(3) take on substance and precision when interpreted in light of the Guiding Principles.

In the context of major development projects, Principle 6(2)(c) sets a high threshold for justification of displacement—"compelling and overriding public interests." This standard could influence the Committee's analysis of such claims.

Principle 15(d), concerning the right not to be forced back to a dangerous home or location, embodies a progressive codification of a norm that was previously implicit in human rights norms defining not only freedom of movement but the rights to life and physical integrity. Thus, the Human Rights Committee might usefully draw upon this standard in interpreting Articles 6 and 7 as well as Article 12 of the ICCPR.

With respect to other aspects of freedom of movement, such as the right to leave any country, the Guiding Principles do not provide much additional detail, except to specify in Principles 2(2) and 15(c) that IDPs enjoy the right to seek asylum. This would obviously entail flight from their state. The ICCPR does not explicitly guarantee the right to seek asylum.

C. Other Liberty Interests

Article 9 prohibits arbitrary detention and Article 10 guarantees humane treatment for persons deprived of their liberty. Principles 12 and 14(2) could guide the Human Rights Committee in assessing whether the internment of IDPs was arbitrary. Principle 4(2) requires that the special needs of vulnerable groups of IDPs be addressed, while Principle 11 protects IDPs against serious abuses such as rape, forced prostitution, and slavery. These provisions can guide interpretation of Article 10 of the ICCPR in appropriate contexts.

D. The Rights to Life and to Physical Integrity

Articles 6, 7, and 8 of the ICCPR contain important non-derogable rights, protecting the right to life, prohibiting torture and cruel treatment, and slavery. The precise terms of Principles 10, 11, 13, 15, 18, 19, 24, 26, 27, 28, and 30 all have a bearing upon the content of these rights with respect to IDPs. For example, Principle 25 directs states to facilitate the provision of humanitarian assistance, which may be vital to the preservation of the lives of the forcibly displaced. Arbitrary denial of access to the means of subsistence could be interpreted as a breach of Article 6. Principle 15(d) draws upon norms relating to the right to life and prohibition on cruel treatment to specify that forced movement of persons into zones of danger is prohibited.

The Human Rights Committee interprets the right to life as having an affirmative dimension, obligating the state to discharge a protective role towards the persons within its jurisdiction. Principle 18, which describes the minimum provisions that must be made for IDPs, could inform interpretation of this obligation in a context of internal displacement.

E. The Rights of the Family and the Child

The ICCPR prohibits arbitrary and unlawful interference with the home and family in Article 17(1), and obliges states parties to protect the family in Article 23(1). The Guiding Principles specify certain obligations to restore and protect the right to family life, to which the Human Rights Committee could turn. Principle 4(2) requires special protection for vulnerable groups, such as mothers with young children. Principle 7(2) requires authorities to avoid separation of family members during a government-ordered displacement. Principle 16 addresses in detail the obligation to trace family members and to protect the bodies of the deceased and their grave sites. Principle 17 provides for the reunification of families.

Article 24 of the ICCPR protects the rights of children. Principles 4(2), 11(2)(b), 13(1), 17(3), and 23 address specific needs of children in situations of internal displacement, and these standards could influence the Committee's application of Article 24. Article 24(2) specifically guarantees that children should be registered upon birth by the authorities, and Article 24(3) protects the child's right to a nationality. The Guiding Principles have constructively addressed the pressing need of IDPs for identity papers in Principle 20, and the prohibition on discrimination based on internal displacement in Principle 1(1) could protect IDP children who suffer denial of their right to a nationality.

F. The Right to Recognition as a Person Before the Law

Principle 20 marks a progressive development in the understanding of human rights norms. The need for identity documents is implicitly addressed in Article 16 of the ICCPR, but Principle 20 brings a clearer understanding of that right. IDPs may suffer additional deprivations of rights protected by the ICCPR because of a lack of documents, such as the right to an effective remedy under Article 2(3) or political rights under Article 25.

G. Derogation

Mass internal displacement is often associated with states of emergency, especially those related to armed conflict or internal strife. Article 4 of the ICCPR sets demanding standards for derogation, requiring *inter alia* that the emergency threaten the life of the nation, that derogation measures be strictly required by the exigencies of the situation and that suspensive measures not discriminate solely on the basis of race, color, sex, language, religion, or social origin. Article 4 essentially adopts a demanding version of the principles of legality, legitimacy, and proportionality that also prevail under the Human Rights Committee's analysis of limitations clauses. In assessing emergency measures (such as suspension of freedom of movement for interned IDPs), the Committee may find it helpful to refer to the more specific framework set out in the Guiding Principles.

H. Other Rights

IDPs often experience additional deprivations of rights protected by the ICCPR, such as freedom of religion and expression or minority rights. The Guiding Principles reiterate many of these rights, but do not really elaborate on them in a manner likely to shape the Human Rights Committee's jurisprudence under the First Optional Protocol.

IV. The Utility of the First Optional Protocol for IDPs

The Human Rights Committee is a highly respected body of experts. Should it be seized of cases involving the rights of IDPs, it is quite possible that the Committee will draw upon the Guiding Principles in the manner described in Section III above. Citation by the Human Rights Committee thus could form a small but noteworthy aspect of the overall project to disseminate the Guiding Principles and to familiarize both governments and IDPs with their content.

But despite the fact that the ICCPR includes a wide array of rights highly relevant to IDPs, it is impossible to identify any reported views of the Human Rights Committee under the First Optional Protocol in which the victim's situation of internal displacement figured in any significant way. As noted above, many states with sizable populations of IDPs accept the Committee's jurisdiction over individual communications. Yet, this mechanism to obtain protection for IDPs is not widely utilized.

The explanations are multiple. The communications procedure is rather legalistic and remote. IDPs who are facing serious risks to their survival may be inclined to seek redress from the Special Representative, other thematic mechanisms of the UN, the High Commissioner for Human Rights, peacekeeping forces, the UNHCR, development agencies, and humanitarian organizations. Unlike the Human Rights Committee, all of these bodies to one degree or another have a field presence. Mailing a written complaint to Geneva may simply not occur to IDP advocates, or they may be skeptical about its utility.

The Human Rights Committee handles communications by mail, and several years elapse between filing and decision. The victim does not appear at a hearing, and there is no face-to-face confrontation with the perpetrators of the violation. It should be noted, however, that Rule 86 of the Committee's Rules of Procedure makes provision for interim measures, where an imminent violation is threatened or the victim's health is at serious risk.

A number of admissibility requirements must be satisfied before the Human Rights Committee's jurisdiction can be invoked under the First Optional Protocol. The victim must exhaust domestic remedies and may not be seeking redress before any other international dispute resolution mechanism, for example. Advocates who are not familiar with the ICCPR may make technical errors that result in delay or dismissal of a communication.

Perhaps the greatest drawback of the First Optional Protocol for IDP advocates is that the Committee's views are not technically legally binding. While some states do conform to the Committee's recommendations to cease or to redress violations of the ICCPR, state compliance is far less uniform than within the European human rights system. The Committee does attempt to follow up on its views to pressure states to comply, but these steps are sometimes ineffectual.

With a grant from the Mellon Foundation, a guide explaining human rights complaints mechanisms such as the First Optional Protocol is being prepared. The Guide will be disseminated to advocates for refugees, asylum-seekers, and internally displaced persons. Possibly greater familiarity with these bodies and their capacity to vindicate the rights of IDPs, at least in the abstract, will induce more advocates for IDPs to invoke the Human Rights Committee's jurisdiction.

V. The Committee Against Torture and Protection of IDPs

The Committee Against Torture (CAT) also supervises an optional individual communications mechanism under Article 22 of the Convention Against Torture. While 28 of the 32 decided cases under Article 22 have involved asylum-seekers, the situation of IDPs has not required the CAT's attention. The Convention Against Torture is of particular interest to asylum-seekers (especially failed asylum-seekers), because Article 3 forbids the *refoulement* of persons who face a substantial risk of torture if returned. This Article, which has generated such a high percentage of cases under Article 22, is of little assistance to IDPs.

The definition of torture in Article 1 is somewhat narrower than that of Article 7 of the ICCPR, and the Guiding Principles do not really provide substantial interpretive detail upon which CAT could rely. Possibly the gross violations listed in Principle 11(2) could guide the CAT's interpretation of torture and cruel treatment in future cases involving IDPs.

Governments often inflict torture as a means to force displacement, especially in contexts of "ethnic cleansing." Article 22 is relevant as a means to prevent displacement by halting violations before displacement results, or to redress violations following flight. The CAT, like the HRC, has the capacity to request states parties to adopt interim measures to prevent or halt an alleged violation during the pendency of the communication.

IDPs may be at heightened risk of torture and cruel treatment following their displacement. For example, IDPs in open relief centers in Sri Lanka reportedly experienced repeated raids by Sri Lankan security forces, who removed persons suspected of having sympathy with or information concerning the insurgents. These persons were subsequently tortured, some fatally.

Situations such as that in Sri Lanka can be addressed in individual communications under Article 22. Alternatively, the CAT itself may undertake an inquiry, when it receives information concerning the systematic practices of torture in a state that accepts its jurisdiction under Article 20. Turkey, a state with a substantial population of IDPs, was the subject of such a CAT inquiry, although internal displacement per se was not a focus of the procedure.

The paucity of cases involving IDPs under Article 22 is explained by essentially the same reasons the Human Rights Committee has been relatively inactive under the First Optional Protocol in confronting violations associated with internal displacement. The process is remote and not well understood by advocates for IDPs. For this reason, it will also be profiled in the Guide.

VI. The Committee on the Elimination of Racial Discrimination and IDPs

Forced displacement, whether internal or transboundary, frequently results from racial or ethnic oppression and violence. Many IDPs experience serious discrimination prior to and following their displacement. The Convention on the Elimination of All Forms of Racial Discrimination prohibits many discriminatory policies that adversely affect the internally displaced.

Indeed, the Committee on the Elimination of Racial Discrimination has recognized that racism and ethnic intolerance are closely linked with displacement, and it has issued General Recommendation XXII in 1996 on refugees and displaced persons (U.N. Doc. A/51/18 (1996)). This recommendation tracks the Guiding Principles on several important points, including the right to return to homes of origin (Principle 28(1)), to compensation or restoration of property (Principles 21 and 29(2)), the right to participate in public affairs following return (Principles 22(d) and 29(1)), and the right to receive rehabilitation assistance (Principle 30).

However, the optional individual complaints mechanism under the Convention has been little used and never to address the specific concerns of IDPs. Only 27 of the 156 states parties to the Convention have accepted CERD's jurisdiction over individual communications. Only 17 cases have ever been registered, resulting so far in nine sets of views finding violations and three decisions of inadmissibility.

Thus, although the Convention contains a wide array of rights that could assist IDPs whose displacement is linked to their race or ethnicity, the individual communications mechanism has not in the past served as a vehicle for their protection. The Guide currently under preparation describes in detail the relevance of the Convention for the protection of refugees, asylum-seekers and IDPs.

VII. The Convention on the Elimination of All Forms of Discrimination Against Women and IDPs

The Guiding Principles address the specific situation of internally displaced women in a number of important provisions. Thus, there is some potential that the Committee on the Elimination of Discrimination Against Women (CEDAW) may in the future be able to draw upon the

Guiding Principles to interpret certain provisions of the Convention on the Elimination of Discrimination Against Women. CEDAW will not be empowered to perform this interpretive task until the Optional Protocol enters into force with a tenth ratification. Like the CAT, CEDAW will also be empowered to launch inquiries into grave or systematic violations, with respect to states that ratify the Optional Protocol and do not opt out of this inquiry procedure.

In its review of state reports (previously the exclusive implementation mechanism under the Convention), CEDAW has repeatedly noted the failure of states to protect displaced women against pervasive violence, and the failure of the state to assist in the reintegration of displaced women. In applying the Convention to future cases involving internally displaced women, CEDAW could draw upon the following Guiding Principles:

> Principle 4(2): The state's obligation to meet the special needs of vulnerable groups, including expectant mothers, women with young children, and female heads of household.
>
> Principle 7(3)(d): The state's obligation, when ordering a displacement, to involve women in the planning and management of their relocation.
>
> Principle 11(2): The state's obligation to protect IDPs against rape, outrages on personal dignity, gender-specific violence, forced prostitution, indecent assault, sale into marriage, and sexual exploitation.
>
> Principle 19(2): The state's obligation to meet the specific health care needs of internally displaced women.
>
> Principle 20(3): The equal right of displaced women to receive identity documents.
>
> Principle 23(3): The rights of internally displaced women and girls to have equal access to education.
>
> Principle 23(4): The rights of women to have access to training facilities, whether in or outside of camps.

These provisions are consistent with CEDAW's interpretation of the Convention. Indeed, the *Annotations* note this Convention as a normative source for these Principles. A reciprocal relationship through which the Principles assist CEDAW in applying the Convention under its Optional Protocol to internally displaced persons could evolve. Because substantial congruence already exists, however, the potential impact of referring to the Guiding Principles may be modest in comparison to the possibilities under the ICCPR, as noted in Section III above.

Appendix 1D
List of States Parties to Selected Human Rights Treaties

International Covenant on Civil and Political Rights (as of June 2001):

Afghanistan, Albania, Algeria (b), Angola (b), Argentina (ab), Armenia (b), Australia (b), Austria (ab), Azerbaijan, Bangladesh, Barbados (b), Belarus (ab), Belgium (ab), Belize, Benin (b), Bolivia (b), Bosnia and Herzegovina (ab), Botswana, Brazil, Bulgaria (ab), Burkina Faso (b), Burundi, Cambodia, Cameroon (b), Canada (ab), Cape Verde, Central African Republic (b), Chad (b), Chile (ab), Colombia (b), Congo (ab), Costa Rica (b), Croatia (ab), Cyprus (b), Czech Republic (ab), Côte d'Ivoire (b), Democratic People's Republic of Korea, Democratic Republic of the Congo (b), Denmark (ab), Dominica, Dominican Republic (b), Ecuador (ab), Egypt, El Salvador (b), Equatorial Guinea (b), Estonia (b), Ethiopia, Finland (ab), France (b), Gabon, Gambia (ab), Georgia (b), Germany (ab), Ghana (b), Greece (b), Grenada, Guatemala (b), Guinea (b), Guyana (ab), Haiti, Honduras, Hong Kong Special Administrative Region, Hungary (ab), Iceland (ab), India, Iran, Iraq, Ireland (ab), Israel, Italy (ab), Jamaica, Japan, Jordan, Kenya, Kuwait, Kyrgyzstan (b), Latvia (b), Lebanon, Lesotho (b), Libyan Arab Jamahiriya (b), Liechtenstein (ab), Lithuania (b), Luxembourg (ab), Madagascar (b), Malawi (b), Mali, Malta (ab), Mauritius (b), Mexico, Monaco, Mongolia (b), Morocco, Mozambique, Namibia (b), Nepal (b), Netherlands (ab), New Zealand (ab), Nicaragua (b), Niger (b), Nigeria, Norway (ab), Panama (b), Paraguay (b), Peru (ab), Philippines (ab), Poland (ab), Portugal (b), Republic of Korea (ab), Republic of Moldova, Romania (b), Russian Federation (ab), Rwanda, Saint Vincent and the Grenadines (b), San Marino (b), Senegal (ab), Seychelles (b), Sierra Leone (b), Slovakia (ab), Slovenia (ab), Somalia (b), South Africa (a), Spain (ab), Sri Lanka (ab), Sudan, Suriname (b), Sweden (ab), Switzerland (a), Syrian Arab Republic, Tajikistan (b), Thailand, The Former Yugoslav Republic of Macedonia (b), Togo (b), Trinidad and Tobago, Tunisia, Turkmenistan (b), Uganda (b), Ukraine (ab), United Kingdom of Great Britain and Northern Ireland (a), United Republic of Tanzania, United States of America (a), Uruguay (b), Uzbekistan (b), Venezuela (b), Viet Nam, Yemen, Yugoslavia, Zambia (b), Zimbabwe (a)

(a) Has recognized the competence of the Human Rights Committee to hear interstate complaints under Article 41.
(b) Has ratified the Optional Protocol permitting individual communications.

International Covenant on Economic, Social and Cultural Rights (as of June 2001):

Afghanistan, Albania, Algeria, Angola, Argentina, Armenia, Australia, Austria, Azerbaijan, Bangladesh, Barbados, Belarus, Belgium, Benin, Bolivia, Bosnia and Herzegovina, Brazil, Bulgaria, Burkina Faso, Burundi, Cambodia, Cameroon, Canada, Cape Verde, Central African Republic, Chad, Chile, China, Colombia, Congo, Costa Rica, Croatia, Cyprus, Czech Republic, Côte D'Ivoire, Democratic People's Republic of Korea, Democratic Republic of the Congo, Denmark, Dominica, Dominican Republic, Ecuador, Egypt, El Salvador, Equatorial Guinea, Eritrea, Estonia, Ethiopia, Finland, France, Gabon, Gambia, Georgia, Germany, Ghana, Greece, Grenada, Guatemala, Guinea, Guinea-Bissau, Guyana, Honduras, Hungary, Iceland, India, Iran, Iraq, Ireland, Israel, Italy, Jamaica, Japan, Jordan, Kenya, Kuwait, Kyrgyzstan, Latvia, Lebanon, Lesotho, Libyan Arab Jamahiriya, Liechtenstein, Lithuania, Luxembourg, Madagascar, Malawi, Mali, Malta, Mauritius, Mexico, Monaco, Mongolia, Morocco, Namibia, Nepal, Netherlands, New Zealand, Nicaragua, Niger, Nigeria, Norway, Panama, Paraguay, Peru, Philippines, Poland, Portugal, Republic of Korea, Republic of Moldova, Romania, Russian Federation, Rwanda, Saint Vincent and the Grenadines, San Marino, Senegal, Seychelles, Sierra Leone, Slovakia, Slovenia, Solomon Islands, Somalia, Spain, Sri Lanka, Sudan, Suriname, Sweden, Switzerland, Syrian Arab Republic, Tajikistan, Thailand, The Former Yugoslav Republic of Macedonia, Togo, Trinidad and Tobago, Tunisia, Turkmenistan, Uganda, Ukraine, United Kingdom of Great Britain and Northern Ireland, United Republic of Tanzania, Uruguay, Uzbekistan, Venezuela, Viet Nam, Yemen, Yugoslavia, Zambia, Zimbabwe

Convention Against Torture and Other Cruel, Inhuman or Degrading Treatment or Punishment (as of June 2001):

Afghanistan, Albania, Algeria (a), Antigua and Barbuda, Argentina (a), Armenia, Australia (a), Austria (a), Azerbaijan, Bahrain, Bangladesh, Belarus, Belgium (a), Belize, Benin, Bolivia, Bosnia and Herzegovina, Botswana, Brazil, Bulgaria (a), Burkina Faso, Burundi, Cambodia, Cameroon (a), Canada (a), Cape Verde, Chad, Chile, China, Colombia, Costa Rica, Croatia (a), Cuba, Cyprus (a), Czech Republic (a), Côte d'Ivoire, Democratic Republic of the Congo, Denmark (a), Ecuador (a), Egypt, El Salvador, Estonia, Ethiopia, Finland (a), France (a),Gabon, Georgia, Germany, Ghana, Greece (a), Guatemala, Guinea, Guyana, Honduras, Hungary (a), Iceland (a), Indonesia, Israel, Italy (a), Japan (b), Jordan, Kazakhstan, Kenya, Kuwait, Kyrgyzstan, Latvia, Lebanon, Libyan Arab Jamahiriya, Liechtenstein (a), Lithuania, Luxembourg (a), Malawi, Mali, Malta (a), Mauritius, Mexico, Monaco (a), Morocco, Mozambique, Namibia, Nepal, Netherlands (a), New Zealand (a), Niger, Norway (a), Panama, Paraguay, Peru, Philippines, Poland (a), Portugal (a), Qatar, Republic of Korea, Republic of Moldova, Romania, Russian Federation (a), Saudi Arabia, Senegal (a), Seychelles, Sierra Leone, Slovakia (a), Slovenia (a), Somalia, South Africa (a), Spain (a), Sri Lanka, Sweden (a), Switzerland (a), Tajikistan, The Former Yugoslav Republic of Macedonia, Togo (a), Tunisia (a), Turkey (a), Turkmenistan, Uganda, Ukraine, United Kingdom of Great Britain and Northern Ireland (b), United States of America (b), Uruguay (a), Uzbekistan, Venezuela (a), Yemen, Yugoslavia (a), Zambia

(a) Has accepted the competence of the Committee Against Torture to consider interstate complaints under Article 21 and individual communications under Article 22.

(b) Has accepted only the competence of the Committee Against Torture to consider interstate complaints under Article 21.

International Convention on the Elimination of All Forms of Racial Discrimination (as of June 2001):

Afghanistan, Albania, Algeria (a), Antigua and Barbuda, Argentina, Armenia, Australia (a), Austria, Azerbaijan, Bahamas, Bahrain, Bangladesh, Barbados, Belarus, Belgium, Bolivia, Bosnia and Herzegovina, Botswana, Brazil, Bulgaria (a), Burkina Faso, Burundi, Cambodia, Cameroon, Canada, Cape Verde, Central African Republic, Chad, Chile (a), China, Colombia, Congo, Costa Rica (a), Croatia, Cuba, Cyprus (a), Czech Republic, Côte d'Ivoire, Democratic Republic of the Congo, Denmark (a), Dominican Republic, Ecuador (a), Egypt, El Salvador, Estonia, Ethiopia, Fiji, Finland (a), France (a), Gabon, Gambia, Georgia, Germany, Ghana, Greece, Grenada, Guatemala, Guinea, Guyana, Haiti, Holy See, Hungary (a), Iceland (a), India, Indonesia, Iran, Iraq, Ireland, Israel, Italy (a), Jamaica, Japan, Jordan, Kazakhstan, Kuwait, Kyrgyzstan, Lao People's Democratic Republic, Latvia, Lebanon, Lesotho, Liberia, Libyan Arab Jamahiriya, Liechtenstein, Lithuania, Luxembourg (a), Madagascar, Malawi, Maldives, Mali, Malta (a), Mauritania, Mauritius, Mexico, Monaco, Mongolia, Morocco, Mozambique, Namibia, Nepal,

Netherlands (a), New Zealand, Nicaragua, Niger, Nigeria, Norway (a), Pakistan, Panama, Papua New Guinea, Peru (a), Philippines, Poland (a), Portugal, Republic of Korea (a), Republic of Moldova, Romania, Russian Federation (a), Rwanda, Saint Lucia, Saint Vincent and the Grenadines, Saudi Arabia, Senegal (a), Seychelles, Sierra Leone, Slovakia (a), Slovenia, Solomon Islands, Somalia, South Africa (a), Spain (a), Sri Lanka, Sudan, Suriname, Swaziland, Sweden (a), Switzerland, Syrian Arab Republic, Tajikistan, The Former Yugoslav Republic of Macedonia (a), Togo, Tonga, Trinidad and Tobago, Tunisia, Turkmenistan, Uganda, Ukraine (a), United Arab Emirates, United Kingdom of Great Britain and Northern Ireland, United Republic of Tanzania, United States of America, Uruguay (a), Uzbekistan, Venezuela, Viet Nam, Yemen, Yugoslavia, Zambia, Zimbabwe

(a) Has accepted the competence of the Committee on the Elimination of Racial Discrimination to consider individual communications under Article 14.

Convention on the Elimination of All Forms of Discrimination Against Women (as of June 2001):

Albania, Algeria, Andorra, Angola, Antigua and Barbuda, Argentina, Armenia, Australia, Austria (a), Azerbaijan, Bahamas, Bangladesh (a), Barbados, Belarus, Belgium, Belize, Benin, Bhutan, Bolivia (a), Bosnia and Herzegovina, Botswana, Brazil, Bulgaria, Burkina Faso, Burundi, Cambodia, Cameroon, Canada, Cape Verde, Central African Republic, Chad, Chile, China, Colombia, Comoros, Congo, Costa Rica, Croatia (a), Cuba, Cyprus, Czech Republic (a), Côte d'Ivoire, Democratic People's Republic of Korea, Democratic Republic of the Congo, Denmark (a), Djibouti, Dominica, Dominican Republic, Ecuador, Egypt, El Salvador, Equatorial Guinea, Eritrea, Estonia, Ethiopia, Fiji, Finland (a), France (a), Gabon, Gambia, Georgia, Germany, Ghana, Greece, Grenada, Guatemala, Guinea, Guinea-Bissau, Guyana, Haiti, Honduras, Hungary (a), Iceland (a), India, Indonesia, Iraq, Ireland (a), Israel, Italy (a), Jamaica, Japan, Jordan, Kazakhstan, Kenya, Kuwait, Kyrgyzstan, Lao People's Democratic Republic, Latvia, Lebanon, Lesotho, Liberia, Libyan Arab Jamahiriya, Liechtenstein, Lithuania, Luxembourg, Madagascar, Malawi, Malaysia, Maldives, Mali (a), Malta, Mauritania, Mauritius, Mexico, Mongolia, Morocco, Mozambique, Myanmar (Burma), Namibia (a), Nepal, Netherlands, New Zealand (a), Nicaragua, Niger, Nigeria, Norway, Pakistan, Panama (a), Papua New Guinea, Paraguay (a), Peru (a), Philippines, Poland, Portugal, Republic of Korea, Republic of Moldova, Romania, Russian Federation, Rwanda, Saint Kitts

List of States Parties to Human Rights Treaties   561

and Nevis, Saint Lucia, Saint Vincent and the Grenadines, Samoa, Saudi Arabia, Senegal (a), Seychelles, Sierra Leone, Singapore, Slovakia (a), Slovenia, South Africa, Spain, Sri Lanka, Suriname, Sweden, Switzerland, Tajikistan, Thailand (a), The Former Yugoslav Republic of Macedonia, Togo, Trinidad and Tobago, Tunisia, Turkey, Turkmenistan, Tuvalu, Uganda, Ukraine, United Kingdom of Great Britain and Northern Ireland, United Republic of Tanzania, Uruguay, Uzbekistan, Vanuatu, Venezuela, Viet Nam, Yemen, Yugoslavia, Zambia, Zimbabwe

(a) Has ratified the 1999 Optional Protocol permitting individual communications.

Convention on the Rights of the Child (as of June 2001):

Afghanistan, Albania, Algeria, Andorra, Angola, Antigua and Barbuda, Argentina, Armenia, Australia, Austria, Azerbaijan, Bahamas, Bahrain, Bangladesh, Barbados, Belarus, Belgium, Belize, Benin, Bhutan, Bolivia, Bosnia and Herzegovina, Botswana, Brazil, Brunei Darussalam, Bulgaria, Burkina Faso, Burundi, Cambodia, Cameroon, Canada, Cape Verde, Central African Republic, Chad, Chile, China, Colombia, Comoros, Congo, Cook Islands, Costa Rica, Croatia, Cuba, Cyprus, Czech Republic, Côte d'Ivoire, Democratic People's Republic of Korea, Democratic Republic of the Congo, Denmark, Djibouti, Dominica, Dominican Republic, Ecuador, Egypt, El Salvador, Equatorial Guinea, Eritrea, Estonia, Ethiopia, Fiji, Finland, France, Gabon, Gambia, Georgia, Germany, Ghana, Greece, Grenada, Guatemala, Guinea, Guinea-Bissau, Guyana, Haiti, Holy See, Honduras, Hungary, Iceland, India, Indonesia, Iran, Iraq, Ireland, Israel, Italy, Jamaica, Japan, Jordan, Kazakhstan, Kenya, Kiribati, Kuwait, Kyrgyzstan, Lao People's Democratic Republic, Latvia, Lebanon, Lesotho, Liberia, Libyan Arab Jamahiriya, Liechtenstein, Lithuania, Luxembourg, Madagascar, Malawi, Malaysia, Maldives, Mali, Malta, Marshall Islands, Mauritania, Mauritius, Mexico, Micronesia, Monaco, Mongolia, Morocco, Mozambique, Myanmar (Burma), Namibia, Nauru, Nepal, Netherlands, New Zealand, Nicaragua, Niger, Nigeria, Niue, Norway, Oman, Pakistan, Palau, Panama, Papua New Guinea, Paraguay, Peru, Philippines, Poland, Portugal, Qatar, Republic of Korea, Republic of Moldova, Romania, Russian Federation, Rwanda, Saint Kitts and Nevis, Saint Lucia, Saint Vincent and the Grenadines, Samoa, San Marino, Sao Tome and Principe, Saudi Arabia, Senegal, Seychelles, Sierra Leone, Singapore, Slovakia, Slovenia, Solomon Islands, South Africa, Spain, Sri Lanka, Sudan, Suriname, Swaziland, Sweden, Switzerland, Syrian Arab Republic, Tajikistan, Thailand, The Former Yugoslav Republic of Macedonia, Togo, Tonga,

Trinidad and Tobago, Tunisia, Turkey, Turkmenistan, Tuvalu, Uganda, Ukraine, United Arab Emirates, United Kingdom of Great Britain and Northern Ireland, United Republic of Tanzania, Uruguay, Uzbekistan, Vanuatu, Venezuela, Viet Nam, Yemen, Yugoslavia, Zambia, Zimbabwe

Optional Protocol to the Convention on the Rights of the Child on the Involvement of Children in Armed Conflicts (as of June 2001):

Andorra, Bangladesh, Canada, Sri Lanka

Optional Protocol to the Convention on the Rights of the Child on the Sale of Children, Child Prostitution and Child Pornography (as of June 2001):

Andorra, Bangladesh, Panama

International Convention on the Protection of the Rights of All Migrant Workers and Members of Their Families (as of June 2001):

Azerbaijan, Bolivia, Bosnia and Herzegovina, Cape Verde, Colombia, Egypt, Ghana, Guinea, Mexico, Morocco, Philippines, Senegal, Seychelles, Sri Lanka, Uganda, Uruguay

African Charter on Human and Peoples' Rights (as of January 2000):

Algeria, Angola, Benin, Botswana, Burkina Faso, Burundi, Cameroon, Cape Verde, Central African Republic, Chad, Comoros, Congo, Côte d'Ivoire, Democratic Republic of the Congo, Djibouti, Egypt, Equatorial Guinea, Eritrea, Ethiopia, Gabon, Gambia, Ghana, Guinea, Guinea-Bissau, Kenya, Lesotho, Liberia, Libyan Arab Jamahiriya, Madagascar, Malawi, Mali, Mauritania, Mauritius, Mozambique, Namibia, Niger, Nigeria, Rwanda, Sao Tome and Principe, Senegal, Seychelles, Sierra Leone, Somalia, South Africa, Sudan, Swaziland, Tanzania, Togo, Tunisia, Uganda, Zambia, Zimbabwe

American Convention on Human Rights (as of May 2001):

Argentina (ab), Barbados (b), Bolivia (b), Brazil (b), Chile (ab), Colombia (ab), Costa Rica (ab), Dominica, Dominican Republic (b), Ecuador (ab), El Salvador (b), Grenada, Guatemala (b), Haiti (b), Honduras (b), Jamaica (a), Mexico (b), Nicaragua (b), Panama (b),

Paraguay (b), Peru (ab), Suriname (b), Trinidad and Tobago (b), Uruguay (ab), Venezuela (ab)

(a) Has filed a declaration under Article 45 accepting interstate complaints.
(b) Has filed a declaration under Article 62 accepting the jurisdiction of the Inter-American Court of Human Rights.

Additional Protocol to the American Convention on Human Rights in the Area of Economic, Social and Cultural Rights (as of May 2001):

Brazil, Colombia, Costa Rica, Ecuador, El Salvador, Guatemala, Mexico, Panama, Paraguay, Peru, Suriname, Uruguay

Inter-American Convention on Forced Disappearance of Persons (as of May 2001):

Argentina, Bolivia, Costa Rica, Ecuador, Guatemala, Mexico, Panama, Paraguay, Peru, Uruguay, Venezuela

Inter-American Convention on the Prevention, Punishment, and Eradication of Violence Against Women (as of May 2001):

Antigua and Barbuda, Argentina, Bahamas, Barbados, Belize, Bolivia, Brazil, Colombia, Costa Rica, Chile, Dominica, Dominican Republic, Ecuador, El Salvador, Grenada, Guatemala, Guyana, Haiti, Honduras, Mexico, Nicaragua, Panama, Paraguay, Peru, Saint Kitts and Nevis, Saint Vincent and the Grenadines, Saint Lucia, Trinidad and Tobago, Uruguay, Venezuela

Inter-American Convention to Prevent and Punish Torture (as of May 2001):

Argentina, Brazil, Colombia, Costa Rica, Chile, Dominican Republic, Ecuador, El Salvador, Guatemala, Mexico, Panama, Paraguay, Peru, Suriname, Uruguay, Venezuela

European Convention for the Protection of Human Rights and Fundamental Freedoms (as of July 2001):

Albania, Andorra, Austria, Belgium, Bulgaria, Croatia, Cyprus, Czech Republic, Denmark, Estonia, Finland, France, Georgia, Germany, Greece, Hungary, Iceland, Ireland, Italy, Latvia, Liechtenstein, Lithuania,

Luxembourg, The Former Yugoslav Republic of Macedonia, Malta, Moldova, Netherlands, Norway, Poland, Portugal, Romania, Russian Federation, San Marino, Slovakia, Slovenia, Spain, Sweden, Switzerland, Turkey, Ukraine, United Kingdom of Great Britain and Northern Ireland

European Convention for the Prevention of Torture and Inhuman or Degrading Treatment or Punishment (as of July 2001):

Albania, Andorra, Austria, Belgium, Bulgaria, Croatia, Cyprus, Czech Republic, Denmark, Estonia, Finland, France, Georgia, Germany, Greece, Hungary, Iceland, Ireland, Italy, Latvia, Liechtenstein, Lithuania, Luxembourg, Malta, Moldova, Netherlands, Norway, Poland, Portugal, Romania, Russian Federation, San Marino, Slovakia, Slovenia, Spain, Sweden, Switzerland, The Former Yugoslav Republic of Macedonia, Turkey, Ukraine, United Kingdom of Great Britain and Northern Ireland

European Social Charter (as of July 2001):

Austria, Belgium, Cyprus, Czech Republic, Denmark, Finland, France, Germany, Greece, Hungary, Iceland, Ireland, Italy, Luxembourg, Malta, Netherlands, Norway, Poland, Portugal, Slovakia, Spain, Sweden, Turkey, United Kingdom of Great Britain and Northern Ireland

Revised European Social Charter (as of July 2001):

Bulgaria, Cyprus, Estonia, France, Ireland, Italy, Lithuania, Norway, Romania, Slovenia, Sweden

Additional Protocol to the European Social Charter Providing for a System of Collective Complaints (as of July 2001):

Cyprus, Finland, France, Greece, Ireland, Italy, Norway, Portugal, Sweden

Framework Convention for the Protection of National Minorities (as of July 2001):

Albania, Armenia, Austria, Azerbaijan, Bosnia and Herzegovina, Bulgaria, Croatia, Cyprus, Czech Republic, Denmark, Estonia, Finland, Germany, Hungary, Ireland, Italy, Liechtenstein, Lithuania, Malta, Moldova, Norway, Poland, Romania, Russian Federation, San Marino, Slovakia, Slovenia, Spain, Sweden, Switzerland, The Former Yugoslav Republic of Macedonia, Ukraine, United Kingdom of Great Britain and Northern Ireland, Yugoslavia

Appendix 2A
Contact Information for UN Treaty Bodies

Applicants may write to three of the UN human rights treaty bodies by addressing letters to the relevant Committee (Human Rights Committee, Committee Against Torture, Committee on the Elimination of Racial Discrimination) at the following address:

> c/o The Office of the High Commissioner for Human Rights
> Palais des Nations
> 8-14 Av. De la Paix
> CH-1211
> Geneva 10
> Switzerland
> Fax to Switzerland (41-22) 917-9022

Applicants may write to the Committee on the Elimination of Discrimination Against Women at the following address:

> Committee on the Elimination of Discrimination Against Women
> c/o Division for the Advancement of Women
> 2 UN Plaza, DC2-12th Floor
> New York, NY 10017
> USA
> Fax (1-212) 963-3463

Appendix 2B
Information on Complaints to the Human Rights Committee

One of the clearest signs of progress in human rights is the fact that individuals who claim that their rights and freedoms have been violated may call the State in question to account for its actions—if it is a *party* to the *Optional Protocol* of the *International Covenant on Civil and Political Rights.*

In the latter part of the 1980s, growing public awareness of the *Human Rights Committee*'s work under the Optional Protocol multiplied the number of communications it received from individuals complaining of violations of their rights.

The Committee considers communications from individuals in private meetings.

Is It Admissible?

Communications must not be anonymous, and cannot be considered unless they come from a person or persons subject to the jurisdiction of a State which is a party to the Optional Protocol.

Normally, a communication should be sent in by the individual who claims that his or her rights have been violated by the State. When it appears that the alleged victim cannot submit the communication, the Committee may consider a communication from another person who must prove that he or she is acting on behalf of the alleged victim. A third party with no apparent links with the person whose rights have allegedly been violated cannot submit a communication.

The complaint cannot be considered if the same problem is being investigated under another international procedure, and all domestic remedies must have been exhausted before it can be taken up by the Committee.

Even before deciding whether a communication is admissible or not, the Committee—or its Working Group on Communications—may ask the alleged victim or the State concerned for additional information or comments and set a time limit. If the State has anything to say at this stage, the person complaining receives a copy of its reply for comment.

If the case is merely referred back to the author for more information before being found inadmissible, nothing will have been transmitted to the State.

The Committee may decide to drop a complaint without a written decision; for example, when the author withdraws it, or shows in some other way that he or she does not want to go on with the matter.

Assessing a Complaint

Once a communication has been declared admissible, the Committee asks the State concerned to explain or clarify the problem and to indicate whether anything has been done to settle it. A time limit of six months is set for the State party's reply. Then the author of the complaint has an opportunity to comment on the State's reply. After that, the Committee expresses its final views and sends them to the State concerned and to the author.

The Committee puts individuals who complain and the States which are alleged to have violated their rights on an equal footing throughout its proceedings. Each has an opportunity to comment on the other's arguments.

The findings of the Committee—its views on communications which have been declared admissible and examined on their merits, as well as decisions declaring other communications inadmissible—are always made public immediately after the session at which the findings were adopted and are reproduced in the Committee's annual report to the General Assembly.

Interim Protection

Usually it takes about 12 to 18 months to declare a case admissible or inadmissible. The examination of the merits of the case may then take a year or two, depending on the degree of co-operation by States parties and the authors of complaints in submitting all the information needed by the Committee.

People who allege that their human rights are being violated may need protection before the Committee adopts it final views. Without prejudging the merits of complaints, the Committee has, for this reason, sometimes addressed urgent requests to the States involved. There have, for example, been cases where the Committee has advised against a threatened expulsion, for the suspension of a death sentence, or the need for an urgent medical examination.

Evidence and Burden of Proof

The Committee has, as yet, no independent fact-finding functions, but it is bound to consider all written information made available by the parties concerned.

In a number of cases dealing with the right to life, torture and ill-treatment, as well as arbitrary arrests and disappearances, the Committee has established that the burden of proof cannot rest alone on the person who is complaining of the violation of rights and freedoms. The Committee also maintains that it is not sufficient to make a refutation in general terms of a complaint of a violation of a person's human rights.

Individual Opinions

The Human Rights Committee works by consensus, but individual members can add their opinions to the views it expresses on the merits of a case or when communications have been declared inadmissible.

Results

Several countries have changed their laws as a result of decisions by the Committee on individual complaints under the Optional Protocol. In a number of cases, prisoners have been released and compensation paid to victims of human rights violations. In 1990, the Committee instituted a mechanism whereby it seeks to monitor more closely whether States parties have given effect to its final decisions on the merits; cooperation from States parties has been encouraged.

Appendix 2C
CAT Fact Sheet and Complaint

Contents:
- Introduction
- A monitoring body
- The Committee at work
- Cooperation with other bodies
- Prevention or cure
- Model communication

Introduction

The eradication of the practice of torture in the world was one of the major challenges taken up by the United Nations only a few years after its establishment. In order to ensure adequate protection for all persons against torture and other cruel, inhuman or degrading treatment or punishment, over the years the United Nations has adopted universally applicable standards. These standards were ultimately embodied in international declarations and conventions. The adoption on 10 December 1984 by the General Assembly of the United Nations of the Convention Against Torture and Other Cruel, Inhuman or Degrading Treatment or Punishment rounded off the codification process to combat the practice of torture.

In developing this valuable instrument, the United Nations did not merely put in writing in a series of articles a body of principles and pious hopes, the implementation and observance of which would not be guaranteed by anything or anyone. It set up also a monitoring body, the Committee Against Torture, whose main function is to ensure that the Convention is observed and implemented. The Committee met for the first time in April 1988 in Geneva and has since carried out intensive activities which, although often discreet, should make it known to the public at large.

A Monitoring Body

The *Convention against Torture and Other Cruel, Inhuman or Degrading Treatment or Punishment* was adopted on 10 December 1984 by the General Assembly of the United Nations. Consisting of 33 articles, this instrument, which 58 States had ratified or acceded to as of 1 January 1992, entered into force on 26 June 1987.

The *Committee against Torture* was established pursuant to article 17 of the Convention and began to function on 1 January 1988.

The Committee consists of 10 experts of high moral standing and recognized competence in the field of human rights. The experts, who must be nationals of States Parties, are elected by those States by secret ballot. They are elected for a term of four years and are eligible for re-election. The present composition of the Committee and the list of States Parties are indicated in the annexes.

The Committee constitutes a new United Nations body, entrusted with the specific su 'pervasion of a multilateral instrument for protection against torture and other inhuman treatment. The Convention sets out a number of obligations designed to strengthen the sphere of protection of human rights and fundamental freedoms, while conferring upon the Committee against Torture broad powers of examination and investigation calculated to ensure their effectiveness in practice.

At their initial meeting held at Geneva in April 1988, the members of the Committee against Torture adopted rules of procedure and defined the Committee's working methods, in conformity with the provisions of the Convention.

The Committee at Work

The Committee normally holds two regular sessions each year. Special sessions, however, may be convened by decision of the Committee itself at the request of a majority of its members or of a State Party to the Convention.

The Committee elects from among its members a Chairman, three Vice-Chairmen and a Rapporteur. These officers are elected for a term of two years and are eligible for re-election.

The Committee may invite specialized agencies, United Nations bodies concerned, regional intergovernmental organizations and non-governmental organizations in consultative status with the Economic and Social Council to submit to it information, documentation and written statements, as appropriate, relevant to the Cornmittee's activities under the Convention. It submits an annual report on its activities to the States Parties and to the General Assembly of the United Nations.

Reports by the States Parties

Submission of Reports by States Parties

Pursuant to article 19 of the Convention, each State Party shall submit to the Committee, through the Secretary-General of the United Nations, reports on the measures taken to give effect to its undertakings under the Convention. The first report must be submitted within one year after the entry into force of the Convention for the State concerned; thereinafter supplementary reports shall be submitted every four years on any subsequent developments. Further reports and additional information may also be requested by the Committee.

At each session, the Secretary-General of the United Nations notifies the Committee of all cases of non-submission of the said reports. In such cases, the Committee may transmit to the State Party concerned a reminder about the submission of such report or reports.

As to the actual formulation of the report, the Committee has prepared general guidelines containing precise instructions on their form and content in order to inform fully the Committee on the situation in each State Party.

Examination of the Reports by the Committee

For the examination of the reports, the Committee invites representatives of the States Parties to attend the meetings when their reports are considered. It may also inform a State Party from which it decides to seek further information that it may authorize its representative to be present at a specified meeting. Such a representative should be able to answer questions which may be put to him by the Committee and clarify, if need be, certain aspects of the reports already submitted by his State.

After its consideration of each report, the Committee, in accordance with article 19, paragraph 3, of the Convention, may make such general comments on the report as it may consider appropriate. It may, in particular, indicate whether it appears to it that some of the obligations of the State concerned under the Convention have not been discharged. The Committee's observations are transmitted to the State Party, which may reply to them.

Some 40 reports had been examined by the Committee by the end of its seventeenth session in November 1991.

Powers of Investigation of the Committee

By virtue of article 20 of the Convention, the Committee is empowered to receive information and to institute inquiries concerning allegations of systematic practice of torture in the States Parties.

The procedure set out in article 20 of the Convention is marked by two features: its confidential character and the pursuit of cooperation with the States Parties concerned.

The competence conferred upon the Committee by this article is optional, which means that, at the time of ratifying or acceding to the

Convention, a State may declare that it does not recognize it. In that case, and so long as that reservation has not been withdrawn, the Committee may not exercise the powers conferred upon it under article 20 in respect of that State Party.

Gathering of Information

In respect of all the States which have accepted the procedure set out in article 20, the Committee is empowered to receive information concerning the existence of the practice of torture. If it appears to the Committee that the information received is reliable and contains well founded indications that torture is being systematically practised in the territory of a State Party to the Convention, the Committee invites that State to cooperate in its examination of the information and, to this end, to submit observations with regard to that information. It may also decide to request additional information either from the representatives of the State concerned or from governmental and non-governmental organizations as well as individuals, for the purpose of obtaining further elements on which to form an opinion.

Inquiry Procedure

If it considers that the information gathered warrants it, the Committee may designate one or more of its members to make a confidential inquiry. In that case, it invites the State Party concerned to cooperate with it in the conduct of the inquiry. Accordingly, the Committee may request the State Party to designate a representative to meet with the members designated to conduct the inquiry in order to provide them with any information they consider necessary. The inquiry may also include, with the agreement of the State Party, a visit to its territory by the designated members, who may then conduct hearings of witnesses.

The designated members submit their findings to the Committee, which transmits them, together with its own comments or suggestions, to the State Party. It invites that State to inform the Committee of the action it takes with regard to the Committee's findings.

After all the proceedings regarding an inquiry have been completed, the Committee may decide to include a summary account of the results of the proceedings in its annual report. Only in that case is the work of the Committee made public; otherwise, all the work and documents relating to its functions under article 20 are confidential.

Inter-State Complaints

The conduct, with respect to the States Parties, of proceedings relating to the inter-State complaints mentioned in article 21 of the Convention is subordinated to the recognition by those States of the competence of the Committee. With respect to those States which have deposited the declaration specified in article 21, the Committee may receive and consider communications in which a State Party alleges that another State Party is not discharging its obligations under the Convention.

Recourse to the Committee

The procedure comprises two stages. If a State Party to the Convention considers that another State Party has violated one of its provisions it may in the first place, by written communication, bring the matter to the attention of that State Party. The State which receives the communication is required to furnish in writing and within three months any explanations necessary to clarify the matter. In the event that the two States Parties concerned are unable to settle the matter between themselves, it may be referred by either State to the Committee, whose meetings are always closed.

All domestic remedies available in the State accused of a violation of the Convention must have been exhausted before the Committee can deal with a matter, except where the application of the remedies is unreasonably prolonged or is unlikely to bring effective relief to the victim of the violation.

Friendly Solution of the Matter

If these conditions are met, the Committee endeavours to arrive at a friendly solution of the matter on the basis of respect for the obligations provided for in the Convention, by making available its good offices to the States Parties concerned and by setting up, when appropriate, an ad hoc conciliation commission. During this phase, any relevant information may be requested by the Committee from the States concerned, which may also make submissions orally or in writing and be represented when the Committee considers the matter.

The Committee shall, within 12 months, submit a report containing a brief statement of the facts and of the solution reached, if a friendly solution is found; otherwise, it submits only the facts with the submissions of the States concerned. The report shall then be communicated, through the Secretary-General of the United Nations, to the States Parties concerned.

Individual Complaints

Like other international instruments relating to human rights, the Convention on Torture gives private individuals, in certain circumstances, the right to lodge with the Committee complaints regarding the violation of one or more of its provisions by a State Party. For the Committee to be able to admit and examine individual communications against a State Party, its competence in that regard must however have been expressly recognized by the State concerned.

Individual complaints are always examined by the Committee in closed meeting.

Submission of Communications

A communication may be submitted by any private individual who claims to be the victim of a violation of the Convention by a State Party which has accepted the competence of the Committee under article 22 and which is subject to its jurisdiction. If the alleged victim is not in a position to submit the communication himself, his relatives or representatives may act on his behalf.

Consideration of Admissibility

In its consideration of the communication, the Committee's first concern is to ascertain its admissibility and, if the conditions for admissibility are met, the Committee then proceeds to examine the merits. The Committee may be assisted, in the exercise of its functions, by a working group comprising not more than five of its members and expressly set up for the purpose.

The conditions for admissibility of communications are specified in the Convention and in the Committee's rules of procedure. For a communication to be declared admissible, it must not:

Be anonymous or incompatible with the provisions of the Convention;

Constitute an abuse of the right to submit a communication under article 22;

Have been examined (or be under examination) under another procedure of international investigation or settlement.

Furthermore, all available domestic remedies must have been exhausted first (under the conditions specified for inter-State complaints).

The Committee may request the State Party concerned or the author of the communication to submit additional information, clarifications or observations relevant to the question of admissibility.

If a communication is declared to be inadmissible, the Committee informs those concerned; the same issue may, however, be reviewed at a later date in the event of the Committee receiving information to the effect that the reasons for inadmissibility no longer apply.

Consideration of the Merits

If the Committee decides that a communication is admissible, after informing the author of the communication and transmitting its decision to the State Party concerned, it then considers the merits. Within six months, the State which has allegedly violated the Convention shall submit to the Committee explanations or statements clarifying the case and indicating any measures that may have been taken to remedy the situation. The author of the communication may also submit his observations or additional information to the Committee. In addition, the author of the communication or his representative may be present at the closed meetings of the Committee, if the latter deems it appropriate, in order to provide clarifications on the merits of the case. The representatives of the State concerned may also be invited to attend in the same way.

Provisional Measures

In the course of the consideration of either the question of inadmissibility or the merits of the communication, and prior to any decision being taken, the Committee may request the State Party concerned to take steps to avoid a possible irreparable damage to the alleged victim of the violation. This provision offers persons who claim a violation of the Convention protection even before the Committee takes a decision on the admissibility or the merits of the case and at the same time does not prejudge the Committee's final decision.

Conclusion of the Proceedings

In the light of all information made available to it by the individual and by the State concerned, the Committee considers the communication and formulates its views thereon. Any member of the Committee may express an individual opinion. The consideration proceedings conclude with the transmission of the final views to the author of the communication and the State concerned, which is also invited by the Committee to inform it of the action it takes in conformity with the Committee's views.

The Committee includes in its annual report a summary of the communications examined, of the explanations and statements of the States Parties concerned, and of its own views.

By the end of its seventh session, the Committee had adopted seven final views on individual communications submitted to it.

Cooperation with Other Bodies

There are other methods of combating torture at either the regional level or the international level. That raises the question of their relationships and the establishment of forms of cooperation to avoid any overlapping of tasks and activities and to strengthen, by means of joint action, the effectiveness of the international campaign against torture.

The Special Rapporteur on Torture

The Committee has considered on a number of occasions the question of cooperation with the Commission on Human Rights Special Rapporteur responsible for issues relating to the practice of torture in the world, as well as the possibility of sharing the tasks as between the Special Rapporteur and the Committee, in order to avoid duplication in the exercise of their respective mandates.

The Committee considers the mandate conferred upon it by the Convention and the mandate conferred on the Special Rapporteur by the Commission on Human Rights to be different but complementary. The Rapporteur is required to report to the Commission on the phenomenon of torture in general. To that end, he asks Governments for information on the legislative and administrative measures taken to prevent torture and to remedy its consequences whenever it occurs. He also visits certain regions of the world to hold consultations with government representatives who express the wish to meet him. His task extends to all States Members of the United Nations and to all States with observer status: from that point of view it is broader than that of the Committee (the functions of the Special Rapporteur on Torture are explained in Fact Sheet No. 4: *Methods of combating torture*).

In view of the complementary nature of their tasks, close contacts have been established between the Committee and the Special Rapporteur for the purpose of exchanging information, reports and documents of common interest.

The European Committee for the Prevention of Torture and the United Nations Voluntary Fund for Victims of Torture

In the course of its work, the Committee has also laid the foundations for establishing working relations with the European Committee for the Prevention of Torture and Inhuman or Degrading Treatment or Punishment, as well as cooperation with the Board of Trustees of the United Nations Voluntary Fund for Victims of Torture set up pursuant to General Assembly resolution 36/151 of 16 December 1981.

The cooperation between the Committee against Torture and the European Committee for the Prevention of Torture and Inhuman or Degrading Treatment or Punishment regarding visits to States which are Parties both to the United Nations Convention and to the European Convention appears, however, limited because of the confidential character of the procedures respectively applicable to those visits.

Prevention or Cure

The machinery provided for by the Convention on Torture for the consideration of communications-whether inter-State or individual-can be set in motion when human rights violations have already occurred. In some sense, it seeks to "remedy" such a violation by recording publicly (in the Committee's annual report) that a State has violated one or more provisions of the Convention, in order to induce the State concerned to remedy the violation. This is also the object of other international instruments on human rights questions established in the United Nations context.

Nevertheless, the establishment of international standards and of monitoring and inquiry procedures, relating to torture and other subjects, is not in itself sufficient to guarantee observance of human rights by the States Members of the United Nations which have undertaken to comply with them.

United Nations activities in this regard can be supplemented in a timely way by its technical assistance and advisory services programme, which operates at two levels.

In the first place, even when a State has accepted international obligations and is willing to respect them, it is not always in a position to do so because of the lack, at the domestic level, of the competent persons and infrastructures necessary for the application of the standards contained in the relevant international instruments. The United Nations can then provide its assistance and its advisory services to help the State concerned to ensure the realization of the rights that have been recognized.

In the second place, through its technical assistance programme, the United Nations also wages a campaign to prevent human rights violations. The setting up of national infrastructures for the protection and promotion of human rights, the organization of courses of study and in-service training for officials responsible for the realization of human rights at the national level (public officials, police forces, personnel of the judiciary) lay down the foundations for creating a human rights culture, which constitutes the best guarantee against the violation of those rights.

Model Communication

_____   Date:

Communication to:
    The Committee against Torture
    c/o Centre for Human Rights
    United Nations Office
    8-14 avenue de la Paix
    1211 Geneva 10
    Switzerland

Submitted for consideration under the Convention against Torture and Other Cruel, Inhuman or Degrading Treatment or Punishment

I.   Information concerning the author of the communication

Name _____   First name(s) _____

Nationality _____   Profession _____

Date and place of birth _____

Present address _____

Address for exchange of confidential correspondence (if other than present address) _____

Submitting the communication as:
    (a) Victim of the violation or violations set forth below
        _____ [ ]
    (b) Appointed representative/legal counsel of the alleged
        victim(s) _____ [ ]
    (c) Other _____ [ ]

If box (c) is marked, the author should explain:

(i) In what capacity he is acting on behalf of the victim(s) (e.g. family relationship or other personal links with the alleged victim(s)): _____
_____

(ii) Why the victim(s) is (are) unable to submit the communication himself (themselves): _____
_____

An unrelated third party having no link to the victim(s) cannot submit a communication on his (their) behalf.

II. Information concerning the alleged victim(s) (if other than author)

Name _____ First name(s) _____

Nationality _____ Profession _____

Date and place of birth _____

Present address or whereabouts _____
_____

III. State concerned/articles violated/domestic remedies

Name of the State party (country) to the Convention against Torture and Other Cruel, Inhuman or Degrading Treatment or Punishment against which the communication is directed:
_____
_____

Articles of the Convention against Torture allegedly violated:
_____
_____

Steps taken by or on behalf of the alleged victim(s) to exhaust domestic remedies-recourse to the courts or other public authorities, when and with what results (if possible, enclose copies of all relevant judicial or administrative decisions):
_____
_____

If domestic remedies have not been exhausted, explain why:
_____
_____

IV. Other international procedures

Has the same matter been submitted for examination under another procedure of international investigation or settlement (e.g. the Inter-American Commission on Human Rights, the European Commission on Human Rights)? If so, when and with what results?

_____

_____

V. Facts of the claim

Detailed description of the facts of the alleged violation or violations (including relevant dates)*

_____

_____

Author's signature: _____

---

* Add as many pages as needed for this description.

Appendix 2D
Information on Complaints to the Committee Against Torture

Like other international instruments relating to human rights, the Convention against Torture gives private individuals, in certain circumstances, the right to lodge with the *Committee against Torture (CAT)* complaints regarding the violation of one or more of its provisions by a State Party. For the Committee to be able to admit and examine individual communications against a State Party, its competence in that regard must however have been *expressly recognized by the State concerned.* Individual complaints are always examined by the Committee in closed meeting.

Submission of Communications

A communication may be submitted by any private individual who claims to be the victim of a violation of the Convention by a State Party which has accepted the competence of the Committee under *article 22* and which is subject to its jurisdiction. If the alleged victim is not in a position to submit the communication himself, his relatives or representatives may act on his behalf.

Consideration of Admissibility

In its consideration of the communication, the Committee's first concern is to ascertain its admissibility and, if the conditions for admissibility are met, the Committee then proceeds to examine the merits. The Committee may be assisted, in the exercise of its functions, by a working group comprising not more than five of its members and expressly set up for the purpose.

The conditions of admissibility of communications are specified in the Convention and in the Committee's rules of procedure. For a communication to be declared admissible, it must not:

- be anonymous or incompatible with the provisions of the Convention;
- constitute an abuse of the right to submit a communication under article 22;
- have been examined (or be under examination) under another procedure of international investigation or settlement.

Furthermore, all available domestic remedies must have been exhausted first (under the conditions specified for inter-State complaints).

The Committee may request the State Party concerned or the author of the communication to submit additional information, clarifications or observations relevant to the question of the admissibility.

If a communication is declared to be inadmissible, the Committee informs those concerned; the same issue may, however, be reviewed at a later date in the event of the Committee receiving information to the effect that the reasons for inadmissibility no longer apply.

Consideration of the Merits

If the Committee decides that a communication is admissible, after informing the author of the communication and transmitting its decision to the State Party concerned, it then considers the merits. Within six months, the State which has allegedly violated the Convention shall submit to the Committee explanations or statements clarifying the case and indicating any measures that may have been taken to remedy the situation. The author of the communication may also submit his observations or additional information to the Committee. In addition, the author of the communication or his representative may be present at the closed meetings of the Committee, if the latter deems it appropriate, in order to provide clarifications on the merits of the case. The representatives of the State concerned may also be invited to attend in the same way.

Provisional Measures

In the course of the consideration of either the question of inadmissibility or the merits of the communication, and prior to any decision being taken, the Committee may request the State Party concerned to take steps to avoid a possible irreparable damage to the alleged victim of the violation. This provision offers persons who claim a violation of the Convention protection even before the Committee takes a decision on the admissibility or the merits of the case and at the same time does not prejudge the Committee's final decision.

Conclusion of the Proceedings

In the light of all information made available to it by the individual and by the State concerned, the Committee considers the communication and formulates its views thereon. Any member of the Committee may express an individual opinion. The consideration proceedings conclude with the transmission of the final views to the author of the communication and the State concerned, which is also invited by the Committee to inform it of the action it takes in conformity with the Committee's views.

The Committee includes in its annual report a summary of the communication examined, of the explanations and statements of the States Parties concerned, and of its own views.

By the end of its 17th session, the Committee had concluded consideration of 35 cases submitted to it.

Appendix 2E
Information on Complaints to the Committee on the Elimination of Racial Discrimination

Article 14 of the International Convention on the Elimination of All Forms Racial Discrimination establishes a procedure which makes it possible for an individual or a group of persons who claim to be victims of racial discrimination to lodge a complaint with the *Committee on the Elimination of Racial Discrimination (CERD)* against their State. This may only be done if the State concerned is a party to the Convention and *has declared that it recognizes the competence of CERD* to receive such complaints.

The Convention also provides that States which have made the declaration may establish or indicate a national body competent to receive petitions from individuals or groups who claim to be victims of violations of their rights and who have exhausted other local remedies. Only if petitioners fail to obtain satisfaction from the body indicated may they bring the matter to the Committee's attention.

In the Programme of action adopted by the Second World Conference to Combat Racism and Racial Discrimination in 1983, States were asked to make access to their national procedures for dealing with complaints of this kind as easy as possible. The procedures should be publicised and victims of racial discrimination should be helped to make use of them. The rules for making complaints should be simple, and complaints should be dealt with promptly. Legal aid should be available for poor victims of discrimination in civil or criminal proceedings and there should be the right to seek reparation for damages suffered.

The procedure for communications from individuals or groups claiming to be the victims of a violation of the Convention to be received by CERD came into operation in 1982 when 10 States parties had declared that they accepted the Committee's competence in this field. The Committee brings such communications confidentially to the attention of the State party in question, but does not—without their consent—reveal the identity of the individual or group claiming a violation. When the State has given an explanation of its views and perhaps suggested a remedy, the Committee debates the matter and may make suggestions and recommendations, which are transmitted both to the individual or group concerned and to the State party.

Appendix 3A
Contact Information (Charter-Based Bodies)

Special Procedures of the UN Commission on Human Rights
1503 Procedure
Sub-Commission on the Promotion and Protection of Human Rights

All of these mechanisms are based at the Office of the High Commissioner for Human Rights and share the following contact details. Always remember to mark clearly which mechanism or mechanisms you wish your information to go to, and if your information requires urgent attention, do not forget to mark this too.

OHCHR—UNOG
8-14 Avenue de la Paix
1211 Geneva 10
Switzerland
Tel: +41-22-917 9000
Fax: +41-22-917 9006 (Special Procedures only)
+4 -22-917 9011 (1503 Procedure and Sub-Commission only)
Email: *webmaster.hchr@unog.ch*
Web-site: <www.unhchr.ch>

Commission on the Status of Women

This body is serviced by the UN Division for the Advancement of Women, based in New York.

UN Division for the Advancement of Women
2 United Nations Plaza
Room DC2-1220
New York, NY 10017
United States
Tel: +1-212-963 5086
Fax: +1-212-963 3463
Email: *daw@un.org*
Web-site: <www.un.org/womenwatch/daw/csw>

Information About the Charter-Based Mechanisms:

The most valuable information you can obtain relating to the Charter-based mechanisms is contained in UN documents. It is through this type of documentation that you can find the reports prepared by the mechanisms themselves, as well as their mandates and any public information produced about them. The easiest source for obtaining such documents is the web-site of the UN High Commissioner for Human Rights, which contains all documents since the mid-1990s as well as a selection of earlier documents. If you do not have access to the Internet, these documents may be found in certain public or academic libraries (known as UN depository libraries), or you could write to the Documentation Section at the OHCHR and request a copy of a particular document. Other NGOs, especially those which are Geneva based, may also be able to help you obtain a particular document.

Finding your way around the OHCHR web-site (<www.unhchr.ch>) can be daunting. The key to navigating it is to go immediately to the "site map" (<www.unhchr.ch/map.htm>), which sets out a list of everything you can find on the web-site. Under the section titled 'Commission on Human Rights,' you will see links to the thematic and country procedures. If you follow these links, you will find that each procedure has its own page which sets out a complete list of all the documents available on the site which are relevant to that procedure, including annual reports, resolutions (which contain the mandate for the procedure), fact-sheets and standard application forms where these exist. If you know what you are looking for, you can also search for a document in the 'Charter bodies database,' which contains all documentation produced by the Charter bodies. Once you become familiar with the "site map," you should be able to find almost anything you need.

Appendix 3B
Model Complaints

3B1 Working Group on Arbitrary Detention

Model questionnaire to be completed by persons alleging arbitrary arrest or detention

I. Identity of the person arrested or detained

1. Family name: _____
2. First name: _____
3. Sex: ☐ (Male)   ☐ (Female)
4. Birth date or age (at the time of detention): _____
5. Nationality/Nationalities: _____
6. (a) Identity document (if any): _____
   (b) Issued by:
   (c) On (date):
   (d) No.:
7. Profession and/or activity (if believed to be relevant to the arrest/detention): _____
8. Address of usual residence: _____

II. Arrest

1. Date of arrest: _____
2. Place of arrest (as detailed as possible): _____
3. Forces who carried out the arrest or are believed to have carried it out: _____
4. Did they show a warrant or other decision by a public authority?

   (Yes) _____   (No) _____
5. Authority who issued the warrant or decision: _____
6. Relevant legislation applied (if known): _____

III. Detention

1. Date of detention: _____

2. Duration of detention (if not known, probable duration):
   _____

3. Forces holding the detainee under custody: _____

4. Places of detention (indicate any transfer and present place of detention): _____

5. Authorities that ordered the detention: _____

6. Reasons for the detention imputed by the authorities: ____
   _____
   _____
   _____

7. Relevant legislation applied (if known): _____
   _____
   _____
   _____

IV. Describe the circumstances of the arrest and/or the detention and indicate precise reasons why you consider the arrest or detention to be arbitrary
   _____
   _____
   _____

V. Indicate internal steps, including, domestic remedies, taken especially with the legal and administrative authorities, particularly for the purpose of establishing the detention and, as appropriate, their results or the reasons why such steps or remedies were ineffective or remedies they were not taken
   _____
   _____
   _____

VI. Full name and address of the person(s) submitting the information (telephone and Fax number, if possible
   _____
   _____
   _____

Date: _____   Signature: _____

This questionnaire should be addressed to the Working Group on Arbitrary Detention, OHCHR-UNOG, 1211 Geneva 10, Switzerland, Fax No. (41-22) 917.90.06.

A separate questionnaire must be completed for each case of alleged arbitrary arrest or detention. As far as possible, all details requested should be given. Nevertheless, failure to do so will not necessarily result in the inadmissibility of the communication.

For the purpose of this questionnaire, "arrest" refers to the initial act of apprehending a person. "Detention" means and includes detention before, during and after trial. In some cases, only section II, or section III may be applicable. None the less, whenever possible, both sections should be filled in.

Copies of documents that prove the arbitrary nature of the arrest or detention, or help to better understand the specific circumstances of the case, as well as any other relevant information, may also be attached to this questionnaire.

If a case is submitted to the Working Group by anyone other than the victim or his family, such person or organization should indicate authorization by the victim or his family to act on their behalf. If, however, the authorization is not readily available, the Working Group reserves the right to proceed without the authorization. All details concerning the persons(s) submitting the information to the Working Group, and any authorization provided by the victim or his family, will be kept confidential.

3B2 Working Group on Enforced or Involuntary Disappearances

Explanatory note for the submission of information on enforced or involuntary disappearances of persons

Reports of enforced or involuntary disappearances of persons may be transmitted to the Working Group on Enforced or Involuntary Disappearances of the Commission of Human Rights, c/o OHCHR-LTNOG, CH-1211 Geneva 10, Switzerland, fax. no. (41-22) 917 9006.

Experience has shown that information on the enforced or involuntary disappearance of a person varies greatly in detail by reason of the nature of each case and the surrounding circumstances. While it is important to receive as much information as possible, missing details should not prevent the submission of reports. However, the Working Group can only deal with clearly identified individual cases containing the following minimum elements of information:

(a) Full name of the missing person (including any available data relevant to the missing person's identification, such as national identity document number, photograph, etc.);

(b) Year, month, day of the disappearance;

(c) Place of arrest or abduction or where the missing person was last seen;

(d) Indication of the persons believed to have carried out the arrest or abduction;

(e) Indication of the action taken by the relatives or others to locate the missing person (inquiries with authorities, *habeas corpus* petitions, etc.);

(f) Identity of the person or organization submitting the report (name and address, which will be kept confidential upon request).

Information on the enforced or involuntary disappearance of a person may be submitted in any written form, in urgent cases preferably by cable or telex. In submitting such reports, consideration may be given to preparing a narrative summary of the events and providing, to the extent possible, the information listed on the attached form. A photograph of the missing person and annexes, such as *habeas corpus* petitions or statements of witnesses, can be sent with the suggested form. Please send only copies of documents, the originals should remain in your files. The person or organization making the reports should be clearly identified and an address should be given at which they can be contacted. If the author of the report is not a relative of the missing person, but acts, directly or indirectly, upon the family's request, he should remain in contact with the family, since any replies obtained by the Working Group on the missing person's fate or whereabouts are for the exclusive information of the relatives.

I. **Identity of the person subjected to enforced or involuntary disappearance**

1. Family name:
2. First name:
3. Sex: Male Female
4. Birth date or age (at time of disappearance):
5. Nationality (ies):
6. Civil status (single, married, etc.):
7. Identity document:
8. Profession:
9. Address of usual residence:
10. Activities: (trade union, political, religious, humanitarian/solidarity, press, etc.)

II. **Date of disappearance**

11. Year, month, day and hour when missing person was arrested or abducted:
12. Year, month, day and hour when missing person was last seen:
13. Other indications relating to date of disappearance:

III. **Place of disappearance**

(Please indicate as precisely as possible country, province, city, location, etc. and if identical with home address)

14. Place where missing person was arrested or abducted:
15. Place where missing person was last seen:
16. If subsequent to the disappearance of the person information was received about him/her being detained, please indicate, if possible, the places (official or others) and period of detention, as well as the source of the information, in particular witnesses who have seen the disappeared person in captivity. (Do you wish the identity of the witnesses or sources to be kept confidential?)
17. Other indications concerning the place of disappearance:

IV. Forces believed to be responsible for the disappearance

18. If the person was arrested or abducted, please indicate who carried out the arrest: military, police, persons in uniform or civilian clothes, agents of security services, unidentified; whether these agents identified themselves (with credentials, orally, etc.); whether they were armed; whether they appeared to act with impunity; whether a vehicle was used (official, with or without licence plages, etc.).
19. If the forces or agents who carried out the arrest or abduction cannot be identified, state why you believe that Government authorities, or persons linked to them, are responsible for the disappearance:
20. If the arrest or abduction took place in the presence of witnesses indicate the names of the witnesses. If the witnesses have not identified themselves or wish to withhold their names, indicate if they are relatives, neighbours, bypassers etc.:
21. If any written evidence of the arrest exists, please describe (arrest order, communiqu6s, official notes, letters, etc.);
22. If a search took place of the missing person's domicile, office of place of work (or that of any other person connected with him/her), before, during or after the disappearance, please indicate and describe the search:
23. If someone was questioned concerning the disappeared person by agents of the security services, official authorities or other persons related to them, before of after the arrest (or disappearance), please indicate and provide available information concerning the questioning:

V. National action (legal or other) on behalf of the missing person

A. *Habeas corpus, amparo or similar*
24. Nature of the action:
25. Date:
26. Tribunal:
27. Result (date and nature):
28. If a judicial decision exists please indicate its contents, if possible:

B. *Criminal complaints*
29. Nature of the action:
30. Date:
31. Tribunal:

32. Result (date and nature):
33. If a judicial decision exists please indicate its contents, if possible:

C. *Other measures taken at the national level*
(Letters, petitions, etc., or other steps taken before the civil or military authorities):

VI. Measures taken at the international level on behalf of the missing, person

34. Organizations addressed
35. Date:
36. Result (date and nature):

VII. Related cases of arrest or disappearance, in particular missing, relatives of children

37. Please give a narrative account indicating relevant names, dates and places:
38. If the missing person was pregnant at the time of disappearance, please indicate the date on which her baby might have been born:

VIII. Information concerning the author of the present report

39. Surname:
40. First name:
41. Nationality(ies):
42. Relationship with the missing person:
43. Present address:
    Telephone:

IX. Confidentiality

44. Please state whether the author of the present report wishes his/her identity to be kept confidential: .

Note: If any information contained in the present report should be kept confidential please print the world "CONFIDENTIAL" beside the relevant entry.

X. Date:

Signature of author: _____

3B3 Special Rapporteur on Freedom of Opinion and Expression

Guidelines for the submission of information to the Special Rapporteur on freedom of opinion and expression

In order for the Special Rapporteur to be able to take action regarding a communication on a case or incident, the following information, as a minimum, must be received.

1. *Allegation regarding a person or persons:*

As detailed a description of the alleged violation as possible, including date, location and circumstances of the event;
Name, age, gender, ethnic background (if relevant), profession;
Views, affiliations, past or present participation in political, social, ethnic or labour group/activity;
Information on other specific activities relating to the alleged violation.

2. *Allegation regarding a medium of communication:*

As detailed a description of the alleged infringement on the right as possible, including date, location and circumstances of the event;
The nature of the medium affected (e.g. newspapers, independent radio); including circulation and frequency of publication or broadcasting, public performances, etc.;
Political orientation of the medium (if relevant).

3. *Information regarding the alleged perpetrators:*

Name, State affiliation (e.g. military, police) and reasons why they are considered responsible;
For non-State actors, description of how they relate to the State (e.g. cooperation with or support by State security forces);
If applicable, State encouragement or tolerance of activities of non-State actors, whether groups or individuals, including threats or use of violence and harassment against individuals exercising their right to freedom of opinion and expression, including the right to seek, receive and impart information.

4. *Information related to State actions:*

If the incident involves restrictions on a medium (e.g. censorship, closure of a news organ, banning of a book, etc.); the identity of the authority involved (individual and/or ministry and/or department), the legal statute invoked, and steps taken to seek domestic remedy;

If the incident involves arrest of an individual or individuals, the identity of the authority involved (individual and/or ministry and/or department), the legal statute invoked, location of detention if known, information on provision of access to legal counsel and family members, steps taken to seek domestic remedy or clarification of person's situation and status;

If applicable, information on whether or not an investigation has taken place and, if so, by what ministry or department of the Government and the status of the investigation at the time of submission of the allegation, including whether or not the investigation has resulted in indictments.

5. Information on the source of the communications:

Name and full address;
Telephone and Fax numbers and e-mail address (if possible);
Name, address, phone/Fax numbers and e-mail address (if applicable) of person or organization submitting the allegation.

Note: In addition to the information requested above, the Special Rapporteur welcomes any additional comments or background notes that are considered relevant to the case or incident.

Follow-up

The Special Rapporteur attaches great importance to being kept informed of the current status of cases and thus very much welcomes updates of previously reported cases and information. This includes both negative and positive developments, including the release of persons detained for exercising their rights to freedom of opinion and expression and to seek, receive and impart information, or the adoption of new laws or policies or changes to existing ones that have a positive impact on the realization of the rights to freedom of opinion and expression and information.

Root causes

In order to carry out his work regarding the root causes of violations, which is of particular importance to the Special Rapporteur, he is very much interested in receiving information on and/or texts of draft laws relating to or affecting the rights to freedom of opinion and expression and to seek, receive and impart information. The Special

Rapporteur is also interested in laws or government policies relating to electronic media, including the Internet, as well as the impact of the availability of new information technologies on the right to freedom of opinion and expression.

Communications

Where requested or considered necessary by the Special Rapporteur, information on the source of the allegations will be treated as confidential.

Any information falling within this description of the mandate of the Special Rapporteur should be sent to:

> Special Rapporteur on the promotion and protection
> of the right to freedom of opinion and expression
> c/o Office of the High Commissioner for
> Human Rights
> United Nations Office at Geneva
> 1211 Geneva 10
> Switzerland
> Fax: +4122 917 9003

3B4 Special Rapporteur on Torture

Model questionnaire to be completed by persons alleging torture or their representatives

Information on the torture of a person should be transmitted to the Special Rapporteur in written form and sent c/o Office of the High Commissioner for Human Rights, United Nations Office at Geneva, CH-1211 Geneva 10, Switzerland. Although it is important to provide as much detail as possible, the lack of a comprehensive accounting should not necessarily preclude the submission of reports. However, the Special Rapporteur can only deal with clearly identified individual cases containing the following minimum elements of information:

a.   Full name of the victim;
b.   Date on which the incident(s) of torture occurred (at least as to the month and year);
c.   Place where the person was seized (city, province, etc.) And location at which the torture was carried out (if known);
d.   Indication of the forces carrying out the torture;
e.   Description of the form of torture used and any injury suffered as a result;
f.   Identify of the person or organization submitting the report (name and address, which will be kept confidential).

Additional sheets should be attached where space does not allow for a full rendering of the information requested. Also, copies of any relevant corroborating documents, such as medical or police records should be supplied where it is believed that such information may contribute to a fuller accounting of the incident. Only copies and not originals of such documents should be sent.

1. Identity of the person(s) subjected to torture

A.   Family Name
B.   First and other names
C.   Sex: Male Female
D.   Birth date or age
E.   Nationality
F.   Occupation
G.   Identity card number (if applicable)
H.   Activities (trade union, political, religious, humanitarian/ solidarity, press, etc.)
I.   Residential and/or work address

2. Circumstances surrounding torture

A. Date and place of arrest and subsequent torture
B. Identity of force(s) carrying out the initial detention and/or torture (police, intelligence services, armed forces, paramilitary, prison officials, other)
C. Were any person, such as a lawyer, relatives or friends, permitted to see the victim during detention? If so, how long after the arrest?
D. Describe the methods of torture used
E. What injuries were sustained as a result of the torture?
F. What was believed to be the purpose of the torture?
G. Was the victim examined by a doctor at any point during or after his/her ordeal? If so, when? Was the examination performed by a prison or government doctor?
H. Was appropriate treatment received for injuries sustained as a result of the torture?
I. Was the medical examination performed in a manner which would enable the doctor to detect evidence of injuries sustained as a result of the torture? Were any medical reports or certificates issued? If so, what did the reports reveal?
J. If the victim died in custody, was an autopsy or forensic examination performed and which were the results?

3. Remedial action

Were any domestic remedies pursued by the victim or his/her family or representatives (complaints with the forces responsible, the judiciary, political organs, etc.)? If so, what was the result?

4. Information concerning the author of the present report:

A. Family Name
B. First Name
C. Relationship to victim
D. Organization represented, if any
E. Present full address

3B5 Special Rapporteur on Violence Against Women

Confidential Violence Against Women Information Form

INFORMER:
Name of person/organization: _____
Address: _____
Fax/Tel/e-mail: _____

VICTIM(S):
Name: _____
Address: _____
Date of birth: _____
Nationality: _____
Sex: _____ female: _____
Occupation: _____
Ethnic background (if relevant): _____
Marital status: _____

THE INCIDENT

Date: _____ Time: _____ Location/country: _____
Number of assailants: _____
Are the assailant(s) known to the victim? _____
Description of the assailant(s) (include any identifiable features):
_____
_____

Description of the incident: _____
Does the victim believe she was specifically targeted because of gender? _____ If yes, why? _____
Has the incident been reported to the relevant State authorities? _____
If so, which authorities and when? _____
Actions taken by the authorities after the incident: _____
WITNESSES: Were there any witnesses? _____
Name/age/relationship/contact address: _____

RETURN TO:

THE SPECIAL RAPPORTEUR ON VIOLENCE AGAINST WOMEN
OHCHR-UNOG
1211 GENEVA 10, SWITZERLAND
(FAX:(41.22) 917.90.03)

Appendix 3C
Guiding Principles on Internal Displacement

E/CN.4/1998/53/Add.2
11 February 1998

Commission on Human Rights
Fifty-fourth session
Item 9 (d) of the provisional agenda

Further Promotion and Encouragement of Human Rights and Fundamental Freedoms, Including the Question of the Programme and Methods of Work of the Commission on Human Rights, Mass Exoduses and Displaced Persons

Report of the Representative of the Secretary-General, Mr. Francis M. Deng, submitted pursuant to Commission resolution 1997/39

Addendum: Guiding Principles on Internal Displacement

Introductory Note to the Guiding Principles

1. Internal displacement, affecting some 25 million people worldwide, has become increasingly recognized as one of the most tragic phenomena of the contemporary world. Often the consequence of traumatic experiences with violent conflicts, gross violations of human rights and related causes in which discrimination features significantly, displacement nearly always generates conditions of severe hardship and suffering for the affected populations. It breaks up families, cuts social and cultural ties, terminates dependable employment relationships, disrupts educational opportunities, denies access to such vital necessities as food, shelter and medicine, and exposes innocent persons to such acts of violence as attacks on camps, disappearances and rape. Whether they cluster in camps, escape into the countryside to hide from potential sources of persecution and violence or submerge into the community of the equally poor and dispossessed, the internally displaced are among the most vulnerable populations, desperately in need of protection and assistance.

2. In recent years, the international community has become increasingly aware of the plight of the internally displaced and is taking steps to address their needs. In 1992, at the request of the Commission on Human Rights, the Secretary-General of the United Nations

appointed a Representative on internally displaced persons to study the causes and consequences of internal displacement, the status of the internally displaced in international law, the extent of the coverage accorded them within existing international institutional arrangements and ways in which their protection and assistance could be improved, including through dialogue with Governments and other pertinent actors.

3. Accordingly, the Representative of the Secretary-General has focused the activities of his mandate on developing appropriate normative and institutional frameworks for the protection and assistance of the internally displaced, undertaking country missions in an ongoing dialogue with Governments and others concerned, and promoting a systemic international response to the plight of internally displaced populations.

4. Since the United Nations initially drew international attention to the crisis of internal displacement, many organizations, intergovernmental and non-governmental, have broadened their mandates or scope of activities to address more effectively the needs of the internally displaced. Governments have become more responsive by acknowledging their primary responsibility of protecting and assisting affected populations under their control, and when they cannot discharge that responsibility for lack of capacity, they are becoming less reticent to seek assistance from the international community. On the other hand, it is fair to say that the international community is more inclined than it is prepared, both normatively and institutionally, to respond effectively to the phenomenon of internal displacement.

5. One area in which the mandate of the Secretary-General's Representative has made significant progress has been in the development of a normative framework relating to all aspects of internal displacement. Working in close collaboration with a team of international legal experts, the Representative prepared a "Compilation and Analysis of Legal Norms" relevant to the needs and rights of the internally displaced and to the corresponding duties and obligations of States and the international community for their protection and assistance. The Compilation and Analysis was submitted to the Commission on Human Rights by the Representative of the Secretary-General in 1996 (E/CN.4/1996/52/Add.2).

6. It is important to note that the Office of the United Nations High Commissioner for Refugees (UNHCR) has developed a manual, based on the Compilation and Analysis, for the practical use of its staff, especially in field operations. There are also indications that other organizations and agencies will follow the example of UNHCR in making use of the document.

7. The Compilation and Analysis examines international human rights law, humanitarian law, and refugee law by analogy, and concludes

that while existing law provides substantial coverage for the internally displaced, there are significant areas in which it fails to provide an adequate basis for their protection and assistance. Besides, the provisions of existing law are dispersed in a wide variety of international instruments which make them too diffused and unfocused to be effective in providing adequate protection and assistance for the internally displaced.

8. In response to the Compilation and Analysis and to remedy the deficiencies in existing law, the Commission on Human Rights and the General Assembly requested the Representative of the Secretary-General to prepare an appropriate framework for the protection and assistance of the internally displaced (see resolutions 50/195 of 22 December 1995 and 1996/52 of 19 April 1996, respectively). Accordingly, and in continued collaboration with the team of experts that had prepared the Compilation and Analysis, the drafting of guiding principles was undertaken. The Commission on Human Rights, at its fifty-third session in April 1997, adopted resolution 1997/39 in which it took note of the preparations for guiding principles and requested the Representative to report thereon to the Commission at its fifty-fourth session. The Guiding Principles on Internal Displacement, completed in 1998, are annexed to the present document.

9. The purpose of the Guiding Principles is to address the specific needs of internally displaced persons worldwide by identifying rights and guarantees relevant to their protection. The Principles reflect and are consistent with international human rights law and international humanitarian law. They restate the relevant principles applicable to the internally displaced, which are now widely spread out in existing instruments, clarify any grey areas that might exist, and address the gaps identified in the Compilation and Analysis. They apply to the different phases of displacement, providing protection against arbitrary displacement, access to protection and assistance during displacement and guarantees during return or alternative settlement and reintegration.

10. The Principles are intended to provide guidance to the Representative in carrying out his mandate; to States when faced with the phenomenon of displacement; to all other authorities, groups and persons in their relations with internally displaced persons; and to intergovernmental and non-governmental organizations when addressing internal displacement.

11. The Guiding Principles will enable the Representative to monitor more effectively situations of displacement and to dialogue with Governments and all pertinent actors on behalf of the internally displaced; to invite States to apply the Principles in providing protection, assistance, reintegration and development support for them; and to mobilize response by international agencies, regional intergovernmental and

non-governmental organizations on the basis of the Principles. The Guiding Principles are therefore intended to be a persuasive statement that should provide not only practical guidance, but also an instrument for public policy education and consciousness-raising. By the same token, they have the potential to perform a preventive function in the urgently needed response to the global crisis of internal displacement.

12. The preparation of the Guiding Principles has benefited from the work, experience and support of many institutions and individuals. In addition to the legal team cited above, many experts from international humanitarian and development organizations, he Office of the United Nations High Commissioner for Human Rights, regional bodies, scholarly institutions, non-governmental organizations and the legal community have made valuable contributions. Appreciation in particular is owed to the Centre for Human Rights and Humanitarian Law of the Washington College of Law of American University, and also to the American Society of International Law, the Faculty of Law of the University of Bern, the Ludwig Boltzmann Institute of Human Rights of the University of Vienna and the International Human Rights Law Group.

13. Support for the development of the Principles was gratefully received from The Ford Foundation, the Jacob Blaustein Institute for the Advancement of Human Rights, the European Human Rights Foundation, the Hauser Foundation, and the John D. and Catherine T. MacArthur Foundation.

14. The development of the Principles also benefited from the Brookings Institution-Refugee Policy Group Project on Internal Displacement, which received generous support from many sources, including the Governments of the Netherlands, Norway and Sweden, and the McKnight Foundation.

15. The Government of Austria hosted an expert consultation in Vienna in January 1998, for the purpose of finalizing the Guiding Principles, which is most gratefully acknowledged.

Annex
Guiding Principles on Internal Displacement

Introduction: Scope and Purpose

1. These Guiding Principles address the specific needs of internally displaced persons worldwide. They identify rights and guarantees relevant to the protection of persons from forced displacement and to their protection and assistance during displacement as well as during return or resettlement and reintegration.

2. For the purposes of these Principles, internally displaced persons are persons or groups of persons who have been forced or obliged to flee or to leave their homes or places of habitual residence, in particular as a result of or in order to avoid the effects of armed conflict, situations of generalized violence, violations of human rights or natural or human-made disasters, and who have not crossed an internationally recognized State border.

3. These Principles reflect and are consistent with international human rights law and international humanitarian law. They provide guidance to:

(a) The Representative of the Secretary-General on internally displaced persons in carrying out his mandate;
(b) States when faced with the phenomenon of internal displacement;
(c) All other authorities, groups and persons in their relations with internally displaced persons; and
(d) Intergovernmental and non-governmental organizations when addressing internal displacement. 4. These Guiding Principles should be disseminated and applied as widely as possible.

Section I—General Principles

Principle 1

1. Internally displaced persons shall enjoy, in full equality, the same rights and freedoms under international and domestic law as do other persons in their country. They shall not be discriminated against in the enjoyment of any rights and freedoms on the ground that they are internally displaced.

2. These Principles are without prejudice to individual criminal responsibility under international law, in particular relating to genocide, crimes against humanity and war crimes.

Principle 2

1. These Principles shall be observed by all authorities, groups and persons irrespective of their legal status and applied without any adverse distinction. The observance of these Principles shall not affect the legal status of any authorities, groups or persons involved.

2. These Principles shall not be interpreted as restricting, modifying or impairing the provisions of any international human rights or international humanitarian law instrument or rights granted to persons under domestic law. In particular, these Principles are without prejudice to the right to seek and enjoy asylum in other countries.

Principle 3

1. National authorities have the primary duty and responsibility to provide protection and humanitarian assistance to internally displaced persons within their jurisdiction.
2. Internally displaced persons have the right to request and to receive protection and humanitarian assistance from these authorities. They shall not be persecuted or punished for making such a request.

Principle 4

1. These Principles shall be applied without discrimination of any kind, such as race, colour, sex, language, religion or belief, political or other opinion, national, ethnic or social origin, legal or social status, age, disability, property, birth, or on any other similar criteria.
2. Certain internally displaced persons, such as children, especially unaccompanied minors, expectant mothers, mothers with young children, female heads of household, persons with disabilities and elderly persons, shall be entitled to protection and assistance required by their condition and to treatment which takes into account their special needs.

Section II—Principles Relating to Protection From Displacement

Principle 5

All authorities and international actors shall respect and ensure respect for their obligations under international law, including human rights and humanitarian law, in all circumstances, so as to prevent and avoid conditions that might lead to displacement of persons.

Principle 6

1. Every human being shall have the right to be protected against being arbitrarily displaced from his or her home or place of habitual residence.
2. The prohibition of arbitrary displacement includes displacement:
   (a) When it is based on policies of apartheid, "ethnic cleansing" or similar practices aimed at/or resulting in altering the ethnic, religious or racial composition of the affected population;
   (b) In situations of armed conflict, unless the security of the civilians involved or imperative military reasons so demand;
   (c) In cases of large-scale development projects, which are not justified by compelling and overriding public interests;

(d) In cases of disasters, unless the safety and health of those affected requires their evacuation; and

(e) When it is used as a collective punishment.

3. Displacement shall last no longer than required by the circumstances.

Principle 7

1. Prior to any decision requiring the displacement of persons, the authorities concerned shall ensure that all feasible alternatives are explored in order to avoid displacement altogether. Where no alternatives exist, all measures shall be taken to minimize displacement and its adverse effects.

2. The authorities undertaking such displacement shall ensure, to the greatest practicable extent, that proper accommodation is provided to the displaced persons, that such displacements are effected in satisfactory conditions of safety, nutrition, health and hygiene, and that members of the same family are not separated.

3. If displacement occurs in situations other than during the emergency stages of armed conflicts and disasters, the following guarantees shall be complied with:

(a) A specific decision shall be taken by a State authority empowered by law to order such measures;

(b) Adequate measures shall be taken to guarantee to those to be displaced full information on the reasons and procedures for their displacement and, where applicable, on compensation and relocation;

(c) The free and informed consent of those to be displaced shall be sought;

(d) The authorities concerned shall endeavour to involve those affected, particularly women, in the planning and management of their relocation;

(e) Law enforcement measures, where required, shall be carried out by competent legal authorities; and

(f) The right to an effective remedy, including the review of such decisions by appropriate judicial authorities, shall be respected.

Principle 8

Displacement shall not be carried out in a manner that violates the rights to life, dignity, liberty and security of those affected.

Principle 9

States are under a particular obligation to protect against the displacement of indigenous peoples, minorities, peasants, pastoralists and other groups with a special dependency on and attachment to their lands.

Section III—Principles Relating to Protection During Displacement

Principle 10

1. Every human being has the inherent right to life which shall be protected by law. No one shall be arbitrarily deprived of his or her life. Internally displaced persons shall be protected in particular against:
    (a) Genocide;
    (b) Murder;
    (c) Summary or arbitrary executions; and
    (d) Enforced disappearances, including abduction or unacknowledged detention, threatening or resulting in death.

Threats and incitement to commit any of the foregoing acts shall be prohibited.

2. Attacks or other acts of violence against internally displaced persons who do not or no longer participate in hostilities are prohibited in all circumstances. Internally displaced persons shall be protected, in particular, against:
    (a) Direct or indiscriminate attacks or other acts of violence, including the creation of areas wherein attacks on civilians are permitted;
    (b) Starvation as a method of combat;
    (c) Their use to shield military objectives from attack or to shield, favour or impede military operations;
    (d) Attacks against their camps or settlements; and
    (e) The use of anti-personnel landmines.

Principle 11

1. Every human being has the right to dignity and physical, mental and moral integrity.
2. Internally displaced persons, whether or not their liberty has been restricted, shall be protected in particular against:
    (a) Rape, mutilation, torture, cruel, inhuman or degrading treatment or punishment, and other outrages upon personal dignity, such as acts of gender-specific violence, forced prostitution and any form of indecent assault;

(b) Slavery or any contemporary form of slavery, such as sale into marriage, sexual exploitation, or forced labour of children; and
(c) Acts of violence intended to spread terror among internally displaced persons.

Threats and incitement to commit any of the foregoing acts shall be prohibited.

Principle 12

1. Every human being has the right to liberty and security of person. No one shall be subjected to arbitrary arrest or detention.
2. To give effect to this right for internally displaced persons, they shall not be interned in or confined to a camp. If in exceptional circumstances such internment or confinement is absolutely necessary, it shall not last longer than required by the circumstances.
3. Internally displaced persons shall be protected from discriminatory arrest and detention as a result of their displacement.
4. In no case shall internally displaced persons be taken hostage.

Principle 13

1. In no circumstances shall displaced children be recruited nor be required or permitted to take part in hostilities.
2. Internally displaced persons shall be protected against discriminatory practices of recruitment into any armed forces or groups as a result of their displacement. In particular any cruel, inhuman or degrading practices that compel compliance or punish non-compliance with recruitment are prohibited in all circumstances.

Principle 14

1. Every internally displaced person has the right to liberty of movement and freedom to choose his or her residence.
2. In particular, internally displaced persons have the right to move freely in and out of camps or other settlements.

Principle 15

Internally displaced persons have:
(a) The right to seek safety in another part of the country;
(b) The right to leave their country;
(c) The right to seek asylum in another country; and

(d) The right to be protected against forcible return to or resettlement in any place where their life, safety, liberty and/or health would be at risk.

Principle 16

1. All internally displaced persons have the right to know the fate and whereabouts of missing relatives.
2. The authorities concerned shall endeavour to establish the fate and whereabouts of internally displaced persons reported missing, and cooperate with relevant international organizations engaged in this task. They shall inform the next of kin on the progress of the investigation and notify them of any result.
3. The authorities concerned shall endeavour to collect and identify the mortal remains of those deceased, prevent their despoliation or mutilation, and facilitate the return of those remains to the next of kin or dispose of them respectfully.
4. Grave sites of internally displaced persons should be protected and respected in all circumstances. Internally displaced persons should have the right of access to the grave sites of their deceased relatives.

Principle 17

1. Every human being has the right to respect of his or her family life.
2. To give effect to this right for internally displaced persons, family members who wish to remain together shall be allowed to do so.
3. Families which are separated by displacement should be reunited as quickly as possible. All appropriate steps shall be taken to expedite the reunion of such families, particularly when children are involved. The responsible authorities shall facilitate inquiries made by family members and encourage and cooperate with the work of humanitarian organizations engaged in the task of family reunification.
4. Members of internally displaced families whose personal liberty has been restricted by internment or confinement in camps shall have the right to remain together.

Principle 18

1. All internally displaced persons have the right to an adequate standard of living.
2. At the minimum, regardless of the circumstances, and without discrimination, competent authorities shall provide internally displaced persons with and ensure safe access to:

(a) Essential food and potable water;
(b) Basic shelter and housing;
(c) Appropriate clothing; and
(d) Essential medical services and sanitation.

3. Special efforts should be made to ensure the full participation of women in the planning and distribution of these basic supplies.

Principle 19

1. All wounded and sick internally displaced persons as well as those with disabilities shall receive to the fullest extent practicable and with the least possible delay, the medical care and attention they require, without distinction on any grounds other than medical ones. When necessary, internally displaced persons shall have access to psychological and social services.

2. Special attention should be paid to the health needs of women, including access to female health care providers and services, such as reproductive health care, as well as appropriate counselling for victims of sexual and other abuses.

3. Special attention should also be given to the prevention of contagious and infectious diseases, including AIDS, among internally displaced persons.

Principle 20

1. Every human being has the right to recognition everywhere as a person before the law.

2. To give effect to this right for internally displaced persons, the authorities concerned shall issue to them all documents necessary for the enjoyment and exercise of their legal rights, such as passports, personal identification documents, birth certificates and marriage certificates. In particular, the authorities shall facilitate the issuance of new documents or the replacement of documents lost in the course of displacement, without imposing unreasonable conditions, such as requiring the return to one's area of habitual residence in order to obtain these or other required documents.

3. Women and men shall have equal rights to obtain such necessary documents and shall have the right to have such documentation issued in their own names.

Principle 21

1. No one shall be arbitrarily deprived of property and possessions.
2. The property and possessions of internally displaced

persons shall in all circumstances be protected, in particular, against the following acts:
  (a) Pillage;
  (b) Direct or indiscriminate attacks or other acts of violence;
  (c) Being used to shield military operations or objectives;
  (d) Being made the object of reprisal; and
  (e) Being destroyed or appropriated as a form of collective punishment.

3. Property and possessions left behind by internally displaced persons should be protected against destruction and arbitrary and illegal appropriation, occupation or use.

Principle 22

1. Internally displaced persons, whether or not they are living in camps, shall not be discriminated against as a result of their displacement in the enjoyment of the following rights:
  (a) The rights to freedom of thought, conscience, religion or belief, opinion and expression;
  (b) The right to seek freely opportunities for employment and to participate in economic activities;
  (c) The right to associate freely and participate equally in community affairs;
  (d) The right to vote and to participate in governmental and public affairs, including the right to have access to the means necessary to exercise this right; and
  (e) The right to communicate in a language they understand.

Principle 23

1. Every human being has the right to education.
2. To give effect to this right for internally displaced persons, the authorities concerned shall ensure that such persons, in particular displaced children, receive education which shall be free and compulsory at the primary level. Education should respect their cultural identity, language and religion.
3. Special efforts should be made to ensure the full and equal participation of women and girls in educational programmes.
4. Education and training facilities shall be made available to internally displaced persons, in particular adolescents and women, whether or not living in camps, as soon as conditions permit.

Section IV—Principles Relating to Humanitarian Assistance

Principle 24

1. All humanitarian assistance shall be carried out in accordance with the principles of humanity and impartiality and without discrimination.
2. Humanitarian assistance to internally displaced persons shall not be diverted, in particular for political or military reasons.

Principle 25

1. The primary duty and responsibility for providing humanitarian assistance to internally displaced persons lies with national authorities.
2. International humanitarian organizations and other appropriate actors have the right to offer their services in support of the internally displaced. Such an offer shall not be regarded as an unfriendly act or an interference in a State's internal affairs and shall be considered in good faith. Consent thereto shall not be arbitrarily withheld, particularly when authorities concerned are unable or unwilling to provide the required humanitarian assistance.
3. All authorities concerned shall grant and facilitate the free passage of humanitarian assistance and grant persons engaged in the provision of such assistance rapid and unimpeded access to the internally displaced.

Principle 26

Persons engaged in humanitarian assistance, their transport and supplies shall be respected and protected. They shall not be the object of attack or other acts of violence.

Principle 27

1. International humanitarian organizations and other appropriate actors when providing assistance should give due regard to the protection needs and human rights of internally displaced persons and take appropriate measures in this regard. In so doing, these organizations and actors should respect relevant international standards and codes of conduct.
2. The preceding paragraph is without prejudice to the protection responsibilities of international organizations mandated for this purpose, whose services may be offered or requested by States.

Section V—Principles Relating to Return, Resettlement and Reintegration

Principle 28

1. Competent authorities have the primary duty and responsibility to establish conditions, as well as provide the means, which allow internally displaced persons to return voluntarily, in safety and with dignity, to their homes or places of habitual residence, or to resettle voluntarily in another part of the country. Such authorities shall endeavour to facilitate the reintegration of returned or resettled internally displaced persons.

2. Special efforts should be made to ensure the full participation of internally displaced persons in the planning and management of their return or resettlement and reintegration.

Principle 29

1. Internally displaced persons who have returned to their homes or places of habitual residence or who have resettled in another part of the country shall not be discriminated against as a result of their having been displaced. They shall have the right to participate fully and equally in public affairs at all levels and have equal access to public services.

2. Competent authorities have the duty and responsibility to assist returned and/or resettled internally displaced persons to recover, to the extent possible, their property and possessions which they left behind or were dispossessed of upon their displacement. When recovery of such property and possessions is not possible, competent authorities shall provide or assist these persons in obtaining appropriate compensation or another form of just reparation.

Principle 30

All authorities concerned shall grant and facilitate for international humanitarian organizations and other appropriate actors, in the exercise of their respective mandates, rapid and unimpeded access to internally displaced persons to assist in their return or resettlement and reintegration.

Appendix 3D
Principles on the Detention of Asylum-Seekers and Immigrants of the Working Group on Arbitrary Detention

The Working Group on Arbitrary Detention has adopted the following set of guidelines to determine whether detention of asylum seekers and immigrants is arbitrary.

Deliberation No. 5
Situation Regarding Immigrants and Asylum-Seekers

By resolution 1997/50, the Working Group was requested by the Commission to devote all necessary attention to reports concerning the situation of immigrants and asylum-seekers who are allegedly being held in prolonged administrative custody without the possibility of administrative or judicial remedy.

For the purposes of the Body of Principles for the Protection of All Persons under Any Form of Detention or Imprisonment:

- The term "a judicial or other authority" means a judicial or other authority which is duly empowered by law and has a status and length of mandate affording sufficient guarantees of competence, impartiality and independence.
- House arrest under the conditions set forth in deliberation No. 1 of the Working Group (E/CN.4/1993/24, para. 20) and confinement on board a ship, aircraft, road vehicle or train are assimilated with custody of immigrants and asylum-seekers.
- The places of deprivation of liberty concerned by the present principles may be places of custody situated in border areas, on police premises, premises under the authority of a prison administration, ad hoc centres (*centres de rétention*), so called international or transit zones in ports or international airports, gathering centres or certain hospital premises (see E/CN.4/1998/44, paras. 28–41).

In order to determine the arbitrary character of the custody, the Working Group considers whether or not the alien is enabled to enjoy all or some of the following guarantees:

I. Guarantees Concerning Persons Held in Custody

Principle 1: Any asylum-seeker or immigrant, when held for questioning at the border, or inside national territory in the case of illegal entry, must be informed at least orally, and in a language which he or she understands, of the nature of and grounds for the decision refusing entry at the border, or permission for temporary residence in the territory, that is being contemplated with respect to the person concerned.

Principle 2: Any asylum-seeker or immigrant must have the possibility, while in custody, of communicating with the outside world, including by telephone, Fax or electronic mail, and of contacting a lawyer, a consular representative and relatives.

Principle 3: Any asylum-seeker or immigrant placed in custody must be brought promptly before a judicial or other authority.

Principle 4: Any asylum-seeker or immigrant, when placed in custody, must enter his or her signature in a register which is numbered and bound, or affords equivalent guarantees, indicating the person's identity, the grounds for the custody and the competent authority which decided on the measure, as well as the time and date of admission into and release from custody.

Principle 5: Any asylum-seeker or immigrant, upon admission to a centre for custody, must be informed of the internal regulations and, where appropriate, of the applicable disciplinary rules and any possibility of his or her being held incommunicado, as well as of the guarantees accompanying such a measure.

II. Guarantees Concerning Detention

Principle 6: The decision must be taken by a duly empowered authority with a sufficient level of responsibility and must be founded on criteria of legality established by the law.

Principle 7: A maximum period should be set by law and the custody may in no case be unlimited or of excessive length.

Principle 8: Notification of the custodial measure must be given in writing, in a language understood by the asylum-seeker or immigrant, stating the grounds for the measure; it shall set out the conditions under which the asylum-seeker or immigrant must be able to apply for a remedy to a judicial authority, which shall decide promptly on the lawfulness of the measure and, where appropriate, order the release of the person concerned.

Principle 9: Custody must be effected in a public establishment specifically intended for this purpose; when, for practical reasons, this is not the case, the asylum-seeker or immigrant must be placed in premises separate from those for persons imprisoned under criminal law.

Principle 10: The Office of the United Nations High Commissioner for Refugees (UNHCR), the International Committee of the Red Cross (ICRC) and, where appropriate, duly authorized non-governmental organizations must be allowed access to the places of custody.

Appendix 4A
Requirements for Complaints to the African Commission on Human and Peoples' Rights

1. Complaints should be submitted to the Secretary General, the Chairman of the Commission and the State party concerned
2. Complaints should be in writing and contain a detailed and comprehensive statement on the actions denounced as well as the provisions of the Charter alleged to have been violated.
3. The notification of the communication to the State party to the Charter, the Secretary General and the Chairman of the Commission shall be done through the most practicable and reliable means.

The Commission, through the Secretary, may request the author of a communication to furnish clarifications on the applicability of the Charter to his/her communication, and to specify in particular:

(a) His name, address, age and profession by justifying his very identity, if ever he/she is requesting the Commission to be kept anonymous;
(b) Name of the State party referred to in the communication;
(c) Purpose of the communication;
(d) Provision(s) of the Charter allegedly violated;
(e) The facts of the claim;
(f) Measures taken by the author to exhaust local remedies, or explanation why local remedies will be futile;
(g) The extent to which the same issue has been settled by another international investigation or settlement body.

When asking for clarification or information, the Commission shall fix an appropriate time limit for the author to submit the communication so as to avoid undue delay in the procedure provided for by the Charter.

Appendix 4B
Useful Addresses

The Organization of African Unity

Secretariat:
P.O. Box 3243
Addis Ababa, Ethiopia
Tel: 251 1 517700
Fax: 251 1 512622
<http://www.oau-oua.org>

African Commission on Human and Peoples' Rights

Secretariat:
Karaiba Avenue
Kombo St Mary Division
P.O. Box 673
Banjul, The Gambia
Tel: 220 392962
Fax: 220 390764
Email: *achpr@achpr.gm*

Division for Refugees, Displaced Persons and Humanitarian Assistance

P.O. Box 3243
Addis Ababa, Ethiopia
Tel: 251 513822
Fax: 251 517844

OAU Center for Conflict Prevention, Management and Resolution

P.O.Box 3243
Addis Ababa, Ethiopia
Tel: 251 513822
Fax: 251 517844
Email: *oau-cmc@telecom.net.et*

The Economic Community of West African States [ECOWAS]

60 Yakubu Gowon Crescent
Asokoro District
Abuja, Nigeria
Tel: 234 9 314 76 47-9; 314 30 05-6
Fax: 234 9 314 76 46
Email: *cedeao@ecowasmail.net* / *info@ecowasmail.net*

L'Union Économique et Monétaire de L'Afrique de l'Ouest [UEMOA]

Secretariat
B.P. 543
Ouagadougou 01
Burkina Faso
Tel: 226 318873 / 76
Fax: 226 318872
<http://www.izf.net>

The Inter-Governmental Authority on Development [IGAD]

IGAD Secretariat
P.O. Box 2653
Djibouti, Republic of Djibouti
Tel: 253 354 050
Fax: 253 356 994 / 356 284 / 353 195
Email: *Igad@intnet.dj* / *igad@igad.org*

The Commission for East African Cooperation [EAC]

Secretariat: AICC Building, Kilimanjaro Wing, 5th Floor
P.O. Box 1096
Arusha, Tanzania
Tel: 255 57 504253/8
Fax: 255 57 504255
Email: *eac@cybernet.co.tz*
<http://www.eachq.org>

Southern African Development Community [SADC]

The Executive Secretary
Private Bag 0095
Gabornone, Botswana
Tel: 267 351 863
Fax: 267 372 848

NGO Liaison Desk
C/o Botswana Council of NGOs
Extension 4, South Ring Road
Maherero Lane, Plot 508
Gaborone, Botswana
Tel/Fax: 267 311 319

Appendix 5A
Requirements for Complaints to the European Court of Human Rights[1]

If you consider that your complaint concerns one of the rights guaranteed by the Convention or its Protocols, and that the conditions are satisfied,[2] you should first send a letter containing the information mentioned below to the Registrar of the Court at the following address:

---

1 <http://www.echr.coe.int/Notices%20for%20Applicants/Notice%20eng.html>

2 I. *What cases can the court deal with?*
1. The European Court of Human Rights is an international institution which, in certain circumstances, can receive complaints from persons claiming that their rights under the European Convention on Human Rights have been violated. This Convention is a treaty by which a number of European States have agreed to secure certain fundamental rights. The rights guaranteed are set out in the Convention itself, and in four supplementary Protocols, Nos. 1, 4, 6 and 7 which some States have accepted. You should read these texts and the accompanying reservations.
2. If you consider that one of the States on the enclosed sheet has to *your personal detriment* violated one of *these* fundamental rights, you may complain to the Court. However, the Court can *only* deal with complaints relating to the rights listed in the Convention and Protocols. It is not a court of appeal from national courts and cannot annul or modify their decisions. Nor can it intervene directly on your behalf with the authority you complain about.
3. The Court can only receive complaints against the States listed on the enclosed sheet and cannot deal with complaints about events before certain dates. The date varies according to the State concerned and according to whether the complaint concerns a right cited in the Convention itself or in one of the Protocols.
4. You can only complain to the Court about matters which are the responsibility of a *public authority* (legislature, administration, courts of law, etc.) of one of these States. The Court cannot deal with complaints against private individuals or private organisations.
5. Before applying to the Court you must have tried *all remedies in the State concerned* which could redress your complaint. This includes bringing your complaint before the highest court which can deal with it. (However if you complain of a court decision such as a conviction or sentence, it is not necessary to try to re-open your case after you have been through the normal appeal procedures in the courts.) You should make correct use of the available remedies and comply with the time limits and

The Registrar
European Court of Human Rights
Council of Europe
F-67075 STRASBOURG CEDEX , FRANCE
In your letter you should:

(a) give a *brief summary* of your complaints;
(b) indicate which of your Convention rights you think have been violated;
(c) state what remedies you have used;
(d) list the official decisions in your case, giving the date of each decision, the court or authority which took it, and brief details of the decision itself.

Attach to your letter *a copy* of these decisions. (No documents will be returned to you, thus it is in your interest only to submit copies, *not* the originals.)

If possible, instruct a lawyer to present your case for you. At a later stage in the proceedings, if you have insufficient means to pay a lawyer's fees, you may be eligible for free legal aid. But legal aid cannot be granted at the time when you lodge your application.

---

procedural rules. If, for instance, your appeal is rejected because it is too late or because you have not used the proper procedure, the Court probably could not examine your case.

6. After decision of the highest competent national court or authority has been given, you have a *six month* period within which you may apply to the Court. If your complaint relates to a court conviction or sentence, this period runs from the final court decision in the ordinary appeal process and not from the date of any later refusal to re-open your case. Unless you have submitted details of your complaint, at least in summary form, within the six month period, the Court will not be able to examine your case.

Appendix 6A
Sample IACHR Complaint Form[1]

Instructions: The following complaint form has been prepared to facilitate the work of human rights organizations and others in assisting victims and family members of victims in the presentation of complaints to the Inter-American Commission on Human Rights.

Please read the instructions and this form carefully before proceeding. It is very important that as much factual detail be supplied as possible. Of course, in cases of emergency, where the alleged victim's life or health might be in danger, do not hesitate to file the complaint even if certain non-essential information may be lacking. Complaints may be filed either by letter, phone or by telex. Incomplete complaints may be supplemented at a later time. In the event that particular information is simply not available or does not exist, write "not applicable" or "none" as appropriate.

Complaints may only be brought against member states of the Organization of American States and should be drafted in a simple and straightforward manner, free of political rhetoric.

Complaints should be sent to:

Emb. Jorge E. Taiana
Executive Secretary
Inter-American Commission on Human Rights
1889 F Street, N.W.
Washington, D.C. 20006
Telephone number: (202) 458-6002
Fax number: (202) 458-3992
E-mail: *cidhoea@oas.org*

Article 32 of the Commission's Rules and Procedure states: Petitions addressed to the Commission shall include:

a. the name, nationality, profession or occupation, postal address, or domicile and signature of the person or persons making the denunciation; or in cases where the petitioner

---

1   This Complaint form may be found at and submitted through the Inter-American Commission on Human Rights website, <http://www.cidh.oas.org/email.htm>.

631

is a nongovernmental entity, its legal domicile or postal address, and the name and signature of its legal representative or representatives;

b. an account of the act or situation that is denounced, specifying the place and date of the alleged violations and, if possible, the name of the victims of such violations as well as that of any official that might have been appraised of the act or situation that was denounced;

c. an indication of the state in question which the petitioner considers responsible, by commission or omission, for the violation of a human right recognized in American Convention on Human Rights in the case of States Parties thereto, even if no specific reference is made to the article alleged to have been violated;

d. information on whether the remedies under domestic law have been exhausted or whether it has been impossible to do so.

Victim:
Name
Age
Nationality
Occupation
Marital status
I.D. No.
Address
Telephone No.
Number of children
Government accused of violation:

Alleged Human Rights violation. Explain what happened in as great a factual detail as possible, specifying place and date of the violation:

The article(s) of the Declaration or Convention which have been violated: _____

Names and titles of persons (authorities) who committed the violation: _____

Witnesses to the violation: _____

Addresses and telephone numbers of witnesses: _____

Documents/proofs (for example, letters, legal documents, photos, autopsies, tape recordings, etc.): _____

Domestic legal remedies pursued (e.g. copies of writs of Habeas Corpus or Amparo): _____

Domestic legal remedies yet to be pursued: _____

I do want my name used by the Commission: _____

yes _____   no _____

Complainant:
   Name
   Address
   Telephone No.
   Telex No.
   Fax No.
   I.D. No.
   Legal Representative if any:
   Is your legal representative a lawyer? yes no
   Address
   Telephone No.
   Telex No.
   Fax No.
   Attach power of attorney designating legal representative:

Signature: _____   Date: _____

Appendix 6B
States Parties to the Organization of American States Charter

Antigua and Barbuda
Argentina
Bahamas
Barbados
Belize
Bolivia
Brazil
Canada
Chile
Colombia
Costa Rica
Cuba
Dominica
Dominican Republic
Ecuador
El Salvador
Grenada
Guatemala
Guyana
Haiti
Honduras
Jamaica
Mexico
Nicaragua
Panama
Paraguay
Peru
Saint Lucia
Saint Vincent
St. Kitts and Nevis
Suriname
Trinidad and Tobago
United States
Uruguay
Venezuela

This information can be obtained through the OAS website at: <http://www.oas.org>.

Appendix 7A
Contact Information (International Criminal Tribunals)

International Criminal Tribunal for the former Yugoslavia (ICTY)

Visiting address:	Churchillplein 1 2517 JW The Hague The Netherlands
Postal address:	P.O. Box 13888 2501 EW The Hague The Netherlands
Telephone numbers:	+31 70 512 5000 (general) +31 70 512 5413 (Office of the Prosecutor, Investigations Sec.) +31 70 512 8877 (Witness hotline in Bosnian/Croatian/Serbian) +31 70 512 5001 (Victims and Witnesses Section) +31 70 512 5233 or 5285 (Public Information Services)
Website:	<http://www.un.org/icty/>

International Criminal Tribunal for Rwanda (ICTR)

Visiting address:	Arusha International Conference Centre Arusha Tanzania
Postal address:	P.O. Box 6016 Arusha Tanzania
Telephone numbers:	+255 57 2504369/72 or +1 212 963 2850 (general)
Website:	<ttp://www.ictr.org/>

Office of the Prosecutor:
>Amahoro Hotel
P.O. Box 749
Kigali
Rwanda

Telephone numbers: +250 84266 or +1 212 963 9906

Bibliography of Cited International Instruments

(in alphabetical order, each section)

Global Instruments

Basic Principles for the Treatment of Prisoners, adopted Dec. 14, 1990, G.A. Res. 45/111 (Annex), U.N. GAOR, 45th Sess., Supp. No. 49, at 199, U.N. Doc. AIRES/45/49 (1991), *reprinted in* 30 I.L.M. 1375 (1991) *and* 3 INTERNATIONAL LAW AND WORLD ORDER: BASIC DOCUMENTS III.M.7 (B. Weston & J. Carlson eds., 5 vole., 1994–) [hereinafter "3 WESTON & CARLSON"]

Basic Principles on the Independence of the Judiciary, adopted by the Seventh United Nations Congress on the Prevention of Crime and the Treatment of Offenders, Aug. 26–Sept. 6, 1985, and endorsed on Nov. 29, 1985 by G.A. Res. 40/32 and on Dec. 13, 1985 by G.A. Res. 40/146, U.N. Doc. A/CONF/121/22/Rev. 1 (1986), *reprinted in* 3 WESTON & CARLSON III.M.6

Basic Principles on the Role of Lawyers, adopted by the Eighth United Nations Congress on the Prevention of Crime and the Treatment of Offenders, Aug. 27–Sept. 7, 1990, U.N. Doc. A/CONF.144/28/Rev.l, at 189 (1990)

Body of Principles for the Protection of All Persons under Any Form of Detention or Imprisonment, adopted Dec. 9, 1988, G.A. Res. 43/173, U.N. GAOR, 43rd Sess., Supp. No. 49, at 298, U.N. Doc. A/RES/43/173 (1988)

Charter of the United Nations, adopted June 26, 1945, *reprinted in* INTERNATIONAL LAW AND WORLD ORDER: BASIC DOCUMENTS I.A.1 (B. Weston & J. Carlson eds., 5 vole., 1994–) [hereinafter "1 WESTON & CARLSON"] (entered into force Oct. 24, 1945)

Code of Conduct for Law Enforcement Officials, adopted Dec. 17, 1979, G.A. Res. 34/169 (Annex), U.N. GAOR, 34th Sess., Supp. No. 46, at 186, U.N. Doc. A/RES134146 (1979), *reprinted in* 3 WESTON & CARLSON III.M.3

Convention Against Torture and Other Cruel, Inhuman or Degrading Treatment or Punishment, opened for signature Dec.10, 1984, G.A. Res. 39/46, U.N. GAOR, 39th Sess., Supp. No. 15, at 197, U.N. Doc. A134146 (Annex), U.N. Doc. A/RES/39/51 (1985), *reprinted in* 23 I.L.M. 1027 (1984) with substantive changes noted in 24 I.L.M. 535 (1985) and 3 WESTON & CARLSON III.K.2 (entered into force June 26, 1987)

Convention on the Elimination of All Forms of Discrimination Against Women, opened for signature Dec. 18, 1979, 1249 U.N.T.S. 13, *reprinted in* 3 WESTON & CARLSON III.C.13 (entered into force Sept. 3, 1981)

Convention on the Rights of the Child, opened for signature Nov. 20, 1989, 1577 U.N.T.S. 44, *reprinted in* 3 WESTON & CARLSON III.D.3 (entered into force Sept. 20, 1990)

Convention Relating to the Status of Refugees, adopted July 28, 1951, 189 U.N.T.S. 150, *reprinted in* 3 WESTON & CARLSON III.G.4 (entered into force Apr. 22, 1954)

Convention Relating to the Status of Stateless Persons, adopted Sept. 28, 1954, 360 U.N.T.S. 117, *reprinted in* 3 WESTON & CARLSON III.G.7 (entered into force June 6, 1960)

Declaration on the Elimination of All Forms of Intolerance and of Discrimination Based on Religion or Belief, adopted Nov. 25, 1981, G.A. Res. 36/55, U.N. GAOR, 36th Sess., Supp. No. 51, at 171, U.N. Doc. AIRES1361684 (1981), *reprinted in* 21 I.L.M. 205 (1982) *and* 3 WESTON & CARLSON III.I.3

Declaration on the Elimination of Violence Against Women, adopted Dec. 20, 1993, G.A. Res. 48/104, U.N. GAOR, 48th Sess., Supp. No. 49, at 261, U.N. Doc. A/RES/48/104 (1994), *reprinted in* 33 I.L.M. 1049 (1994) *and* 3 WESTON & CARLSON III.C. 14

Declaration on the Protection of All Persons from Being Subjected to Torture and Other Cruel, Inhuman or Degrading Treatment or Punishment, adopted Dec. 9, 1975, G.A. Res. 3452, U.N. GAOR, 30th Sess., Supp. No. 34, at 91, U.N. Doc. A/RES/10034 (1976)

Declaration on the Protection of All Persons from Enforced Disappearance, adopted Dec. 18, 1992, G.A. Res. 47/133, U.N. GAOR, 47th Sess., Supp. No. 49, at 207, U.N. Doc. A/RES/47/133 (1993), *reprinted in* 3 WESTON & CARLSON III.K.5

Declaration on the Right and Responsibility of Individuals, Groups and Organs of Society to Promote and Protect Universally Recognized Human Rights and Fundamental Freedoms, adopted Dec. 9, 1998, G.A. Res. 53/144, U.N. GAOR, 53rd Sess., Supp. No. 49, Vol. 1, at 261, U.N. Doc. A/RES/53/144 (1998)

Declaration on the Rights of Persons Belonging to National or Ethnic, Religious and Linguistic Minorities, adopted Dec. 18, 1992, G.A. Res. 47/135, U.N. GAOR, 47th Sess., Supp. No. 49, at 210, U.N. Doc. A/RES/47/135 (1993), *reprinted in* 3 WESTON & CARLSON III.I.5

I.L.O. Convention (No. 169) Concerning Indigenous and Tribal Peoples in Independent Countries, adopted June 27, 1989, International Labour Conference Draft Report of the Committee on Convention

No. 107, Appendix I, C.C. 107/D.303 (June 1989), *reprinted in* 28 I.L.M. 1382 (1989) *and* 3 WESTON & CARLSON III.F.2 (entered into force Sept. 5, 1991)

Geneva Convention Relative to the Protection of Civilian Persons in Time of War, adopted Aug. 12, 1949, 75 U.N.T.S. 287, 2 INTERNATIONAL LAW AND WORLD ORDER: BASIC DOCUMENTS II.B.14 (B. Weston & J. Carlson eds., 5 vole., 1994–) [hereinafter "2 WESTON & CARLSON"] (entered into force Oct. 21, 1950)

Guidelines on the Role of Prosecutors, Adopted by the Eighth United Nations Congress on the Prevention of Crime and the Treatment of Offenders, Aug. 27–Sept. 7, 1990, U.N. Doc. A/CONF.144/28/Rev.1, at 189 (1990)

International Convention on the Elimination of All Forms of Racial Discrimination, opened for signature Dec. 21, 1965, 660 U.N.T.S. 195, *reprinted in* 3 WESTON & CARLSON III.I.1 (entered into force Jan. 4, 1969)

International Convention on the Protection of the Rights of All Migrant Workers and Their Families, adopted Dec. 18, 1990, G.A. Res. 45/158 (Annex), U.N. GAOR, 45th Sess., Supp. No. 49, at 262, U.N. Doc. A/RES/45/49 (1991), *reprinted in* 30 I.L.M. 1521 (1991) *and* 3 WESTON & CARLSON III.0.6

International Covenant on Civil and Political Rights, opened for signature Dec. 16, 1966, 999 U.N.T.S. 171, *reprinted in* 3 WESTON & CARLSON III.A.3 (entered into force Mar. 23, 1976)

International Covenant on Economic, Social and Cultural Rights, opened for signature Dec. 16, 1966, 999 U.N.T.S. 3, *reprinted in* 3 WESTON & CARLSON III.A.2 (entered into force Jan. 3, 1976)

Optional Protocol to the Convention on the Elimination of All Forms of Discrimination Against Women, opened for signature Oct. 6, 1999, G.A. Res. 54/4, U.N. GAOR, 54th Sess., Supp. No. 49, Vol. I, at 4, U.N. Doc. A/RES/54/4 (1999), *reprinted in* 38 I.L.M. 763 (1999) *and* 3 WESTON & CARLSON III.C.16 (entered into force Dec. 22, 2000)

Optional Protocol to the Convention on the Rights of the Child on the Involvement of Children in Armed Conflicts, opened for signature May 25, 2000, G.A. Res. A/54/263 (Annex b, U.N. GAOR, 54th Sess., Supp. No. 49, Vol. III, at 6, U.N. Doc. A/RES/54/263 (2000), *reprinted in* 39 I.L.M. 1285 (2000) *and* 3 WESTON & CARLSON III.D.5

Optional Protocol to the Convention on the Rights of the Child on the Sale of Children, Child Prostitution and Child Pornography, opened for signature May 25, 2000, G.A. Res. A/54/263 (Annex II), U.N. GAOR, 54th Sess., Supp. No. 49, Vol. III, at 6, U.N. Doc.

A/RES/54/4 (2000), *reprinted in* 39 I.L.M. 1285 (2000) *and* 3 WESTON & CARLSON III.D.6

Optional Protocol to the International Covenant on Civil and Political Rights, adopted Dec. 16, 1966, 999 U.N.T.S. 171, *reprinted in* 3 WESTON & CARLSON III.A.4 (entered into force Mar. 23, 1976)

Protocol relating to the Status of Refugees, adopted Jan. 31, 1967, 606 U.N.T.S. 267, *reprinted in* 3 WESTON & CARLSON III.G.8 (entered into force Oct. 4, 1967)

Protocol Additional (No. II) to the Geneva Conventions of August 12, 1949, and relating to the Protection of Victims of Non-International Armed Conflicts, opened for signature Dec. 12, 1977, 1125 U.N.T.S. 609, *reprinted in* 2 WESTON & CARLSON II.B.21 (entered into force Dec. 7, 1978)

Rome Statute of the International Criminal Court, adopted July 17, 1998, U.N. Doc. A/CONF.183/9 (1998), *reprinted in* 37 I.L.M. 999 (1998), *and* 1 WESTON & CARLSON I. M.13

Standard Minimum Rules for the Treatment of Prisoners, adopted Aug. 30, 1955, by the First United Nations Congress on the Prevention of Crime and the Treatment of Offenders, U.N. Doc. A/CONF/6/1, Annex I, A (1956); adopted July 31, 1957 by the Economic and Social Council, E.S.C. Res. 663C (1957), amended E.S.C. Res. 2076 (1977), *reprinted in* 3 WESTON & CARLSON III.M.1

United Nations Rules for the Protection of Juveniles Deprived of Their Liberty, adopted Dec. 14, 1990, G.A. Res. 45/113, U.N. GAOR, 45th Sess., Supp. No. 49A, at 205, U.N. Doc. A/RES/45/113 (1990)

United Nations Standard Minimum Rules for the Administration of Juvenile Justice (The Beijing Rules), adopted Nov. 29, 1985, G.A. Res. 40/33, U.N. GAOR, 40th Sess., Supp. No. 53, at 207, U.N. Doc. A/RES/40/33 (1985)

Universal Declaration of Human Rights, adopted Dec. 10, 1948, G.A. Res. 217 A (III), U.N. GAOR 3rd Sess., Pt. I, Resolutions, at 71, U.N. Doc. A/RES/810 (1948), *reprinted in* 3 WESTON & CARLSON III.A.1

Regional Instruments

Additional Protocol to the American Convention on Human Rights in the Area of Economic, Social and Cultural Rights ("Protocol of San Salvador"), opened for signature Nov. 17, 1988, O.A.S. T.S. No. 69, *reprinted in* BASIC DOCUMENTS PERTAINING TO HUMAN RIGHTS IN THE INTERAMERICAN SYSTEM, OAS/Ser.L/V/I.4 Rev.7 (Jan. 2000) *and* 3 INTERNATIONAL LAW AND WORLD ORDER: BASIC DOCUMENTS III.B.25 (B. Weston & J. Carlson eds., 5 vole., 1994–)

[hereinafter "3 WESTON & CARLSON"] (entered into force Nov. 16, 1999)

Additional Protocol to the European Social Charter Providing for a System of Collective Complaints, adopted Nov. 9, 1995, Eur. T.S. No. 158, *reprinted in* 34 I.L.M. 1453 (1995) *and* 3 WESTON & CARLSON III.B.16c (entered into force Jan. 7, 1998)

African Charter on Human and Peoples' Rights, adopted June 27, 1981, OAU Doc. CAB/LEG/67/3 Rev. 5, *reprinted in* 21 I.L.M. 58 (1982) *and* 3 WESTON & CARLSON III.B.1 (entered into force Oct. 21, 1986)

African Charter on the Rights and Welfare of the Child, adopted July 1990, OAU Doc. CAB/LEG/153/Rev.2 (1990) (entered into force Nov. 29, 1999)

Agreement Establishing the Inter-Governmental Authority on Development (IGAD), adopted Mar. 21, 1996 by the Assembly of Heads of State and Government in Nairobi, *available at* <http://www.alliancesforafrica.org/default.asp?format=39>

American Convention on Human Rights, Nov. 22, 1969, O.A.S. T.S. No. 36, *reprinted in* BASIC DOCUMENTS PERTAINING TO HUMAN RIGHTS IN THE INTERAMERICAN SYSTEM, OAS/Ser.L/V/I.4 Rev.7 (January 2000) *and* 3 WESTON & CARLSON III.B.24 (entered into force July 18, 1978)

American Declaration of the Rights and Duties of Man, OAS res. XXX, adopted by the Ninth International Conference of American States, Bogota (1948), *reprinted in* BASIC DOCUMENTS PERTAINING TO HUMAN RIGHTS IN THE INTERAMERICAN SYSTEM, OAS/Ser.L/V/I.4 Rev. 7 (January 2000)) *and* 3 WESTON & CARLSON III.B.23

Cartagena Declaration on Refugees, adopted by the Colloquium on the International Protection of Refugees in Central America, Mexico and Panama, held in Cartagena Nov. 19–22, 1984, *reprinted in* UNITED NATIONS HIGH COMMISSIONER FOR REFUGEES, COLLECTION OF INRERNATIONAL INSTRUMENTS AND OTHER LEGAL TEXTS CONCERNING REFUGEES AND DISPLACED PERSONS 206 (1995)

Charter of Fundamental Rights of the European Union, adopted Dec. 7, 2000, OFFICIAL JOURNAL OF THE EUROPEAN COMMUNITIES, C 364/8 (Dec. 18, 2000), *reprinted in* 40 I.L.M. 266 (2001) *and* 3 WESTON & CARLSON III.B.16g

Charter of the Organization of African Unity, adopted May 25, 1963, 479 U.N.T.S. 39, *reprinted in* 2 I.L.M. 766 (1963)) *and* 1 INTERNATIONAL LAW AND WORLD ORDER: BASIC DOCUMENTS I.B.1 (B. Weston & J. Carlson eds., 5 vole., 1994–) [hereinafter "1 WESTON & CARLSON',] (entered into force Sept. 13, 1963)

Charter of the Organization of American States, signed in Bogota in 1948 and amended by the Protocol of Buenos Aires (1967), the

Protocol of Cartagena de Indias (1985), the Protocol of Washington (1992), and the Protocol of Managua (1993), *reprinted in* 1 WESTON & CARLSON I.B.14 (in force as of Sept. 25, 1997)

Constitutive Act of the African Union, adopted July 11, 2000, OAU/CAB/LEG/23.15 (entered into force May 26, 2001)

Draft Protocol to the African Charter on Human and Peoples Rights on the Rights of Women in Africa, OAU Doc. CAB/LEG/66.6 (Sept. 2000)

European Convention for the Prevention of Torture and Inhuman or Degrading Treatment, adopted Nov. 26, 1987, Eur. T.S. No. 126, *reprinted in* 3 WESTON & CARLSON III.K.4 (entered into force Feb. 1, 1989)

European Convention for the Protection of Human Rights and Fundamental Freedoms, adopted Nov. 4, 1950, Eur. T.S. No. 5, 213 U.N.T.S. 221, *reprinted in* 3 WESTON & CARLSON III.B.2 (entered into force Sept. 3, 1953)

European Social Charter, adopted Oct. 18, 1961, Eur. T.S. No. 35, *reprinted in* 3 WESTON & CARLSON III.B.4 (entered into force Feb. 26, 1965)

Final Act of the Conference on Security and Cooperation in Europe, adopted Aug. 1, 1975, *reprinted in* 14 I.L.M. 1292(1975) *and* WESTON & CARLSON I.D.9

Framework Convention for the Protection of National Minorities, opened for signature Feb. 1, 1995, Eur. T.S. No. 157, *reprinted in* 34 I.L.M. 351 (1995) *and* 3 WESTON & CARLSON III.I.7 (entered into force Feb. 1, 1998)

General Framework Agreement for Peace in Bosnia and Herzegovina, Dec.14, 1995, *reprinted in* 35 I.L.M. 75 (1996)) *and* 2 INTERNATIONAL LAW AND WORLD ORDER: BASIC DOCUMENTS II.D.17b (B. Weston & J. Carlson eds., 5 vole., 1994–)

Inter-American Convention on Forced Disappearance of Persons, adopted June 9, 1994, *reprinted in* BASIC DOCUMENTS PERTAINING TO HUMAN RIGHTS IN THE INTER-AMERICAN SYSTEM, OAS/Ser.L/V/I.4 Rev.7 (January 2000), *reprinted in* 33 I.L.M. 1530 (1994) (entered into force Mar. 28, 1996)

Inter-American Convention on the Prevention, Punishment and Eradication of Violence Against Women (Convention of Belem Do Para, adopted June 9, 1994, *reprinted in* BASIC DOCUMENTS PERTAINING TO HUMAN RIGHTS IN THE INTER-AMERICAN SYSTEM, OAS/Ser.L/V/I.4 Rev.7 (January 2000) and 33 I.L.M. 1535 (1994) (entered into force Mar. 5, 1995)

Inter-American Convention to Prevent and Punish Torture, adopted Dec. 9, 1985, O.A.S. T.S. No. 67, *reprinted in* BASIC DOCUMENTS PER-

TAINING TO HUMAN RIGHTS IN THE INTER-AMERICAN SYSTEM, OAS/ Ser.L/V/I.4 Rev.7 (January 2000), reprinted in 25 I.L.M. 519 (1986) *and* 3 WESTON & CARLSON III.K.3 (entered into force Feb. 28, 1987)

Organization of African Unity Convention on the Specific Aspects of Refugee Problems in Africa, adopted Sept. 10, 1969, 1000 U.N.T.S. 46, *reprinted in* 8 I.L.M. 1288 (1969) (entered into force June 20, 1974)

Protocol No. 11 to the 1950 European Convention for the Protection of Human Rights and Fundamental Freedoms, Restructuring the Control Machinery Established Thereby, adopted May 11, 1994, Eur.T.S. No. 155, *reprinted in* 33 I.L.M. 943 (1994) *and* 3 WESTON & CARLSON III.B.16a (entered into force Nov. 1, 1998)

Protocol No. 12 to the 1950 European Convention for the Protection of Human Rights and Fundamental Freedoms, adopted Nov. 4, 2000, Eur. T.S. No. 177, *reprinted in* 3 WESTON & CARLSON III.B.16f

Protocol on the Community Court of Justice (ECOWAS), adopted July 6, 1991, A/Pl117191

Protocol on Tribunal in the Southern African Development Community with Rules of Procedure of the Southern African Development Community Tribunal, adopted by the Summit of the Southern African Development Community (SADC), Windhoek, Namibia, Aug. 6–7, 2000 (on file with the editor)

Protocol Relating to the Definition of Community Citizen (ECOWAS), adopted May 29, 1982, AIP315182

Protocol Relating to Free Movement of Persons and the Right of Residence and Establishment (ECOWAS), adopted May 1979, A/P115179

Protocol Relating to Mutual Assistance in Defense (ECOWAS), adopted May 29, 1981, AISP31S18 1

Protocol to the African Charter on Human and Peoples Rights on the Establishment of an African Court on Human and Peoples Rights, OAU/LEG/EXP/AFCHPR/PROT (III), adopted June 9, 1998, *reprinted in* 9 AFR. J. INT & COMP. L. 953 (1997) *and* 3 WESTON & CARLSON III.B. la

Revised European Social Charter, adopted May 3, 1996, Eur. T.S. No. 163, *reprinted in* 3 WESTON & CARLSON III.B.16d (entered into force July 1, 1999)

Revised Treaty of the Economic Community of West African States, adopted July 24, 1993, *reprinted in* 35 I.L.M. 660 (1996) *and* 4 International Law and World Order: Basic Documents IV.B.2a (B. Weston & J. Carlson eds., 5 vols, 1994–) [hereinafter "4 WESTON & CARLSON"]

Supplementary Protocol on the Code of Conduct for the Implementation of the Protocol on Free Movement of Persons, the Right of Residence and Establishment (ECOWAS), adopted July 6, 1985, A/SP.1/7/85

Supplementary Protocol on the Implementation of the Third Phase (Right of Establishment) of the Protocol on Free Movement of Persons, Right of Residence and Establishment (ECOWAS), adopted May 29, 1990, A/SP2/5/90

Traite de ['Union Economique et Monetaire de L'Afrique de L'Ouest, adopted Jan. 10, 1994 (entered into force Jan. 1995), *available at* <http://v-vww.uemoa.int/actes/Default.htm>

Treaty Establishing the Economic Community of West African States (ECOWAS), adopted May 28, 1975, 1010 U.N.T.S.17

Treaty Establishing the European Community, adopted Mar. 25, 1957, 298 U.N.T.S. 11, as amended by the Treaty of Amsterdam, adopted Oct. 2, 1997, O.J. (C 340) 1 (1997), *reprinted in* 37 I.L.M. 56, 82 (1998) *and* 4 WESTON & CARLSON IV.B.12d

Treaty Establishing the Southern African Development Community, adopted Aug. 17, 1992, *reprinted in* 32 I.L.M. 116 (1993)

Treaty for the Establishment of East African Community, adopted Nov. 30, 1999, *available at* <http: llwww. newaf rice. com/eac/treaty>

Index

ADDRESSES, 589–590, 625–627
  See also INTERNET
ADVOCACY AND LOBBYING, 235–248
  Consultative status, 241–244
AFRICAN CHARTER ON HUMAN AND PEOPLES' RIGHTS, 263–267
  Rights of refugees as human persons, 264–266
AFRICAN COMMISSION ON HUMAN AND PEOPLES'S RIGHTS, 267–275
  Exhaustion of local remedies, 271–274
  Mandate, 267–269
  Procedure
    Admissibility conditions, 274–275
    Non-state complaints, 269–271
    Requirements for complaints to, 623
AFRICAN COMMITTEE OF EXPERTS
  Rights and Welfare of the child, 277–279
AFRICAN COURT OF HUMAN AND PEOPLES' RIGHTS, 275–279

Jurisdiction, 276–277
AFRICAN ECONOMIC COMMUNITY (AEC), 308–309
AFRICAN REGIONAL MECHANISMS, 259–314
  African Economic Community
    Aims and objectives of, 308–309
  Asylum, rights during flight, 266–267
  Community Court of Justice, 289–290, 293–295, 301
  East African Community, 299–301
  Human and People's Rights, African Commission on, 267–275
  In general, 18–20
  Inter-Governmental Authority on Development, 297–299
  Introduction, 259–262
  OAU Division for Refugees, Displaced Persons and Humanitarian @AAAA:Assistance, 279–282, 279–282
  OAU Mechanism for Conflict Prevention, etc., 282–283

AFRICAN REGIONAL
MECHANISMS *(continued)*
L'Union Economique et
Monetaire de l'Afrique,
290-296
Organization of African Unity,
262-279
South African Development
Community, 302-308
Aims and objectives of,
302-308, 351-352
Gender, 305-306
Human rights and migration, 304-305
Institutions of, 303
SADC Tribunal, 306-308
Statistics, 259
Sub-regional mechanisms,
283-290
AFRICAN UNION, 309-310
ALIENS
Collective expulsion of, 404
AMERICAN DECLARATION ON
THE RIGHTS AND DUTIES
OF MAN, 19, 462
AMICUS CURIAE, 485
ANONYMITY, 43
ARREST OR DETENTION
Arbitrary, 56-58
ASKIN, KELLY
International Criminal
Tribunals
Witnesses before, 495-520
ASYLUM-SEEKERS
See also specific entries
African Regional Mechanisms,
259-314
See also AFRICAN
REGIONAL MECHA-
NISMS
Human rights of
Basic introduction, 1-22
Right to asylum, 68, 84, 91

ATKINSON-SANFORD, DIANE
European Human Rights
Mechanisms, 315-437

BAYEFSKY, ANNE
Protection Under the
Complaint Procedures of
the UN Treaty Bodies,
23-135
BIBLIOGRAPHY
African regional mechanisms,
310-314
Cases, 313
Internet, 314
Basic introduction, 21-22
Complaint procedures,
248-257
European human rights
mechanisms, 431-437
Cases, 432-437
Internally displaced persons,
538-540
Cases, 540
Internet, 540
Individual complaints, 128-135
Cases, 131-135
Internet sources, 135
Inter-American mechanisms,
485-493
Cases, 488492
International criminal tribunals. 518-520
Cases, 520
International instruments,
639-646
Global instruments,
639-642
Regional instruments,
642-646
International Law Monograph
Series, 651-652
PAIL Institute Publications,
651-653

Relevant human rights manuals/resources, 541–542
BOSNIA-HERZEGOVINA, 19, 536–537

CAPITAL PUNISHMENT, 380–381
CENTER FOR JUSTICE AND INTERNATIONAL LAW (CEJIL), 468
CHARTER-BASED MECHANISMS (UN), 137–257
  Assessing effectiveness of, 222–226
  Asylum-seekers and IDPs, 143–144
  Case studies, 156–163
  Commission on Human Rights and, 140–141, 169–221
    Arbitrary detention, 169–173
    Country-specific procedures, 220–221
    Fact-finding, 147–148
    Special procedures of, 145–149
    Thematic procedures, 169–220
  Commission on the Status of Women, 141
  Common aspects, 163–169
  Country-specific procedures, 155–156, 220–221, 226
  Distinguished from treaty-based, 138–143
  Economic and Social Council, 139–140
  Effectiveness of, 222–226
  Enforced and involuntary disappearance, 174–177
    Examples, 175
  Executions, 177–182
  Fact-finding, 147
  General Assembly, 138–139
  In general, 18–20
  Introduction, 137–138
  Languages, 163
  Mechanisms available, 150–163
  Procedures, 144–149, 163–221
    Communications
      Content, 166–168
      Form of, 165–166
      Style, 166
    Imminent deportation, 168–169
    Practical considerations, 163–165
  Purpose of, 144–149
  Relevancy for refugees, etc., 143–144
  Secretariat, 142–143
  Security Council, 139
  Thematic procedures, 150–154, 169–220, 222–225
  Torture, 182–188
CID (cruel, inhuman and degrading (treatment of punishment), 9
COMMISSION ON HUMAN RIGHTS (CHR)
1503 Procedure, 227–232
CHILDREN
  African Committee on Rights and Welfare of, 277–279
  Children in the armed conflict, 207–210
  Definition of child, 108
  Economic and social rights of the child, 72–73
  Rights at a glance, 109
  Special Rapporteur on the Sale of Children, 205–207
CIVIL AND POLITICAL RIGHTS, 462–468

COMMISSION FOR REAL
  PROPERTY CLAIMS OF
  DISPLACED PERSONS AND
  REFUGEES (CRPC), 529–530
COMMISSION ON THE
  STATUS OF WOMEN (CSW)
  See also WOMEN
  Address, 589–590
  Individual complaint procedure,
    234–235
COMMITTEE AGAINST
  TORTURE (CAT)
  See TORTURE CONVENTION
COMMITTEE ON THE
  ELIMINATION OF DISCRIMI-
  NATION AGAINST WOMEN
  (CEDAW)
  See also WOMEN
  Guiding Principles and, 555
COMMITTEE ON THE
  ELIMINATION OF RACIAL
  DISCRIMINATION (CERD), 26
  Exhaustion of remedies, 39–41
  Guiding Principles and, 555
  Information on complaints to,
    587
  Victim under, 29
COMMITTEE ON THE RIGHTS
  OF THE CHILD (CRC), 108
  See also CHILDREN
COMPLAINT PROCEDURE
  Confidentiality, 118–119
  Charter-based
    Distinguished from treaty-
      based, 138–143
  Checklist, 44–45
  Filing and decision
    Inordinate time and, 122
  Guiding principles, 545–556
  Incompatibility, 44
  Individual complaints
    See also INDIVIDUAL COM-
      PLAINTS
  Admissibility criteria, 26–45
  Overview of, 23–25
  Information on complaints to
    the Human Rights
    Committee, 567–569
  Interim measure, 111–114
  Legal aid, 119
  Model complaints, 591–593
  Participants at Consultation,
    543–544
  Remedies, 114–117
  Strengths and weaknesses of,
    119–123
  Substantive rights and signifi-
    cant jurisprudence,
    45–111
    Rights at a glance, 46
  Time limits, 41
  United National treaty bodies,
    23–135
CONFIDENTIALITY, 118–119,
  483–484
CONFLICT RESOLUTION
  MECHANISM (of the
  Organization of African Unity)
  (CRM), 282–283
  IGAD and, 299
COUNCIL OF EUROPE
  Commissioner for Human
    Right, 425
COX, MARCUS
  Internationalized legal struc-
    tures and IDP, 521–540
CRIMINAL TRIBUNALS
  See INTERNATIONAL
    CRIMINAL TRIBUNALS
CUSTOMARY LAW
  Primer on, 18

DEPORTATION, 376, 408–411
DEROGATION, 552
DETENTION
  Refugees and, 83

Working Group on Arbitrary Detention, 169–173
Principles, 619–621
DISCRIMINATION
See also as subhead to other topics
Equality and non-discrimination, 382–384
IDPs and, 525–526
DISPLACED PERSON
See IDP
DIVISION OF THE ADVANCEMENT OF WOMEN (DAW)
See WOMEN
DOCUMENTS
Seizure of, 14–15
DUE PROCESS OF LAW, 59, 83, 89, 457
EAST AFRICAN COMMUNITY (EAC), 299–301
Human rights and migration, 300–301
Institutions, 300
ECONOMIC AND SOCIAL COUNCIL (ECOSOC), 138
ECONOMIC COMMUNITY OF WEST AFRICAN STATES (ECOWAS), 283–290
Aims and objectives, 285–286
Human rights and migration, 287–289
ECONOMIC COMMUNITY OF WEST AFRICAN STATES MONITORING GROUP (ECOMOG), 284, 287
EDUCATION
Right to, 92, 415–416
EQUALITY AND NON-DISCRIMINATION
Economic and social rights, 73
Right to, 9–10, 52–53, 82–83, 88

EUROPEAN COMMITTEE FOR THE PREVENTION OF TORTURE AND INHUMAN OR DEGRADING TREATMENT OR PUNISHMENT (CPT), 422–424
EUROPEAN CONVENTION FOR THE PROTECTION OF HUMAN RIGHTS AND FUNDAMENTAL FREEDOMS (ECHR), 316
EUROPEAN COURT OF HUMAN RIGHTS (ECHR)
See also EUROPEAN HUMAN RIGHTS MECHANISMS
Abuse of process, 353
Admissibility criteria, 334–344
Against whom claim can be brought, 342–344
Groups of individuals, 340–341
Indirect victims, 334–338
Individual victims, 334
Loss of victim status, 341–342
Potential victims, 339
Anonymity, 353
Application to the Court
Procedure, 353–359
Timeline, 354–359
Belief, right to holding of, 392–394
Capital punishment, 380–381
Checklist, 320–321
Criminal law
Extradition, expulsion, 373
Failure to enforce, 369–371
Failure to investigate or prosecute, 371–373
Damages, 332
Deportation and expulsion, 408–411
Education, 415

EUROPEAN COURT OF
  HUMAN RIGHTS (ECHR)
  (continued)
    Equality and non-discrimination, 382–384
    Exhaustion of remedies, 347–353
      Burden of proof, 349–352
    Expulsions, 404–405
    Extradition, expulsion, deportation, 376–380
    Fact-finding, 357
    Fair trial and due process of law, 388–391
    Family and private life, right to, 68–69, 405
    Food, clothing, social support and shelter, 415
    Freedom of assembly and association, 401–404
    Freedom of expression, 394–397
    Freedom of movement, 11, 404–405
    Freedom of religion, thought and conscience, 11, 392–394
    Freedom of the press, 397–401
    Health care, 381–382
    Home, right to, 406–407
    Individual petition mechanisms, 318
    Institutional framework of the Court, 319–320
    Interim measures, 321–322
    Judgment
      Enforcement of, 332–333, 359
    Jurisdiction, 344–347
    Jurisprudence and refugees, 359–373
    Just compensation, 324–330
    Lack of binding legal obligations, 17
    Legal aid, 330–331
    Marriage, rights as to, 413–414
    National legislation
      Interpreting, 339
    Personal identity, right to, 407–408
    Personal liberty, 385–388
    Prohibition on taking of life, 363–369
      Death in custody, 366369
      Forced disappearances, 365–366
      Lethal force, 364–365
      Use of force, 363–364
    Property rights, 416–420
    Refugees, asylum-seekers, and IDPs, 359–362
    Requirement for complaints to, 629–630
    Reunification, right to, 411–413
    Right to life and physical integrity, 362–363
    Right to private life, 382
    Settlements, 322–324, 357
    Slavery, servitude, compulsory labor, 414–415
    Torture and inhuman and degrading treatment, 373–382
    Vote, right to, 391–392
EUROPEAN COURT OF
  JUSTICE (ECJ), 429–430
EUROPEAN HUMAN RIGHTS
  MECHANISMS, 315–437
  See also specific topics and institutions
  Admissibility criteria, 334–359
  Advocacy, 318–359
  Collective complaint mechanisms, 422
  Convention on Torture, etc. 422–424

European Convention for the
Prevention of Torture,
etc. 422–424
European Court of Human
Rights
See also EUROPEAN COURT
OF HUMAN RIGHTS
Background, 318–319
Checklist for bringing action,
320–321
Friendly settlement, 322–324
Institutional framework of the
Court, 319–320
Interim measures, 321–322
Just satisfaction, 324–420
European Social Charter,
420–422
European Union, 427–431
Human rights and,
428–429
Framework Convention for the
Protection of National
Minorities, 424
In general, 18–20
Individual petition mechanisms, 318–319
Introduction, 315–318
Organization for Security and
Cooperation in Europe,
425–427
EUROPEAN UNION (EU),
427–429
Charter of Fundamental Rights
of, 316–317
Human rights and, 428–429
Refugees and asylum-seekers,
430–431
Treaty of (TEU)
EXECUTIONS, 177–182
Examples, 179–180
EXPULSION, 373, 376, 408–411
Collective or mass expulsions,
65–66

Prohibition on and removal
from country, 64–65,
83–84, 90
EXTRADITION, 373, 376

FAIR TRIAL, 59, 83, 89
FAMILY LIFE
Family reunification, 69–70
Guiding Principles and, 551
Right to, 13, 68–69, 91,
473–474
FARRIOR, STEPHANIE
Protection Under the
Complaint Procedures of
the UN Treaty Bodies,
23–135
FIFTEEN HUNDRED AND
THREE PROCEDURE (1503),
227–232
FITZPATRICK, JOAN
The Human Rights of
Refugees, Asylum-seekers,
and Internally
Displaced Person, 1–22
FOOD, CLOTHING, SOCIAL
SUPPORT, AND SHELTER,
415, 474
FREEDOM OF ASSEMBLY AND
ASSOCIATION, 90,
401–404
FREEDOM OF EXPRESSION
AND ASSOCIATION
Advertising, 401
Broadcasting, 400–401
Freedom of the press,
397–399
Literary works, 400
Political parties, 403
Political figures, 399–400
Right to, 11, 61–62, 89,
394–401
Special Rapporteur on,
191–194, 598–600

FREEDOM OF MOVEMENT
  Guiding Principles and,
    549–560
  Right to, 11–13, 63–64, 83, 404
FREEDOM OF RELIGION,
  60–61, 89, 392–394
  Special Rapporteur on
    Religious Intolerance,
    195–199

GENDER
  SADC and, 305306
GENERAL ASSEMBLY (GA),
  138–139
GIFFARD, CAMILLE
  The Un Charter-Based
    Mechanisms, 137–257

HAITIAN INTERDICTION
  CASE, 466
HANRAHAN, KAREN
  Protection Under the
    Complaint Procedures of
    the UN Treaty Bodies,
    23–135
HARLAND, CHRISTOPHER
  Internationalized legal struc-
    tures and IDP, 521–540
HEALTH
  Right to health care, 92, 475
HRLE, MEAGAN
  The UN Charter-Based
    Mechanisms, 137–257
HOUSING
  Municipal housing offices,
    535–536
  Right to, 92
  Right to return home,
    523–524
HUMAN RIGHTS
  Basic introduction, 1–22
    International human rights
      law, 15–20

Human rights mechanisms,
  18–20
Nature of international human
  rights law, 16
HUMAN RIGHTS CHAMBER,
  530
HUMAN RIGHTS COMMITTEE
  (HRC), 28, 38

IDP (internally displaced
  person), 1
  See also specific topics
  Discrimination, 525–526
  Federation ombudsmen,
    533–534
  Freedom to enter another
    country, 91
  Freedom to leave one's country,
    66–67, 90
    Right to return to one's
      country, 67–68, 90
  Guiding Principles, 605–618
    Relevance of, 545–556
  Human rights advocacy,
    533–534
  Institutional choices
    Assessing, 536–538
  Institutional model for the
    protection of IDPs,
    528–536
  Internationalized legal
    structures and,
    521–540
  Internationally displaced
    persons, 521–548
  Human Rights Chamber and
    ombudsman, 530–533
  Human rights of
    Basic introduction, 1–22
  Institutional models for the
    protection of, 528–536
    Critique of, 536–538
  Mass displacement, 522–523

Mass property title determination, 529–530
Municipal housing offices, 535–536
Personal security, 525
Population displacement
  Human right issues in, 523–528
Property rights, 525
Protection of, 521–540
  Introduction, 521–523
  Restitution and transitional justice, 526–528
  Right to return home, 523–524
  Special Representative on, 210–217
INDIVIDUAL COMPLAINTS
See also COMPLAINT PROCEDURE
Admissibility criteria, 2–45
Brief overview, 23–25
Checklist for submissions, 44–45
Confidentiality, 118–119
Convention Against Torture, etc. 73–84
Convention on the Elimination Discrimination Against women
  Protection under, 95–111
  Victim under, 29
  Women's Convention), 24
Convention on the Elimination of All Forms of Racial Discrimination
  Protection under, 84–94
  Racial Discrimination Convention, 24
Exhaustion of domestic remedies, 36–41
Interim measures, 111–114
Jurisdiction, 26–36
Legal aid, 119

Procedures other than, 123–128
Remedies, 114–117
Strengths and weaknesses of system, 119–123
  Binding nature of opinions, 123
Substantive rights, 45–73
INTER-AMERICAN COMMISSION ON HUMAN RIGHTS (IACHR), 3, 19, 440–441, 470
Complaint form, 631–633
Inter-institutional coordination, 442–443
INTER-AMERICAN COURT OF HUMAN RIGHTS, 441–442
Lack of binding legal obligations, 17
INTER-AMERICAN MECHANISMS, 439–493
Admissibility criteria, 461
Advisory opinions, 482
Advocacy, 481–485
Amicus curiae, 485
Asylum
  Right to seek and receive, 462–468
Civil and political rights, 462–474
Complaint, framing of, 483
Confidentiality, 483–484
Country reports, 469–473
Due process of law, 457
Education, 475
Effectiveness of, 477–480
Exhaustion of local remedies, 453–461
Family and private life, right to, 473–474
Food, clothing and shelter, access to, 474
Health care, 475
In general, 18–20

INTER-AMERICAN MECHA-
NISMS (continued)
  Individual complaints
    Admissibility criteria,
      443–449
    Inter-American Commission
      on Human Rights,
      440–441
    Inter-American Court of
      Human Rights, 441–442
    Inter-institutional coordination,
      442–443
  Jurisdiction, 450–453
    Concurrent, 460–461
    Jurisdiction ratione loci, 453
    Jurisdiction ratione materiae,
      450
    Jurisdiction ratione temporis,
      452–453
  On-site visits and country
    reports, 481–482
  Property rights, 475–477
  Right to seek and receive
    asylum, 462–473
  Organization of American
    States, 439–440
  Protective orders, 484–485
  Remedies, 458–459
    Unwarranted delay of, 458
  Settlements, 484
  Social and economic rights,
    474–477
  Substantive rights, 462–477
INTER-GOVERNMENTAL
  AUTHORITY ON DEVELOP-
  MENT (IGAD), 297–299
  Human rights and migration,
    298–299
  IGAD institutions, 297–298

INTER-STATE DEFENCE AND
  SECURITY COMMITTEE (of
  the Southern

African Development
  Community) (ISDSC)
INTERNATIONAL COMMIT-
  TEE OF THE RED CROSS, 13
INTERNATIONAL COVENANT
  ON CIVIL AND POLITICAL
  RIGHTS (ICCPR), 11, 12, 23, 23
  Article 4, 47
  Article 7, 50
  Complaint, 32
  Equal protection of the law, 54
  Equality before the law, 54
  Substantive rights and signifi-
    cant jurisprudence, 45–73
  Using Guiding Principles to
    interpret provisions of,
    547–552
  Victim under, 27, 30
INTERNATIONAL COVENANT
  ON ECONOMIC, SOCIAL
  AND CULTURAL RIGHTS
  (ICESCR), 110
  Rights at a glance, 110
INTERNATIONAL CRIMINAL
  COURT (ICC), 495, 514–518
INTERNATIONAL CRIMINAL
  TRIBUNAL FOR RWANDA
  (ICTR), 496 ET SEQ.
  Contact information, 637–638
  Office of the Prosecutor (OTP)
  Victims and Witnesses Section
    (VWS)
INTERNATIONAL CRIMINAL
  TRIBUNAL FOR THE FOR-
  MER YUGOSLAVIA (ICTY),
  495, 496 ET SEQ.
  Contact information, 637–638
  Office of the Prosecutor
    (OTP), 502 et seq.
  Victims and Witnesses Section
    (VWS), 503–504
INTERNATIONAL CRIMINAL
  TRIBUNALS

Ad Hoc Tribunals, 497–499
International Criminal Court, 514–518
Introduction, 495–497
Investigation and pre-trial stages, 499–503
Indictments, 500
Post trial phase, 512–513
Restitution of property and victim compensation, 513–514
Sexual violence, 511
Trial phase, 504–512
Evidence, 507–508
Victims and witnesses section (VSW), 503–504
Witnesses before, 495–520
Confidentiality, 509
Expunging name of, 508
Protective measure, 508–510
Voice obscuring, 508
INTERNATIONAL LABOR ORGANIZATION (ILO)
Convention Concerning Indigenous & Tribal Peoples.., 12
ILO Convention No. 169, 12
INTERNET
See also BIBLIOGRAPHY, and as subheading
Complaint procedures, 256–257
UNHCR News, 259
UN Division for the Advancement of Women, 235
UN High Commissioner for Human Rights, 135
UN High Commissioner for Refuges, 22

JUDGES AND LAWYERS
Special Rapporteur on Independence of, 188–191

JURISDICTION
See also as subhead to other topics
Concurrent and successive, 41–43, 460
Ratione loci, 35, 346, 43
Ratione materiae, 31, 344, 450
Ratione personae, 334, 444
Ratione temporis, 33–34, 345, 452–43
JUST SATISFACTION, 324–330

KOSOVO, 14, 521, 524

LABOR
Prohibition against compulsory labor, 414–415
LANGHAM, ANDREW
Protection Under the Complaint Procedures of the UN Treaty Bodies, 23–135
LANGUAGES, 163
Official language, 331–332
LAWYERS
Legal representation, 331
Special Rapporteur on Independence of, 188–191
LEGAL AID, 119, 330–331
LIFE AND PHYSICAL INTEGRITY
Guiding Principles and, 551
Right to, 8–9, 48–50, 87
LYON, BETH
Inter-American Mechanisms, 439–493

MARRIAGE
Rights as to, 413–414
MIGRANTS
Special Rapporteur on the Human Rights of, 217–221

MINORITIES
Framework Convention for Protection of, 424
Rights of racial, ethnic, and linguistic minorities, 55

NATIONALITY
Right to, 70, 91
NON-DISCRIMINATION
Guiding Principles and, 547–548
NON-GOVERNMENTAL ORGANIZATION (NGO), 448
Consultative status, 244
European Court of Justice and, 340–341
Formal interventions by, 246–247
Oral interventions by, 247
State reporting procedures and, 124–125

ODINKALU, CHIDI
African Regional Mechanisms, 259–314
OFFICE OF THE HIGH COMMISSIONER FOR HUMAN RIGHTS (OHCHR)
Address, 589
OMBUDSMAN, 530–534
ON-SITE VISITS, 481–482
OPTIONAL PROTOCOL TO THE CONVENTION ON THE ELIMINATION OF ALL FORMS OF DISCRIMINATION AGAINST WOMEN (CEDAW OP), 24, 24
See also WOMEN
ORGANIZATION FOR SECURITY AND COOPERATION IN EUROPE (OSCE), 425–427
ORGANIZATION OF AFRICAN UNITY (OAU), 259 et seq.

See also AFRICAN REGIONAL MECHANISMS
Organization of, 262
ORGANIZATION OF AMERICAN STATES (OAS), 439–440
State parties to, 635

PERSON
Recognition as a person before the law, 70
PERSONAL LIBERTY
Right to, 10, 89
PROPERTY RIGHTS, 15, 93, 475–477
Compensation for taking, 419–420
Deprivation of, 416–417
Expropriation, 419
IDPs and, 525
Possessions, meaning of, 416
Right to enjoyment of, 416–420
State control of, 418–419
PROTECTIVE ORDERS, 484–485

RACIAL DISCRIMINATION, 94
Elimination of all forms of, 84–87
Humiliation, 88
Racist propaganda, 87
Rights at a glance, 86
Special Rapporteur on, 203–205
RECOGNITION AS A PERSON BEFORE THE LAW
Right to, 552
REFUGEES
See also specific entries
African Regional Mechanisms, 259–314
See also AFRICAN REGIONAL MECHANISMS

Definition, 4, 5, 260
Human rights of
 Basic introduction, 1–22
RELIGION
 Right to holding of belief, 392–394
REPORTING PROCEDURE
 State reporting procedure, 124–125
RESTITUTION
 Restitution and transitional justice, 526–528
REUNIFICATION
 Right to, 411–413
ROTTMAN, SOREN
 Inter-American Mechanisms, 439–493
RYDBERG, ASA
 International Criminal Tribunals
  Witnesses before, 495–520

SCENARIOS
 Scenario 1 (Chen), 7, 156–158, 326, 341, 363, 373, 382, 411, 448, 452, 474
 Scenario 2 (Ibrahim), 7–8, 158–160, 323–324, 326, 345, 373, 376
 Scenario 3 (Maria), 8, 50, 47, 160–162, 330, 407, 445, 470, 471, 474, 475, 477
 Scenario 4 (Chen, mass influx), 8, 162
 Scenario 5 (Ibrahim, mass influx), 8, 162, 343, 446
 Scenario 6 (Maria, mass internal displacement), 8, 162, 326, 337, 343, 373
SECURITY
 Personal security, 525
SETTLEMENT, 484
 Friendly settlement, 322–324

SHELTER
 Right to, 92
SLAVERY
 Prohibition against, 414–415
SOCIAL AND ECONOMIC RIGHTS, 14
SOCIAL SECURITY
 Right to, 93
SOUTH AFRICAN DEVELOPMENT COMMUNITY (SADC), 302–308
 See also AFRICAN REGIONAL MECHANISMS
SPECIAL REPRESENTATIVE OF THE SECRETARY-GENERAL (SRSG), 207–217
SUB-COMMISSION ON THE PROMOTION AND PROTECTION OF HUMAN RIGHTS, 141–142
 1503 Procedure, 227–232
 Studies of, 232–234

TORTURE
 ECHR and, 373–376
 European Convention on Torture, 422–424
 Inquiry procedure, 126–127
 Physical and mental integrity, 76–81
 Prohibition against torture, etc., 50–52, 73–75
 Rights at a glance, 74
 Special Rapporteur on Torture, 182–188, 601–602
  Example, 185
 Specialized training to prevent, 82, 94
TORTURE CONVENTION, 23–24
 CAT fact sheet and complaint, 571–582

TORTURE CONVENTION
(continued)
   Complaint, 32–33
   Exhaustion of remedies, 38–39
   Guiding Principles and, 554–555
   Information on complaints to CAT, 583–585
   Victim under, 28–29, 31
TREATIES
   Basic information as to, 16–18
   Comments and recommendations, 125–126
   Complaint procedures under UN treaty bodies, 23–135
      See also COMPLAINT PROCEDURE and specific entries
   Contact information for UN treaty bodies, 565
   Inquiry procedure, 126
   List of state parties to, 557–564
   Strengths and weaknesses of UN treaty mechanisms, 119–123

L'UNION ECONOMIQUE ET MONETAIRS DE L'AFRIQUE DE L'OUEST (UEMOA), 290–296
   See also AFRICAN REGIONAL MECHANISMS
   Aims and objectives, 291
   Human rights and migration, 292–293
   Institutions of, 291–292
   Procedure before, 296
UNITED NATIONS (UN)
   Charter-based mechanisms, 137–257
      See also CHARTER-BASED MECHANISMS
   Complaint procedures
      See also COMPLAINT PROCEDURE and specific entries
   Protection under UN treaty bodies, 23–135
UNITED NATIONS HIGH COMMISSIONER FOR REFUGEE (UNHCR), 1, 4
   Internet source, 22
UNITED STATES COMMITTEE FOR REFUGEES (USCR), 479

VICTIMS
   See also as subhead to other topics
   Indirect victims, 334–335, 447
   Individual victims, 334, 446
   Loss of victim status, 341–342
   Optional Protocol and, 27–28
   Potential victims, 339–340
   Reparations to, 517
VOTE, RIGHT TO, 11, 60

WOMEN
Commission on the Status of women
   Complaint procedure, 234–235
   Discrimination against
   Definition, 95–96
   Education, 105–106
   Employment rights, 106
   Equal enjoyment of rights by men and women, 53–54
   Equal rights in economic life, 107
   Equality and non-discrimination, 99–100
   Equality before the law, 100–101
      Acceleration of, 107
   Fair trial and due process, 101
   Food, clothing and shelter, 104

Freedom of
  Association, 102
  Expression, 102
  Family and private life, 102–103
  Movement, 102
  Religion, 101–102
Health care, 104–105
Inquiry procedure, 127–128
Nationality and, 103
Property rights, 107
Protections under Convention and Optional Protocol, 95–109
Rights at a glance, 96
Social and cultural patterns of conduct, 108
Special Rapporteur on Violence Against Women, 197–203
  Complaint form, 603
Trafficking of women and girls and prostitution, 71–72, 98–99
Violence, 97–98
Voting, 101

WORK
  Right to, 92
WORKING GROUP (WG)
  See DETENTION
WORKING GROUP ON ARBITRARY DETENTION (WGAD), 169–173
WORKING GROUP ON ENFORCED AND INVOLUNTARY DISAPPEARANCES (WGEID), 174–177, 594–598

XENOPHOBIA, 203–205

ZARD, MONETTE
  African Regional Mechanisms, 259–314

About The Procedural Aspects of International Law Institute

The Procedural Aspects of International Law Institute is a nonprofit organization devoted to furthering the observance of international law through research, consulting, and publishing monographs and other educational materials. Established in 1965 by academic lawyers, government officials, and private practitioners, the Institute's activities include work in areas as diverse as international claims settlements, a draft convention on terrorism, the concept of autonomy in international law, the reform of international organizations and institutions and the international protection of human rights. The twenty-five volumes of the PAIL Monograph Series represent the only continuously-edited series of books and monographs on international law in the United States. The Institute has consultative status with the Economic and Social Council (ECOSOC) of the United Nations. For further information on the Institute and its activities, write PAIL Institute, P.O. Box 33016, Farragut Station, Washington, D.C. 20033-0016 or send e-mail to *advice@fedcounsel.com*.

Procedural Aspects of International Law Monograph Series

Burns H. Weston, Series Editor (1994–   )
Robert Kogod Goldman, Editor (1977–1994)
Richard B. Lillich, Editor (1964–1977)

[Volumes 1–18 are available from William S. Hein & Company, 1285 Main Street, Buffalo, NY 14209-1987 (Tel: +800-828-7571; Fax: +716-883-8100; email: *wsheinco@class.org*). Volumes 19–21 are available from The University of Pennsylvania Press, Blockley Hall, 418 Service Drive, Philadelphia, PA 19104-6097 (Tel: +800-445-9880; Fax: +40-516-6998). All other volumes are available from Transnational Publishers, Inc., 410 Saw Mill River Road, Ardsley, NY 10502 (Tel: +914-693-5100; Fax: +914-693-4430; email: *info@transnationalpubs.com*).].

1. Richard B. Lillich. *International Claims: Their Adjudication by National Commissions.* 1962

2. Richard B. Lillich and Gordon A. Christenson. *International Claims: Their Preparation and Presentation.* 1962

3. Richard A. Falk. *The Role of Domestic Courts in the International Legal Order.* 1964

4. Gillian M. White. *The Use of Experts by International Tribunals.* 1965

5. Richard B. Lillich. *The Protection of Foreign Investment: Six Procedural Studies.* 1965

6. Richard B. Lillich. *International Claims: Postwar British Practice.* 1967

7. Thomas Buergenthal. *Law-Making in the International Civil Aviation Organization.* 1969
8. John Carey. *UN Protection of Civil and Political Rights.* 1970
9. Burns H. Weston. *International Claims: Postwar French Practice.* 1971
10. Frank Griffith Dawson and Ivan L. Head. *International Law, National Tribunals, and the Rights of Aliens.* 1971
11. Ignaz Seidl-Hohenveldern. *The Austrian-German Arbitral Tribunal.* 1972
12. Richard B. Lillich and Burns H. Weston. *International Claims: Their Settlement by Lump Sum Agreements.* 1975
13. Durward V. Sandifer. *Evidence Before International Tribunals* (Revised Edition). 1975
14. Roger Fisher, *Improving Compliance with International Law.* 1981
15. Richard B. Lillich and Burns H. Weston, eds. *International Claims: Contemporary European Practice.* 1982
16. Frederic L. Kirgis, Jr. *Prior Consultation in International Law: A Study of State Practice.* 1983
17. David Harris. *The European Social Charter.* 1984
18. Richard A. Falk. *Reviving the World Court.* 1986
19. Joan Fitzpatrick. *Human Rights in Crisis: The International System for Protecting Rights During States of Emergency.* 1993
20. Roger S. Clark. *The United Nations Crime Prevention and Criminal Justice Program: Formulation of Standards and Efforts at Their Implementation.* 1994
21. Sean D. Murphy. *Humanitarian Intervention: The United Nations in an Evolving World Order.* 1996
22. Douglas M. Johnston. *Consent and Commitment in the World Community: The Classification and Analysis of International Instruments.* 1997
23. Burns H. Weston, Richard B. Lillich, and David J. Bederman. *International Claims: Their Settlement by Lump Sum Agreements, 1975–1995.* 1999
24. Paul Conlon, *United Nations Sanctions Management: A Case Study of the Iraq Santions Committee, 1990–1994.* 2000
25. David Harris and John Darcy, *The European Social Charter (Second Edition).* 2001

Other PAIL Institute Publications

Transnational Publishers, Inc.

    Hannum, Hurst. *Guide to International Human Rights Practice—Third Edition.* (1999).

    Joan Fitzpatrick, ed. *Human Rights Protection for Refugees, Asylum-Seekers, and Internally Displaced Persons: A Guide to International Mechanisms and Procedures* (2001).

William S. Hein & Co., Inc.

    Hannum, Hurst. *Materials on International Human Rights and U.S. Constitutional Law.* (1985).

    Hannum, Hurst. *Materials on International Human Rights and U.S. Criminal Law.* (1989).

    Lillich, Richard B., ed. *Humanitarian Intervention and the United Nations.* (1973).

    Lillich, Richard B., ed. *Economic Coercion and the New International Economic Order.* (1976).

    Lillich, Richard B. *Transnational Terrorism: Conventions and Commentary.* (1982) together with 1986 Supp.

    Lillich, Richard B. *The Human Rights of Aliens in Contemporary International Law.* (1984).

University of Pennsylvania Press

    Hannum, Hurst. *Autonomy, Sovereignty and Self-Determination: The Accommodation of Conflicting Rights.* (1990).

Kluwer Academic Publisher

    Hannum, Hurst. *The Right to Leave and Return in International Law and Practice.* (1987).